에듀윌 토익

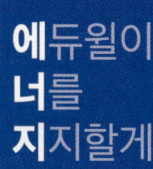

세상을 움직이려면
먼저 나 자신을 움직여야 한다.

– 소크라테스(Socrates)

머리말

이 책은 토익을 처음 접하는 학생들이 RC의 최신 경향을 파악하고 단기에 700~900점을 획득할 수 있게 하는 데 목표를 두고 있다. 시중의 기본서나 종합서들이 최대한 많은 내용을 담는 데 열중했다면, 이 책은 반대로 핵심에서 벗어나는 것을 솎아 내고 오직 빈출 유형에만 집중하여 초급자가 단기간에 목표하는 점수를 얻게 하는 데 초점을 맞췄다.

각 챕터는 RC의 세 개 파트(Part 5, 6, 7)를 기준으로 하되 Part 5는 문법과 어휘 챕터로 분류했다. 문법이 RC의 바탕이 되는 만큼 가장 큰 비중을 할애했으며, 최근 3년간의 기출 유형을 세분화한 다음, 그중 출제 빈도가 하위 10%에 해당하는 유형은 과감히 배제함으로써 오직 핵심을 담는다는 원칙을 견지했다. 그렇게 해서 총 52개의 대표 빈출 유형을 선정했고, 그것들을 제대로 익혀 어떤 변형 문제가 나와도 틀리지 않게 하는 데 집중했다. 문법 챕터 앞에는 52개 빈출 유형에 기반한 진단 테스트를 제공하여 사전에 자신의 문법 수준을 정확히 측정하고, 진단 결과에 따라 취약 유형으로 곧장 갈 수 있게 했다.

문법에서 상당수의 빈출 유형은 굳이 문장 전체를 읽고 해석하지 않아도 단 몇 초 만에 정답을 찾아낼 수 있는 규칙들이 존재한다. 그런 규칙들을 제대로 알고 적용할 수 있다면 Part 5에서 시간을 벌어 Part 7 독해에 더 많은 시간을 할애할 수 있다. 그 규칙들을 정교하게 다듬어 실전에 바로 써먹을 수 있게 만든 것이 바로 '**쉬운 토익 공식**'이다.

문법과 어휘, 독해가 결합된 Part 6는 Part 5와 겹치는 문제 유형을 배제하고 문맥을 통해 풀어야 하는 내용만을 짧게, 집중 연습하게 했다. Part 7 독해는 단순한 요령만으로는 고득점을 얻을 수 없다. 따라서 기본적인 문제 유형과 독해 전략을 제시하되 다양한 양식과 내용의 지문들을 최대한 많이 다루어 전반적인 독해 능력을 끌어올리는 데 목표를 두었다.

교재 끝에는 최신 기출 유형을 반영한 총 3회분의 모의고사를 수록했으며, 이를 통해 RC 전체 파트를 종합적으로 점검하고 자신의 실력을 정확하게 파악할 수 있는 충분한 기회를 제공했다.

부디 이 책을 통해 빠른 시일 안에 원하는 목표 점수를 달성하여 더 원대한 꿈에 한 걸음 더 가까이 다가갈 수 있기를 바란다.

에듀윌 어학연구소

목차

CHAPTER 1　PART 5&6 문법

UNIT 01　명사　28
- 빈출 유형 공략 01　관사/한정사/형용사 + 명사
- 빈출 유형 공략 02　주어와 목적어 역할을 하는 명사
- 빈출 유형 공략 03　사람 명사와 사물/추상 명사
- 빈출 유형 공략 04　복합 명사

UNIT 02　대명사와 한정사　38
- 빈출 유형 공략 01　인칭대명사
- 빈출 유형 공략 02　재귀대명사
- 빈출 유형 공략 03　these와 those
- 빈출 유형 공략 04　one, other, another
- 빈출 유형 공략 05　some과 any
- 빈출 유형 공략 06　수량을 나타내는 대명사와 한정사

UNIT 03　형용사와 부사　50
- 빈출 유형 공략 01　형용사 자리
- 빈출 유형 공략 02　혼동하기 쉬운 형용사
- 빈출 유형 공략 03　부사 자리
- 빈출 유형 공략 04　주의해야 할 부사
- 빈출 유형 공략 05　원급과 비교급 비교
- 빈출 유형 공략 06　최상급 비교

UNIT 04　전치사　62
- 빈출 유형 공략 01　시간을 나타내는 전치사
- 빈출 유형 공략 02　장소를 나타내는 전치사
- 빈출 유형 공략 03　기타 빈출 전치사
- 빈출 유형 공략 04　빈출 전치사구
- 빈출 유형 공략 05　동사/명사/형용사 + 전치사
- 빈출 유형 공략 06　전치사 관용 표현

UNIT 05　수 일치　74
- 빈출 유형 공략 01　수량 표현이 쓰인 주어와 동사의 수 일치
- 빈출 유형 공략 02　등위 접속사가 있는 주어와 동사의 수 일치
- 빈출 유형 공략 03　수식어가 긴 주어와 동사의 수 일치
- 빈출 유형 공략 04　수 일치 복합 문제

UNIT 06　수동태　84
- 빈출 유형 공략 01　수동태 vs. 능동태
- 빈출 유형 공략 02　be p.p. + 명사/형용사
- 빈출 유형 공략 03　be p.p. + to부정사/전치사
- 빈출 유형 공략 04　태와 시제 복합 문제

UNIT 07　시제　94
- 빈출 유형 공략 01　단순 시제
- 빈출 유형 공략 02　진행 시제
- 빈출 유형 공략 03　완료 시제
- 빈출 유형 공략 04　주절-종속절의 시제 일치와 예외
- 빈출 유형 공략 05　시간과 조건 부사절의 시제
- 빈출 유형 공략 06　if 가정법

UNIT 08　to부정사와 동명사　108
- 빈출 유형 공략 01　to부정사 자리와 역할
- 빈출 유형 공략 02　동명사 자리와 역할
- 빈출 유형 공략 03　동명사 vs. 명사
- 빈출 유형 공략 04　to부정사와 동명사 관용 표현

UNIT 09　분사　118
- 빈출 유형 공략 01　과거분사/현재분사 + 명사
- 빈출 유형 공략 02　명사 + 과거분사/현재분사
- 빈출 유형 공략 03　접속사 + 분사
- 빈출 유형 공략 04　관용적 분사구문

UNIT 10　접속사　128
- 빈출 유형 공략 01　등위 접속사와 상관 접속사
- 빈출 유형 공략 02　부사절 접속사
- 빈출 유형 공략 03　명사절 접속사
- 빈출 유형 공략 04　접속사 vs. 전치사

UNIT 11　관계사　138
- 빈출 유형 공략 01　관계대명사
- 빈출 유형 공략 02　관계대명사의 생략
- 빈출 유형 공략 03　관계부사
- 빈출 유형 공략 04　복합관계사

| CHAPTER 2 | PART 5 어휘 |

UNIT 01	명사❶+TEST	150
UNIT 02	명사❷+TEST	154
UNIT 03	형용사❶+TEST	158
UNIT 04	형용사❷+TEST	162
UNIT 05	동사❶+TEST	166
UNIT 06	동사❷+TEST	170
UNIT 07	부사❶+TEST	174
UNIT 08	부사❷+TEST	178

| CHAPTER 3 | PART 6 장문 빈칸 채우기 |

UNIT 01	시제	188
UNIT 02	어휘	190
UNIT 03	접속부사	192
UNIT 04	문맥에 맞는 문장 고르기	194

| CHAPTER 4 | PART 7 독해 |

PART 7 질문 유형별 풀이 전략 208
❶ 주제/목적/대상 문제
❷ NOT/True 문제
❸ 추론/암시 문제
❹ 세부 사항 문제
❺ 문장 삽입 문제
❻ 동의어 찾기 문제

UNIT 01 이메일, 편지 222
빈출 유형 공략 01   이메일: 주제/목적 문제
빈출 유형 공략 02   편지: 문장 삽입 문제

UNIT 02 문자 메시지, 온라인 채팅 232
빈출 유형 공략 01   문자 메시지: 의도 파악 문제
빈출 유형 공략 02   온라인 채팅: 추론/암시 문제

UNIT 03 기사, 안내문 242
빈출 유형 공략 01   기사: 주제/목적 문제
빈출 유형 공략 02   안내문: 세부 사항 문제

UNIT 04 공지, 회람 252
빈출 유형 공략 01   공지: 주제/목적 문제
빈출 유형 공략 02   회람: 세부 사항 문제

UNIT 05 광고 262
빈출 유형 공략 01   상품/서비스 광고: NOT/True 문제
빈출 유형 공략 02   구인 광고: 세부 사항 문제

UNIT 06 웹페이지, 양식, 후기 272
빈출 유형 공략 01   웹페이지: 추론/암시 문제
빈출 유형 공략 02   양식: 세부 사항 문제

UNIT 07 다중 지문 282
빈출 유형 공략   이메일을 포함하는 삼중 지문 문제

실전 모의고사 1회   294
실전 모의고사 2회   322
실전 모의고사 3회   350

정답 및 해설

이 책의 구성과 특징

PART 5&6 문법

최신 토익 출제 경향을 완벽하게 분석 및 반영하여 토익에 출제되는 핵심 문법만 학습할 수 있도록 구성했다.

❶ 토익 기초 문법 OVERVIEW
해당 UNIT을 본격적으로 학습하기 전에 꼭 알아야 하는 문법 개념을 짚고 넘어간다.

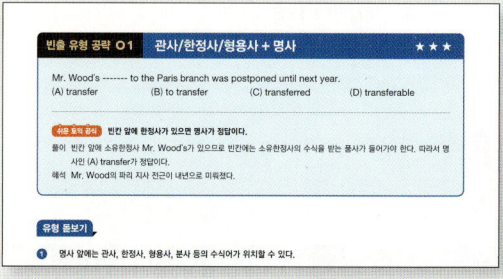

❷ 빈출 유형 공략
토익 문법 문제 풀이에는 대단한 문법 지식이 필요하지 않다. 한 UNIT에 4~6개로 정리한 빈출 유형만 제대로 학습하면 토익 졸업은 시간 문제! 대표 문제의 오른쪽 상단에 있는 별은 빈출도를 나타낸다. 하얀 별이 많을 수록 빈출도가 높다는 걸 뜻한다.
알아 두면 정답이 5초 만에 보이는 쉬운 토익 공식과 더불어 고득점 전략까지 덤으로 얻어 가자.

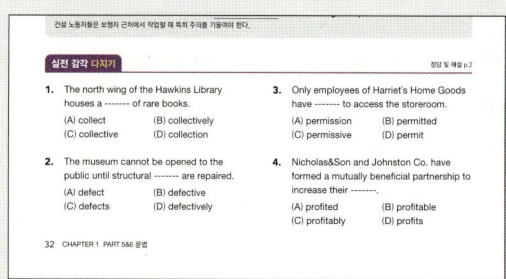

❸ 실전 감각 다지기
최신 경향을 반영한 토익 기출 변형 문제를 풀면서 학습한 내용을 실전에 적용하는 연습을 한다.

PART 5 어휘

핵심 기출 어휘만 집중 학습할 수 있도록 최근 3년간 PART 5에서 어휘 문제로 출제된 어휘들만 모았다.

품사별 빈출 어휘 학습
한 UNIT에 약 30개 어휘를 콜로케이션, 파생어와 함께 학습한다.

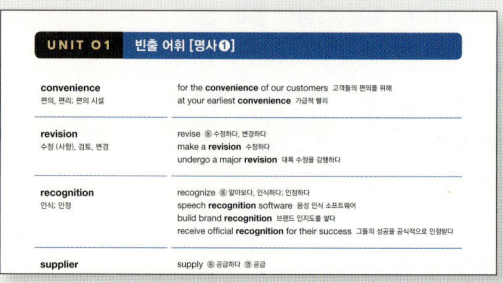

PART 6

PART 6의 특정 문법(시제)과 어휘 문제는 지문의 맥락을 알아야 풀 수 있다. 이러한 출제 특징에 맞춰 PART 6를 전략적으로 학습할 수 있도록 PART 6에 빈출되는 문법, 어휘, 문맥에 맞는 문장 고르기 유형을 제시했다.

빈출 유형 공략
PART 6에서 출제되는 대표 문제 유형을 다양한 지문에 제시하여 학습자가 충분히 연습할 수 있도록 구성했다.

PART 7

질문 유형별 풀이 전략을 익히고, 토익 빈출 지문을 구조적으로 분석하여 지문 맞춤형 학습 방향을 제시했다.

문제 풀이 전략
기초적인 PART 7 문제 풀이 순서와 방법, 지문 속 단서를 찾는 스킬 등을 시뮬레이션으로 제시하여 토익 초급자도 쉽게 따라할 수 있도록 했으며, 더 나아가 질문 유형별 특징과 문제 풀이 전략 등을 제시했다.

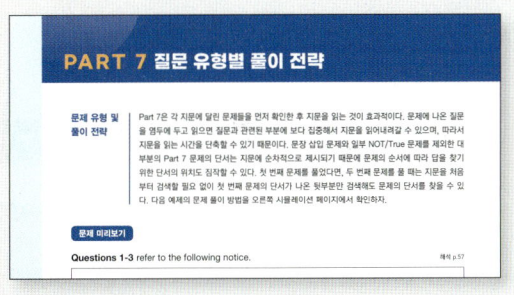

지문 유형별 공략
지문 유형에서는 토익에 자주 나오는 지문 양식들을 크게 7개의 카테고리로 분류하고, 각 카테고리별 지문의 기본 구조와 특징, 빈출 표현, 질문 유형별 풀이 전략을 집중적으로 학습하여 PART 7 문제에 효과적으로 대응할 수 있도록 구성했다.

학습 일정표

PART 5, 6, 7을 순차적으로 학습하는
4주 완성 A코스

1주	**DAY 1** PART 5&6 문법 UNIT 01 월 일	**DAY 2** PART 5&6 문법 UNIT 02 월 일	**DAY 3** PART 5&6 문법 UNIT 03 월 일	**DAY 4** PART 5&6 문법 UNIT 04 월 일	**DAY 5** PART 5&6 문법 UNIT 05 월 일	**DAY 6** PART 5&6 문법 UNIT 06 월 일
2주	**DAY 7** PART 5&6 문법 UNIT 07 월 일	**DAY 8** PART 5&6 문법 UNIT 08 월 일	**DAY 9** PART 5&6 문법 UNIT 09 월 일	**DAY 10** PART 5&6 문법 UNIT 10 월 일	**DAY 11** PART 5&6 문법 UNIT 11 월 일	**DAY 12** PART 5 어휘 UNIT 01~02 월 일
3주	**DAY 13** PART 5 어휘 UNIT 03~04 월 일	**DAY 14** PART 5 어휘 UNIT 05~06 월 일	**DAY 15** PART 5 어휘 UNIT 07~08 월 일	**DAY 16** PART 6 장문 빈칸 채우기 UNIT 01~04 월 일	**DAY 17** PART 7 질문 유형별 풀이 전략 월 일	**DAY 18** PART 7 독해 UNIT 01 월 일
4주	**DAY 19** PART 7 독해 UNIT 02 월 일	**DAY 20** PART 7 독해 UNIT 03 월 일	**DAY 21** PART 7 독해 UNIT 04 월 일	**DAY 22** PART 7 독해 UNIT 05 월 일	**DAY 23** PART 7 독해 UNIT 06 월 일	**DAY 24** PART 7 독해 UNIT 07 월 일

PART 5, 6, 7을 동시에 학습하는

4주 완성 B코스

	DAY 1	DAY 2	DAY 3	DAY 4	DAY 5	DAY 6
1주	PART 5&6 문법 UNIT 01 월 일	PART 5 어휘 UNIT 01~02 월 일	PART 5&6 문법 UNIT 02 월 일	PART 5 어휘 UNIT 03~04 월 일	PART 5&6 문법 UNIT 03 월 일	PART 5 어휘 UNIT 05~06 월 일

	DAY 7	DAY 8	DAY 9	DAY 10	DAY 11	DAY 12
2주	PART 5&6 문법 UNIT 04 월 일	PART 5 어휘 UNIT 07~08 월 일	PART 5&6 문법 UNIT 05 월 일	PART 6 장문 빈칸 채우기 UNIT 01~04 월 일	PART 5&6 문법 UNIT 06 월 일	PART 7 질문 유형별 풀이 전략 월 일

	DAY 13	DAY 14	DAY 15	DAY 16	DAY 17	DAY 18
3주	PART 5&6 문법 UNIT 07 월 일	PART 7 독해 UNIT 01 월 일	PART 5&6 문법 UNIT 08 월 일	PART 7 독해 UNIT 02 월 일	PART 5&6 문법 UNIT 09 월 일	PART 7 독해 UNIT 03 월 일

	DAY 19	DAY 20	DAY 21	DAY 22	DAY 23	DAY 24
4주	PART 5&6 문법 UNIT 10 월 일	PART 7 독해 UNIT 04 월 일	PART 5&6 문법 UNIT 11 월 일	PART 7 독해 UNIT 05 월 일	PART 7 독해 UNIT 06 월 일	PART 7 독해 UNIT 07 월 일

TOEIC 소개

토익이란?

TOEIC은 Test of English for International Communication(국제적인 의사소통을 위한 영어 시험)의 약자로, 영어가 모국어가 아닌 사람들이 비즈니스 현장 및 일상생활에서 필요한 실용 영어 능력을 갖추었는가를 평가하는 시험이다.

시험 구성

구성	파트		문항 수		시간	배점
Listening Comprehension	Part 1	사진 묘사	6	100	45분	495점
	Part 2	질의 응답	25			
	Part 3	짧은 대화	39			
	Part 4	짧은 담화	30			
Reading Comprehension	Part 5	단문 빈칸 채우기	30	100	75분	495점
	Part 6	장문 빈칸 채우기	16			
	Part 7	독해	단일 지문 29			
			이중 지문 10			
			삼중 지문 15			
합계	7 Parts		200문항		120분	990점

출제 범위 및 주제

업무 및 일상생활에서 쓰이는 실용적인 주제들이 출제된다. 특정 문화나 특정 직업 분야에만 해당되는 주제는 출제하지 않으며, 듣기 평가의 경우 미국, 영국, 호주 등 다양한 국가의 발음이 섞여 출제된다.

일반 업무	계약, 협상, 영업, 홍보, 마케팅, 사업 계획
금융 / 재무	예산, 투자, 세금, 청구, 회계
개발	연구, 제품 개발
제조	공장 경영, 생산 조립 라인, 품질 관리
인사	채용, 승진, 퇴직, 직원 교육, 입사 지원
사무실	회의, 메모 / 전화 / 팩스 / 이메일, 사무 장비 및 가구
행사	학회, 연회, 회식, 시상식, 박람회, 제품 시연회
부동산	건축, 부동산 매매 / 임대, 기업 부지, 전기 / 수도 / 가스 설비
여행 / 여가	교통수단, 공항 / 역, 여행 일정, 호텔 및 자동차 예약 / 연기 / 취소, 영화, 전시, 공연

접수 방법

- 한국 TOEIC 위원회 사이트(www.toeic.co.kr)에서 인터넷 접수 기간을 확인하고 접수한다.
- 시험 접수 시 최근 6개월 이내에 촬영한 jpg 형식의 사진 파일이 필요하므로 미리 준비한다.
- 시험 10~12일 전부터는 특별 추가 접수 기간에 해당하여 추가 비용이 발생하므로, 접수 일정을 미리 확인하여 정기 접수 기간 내에 접수하도록 한다.

시험 당일 준비물

- 신분증: 주민등록증, 운전면허증, 기간 만료 전 여권, 공무원증 등 규정 신분증만 인정
  (중·고등학생의 경우 학생증, 청소년증도 인정)
- 필기구: 연필, 지우개 (볼펜, 사인펜은 사용 불가)

시험 진행

오전 시험	오후 시험	진행 내용
09:30 – 09:45	02:30 – 02:45	답안지 작성 오리엔테이션
09:45 – 09:50	02:45 – 02:50	쉬는 시간
09:50 – 10:05	02:50 – 03:05	신분증 확인
10:05 – 10:10	03:05 – 03:10	문제지 배부 및 파본 확인
10:10 – 10:55	03:10 – 03:55	듣기 평가 (LC)
10:55 – 12:10	03:55 – 05:10	독해 평가 (RC)

성적 확인

- 미리 안내된 성적 발표일(시험일로부터 약 12일 후)에 한국 TOEIC 위원회 사이트(www.toeic.co.kr) 및 공식 애플리케이션을 통해 성적을 확인할 수 있다.
- 성적표 수령은 온라인 출력 또는 우편 수령 중에서 선택할 수 있다.
- 온라인 출력과 우편 수령 모두 1회 발급만 무료이며, 그 이후에는 유료로 발급된다.

RC 파트별 문제 유형

PART 5 단문 빈칸 채우기

파트 소개	빈칸이 포함된 하나의 문장이 주어지고, 빈칸에 알맞은 단어나 구를 4개의 선택지 중에서 고르는 파트
문항 수	30문항
문제 유형	• 문법 문제 (문법의 적절한 쓰임을 묻는 문제) • 어휘 문제 (문맥에 어울리는 어휘를 묻는 문제)

문제지 형태

READING TEST

In the Reading test, you will read a variety of texts and answer several different types of reading comprehension questions. The entire Reading test will last 75 minutes. There are three parts, and directions are given for each part. You are encouraged to answer as many questions as possible within the time allowed.

You must mark your answers on the separate answer sheet. Do not write your answers in your test book.

PART 5

Directions: A word or phrase is missing in each of the sentences below. Four answer choices are given below each sentence. Select the best answer to complete the sentence. Then mark the letter (A), (B), (C), or (D) on your answer sheet.

101. All valuables are stored ------- in the hotel's safe.
(A) secures
(B) securely
(C) security
(D) secure

102. Following an intense -------, the Alvarado Inc. managers were able to finalize the contract's terms.
(A) negotiate
(B) negotiated
(C) negotiating
(D) negotiation

103. A reception was held to welcome Ms. Dennis and ------- team.
(A) her
(B) hers
(C) she
(D) herself

104. The human resources department ------- the compliance records required by the federal government.
(A) maintains
(B) cultivates
(C) persuades
(D) associates

105. Fairway Shipping cannot issue refunds for delays caused by circumstances ------- its control.
(A) below
(B) before
(C) behind
(D) beyond

106. ------- can be spent on repairs without the written consent of the building manager.
(A) Nothing
(B) Never
(C) Somebody
(D) Another

107. Under the new policy, salespeople are responsible for ------- their own clients.
(A) to find
(B) find
(C) found
(D) finding

108. The shuttle bus was running behind schedule due to getting ------- in rush-hour traffic.
(A) forced
(B) stuck
(C) rejected
(D) stood

PART 6 장문 빈칸 채우기

파트 소개	4개의 빈칸이 포함된 지문이 주어지고, 각각의 빈칸에 들어갈 알맞은 단어나 구, 문장을 고르는 파트
문항 수	16문항 (4개 지문 × 4문항)
문제 유형	• 문법 문제 (문법의 적절한 쓰임을 묻는 문제) • 어휘 문제 (문맥에 어울리는 어휘를 묻는 문제) • 문장 삽입 문제 (문맥에 어울리는 문장을 묻는 문제)

문제지 형태

PART 6

Directions: Read the texts that follow. A word, phrase, or sentence is missing in parts of each text. Four answer choices for each question are given below the text. Select the best answer to complete the text. Then mark the letter (A), (B), (C), or (D) on your answer sheet.

Questions 131-134 refer to the following article.

BEAUMONT, TX (April 20)—As part of the celebration of our city's history, Centennial Hall ------- an orchestra concert featuring the work of local composer Emilia Oyola. Tickets go on
131.
sale at the box office and online tomorrow. The show is set for June 3 at 7:30 P.M.

While Ms. Oyola will be the conductor, some of the pieces will not be ------- . Two songs
132.
written by other local composers are also part of the lineup. ------- .
133.
The concert will mark the first performance of the Beaumont City Orchestra since the

concert hall was renovated. ------- attendees to Centennial Hall will certainly notice a vast
134.
improvement in sound quality thanks to sound reflectors added to the ceiling.

131. (A) host
(B) hosted
(C) will host
(D) has hosted

132. (A) hers
(B) ours
(C) theirs
(D) its

133. (A) Ms. Oyola grew up just outside of Beaumont.
(B) The orchestra is looking for new members.
(C) Ms. Oyola plays the piano and violin.
(D) It is these composers' official debut.

134. (A) Authorized
(B) Sensible
(C) Preceding
(D) Regular

PART 7 독해

파트 소개	지문을 읽고, 지문 내용과 관련된 2~5개 문제에 대해 가장 적절한 답을 고르는 파트
지문/문항 수	• 단일 지문 10개 (지문당 2~4문항; 총 29문항) • 이중 지문 2개 (지문당 5문항; 총 10문항) ┐ 총 15개 지문 (54문항) • 삼중 지문 3개 (지문당 5문항; 총 15문항) ┘
지문 유형	이메일·편지, 광고, 공지·회람, 기사, 양식(웹페이지, 설문지, 청구서 등), 문자 메시지 대화문 등
문제 유형	주제·목적, 세부 사항, 사실 확인, 추론, 문장 넣기, 의도 파악, 동의어 찾기

문제지 형태 (단일 지문)

PART 7

Directions: In this part you will read a selection of texts, such as magazine and newspaper articles, e-mails, and instant messages. Each text or set of texts is followed by several questions. Select the best answer for each question and mark the letter (A), (B), (C), or (D) on your answer sheet.

Questions 147-148 refer to the following memo.

MEMO

To: Prolance Customer Service Team
From: Olivia Cronin
Re: Customer complaints
Date: September 2

The August electricity bills were calculated incorrectly, so customers received bills that were too high. We're issuing new bills this week, so please explain this to customers if needed.

Additionally, we are receiving a lot of positive feedback from customers. Therefore, starting next month, we will make printouts of what customers are saying and hang them up in the break room to help motivate the staff.

147. Why did Ms. Cronin send the message?
(A) To describe a policy
(B) To explain a problem
(C) To introduce new equipment
(D) To announce a staff change

148. When can employees start to see comments from customers?
(A) In September
(B) In October
(C) In November
(D) In December

문제지 형태 (삼중 지문)

E-Mail Message

From: Rhonda Fitch ⟨rfitch@diazandassoc.com⟩
To: William Austell ⟨waustell@diazandassoc.com⟩
Subject: Interview
Date: October 3

Hi William,

I would like you to cover one of the interviews for the marketing coordinator position, as I don't want to reschedule it. Please interview Mr. Trevino on my behalf, as I've been invited to give a speech at a small business luncheon in Westerville on that day, and I think this would be great exposure for our company. We can meet when I get back to discuss what you thought of the candidate.

Thank you so much!

Rhonda

---

186. What is indicated about Dia in the job posting?
(A) It is entering a new field.
(B) It was founded two year
(C) It will open a new branc
(D) It specializes in security.

187. What is one responsibility m the job posting?
(A) Finding new customers
(B) Creating online content
(C) Traveling for events
(D) Conducting staff training

188. Who best matches the com requirements and preferenc
(A) Ms. Geiger
(B) Mr. Kim
(C) Mr. Trevino
(D) Ms. Echols

Questions 186-190 refer to the following job posting, interview schedule, and e-mail.

Marketing Coordinator Position at Diaz&Associates

Diaz&Associates, a Seattle-based firm dedicated to providing financial planning services, is looking for a new marketing coordinator. We have been in operation for two decades, and, for the first time in our company's history, we are expanding our business into the insurance industry. Therefore, effective marketing will be crucial.

Position description: The marketing coordinator is primarily responsible for managing our social media accounts, writing articles for our online newsletter, and organizing in-person and virtual events.

Requirements: A bachelor's or master's degree in marketing, business administration, or advertising is required along with three years of project management experience. Proficiency in GoCreate design software is a plus.

Interested applicants should send a résumé to hr@diazandassoc.com.

Marketing Coordinator Interviews		
Applicant	Date & Time	Employment Details
Corina Geiger	October 8, 2:00 P.M.	Bachelor's degree in marketing; 2 years project management; proficient in GoCreate
Byoungmin Kim	October 8, 4:00 P.M.	Master's degree in business administration; 3 years project management; proficient in GoCreate
Darrell Crawford	October 9, 1:00 P.M.	Bachelor's degree in advertising; operates personal blog; 3 years project management
Sebastian Trevino	October 10, 3:30 P.M.	Master's degree in advertising; winner of Campaign Creativity Award; proficient in GoCreate
Margaret Echols	October 11, 10:00 A.M.	Master's degree in literature; 4 years project management; proficient in GoCreate

절과 문장

두 개 이상의 단어가 모이되 주어와 동사의 구조를 갖추고 있을 경우 절이라 한다. 하나의 절은 하나의 문장(단문)을 이루기도 하며, 두 개 이상의 절이 모여 복문, 중문을 이룬다.

복문(complex sentence)은 독립적으로 쓸 수 있는 주절과 독립적으로 쓸 수 없는 종속절로 이루어진다. 종속절은 시간이나 이유 등을 나타내는 부사절로 쓰이거나, 주어/보어/목적어 구실을 하는 명사절, 명사를 수식하는 형용사절 역할을 한다. 중문(compound sentence)은 독립해서 쓸 수 있는 두 개 이상의 대등한 절로 이루어지며, and, but, so 등의 등위 접속사가 절과 절을 이어 준다.

단문

Gasoline prices **have risen** **steadily** **over the past year**.
　주어　　　　　동사　　　　부사　　　　전치사구

기름값이 지난 한 해 동안 지속적으로 올랐다.

복문

Since the flight was delayed, **he didn't attend the meeting**.
　　　　부사절　　　　　　　　　　주절(main clause)

비행기가 지연되었기 때문에 그는 회의에 참석하지 못했다.

➡ 부사절은 시간, 이유, 조건 등을 설명한다. 여기에서는 since가 이끄는 절이 이유를 나타내는 부사어 역할을 한다.

Some customers **complained** **that they received the wrong items**.
　　주어　　　　　　동사　　　　　　　　　　명사절

몇몇 고객들은 그들이 엉뚱한 물건을 받았다고 항의했다.

➡ 명사절은 문장에서 주어, 보어, 목적어 역할을 한다. 여기에서는 that이 이끄는 절이 목적어 역할을 한다.

They **hired** **a lawyer** **who specializes in corporate law**.
　주어　동사　목적어　　　　　　형용사절

그들은 기업 법을 전문으로 하는 변호사를 고용했다.

➡ 형용사절은 명사를 수식하는 역할을 한다. 여기에서는 who 이하의 관계사절이 a lawyer라는 명사를 수식한다.

중문

Our production schedule is tight and **we need extra staff**.
　　독립해서 쓸 수 있는 절　　　　　　독립해서 쓸 수 있는 절

생산 일정이 빠듯해서 추가 인력이 필요하다.

➡ 두 개의 완전한 문장이 and라는 접속사에 의해 대등하게 연결되어 있다.

문장 성분 및 구조

주어 + 동사

She moved to London last year. 그녀는 작년에 런던으로 이사했다.
주어 동사 부사어(장소) 부사어(시간)

➡ 주어 자리에는 명사, 대명사 및 명사 역할을 하는 어구가 온다. 부사어는 주로 동작이나 상황에 대한 추가적인 정보(시간, 장소, 방법, 정도, 빈도, 태도)를 제공하며, 필수 성분은 아니지만 부사어가 빠졌을 때 의미가 제대로 전달되지 않을 수 있다.

주어 + 동사 + 주격 보어

The merger was successful. 합병은 성공적이었다.
주어 동사 보어(형용사)

The book soon became a bestseller. 그 책은 금세 베스트셀러가 되었다.
주어 부사어 동사 보어(명사)

➡ 보어는 주어와 동사만으로는 뜻이 완전하지 못할 때, 그 불완전한 의미를 보충해 준다. 보어 자리에는 형용사, 전치사구, 명사, 대명사, to부정사, 동명사, 명사절 등이 올 수 있다.

주어 + 동사 + 목적어

Ms. Lewis received a damaged package. Ms. Lewis는 파손된 소포를 받았다.
주어 동사 목적어

Bluestar Airlines began operating last month. Bluestar Airlines는 지난달에 운영을 시작했다.
주어 동사 목적어 부사어

➡ 타동사는 목적어를 취하며, 목적어 자리에는 명사, 대명사, to부정사, 동명사, 명사절 등이 올 수 있다.

주어 + 동사 + 간접목적어 + 직접목적어

Mr. Miller sent me the proposal yesterday. Mr. Miller가 어제 제게 제안서를 보냈습니다.
주어 동사 간목 직목 부사어

Your assistant gave me your e-mail address. 당신의 비서가 저에게 당신의 이메일 주소를 주었습니다.
주어 동사 간목 직목

➡ 간접목적어는 '~에게', 직접목적어는 '~을/를'로 해석되며, give, send, tell, offer 등의 동사가 토익에 주로 쓰인다.

주어 + 동사 + 목적어 + 목적격 보어

She found the work rewarding. 그녀는 그 일이 보람 있다고 느꼈다.
주어 동사 목적어 목적격 보어

She asked all sales staff to attend the meeting. 그녀는 모든 영업 사원에게 회의에 참석하도록 요청했다.
주어 동사 목적어 목적격 보어

➡ 목적격 보어는 목적어를 보완해 주며, 형용사, 분사, 명사, to부정사, 원형동사 등이 쓰인다.

실전에서 바로 써먹는
쉬운 토익 공식 인강

toeic.eduwill.net

CHAPTER 1

PART 5&6 문법

문법 진단 테스트 [빈출 유형 52]

자신이 취약한 문법 유형을 파악하고 그 유형만 선택적으로 학습하고 싶다면, 진단 테스트를 풀고 난 다음 틀린 문제의 해당 유형으로 바로 가세요! 정답은 문법 진단 테스트의 마지막 페이지(p.27)에 실려 있습니다.

쉬 운 토 익 공 식

UNIT 01 빈출 유형 공략 01

1. Mr. Wood's ------- to the Paris branch was postponed until next year.
   (A) transfer
   (B) to transfer
   (C) transferred
   (D) transferable

빈칸 앞에 한정사가 있으면 명사가 정답이다.

UNIT 01 빈출 유형 공략 02

2. Mr. Meyers was happy to receive ------- that his logo design was well liked among company executives.
   (A) notify
   (B) notification
   (C) notifying
   (D) notifies

빈칸 앞에 타동사가 있으면 명사가 정답이다.

UNIT 01 빈출 유형 공략 03

3. Fleming Institute's time management seminar teaches ------- how to use their time productively.
   (A) participatory
   (B) participants
   (C) participation
   (D) participated

UNIT 01 빈출 유형 공략 04

4. Our system sends an e-mail ------- to online shoppers who haven't completed their purchases.
   (A) remind
   (B) reminding
   (C) reminded
   (D) reminder

UNIT 02 빈출 유형 공략 01

5. Faraway Travel can book various accommodations for ------- stay, either at a hotel or at a hostel.
   (A) you
   (B) your
   (C) yours
   (D) yourself

명사 앞에 빈칸이 있으면 소유한정사가 정답이다.

UNIT 02 빈출 유형 공략 02

6. Ms. Smith likes to handle the finer details ------- to ensure that they are done right.
   (A) she
   (B) herself
   (C) her
   (D) hers

빈칸이 없어도 모든 문장 구조를 갖춘 완전한 문장이라면 재귀대명사가 정답이다.

20 CHAPTER 1 PART 5&6 문법

UNIT 02 빈출 유형 공략 03

7. ------- who take a vacation for over a week should make sure their work is covered by their colleagues.

    (A) These (B) Those
    (C) That   (D) They

> 빈칸이 주격 관계대명사절의 수식을 받으면 those가 정답이다.

UNIT 02 빈출 유형 공략 04

8. The editor-in-chief will review the garments and choose the best ------- to put on the cover.

    (A) it   (B) that
    (C) one   (D) other

UNIT 02 빈출 유형 공략 05

9. Please make sure you report ------- abnormalities with the software to the IT department.

    (A) another (B) each
    (C) any   (D) something

UNIT 02 빈출 유형 공략 06

10. Belladonna Makeup is giving away ------- free items with purchases of $100 or more.

    (A) each   (B) much
    (C) several (D) every

UNIT 03 빈출 유형 공략 01

11. Hiring an outside firm to perform the inspection will help to guarantee an ------- assessment.

    (A) object   (B) objection
    (C) objective (D) objecting

> 빈칸 앞에 관사가 있고 뒤에는 명사가 있으면 형용사가 정답이다.

UNIT 03 빈출 유형 공략 02

12. ------- experience in logistics is required for the position at Tribebolt Ltd.

    (A) Managed   (B) Managers
    (C) Manageable (D) Managerial

UNIT 03 빈출 유형 공략 03

13. Ms. Wheeler ------- encouraged her team members to attend the technology seminar.

    (A) stronger (B) strengthen
    (C) strongly (D) strength

> 빈칸 뒤에 타동사가 있으면 부사가 정답이다.

UNIT 03 빈출 유형 공략 04

14. Human Resources has not ------- decided which candidate to hire for the position.

(A) already (B) soon
(C) still (D) yet

> **쉬운 토익 공식**
>
> not 뒤에 위치하는 빈칸이 부사 자리일 경우 yet이 정답이다.

UNIT 03 빈출 유형 공략 05

15. Now under new ownership, department heads are monitoring their spending ------- than before.

(A) closely (B) close
(C) more closely (D) closest

> 빈칸 뒤에 than이 있으면 비교급이 정답이다.

UNIT 03 빈출 유형 공략 06

16. Jimberland is pleased to release the ------- shoe in its limited edition line: the brogue Oxford shoe.

(A) popularity of (B) as popular as
(C) most popular (D) popular than

UNIT 04 빈출 유형 공략 01

17. Tour participants must be on time because the boat departs promptly ------- 7:00 A.M. tomorrow.

(A) for (B) from
(C) on (D) at

UNIT 04 빈출 유형 공략 02

18. Our carefully harvested coffee beans can be found ------- coffee shops all over the world.

(A) in (B) around
(C) from (D) on

UNIT 04 빈출 유형 공략 03

19. ------- the nice weather, the beach at Toto Resort had a lower-than-average number of visitors yesterday.

(A) Despite (B) Besides
(C) Concerning (D) However

UNIT 04 빈출 유형 공략 04

20. ------- growing public interest in healthy food products, Organic Grocery has seen increased profits.

(A) Aside from (B) On behalf of
(C) Owing to (D) Instead of

22 CHAPTER 1 PART 5&6 문법

UNIT 04 빈출 유형 공략 05

21. Plymouth Supplies can provide your staff ------- stylish and comfortable uniforms in a wide range of colors.

(A) besides
(B) inside
(C) from
(D) with

UNIT 04 빈출 유형 공략 06

22. The manager told Ms. Farrow to proofread these documents ------- her earliest convenience.

(A) in
(B) at
(C) on
(D) by

UNIT 05 빈출 유형 공략 01

23. About half of our packaging centers ------- in the UK.

(A) location
(B) is locating
(C) are located
(D) locates

UNIT 05 빈출 유형 공략 02

24. Both the manager and the director ------- to take business trips whenever necessary.

(A) are allowed
(B) was allowed
(C) has been allowed
(D) to allow

> 빈칸이 동사 자리이고 주어가 and로 연결되어 있으면 복수 동사가 정답이다.

UNIT 05 빈출 유형 공략 03

25. A new company policy that affords workers more rights ------- last week.

(A) have been enacted
(B) were enacted
(C) enacting
(D) was enacted

UNIT 05 빈출 유형 공략 04

26. The schedule for next month's training sessions ------- to this e-mail.

(A) were attaching
(B) is attaching
(C) are attached
(D) has been attached

UNIT 06 빈출 유형 공략 01

27. This new tablet ------- with the needs of digital artists in mind.

(A) to create
(B) has created
(C) will be creating
(D) was created

> 빈칸 뒤에 목적어가 없으면 수동태가 정답이다.

UNIT 06 빈출 유형 공략 02

28. Each passenger whose flight is delayed by more than three hours ------- a voucher for a free meal at the airport.

(A) giving
(B) will be given
(C) has given
(D) is giving

UNIT 06 빈출 유형 공략 03

29. The total cost of the renovation project ------- to be about half a million dollars over the initial budget.

(A) was expecting
(B) is expected
(C) has expected
(D) expects

UNIT 06 빈출 유형 공략 04

30. The proposal ------- to the executives tomorrow, so it should be completed by today.

(A) is being given
(B) was given
(C) had been given
(D) will give

UNIT 07 빈출 유형 공략 01

31. The schedule for the career fair ------- to participants later this week.

(A) will be e-mailed
(B) had been e-mailed
(C) was e-mailed
(D) to e-mail

문장에 미래를 나타내는 표현이 있으면 미래 시제가 정답이다.

UNIT 07 빈출 유형 공략 02

32. Next week, Jack's Hardware ------- a special event for its 10th anniversary.

(A) has hosted
(B) hosted
(C) will be hosting
(D) hosting

UNIT 07 빈출 유형 공략 03

33. Our customer service center ------- nearly 3,000 people over the past six months.

(A) assists
(B) is assisting
(C) will assist
(D) has assisted

문장에 for(~ 동안), since(~ 이래로), over(~에 걸쳐) 등이 있으면 현재완료 시제가 정답이다.

UNIT 07 빈출 유형 공략 04

34. Casablanca was forced to reschedule its grand opening when the furniture and silverware for the restaurant ------- on time.

(A) did not arrive
(B) not to arrive
(C) not to have arrived
(D) will not be arriving

24　CHAPTER 1　PART 5&6 문법

UNIT 07 빈출 유형 공략 05

35. Please mute your cell phone once the movie -------.

(A) will begin (B) was beginning
(C) begins (D) began

UNIT 07 빈출 유형 공략 06

36. If Ms. Melo had known Mr. Kao was feeling unwell, she ------- to go to the conference instead.

(A) would have offered (B) has offered
(C) is being offered (D) will offer

UNIT 08 빈출 유형 공략 01

37. A technician from the software company will be here tomorrow morning ------- a new word processor.

(A) be installing (B) installs
(C) to install (D) install

UNIT 08 빈출 유형 공략 02

38. Factory supervisors are responsible for ------- a safe work environment.

(A) maintain (B) to maintain
(C) maintaining (D) maintained

UNIT 08 빈출 유형 공략 03

39. The Seattle Zoo offers internships to undergraduates thinking about ------- a career in zoology.

(A) pursuing (B) pursuit
(C) pursues (D) pursued

UNIT 08 빈출 유형 공략 04

40. Home Medica's customers are eligible ------- a 25% off coupon if their purchase is over $50.

(A) receiving (B) to receive
(C) received (D) receiver

UNIT 09 빈출 유형 공략 01

41. All elevators in the building will be out of service for one hour from 10 A.M. in order to perform ------- maintenance.

(A) required (B) requiring
(C) require (D) requires

쉬운 토익 공식

빈칸이 시간 부사절의 동사 자리이고 문맥상 미래의 일을 나타내면 현재 시제가 정답이다.

선택지가 동사의 활용형으로 구성되어 있고 빈칸 앞에 전치사가 있으면 동명사가 정답이다.

빈칸 앞에 전치사가 있고 뒤에는 명사(구)가 있으면 동명사가 정답이다.

분사가 뒤에 오는 명사와 수동의 관계일 때는 과거분사가 정답이다.

UNIT 09 빈출 유형 공략 02

42. Every travel package ------- over $1,500 comes with a 15% discount on car rentals.

(A) prices (B) priced
(C) pricey (D) pricing

UNIT 09 빈출 유형 공략 03

43. When ------- in, conference attendees will need to present a valid form of identification.

(A) check (B) checked
(C) checking (D) to check

UNIT 09 빈출 유형 공략 04

44. ------- on January 2, the main entrance will be closed for one month while new doors are installed.

(A) Began (B) Beginning
(C) Begins (D) Begin

UNIT 10 빈출 유형 공략 01

45. The event is sold out online, ------- a few seats may be available for purchase at the venue.

(A) but (B) if
(C) nor (D) also

UNIT 10 빈출 유형 공략 02

46. Tardiness at Wednesday's staff meeting will not be accepted ------- we have an important visitor.

(A) because (B) until
(C) although (D) nevertheless

UNIT 10 빈출 유형 공략 03

47. The city government is analyzing the budget to determine ------- funding should go to public parks or libraries.

(A) another (B) into
(C) whether (D) elsewhere

UNIT 10 빈출 유형 공략 04

48. ------- some materials arrived late, the contractor was able to have the renovations completed ahead of schedule.

(A) Prior to (B) When
(C) Even though (D) Despite

쉬운 토익 공식

분사가 앞에 있는 명사와 수동의 관계일 때는 과거분사가 정답이다.

[접속사+분사] 구문에서 생략된 주어와 분사로 쓰인 동사가 능동의 관계이면 현재분사가 정답이다.

빈칸 뒤에 절이 있으면 접속사, 명사(구)가 있으면 전치사가 정답이다.

UNIT 11 빈출 유형 공략 01

49. Passengers ------- would like to upgrade their tickets to first class may do so on the Web site.

(A) who
(B) whose
(C) whoever
(D) to whom

> **쉬운 토익 공식**
>
> 빈칸 앞에 사람 명사가 있고 뒤에는 동사가 바로 이어지면 주격 관계대명사 who가 정답이다.

UNIT 11 빈출 유형 공략 02

50. According to sales figures ------- by Jerome's Technologies, company profits rose 3% last quarter.

(A) to release
(B) releasing
(C) released
(D) have released

> [주격 관계대명사+be동사]가 생략된 구조라면 과거분사가 정답이다.

UNIT 11 빈출 유형 공략 03

51. Raw milk is sanitized in steel pipes, ------- it is heated until safe to drink.

(A) who
(B) which
(C) when
(D) where

UNIT 11 빈출 유형 공략 04

52. The manager on duty should be notified ------- a customer makes a complaint.

(A) whenever
(B) which
(C) however
(D) in spite of

문법 진단 테스트 정답

1. (A)	**2.** (B)	**3.** (B)	**4.** (D)	**5.** (B)	**6.** (B)	**7.** (B)	**8.** (C)	**9.** (C)	**10.** (C)
11. (C)	**12.** (D)	**13.** (C)	**14.** (D)	**15.** (C)	**16.** (C)	**17.** (D)	**18.** (A)	**19.** (A)	**20.** (C)
21. (D)	**22.** (B)	**23.** (C)	**24.** (A)	**25.** (D)	**26.** (D)	**27.** (D)	**28.** (B)	**29.** (B)	**30.** (A)
31. (A)	**32.** (C)	**33.** (D)	**34.** (A)	**35.** (D)	**36.** (A)	**37.** (C)	**38.** (C)	**39.** (A)	**40.** (B)
41. (A)	**42.** (B)	**43.** (C)	**44.** (B)	**45.** (A)	**46.** (A)	**47.** (C)	**48.** (C)	**49.** (A)	**50.** (C)
51. (D)	**52.** (A)								

CHAPTER 1
PART 5 & 6
문법

실전에서 바로 써먹는
쉬운 토익 공식 인강

UNIT 01

명사

토익 기초 문법 OVERVIEW

빈출 유형 공략 01 관사/한정사/형용사 + 명사

빈출 유형 공략 02 주어와 목적어 역할을 하는 명사

빈출 유형 공략 03 사람 명사와 사물/추상 명사

빈출 유형 공략 04 복합 명사

ACTUAL TEST

UNIT 01 | 명사

토익 기초 문법 OVERVIEW

A 일반 명사에는 '가산명사(셀 수 있는 명사)'와 '불가산명사(셀 수 없는 명사)'가 있다. 가산명사는 하나를 나타낼 때에는 a/an과 함께 쓰이고, 여럿을 나타낼 때에는 복수형으로 쓰인다.

A car was parked in **a** no-parking **area**.
차 한 대가 주차 금지 구역에 주차되어 있었다.

Cars parked next to pedestrian **areas** will be towed.
인도 옆에 주차된 차량들은 견인됩니다.

B 불가산명사는 a/an과 함께 쓰이지 않으며, 복수로 쓰이지 않는다.

For further **information** / ~~**informations**~~, call 202-555-0123.
자세한 내용은 202-555-0123으로 문의하십시오.

The Savoy Theater will soon have new **equipment** / ~~**equipments**~~ installed.
Savoy Theater는 곧 새로운 장비를 설치할 것이다.

Thank you for your **cooperation** / ~~**cooperations**~~ and **support** / ~~**supports**~~.
귀하의 협조와 후원에 감사드립니다.

C 추상 명사는 대개 불가산명사이지만, 개별적이고 구체적인 의미로 쓰일 경우 가산명사로 쓰인다.

불가산명사	가산명사
Many flights are subject to **cancellation** due to the storm. 폭풍우로 인해 많은 항공편이 결항될 수 있다.	We will let you know if there are any **cancellations**. 취소가 생기면 알려 드리겠습니다.
Herb Cabinets has a reputation for **quality**. Herb Cabinets는 품질로 정평이 나 있다.	She has strong leadership **qualities**. 그녀는 강력한 지도자로서의 자질들을 지니고 있다.
He retired from the company after 25 years of **service**. 그는 그 회사에서 25년을 근무한 후 퇴직했다.	They offer **a** delivery **service** that ships to over 50 countries. 그들은 50개국 이상에 수송하는 배송 서비스를 제공한다.

D 한 단어가 명사와 동사로 쓰일 수 있다.

supply 공급; 공급하다	offer 제안, 할인; 제공하다	order 주문(품); 주문하다
pay 급여; 지불하다	access 접속; 접속하다	request 요구; 요구하다
transfer 이동; 이동하다	produce 농작물; 생산하다	launch 출시; 출시하다

Sign up to receive special **offers** by e-mail. 가입하셔서 이메일로 특별 할인을 받으세요.

He was **offered** the position of vice president. 그는 부사장직을 제안받았다.

특정 명사들은 항상 복수로만 쓰인다.

| belongings 소지품 | instructions 설명서; 지시 | savings 저축한 돈 | headquarters 본사 |

City Air is not responsible for any **belongings** / ~~belonging~~ left behind on the aircraft.
City Air는 기내에 남겨진 어떤 소지품에 대해서도 책임을 지지 않습니다.

He used his life **savings** / ~~saving~~ to start his own e-commerce company.
그는 평생 모은 돈을 자신의 전자 상거래 회사를 설립하는 데 사용했다.

 동사 또는 형용사에 접미사가 붙어 다양한 명사가 만들어질 수 있다.

접미사	명사		
-ment	pay**ment** 지불 supple**ment** 보충; 부록	employ**ment** 고용 assess**ment** 평가	invest**ment** 투자 arrange**ment** 약속
-ion	participat**ion** 참가 applicat**ion** 적용; 지원서	construct**ion** 건설, 공사 inspect**ion** 검사	submiss**ion** 제출 expans**ion** 확장
-ance	attend**ance** 참석 mainten**ance** 유지	assist**ance** 도움 perform**ance** 공연; 성과	allow**ance** 허용 accept**ance** 수락; 승인
-al	approv**al** 승인	renew**al** 갱신; 재개	arriv**al** 도착
-ee/-er/-or/-ant	employ**ee** 직원 employ**er** 고용주	attend**ee** 참석자 attend**ant** 안내원	visit**or** 방문객 applic**ant** 지원자
-ty/-ity	safe**ty** 안전 abil**ity** 능력, 재능	securi**ty** 보안 activi**ty** 활동	productiv**ity** 생산성 publici**ty** 홍보; 매스컴의 주목

기초 문법 CHECK

정답 및 해설 p.2

1~6. 밑줄 친 부분 중 가장 적절한 것을 고르세요.

1. I have attached information / informations about both car leasing companies.
2. We appreciate your support / supports and look forward to continuing to serve you.
3. Only those with valid licenses are authorized to operate heavy equipment / equipments.
4. Always use the tools specified in the instruction / instructions when installing.
5. A late pay / payment incurs a $50 fee.
6. The Hudson Hotel offers a special room rate for conference attendance / attendees.

빈출 유형 공략 01 관사/한정사/형용사 + 명사

Mr. Wood's ------- to the Paris branch was postponed until next year.
(A) transfer　　(B) to transfer　　(C) transferred　　(D) transferable

쉬운 토익 공식 빈칸 앞에 한정사가 있으면 명사가 정답이다.

풀이　빈칸 앞에 소유한정사 Mr. Wood's가 있으므로 빈칸에는 소유한정사의 수식을 받는 품사가 들어가야 한다. 따라서 명사인 (A) transfer가 정답이다.

해석　Mr. Wood의 파리 지사 전근이 내년으로 미뤄졌다.

유형 돋보기

① 명사 앞에는 관사, 한정사, 형용사, 분사 등의 수식어가 위치할 수 있다.

관사 + 명사　City council members voted on **the amendment** to the safety regulations.
시 의회 의원들은 안전 규정 수정안에 대해 투표를 진행했다.

형용사 + 명사　The product demonstration earned **huge applause**. 그 제품 시연회는 큰 찬사를 받았다.

② 가산명사 단수형과 복수형을 판별할 때는 빈칸 앞 부정관사의 유무와 동사의 단/복수형을 확인한다.

To cater to **a** larger customer **base** / ~~bases~~, Spring Café will soon add vegan dishes to its menu.
다양한 고객층을 만족시키기 위해 Spring Café는 곧 메뉴에 채식 요리를 추가할 것이다.

Extensive ~~repair~~ / **repairs** to the building **are** being carried out. 그 건물에 광범위한 수리가 진행되고 있다.

고득점 POINT

불가산명사로 착각하기 쉬운 가산명사		형태가 유사한 가산명사와 불가산명사	
an opening 공석	an appointment 약속, 예약	a permit 허가증	permission 허가
results 성과	precautions 예방책	a process 과정	processing 처리
instructions 설명(서)	benefits (급여 외) 수당	a cause 원인	caution 주의, 조심

Construction workers must use extreme ~~cause~~ / **caution** when working near pedestrians.
건설 노동자들은 보행자 근처에서 작업할 때 특히 주의를 기울여야 한다.

실전 감각 다지기

정답 및 해설 p.2

1. The north wing of the Hawkins Library houses a ------- of rare books.
   (A) collect　　(B) collectively
   (C) collective　　(D) collection

2. The museum cannot be opened to the public until structural ------- are repaired.
   (A) defect　　(B) defective
   (C) defects　　(D) defectively

3. Only employees of Harriet's Home Goods have ------- to access the storeroom.
   (A) permission　　(B) permitted
   (C) permissive　　(D) permit

4. Nicholas&Son and Johnston Co. have formed a mutually beneficial partnership to increase their -------.
   (A) profited　　(B) profitable
   (C) profitably　　(D) profits

빈출 유형 공략 02   주어와 목적어 역할을 하는 명사

Mr. Meyers was happy to receive ------- that his logo design was well liked among company executives.

(A) notify   (B) notification   (C) notifying   (D) notifies

쉬운 토익 공식 빈칸 앞에 타동사가 있으면 명사가 정답이다.

풀이   빈칸은 타동사 receive의 목적어 자리이므로 명사인 (B) notification이 정답이다.
해석   Mr. Meyers는 자신의 로고 디자인이 회사 중역들에게 좋은 반응을 얻었다는 얘기를 들어서 기분이 좋았다.

유형 돋보기

토익에서는 주어나 목적어 자리에 위치하는 명사 문제가 출제되기도 한다. 관사, 한정사, 형용사 등으로 빈칸이 명사 자리임을 판단할 수 있는 힌트가 없다면 빈칸이 문장에서 어떤 역할을 하는지 파악해야 한다.

주어   **Renovations** would give Carlos's Mexican Paradise an interior design upgrade.
리모델링 작업으로 Carlos's Mexican Paradise의 인테리어가 업그레이드될 것이다.

목적어   This shea butter cream provides **relief** from extreme dryness.
이 시어 버터 크림은 악건성 피부를 진정시켜 준다.

전치사의 목적어   Restaurant owners should make sure their kitchens are ready **for inspection** at all times.
식당 주인들은 주방이 언제든 점검받을 수 있도록 준비해 놓아야 한다.
→ 명사는 전치사 뒤에 위치하여 전치사의 목적어 역할을 할 수 있다.

고득점 POINT 빈칸 앞이나 뒤에 명사가 이미 있다고 해서 빈칸을 다른 품사 자리라고 속단해서는 안 된다. [명사 + 명사] 구조로 된 명사구도 주어나 목적어 역할을 할 수 있다.

Coral Construction sought city **approval** / ~~approved~~ to build a new apartment complex.
Coral Construction은 새 아파트 단지를 조성하기 위해 시 승인을 구했다.
→ city approval이 sought(seek의 과거형)의 목적어 역할을 하고 있다.

실전 감각 다지기

정답 및 해설 p.2

1. ------- to the law firm's internship depends on university transcripts, interview skills, and recommendations.

(A) Accept   (B) Acceptance
(C) Acceptable   (D) Acceptably

2. O'Brian's has no problem with restaurant guests who want to make menu -------.

(A) substituted   (B) substituting
(C) substitutions   (D) to substitute

3. With its new logo and marketing strategy, Sistema Inc. is headed in the direction of -------.

(A) successful   (B) successfully
(C) succeed   (D) success

4. Ms. Nolan offers her workers ------- in their maternity and paternity leave.

(A) flexible   (B) flex
(C) flexibility   (D) flexed

빈출 유형 공략 03 — 사람 명사와 사물/추상 명사

Fleming Institute's time management seminar teaches ------- how to use their time productively.
(A) participatory (B) participants (C) participation (D) participated

풀이 빈칸은 타동사 teach의 목적어 역할을 하는 명사 자리이다. 명사인 (B) participants와 (C) participation 중에서 문맥상 '참가자'를 뜻하는 (B)가 정답이다.
해석 Fleming Institute의 시간 관리 세미나는 참가자들에게 시간을 생산적으로 쓰는 방법을 알려 준다.

유형 돋보기

빈칸이 명사 자리이고 선택지에 명사가 두 개라면 문맥에 어울리는 명사를 골라야 한다. 다음은 토익에 세트로 출제되는 사람 명사와 사물/추상 명사들이다.

사람 명사	사물/추상 명사	사람 명사	사물/추상 명사
publisher 출판인, 출판사	publication 출판(물), 발행	depositor 예금주	deposit 보증금
subscriber 구독자	subscription 구독(료)	communicator 전달자	communication 의사소통; 연락
producer 생산자, 제작자	production 생산	collector 징수원; 수집가	collection 수집
manager 관리자	management 관리	competitor 경쟁자, 경쟁사	competition 경쟁(자); 대회
accountant 회계사	account 계좌; 거래처; 거래	contributor 기여자	contribution 기여
applicant 지원자	application 지원(서), 신청(서)	committee 위원회	commitment 의무, 책무; 약속; 헌신
participant 참가자	participation 참가	representative 대표자	representation 대표; 표현, 묘사

Unfortunately, that service is only available to **subscribers** / ~~subscription~~.
아쉽지만 그 서비스는 구독자만 이용할 수 있습니다.

고득점 POINT 추상 명사를 불가산명사로 단정하여 부정관사만 보고 사람 명사를 정답으로 선택해서는 안 된다. 추상 명사도 셀 수 있는 경우가 많으므로 반드시 문맥도 살펴서 정답을 골라야 한다.
The voluntary organizations made a **contributor** / contribution to the safety of the town.
그 봉사 단체들은 도시의 안전에 이바지했다.

실전 감각 다지기

정답 및 해설 p.3

1. The city government has formed a ------- to help deal with citizens' complaints.
(A) committee (B) commit
(C) committed (D) commitment

2. An ------- to film a movie scene at Kingsdale High School was submitted to its principal.
(A) apply (B) applicable
(C) application (D) applicant

3. The photography in this ------- is considered some of the best in the magazine industry.
(A) publish (B) publisher
(C) publishing (D) publication

4. Trust Bank informs ------- of new savings account rates and available credit cards.
(A) depositing (B) deposit
(C) depositors (D) deposits

빈출 유형 공략 04 복합 명사

Our system sends an e-mail ------- to online shoppers who haven't completed their purchases.
(A) remind (B) reminding (C) reminded (D) reminder

풀이 빈칸 앞의 e-mail과 어울려 '이메일 알림'을 의미하는 게 문맥상 자연스러우므로 (D) reminder가 정답이다.
해석 우리는 시스템상 구입을 완료하지 않은 온라인 고객에게 이메일 알림을 보냅니다.

유형 돋보기

복합 명사는 두 개의 명사가 결합하여 하나의 명사로 쓰이는 것을 말한다. 토익에서는 복합 명사의 첫 번째나 두 번째 자리에 명사를 채우는 문제로 출제된다.

tourist attraction 관광지, 관광 명소	flight arrangements 항공편 일정
security/vacation policy 보안/휴가 정책	earnings growth 수익 성장
cancellation fee 취소 수수료	job creation 일자리 창출
expiration date 유효 기간, 만기일	sales event 할인 행사
building management 건물 관리	warranty certificate 품질 보증서
e-mail reminder (약속, 일정 등을) 상기시키기 위한 이메일	budget surplus/deficit 예산 흑자/적자
service fee[charge] 서비스 요금	safety regulation 안전 규정
baggage allowance 수하물 허용량	price reduction 가격 인하

Employees can now take more time off thanks to the company's new **vacation policy**.
회사의 새로운 휴가 정책 덕분에 직원들은 이제 더 많은 휴가를 쓸 수 있다.

The **budget deficit** has led the company to pull back its latest advertising campaign.
예산 적자로 인해 그 회사는 최신 광고를 중단하게 되었다.

고득점 POINT 빈칸이 복합 명사의 첫 번째 자리에 있을 경우 형용사나 분사를 정답으로 선택하지 않도록 주의해야 한다.
The botanic garden is the most popular **tourist** / ~~touristic~~ attraction in Cincinnati.
그 식물원은 신시내티에서 가장 인기 있는 관광지이다.

실전 감각 다지기

1. Restaurant managers should always check ------- dates when restocking their kitchens.
   (A) expire (B) expiring
   (C) expiration (D) to expire

2. ------- regulations at the local factory have prevented countless injuries.
   (A) Safe (B) Safer
   (C) Safely (D) Safety

3. There is a significant service ------- if your checked luggage is over 25 kilograms.
   (A) charge (B) charges
   (C) charging (D) chargeable

4. The new tax incentives in Blissfield are expected to encourage job ------- among small businesses.
   (A) create (B) creating
   (C) creation (D) created

ACTUAL TEST

1. The written ------- between HC Media and the band clearly outlined the terms for licensing the music.
   (A) agrees
   (B) agreement
   (C) agreeable
   (D) agreeably

2. The company's ------- policy mandates that employees create strong passwords to protect their data.
   (A) secure
   (B) security
   (C) securely
   (D) secured

3. Because of unexpected competition, the store still had an ------- of one hundred televisions left in stock.
   (A) excessive
   (B) excess
   (C) exceedingly
   (D) exceeding

4. We would like to congratulate Ms. Kent for her great work on the Norbert -------.
   (A) accounted
   (B) account
   (C) accountant
   (D) accountable

5. Because of a broken dental drill, all dentist ------- made for today must be rescheduled.
   (A) appointed
   (B) appoint
   (C) appointment
   (D) appointments

6. Many ------- to *EcoFriendly Magazine* have opted to receive digital copies in order to reduce their environmental impact.
   (A) subscribers
   (B) subscriptions
   (C) subscribing
   (D) subscribed

7. Mr. Kumar, the head of building -------, sent employees an e-mail to notify them about potential noise from next week's construction.
   (A) manage
   (B) managing
   (C) management
   (D) manageable

8. Housekeeping ------- are free for all guests and will be performed once a day.
   (A) service
   (B) serviced
   (C) services
   (D) servicing

9. Murphy Co.'s extensive market research gives its clients ------- of trends that may affect their business.
   (A) predicted
   (B) predictions
   (C) predictable
   (D) predict

10. Despite being the largest ------- of textiles in the country, Grenadine's Fabrics has seen a steady decline in profits.
    (A) productive
    (B) producing
    (C) production
    (D) producer

Questions 11-14 refer to the following advertisement.

Cordova Realty is ------- a full-time administrative assistant for its Roxbury branch. The role mainly consists of filing documents, updating its property database, ------- answering incoming phone calls, as outlined in our standard contract. Paid vacation time and quarterly performance bonuses are also guaranteed for the -------. A minimum of two years' experience in office work is preferred. We will provide training on how to use our specialized software. -------. Applications should be sent to hr@cordova-realty.com no later than October 3.

11. (A) suggesting
    (B) applying
    (C) hiring
    (D) offering

12. (A) and
    (B) so
    (C) yet
    (D) once

13. (A) employ
    (B) employment
    (C) employee
    (D) employing

14. (A) The office manager has chosen the most qualified person for the job.
    (B) Similarly, most of our employees commute to work by public transportation.
    (C) The new policy will go into effect on the first of next month.
    (D) Furthermore, professional development workshops are held throughout the year.

CHAPTER 1
—
PART 5&6
문법

실전에서 바로 써먹는
쉬운 토익 공식 인강

UNIT 02

대명사와 한정사

토익 기초 문법 OVERVIEW

빈출 유형 공략 01 인칭대명사

빈출 유형 공략 02 재귀대명사

빈출 유형 공략 03 these와 those

빈출 유형 공략 04 one, other, another

빈출 유형 공략 05 some과 any

빈출 유형 공략 06 수량을 나타내는 대명사와 한정사

ACTUAL TEST

UNIT 02 | 대명사와 한정사

토익 기초 문법 OVERVIEW

A 대명사에는 인칭대명사, 지시대명사, 부정대명사가 있다.

인칭대명사	자신이나 상대방, 제삼자를 구별함 (I, we, you, he, she, they 등)
지시대명사	사람이나 사물 등 특정한 대상을 가리킴 (this, these, that, those)
부정대명사	정해지지 않은 불특정한 대상을 대신함 (one, others, the others, another 등)

B 인칭대명사는 사람이나 사물을 가리키는 대명사로, 수와 성별, 격에 따라 형태가 달라진다.

인칭/수		격 주격 (~은/~는/~이/~가)	목적격 (~을/~를/~에게)	소유한정사 (~의)	소유대명사 (~의 것)	재귀대명사 (~자신/~스스로)
1인칭	단수	I	me	my	mine	myself
	복수	we	us	our	ours	ourselves
2인칭	단수	you	you	your	yours	yourself
	복수	you	you	your	yours	yourselves
3인칭	단수	he	him	his	his	himself
		she	her	her	hers	herself
		it	it	its	-	itself
	복수	they	them	their	theirs	themselves

C 3인칭 대명사 it은 앞에 이미 언급되었거나 현재 이야기되고 있는 사물, 동물, 또는 상황을 가리킨다.

Please sign **the attached contract** and return **it** to me at your earliest convenience.

첨부된 계약서에 서명하시고 빠른 시일 내에 저에게 돌려주시기 바랍니다.

Miki Travel has focused on a unique type of tourism and **it** has paid off.

Miki Travel은 독특한 형태의 관광에 초점을 맞췄고 그 효과를 봤다.

Giant Technologies offers **its** employees flexibility in their working hours.
　　　　　　　　= Giant Technologies'
Giant Technologies는 직원들이 근무 시간을 융통성 있게 쓰도록 해 준다.

D 지시대명사 those는 종종 뒤에 오는 분사구나 관계사절의 수식을 받는다.

Those interested in transferring to the Leesburg branch should contact Ms. Grant.
리즈버그 지점으로 옮기고 싶은 분들은 Ms. Grant에게 연락해야 합니다.

Those who wish to join the 3:00 P.M. seminar should register by noon today.
오후 3시 세미나에 참석하고자 하는 분은 오늘 정오까지 등록하셔야 합니다.

E 부정대명사 one은 앞에 언급된 명사를 대신하여 사용하며, 반드시 앞에 한정사(a/an, the, this, your 등)가 온다. (단, ones는 한정사 없이 사용 가능하다.)

Negotiating is a critical **skill**, yet many people find it <u>a</u> difficult **one** to master.
협상은 중요한 능력이지만 많은 사람들은 그것을 숙달하기 어려운 능력으로 여긴다. (one = skill)

New **washing machines** are more energy efficient than <u>the</u> old **ones**.
새 세탁기는 오래된 세탁기보다 에너지 효율이 더 높다. (ones = washing machines)

We suggest substituting natural **sweeteners** for artificial **ones** in your favorite recipes.
우리는 당신이 좋아하는 요리법에서 인공 감미료를 천연 감미료로 대체할 것을 제안합니다. (ones = sweeteners)

F 한정사는 명사 앞에 쓰이며, 명사의 의미를 한정하거나 수 또는 양을 한정하는 역할을 한다.

명사의 의미를 한정	관사	a, an, the	+ 명사
	지시한정사	this, these, that, those	
	소유한정사	my, our, your, his, her, its, their	
수 또는 양을 한정	수량한정사	(a) few, fewer, (a) little, many, much, more, most, some, any, every, all, both 등	

G 한정사 all과 every는 같은 뜻이지만 쓰임이 다르다.

- □ all + 복수 명사, every + 단수 명사 → **all** employee**s**   **every** employee
- □ all 다음에는 다른 한정사가 올 수 있다. → <u>**all**</u> / ~~every~~ his files   <u>**all**</u> / ~~every~~ this food
- □ every 다음에는 불가산명사를 쓸 수 없다. → <u>**all**</u> / ~~every~~ (the) information

기초 문법 CHECK

정답 및 해설 p.5

1~6. 밑줄 친 부분 중 가장 적절한 것을 고르세요.

1. The sales team should use the accounting department's printer while <u>theirs / their</u> is being replaced.
2. Lillard Ltd. announced today that <u>it / he</u> will be merging with Quester Inc.
3. The Kadiri Hotel is centrally located and has <u>its / other</u> own restaurant.
4. The course is intended for <u>those / these</u> interested in medical careers.
5. For one week only, Yellow Coffee is giving away a free coffee mug with <u>all / every</u> order of 30 dollars or more.
6. Burpee is the exclusive provider for <u>all / every</u> his restaurants.

빈출 유형 공략 01 인칭대명사

Faraway Travel can book various accommodations for ------- stay, either at a hotel or at a hostel.
(A) you   (B) your   (C) yours   (D) yourself

쉬운 토익 공식 명사 앞에 빈칸이 있으면 소유한정사가 정답이다.

풀이 빈칸 앞에 전치사 for가 있고 뒤에는 명사 stay가 있으므로 빈칸에는 명사를 수식하는 말이 들어가야 한다. 따라서 소유한정사인 (B) your가 정답이다.

해석 Faraway Travel에서는 귀하가 머물 다양한 숙소를 호텔이든 호스텔이든 예약해 드릴 수 있습니다.

유형 돋보기

1. 주어 자리에는 주격, 목적어 자리에는 목적격, 명사 앞에는 소유한정사를 쓴다.

- **주격** The Web site is now unavailable as **it** is undergoing routine maintenance.
  그 웹사이트는 정기 점검을 하고 있기 때문에 현재 이용할 수 없다.

- **목적격** The committee elected **him** as their representative. 그 위원회는 그를 대표로 선출했다.

- **소유한정사** Before signing **her** contract with Core Design, Ms. Lee carefully read the fine print.
  Core Design과의 계약서에 서명하기 전에 Ms. Lee는 세세한 항목들도 꼼꼼하게 읽었다.

2. 소유대명사는 주어, 보어, 목적어 자리에 위치할 수 있다.

- **주어** Ms. Powell asked her coworker to lend her a laptop because **hers** is under repair.
  Ms. Powell은 자신의 노트북이 수리 중이어서 동료 직원에게 노트북을 빌려 달라고 했다.

- **보어** If you create an account with Kashata Bank, this planner is **yours**, free of charge.
  Kashata Bank에 계좌를 개설하시면 이 다이어리를 무료로 고객님께 드립니다.

- **목적어** After completing her report, Ms. Boyd helped Mr. Ward finish **his**.
  자신의 보고서 작성을 완료한 후에 Ms. Boyd는 Mr. Ward가 보고서를 마무리하는 걸 도왔다.

- **전치사의 목적어** Our interest rates are lower **than theirs**.
  우리의 이율은 그들의 이율보다 낮습니다.

실전 감각 다지기

정답 및 해설 p.5

1. The department manager will give ------- the new schedule for the summer season.
   (A) we   (B) us
   (C) our   (D) ourselves

2. The presenters were surprised because ------- slides were in black and white instead of color.
   (A) their   (B) them
   (C) they   (D) themselves

3. A coworker of ------- will be taking a business trip to Ulaanbaatar in a few weeks.
   (A) my   (B) myself
   (C) me   (D) mine

4. As soon as the permit for the stadium was approved, residents started wondering how ------- might affect the community.
   (A) us   (B) it
   (C) theirs   (D) yours

빈출 유형 공략 02 재귀대명사

Ms. Smith likes to handle the finer details ------- to ensure that they are done right.
(A) she (B) herself (C) her (D) hers

쉬운 토익 공식 빈칸이 없어도 모든 문장 구조를 갖춘 완전한 문장이라면 재귀대명사가 정답이다.

풀이 빈칸 앞에 [주어(Ms. Smith) + 동사(likes) + 목적어(to ~ details)] 구조의 완전한 문장이 있으므로 빈칸에는 생략해도 문장이 성립할 수 있는 말이 들어가야 한다. 따라서 재귀대명사인 (B) herself가 정답이다.

해석 Ms. Smith는 모든 걸 확실히 하기 위해 아주 세세한 부분도 직접 처리하고 싶어 한다.

유형 돋보기

① 주어와 목적어가 동일한 대상일 때 목적어 자리에 재귀대명사를 쓴다. 이때 재귀대명사는 문장의 구성 성분이므로 생략할 수 없다.

William's Groceries transformed **itself** from a small business into a huge enterprise in only two years.
William's Groceries는 단 2년 만에 작은 사업체에서 거대한 기업으로 변모했다.

② 주어나 목적어를 강조하기 위해 재귀대명사를 쓰기도 한다. 이때 재귀대명사는 생략할 수 있다.

Ms. Reid was proud of her new luxury clothing line because she made all the designs **(herself)**.
Ms. Reid는 모든 디자인을 그녀가 직접 했기 때문에 자신의 새로운 럭셔리 의류 브랜드에 자부심이 있었다.

③ 꼭 알아야 하는 재귀대명사 관용 표현

by oneself 혼자서 (= alone, on one's own)

Ms. Watson will lead the meeting **by herself** since her partner suddenly called in sick today.
오늘 Ms. Watson의 동료가 갑자기 병가를 내서 그녀 혼자 회의를 주관할 것이다.

Mr. Haslam tried solving the problem **on his own** before asking an IT consultant for help.
Mr. Haslam은 IT 컨설턴트에게 도움을 요청하기 전에 혼자 문제 해결을 시도했다.

for oneself 혼자 힘으로, 스스로, 직접

The manager wanted to check the new products **for herself**.
관리자는 신상품들을 직접 확인하길 원했다.

실전 감각 다지기

1. For the team building exercises, workers were asked to organize ------- into groups of four.
   (A) their (B) them
   (C) themselves (D) they

2. Staying past work hours, Ms. Shaw finished the assignment -------.
   (A) she (B) hers
   (C) herself (D) her own

3. Thousands of comments have been posted on the topic, while the article ------- was only one paragraph long.
   (A) its (B) itself
   (C) they (D) themselves

4. Mr. Wilson was determined to take on this task by -------, but he realized he needed some assistance.
   (A) his (B) himself
   (C) him (D) he

빈출 유형 공략 03 — these와 those

------- who take a vacation for over a week should make sure their work is covered by their colleagues.
(A) These   (B) Those   (C) That   (D) They

쉬운 토익 공식 빈칸이 주격 관계대명사절의 수식을 받으면 those가 정답이다.

풀이 빈칸은 주격 관계대명사절(who ~ a week)의 수식을 받는 자리이다. 따라서 선택지 중 관계사절의 수식을 받을 수 있는 (B) Those가 정답이다.

해석 일주일 이상 휴가를 내는 사람은 반드시 동료 직원이 자신의 업무를 대신할 수 있도록 해야 한다.

유형 돋보기

1 these와 those는 각각 this와 that의 복수형으로, 지시대명사나 지시한정사로 쓰인다.

Marketers know that advertisements with bright colors and catchy slogans do better than **those** without **these** elements.
마케터들은 밝은 색과 기억하기 쉬운 문구가 있는 광고가 이러한 요소들이 없는 것보다 더 효과가 있다는 걸 안다.
→ those는 advertisements를 대신하는 지시대명사로, these는 elements를 수식하는 지시한정사로 쓰였다.

2 those는 분사구나 주격 관계대명사절의 수식을 받는다.

This program is intended for **those interested in social media management**.
이 프로그램은 소셜 미디어 관리에 관심 있는 사람들을 위한 것이다.

Those who wish to sign up for the workshop should let Ms. Jones know.
워크숍 신청을 원하는 사람들은 Ms. Jones에게 알려야 한다.
→ those who 뒤에는 복수 동사가 이어지고, anyone과 everyone은 who 뒤에 단수 동사가 이어진다는 걸 함께 알아 두자.

실전 감각 다지기

정답 및 해설 p.6

1. Mr. Kroll asked ------- who want to attend the product demonstration to contact him directly.
   (A) they   (B) those
   (C) them   (D) everyone

2. The research showed that stores which have a rewards program had more repeat customers than ------- that did not.
   (A) this   (B) itself
   (C) those   (D) fewer

3. Please wrap ------- vases in additional packaging material as they are extremely fragile.
   (A) each   (B) these
   (C) else   (D) this

4. The commercial real estate prices in Southfield are significantly lower than ------- in Sherwood.
   (A) another   (B) few
   (C) those   (D) that

빈출 유형 공략 04 — one, other, another

The editor-in-chief will review the garments and choose the best ------- to put on the cover.
(A) it   (B) that   (C) one   (D) other

풀이 빈칸에는 최상급 the best의 수식을 받는 동시에 앞에서 언급된 garment를 대신할 수 있는 말이 들어가야 한다. 문맥상 정해지지 않은 대상을 나타내야 하므로 부정대명사인 (C) one이 정답이다.

해석 편집장은 의상들을 검토하고 나서 표지에 실을 최고의 의상을 선택할 것이다.

유형 돋보기

❶ one vs. it

The tire was replaced with a new **one** because **it** was flat. 그 타이어는 펑크가 나서 새 타이어로 교체되었다.
→ one은 앞에 언급된 타이어와 종류는 같지만 전혀 다른 타이어를 말하며, it은 펑크가 나서 교체가 필요한 바로 그 타이어를 가리킨다.

❷ (the) other vs. another

While **other companies** tend to follow trends, the handbags at LACY are always classic styles.
다른 회사들은 유행을 따르는 경향이 있는 반면에, LACY의 핸드백은 항상 고전적인 스타일을 고수한다.
→ other는 '(이미 언급된 것 외에) 불특정한 나머지 몇몇'을 의미하는 한정사로 복수 명사나 불가산명사를 수식한다.

Journalism experience separates Mr. Garrison from **the other candidates** for the position.
언론계 경력은 Mr. Garrison을 그 직책의 다른 후보들과 차별화하는 요소이다.
→ the other는 '(이미 언급된 것 외에) 나머지 전부'를 의미하며, 한정사로 쓸 때는 단수나 복수 명사를 수식한다.

Mr. Lee couldn't join the meeting because of **another appointment** he had.
Mr. Lee는 또 다른 일정 때문에 그 회의에 참석할 수 없었다.
→ another는 '(이미 언급된 것과 같은 종류의) 또 다른 하나'를 의미하며, 한정사로 쓸 때는 단수 명사를 수식한다.

고득점 POINT '서로'를 뜻하는 each other와 one another는 목적어 자리에만 쓰며, 's를 붙여 소유한정사 형태로도 쓸 수 있다.

The manufacturers are in competition with **each other(= one another)** on electric mobility.
그 제조사들은 전기 자동차 분야에서 서로 경쟁 관계이다.

실전 감각 다지기

1. After getting positive reviews on her new coffee blend, Ms. Darden decided to formulate -------.
   (A) every   (B) other
   (C) anyone   (D) another

2. To distinguish itself from ------- companies, Lance's Electronics uses a unique logo and color scheme.
   (A) other   (B) each
   (C) another   (D) every

3. The sales team members do their best to help ------- close deals and increase the overall revenue for the company.
   (A) another one   (B) each other
   (C) yourself   (D) everything

4. We will consider all candidates and pick the ------- who is best suited for the role of lead designer.
   (A) one   (B) one another
   (C) each other   (D) others

빈출 유형 공략 05 — some과 any

Please make sure you report ------- abnormalities with the software to the IT department.
(A) another   (B) each   (C) any   (D) something

풀이 빈칸은 복수 명사 abnormalities를 수식하는 자리이므로 (C) any가 정답이다. (A) another와 (B) each는 단수 명사를 수식하기 때문에 답이 될 수 없다.

해석 그 소프트웨어에 발생하는 오류는 무엇이든 반드시 IT 부서에 보고해 주세요.

유형 돋보기

1 some은 '몇몇(의), 약간(의)'라는 의미로 대명사나 한정사로 쓰이며, 불명확한 양이나 수를 나타낸다. 한정사일 때는 가산명사 단수형과 복수형, 그리고 불가산명사를 모두 수식할 수 있다.

대명사 Only **some** of the applicants will be interviewed for the position.
지원자 중 일부만 그 직무의 면접을 볼 것이다.

한정사 **Some international events** take place at the McLean Convention Center.
몇몇 국제 행사들은 McLean Convention Center에서 개최된다.

Mr. Tsunoda recommended adding **some upscale furniture** to the main lobby.
Mr. Tsunoda는 중앙 로비에 고급 가구 몇 채를 추가할 것을 권했다.

2 any는 긍정문에서는 '모든'의 의미를, 부정문에서는 '전혀'의 의미를 강조하며, 조건문에서는 '어떤 ~라도'의 의미로 쓰인다. some과 마찬가지로 any도 한정사일 때는 가산명사 단/복수형과 불가산명사를 모두 수식할 수 있다.

긍정문 **Any** of these logos would suit our new line of automobiles.
이 로고들은 어느 것이라도 우리의 새로운 자동차 라인에 잘 어울릴 것이다.

부정문 Mr. Kamau tried to get a ticket but there weren't **any** left.
Mr. Kamau는 표를 구하려고 노력했지만 남은 표가 전혀 없었다.

3 someone 누군가, something 무언가 vs. anyone 누구든, anything 어느 것이든

We need **something** that draws consumers' attention. 우리는 소비자의 주목을 끌 무언가가 필요하다.

Anyone wishing to attend the AI conference should contact Ms. McCracken.
AI 콘퍼런스에 참석하고자 하는 사람은 누구든 Ms. McCracken에게 연락해야 한다.

실전 감각 다지기

정답 및 해설 p.7

1. The annual performance reviews didn't reveal ------- negative about the people working in our department.
   (A) itself   (B) anything
   (C) each   (D) someone

2. ------- will have to supervise the kitchen at Bistrona while the executive chef is away.
   (A) Something   (B) Any
   (C) Each other   (D) Someone

3. Management will offer special perks for ------- of the staff who clearly demonstrate excellent sales capabilities.
   (A) everyone   (B) everywhere
   (C) some   (D) anything

4. A safety label is attached to the product to prevent ------- accidents with children.
   (A) another   (B) each
   (C) any   (D) something

빈출 유형 공략 06   수량을 나타내는 대명사와 한정사

Belladonna Makeup is giving away ------- free items with purchases of $100 or more.
(A) each   (B) much   (C) several   (D) every

풀이   빈칸은 복수 명사 free items를 수식하는 자리이므로 (C) several이 정답이다. (A) each와 (D) every는 단수 명사를 수식하고, (B) much는 불가산명사를 수식하기 때문에 답이 될 수 없다.
해석   Belladonna Makeup은 100달러 이상을 구매하면 몇 가지 사은품을 준다.

유형 돋보기

❶ each/every + 단수 명사 ➜ 단수 동사
Each/Every product comes with a five-year warranty.   각/모든 제품에는 5년 품질 보증서가 딸려 온다.

❷ each of + 복수 명사 ➜ 단수 동사
Each of the sessions **lasts** approximately 40 minutes.   각 세션은 대략 40분간 진행됩니다.

❸ several, many (+ of the) + 복수 명사 ➜ 복수 동사
Several complaints about the product **were** posted online.   그 제품에 대한 여러 불만이 온라인에 게시되었다.

❹ all, more, most (+ of the) + 복수 명사/불가산명사 ➜ 복수 동사/단수 동사
All items **are** 30% off this week.   이번 주에 모든 제품은 30% 할인됩니다.
Most equipment in the laboratory **is** 10 years old or more.
그 실험실에 있는 기구 대부분은 10년 이상 된 것들이다.

고득점 POINT   every와 all은 명사를 수식하는 한정사이므로 앞에 관사나 소유한정사가 위치하지 않는다. 그러나 whole과 entire는 형용사이므로 명사를 수식할 때 반드시 앞에 관사나 소유한정사가 있어야 한다.
Every investment firm is interested in the software company.   모든 투자 회사가 그 소프트웨어 회사에 관심이 있다.
The **whole** process will take a week to complete.   모든 과정은 완료하는 데 일주일이 걸릴 것이다.

실전 감각 다지기

1. After the HR department does its initial screening, the executives will choose ------- candidates to interview with the CEO.
   (A) another   (B) several
   (C) either   (D) whichever

2. Our managers ensure that ------- product is of the highest quality.
   (A) complete   (B) all
   (C) every   (D) entire

3. Mr. Lambert was surprised that ------- of his coworkers wrote him a letter for his retirement party.
   (A) every   (B) anyone
   (C) all   (D) other

4. The Dove Hotel is within walking distance of ------- fine shopping and dining options.
   (A) another   (B) much
   (C) every   (D) many

ACTUAL TEST

1. Tour participants should not leave ------- items of value on the bus.
   (A) any
   (B) each
   (C) whether
   (D) every

2. The CEO of Stockton Tech usually gives new employees a building tour -------.
   (A) he
   (B) his
   (C) him
   (D) himself

3. On the production line, quality control managers ensure that ------- product meets the necessary safety standards.
   (A) all
   (B) most
   (C) each
   (D) several

4. The office was having electrical issues, and the electrician believed ------- were due to last night's storm.
   (A) it
   (B) them
   (C) they
   (D) any

5. One of the candidates had a strong résumé, but the ------- had better interpersonal skills.
   (A) each
   (B) it
   (C) other
   (D) them

6. Ms. Duda is trying to persuade the executives to postpone the product launch until ------- team is ready.
   (A) she
   (B) her
   (C) hers
   (D) herself

7. For this month only, Whitetail is offering free delivery and installation on ------- kitchen appliances.
   (A) every
   (B) anyone
   (C) each
   (D) all

8. ------- are the mid-year goals that we need to reach by the end of the month.
   (A) These
   (B) Another
   (C) That
   (D) Something

9. The workers at the construction site forgot to label their tools, so they are not sure which are -------.
   (A) themselves
   (B) theirs
   (C) their
   (D) they

10. The shuttle bus is unavailable for now, so ------- who want to get a ride to the event will not be able to do so.
    (A) the other
    (B) everyone
    (C) someone
    (D) those

Questions 11-14 refer to the following information.

Graystone Publishing House is holding its annual Graystone Creative Writing Competition. This competition is open to amateur writers. In previous years, our firm ------- many new talented writers through this event. Some of those writers are now working full-time as professional authors. Submissions will be accepted through our Web site, www.graystonepublishing.com, from April 1 to 15. We offer three categories—short stories, poetry, and essays—so that writers can express ------- fully. The ------- for each category differ, so be sure to check the word count and other details carefully. Writers can submit up to three pieces of writing for consideration. Unlike many other writing contests, there is no fee for entry. -------.

11. (A) occupied
    (B) preserved
    (C) discovered
    (D) entered

12. (A) their
    (B) theirs
    (C) them
    (D) themselves

13. (A) identifications
    (B) locations
    (C) requirements
    (D) warranties

14. (A) This author has another novel coming soon.
    (B) It's a great time to put your writing to the test.
    (C) Your enthusiasm really impressed the judging panel.
    (D) The publishing industry has a few market leaders.

CHAPTER 1
—
PART 5 & 6
문법

실전에서 바로 써먹는
쉬운 토익 공식 인강

UNIT 03

형용사와 부사

토익 기초 문법 OVERVIEW

빈출 유형 공략 01 형용사 자리

빈출 유형 공략 02 혼동하기 쉬운 형용사

빈출 유형 공략 03 부사 자리

빈출 유형 공략 04 주의해야 할 부사

빈출 유형 공략 05 원급과 비교급 비교

빈출 유형 공략 06 최상급 비교

ACTUAL TEST

UNIT 03 | 형용사와 부사

토익 기초 문법 OVERVIEW

A 형용사는 명사 앞에서 명사를 꾸며 주거나, be동사/연결동사 뒤에 오는 보어 역할을 한다.

형용사 + 명사	It was a highly **successful** campaign. 그것은 매우 성공적인 캠페인이었다.
be동사 + 형용사	The roads were **crowded** with holiday traffic. 도로는 휴일 차량으로 붐볐다.
연결동사 + 형용사	Its sales have remained **steady** for the last three years. 그것의 매출은 지난 3년간 꾸준히 유지되어 왔다. Mr. Brown couldn't stay **long** because he had a meeting at three. Mr. Brown은 세 시에 회의가 있어 오래 있을 수가 없었다.

B -thing, -one으로 끝나는 단어는 형용사가 뒤에서 수식한다.

They wanted to do **something special** for the retiring director.
그들은 퇴직하는 본부장을 위해 뭔가 특별한 것을 해 주고 싶었다.

It's the perfect way to create a memorable gift for **someone special**.
그것은 특별한 사람을 위해 기억에 남는 선물을 만드는 완벽한 방법입니다.

C [find, have, make + 목적어 + 목적격 보어] 구조에서, 형용사는 목적격 보어로 쓰일 수 있다.

> Many employees **found** the program quite **easy** to use.
>   동사   목적어   목적격 보어
> 많은 직원들이 그 프로그램이 상당히 사용하기 편리하다고 여겼다.

We aim to **have** the mobile libraries **ready** for use as early as next May.
우리는 빠르면 내년 5월에 이동 도서관을 이용할 수 있도록 하는 것을 목표로 하고 있다.

We require bolder investments to **make** the business **profitable**.
그 사업을 수익성 있게 만들려면 더 과감한 투자가 필요하다.

D 혼동하기 쉬운 분사(-ing/-ed) 형태의 형용사들

현재분사(-ing) 형태의 형용사들	과거분사(-ed) 형태의 형용사들
remaining candidates 남아 있는 후보들 **aspiring** writers 작가 지망생들 a **promising** young artist 촉망받는 젊은 예술가 a **surrounding** area 주변 지역 a **convincing** argument 설득력 있는 주장 a **rewarding** job 보람 있는 일 a **leading** supplier 선도적인 공급업체	**qualified** employees 자격을 갖춘 직원들 **detailed** information 구체적인 정보 **assorted** beverages 여러 가지 음료 an **accomplished** author 뛰어난 작가 a **balanced** diet 균형 잡힌 식사 a **licensed** institution 인가받은 기관 an **experienced** photographer 노련한 사진작가

부사는 동사, 형용사, 다른 부사(구), 문장 전체를 꾸민다.

동사 수식	The main hall was **completely** renovated last spring. 본관은 지난봄에 완전히 개축되었다.
형용사 수식	Wholesale food stores are becoming **increasingly** popular. 도매 식품점이 점점 더 인기를 끌고 있다.
부사 수식	Once the program is installed, it runs **completely** automatically. 일단 프로그램이 설치되면 완전히 자동으로 실행됩니다.
문장 수식	**Unfortunately**, our policies do not allow refunds. 안타깝게도 정책상 환불을 허용하지 않습니다.

 -ly가 붙었지만 형용사인 단어들

timely 시기적절한, 때맞춘	likely ~할 것 같은 (↔ unlikely)	costly 비싼, 비용이 많이 드는
friendly 친절한, 상냥한	orderly 정돈된, 질서 있는	neighborly (이웃 간에) 우호적인
oily 기름진	lively 활발한	elderly 나이 든

We respond to all e-mails in a **timely** manner. 우리는 모든 이메일에 늦지 않게 답한다.
The building repairs will be **costly**. 건물 수리 비용이 많이 들 것이다.

기초 문법 CHECK

정답 및 해설 p.9

1~8. 밑줄 친 부분 중 가장 적절한 것을 고르세요.

1. <u>Successful / Success</u> candidates will be posted to either Maryland or New Jersey.
2. The fitness center will stay <u>open / opening</u> three extra hours Monday through Friday.
3. It'll take us some time to find someone <u>suitable / suitably</u>.
4. Long presentations will make the audience <u>restless / restlessly</u>.
5. The bookstore will host a book signing event with <u>accomplished / accomplishing</u> author Jonathan Bate.
6. The Web site is an incredibly useful resource for <u>aspired / aspiring</u> architects.
7. The new location of the Vien Art Museum is <u>easy / easily</u> accessible by car or bus.
8. In the <u>unlikeness / unlikely</u> event that you are not satisfied with your delivery, returns can be made within 14 days of purchase.

빈출 유형 공략 01 형용사 자리

Hiring an outside firm to perform the inspection will help to guarantee an ------- assessment.
(A) object	(B) objection	(C) objective	(D) objecting

쉬운 토익 공식 빈칸 앞에 관사가 있고 뒤에는 명사가 있으면 형용사가 정답이다.

풀이 빈칸 앞에 부정관사 an이 있고 뒤에는 명사 assessment가 있으므로 빈칸은 명사를 수식하는 형용사 자리이다. 따라서 (C) objective가 정답이다.

해석 그 조사를 수행하기 위해 외부 회사를 고용하는 것은 객관적인 결과를 보장하는 데 도움이 될 것이다.

유형 돋보기

❶ 형용사는 명사 앞에 위치한다.

Retro Luxury is an **excellent place** to browse antiques, collectibles, and vintage items.
Retro Luxury는 골동품과 소장 가치가 있는 물건, 그리고 빈티지 제품들을 둘러보기에 아주 좋은 장소이다.

The prizes are awarded for the most **creative business ideas**.
그 상은 가장 창의적인 사업 아이디어에 수여된다.

❷ 형용사는 보어 자리에 위치하여 주어나 목적어를 보충 설명한다.

주격 보어 The new traffic signals at the intersection are now fully **functional**.
그 교차로의 새로운 신호등은 현재 완전히 제대로 작동하고 있다.

목적격 보어 Attention to detail makes Ms. Rose **reliable** and **easy** to work with.
꼼꼼한 성격 덕분에 Ms. Rose는 믿을 만하고 함께 일하기 편한 사람이다.

고득점 POINT 빈칸이 형용사 자리이고 선택지에 형용사와 분사가 있으면 형용사가 정답일 확률이 높다.

Key Corporation has developed into a highly **profitable** / **profiting** business over the last few years.
Key Corporation은 지난 몇 년 사이에 매우 수익성이 좋은 회사로 발전했다.

실전 감각 다지기

정답 및 해설 p.9

1. New employees will watch an ------- video about how to assemble the device.
   (A) instruct	(B) instructing
   (C) instructional	(D) instructed

2. The safe in your hotel room is designed to keep your valuables -------.
   (A) securing	(B) security
   (C) secures	(D) secure

3. The LED lights outside this boutique are extremely ------- to persuade pedestrians to enter the shop.
   (A) bright	(B) brightest
   (C) brightly	(D) brightness

4. The Malaysian branch of our company has had continuous growth because of several ------- advertising campaigns.
   (A) successful	(B) success
   (C) succeed	(D) to succeed

빈출 유형 공략 02 혼동하기 쉬운 형용사

------- experience in logistics is required for the position at Tribebolt Ltd.
(A) Managed (B) Managers (C) Manageable (D) Managerial

풀이 빈칸 뒤에 명사가 있으므로 빈칸은 형용사 자리이다. 선택지 중에서 의미상 experience를 수식하기에 가장 적절한 것은 '경영[관리]의'를 뜻하는 (D) Managerial이다.

해석 물류 관리 경험은 Tribebolt Ltd.의 그 직책에 필요하다.

유형 돋보기

형태는 비슷하지만 뜻이 달라서 혼동하기 쉬운 형용사를 주의해야 한다.

manageable 처리하기 쉬운	respective 각자의, 각각의	beneficial 유익한
managerial 경영[관리]의	respectable 존경할 만한	beneficent 인정 많은
responsible 책임이 있는	successful 성공한	complimentary 무료의; 칭찬하는
responsive 즉각 반응하는	successive 연속의	complementary 보완하는
favorable 호의적인; 유리한	confidential 기밀의	sensitive 세심한; 예민한
favorite 가장 좋아하는	confident 자신감 있는	sensible 분별 있는
considerable 상당한	economic 경제의	comprehensive 종합적인
considerate 사려 깊은	economical 경제적인	comprehensible 이해할 수 있는
prospective 장래의; 곧 있을	dependent 의존하는	appreciative 고마워하는
prosperous 번영하는	dependable 믿을 만한	appreciable 상당한
advisable 바람직한	reliable 믿을 수 있는	arguable 논쟁의 여지가 있는
advisory 자문의	reliant 의존적인	argumentative 따지고 드는

Please take great care when handling **confidential** / ~~confident~~ information from clients.
고객들의 기밀 정보를 취급할 때는 각별히 주의해 주세요.

The cafeteria in Boros Hall offers **complimentary** / ~~complementary~~ lunch for conference attendees.
Boros Hall에 있는 식당에서 학회 참석자들에게 무료 점심 식사를 제공한다.

실전 감각 다지기

정답 및 해설 p.10

1. According to recent surveys, most guests' ------- part of the resort is the rooftop lounge.
   (A) favors (B) favorable
   (C) favorite (D) favorably

2. Without ------- information, stock traders would not be able to handle their clients' investments in a responsible manner.
   (A) relying (B) reliable
   (C) reliant (D) reliability

3. The success of our new product is ------- on our marketing team's strategy.
   (A) depends (B) depended
   (C) dependable (D) dependent

4. KL Sneakers expects a ------- turnout for their new sneaker launch.
   (A) considerable (B) considerate
   (C) considerately (D) consideration

빈출 유형 공략 03 부사 자리

Ms. Wheeler ------- encouraged her team members to attend the technology seminar.
(A) stronger   (B) strengthen   (C) strongly   (D) strength

쉬운 토익 공식 빈칸 뒤에 타동사가 있으면 부사가 정답이다.

풀이 빈칸 앞에 주어 Ms. Wheeler가 있고 뒤에는 타동사 encourage가 있으므로 빈칸은 부사 자리이다. 따라서 (C) strongly가 정답이다.

해석 Ms. Wheeler는 팀원들이 그 기술 세미나에 참석하도록 적극 독려했다.

유형 돋보기

토익에 빈출되는 부사 자리 문제는 아래와 같이 크게 여섯 가지 유형으로 정리할 수 있다.

부사 + 타동사	The food critic **favorably reviewed** the chef's special dishes served at Franco's Italian Restaurant. 그 음식 비평가는 Franco's Italian Restaurant에서 내놓은 그 요리사의 특선 요리들을 좋게 평했다.
자동사 + 부사	Bing Motors' sales figures **increased significantly**. Bing Motors의 판매량이 상당히 증가했다.
부사 + 형용사	The local bookstore has a **surprisingly large** selection of children's books. 그 지역 서점에는 놀라울 정도로 많은 아동 도서가 있다.
be동사 + 부사 + p.p.	The heater temperature **is easily adjusted** by a remote control. 히터 온도는 리모컨으로 쉽게 조절된다.
조동사 + 부사 + 동사	The Grand Ballroom **can comfortably accommodate** up to 300 people. Grand Ballroom은 300명까지 무리 없이 수용할 수 있다.
have + 부사 + p.p.	The sales manager **has successfully negotiated** contracts with a wide variety of corporate clients. 그 판매 담당자는 다양한 분야의 기업 고객들과 성공적으로 계약을 협상해 왔다.

실전 감각 다지기

정답 및 해설 p.10

1. Managers have been facing ------- difficult decisions regarding hiring temporary workers.
   (A) increases   (B) increase
   (C) increasingly   (D) to increase

2. This project will only be successful if team leaders can get everyone to work -------.
   (A) collaborate   (B) collaboratively
   (C) collaboration   (D) collaborating

3. After the reading, the author will ------- sign copies of his new novel for fans.
   (A) personality   (B) personalization
   (C) personally   (D) personal

4. The store's refund policy is ------- stated on its Web site.
   (A) clear   (B) clearing
   (C) clearest   (D) clearly

빈출 유형 공략 04 주의해야 할 부사 ★★★

Human Resources has not ------- decided which candidate to hire for the position.
(A) already (B) soon (C) still (D) yet

쉬운 토익 공식 not 뒤에 위치하는 빈칸이 부사 자리일 경우 yet이 정답이다.

풀이 빈칸은 조동사 have와 과거분사 decided 사이의 부사 자리이다. 문맥상 아직 결정하지 못했다는 의미가 되어야 하는데, 빈칸 앞에 not이 있으므로 (D) yet이 정답이다.

해석 인사 팀은 그 직책에 어떤 후보를 채용할지 아직 결정하지 못했다.

유형 돋보기

1 still vs. yet

still과 yet은 모두 '아직'을 의미하는데, still은 not 앞에 위치하고 yet은 not 뒤에 위치한다.

The price for the new laptop **still** has**n't** been decided. 새 노트북의 가격은 아직 정해지지 않았다.

The items have**n't** arrived **yet** because of stock shortages. 재고 부족 때문에 그 제품들은 아직 도착하지 않았다.

2 quite vs. enough

quite는 동사, 형용사, 부사를 앞에서 수식하고 enough는 뒤에서 수식한다.

The training session was **quite** informative and motivating. 그 연수는 꽤 유익하고 동기 부여가 되었다.

The venue is large **enough** to hold 50 audience members. 그 장소는 관객 50명을 수용할 정도로 충분히 넓다.

3 very vs. so

very와 so는 둘 다 형용사, 부사를 수식할 수 있는데, so는 뒤에 that절이 이어질 수 있다.

The advertisement is in the middle of Times Square, making it **very** visible to onlookers.
그 광고는 타임스 스퀘어 한복판에 있어서 구경하는 사람들의 눈에 잘 띈다.

Juicy Co.'s new flavor was **so** popular **that** it sold out of every store within hours.
Juicy Co.가 선보인 새로운 맛은 매우 인기가 많아서 몇 시간 만에 모든 매장에서 매진되었다.

실전 감각 다지기

정답 및 해설 p.10

1. Organizing a company-wide conference is ------- difficult for a relatively new employee.
   (A) how   (B) early
   (C) quite   (D) enough

2. Even though the price of ingredients increased, Mike's Pizzeria ------- won't raise its menu prices.
   (A) finally (B) yet
   (C) since   (D) still

3. The advertising campaign was ------- successful that the sales goals were achieved faster than anticipated.
   (A) so   (B) such
   (C) very   (D) many

4. Members of the publicity team need to be organized ------- to work on multiple projects throughout the workday.
   (A) already (B) quite
   (C) neither (D) enough

빈출 유형 공략 05 — 원급과 비교급 비교

Now under new ownership, department heads are monitoring their spending ------- than before.
(A) closely (B) close (C) more closely (D) closest

쉬운 토익 공식 빈칸 뒤에 **than**이 있으면 비교급이 정답이다.

풀이 빈칸은 동사구 are monitoring을 수식하는 부사 자리이며, 빈칸 뒤에 비교 대상을 나타내는 전치사 than이 있으므로 closely의 비교급인 (C) more closely가 정답이다.

해석 이제 새로운 소유주의 체제 아래에서 부서장들은 지출을 전보다 더 주의 깊게 관리하고 있다.

유형 돋보기

1. 원급 비교

The new laptop is nearly **as thin** / ~~thinly~~ **as** the previous one.
새 노트북은 거의 예전 것만큼 두께가 얇다.
→ as와 as 사이에 들어갈 말이 주격 보어 역할을 하면 형용사를 쓰고, 동사를 수식하면 부사를 쓴다.

2. 비교급 비교

The latest SUV by Eighto Motors is **more spacious** / ~~spaciously~~ **than** it looks.
Eighto Motors의 신형 SUV는 보이는 것보다 공간이 넓다.
→ is의 주격 보어 역할을 해야 하므로 형용사인 spacious를 쓴다.

Buses to downtown run **less** ~~frequent~~ / **frequently than** they used to.
시내로 가는 버스는 예전보다 덜 자주 운행한다.
→ 동사 run을 수식해야 하므로 부사인 frequently를 쓴다.

Owing to the closure of Macon Bridge, traffic congestion in the city was **far worse than** usual.
Macon Bridge의 폐쇄로 인해 그 도시의 교통 체증은 평소보다 훨씬 더 심해졌다.
→ 비교급 강조 부사인 much, even, still, far, a lot은 비교급 앞에 위치하여 '훨씬 더 ~한'의 의미를 더한다.

Clothery produces cotton T-shirts that are **noticeably softer than** its competitors.
Clothery는 경쟁사들보다 현저히 더 부드러운 면 티셔츠를 생산한다.
→ noticeably(두드러지게), considerably(상당히), significantly(상당히)도 비교급을 강조할 수 있다.

실전 감각 다지기

정답 및 해설 p.11

1. Because employees here feel valued, their productivity levels are ------- than average.
(A) higher (B) highness
(C) highly (D) highest

2. Few companies can advertise a product as ------- as PW Marketing Firm can.
(A) efficiency (B) efficiently
(C) more efficiently (D) more efficient

3. To draw more attention to the poster, the designers decided to make the colors even -------.
(A) boldness (B) bold
(C) boldly (D) bolder

4. The newly released Voyager Prime Phone is ------- larger than its five-year-old counterpart.
(A) better (B) very
(C) ever (D) much

빈출 유형 공략 06 최상급 비교

Jimberland is pleased to release the ------- shoe in its limited edition line: the brogue Oxford shoe.

(A) popularity of   (B) as popular as   (C) most popular   (D) popular than

풀이 빈칸 앞에 정관사 the가 있고 뒤에는 명사 shoe가 있으므로 빈칸은 명사를 수식하는 형용사 자리이다. 문맥상 '가장 인기 있는 신발'이라고 하는 게 자연스러우며, 이때 최상급 표현을 위해 정관사 the와 함께 쓸 수 있어야 하므로 (C) most popular가 정답이다.

해석 Jimberland는 한정판 제품으로 가장 인기 있는 신발인 브로그 옥스퍼드화를 선보이게 되어 기쁩니다.

유형 돋보기

1 최상급 비교

Of the four new turtleneck designs, the one with white polka dots is **the most popular**.
새로운 터틀넥 디자인 네 개 중에서 하얀 물방울무늬가 있는 것이 가장 인기 있다.

Steelswitch became **the largest** steel company in the country.
Steelswitch는 그 나라에서 제일 큰 철강 회사가 되었다.

2 최상급 강조 부사와 위치

Strong interpersonal skills are **by far the most important** qualifications for the position.
뛰어난 대인 관계 기술은 그 직책에서 단연코 가장 중요한 자질이다.
→ by far, even, much, quite는 최상급 앞에 위치한다.

Road Plex offers **the very latest** traffic conditions on its Web site.
Road Plex는 웹사이트에 가장 최신 교통 상황을 제공한다.
→ very는 [the + very + 최상급] 구조로 쓴다.

An influx of investors has made this **the most prosperous** year **yet** for Infot Technologies.
투자자의 유입으로 올해는 Infot Technologies의 역사상 가장 번창하는 해가 되었다.
→ ever와 yet은 최상급 뒤에 위치한다.

실전 감각 다지기

정답 및 해설 p.11

1. The ------- health benefit of this supplement is its ability to breakdown fat.

(A) greater   (B) greatest
(C) greatly   (D) most greatly

2. The advertisement emphasized the fact that Glit's new laptop is the slimmest ------- to be released.

(A) ever   (B) very
(C) quite   (D) well

3. ------- the newest interns have the opportunity to take part in significant projects.

(A) Following   (B) Including
(C) Similar   (D) Even

4. Though customer satisfaction is crucial to any restaurant, food safety is actually the ------- element of a successful establishment.

(A) as essential   (B) most essential
(C) essentially   (D) more essentially

ACTUAL TEST

1. BT News gets a lot of traffic to its Web site because it advertises ------- on social media.
   (A) heavy
   (B) heavily
   (C) heavier
   (D) heaviest

2. The recruits seem ------- to start their first day on the job.
   (A) eagerly
   (B) more eagerly
   (C) eager
   (D) eagerness

3. The Mumbai branch had the ------- sales numbers out of the whole global sales team.
   (A) highest
   (B) higher
   (C) highly
   (D) height

4. Because she was unfamiliar with the software, one of the trainees ------- printed 10 extra banners for Traylyn Inc.
   (A) accident
   (B) accidental
   (C) accidents
   (D) accidentally

5. Tony's Electronics always has generous discounts so customers can feel ------- they are not being overcharged for their purchases.
   (A) confide
   (B) confidential
   (C) confident
   (D) confiding

6. Though he seems intimidating, the CEO is a ------- understanding leader.
   (A) remarks
   (B) remarked
   (C) remarkable
   (D) remarkably

7. Gracie's Fashions' ------- manufacturing process allows it to pay workers fairly and pass discounts on to consumers.
   (A) economics
   (B) economize
   (C) economical
   (D) economies

8. The company's president and vice president both gave excellent speeches, although their styles were ------- different.
   (A) quite
   (B) concerning
   (C) enough
   (D) such

9. Investgain's new CEO, Rachel Fendley, has made ------- improvements since taking on her current role.
   (A) notices
   (B) noticeable
   (C) notice
   (D) noticeably

10. To the average buyer, the mini tablet is ------- more attractive than the extra-large one.
    (A) very
    (B) quite
    (C) strongly
    (D) considerably

Questions 11-14 refer to the following e-mail.

To: All staff
From: Jin Baek
Date: March 24
Subject: Urgent

On March 28, Avery Investments will move its offices to the Murphy Building. This ------- will
                                                                                  11.
ensure that we have enough space to take on more employees as our business grows. It will be
convenient for employees to use the café on the building's ground floor. I think you'll also enjoy
the ------- meeting rooms in our unit. Sorry that we have ------- time to make the necessary
    12.   **13.**
preparations. On March 27, all employees will be packing up the office rather than performing
their regular business duties. -------.
                               14.

Sincerely,

Jin Baek
Support Services Manager

11. (A) addition
(B) supplement
(C) treatment
(D) relocation

12. (A) privately
(B) private
(C) privacy
(D) privatize

13. (A) each
(B) both
(C) few
(D) little

14. (A) Please find attached the vacation schedule.
(B) You are thus encouraged to wear casual clothing.
(C) Each year, we recognize hard-working employees.
(D) Some branches may hold their own training.

CHAPTER 1
PART 5 & 6
문법

실전에서 바로 써먹는
쉬운 토익 공식 인강

UNIT 04

전치사

토익 기초 문법 OVERVIEW

빈출 유형 공략 01 시간을 나타내는 전치사

빈출 유형 공략 02 장소를 나타내는 전치사

빈출 유형 공략 03 기타 빈출 전치사

빈출 유형 공략 04 빈출 전치사구

빈출 유형 공략 05 동사/명사/형용사 + 전치사

빈출 유형 공략 06 전치사 관용 표현

ACTUAL TEST

UNIT 04 | 전치사

토익 기초 문법 OVERVIEW

A 전치사 뒤에는 명사, 대명사, 동명사, 명사절이 온다.

전치사 + 명사	JD Motors has not experienced any delays **in production**. JD Motors는 어떠한 생산 지연도 겪은 적이 없었다.
전치사 + 대명사	Ms. Lewis had to reschedule an appointment **with them**. Ms. Lewis는 그들과 약속 시간을 다시 정해야 했다.
전치사 + 동명사	Many local artists are interested **in participating** in the fair. 지역의 많은 예술가들이 그 박람회 참가에 관심을 가지고 있다.
전치사 + 명사절	Ms. Lee will present an overview **of what the Web site will look like**. Ms. Lee는 그 웹사이트가 어떤 모습일지에 대해 대략적으로 발표할 것이다.

B 전치사구는 [전치사 + 명사/대명사/동명사]로 이루어진 구로서, 문장 내에서 명사를 수식하는 형용사 또는 동사 및 문장을 수식하는 부사 역할을 한다.

• 형용사 역할: 명사 수식

Ms. Lopez will arrange **the schedule of events**.
Ms. Lopez가 이벤트들의 일정을 조정할 것이다.

Cannon Corporation is exploring **the possibility of extending** its market to Asia.
Cannon Corporation은 아시아로 시장을 확대할 수 있는 가능성을 모색하고 있다.

• 부사 역할: 동사 및 문장 수식

The opening of the restaurant **was postponed until September**.
그 식당의 개업은 9월로 연기되었다.

As a result, Shop City has closed its flagship store after only two years in Belgium.
그 결과, Shop City는 벨기에에서 불과 2년 만에 주력 매장의 문을 닫았다.

C 동사가 전치사와 결합하여 하나의 동사처럼 쓰이는 구동사의 경우, 전치사 뒤에 명사가 오더라도 전치사구로 묶을 수 없다. 이때 전치사 뒤의 명사는 구동사의 목적어가 된다.

Rosetown is **looking for ways** to attract tourists. 로즈타운은 관광객을 유치할 방법을 찾고 있다.
                     구동사 + 목적어

Mr. Miller is **going over the budget proposal**. Mr. Miller가 그 예산안을 검토할 것이다.
              구동사 + 목적어

D 전치사 at, on, in은 시간을 나타낸다.

at	**at** 6 o'clock 6시 정각에 **at** 6 A.M./P.M. 오전/오후 6시에 **at** noon/night 정오에/밤에	**at the** time of registration 등록 시점에 **at the** beginning of the week 주초에 **at the** end of the year 연말에
on	**on** July 20 7월 20일에 **on** Monday(s) 월요일에/월요일마다 **on** opening day 개업식에	**on the** weekends 주말에 **on the** day of the event 이벤트 당일에 **on the** date of issue 발행일에
in	**in** 2021 2021년에 **in** (the) summer/winter 여름에/겨울에 **in** the summer months 여름철에 **in** (early/late) July 7월(초/말)에	**in the** morning/evening 아침에/저녁에 **in the** past/future 과거에/미래에 **in the** near future 가까운 미래에 **in his** absence 그가 부재중일 때에

E 전치사 at, on, in은 장소를 나타낸다.

at 특정 지점 및 장소	Recycling receptacles will be placed **at** the entrances of the park. 재활용 휴지통이 공원 입구에 놓일 것이다. The conference will be held **at** the Volos Hotel. 그 콘퍼런스는 Volos Hotel에서 열릴 것이다.
on ~의 위에 또는 표면에	The ceremony will be held **on** the third floor of the Hillside Hotel. 그 행사는 Hillside Hotel 3층에서 열릴 예정이다. Any schedule changes will be posted **on** the boards down the hall. 일정 변경 사항은 복도 게시판에 게시됩니다.
in 넓은 장소나 영역, 위치, 내부	Our hotel is located **in** the heart of Rome. 우리 호텔은 로마의 중심가에 위치해 있습니다. We offer Internet access **in** every room. 우린 모든 방에 인터넷을 제공합니다.

기초 문법 CHECK

정답 및 해설 p.13

1~6. 밑줄 친 부분 중 가장 적절한 것을 고르세요.

1. The new branch will not be in operate / operation until July 1.
2. Mr. Scott will finalize his agreement with our / us this Friday.
3. Many employees are interested in attend / attending the conference.
4. The Lotus Restaurant offers a special dinner in / on Saturdays.
5. Employees get paid at / on the end of every month.
6. The store is located in / on the shopping center at the corner of Lakeview Avenue.

빈출 유형 공략 01   시간을 나타내는 전치사   ★★★

Tour participants must be on time because the boat departs promptly ------- 7:00 A.M. tomorrow.

(A) for   (B) from   (C) on   (D) at

풀이   빈칸 뒤에 구체적인 시각을 나타내는 7:00 A.M.이 있으므로 (D) at이 정답이다.
해석   배가 내일 오전 7시 정각에 출발하기 때문에 투어에 참석하시는 분들은 반드시 늦지 않게 오셔야 합니다.

유형 돋보기

1

at
at은 구체적인 시각을 나타낼 때 쓰고 특정 시각이나 시점을 나타내는 말이 이어진다.
every evening **at** 6:00 P.M.
매일 오후 6시에
at the beginning of the month
월초에

on
on은 at보다 넓은 범위의 시간 개념을 나타내며, 뒤에 날짜, 요일, 특정일을 나타내는 말이 이어진다.
on February 25
2월 25일에
on the first day of class
수업 첫날에

in
in은 연도, 계절, 월, 오전/오후 등을 나타낼 때 쓴다. 또한 in 뒤에 숫자가 포함된 시간 표현이 오면 '~ 후에'를 의미할 수 있다.
in winter/March/the evening
겨울/3월/저녁에
start **in** 10 minutes
10분 후에 시작하다

2 시점을 나타내는 전치사

by ~까지   submit **by** 3:00 P.M. today 오늘 오후 3시까지 제출하다[제출을 완료하다]
until ~까지   be open **until** 9:00 P.M. 오후 9시까지 (계속) 열려 있다
                   → by는 특정 시점까지 행위가 '완료됨'을, until은 특정 시점까지 행위가 '지속됨'을 나타낼 때 쓴다.
from ~부터   **from** mid-March **to** the end of April 3월 중순부터 4월 말까지
since ~ 이래로   **since** October of last year 작년 10월 이래로

3 기간을 나타내는 전치사

during ~ 동안   **during** the previous quarter 지난 분기 동안   **during** the presentation 발표 동안
for ~ 동안   **for** approximately two days 대략 이틀 동안   **for** the past three years 지난 3년간
                   → during 뒤에는 특정 활동/사건이나 시점(the event, the meeting, the night, …)을 나타내는 말을 쓰고, for 뒤에는 구체적인 숫자로 표현된 기간을 쓴다.
within ~ 내에   **within** two weeks of purchase 구매 후 2주 내에
throughout ~ 내내   **throughout** the entire construction period 전체 공사 기간 내내

실전 감각 다지기

정답 및 해설 p.13

1. Visitors to La Tortilla ------- Saturday were pleased with the Super Salsa Special.

    (A) beside   (B) in
    (C) on   (D) also

2. Because of slow business in the winter months, Polly's Ice Cream Parlor will not reopen ------- May.

    (A) until   (B) always
    (C) by   (D) into

빈출 유형 공략 02 장소를 나타내는 전치사

Our carefully harvested coffee beans can be found ------- coffee shops all over the world.
(A) in   (B) around   (C) from   (D) on

풀이 빈칸 뒤에 장소를 나타내는 명사구 coffee shops가 있으므로 비교적 넓은 장소 및 내부를 나타낼 때 쓰는 전치사인 (A) in이 정답이다.
해석 저희가 심혈을 기울여 수확한 커피콩을 전 세계 커피숍에서 만나 보실 수 있습니다.

유형 돋보기

1

at	on	in
at은 특정 지점이나 위치를 구체적으로 나타낼 때 쓴다.	on은 거리, 층수, 표면 위 등을 나타낼 때 쓴다.	in은 넓은 지역이나 장소, 무언가의 내부를 나타낼 때 쓴다.
at the counter 카운터에서	**on** Minerva Street 미네르바가에	**in** the world 세계에서
at the bus stop 버스 정류장에서	**on** the second floor 2층에	**in** the city 도시에서
at the job fair 취업 박람회에서	**on** the bulletin board 게시판에	**in** the library 도서관에서

2 장소/위치를 나타내는 전치사

between (둘) 사이에 — be situated **between** the mountains and the sea 산과 바다 사이에 위치해 있다
among (셋 이상) 사이에 — find the letter **among** the papers 서류들 사이에서 그 편지를 발견하다
within ~ 내에 — **within** walking distance 걸어서 갈 수 있는 거리 내에
throughout ~ 전역에 — be located **throughout** the airport 공항 전역에 위치해 있다
above ~ 위에; ~을 넘는 — be posted **above** the window 창문 위에 붙어 있다
around ~ 주변에 — the hiking trail **around** Lake Raven 레이븐 호수 주변의 등산로

3 이동/방향을 나타내는 전치사

from ~로부터, ~에서부터 — **from** different regions of the world 세계 각지로부터
through ~을 통하여; ~을 거쳐 — enter **through** the main entrance 정문을 통하여 입장하다
across ~을 가로질러; ~ 전역에 — directly **across** the street 도로 바로 맞은편에
along ~을 따라서 — roadwork **along** Highway 57 57번 고속 도로를 따라 진행되는 도로 공사

실전 감각 다지기

정답 및 해설 p.13

1. Highland Tower is a well-known tourist spot, and it is only four miles away ------- the airport.

   (A) from   (B) since
   (C) under   (D) besides

2. This apartment is ------- walking distance of many popular attractions, making it prime real estate.

   (A) under   (B) within
   (C) along   (D) among

빈출 유형 공략 03 | 기타 빈출 전치사

------- the nice weather, the beach at Toto Resort had a lower-than-average number of visitors yesterday.
(A) Despite (B) Besides (C) Concerning (D) However

풀이 빈칸 뒤에 명사구 the nice weather가 있고, 문맥상 날씨가 좋았음에도 해변 방문객이 적었다는 내용이 되는 게 자연스러우므로 '~에도 불구하고'를 뜻하는 전치사 (A) Despite가 정답이다.
해석 화창한 날씨에도 불구하고 어제 Toto Resort의 해변은 방문객이 평소보다 적었다.

유형 돋보기

도구/방법/수단 with ~와 함께; ~을 가지고   without ~ 없이   by (방법, 수단 등)으로
With its exquisite seasonal menus, Mucho Gusto is the most popular restaurant in town.
최고의 계절 메뉴로 Mucho Gusto는 시내에서 가장 유명한 식당이다.

대상/주제 about, on, over ~에 대하여   regarding, concerning ~에 대하여
If you need more information **about** the new product, please visit our Web site.
그 신제품에 대한 정보가 더 필요하면 저희 웹사이트를 방문해 주세요.

양보 despite ~에도 불구하고   notwithstanding ~에도 불구하고
Despite being located in a desolate area, Clara's business has been thriving in its first year.
외진 지역에 위치해 있음에도 불구하고 Clara의 사업은 첫해에 굉장히 잘 되었다.

추가/제외 besides ~ 외에도   including ~을 포함하여   excluding ~을 제외하고
Besides teaching finance at a college, Mr. Liu writes a weekly column for a local newspaper.
Mr. Liu는 대학에서 금융학 수업을 하는 것 외에 지역 신문에 주간 칼럼 연재도 한다.

기타 following ~을 따라; ~ 후에   like/unlike ~처럼/~와 달리   as ~로서
Willard Carswell was hired **as** a representative of Hype Consultancy.
Willard Carswell은 Hype Consultancy의 대표로 채용되었다.

실전 감각 다지기

1. Next week, our manager plans to inform us of issues ------- client confidentiality.
   (A) concerning (B) throughout
   (C) above   (D) following

2. Ms. Almaraz was offered the promotion mainly because of her remarkable skills ------- a corporate trainer.
   (A) in   (B) to
   (C) as   (D) at

빈출 유형 공략 04 빈출 전치사구

------- growing public interest in healthy food products, Organic Grocery has seen increased profits.

(A) Aside from (B) On behalf of (C) Owing to (D) Instead of

풀이 문맥상 대중의 관심이 높아져서 Organic Grocery의 이익이 증가했다는 내용이 되는 게 자연스러우므로 '~ 때문에'를 뜻하는 (C) Owing to가 정답이다.

해석 몸에 좋은 식품에 대한 대중의 관심이 높아진 덕분에 Organic Grocery는 이익이 증가했다.

유형 돋보기

이유/양보
- because of ~ 때문에
- due to ~ 때문에
- owing to ~ 때문에
- on account of ~ 때문에
- thanks to ~ 덕분에
- in spite of ~에도 불구하고

Because of transportation delays, some conference participants arrived late.
교통이 지연되어 학회 참석자 몇 명이 늦게 도착했다.

추가/제외
- in addition to ~ 외에도
- on top of ~ 외에도
- except (for) ~을 제외하고
- apart[aside] from ~ 외에도, ~ 뿐만 아니라(= in addition to); ~을 제외하고(= except (for))

Apart from his success as a chef, Francis also has several bestselling books.
Francis는 요리사로 성공했을 뿐만 아니라 베스트셀러 책도 몇 권 냈다.

Most mall employees left early for Christmas **apart from** the security guards.
보안 직원들을 제외하고 쇼핑센터 직원들은 대부분 크리스마스에 일찍 퇴근했다.

기타
- in front of (위치상) ~의 앞에
- prior to (시간상) ~ 전에
- according to ~에 따르면
- regardless of ~에 관계없이
- instead of ~ 대신에
- on behalf of ~을 대표[대신]하여
- along with ~와 함께, ~을 비롯하여
- rather than ~라기 보다는

On weekends during the winter months, the store closes at 5:30 P.M. **instead of** 7:00 P.M.
그 가게는 겨울 주말에 오후 7시 대신 오후 5시 30분에 문을 닫는다.

실전 감각 다지기

1. Mr. Benton decided to keep his new restaurant's grand opening date ------- opposition from the interior designer.
   (A) in spite of (B) even so
   (C) along with (D) in addition to

2. The last person to leave the office must make sure the security alarm is set ------- locking the door.
   (A) according to (B) in front of
   (C) prior to (D) due to

빈출 유형 공략 05   동사/명사/형용사 + 전치사

Plymouth Supplies can provide your staff ------- stylish and comfortable uniforms in a wide range of colors.

(A) besides   (B) inside   (C) from   (D) with

풀이 문맥상 직원들에게 유니폼을 제공한다는 내용이 되어야 하는데, provide는 목적어 뒤에 with를 써서 무엇을 제공하는지 나타내므로 (D)가 정답이다.

해석 Plymouth Supplies는 귀하의 직원들에게 다양한 색상의 세련되고 편안한 유니폼을 제공합니다.

유형 돋보기

1 동사 + 전치사

to	send A **to** B A를 B에게 보내다	move A **to** B A를 B로 옮기다	offer A **to** B A를 B에게 제안하다	adapt **to** ~에 적응하다
with	provide A **with** B A에게 B를 제공하다	supply A **with** B A에게 B를 공급하다	replace A **with** B A를 B로 대체하다	partner **with** ~와 협력[제휴]하다
for	provide A **for** B B에게 A를 제공하다	praise A **for** B B에 대해 A를 칭찬하다	register **for** ~에 등록하다	search **for** ~을 찾다

The Linsey Hotel **provides** excellent service **for** all of its guests.
Linsey Hotel은 모든 투숙객에게 최상의 서비스를 제공한다.

2 명사 + 전치사

of	approval **of** ~의 승인	importance **of** ~의 중요성	lack **of** ~의 부족	awareness **of** ~에 대한 인식[관심]
in	interest **in** ~에 갖는 관심	role **in** ~에서의 역할	increase/decrease/decline **in** ~에서의 상승/하락/감소	

3 be동사 + 형용사/과거분사 + 전치사

with	be equipped **with** ~을 갖추다	be compatible **with** ~와 호환되다	be consistent **with** ~와 일치하다	be associated **with** ~와 연관되다
for	be eligible **for** ~할 자격이 있다	be responsible **for** ~에 책임이 있다	be grateful **for** ~에 감사하다	be ideal **for** ~에 이상적이다

Our restaurant's new kitchen **is equipped with** state-of-the-art ovens and burners.
우리 식당의 새 주방에는 최신 오븐과 버너가 갖춰져 있습니다.

실전 감각 다지기

정답 및 해설 p.14

1. Anyone who has been working with the company for over six months is eligible ------- a holiday bonus.

   (A) for   (B) to
   (C) with   (D) in

2. CoolBeats Tech saw a huge increase ------- sales after getting free promotion from a famous blogger.

   (A) under   (B) in
   (C) for   (D) at

빈출 유형 공략 06 전치사 관용 표현

The manager told Ms. Farrow to proofread these documents ------- her earliest convenience.
(A) in   (B) at   (C) on   (D) by

풀이 문맥상 가급적 빨리 서류를 검토하라고 말했다는 내용이 되어야 하는데, one's earliest convenience는 전치사 at과 함께 쓰이므로 (B)가 정답이다.
해석 그 부장은 Ms. Farrow에게 가급적 빨리 이 서류들을 검토하라고 말했다.

유형 돋보기

at	**at** once 즉시, 지체 없이	**at** no cost 무료로	**at** a discount 할인하여
	at one's earliest convenience 가급적 빨리		
on	**on** time 정각에, 제때	**on** vacation 휴가 중인	**upon** request 요청에 따라
	(up)on -ing ~하자마자	**(up)on** completion of ~을 마치고 나서	
in	**in** time (for) ~에 늦지 않게	**in** that + 절 ~라는 점에서	**in** preparation for ~에 대비하여
	in advance 미리, 사전에	**in** particular 특히	**in** a timely manner 시기적절하게
	in writing 서면으로	**in** the near future 가까운 미래에	
	in one's absence ~가 부재 시에	**in** effect (정책 등이) 시행되는; 실제로는	
for	**for** free 무료로	**for** sale 판매 중인	**for** future use 나중에 사용하기 위해
	for one's convenience ~의 편의를 위해		
under	**under** construction 공사 중인	**under** way 진행 중인	**under** warranty 보증 기간 중인
	under pressure 압박을 받고 있는	**under** one's leadership/supervision ~의 지휘/감독하에	
beyond	**beyond** repair 수리가 불가능한	**beyond** expectation 기대 이상으로	
out of	**out of** service 이용할 수 없는	**out of** stock 재고가 없는	**out of** town 다른 지역에 있는
by	**by** -ing ~함으로써		

실전 감각 다지기

정답 및 해설 p.14

1. Our former intern excelled ------- our expectations and is now a permanent employee.
   (A) because   (B) beyond
   (C) between   (D) behind

2. ------- Ms. Keaton's supervision, the sales team was able to reach its target.
   (A) As if   (B) Under
   (C) Instead   (D) Rather than

ACTUAL TEST

1. Today's meeting with the client has been moved ------- 2:30 P.M.
   (A) on
   (B) with
   (C) to
   (D) along

2. ------- the release of its virtual car racing video game, Popka Inc. has become the country's most profitable gaming company.
   (A) Together
   (B) With
   (C) Notwithstanding
   (D) Except

3. The vendors in the weekly farmer's market prefer cash, but customers can also pay ------- credit card.
   (A) of
   (B) to
   (C) by
   (D) on

4. ------- coming to work early, Mr. Earl sometimes works on weekends to make sure he meets deadlines.
   (A) As long as
   (B) After
   (C) In addition to
   (D) However

5. This winter's new boot collection will be released ------- three weeks.
   (A) since
   (B) on
   (C) in
   (D) as

6. ------- conducting the Philadelphia Orchestra, Mr. Graham also teaches piano lessons to university students and other adults.
   (A) On behalf of
   (B) Neither
   (C) Besides
   (D) Additionally

7. Most workers left early for the holiday break ------- those who needed to finish last-minute assignments.
   (A) already
   (B) except for
   (C) in case of
   (D) following

8. Pearl Cosmetics is successful because it adapts ------- new trends quickly.
   (A) to
   (B) for
   (C) by
   (D) with

9. Alex's Diamonds will be shut down ------- about two months while renovations are being completed.
   (A) at
   (B) until
   (C) for
   (D) of

10. Despite the busy wedding season, Marcy's Cakes promised to deliver their confections ------- time.
    (A) on
    (B) at
    (C) out of
    (D) under

Questions 11-14 refer to the following notice.

NOTICE

In order to maintain high ------- here at Jamestown Hotel, our rooftop pool will be deep cleaned
                               11.
this Monday, June 7. ------- that date, guests will not have access to the rooftop, so we
                     12.
encourage those wishing to go for a swim to take advantage of the outdoor pool just beside the hotel.

-------. Please direct any ------- to the front desk staff.
13.   **14.**

Jamestown Hotel Management

11. (A) standards
    (B) standardization
    (C) standardizing
    (D) standardized

12. (A) Between
    (B) Before
    (C) On
    (D) In

13. (A) We are sincerely sorry for any trouble this may cause.
    (B) Please enjoy the rooftop pool at any time during your stay.
    (C) Our hotel has been running for over 150 years.
    (D) If you are qualified to teach swimming lessons, contact us today.

14. (A) recommendations
    (B) questions
    (C) applications
    (D) disputes

CHAPTER 1
─
PART 5&6
문법

실전에서 바로 써먹는
쉬운 토익 공식 인강

UNIT 05

수 일치

토익 기초 문법 OVERVIEW

빈출 유형 공략 01 수량 표현이 쓰인 주어와 동사의 수 일치

빈출 유형 공략 02 등위 접속사가 있는 주어와 동사의 수 일치

빈출 유형 공략 03 수식어가 긴 주어와 동사의 수 일치

빈출 유형 공략 04 수 일치 복합 문제

ACTUAL TEST

UNIT 05 | 수 일치

토익 기초 문법 OVERVIEW

A 단수 주어 뒤에는 am/is(현재), was(과거)를 쓴다.

I am writing to report an error on my bill. 제 청구서에 오류가 있어 편지를 씁니다.
She/He is the CEO of CN&T. 그녀/그는 CN&T의 대표다.
Your satisfaction is our top priority. 귀하의 만족은 우리의 최고 우선순위입니다.
The company was founded last year. 그 회사는 작년에 설립되었다.

B 복수 주어 뒤에는 are(현재), were(과거)를 쓴다.

Some item**s are** currently not in stock. 일부 품목들은 현재 재고가 없습니다.
Some order**s were** delivered late. 일부 주문품들이 늦게 배송되었다.
They are scheduled to meet on Friday. 그들은 금요일에 만나기로 예정되어 있다.

C 일반 동사 단수는 끝에 -(e)s를 붙인다. have의 단수 동사는 has를 쓴다.

-s	This manual **provides** guidelines for inventory control. 본 설명서는 재고 관리에 대한 지침을 제공한다.
-es	Mr. Martin **wishes** to modify some terms of his contract before signing it. Mr. Martin은 서명 전에 계약서의 몇 가지 조건들을 수정하기를 원한다.
-ies	The attached coupon **specifies** the discount code that you can use online. 첨부된 쿠폰은 귀하가 온라인에서 사용하실 수 있는 할인 코드를 명시하고 있습니다.
has	He **has** a lot of experience laying tiles. 그는 타일을 깔아 본 경험이 많다.

D 기업의 이름에 -s가 붙어도 단수 동사를 쓴다. 기업명은 대문자로 시작한다.

NT&Y **Technologies is** planning to merge with Frey in early May.
NT&Y Technologies는 5월 초에 Frey와 합병할 계획이다.

Humax **Electronics has** been our most reliable supplier for the past 20 years.
Humax Electronics는 지난 20년간 우리의 가장 믿음직스러운 공급업체였다.

기타: XXX Motors/Vehicles/Logistics/Pharmaceuticals/Industries/Services/Enterprises

E 하나의 주어에 두 개의 동사가 접속사 and, but으로 연결되었을 때 수를 일치시킨다.

This warranty **lasts** 36 months **and is** not transferable to other owners.
이 보증서는 36개월간 유효하며 다른 사람에게 양도할 수 없다.

The interns **are** working hard **but find** themselves somewhat overwhelmed by the process.
인턴들은 열심히 일하고 있지만 그 과정에 다소 부담을 느끼고 있다.

F 주어 뒤에 수식어구나 수식절이 올 때, 동사 바로 앞에 오는 명사를 주어로 혼동해서는 안 된다.

Buses [leaving the Hamilton **terminal**] **are being delayed because of icy roads**.
주어 (복수)　　　　　현재분사구　　　　　　be동사 (복수)　　　　　　← 주어 아님 (terminal)
해밀턴 역을 떠나는 버스들이 빙판길로 인해 지체되고 있다.

Vehicles [parked on the side of the **roadway**] **are causing traffic issues**.
주어 (복수)　　　　　과거분사구　　　　　　be동사 (복수)
길가에 주차된 차량들이 교통 혼잡을 일으키고 있다.

Some information [which is contained in the **documents**] **is outdated**.
주어 (단수)　　　　　　관계사절　　　　　　be동사 (단수)
그 문서들에 포함되어 있는 일부 정보들은 오래되었다.

The plan [to replace underground **pipelines**] **is being reviewed**.
주어 (단수)　　　　　to부정사구　　　　　be동사 (단수)
지하 파이프라인을 교체하려는 계획이 검토되고 있는 중이다.

Anyone [with a passion for video **games**] **is encouraged to apply**.
주어 (단수)　　　　　전치사구　　　　　be동사 (단수)
비디오 게임에 열정이 있는 누구든 지원해 주세요.

기초 문법 CHECK

정답 및 해설 p.16

1~7. 밑줄 친 부분 중 가장 적절한 것을 고르세요.

1. The company is / are planning to expand distribution statewide.
2. The employment contract specify / specifies that employees must give a month's notice if they wish to leave their job.
3. Chowlan Pharmaceuticals has / have increased its stock of preventative medicine.
4. Ms. Walters has served as Vice President of Phoenix for the past five years and is / are retiring next month.
5. Several properties on this street is / are for sale.
6. Prices for kitchen items listed on our Web site is / are subject to change without notice.
7. The schedule of tomorrow's opening events is / are attached.

빈출 유형 공략 01 수량 표현이 쓰인 주어와 동사의 수 일치

About half of our packaging centers ------- in the UK.
(A) location (B) is locating (C) are located (D) locates

풀이 주어가 [half of + 명사]이므로 of 뒤의 명사 our packaging centers에 동사를 수 일치해야 한다. 따라서 복수 동사인 (C) are located가 정답이다.
해석 우리의 포장 센터 절반가량은 영국에 위치해 있다.

유형 돋보기

❶ 단수 동사로 수 일치하는 수량 표현

> a(n), one, another, each, every, either, neither + 단수 명사
> each of, either of, neither of, the number of + 복수 명사

Neither of the budget proposals **was** approved. 그 예산안들은 어느 것도 승인되지 않았다.

❷ 복수 동사로 수 일치하는 수량 표현

> (a) few, several, many, both (+ of the) + 복수 명사
> a number of, a couple of + 복수 명사

Both of the candidates **hold** a master's degree in business administration.
후보자 둘 다 경영학 석사 학위가 있다.

❸ of 뒤의 명사에 동사를 수 일치하는 수량 표현

> all, most, a lot, lots, half, part, the rest,   단수/불가산명사 → 단수 동사
> the majority, some, any, percent, 분수 + of + 복수 명사 → 복수 동사

All of the furniture we ordered last week **has** not arrived yet.
우리가 지난주에 주문한 가구는 모두 아직 도착하지 않았다.
All of the meeting rooms in the Wilkinson Convention Center **are** equipped with a projector.
Wilkinson Convention Center의 모든 회의실에는 프로젝터가 구비되어 있다.

실전 감각 다지기

정답 및 해설 p.16

1. The number of coffee bean ------- has grown steadily over the past few years.
   (A) productive (B) producing
   (C) producers   (D) production

2. Roughly 40% of KLP&Co.'s business ------- from overseas clients.
   (A) come   (B) coming
   (C) comes (D) to come

3. Several managers ------- an important meeting in the conference room right now.
   (A) are having (B) having
   (C) has   (D) was having

4. According to survey data, a significant number of returning guests ------- the new menu is an improvement.
   (A) believe   (B) believes
   (C) is believing (D) belief

78 CHAPTER 1 PART 5&6 문법

빈출 유형 공략 02 등위 접속사가 있는 주어와 동사의 수 일치

Both the manager and the director ------- to take business trips whenever necessary.
(A) are allowed   (B) was allowed   (C) has been allowed   (D) to allow

쉬운 토익 공식 빈칸이 동사 자리이고 주어가 and로 연결되어 있으면 복수 동사가 정답이다.

풀이 주어가 [both A and B]이므로 복수 동사로 수 일치해야 한다. 따라서 (A) are allowed가 정답이다.
해석 부장과 이사 모두 필요할 때마다 출장을 가는 것이 허용된다.

유형 돋보기

1 and로 연결된 주어는 복수 동사로 수 일치하고, (n)or로 연결된 주어는 (n)or 뒤의 명사에 수 일치한다.

Prior experience and a master's degree in accounting are preferred.
회계 분야에서 일했던 경험과 석사 학위는 우대 사항입니다.

Coding skills **or experience is** needed to attend the software development courses.
그 소프트웨어 개발 과정을 수강하려면 코딩 기술과 경력이 있어야 한다.

Neither Cailco's partners **nor Cailco itself takes** any responsibility for defects after one year of purchase.
Cailco의 협력사와 Cailco는 구입 후 1년이 지나고 발생한 결함에는 어떤 책임도 지지 않습니다.

2 [A of B] 주어는 A에 수 일치한다.

Sales figures of the energy drink **have** risen considerably. 그 에너지 드링크의 매출액이 상당히 늘었다.

고득점 POINT not only A but also B(= B as well as A)는 B에 수 일치한다.
Not only high-end kitchen appliances **but also marble flooring is** a key feature of the apartment.
고급 주방 기기뿐만 아니라 대리석 바닥재도 그 아파트의 주요한 특징이다.

실전 감각 다지기

정답 및 해설 p.16

1. Not only Procon Company but also its competitors ------- products directly to the consumers.

(A) distributing   (B) is distributing
(C) distribute   (D) has distributed

2. Its innovation and risk-taking ------- Yonder Technologies from traditional electronics companies.

(A) have separated
(B) is separating
(C) separates
(D) separating

3. Neither Mr. Herbert nor his ------- were aware of the safety issues at the amusement park.

(A) employer   (B) employ
(C) employing   (D) employees

4. Many projects of market research ------- to identify our customer base.

(A) are being conducted
(B) has been conducted
(C) was conducted
(D) to conduct

빈출 유형 공략 03 — 수식어가 긴 주어와 동사의 수 일치

A new company policy that affords workers more rights ------- last week.
(A) have been enacted (B) were enacted (C) enacting (D) was enacted

풀이 주어 A new company policy가 주격 관계대명사절(that ~ rights)의 수식을 받는 구조이며 빈칸은 동사 자리이다. 따라서 빈칸에는 단수 동사가 들어가야 하므로 (D) was enacted가 정답이다.
해석 직원들에게 더 많은 권리를 주는 회사의 새 정책이 지난주에 제정되었다.

유형 돋보기

1 주어와 동사 사이에 위치한 수식어구는 수 일치와 관계없는 요소이므로 혼동하지 않도록 주의한다.

| 분사구 | **Cancellations** (made 10 days prior to the concert) **are** eligible for a full refund.
공연 시작 열을 전에 취소하면 전액 환불됩니다.

| 관계사절 | **The number of** customers (who bring their own tumblers) **has** increased greatly.
개인 텀블러를 갖고 오는 고객의 수가 많이 늘었다.

| to부정사구 | **The strategy** (to market our new products) **is** under development.
신제품들을 광고하기 위한 전략은 개발 중이다.

| 전치사구 | **Facilities** (at the Magnolia Hotel) **include** an indoor swimming pool.
Magnolia Hotel의 시설에는 실내 수영장이 포함되어 있다.

2 주격 관계대명사절의 동사는 선행사에 수 일치한다.
All employees of Brad's Bistro (**who handle** food) must have a food hygiene training certificate.
Brad's Bistro에서 음식을 다루는 모든 직원은 식품 위생 교육 수료증이 있어야 한다.

실전 감각 다지기

1. Clothes made by Vincenzo ------- to appeal to younger consumers.
(A) are designed (B) having designed
(C) to be designed (D) is designed

2. All the sculptures at Central Museum ------- to be displayed in the garden within this month.
(A) scheduling
(B) are scheduled
(C) was scheduled
(D) has been scheduled

3. Watches from Walencia come with a quality guarantee that ------- for five years.
(A) lasts (B) to last
(C) lasting (D) last

4. Many painters who visit the city hall for the first time ------- to recreate it as an object of art.
(A) is being inspired
(B) to inspire
(C) are inspired
(D) has been inspired

빈출 유형 공략 04 수 일치 복합 문제

The schedule for next month's training sessions ------- to this e-mail.
(A) were attaching   (B) is attaching   (C) are attached   (D) has been attached

풀이 주어 The schedule이 전치사구 for next month's training sessions의 수식을 받는 구조이다. 따라서 빈칸에는 단수 동사가 들어가야 하는데 빈칸 뒤에 목적어가 없으므로 수동태인 (D) has been attached가 정답이다.
해석 다음 달 교육 일정은 이 이메일에 첨부되었다.

유형 돋보기

수 일치가 태 또는 시제와 결합된 문제를 풀 때는 수 일치를 먼저 판별한 다음 태 또는 시제를 따진다.

❶ 수 일치와 태 복합

This document is explained / explains / explain essential HR policies.
이 문서에는 필수적인 인사 정책이 나와 있다.
[1] 수 일치 판별: 주어(This document)가 단수이므로 복수 동사인 explain은 오답으로 소거한다.
[2] 능동태/수동태 판별: 뒤에 목적어(essential HR policies)가 있으므로 능동태인 explains가 정답이다.

❷ 수 일치와 시제 복합

Sonora Trucking is delivering / has delivered / deliver refrigerated goods across the country for the past two decades.
Sonora Trucking은 지난 20년간 냉장 제품을 전국 각지로 배달했다.
[1] 수 일치 판별: 주어(Sonora Trucking)가 단수이므로 복수 동사인 deliver는 오답으로 소거한다.
[2] 시제 판별: 뒤에 현재완료 시제와 어울려 쓰이는 표현(for the past two decades)이 있으므로 현재완료 시제인 has delivered가 정답이다.

실전 감각 다지기

1. Nearly half of the country's luxury hotels ------- along the coast.
   (A) situates
   (B) are situated
   (C) have situated
   (D) situating

2. Please look over the proposed budget changes that ------- on the screen.
   (A) were displaying
   (B) are displayed
   (C) to be displayed
   (D) has been displayed

3. An increase in profits ------- Warren Industries to hire more employees.
   (A) has allowed
   (B) allowing
   (C) allow
   (D) was allowed

4. A retirement party will be held next week for Mr. Schmidt, who ------- for Melon Technologies for over 30 years.
   (A) works
   (B) was worked
   (C) have worked
   (D) has been working

ACTUAL TEST

1. The customers in line ------- to get restless because they have been waiting for so long.
   (A) are starting
   (B) starting
   (C) has been starting
   (D) is starting

2. Those who wish to participate in next month's Open Slate festival ------- to sign up early.
   (A) encourage
   (B) are encouraged
   (C) has been encouraging
   (D) to encourage

3. The robots on this assembly line ------- remotely, preventing worker injuries.
   (A) was being controlled
   (B) are controlled
   (C) controlling
   (D) has been controlled

   고득점 도전
4. Since Henry's Café built a drive-through window, the number of visitors to the coffee shop -------.
   (A) increasing
   (B) increases
   (C) has increased
   (D) have been increasing

5. About half of the employees at Tuscana ------- to and from work every day.
   (A) has driven
   (B) is driving
   (C) drives
   (D) drive

6. Customers ------- Mantique Furniture for decades because of its commitment to quality.
   (A) trusts
   (B) is trusting
   (C) have trusted
   (D) trust

7. Koolie Co. is searching for an ideal marketing format that ------- to older consumers.
   (A) appeals
   (B) appeal
   (C) appealing
   (D) are appealing

   고득점 도전
8. As soon as the buses -------, the cleaning crew begin preparing them for the next passengers.
   (A) arrive
   (B) will arrive
   (C) has arrived
   (D) is arriving

9. Feedback from employees ------- the management team to make necessary improvements at the office.
   (A) allow
   (B) allows
   (C) allowing
   (D) have allowed

10. Please note the key points in the presentation files that ------- to my e-mail.
    (A) were attaching
    (B) attachment
    (C) has been attached
    (D) are attached

Questions 11-14 refer to the following article.

WOOSTER (January 28)—Sparkle Dance Studio ------- its third anniversary this weekend. Owner
                                              11.
Rachel Chapman had concerns about opening a studio in such a small town. Fortunately, the classes of the first semester were nearly at full capacity, so she was relieved. A dance recital was held at the end of the semester to show the students' progress. -------.
                                                                                              12.
Ms. Chapman then posted an instructional dance video online ------- went viral. The publicity
                                                              13.
from that video resulted in a sudden surge of interest in her business. Ms. Chapman took advantage of the opportunity and hired more instructors. She also moved to a larger location to accommodate the ------- of her business.
                    14.

11. (A) celebrate
(B) were celebrated
(C) is celebrating
(D) will have celebrated

12. (A) Its tickets go on sale next week on the studio's Web site.
(B) It also helped audience members learn about the studio.
(C) She decided to change her career path dramatically.
(D) She designed them herself with a software program.

13. (A) what
(B) whose
(C) how
(D) which

14. (A) innovation
(B) vacancy
(C) supervision
(D) growth

CHAPTER 1

PART 5 & 6
문법

실전에서 바로 써먹는
쉬운 토익 공식 인강

UNIT 06

수동태

토익 기초 문법 OVERVIEW

빈출 유형 공략 01 수동태 vs. 능동태

빈출 유형 공략 02 be p.p. + 명사/형용사

빈출 유형 공략 03 be p.p. + to부정사/전치사

빈출 유형 공략 04 태와 시제 복합 문제

ACTUAL TEST

UNIT 06 | 수동태

토익 기초 문법 OVERVIEW

A 주어가 행위를 하는 주체이면 능동태를, 주어가 동사의 행위를 받는 대상이면 [be + 과거분사] 형태의 수동태를 쓴다.

능동태	ESC Ltd. **will build** the shopping mall. ESC Ltd.가 그 쇼핑몰을 지을 것이다.
수동태	The shopping mall **will be built** by ESC Ltd. 그 쇼핑몰은 ESC Ltd.에 의해 지어질 것이다.

be + 과거분사

B 수동태에서 행위의 주체는 [by + 명사]로 나타내며, 행위자가 불분명하거나 굳이 언급할 필요가 없을 때는 생략한다.

의미상 [by + 행위 주체]가 필요한 경우	의미상 [by + 행위 주체]가 불필요한 경우
The project **was affected** by bad weather. 그 프로젝트는 나쁜 날씨의 영향을 받았다.	All confidential files should **be shredded**. 모든 기밀문서는 파쇄되어야 한다.

C 토익에 자주 쓰이는 수동태 시제

현재	The interns **are paid** on an hourly basis. 인턴들은 시간당 급여를 받는다.
과거	The house **was sold** at auction last week. 그 집은 지난주에 경매에서 팔렸다.
미래	The main entrance **will be closed** for repairs. 정문은 수리를 위해 폐쇄될 것이다.
현재진행	The Brunswick Mall **is being renovated**. Brunswick Mall은 개조 중이다.
과거진행	His car **was being repaired**. 그의 차는 수리 중이었다.
현재완료	Building renovations **have been completed**. 건물 수리가 완료되었다.
과거완료	The merger was not made public until it **had been finalized**. 합병은 최종 확정될 때까지 공개되지 않았다.
미래완료	The car **will have been fixed** by 3 P.M. 그 차는 오후 3시까지는 수리가 끝날 것이다.

D 수동태 뒤에는 부사, 전치사구, to부정사구, 부사절 등이 올 수 있다.

수동태 + 부사	The program **is run** year-round. 그 프로그램은 일 년 내내 운영된다. Your order will **be processed** promptly. 귀하의 주문은 신속히 처리될 것입니다.
수동태 + 전치사구	The printer **is offered** at 50% off. 그 프린터는 50% 할인된 가격에 판매된다.
수동태 + to부정사구	Library patrons **are encouraged** to complete the survey. 도서관 이용객들은 설문 조사를 완료하도록 권유받는다.
수동태 + 절	Training will **be postponed** until everyone returns from vacation. 교육은 모두 휴가에서 복귀할 때까지 연기될 것입니다.

E 간접목적어와 직접목적어를 취하는 일부 동사는 간접목적어와 직접목적어가 각각 수동태의 주어로 전환될 수 있다.

능동태	The company **will give** all salespeople a bonus. _{간접목적어　　　직접목적어}	그 회사는 모든 영업 사원들에게 보너스를 줄 것이다.
수동태	All salespeople **will be given** a bonus. _{직접목적어}	모든 영업 사원들이 보너스를 받을 것이다.
수동태	A bonus **will be given** to all salespeople. _{전치사 + 간접목적어}	보너스는 모든 영업 사원들에게 주어질 것이다.

F 수동태 뒤에 직접목적어가 오는 동사들 중 토익에 자주 등장하는 단어들은 다음과 같다.

award ~에게 …을 수여하다	All factory employees **were awarded** a 5% pay increase. 모든 공장 직원들은 5%의 임금 인상을 받았다.
grant ~에게 …을 승인하다	MC Corporation **was granted** permission to build on the site. MC Corporation은 그 부지에 건축 허가를 받았다.
assign ~에게 …을 배정하다	You'll **be assigned** your own personal parking space tomorrow. 내일 개인 주차 공간을 배정받으실 겁니다.
charge ~에게 …을 청구하다	You will not **be charged** a shipping fee. 배송비는 청구되지 않습니다.
offer ~에게 …을 제안하다	He **was offered** a job at the interview. 그는 면접에서 일자리를 제의받았다.

기초 문법 CHECK

정답 및 해설 p.19

1~7. 밑줄 친 부분 중 가장 적절한 것을 고르세요.

1. The Tokyo store is run / running by Ms. Saito.
2. Ms. Allen is considering / being considered for a managerial position.
3. A 10% cancellation fee will charge / be charged if the booking is cancelled.
4. Ms. Hall called this morning to see if the package she sent yesterday had delivered / had been delivered.
5. Every employee is encouraging / encouraged to attend the AI conference.
6. The new apartment complex is moderately pricing / priced.
7. Ticket-holders for the performances will give / be given a refund.

빈출 유형 공략 01 : 수동태 vs. 능동태 ★ ★ ★

This new tablet ------- with the needs of digital artists in mind.
(A) to create (B) has created (C) will be creating (D) was created

쉬운 토익 공식 빈칸 뒤에 목적어가 없으면 수동태가 정답이다.

풀이 빈칸 뒤에 목적어가 없으므로 수동태인 (D) was created가 정답이다.
해석 이 신형 태블릿은 디지털 예술가들의 수요를 염두에 두고 만들어졌다.

유형 돋보기

토익은 태를 판별하는 문제가 의외로 까다롭지 않게 출제된다. 다음 대전제만 알고 있으면 수동태와 능동태를 가려내는 문제는 어렵지 않게 풀 수 있다.

① 빈칸 뒤에 목적어가 없으면 수동태를, 목적어가 있으면 능동태를 쓴다.

All items will ~~discount~~ / **be discounted** during the upcoming holiday sale.
곧 있을 연휴 세일 기간 동안에는 모든 제품이 할인될 것이다.

Mr. Trent **completed** / ~~was completed~~ an internship at a local business last week.
Mr. Trent는 지난주에 지역 사업체에서 인턴십을 마쳤다.

② 주격 관계대명사절과 to부정사의 동사, 그리고 동명사도 목적어 유무에 따라 능동태와 수동태를 구별한다.

The Montreal Theatre, which ~~is constructing~~ / **is being constructed** on an unused lot, will have two floors for audience seating.
Montreal Theatre는 공터에 건설되는 중인데, 객석은 두 개의 층으로 될 것이다.

Customers are asked **to fill out** / ~~to be filled out~~ a survey after shopping at the mall.
고객들은 그 쇼핑몰에서 쇼핑을 하고 난 후에 설문지를 작성하도록 요청받는다.

Please update your passwords regularly to prevent data from ~~stealing~~ / **being stolen**.
데이터가 유출되는 것을 방지하기 위해 비밀번호를 주기적으로 변경하세요.

실전 감각 다지기

정답 및 해설 p.20

1. A special training course will be held for employees that ------- in conducting video conferences with clients.
   (A) involvement (B) are involved
   (C) had involved (D) were involving

2. Each vase is wrapped and secured carefully to prevent it from ------- while in transit.
   (A) damaged (B) is damaged
   (C) damaging (D) being damaged

3. Ms. Delacruz's bronze statue at the exhibition ------- as an important piece of contemporary art.
   (A) to praise (B) has praised
   (C) praises (D) was praised

4. All merchandise ------- to guarantee it meets our quality standards.
   (A) has inspected (B) inspected
   (C) is inspected (D) inspecting

빈출 유형 공략 02 — be p.p. + 명사/형용사

Each passenger whose flight is delayed by more than three hours ------- a voucher for a free meal at the airport.

(A) giving (B) will be given (C) has given (D) is giving

풀이 빈칸 뒤에 목적어가 있지만 give는 목적어를 두 개 취하는 동사이므로 주어가 행위를 하는 주체인지, 행위를 당하는 대상인지 확인해 봐야 한다. 문맥상 각 승객이 무료 식사 이용권을 받는 대상이 되는 게 자연스러우므로 수동태인 (B) will be given이 정답이다.

해석 비행기가 3시간 이상 지연된 각 승객은 공항 무료 식사 이용권을 받게 될 것이다.

유형 돋보기

1 be p.p. + 명사

Ms. Rodriguez **was assigned** Mr. Li's responsibilities while he was on a business trip to Tokyo.
Mr. Li가 도쿄로 출장을 가 있는 동안 Ms. Rodriguez에게 그의 업무가 맡겨졌다.

→ [동사 + 간접목적어 + 직접목적어]의 수동태는 간접목적어가 주어 자리에 위치할 때 [be p.p. + 직접목적어]로 쓴다. 직접목적어가 주어 자리에 위치할 때는 [be p.p. + 전치사(to/for) + 간접목적어]로 쓴다.

☑ **목적어를 두 개 취하는 동사**: give 주다, award (상을) 수여하다, grant 승인하다, 주다, assign 배정하다, 맡기다, charge (요금 등을) 청구하다, offer 제안하다, 제공하다, send 보내다, lend 빌려주다, pay 지불하다, issue 발급하다

Jane Hamilton **was elected** chairperson of the meeting. Jane Hamilton은 그 회의의 의장으로 선출되었다.

→ [동사 + 목적어 + 목적격 보어(명사)]의 수동태는 [be p.p. + 목적격 보어(명사)]로 쓴다.

☑ **목적격 보어 자리에 명사를 쓰는 동사**: consider 여기다, appoint 임명하다, name 임명하다, elect 선출하다

2 be p.p. + 형용사

Hosto Corp. **is considered** responsible for the great expansion of the wireless industry.
Hosto Corp.는 무선 산업의 엄청난 확장에 기여한 것으로 여겨진다.

It is imperative that client information **be kept** confidential. 고객 정보는 철저하게 기밀을 유지해야 한다.

→ [동사 + 목적어 + 목적격 보어(형용사)]의 수동태는 [be p.p. + 목적격 보어(형용사)]로 쓴다.

☑ **목적격 보어 자리에 형용사를 쓰는 동사**: consider 여기다, keep 유지하다, make 만들다, find 발견하다; 느끼다

실전 감각 다지기

정답 및 해설 p.20

1. An employment offer ------- to you once the details of your contract are finalized.
(A) sent (B) will be sent
(C) has sent (D) is sending

2. Account holders who spend more money than the amount available in their account ------- an overdraft fee.
(A) charged (B) are charging
(C) have charged (D) will be charged

3. To maintain transparency, any changes to our formula ------- public and announced on the company Web site.
(A) to be making (B) were making
(C) should be made (D) would have made

4. Since developing the new standard for semiconductors, Newman Tech ------- innovative by many.
(A) considers (B) to consider
(C) has considered (D) was considered

빈출 유형 공략 03 be p.p. + to부정사/전치사

The total cost of the renovation project ------- to be about half a million dollars over the initial budget.

(A) was expecting (B) is expected (C) has expected (D) expects

풀이 선택지가 expect의 활용형으로 구성되어 있고 빈칸 뒤에 to부정사가 있는 것으로 보아 빈칸에는 뒤에 to부정사를 취할 수 있는 expect의 활용형이 들어가야 한다. 따라서 (B) is expected가 정답이다.

해석 그 수리 계획의 총 비용은 초기 예산에서 약 50만 달러가 넘을 것으로 예상된다.

유형 돋보기

1 be p.p. + to부정사

be expected to	be asked to	be invited to	be requested to
~할 것으로 예상되다	~하도록 요청받다	~하도록 (정식으로) 요청받다	~하도록 요청받다
be required to	be encouraged to	be pleased to	be scheduled to
~하도록 요구받다	~하도록 장려되다	~해서 기뻐하다	~하기로 예정되다
be reminded to	be instructed to	be intended to	be prepared to
~하라고 (상기시키는 말을) 듣다	~하라고 지시받다	~하기 위한 의도이다	~할 준비가 되다
be allowed to	be permitted to	be advised to	
~하도록 허락되다	~하도록 허락되다	~하도록 조언받다	

Managers **are invited to** nominate two deserving team members for Employee of the Month.
부장들은 이달의 사원에 적합한 부서원 두 명을 지명하도록 요청받는다.

2 be p.p. + 전치사

be based on	be based in	be interested in	be satisfied with
~에 근거하다	(장소)에 기반을 두다	~에 관심이 있다	~에 만족하다
be directed to	be pleased with	be scheduled for	be equipped with
~에 안내되다, ~로 향하다	~에 기뻐하다	~로 예정되어 있다	~을 갖추다
be related to	be involved in	be exposed to	be credited with
~와 관련되다	~에 관여하다	~에 노출되다	~로 공로를 인정받다

The job interview **is scheduled for** next Friday. 면접은 다음 주 금요일로 예정되어 있다.

실전 감각 다지기

정답 및 해설 p.20

1. After checking in at the security desk, visitors are ------- to visit select areas of the factory.
   (A) permissive   (B) permitted
   (C) permitting   (D) permit

2. Those who want to donate to the holiday food drive ------- to bring their food items to work this Monday.
   (A) asking   (B) are asked
   (C) ask   (D) have asked

3. This luxury vehicle ------- with a heated steering wheel, massage seats, and a built-in umbrella holder.
   (A) has equipped   (B) was equipping
   (C) equipment   (D) is equipped

4. The CEO is extremely ------- with the steady growth the company has experienced over the past few years.
   (A) pleasing   (B) pleasure
   (C) pleased   (D) to please

빈출 유형 공략 04   태와 시제 복합 문제

The proposal ------- to the executives tomorrow, so it should be completed by today.
(A) is being given   (B) was given   (C) had been given   (D) will give

풀이   빈칸 뒤에 목적어가 없으므로 빈칸에는 수동태가 들어가야 한다. 또한 '내일'을 뜻하는 tomorrow가 있으므로 가까운 미래를 나타낼 수 있는 현재진행 시제인 (A) is being given이 정답이다.

해석   그 제안서는 내일 임원들에게 전달되기 때문에 오늘까지 마무리되어야 한다.

유형 돋보기

① 시제를 나타내는 부사(구)가 있을 때는 시제를 먼저 판단한 다음에 태를 판단한다.

The new sales manager is introducing / was introduced / will be introduced at next week's team meeting.
새 판매 담당자는 다음 주 팀 회의에서 소개될 것이다.

[1] 시제 판별: 미래를 나타내는 표현(next week)이 있으므로 과거 시제인 was introduced는 오답으로 소거한다.
[2] 능동태/수동태 판별: 뒤에 목적어가 없으므로 수동태인 will be introduced가 정답이다.

② 시제를 파악할 수 있는 요소가 없으면 태를 먼저 판단하고 문맥으로 시제를 따져 본다.

None of the project proposals submitted to the director accept / were accepted / had been accepted.
부장에게 제출된 프로젝트 제안서들은 어느 것도 받아들여지지 않았다.

[1] 능동태/수동태 판별: 뒤에 목적어가 없으므로 능동태인 accept는 오답으로 소거한다.
[2] 시제 판별: 과거완료는 어떤 일이 과거보다 앞선 때에 발생했음을 나타내기 위해 쓴다. 이 문장은 굳이 일의 선후 관계를 밝힐 필요가 없기 때문에 과거완료를 쓰는 건 적절하지 않다. 따라서 단순 과거 시제인 were accepted가 정답이다.

실전 감각 다지기

정답 및 해설 p.21

1. For the past few weeks, sales of high heels ------- sneakers at Shoe Emporium.

(A) are outperformed
(B) will be outperforming
(C) have been outperforming
(D) would have been outperformed

2. Ms. Lai was supposed to arrive today, but her flight ------- because of dangerous weather conditions.

(A) to delay
(B) has been delayed
(C) will be delaying
(D) would have been delayed

3. Although he ------- every step of the process, Mr. Cameron was pleased with the development team's new prototype.

(A) was not overseen
(B) had not overseen
(C) is not overseen
(D) will not oversee

4. Former floor manager Mr. Nyman ------- the newest director of quality control last week.

(A) to appoint
(B) will be appointed
(C) appoints
(D) was appointed

ACTUAL TEST

1. Mongoose LTC ------- a new branch in Bangkok to cover the Southeast Asian market last month.
   (A) establishes
   (B) established
   (C) was established
   (D) will have established

2. The latest sculpture by Daniel Kirkpatrick ------- as his most ambitious piece.
   (A) regards
   (B) to be regarded
   (C) regarding
   (D) is regarded

3. A maintenance worker ------- the trash cans and recycling bins on the third floor.
   (A) emptying
   (B) emptied
   (C) had been emptied
   (D) was emptied

4. Marsh&Sons is holding a contest for a new logo design and each branch ------- to submit their best concept.
   (A) to invite
   (B) invites
   (C) inviting
   (D) is invited

5. Further studies ------- on the medication to better understand its side effects.
   (A) are performing
   (B) have performed
   (C) to perform
   (D) will be performed

6. The tasks that ------- to the marketing team had been given to the new interns to assess their skills.
   (A) were assigned
   (B) are assigning
   (C) assigned
   (D) will have assigned

7. The final blueprint for the new city hall building ------- to be completed by the end of September.
   (A) is expected
   (B) expecting
   (C) had expected
   (D) expects

8. Suggestions for improvement should ------- to Ms. Loggia, who will organize and send the comments to Human Resources.
   (A) to direct
   (B) be directed
   (C) direct
   (D) have directed

9. At the awards ceremony, Robin Kelton ------- for her 20 years of service to McEvoy Engineering.
   (A) has been recognizing
   (B) recognized
   (C) was recognized
   (D) recognizing

10. Mr. Dixon ------- to act as team leader while Ms. Parson was on maternity leave.
    (A) had selected
    (B) will have been selected
    (C) had been selected
    (D) selected

Questions 11-14 refer to the following memo.

To: All Camden Inc. Staff
From: Jeremy Schubert
Subject: Web site
Date: January 8

Dear Staff,

Upgrades to the company Web site will be completed next week. The upgraded Web site will still have our usual catalog and online shopping portal for customers. -------, there will be a newly added section for employees only.
11.

Through the employee portal, you can report your working hours, make vacation requests, and get the latest company news. Members of the public cannot access this part of the Web site.

A unique username and password ------- for you by the system. You can easily change the
12.
password on your own by following the prompts. You can also change your username, but ------- to do so must be given by your department head.
13.
Executives at Camden Inc. have always placed utmost importance in keeping the staff well informed, so this has led to developing new employee portal. -------.
14.

Jeremy Schubert, Vice President

---

11. (A) For example
(B) In fact
(C) However
(D) Even though

12. (A) generated
(B) will have generated
(C) had been generated
(D) will be generated

13. (A) failure
(B) creation
(C) resistance
(D) permission

14. (A) Thank you for providing immediate feedback.
(B) We hope this change will contribute to that goal.
(C) I look forward to seeing you there.
(D) Please let me know if it is missing.

CHAPTER 1

PART 5&6
문법

실전에서 바로 써먹는
쉬운 토익 공식 인강

UNIT 07

시제

토익 기초 문법 OVERVIEW

빈출 유형 공략 01 단순 시제

빈출 유형 공략 02 진행 시제

빈출 유형 공략 03 완료 시제

빈출 유형 공략 04 주절-종속절의 시제 일치와 예외

빈출 유형 공략 05 시간과 조건 부사절의 시제

빈출 유형 공략 06 if 가정법

ACTUAL TEST

UNIT 07 | 시제

토익 기초 문법 OVERVIEW

A 현재, 미래, 과거 시제는 종종 특정 부사(구)와 어울려 쓰인다.

현재	Delivery **usually takes** one to two weeks. 배송은 보통 1~2주가 걸립니다. The shop **is always** crowded. 그 가게는 항상 붐빈다. The shuttle bus **leaves every** 15 minutes. 셔틀버스는 15분마다 떠납니다.
미래	Highway 11 **will soon be widened** from two lanes to four. 11번 고속 도로는 곧 2개 차선에서 4개 차선으로 확대될 것이다. Ms. Mitchell **will be moving** to the Bristol office **next week**. Ms. Mitchell은 다음 주에 브리스톨 사무실로 옮길 것입니다.
과거	Mr. Brown **transferred** to the London headquarters **last week**. Mr. Brown은 지난주에 런던 본사로 전근했다. Fresh Fridays **was founded** six years **ago**. Fresh Fridays는 6년 전에 설립되었다.

B 현재 시제가 가까운 미래를 나타내는 표현과 함께 쓰이면 확정된 미래의 일을 나타낼 수 있다.

The bus bound for the Evergreen Zoo **departs** at 8:10 A.M. **tomorrow**.
Evergreen Zoo로 향하는 버스는 내일 오전 8시 10분에 출발한다.

Registration **begins** this Friday and **continues** until the end of **next month**.
등록은 이번 주 금요일에 시작해서 다음 달 말까지 계속된다.

C 현재완료 시제는 경험이나 완료, 계속의 의미로 쓰인다.

경험 현재완료는 특정 기간 동안의 경험을, 단순 과거는 특정 시점의 일회적 사건을 나타낸다.

현재완료		단순 과거
He **has visited** London **many times**. 그는 여러 번 런던을 방문했다. ➜ 과거 특정 시점부터 현재까지의 경험을 나타내고 있으므로 현재완료 시제를 써야 한다.	vs.	He **visited** London **in 2010**. 그는 2010년에 런던을 방문했다. ➜ 명확한 과거를 나타내는 표현(in 2010)이 있으므로 과거 시제를 써야 한다.

완료 계속되던 일이 방금 완료되었을 때, 혹은 새로운 소식이나 정보를 전할 때 쓰인다.
Harrolds Department Store **has just opened** its first overseas branch in Sydney.
Harrolds Department Store가 (지금 막) 시드니에 첫 해외 지점을 열었다.

계속 사건이나 행위가 특정 기간 동안 계속됨을 나타낸다.
Maria Jones **has been** the chief curator of the Birkdale Museum **since 2010**.
Maria Jones는 2010년부터 Birkdale Museum의 수석 큐레이터를 맡고 있다.

D 현재완료진행은 과거부터 현재 시점까지 계속되어 왔던 일이 지금도 진행 중임을 나타낸다.

Sales of Awake Organics **have been increasing** steadily **over the past three years**.
Awake Organics는 최근 3년간 매출이 꾸준히 증가하고 있다.

I **have been working** as an editor at Egmont Publishing House **for six years**.
저는 Egmont Publishing House에서 6년간 편집자로 일해 왔습니다.

E 과거완료는 어떤 일이 과거보다 앞선 때에 발생했음을 나타낸다.

He **had been finished** with the assignment weeks before it **was** due.
그는 마감일 몇 주 전에 그 과제를 끝낸 상태였다.

The old house **had been neglected** for years before it **was** recently renovated.
그 오래된 집은 최근에 개축되기 전에 몇 년 동안 방치되어 있었다.

F 시제 문제의 선택지들을 보면 단순히 여러 개의 시제 중 하나를 고르는 형태보다는 동사 자리인지 아니면 to부정사나 동명사, 분사 자리인지를 먼저 판별해야 하는 경우가 많으며, 나아가 수 일치, 태를 동시에 고려해야 하는 문제도 빈번하게 출제된다.

> **101.** **The appointment** of a new chief financial officer at Arran Aromatics ------- **yesterday**.
> (A) to announce → 동사 자리이므로 to부정사는 소거
> (B) announced → 시제: 과거(yesterday) → 태: 능동태 (오답)
> (C) was announced → 시제: 과거(yesterday) → 태: 수동태 (정답)
> (D) had been announced → 시제: 과거완료
> 해석 Arran Aromatics의 새로운 최고 재무 책임자 임명이 어제 발표되었다.

기초 문법 CHECK

정답 및 해설 p.23

1~6. 밑줄 친 부분 중 가장 적절한 것을 고르세요.

1. The restaurants on Main Street usually open / will open early on Fridays.
2. Sedwick Electronics relocates / relocated its main factory to Dublin last year.
3. White Fox ran / will be running a special sale next month to celebrate its fifth anniversary.
4. The market for minivans is growing / has grown exponentially for the past three years.
5. The number of tourists in Kingham increased / has been increasing steadily since 2019.
6. The building has been left / had been left unoccupied for almost two decades before it was purchased two years ago by Steffan Young.

빈출 유형 공략 01 단순 시제

The schedule for the career fair ------- to participants later this week.
(A) will be e-mailed   (B) had been e-mailed   (C) was e-mailed   (D) to e-mail

쉬운 토익 공식 문장에 미래를 나타내는 표현이 있으면 미래 시제가 정답이다.

풀이 빈칸 뒤에 미래를 나타내는 표현(later this week)이 있으므로 미래 시제인 (A) will be e-mailed가 정답이다.
해석 채용 박람회의 일정표는 이번 주 후반에 참가자들에게 이메일로 발송될 것이다.

유형 돋보기

토익의 단순 시제 문제는 출제 빈도와 난이도가 낮은 편이고 기본 개념을 벗어나지 않는 범위에서 출제된다. 특히 특정 표현과 어울려 출제되는 경우가 대부분이므로 주어진 표현을 함께 알아 두면 문제 풀이에 도움이 된다.

① 현재 시제

New employees **are usually** required to serve a probationary period.
대개 신규 직원들은 수습 기간을 거칠 것을 요구받는다.
☑ 현재 시제와 어울려 쓰이는 표현: usually, generally, every week/month/year 등

② 미래 시제

Magazine subscription requests made after May 20 **will be** fulfilled by **early next month**.
5월 20일 이후에 들어온 잡지 구독 요청은 다음 달 초에 처리될 것이다.
☑ 미래 시제와 어울려 쓰이는 표현: next week/month/year, tomorrow, soon, later today/this week 등

③ 과거 시제

The bridge **was** closed for repair work two weeks **ago**.
그 다리는 보수 작업으로 인해 2주 전에 폐쇄되었다.
☑ 과거 시제와 어울려 쓰이는 표현: ago, yesterday, recently, lately, last week/month/year, in + 연도 등

실전 감각 다지기

정답 및 해설 p.23

1. Both employees and their family members ------- tomorrow's banquet, so we need 146 servings altogether.
   (A) attending   (B) attended
   (C) have attended (D) will attend

2. Diesel Motors ------- to open a new factory in Colorado last month but faced a labor shortage.
   (A) expects   (B) is expecting
   (C) expected   (D) will expect

3. The secretary ------- office supplies every Thursday, so please e-mail him any requests you have before then.
   (A) had ordered   (B) orders
   (C) ordering   (D) ordered

4. A television show with chef Eva Santiago ------- on Channel 4 next Friday.
   (A) will air   (B) airing
   (C) has aired   (D) aired

빈출 유형 공략 02 진행 시제

Next week, Jack's Hardware ------- a special event for its 10th anniversary.
(A) has hosted (B) hosted (C) will be hosting (D) hosting

풀이 빈칸 앞에 미래를 나타내는 표현(Next week)이 있으므로 미래진행 시제인 (C) will be hosting이 정답이다.
해석 다음 주에 Jack's Hardware는 10주년을 맞아 특별 이벤트를 개최할 것이다.

유형 톺아보기

현재와 미래, 그리고 과거의 특정 시점에 진행되는 일을 나타낼 때는 진행 시제를 쓴다.

1 현재진행 시제

The company **is currently seeking** experienced market analysts.
그 회사는 현재 경력이 있는 시장 분석가를 구하고 있다.

2 미래진행 시제

Later today, Mr. Klein **will be preparing** a training session on a new design program.
오늘 오후에 Mr. Klein은 새 디자인 프로그램에 관한 교육을 준비하고 있을 것이다.

3 과거진행 시제

Ms. Maiden **was making** training materials for the interns **yesterday**.
Ms. Maiden은 어제 인턴들을 위해 교육 자료를 만들고 있었다.

> **고득점 POINT** 현재진행 시제가 가까운 미래를 나타내는 표현과 함께 쓰이면 예정된 미래의 일을 나타낼 수 있다.
> The ingredients **are being shipped** to the restaurant **later this afternoon**.
> 그 재료들은 오늘 오후 늦게 그 식당에 배송될 것이다.

실전 감각 다지기

1. Cup of Joe's coffee ------- popularity right now for its rare blend and unique scent.
   (A) gained (B) is gaining
   (C) to gain (D) will gain

2. The Shanghai branch ------- for the online meeting soon, so gather in the meeting room.
   (A) was calling (B) will be calling
   (C) has called (D) calling

3. Next Saturday, Kenny's Sporting Goods ------- out free baseballs to customers who purchase the Gibson bat.
   (A) to give (B) gave
   (C) was giving (D) is giving

4. Headquarters ------- out invitations for the company-wide holiday party in New York via e-mail next week.
   (A) will be sending (B) was sending
   (C) had sent (D) having sent

빈출 유형 공략 03 완료 시제

Our customer service center ------- nearly 3,000 people over the past six months.
(A) assists   (B) is assisting   (C) will assist   (D) has assisted

쉬운 토익 공식 문장에 for(~ 동안), since(~ 이래로), over(~에 걸쳐) 등이 있으면 현재완료 시제가 정답이다.

풀이 지난 6개월 동안(over the past six months), 즉 6개월 전부터 현재까지 계속 돕고 있다는 것을 나타내야 하므로 현재완료 시제가 적절하다. 따라서 (D) has assisted가 정답이다.
해석 우리의 고객 서비스 센터는 지난 6개월 동안 거의 3천 명의 고객을 도왔다.

유형 돋보기

토익에서는 완료 시제, 그중에서도 현재완료 시제 문제가 다른 시제들에 비해 압도적으로 많이 출제된다. 특히 현재완료와 미래완료 시제를 묻는 문제는 특정 표현이 항상 문제 풀이 단서로 나오기 때문에 반드시 알아 두어야 한다.

1 현재완료

A crew from Martin Builders **has already begun** construction on the new Batholomew Bridge.
Martin Builders의 작업조는 새로운 Batholomew Bridge 공사에 이미 착수했다.

☑ 현재완료 시제와 어울려 쓰이는 표현: for ~ 동안, since ~ 이래로, already 이미, just 막, yet 아직, so far 지금까지, over ~에 걸쳐, in recent weeks 최근 몇 주간, in just one year 1년 만에

2 과거완료

By the time Ms. Yamada arrived at the auditorium, the opening remarks **had** already **started**.
Ms. Yamada가 강당에 도착했을 무렵에 개회사는 이미 시작한 상태였다.

☑ 과거완료 시제와 어울려 쓰이는 표현: by the time + 주어 + 동사의 과거형 ~했을 무렵에는

3 미래완료

Mr. Russell **will have worked** at Lilimelon Construction for 20 years **by next month**.
Mr. Russell은 다음 달이면 Lilimelon Construction에서 일한 지 20년이 된다.

☑ 미래완료 시제와 어울려 쓰이는 표현: by the time + 주어 + 동사의 현재형 ~한 무렵에는, by ~쯤에는, at/by the end of ~의 말에/말까지

실전 감각 다지기

정답 및 해설 p.24

1. VitaMint ------- some major improvements in their new supplement formula in recent weeks.
   (A) had made   (B) has made
   (C) will make   (D) making

2. By the time Ms. Coleman joined our department as the head of finances, she ------- client accounting for many years.
   (A) has managed   (B) had managed
   (C) managing   (D) manages

3. By the end of this month, our store ------- half a million dollars' worth of jewelry.
   (A) sold   (B) selling
   (C) will have sold (D) had sold

4. Since Calvin's Coffee started offering frequency rewards, the amount of returning customers -------.
   (A) has increased   (B) is increasing
   (C) increasing   (D) increases

빈출 유형 공략 04   주절 – 종속절의 시제 일치와 예외

Casablanca was forced to reschedule its grand opening when the furniture and silverware for the restaurant ------- on time.
(A) did not arrive   (B) not to arrive   (C) not to have arrived   (D) will not be arriving

풀이   주절의 시제가 과거 시제이므로 종속절인 when절도 과거 시제로 써야 한다. 따라서 (A) did not arrive가 정답이다.
해석   식당에 들어갈 가구와 은 식기가 제때 도착하지 않아서 Casablanca는 어쩔 수 없이 개업식 일정을 다시 잡아야 했다.

유형 돋보기

주절이나 종속절에 들어갈 알맞은 시제를 고르는 문제가 간혹 출제된다. 이때는 특정 시제와 어울려 쓰이는 표현을 보고 시제를 판별하면 된다. 단, 문장 안에 시제를 유추할 수 있는 특정 표현이 없다면 문맥으로 알맞은 시제를 파악해야 한다.

① 대부분의 경우에 주절의 동사가 과거 시제면 종속절의 동사는 과거 또는 과거완료로 쓴다.

The customer **inquired** about a paint color that the manufacturer **had discontinued**.
그 고객은 제조사가 생산을 중단한 페인트 색깔을 문의했다.

② 주절이 과거 시제이더라도 문맥에 따라 종속절에 현재(완료)나 미래 시제를 쓸 수 있다.

Mr. Fisher **told** his team members that the departmental meeting **will be held** next Friday.
Mr. Fisher는 팀원들에게 부서 회의가 다음 주 금요일에 있을 것이라고 말했다.
→ 주절이 과거 시제(told)이지만 종속절에서는 '다음 주 금요일(next Friday)'이라는 미래 상황을 이야기하고 있으므로 미래 시제(will be held)를 썼다.

③ 주절이 현재나 미래 시제일 때는 종속절에 어떤 시제든 들어갈 수 있다. 따라서 이때는 문맥을 보고 적절한 시제를 선택해야 한다.

ActiveWhere plans to introduce a new sneaker that **will offer** / ~~had offered~~ amazing comfort.
ActiveWhere는 놀라운 편안함을 제공하게 될 새로운 스니커즈를 선보일 계획이다.
→ 새로 선보일 스니커즈의 특징을 묘사하고 있으므로 미래 시제(will offer)가 알맞다.

실전 감각 다지기

정답 및 해설 p.24

1. After Mr. Han ------- his presentation, the staff understood the new software more clearly.
(A) has been giving   (B) giving
(C) gave   (D) will give

2. Because the air conditioning has still not been fixed, employees ------- to work from home tomorrow.
(A) will be allowed
(B) had been allowed
(C) being allowed
(D) to allow

3. Eco-Green will choose which poster proposal ------- their company's marketing campaign best.
(A) suiting   (B) suits
(C) had suited   (D) was suiting

4. The Mexico City branch was closed yesterday as the country ------- its Independence Day.
(A) will have celebrated
(B) to celebrate
(C) is celebrating
(D) had celebrated

빈출 유형 공략 05 — 시간과 조건 부사절의 시제

Please mute your cell phone once the movie -------.
(A) will begin (B) was beginning (C) begins (D) began

쉬운 토익 공식 빈칸이 시간 부사절의 동사 자리이고 문맥상 미래의 일을 나타내면 현재 시제가 정답이다.

풀이 시간 부사절에서는 미래의 일을 현재 시제로 나타내므로 (C) begins가 정답이다.
해석 영화가 시작되면 휴대 전화를 반드시 무음으로 설정해 주세요.

유형 돋보기

시간과 조건 부사절에서는 미래 시제 대신 현재 시제를 쓴다.

① 시간 부사절

The mobile application will notify you **when** the delivery driver **is** / ~~will be~~ at your doorstep.
그 휴대 전화 애플리케이션은 배달원이 문 앞에 오면 당신에게 알려 줍니다.

② 조건 부사절

if 조건절은 현재나 미래에 일어날 가능성이 높은 사실을 말할 때 쓴다. 토익에 출제되는 if 문제는 대부분 if 조건절인데 if절이나 주절에 들어갈 알맞은 시제를 묻는 문제가 출제된다.

Passengers on Grand Northern Railway **receive** compensation **if** their train **is** / ~~will be~~ delayed.
Grand Northern Railway 승객은 기차가 지연되면 보상을 받습니다.

If you **get** / ~~will get~~ an annual subscription, you **will** also **receive** a free tote bag with your first issue of the magazine.
연간 구독을 하신다면 첫 번째 구독 잡지에 무료 토트백도 받게 되실 겁니다.

If it **should** rain, the festival **will be** rescheduled. (= Should it rain, the festival will be rescheduled.)
혹시라도 비가 오면 축제 일정이 변경될 것이다.

→ if절에 동사 현재형 대신 should를 써서 '혹시라도'의 의미를 나타낼 수 있다. 단, 이때는 주로 if를 생략하고 주어와 동사를 도치하여 [Should + 주어 + 동사원형] 구조로 쓴다.

실전 감각 다지기

정답 및 해설 p.25

1. Mr. Grantham will announce the good news to his employees when they ------- from winter break next week.
   (A) will return (B) return
   (C) returned (D) have returned

2. The watercolor painting class ------- if registration includes fewer than 10 people.
   (A) canceled (B) was canceled
   (C) will be canceled (D) had been canceled

3. Payments to your credit card balance will be carried over to the next billing cycle if they ------- after the payment due date.
   (A) will be transferred (B) were transferred
   (C) transferred (D) are transferred

4. Once the marketing team ------- its current advertising campaign, it will go public within a few weeks.
   (A) perfected (B) has perfected
   (C) will perfect (D) perfects

빈출 유형 공략 06 if 가정법

If Ms. Melo had known Mr. Kao was feeling unwell, she ------- to go to the conference instead.
(A) would have offered (B) has offered (C) is being offered (D) will offer

풀이 if절의 동사(had known)가 [had p.p.]인 것으로 보아 가정법 과거완료 문장임을 알 수 있다. 따라서 주절의 동사는 [would/could/might + have p.p.]가 되어야 하므로 (A) would have offered가 정답이다.
해석 Mr. Kao가 아프다는 걸 Ms. Melo가 알았더라면 그녀는 학회에 대신 가겠다고 제안했을 것이다.

유형 돋보기

if 가정법은 사실이 아닌 상황을 설정하여 실현 가능성이 낮은 일을 나타낼 때 쓴다. if 조건절과 마찬가지로 if 가정법도 if절이나 주절에 들어갈 알맞은 시제를 묻는 문제가 출제되고 가정법 과거보다 가정법 과거완료의 출제 빈도가 훨씬 높은 편이다.

❶ 가정법 과거: If + 주어 + 동사 과거형 ~, 주어 + would/could/might + 동사원형 ~

If Ms. Weber **were** not busy, she **would attend** the training session.
Ms. Weber는 바쁘지 않다면 그 교육 과정에 참석할 텐데. (바빠서 참석하지 못한다.)
→ if절의 동사가 be동사면 주어의 수에 상관없이 were를 쓴다. (다만 구어체 영어에서는 was도 허용한다.)

❷ 가정법 과거완료: If + 주어 + had p.p. ~, 주어 + would/could/might + have p.p. ~

If user testing **had been** more thorough, the product launch **would have been** successful.
사용자 검증이 더 철저했다면 그 제품 출시는 성공적이었을 텐데. (성공적이지 않았다.)
→ 과거 사실과 반대되는 상황을 가정할 때 쓰며, '~했다면 …했을 텐데'라고 해석한다. if절의 동사가 과거완료형이어서 흔히 '가정법 과거완료'라고 한다.

고득점 POINT if를 생략하면 주어와 동사가 도치된다.
Had we **taken** the subway instead of a taxi, we might have caught our flight.
택시 대신 지하철을 탔다면 우리는 비행기를 탔을 것이다.

실전 감각 다지기

정답 및 해설 p.25

1. If the salt content ------- any further, Haier's chips would not have the same taste.
   (A) is reduced (B) has been reduced
   (C) will be reduced (D) were reduced

2. Had a sudden miscommunication not interrupted the negotiation, the two companies ------- peacefully.
   (A) would have merged
   (B) have merged
   (C) had merged
   (D) will have merged

3. Ms. Ferebee would not have been late for the conference if her flight ------- as scheduled.
   (A) arrives (B) will arrive
   (C) had arrived (D) arriving

4. The distributor ------- with as much criticism if it had properly followed all necessary health regulations.
   (A) had not been confronted
   (B) would not have been confronted
   (C) is not confronted
   (D) not to be confronted

ACTUAL TEST

1. Ms. Bax ------- today's board meeting, since Mr. Gonzalez is out of town for the International Marketing Conference.
   (A) having led
   (B) to lead
   (C) will be leading
   (D) had led

2. Nearly 40 new jobs will be created when Brentwood Mills ------- a new logging factory in town.
   (A) was opening
   (B) opens
   (C) has opened
   (D) will have opened

3. LP Law Firm ------- over 30 cases in just one year.
   (A) winning
   (B) wins
   (C) will have won
   (D) has won

4. The IT department completed the project even though they ------- working on it just last week.
   (A) start
   (B) will start
   (C) to start
   (D) had started

5. If the granulated sugar shortage continues, it ------- lemonade sales at our restaurant.
   (A) will affect
   (B) to affect
   (C) was affecting
   (D) affected

6. So far, Alliance Foods ------- with two shipping companies to manage the distribution of its products.
   (A) was partnering
   (B) to partner
   (C) partners
   (D) has partnered

7. Until the WiFi connection in the office -------, please use an Ethernet cable to access the Internet.
   (A) reestablished
   (B) has been reestablished
   (C) is reestablished
   (D) will be reestablished

8. Later this week, Ms. Harden ------- job applicants who passed the written test.
   (A) has been interviewing
   (B) interviewing
   (C) had interviewed
   (D) will be interviewing

9. If BND Technology ------- on innovation, it would not have been as profitable.
   (A) does not focus
   (B) had not focused
   (C) is not focusing
   (D) will not focus

10. At the end of the month, night shift manager Rolan Mojica ------- at La Suprema Tacos for 20 years.
    (A) served
    (B) will have served
    (C) to serve
    (D) was serving

Questions 11-14 refer to the following advertisement.

Zielo Tours Seeks Guide

Zielo Tours is hiring a tour guide for people ------- sign up for group tours to Barcelona and
                                              11.
Madrid. The tour guide ------- the pace of the tour to ensure that the appropriate amount of time
                        12.
is spent at each stop. The guide must be fluent in both English and Spanish. -------. Benefits of
                                                                              13.
the job include competitive wages as well as free and discounted travel. To apply, please upload
your résumé to zielotours.com. We also ask that you provide professional ------- from two
                                                                          14.
previous employers should you pass the initial screening phase.

---

11. (A) rarely
(B) who
(C) securely
(D) what

12. (A) was managing
(B) managed
(C) will manage
(D) will have managed

13. (A) We have been growing steadily since opening.
(B) This step of the process cannot be skipped.
(C) You can select the size of your hotel room.
(D) Knowledge of the local area is also highly desired.

14. (A) references
(B) questions
(C) negotiations
(D) characteristics

에듀윌이
너를
지지할게

ENERGY

쉼 없는 분주함은 소란스럽고,
분주함 없는 쉼은 게으릅니다.

— 조정민, 『인생은 선물이다』, 두란노

CHAPTER 1

PART 5 & 6
문법

실전에서 바로 써먹는
쉬운 토익 공식 인강

UNIT 08

to부정사와 동명사

토익 기초 문법 OVERVIEW

빈출 유형 공략 01 to부정사 자리와 역할

빈출 유형 공략 02 동명사 자리와 역할

빈출 유형 공략 03 동명사 vs. 명사

빈출 유형 공략 04 to부정사와 동명사 관용 표현

ACTUAL TEST

UNIT 08 | to부정사와 동명사

토익 기초 문법 OVERVIEW

A to부정사는 명사, 형용사, 부사 역할을 한다.

명사 (~하는 것)	A large part of her job is **to negotiate** contracts with manufacturers. 그녀가 하는 일의 상당 부분은 제조업자들과 계약을 협상하는 것이다.
형용사 (~하려는, ~할)	Plans **to turn** the factory into a park are under consideration. 그 공장을 공원으로 바꾸려는 계획이 검토되고 있다.
	She couldn't find any place **to park**. 그녀는 주차할 곳을 찾을 수 없었다.
부사 (~하기 위해, ~하기에, ~하는 데)	Many staffers are working overtime **to complete** projects on time. 많은 직원들이 프로젝트를 제시간에 끝내기 위해 초과 근무를 하고 있다.
	Such a database will be extremely costly **to set up**. 그런 데이터베이스는 구축하는 데 매우 많은 비용이 들 것이다.

B 특정 동사는 to부정사를 목적어로 취한다. 특히 계획이나 희망을 의미하는 동사들이 여기에 속한다.

plan 계획하다	hope 희망하다	agree 동의하다	promise 약속하다
aim 목표하다	expect 기대하다	refuse 거절하다	fail ~하지 못하다
would like 원하다	wish 바라다	offer 제안하다	need ~할 필요가 있다
want 원하다	decide 결정하다	afford 여유가 있다	tend 경향이 있다

The initiative **aims to** **minimize** the impact on the environment.
그 계획은 환경에 미치는 영향을 최소화하는 것을 목표로 한다.

Mr. Carter **plans to** **make** a donation to the Maughan Library.
Mr. Carter는 Maughan Library에 기부할 계획이다.

C 특정 동사는 [동사 + 목적어 + to부정사]의 형태로 쓸 수 있으며, [be p.p. + to부정사]의 수동태로 전환될 수 있다.

Mr. Hall **asked** all sales staff **to** attend the meeting. Mr. Hall은 모든 영업 사원들이 회의에 참석할 것을 요청했다.	All sales staff **were asked to** attend the meeting. 모든 영업 사원은 회의에 참석하도록 요청되었다.

The software **allows** users **to customize** designs.
그 소프트웨어는 사용자가 디자인을 개별적으로 바꿀 수 있게 한다.

We don't **expect** the meeting **to last** longer than one hour.
우리는 그 회의가 한 시간 이상 걸릴 거라고 예상하지 않습니다.

D 동명사는 명사의 역할을 하지만 동사의 성질을 가지고 있기에 뒤에 목적어를 취할 수 있고, 부사의 수식을 받을 수 있다.

> Thank you for **promptly submitting** your quarterly report.
> 　　　　　　　　부사　　　동명사　　　　　목적어
> 분기별 보고서를 신속히 제출해 주셔서 감사합니다.

E 동명사는 전치사의 목적어로 쓰일 수 있다.

The training session is aimed **at improving** productivity.
그 교육은 생산성 향상을 목표로 한다.

Mr. Smith was a professor **before starting** his own company.
Mr. Smith는 창업을 하기 전에는 교수였다.

Venturi Financial is well aware of the importance **of protecting** customer information.
Venturi Financial은 고객 정보 보호의 중요성을 잘 인식하고 있습니다.

F 특정 동사는 동명사를 목적어로 취한다.

| consider 고려하다 | suggest 제안하다 | finish 마치다 |
| enjoy 즐기다 | recommend 추천하다 | avoid 피하다 |

Mr. Wilson **suggested postponing** the meeting.
Mr. Wilson은 그 회의를 연기할 것을 제안했다.

She **finished designing** the new corporate logo yesterday.
그녀는 어제 회사의 새로운 로고 디자인을 끝냈다.

The mechanic **recommended replacing** some worn parts.
정비사는 일부 마모된 부품을 교체하라고 권했다.

기초 문법 CHECK

정답 및 해설 p.27

1~7. 밑줄 친 부분 중 가장 적절한 것을 고르세요.

1. Cavendish Conference Centre is the perfect place to hold / holding corporate events.
2. We plan to replace / replacing the carpet in your office on Friday.
3. I would like to cancel / canceling the order for item D12.
4. This software allows you to access / accessing files anywhere you need them.
5. The project is expected to create / creating more than 200 new jobs.
6. The new system is aimed at improve / improving company security.
7. Ms. Lopez had to work late to finish to draw / drawing up the budget.

빈출 유형 공략 01 　 to부정사 자리와 역할　

A technician from the software company will be here tomorrow morning ------- a new word processor.
(A) be installing　　(B) installs　　(C) to install　　(D) install

풀이　빈칸 앞이 완전한 절이므로 빈칸 이하는 부사 역할을 해야 한다. 선택지 중에서 부사 역할을 할 수 있는 것은 to부정사이므로 (C) to install이 정답이다.
해석　그 소프트웨어 회사의 기술자가 새 워드 프로세서를 설치하기 위해 내일 오전에 이곳에 올 것이다.

유형 돋보기

① to부정사는 주어, 보어, 목적어 자리에 위치하여 명사 역할을 하며, 토익에서는 주로 보어나 목적어 자리에 to부정사를 채우는 문제가 출제된다.

주격 보어	One of our main goals this year is **to attract** more customers. 올해 우리의 주요 목표 중 하나는 더 많은 고객을 유치하는 것이다.
목적격 보어	The manager asked Ms. Horrocks **to review** the report and add her comments. 그 부장은 Ms. Horrocks에게 보고서를 검토해서 의견을 추가해 달라고 요청했다. → [동사 + 목적어 + to부정사]는 [be p.p. + to부정사] 형태로도 자주 쓰인다.
목적어	We expect **to see** a profit increase with the upcoming holiday season. 우리는 다가오는 휴가 시즌에 수익 증가를 보길 기대한다.

② to부정사는 명사를 뒤에서 수식하는 형용사 역할을 한다.

The IT consultant for Alabaster Co. has decided that it is **time to upgrade** its wireless network.
Alabaster Co.의 IT 컨설턴트는 이제 무선 네트워크를 업그레이드해야 할 시기라고 결론을 내렸다.

③ to부정사는 부사 역할을 한다.

The CEO does everything she can **to support**(= in order to support) her employees.
그 대표 이사는 직원들을 지원하기 위해 그녀가 할 수 있는 모든 것을 한다.

실전 감각 다지기

정답 및 해설 p.27

1. Ichihara Solutions is searching for new ways ------- packages to its customers even faster.
(A) deliver　　(B) have delivered
(C) to deliver　　(D) delivers

2. The objective for this month is ------- 5% more than we did last month.
(A) to sell　　(B) sell
(C) sold　　(D) being sold

3. Tourists are invited ------- the information center to learn more about the town's best attractions.
(A) visiting　　(B) to visit
(C) visits　　(D) having visited

4. Moussa TV, after critical acclaim in Kenya, plans ------- its coverage across East Africa.
(A) broad　　(B) to broaden
(C) have broadened　　(D) broader

빈출 유형 공략 02 동명사 자리와 역할

Factory supervisors are responsible for ------- a safe work environment.
(A) maintain   (B) to maintain   (C) maintaining   (D) maintained

쉬운 토익 공식 선택지가 동사의 활용형으로 구성되어 있고 빈칸 앞에 전치사가 있으면 동명사가 정답이다.

풀이 빈칸에는 전치사 for의 목적어 역할을 하는 동명사가 들어가야 한다. 따라서 (C) maintaining이 정답이다.
해석 공장 감독자들은 안전한 작업 환경을 유지해야 하는 책임이 있다.

유형 돋보기

1 동명사는 전치사 뒤에 위치한다.

All visitors must check in at the security desk **before entering** the building.
모든 방문객은 건물에 들어가기 전에 보안 창구에서 방문자 등록을 해야 한다.

Since switching offices, Prowler Co. has reported a 5% increase in productivity.
사무실을 바꾼 이후로 Prowler Co.는 생산성이 5% 증가했다고 보고했다.

2 동명사는 주어, 보어, 목적어 자리에 위치하여 명사 역할을 한다.

주어	**Opening** a branch in Singapore will give the company more influence abroad. 싱가포르에 지사를 열면 그 회사는 해외에서 더 큰 영향력을 갖게 될 것이다.
보어	One of the receptionist's duties is **answering** every incoming call. 접수원의 업무 중 하나는 걸려 오는 전화를 모두 받는 것이다.
목적어	If there are technical issues with the projector, we suggest **contacting** Mr. Yi in the maintenance department. 프로젝터에 기술적인 문제가 생기면 유지 관리 부서의 Mr. Yi에게 연락하세요.

실전 감각 다지기

정답 및 해설 p.27

1. Ms. Kirk is in charge of ------- everything that happens on the assembly line.
   (A) oversee   (B) overseen
   (C) overseeing   (D) will oversee

2. Before ------- the office, please make sure all the lights and computers have been shut off.
   (A) leaving   (B) are leaving
   (C) to leave   (D) leave

3. The board of trustees will consider ------- the business into other ventures if profits remain high.
   (A) expand   (B) expanding
   (C) to expand   (D) has expanded

4. ------- an impressive portfolio that shows your technical skills will help you get jobs in graphic design.
   (A) Create   (B) Creating
   (C) Creates   (D) Created

빈출 유형 공략 03 — 동명사 vs. 명사

The Seattle Zoo offers internships to undergraduates thinking about ------- a career in zoology.

(A) pursuing (B) pursuit (C) pursues (D) pursued

쉬운 토익 공식 빈칸 앞에 전치사가 있고 뒤에는 명사(구)가 있으면 동명사가 정답이다.

풀이 빈칸 앞에 전치사 about이 있고 뒤에는 명사구 a career in zoology가 있으므로 빈칸에는 명사를 목적어로 취할 수 있는 동명사가 들어가야 한다. 따라서 (A) pursuing이 정답이다.

해석 Seattle Zoo는 동물학에서 경력을 쌓을 생각이 있는 학부생들에게 인턴십 기회를 제공한다.

유형 돋보기

① 동명사는 목적어를 취할 수 있다.

The team leader thanked Ms. Reece for **bringing the building security issue** to his attention.
팀장은 그 건물의 보안 문제를 알려 준 것에 대해 Ms. Reece에게 감사를 표했다.

② 동명사는 관사의 수식을 받을 수 없다.

Every Sunday, the restaurant offers a ~~selecting~~ / **selection** of delicious desserts at its buffet.
매주 일요일 그 레스토랑은 뷔페 메뉴에 맛있는 디저트를 다양하게 제공한다.

③ 동명사는 부사(구)의 수식을 받고, 명사는 형용사나 분사의 수식을 받는다.

Pristine Hair will begin **shipping internationally** only if there is enough demand.
Pristine Hair는 충분한 수요가 있어야 국제 배송을 시작할 것이다.

Because of the **delayed shipment**, the product launch didn't take place as scheduled.
지연된 배송 때문에 제품 출시 행사는 예정된 대로 열리지 않았다.

고득점 POINT -ing형 명사는 일반 명사처럼 관사나 형용사의 수식을 받을 수 있다.

planning 계획 (수립)	processing 처리	funding 자금 조달	seating 좌석 배치
wording 단어 선택, 표현	packaging 포장	offering 제공된 것	opening 개시, 개막; 공석

Pinglet Bistro expanded its **seasonal** menu **offerings**. Pinglet Bistro는 계절 메뉴를 확대했다.

실전 감각 다지기

정답 및 해설 p.28

1. The marketing research shows that ------- wording does a great job of attracting the audience's attention.

(A) describe (B) describing
(C) descriptive (D) descriptively

2. Staff members are hurriedly preparing for the ------- of the new coffee shop.

(A) opening (B) openness
(C) openly (D) opens

3. The owner of the Lucier Theater made a rare ------- and allowed a private party to be hosted there.

(A) exception (B) excepts
(C) excepting (D) excepted

4. After ------- the downtown area, Mr. Tait chose not to move his restaurant to Clifton.

(A) evaluation (B) evaluate
(C) evaluating (D) evaluated

빈출 유형 공략 04 — to부정사와 동명사 관용 표현

Home Medica's customers are eligible ------- a 25% off coupon if their purchase is over $50.
(A) receiving   (B) to receive   (C) received   (D) receiver

풀이 형용사 eligible은 to부정사와 어울려 쓰이므로 (B) to receive가 정답이다.
해석 Home Medica의 고객은 구매 금액이 50달러가 넘으면 25% 할인 쿠폰을 받을 수 있다.

유형 돋보기

① [be동사 + 형용사 + to부정사] 관용 표현

be[make] sure to 확실히 ~하다	be able to ~할 수 있다	be eligible to ~할 자격이 되다
be willing to 기꺼이 ~하다	be hesitant to ~하는 것을 주저하다	be advisable to ~하는 것을 권하다
be eager to ~하기를 간절히 바라다	be ready to ~할 준비가 되다	be proud to ~해서 자랑스럽다
be likely to ~할 가능성이 있다	be available to ~하는 것이 가능하다; (시간적으로) ~할 여유가 되다	

Ms. Craig will **be able to** cope with the work.
Ms. Craig는 그 일을 잘 처리할 수 있을 겁니다.

Mr. Juan **was** not **available to** work last week, so Mr. Vettel filled in for him.
Mr. Juan은 지난주에 근무를 할 수 없어서 Mr. Vettel이 그를 대신하여 근무했다.

② 동명사 관용 표현

have difficulty (in) -ing ~하는 데 어려움이 있다	have trouble (in) -ing ~하는 데 곤란을 겪다
spend 시간/돈 (on) -ing ~하는 데 시간/돈을 쓰다	be busy -ing ~하느라 바쁘다
be worth -ing ~할 가치가 있다	be accustomed to -ing ~하는 데 익숙하다

Let us know if customers **had any difficulty placing** orders on the Web site.
고객들이 그 웹사이트에서 주문을 하는 데 어려움을 겪었다면 우리에게 알려 주세요.

실전 감각 다지기

정답 및 해설 p.28

1. Ms. Presley was willing to ------- operations at the Boston branch in Mr. Morgan's absence.
   (A) supervising   (B) supervision
   (C) supervise   (D) supervises

2. Customers seem to have trouble ------- their accounts from our Web site.
   (A) accessible   (B) accessing
   (C) accessed   (D) to access

3. It is advisable to ------- with recruiters to get advice on how to find the best opportunities.
   (A) communicated   (B) communication
   (C) communicating   (D) communicate

4. Fresh Park fans who are accustomed to ------- to the band's rock ballads will be surprised by the new album.
   (A) listen   (B) be listening
   (C) listening   (D) listened

ACTUAL TEST

1. The Business Writing Workshop will teach participants ways ------- their ideas clearly and effectively.
   (A) are communicating
   (B) to communicate
   (C) communicates
   (D) have communicated

2. Please save documents regularly when working on them to prevent important information from -------.
   (A) is lost
   (B) lost
   (C) being lost
   (D) losing

3. MaryAnn's Coffee increased the price of drinks with paper cups ------- encourage customers to bring their own.
   (A) for
   (B) so that
   (C) because
   (D) in order to

4. If you have a mechanical problem with the product, we suggest ------- the manufacturer directly first for support.
   (A) contacted
   (B) contacting
   (C) contacts
   (D) to contact

5. Paris Museum Tour tickets are available to ------- online or at any participating museum.
   (A) purchasing
   (B) purchased
   (C) being purchased
   (D) purchase

6. With his excellent leadership skills, Mr. Rangel will have no trouble ------- the team.
   (A) manager
   (B) managing
   (C) manage
   (D) managed

7. Because of supply chain issues, the price of raw materials is expected ------- this month.
   (A) increases
   (B) to increase
   (C) increasingly
   (D) increased

8. There will be some noise disruptions as the crew works ------- the cracked section of the road.
   (A) repaired
   (B) repair
   (C) had repaired
   (D) to repair

9. Since ------- on the television talent show, Nori Shibutani's singing career has taken off.
   (A) performers
   (B) performance
   (C) performable
   (D) performing

10. Please make sure ------- patients' health matters in confidence.
    (A) can address
    (B) having addressed
    (C) to address
    (D) addressing

Questions 11-14 refer to the following press release.

Queenstown is happy to announce that the construction of a brand-new public library has been completed. Residents are encouraged ------- the library, which is located on Third Street, for its grand opening on June 18. Throughout the day, librarians will be giving tours of the newly ------- facilities. The library features a computer lab, children's playroom, and printing center. -------, Queenstown residents who sign up for a library card will have access to our e-book collection. -------. You're certain to find something you will enjoy reading.

We hope to see you there!

11. (A) to visit
(B) visiting
(C) visited
(D) they visited

12. (A) development
(B) develop
(C) developed
(D) developing

13. (A) Additionally
(B) However
(C) Therefore
(D) Unfortunately

14. (A) Please direct questions to the front desk.
(B) The lobby was designed by a famous architect.
(C) The library staff is incredibly friendly.
(D) This includes over 10,000 books for you to borrow electronically.

CHAPTER 1

PART 5 & 6
문법

실전에서 바로 써먹는
쉬운 토익 공식 인강

UNIT 09

분사

토익 기초 문법 OVERVIEW

빈출 유형 공략 01 과거분사/현재분사 + 명사

빈출 유형 공략 02 명사 + 과거분사/현재분사

빈출 유형 공략 03 접속사 + 분사

빈출 유형 공략 04 관용적 분사구문

ACTUAL TEST

UNIT 09 | 분사

토익 기초 문법 OVERVIEW

A 분사는 동사에 -ed, -ing가 붙은 형태로서, 형용사처럼 명사를 수식할 수 있다. 이때, 과거분사는 수동의 의미, 현재분사는 능동의 의미를 나타낸다.

수동: Please see the **attached** document and respond with your comments.
첨부된 문서를 보시고 의견을 주시기 바랍니다.

능동: **Returning** customers receive 10% off all future lawn maintenance.
재방문하는 고객들은 향후 모든 잔디 정비에 대해 10% 할인을 받습니다.

B 과거분사가 하나의 형용사로 굳어져 쓰일 수 있다. 이때, 과거분사 형태의 형용사가 항상 수동을 의미하지는 않으며, 사람 앞에 올 때는 주로 자질을 의미한다.

acclaim ~을 칭송하다 → an **acclaimed** writer 호평 받는 작가 (형용사: 수동 의미)

accomplish ~을 성취하다 → an **accomplished** writer 뛰어난 작가 (형용사: 수동 의미 아님)

> a **distinguished** scholar 뛰어난 학자 　　an **experienced** employee 경력 직원
> a **qualified** applicant 적격인 지원자 　　a **motivated** worker 적극적인 직원
> a **noted** composer 유명한 작곡가 　　　an **established** company 저명한 회사

C 분사는 명사의 뒤에서 명사를 수식할 수 있다. 이것을 축약된 관계사절로 볼 수 있다.

Some information **(which is) contained** in the documents is confidential.
그 문서들에 포함되어 있는 일부 정보들은 기밀이다.

Ms. Stevenson is a designer **working** with Sam at Design Tech.
　　　　　　　　　　　　　　　= who worked/works/is working
Ms. Stevenson은 Design Tech에서 Sam과 함께 일했던/일하는/일하고 있는 디자이너다.

☑ 과거의 일회적인 사건의 경우 현재분사를 쓸 수 없다.
Passengers ~~missing~~ / **who missed** the train were making complaints.
기차를 놓친 승객들이 항의를 하고 있었다.

D 주어를 수식하는 분사(주로 과거분사)구는 문장 앞에 위치할 수 있다.

Born and raised in Westport, Richard Meier started writing short stories in high school.
웨스트포트에서 태어나고 자란 Richard Meier는 고등학교 때 단편 소설을 쓰기 시작했다.

Scheduled for release by mid-March, the novel is sure to appeal to a wide audience.
3월 중순까지 발매될 예정인 그 소설은 분명 많은 독자들에게 어필할 것이다.

E 부사절이 시간, 이유를 나타낼 경우, 주절과 부사절의 주어가 동일하면 부사절은 분사구문으로 대체될 수 있다.

Arriving at the airport, Mr. Smith called his assistant. 공항에 도착하자마자 Mr. Smith는 그의 비서에게 연락했다.
= As soon as / When he arrived at the airport

Written in chronological order, the book is easy to follow. 그 책은 시간 순으로 쓰여서 따라가기 쉽다.
= Because it is written in chronological order

F 감정을 나타내는 동사들의 분사는 형용사로 굳어져 쓰이는 경우가 많다.

동사	The hair-care product might **interest** many middle-aged men. 그 모발 관리 상품은 많은 중년 남성들의 관심을 끌 수도 있을 것이다.
-ing 형용사	Mr. Taylor's presentation was **interesting**. → 주어(presentation)가 감정을 일으킴 Mr. Taylor의 발표는 흥미로웠다.
-ed 형용사	Ms. Lee was **interested** in the conference. → 주어(Ms. Lee)가 감정을 느낌 Ms. Lee는 그 콘퍼런스에 관심 있었다.

satisfying — satisfied 만족할 만한 — 만족하는	fascinating — fascinated 흥미진진한 — 흥미를 느낀	surprising — surprised 놀라운 — 놀란
pleasing — pleased 기분 좋게 하는 — 기쁜	concerning — concerned 걱정스러운 — 걱정하는	disappointing — disappointed 실망스러운 — 실망한

기초 문법 CHECK

정답 및 해설 p.30

1~7. 밑줄 친 부분에서 옳은 것을 고르세요.

1. The ventilation system helps to freshen enclosing / enclosed spaces by pumping in air from outside.

2. Risen / Rising labor costs have forced us to raise our prices by 5%.

3. The Senior Planning Committee is composed of highly accomplished / accomplishing executives.

4. All employees wished / wishing to take time off must submit their requests one week in advance.

5. A list of the customers who received e-mails containing / contained errors is attached.

6. Founded / Founding and headquartered in Belgium, the cookware company is currently in the process of launching operations in Asia.

7. If you are not satisfied / satisfying with an item, return it for a full refund within 10 days of purchase.

빈출 유형 공략 01 과거분사/현재분사 + 명사

All elevators in the building will be out of service for one hour from 10 A.M. in order to perform ------- maintenance.

(A) required (B) requiring (C) require (D) requires

쉬운 토익 공식 분사가 뒤에 오는 명사와 수동의 관계일 때는 과거분사가 정답이다.

풀이 타동사 perform과 명사 maintenance 사이에 빈칸이 왔으므로, 선택지 중 빈칸에 들어갈 수 있는 것은 명사를 수식하는 분사나 형용사밖에 없다. maintenance(유지 보수)는 '요구하는' 주체가 아니라 '요구되는' 대상이므로 수동의 의미를 나타내는 과거분사 (A) required가 정답이다.

해석 건물 내의 모든 승강기는 필요한 유지 보수를 수행하기 위해 오전 10시부터 한 시간 동안 작동이 중지됩니다.

유형 돋보기

❶ 과거분사 + 명사: 분사가 뒤에 오는 명사와 수동의 관계이면 과거분사를 쓴다.

Visitors must return all **borrowed** roller skates to the front desk.
방문객들은 빌린 롤러스케이트를 모두 프런트 데스크에 반납해야 합니다. (borrow 빌리다 → borrowed 빌려진)

The publisher will release a **revised** edition of the book early next month.
그 출판사는 다음 달 초에 그 책의 개정판을 출간할 것이다. (revise 개정하다 → revised 개정된)

The **selected** candidates will first complete a paid month-long training course during May.
선발된 지원자들은 우선 5월 중에 한 달간의 유급 교육 과정을 이수할 것이다. (select 선발하다 → selected 선발된)

The document contains details about **anticipated** expenditures and profits.
그 서류에는 예상 지출과 이익에 대한 세부 사항이 포함되어 있다. (anticipate 예상하다 → anticipated 예상되는)

❷ 현재분사 + 명사: 분사가 뒤에 오는 명사와 능동의 관계이면 현재분사를 쓴다.

Rainbow Travel has formed a partnership with Blue Airways, a **growing** international airline.
Rainbow Travel은 성장하는 국제 항공사인 Blue Airways와 파트너십을 맺었다. (grow 성장하다 → growing 성장하는)

Micro Products seeks ways of meeting rapidly **changing** consumer demand.
Micro Products는 급변하는 소비자 수요를 충족시킬 방법을 모색하고 있다. (change 변하다 → changing 변화하는)

Executives have **differing** views on the issue.
임직원들은 그 문제에 대해 다른 견해를 가지고 있다. (differ 다르다 → differing 다른)

실전 감각 다지기

정답 및 해설 p.30

1. The mayor believes the ------- 100-foot sculpture will attract tourists to the city.
(A) propose (B) proposed
(C) proposing (D) proposal

2. Please contact Mr. Jones immediately and e-mail him the ------- agreement.
(A) correction (B) corrected
(C) correcting (D) correctly

3. ------- passengers must complete a security check in order to fly.
(A) Depart (B) Departed
(C) Departing (D) Departure

4. The sales department has already spent more than its ------- budget.
(A) allot (B) allotted
(C) allotting (D) allotments

빈출 유형 공략 02 : 명사 + 과거분사/현재분사 (축약된 관계사절)

Every travel package ------- over $1,500 comes with a 15% discount on car rentals.
(A) prices (B) priced (C) pricey (D) pricing

쉬운 토익 공식 분사가 앞에 있는 명사와 수동의 관계일 때는 과거분사가 정답이다.

풀이 빈칸에는 주어 Every travel package를 수식하는 형용사 또는 분사가 들어갈 수 있다. price는 '가격을 정하다'라는 뜻의 타동사이며, travel package는 가격을 정하는 주체가 아니라 '가격이 매겨지는' 대상이 되므로 수동의 의미를 지닌 과거분사 (B) priced가 정답이다.
= Every travel package (which is) priced over $1,500...

해석 가격이 1,500달러가 넘는 모든 여행 패키지에는 자동차 렌트 15% 할인 혜택이 있습니다.

유형 돋보기

1 명사 + 과거분사

명사 뒤에 오는 과거분사는 수동의 의미를 지니며, 명사와 과거분사 사이에는 주격 관계대명사와 be동사가 생략되어 있다.

Weardale Ski Club is a beautiful ski resort **(which is) located** near Durham.
Weardale Ski Club은 더럼 근처에 위치한 아름다운 스키 리조트입니다.

Full refunds are available for reservations **(which were) canceled** 24 hours or more before the event date.
행사일 24시간 전까지 취소된 예약에 대해서는 전액 환불이 가능하다.

2 명사 + 현재분사

명사 뒤에 오는 현재분사는 능동의 의미를 지니며, 대개 [관계대명사 + 동사]를 축약한 형태라고 볼 수 있다.

Anyone **wishing** to attend the quarterly meeting should contact Mr. Jackson.
　　　　= who wishes
분기 회의에 참석하고자 하는 사람은 Mr. Jackson에게 연락하세요.

The spreadsheet **containing** data on retail sales during the fourth quarter is attached.
　　　　　　　= which contains
4분기 동안의 소매 매출에 대한 데이터를 포함하고 있는 스프레드 시트가 첨부되어 있습니다.

실전 감각 다지기

정답 및 해설 p.31

1. Even the company lawyers were confused about several of the conditions ------- in the proposed merger.
   (A) list   (B) listing
   (C) listed (D) to list

2. The warranty does not cover damages ------- from improper use of medical equipment.
   (A) results   (B) resulted
   (C) resulting (D) to result

3. This year, Louis and Son Contracting signed several new deals ------- 16 million pounds.
   (A) totaled (B) total
   (C) totals   (D) totaling

4. Management sent an e-mail to all staff ------- them of the new company policy.
   (A) informative (B) informs
   (C) informing   (D) informed

빈출 유형 공략 03 접속사 + 분사

When ------ in, conference attendees will need to present a valid form of identification.
(A) check   (B) checked   (C) checking   (D) to check

쉬운 토익 공식 [접속사 + 분사] 구문에서 생략된 주어와 분사로 쓰인 동사가 능동의 관계이면 현재분사가 정답이다.

풀이 빈칸이 포함된 접속사절에 주어와 동사가 없으므로 [접속사 + 분사] 구조의 분사구문임을 알 수 있다. 과거분사인 (B) checked와 현재분사인 (C) checking이 정답 후보인데, 생략된 주어(conference attendees)는 '입장을 하는' 주체이기 때문에 빈칸과 능동 관계이므로 (C)가 정답이다.
When conference attendees check in... → When checking in...

해석 콘퍼런스에 입장할 때, 참석자들은 유효한 신분증을 제시해야 합니다.

유형 돋보기

1 접속사절의 주어와 주절의 주어가 동일할 때 접속사절은 [접속사 + 분사]로 대체할 수 있다.

While not as well-known as Taylor, Caroline is an equally accomplished designer.
= While she is not as well-known as Taylor
Taylor만큼 잘 알려져 있지는 않지만, Caroline 역시 다를 바 없이 뛰어난 디자이너이다.

Though pleasing to the eye, the building is drafty and cold.
= Though it is pleasing to the eye
그 건물은 겉보기에는 좋지만 외풍이 심하고 춥다.

☑ Because절은 분사구문으로 전환할 수 없다.
Because ~~arriving~~ / **he arrived** early, Mr. Brown had to wait an hour.
Mr. Brown은 일찍 도착했기 때문에 한 시간을 기다려야 했다.

2 관용적으로 쓰이는 [as + 과거분사]: ~한 바와 같이

As reported last month, All-Fresh is opening a regional distribution center in London.
지난달 보도된 바와 같이 All-Fresh는 런던에 지역 물류 센터를 개설할 예정입니다.

Factory workers must follow the safety guidelines **as outlined** in the company manual.
공장 근로자는 회사 편람에 나와 있는 대로 안전 지침을 따라야 합니다.

실전 감각 다지기

정답 및 해설 p.31

1. When recently ------, residents of Pleasantville said that improving public schools is their top concern.
   (A) polled   (B) polling
   (C) be polling   (D) to poll

2. While ------ faithful to the founder's original goal, the new CEO plans to make big changes in the company.
   (A) remain   (B) to remain
   (C) remaining   (D) remained

3. As ------, Paul Young's retirement party will be held at 2 P.M. on Friday, May 10.
   (A) discuss   (B) discussion
   (C) discussing   (D) discussed

4. Thankfully, the new prototype seems to be working as ------.
   (A) intentionally   (B) to intend
   (C) intending   (D) intended

빈출 유형 공략 04 관용적 분사구문

------ on January 2, the main entrance will be closed for one month while new doors are installed.
(A) Began (B) Beginning (C) Begins (D) Begin

풀이 특정 분사구문은 형태나 의미가 굳어져 관용적으로 쓰인다. Beginning은 주로 문장의 앞에 사용되며, 어떤 일의 시작 시점을 나타내는 표현으로 항상 현재분사로 사용한다.
해석 1월 2일부터 정문은 새로운 문이 설치되는 동안 약 한 달 정도 폐쇄됩니다.

유형 돋보기

① 관용적 현재분사구문

Starting this month, Chris's Coffee will be offering a 10% discount on all purchases by local college students.
이번 달부터 Chris's Coffee는 지역 대학교 학생들에게 모든 구매에 대해 10%의 할인을 제공합니다.

Considering how successful this new advertising campaign is, we should hire the same marketing firm for our next project.
이 새로운 광고 캠페인이 얼마나 성공적이었는지를 고려해 본다면, 다음 프로젝트에도 동일한 마케팅 업체를 이용해야 할 것입니다.

Your delivery will arrive in five to seven business days, **depending on** the shipping method you selected at checkout.
결제 단계에서 선택하신 배송 방법에 따라 배송품은 영업일 기준 5일에서 7일 후에 도착할 것입니다.

② 결과를 나타내는 관용적 현재분사구문

Production capacity expanded by 30%, **thus bringing** down prices.
생산성이 30%까지 증가해서 가격을 떨어뜨렸다.

③ 관용적 과거분사구문

Based on how many units were pre-ordered, the company anticipates its new game console launch to be a huge success.
많은 예약 판매 대수를 바탕으로 이 회사는 새로운 게임기 출시가 큰 성공을 거둘 것으로 예상하고 있다.

실전 감각 다지기

정답 및 해설 p.32

1. ------ this April, Greenwood Retails will no longer sell office desks.
(A) Start (B) Starting
(C) Started (D) To start

2. Lacy's Cosmetics offers returning customers generous discounts ------ on how much they spend.
(A) depend (B) depending
(C) depended (D) to depend

3. ------ on her own experience, Ms. Keenan offers expert guidance on creating a business plan.
(A) Base (B) Based
(C) Basing (D) Having based

4. The local supermarket added another checkout lane, thus ------ customers to finish their grocery shopping quicker.
(A) allowed (B) to allow
(C) allows (D) allowing

ACTUAL TEST

1. There are many factors ------- to the decrease in interest in print newspapers.
   (A) contribute
   (B) contribution
   (C) contributing
   (D) contributed

2. Sales at Noble Gardener fluctuate ------- on the weather.
   (A) depends
   (B) dependable
   (C) depending
   (D) depended

3. Enjoy your stay at the Bizmark Hotel and be sure to try the delicious cookies ------- in the executive lounge.
   (A) offered
   (B) to offer
   (C) offering
   (D) offers

4. The ------- applications for the managing editor position will be reviewed on Monday.
   (A) remains
   (B) remained
   (C) remainders
   (D) remaining

5. Tesmi House has been the ------- publisher of autobiographies for the past five years.
   (A) leadership
   (B) led
   (C) leader
   (D) leading

6. While investing in startup businesses comes with ------- risks, it also comes with the potential to make millions.
   (A) increased
   (B) increase
   (C) increasingly
   (D) increases

7. ------- in France for over 10 years, Mr. Barreto was put in charge of consulting for our French clientele.
   (A) Lived
   (B) Was living
   (C) Having lived
   (D) To live

8. Visitors under 12 years of age may enter the museum only when ------- by an adult.
   (A) accompany
   (B) accompanying
   (C) accompanied
   (D) to accompany

9. The university's main library will be open during winter break with ------- hours.
   (A) limited
   (B) limiting
   (C) limits
   (D) to limit

10. Most applicants to HM Technology have completed a ------- internship at the company's headquarters.
    (A) pay
    (B) paying
    (C) paid
    (D) to pay

Questions 11-14 refer to the following e-mail.

To: Katie Kitson <katiekitson@sunshinefabrics.net>
From: Estevan Oliveira <e.oliveira@caval-inc.com>
Date: September 30
Subject: Caval Inc.

Dear Ms. Kitson,

It was a pleasure meeting you at last week's International Textiles Expo. I know that you are ------- new to the business, so I believe my firm would be an excellent asset in helping you export goods to Brazil.
   11.

-------. We are the longest-running firm of our kind, and most of our employees have been
12.
working in this field for at least five years. We can help you navigate the ------- import and export
                                                                              13.
regulations and avoid making costly mistakes. We also keep up on the latest policy changes to ensure that you don't waste time sending items ------- by the government. I would welcome the
                                                                                14.
opportunity to discuss our services further.

Sincerely,

Estevan Oliveira

11. (A) diligently
(B) thoroughly
(C) relatively
(D) incidentally

12. (A) Please feel free to contact my office about the change.
(B) I hope to see you again at next year's event.
(C) We have a high level of expertise that you can trust.
(D) The quoted fee is an estimate that can be negotiated.

13. (A) strict
(B) identical
(C) emerged
(D) optional

14. (A) prohibition
(B) prohibited
(C) prohibiting
(D) prohibits

CHAPTER 1

PART 5 & 6
문법

실전에서 바로 써먹는
쉬운 토익 공식 인강

UNIT 10

접속사

토익 기초 문법 OVERVIEW

빈출 유형 공략 01 등위 접속사와 상관 접속사

빈출 유형 공략 02 부사절 접속사

빈출 유형 공략 03 명사절 접속사

빈출 유형 공략 04 접속사 vs. 전치사

ACTUAL TEST

UNIT 10 | 접속사

토익 기초 문법 OVERVIEW

A 등위 접속사(and, but, or, so)는 단어와 단어, 구와 구, 절과 절을 대등하게 이어 준다.

• 단어와 단어의 연결

Programs and schedules are subject to change. 프로그램과 스케줄은 변경될 수 있습니다.

Investing in property is **risky but lucrative**. 부동산에 투자하는 것은 위험하지만 수익성이 있다.

• 구와 구의 연결

His duties mainly involve **revising articles and creating content** for the magazine.
그의 업무는 주로 기사를 수정하고 잡지의 내용을 만드는 것이다.

Visit our Web site **to read reviews or to schedule a tour**.
저희 웹사이트에 방문하셔서 후기를 확인하거나 투어를 예약하세요.

• 절과 절의 연결

The rooms were comfortable, **and** the breakfast buffet was well worth the price.
방은 편안했고, 조식 뷔페는 충분히 제값을 했다.

The venue is small, **so** not every member will be able to attend.
행사장이 협소해서 모든 회원들이 참석할 수 있는 것은 아니다.

B 등위 접속사가 두 개의 절을 연결할 때, 동일한 [주어 + 조동사/be동사]는 생략된다.

We can provide existing courses **or** customize them to meet your needs.
저희는 기존 과정을 제공하거나 귀사의 요구에 맞춰 과정을 수정해 드릴 수 있습니다.

The repair work was completed on time **and** priced as in the initial quote.
그 수리 작업은 제시간에 완료되었고 가격은 최초의 견적과 동일했다.

C 주어가 등위 접속사 and로 연결되면 복수 동사를 쓴다. (Unit 05 빈출 유형 공략 02 참고)

Passenger check-in **and** security screening **are** subject to unexpected delays.
승객 탑승 수속과 보안 심사는 예상치 못한 지연을 겪을 수 있다.

The branch manager **and** her assistant **are** on a business trip to Brisbane.
지점장과 그녀의 비서가 브리즈번에 출장 중이다.

D 세 개 이상의 단어나 구를 나열할 때, 마지막 단어나 구 앞에 and나 or를 쓴다.

For **registration, fees, and payment information**, please see page 2 of this brochure.
등록, 수수료 및 결제 정보는 이 브로슈어의 2페이지를 참조하십시오.

Membership is available on **a monthly, quarterly, or annual basis**.
회원 자격은 월별, 분기별 또는 연간 단위로 이용할 수 있습니다.

E 부사절 접속사는 시간, 이유, 조건, 양보 등의 의미를 지닌 종속절을 이끈다.

Please only use the back door **while** the lobby is being painted.
　　　　　　　주절　　　　　　　　　　　종속절 (부사절)
로비에 페인트칠을 하는 동안에는 후문만 이용해 주세요.

시간	The RedRock Hotel collects payment **when** the guests check in. RedRock Hotel은 투숙객이 체크인할 때 요금을 받습니다.
이유	The copier is unavailable **because** it broke down. 복사기가 고장 나서 사용할 수 없다.
조건	Orders may be delayed **if** the item is temporarily out of stock. 일시적으로 재고가 없을 경우 주문이 지연될 수 있습니다.
양보	**Though** the AK5 mixer is similar to other models, it costs only half as much. AK5 믹서는 다른 모델과 비슷하지만, 가격은 절반밖에 안 한다.

F 명사절 접속사(that, if, whether)는 문장에서 주어, 보어, 목적어 역할을 한다.

　　　　　　　　　　　　　주격 보어
The expectation is **that** more than 50 companies will attend this year's fair.
올해 박람회에는 50여개 업체가 참석할 것으로 예상된다.

　　　　　　　note의 목적어
Please note **that** the cost of return shipping is the responsibility of the customer.
반품 배송료는 고객 부담임을 알려 드립니다.

　　　　　　　　　　　　　　　　　　　　determine의 목적어
The agency is investigating diet products to determine **if** they pose a health hazard.
그 기관은 다이어트 제품들이 건강에 해를 끼치는지를 판단하기 위해 조사하고 있다.

　　　　　　　　　　　be sure의 목적어
Ms. Chomley was not sure **whether** the CFO position would be right for her.
Ms. Chomley는 CFO 직책이 자신에게 맞을지 확신할 수 없었다.

기초 문법 CHECK　　　　　　　　　　　　　　　정답 및 해설 p.34

1~5. 밑줄 친 부분 중 가장 적절한 것을 고르세요.

1. Please call 555-1230 to receive further information or <u>scheduling / to schedule</u> an appointment.
2. We have processed your request, <u>and / but</u> your membership will be continued for another year.
3. Luggage often looks very similar, <u>so / or</u> please check the luggage ID tag.
4. <u>Although / If</u> it has a high admission fee, the golf club has a reasonable monthly rate.
5. Note <u>that / whether</u> reservations are on a first-come, first-served basis.

빈출 유형 공략 01 등위 접속사와 상관 접속사

The event is sold out online, ------- a few seats may be available for purchase at the venue.
(A) but (B) if (C) nor (D) also

풀이 빈칸을 기준으로 두 개의 절이 연결된 것으로 보아 빈칸은 등위 접속사 자리이다. 문맥상 빈칸 앞뒤 내용이 서로 대립되므로 '그러나'를 뜻하는 (A) but이 정답이다.

해석 그 행사는 온라인에서는 표가 다 팔렸지만 현장에서는 몇 좌석 정도 구입할 수 있을 것이다.

유형 돋보기

1 등위 접속사

and 그리고	but 그러나	yet 그렇지만, 그런데도	or 또는	so 그래서

The manufacturing process is simple **yet** efficient. 그 제조 과정은 간단하지만 효율적이다.

The elevator will be out of service for a few days, **so** visitors are asked to take the stairs instead.
그 엘리베이터는 며칠간 운행되지 않을 것이다. 그래서 방문객은 대신에 계단을 이용하라고 요청받는다.
→ so는 절만 연결한다.

2 상관 접속사

either A or B A 또는 B	neither A nor B A와 B 둘 다 아닌
both A and B A와 B 둘 다	not A but B A가 아니라 B
not only A but (also) B A뿐만 아니라 B도	B as well as A A뿐만 아니라 B도

Neither the manager **nor** the staff were familiar with the new tablets.
그 매니저와 직원 모두 새로운 태블릿에 익숙하지 않았다.

The design of the product is **not only** sleek **but also** functional.
그 제품의 디자인은 세련될 뿐만 아니라 실용적이다.

실전 감각 다지기

정답 및 해설 p.34

1. HF Law Firm is currently looking for lawyers who have deep knowledge of patent ------- copyright law.
   (A) and (B) but
   (C) nor (D) for

2. Girvan Tran has clearly demonstrated his ability to develop unique concepts, ------- in fashion and interior design.
   (A) either (B) those
   (C) both (D) many

3. ------- CFG&Son nor Hardknocks Co. could figure out how to make a fair contract to merge the two companies.
   (A) Both (B) None
   (C) Neither (D) Whoever

4. Suggestions for improvement can be ------- sent to the company e-mail or placed anonymously in the feedback box.
   (A) each (B) both
   (C) either (D) whom

빈출 유형 공략 02   부사절 접속사

Tardiness at Wednesday's staff meeting will not be accepted ------- we have an important visitor.

(A) because   (B) until   (C) although   (D) nevertheless

풀이 빈칸을 기준으로 두 개의 절이 연결된 것으로 보아 빈칸은 접속사 자리이다. 문맥상 손님이 오기 때문에 회의에 늦으면 안 된다는 내용이 되는 게 자연스러우므로 '~하기 때문에'를 뜻하는 (A) because가 정답이다. (D) nevertheless는 '그럼에도 불구하고'를 뜻하는 접속부사이며, 말 그대로 부사이기 때문에 절과 절을 연결하는 역할을 할 수 없다.

해석 중요한 손님이 오기 때문에 수요일 직원회의에 지각해서는 안 됩니다.

유형 돋보기

시간 부사절 접속사	조건 부사절 접속사	이유 부사절 접속사	기타 부사절 접속사
until ~할 때까지	if 만약 ~라면	because ~하기 때문에	except ~라는 점만 제외하면
before ~하기 전에	provided (that) 만약 ~라면	since ~하기 때문에; ~한 이래로	so that ~하기 위해서
after ~한 후에	unless 만약 ~가 아니라면	now (that) 이제 ~이므로	whether ~이든 (아니든)
when ~할 때	once 일단 ~하면; ~하자마자	as ~하기 때문에; ~할 때	
while ~하는 동안; ~한 반면에	in case ~한 경우에 대비하여		
whenever ~할 때마다	as if 마치 ~인 것처럼	**양보/대조 부사절 접속사**	
as soon as ~하자마자	only if (오직) ~해야만	whereas ~한 반면에	
		although 비록 ~일지라도(= even though)	

Although the toner cartridges were scheduled to come today, the package still hasn't arrived.
토너 카트리지가 오늘 오기로 예정되어 있음에도 불구하고 택배는 여전히 도착하지 않은 상태이다.

Mr. Rocha will be traveling to São Paulo **so that** he can see the new factory in person.
Mr. Rocha는 새 공장을 직접 보기 위해 상파울루에 갈 것이다.

Our gift wrap service is complimentary **whether** you shop in store or online.
매장에서 구입하든 온라인으로 구입하든 선물 포장 서비스는 무료입니다.

실전 감각 다지기

정답 및 해설 p.34

1. ------- the main entrance is being renovated, everyone must use the back entrance to report to work.
   (A) Therefore   (B) Before
   (C) While   (D) As if

2. Visitors should not leave the lobby ------- they are given specific permission.
   (A) unless   (B) only if
   (C) instead   (D) whereas

3. ------- the executives come to a unanimous decision, they will spend the next few hours trying to figure out how to solve the issue.
   (A) Since   (B) In case
   (C) Besides   (D) Until

4. ------- the production process is streamlined, goods can be made more efficiently.
   (A) When   (B) Above all
   (C) Except   (D) So that

빈출 유형 공략 03 명사절 접속사

The city government is analyzing the budget to determine ------- funding should go to public parks or libraries.

(A) another   (B) into   (C) whether   (D) elsewhere

풀이 빈칸은 determine의 목적어인 명사절을 이끄는 접속사가 들어갈 자리이므로 (C) whether가 정답이다.
해석 시 정부는 자금을 공원에 써야 할지 도서관에 써야 할지 결정하기 위해 예산을 분석하고 있다.

유형 돋보기

명사절 접속사는 주어, 보어, 목적어 자리에 위치할 수 있다. 명사절 접속사 문제는 출제 빈도가 그리 높지 않은데, 주로 동사 뒤에 명사절 접속사를 채우는 유형으로 출제되어 문제 난이도 역시 그리 높지 않은 편이다.

① whether

Joe Bake's action movie was certainly popular, but he is unsure **whether** he will make a sequel.
Joe Bake의 액션 영화는 확실히 흥행했지만 그는 후속작을 만들어야 할지 확신이 없다.

A technician is coming to the office this afternoon to see **whether(= if)** the copier can be repaired.
그 복사기가 수리될 수 있을지 확인하기 위해 오늘 오후에 기사가 사무실을 방문할 것이다.
→ whether가 동사의 목적어 역할을 할 때는 if로 바꿔 쓸 수 있다.

② that

Most retailers have reported **that** the new A5 smartphone is already sold out.
소매점 대부분은 새로 나온 A5 스마트폰이 이미 품절되었다고 알렸다.

> **고득점 POINT** 제안(suggest, propose), 권고(recommend), 요구/요청(request, insist, ask, require)의 의미가 있는 동사는 that절에 '(should) 동사원형'을 쓴다.
> We **ask that** any defective goods **(should) be** returned within 14 days of receipt.
> 불량품은 수령 후 14일 내에 반송해 주실 것을 요청 드립니다.

실전 감각 다지기

정답 및 해설 p.35

1. Please specify ------- you would prefer a physical copy or an electronic version of your receipt.
   (A) even   (B) whether
   (C) although   (D) including

2. Consumers believe ------- hiring a technician is easier than installing equipment themselves.
   (A) that   (B) for
   (C) and   (D) when

3. Nard LTE requires ------- new employees sign a confidentiality agreement so they do not share any company secrets.
   (A) with   (B) again
   (C) that   (D) about

4. The client has requested that their print advertisements ------- to several prominent newspapers.
   (A) sending   (B) were sent
   (C) to send   (D) be sent

빈출 유형 공략 04 접속사 vs. 전치사

------- some materials arrived late, the contractor was able to have the renovations completed ahead of schedule.

(A) Prior to (B) When (C) Even though (D) Despite

쉬운 토익 공식 빈칸 뒤에 절이 있으면 접속사, 명사(구)가 있으면 전치사가 정답이다.

풀이 빈칸 뒤에 완전한 절이 있으므로 빈칸은 절을 이끌 수 있는 접속사 자리이다. 문맥상 자재가 늦게 도착하긴 했지만 작업을 일찍 마쳤다는 내용이 되는 게 자연스러우므로 '비록 ~일지라도'를 뜻하는 (C) Even though가 정답이다.

해석 비록 몇몇 자재가 늦게 도착하긴 했지만 그 시공사는 수리 작업을 예정보다 일찍 마칠 수 있었다.

유형 돋보기

접속사는 뒤에 절이 이어지고, 전치사는 명사(구)가 이어진다. 이때 의미가 유사한 접속사와 전치사에 유의한다.

뜻	접속사	전치사
~하기 전에	before	before, prior to
~한 후에	after	after, following
~하는 동안	while	during
~하자마자	as soon as, once	(up)on -ing
만약 ~가 아니라면	unless	without
~하기 때문에	because, as	because of, due to, owing to, on account of
비록 ~일지라도	although, even though	despite, in spite of
~라는 점만 제외하면	except	except for

~~Because~~ / **Owing to** some scheduling confusion, the VIP guests arrived at the conference a bit later than expected.
일정에 혼선이 있어서 VIP 손님들은 예상보다 조금 늦게 콘퍼런스장에 도착했다.

실전 감각 다지기

1. Please do not go on to the next step in the process ------- the instructor says it is okay.
   (A) except for   (B) once
   (C) unless   (D) without

2. The assembly line resumed operation about one hour ------- the faulty equipment was discovered and replaced.
   (A) either   (B) while
   (C) after   (D) following

3. Contact the IT department if you encounter any technical problems ------- the online meeting.
   (A) even though   (B) or
   (C) while   (D) during

4. Proper maintenance of your pool equipment will ensure that minor problems can be found ------- they become major ones.
   (A) although   (B) before
   (C) prior to   (D) in addition

ACTUAL TEST

1. Intercity bus services will resume ------- the snow from last night's blizzard is cleared.
   (A) as soon as
   (B) such as
   (C) whether
   (D) since

2. The advertising team will get started on their new campaign ------- they finish conducting market research.
   (A) within
   (B) during
   (C) whereas
   (D) after

3. ------- the printer is out of ink, please report it to the maintenance department, and they will send someone.
   (A) Whenever
   (B) As if
   (C) Besides
   (D) Prior to

4. Pulaski Theater requests ------- audience members turn off all mobile devices before entering the auditorium.
   (A) what
   (B) which
   (C) that
   (D) or

5. Cafeteria B will be closed on Wednesday for a deep cleaning, ------- please use Cafeteria A or bring your own lunch.
   (A) except that
   (B) or
   (C) so
   (D) if

6. ------- the design team and the marketing team work together to make the most eye-catching book covers.
   (A) Each
   (B) Either
   (C) Both
   (D) Whoever

7. ------- the new product launch is successful or not, it is important to keep taking risks with our designs.
   (A) Whether
   (B) Because
   (C) Despite
   (D) Even

8. Carol's Cabinets is known for its outstanding quality and offers products in either hardwood ------- plywood.
   (A) or
   (B) but
   (C) so
   (D) as

9. The bank will be closed tomorrow after lunch ------- the vault is being repaired.
   (A) during
   (B) yet
   (C) although
   (D) while

10. Issuing store credit encourages the customer to come back, ------- providing a refund does not create a reason to return.
    (A) unless
    (B) furthermore
    (C) so that
    (D) whereas

136 CHAPTER 1 PART 5&6 문법

Questions 11-14 refer to the following customer review.

My wife and I recently decided to get married. Since we wanted to have the ceremony before the weather gets too cold, we had to prepare everything -------. I was tasked with finding the
                                                                                                                11.
wedding cake, so I was happy to stumble upon Grace's Baking Company on a review Web site.
------- I am somewhat skeptical of online reviews, I was impressed by the pictures I saw. I visited
  12.
Grace two weeks before the big event and she assured me that she could have it done by my

wedding day. -------.
              13.
Grace is truly a ------- at her craft. I can't believe how beautiful the cake looked at the wedding.
                14.
If I ever need another cake, I will only take her expert advice on what to get.

Adio Clarke, Jamestown

11. (A) hastiness
    (B) haste
    (C) hastily
    (D) hastier

12. (A) Although
    (B) In case
    (C) Despite
    (D) Now that

13. (A) She even figured out the entire cake design by herself.
    (B) Chocolate cakes are my favorite dessert.
    (C) It was difficult to find someone to listen to my complaints.
    (D) I will gladly return to try out other cake flavors.

14. (A) competitor
    (B) novice
    (C) master
    (D) pupil

CHAPTER 1

PART 5 & 6
문법

실전에서 바로 써먹는
쉬운 토익 공식 인강

UNIT 11

관계사

토익 기초 문법 OVERVIEW

빈출 유형 공략 01 관계대명사

빈출 유형 공략 02 관계대명사의 생략

빈출 유형 공략 03 관계부사

빈출 유형 공략 04 복합관계사

ACTUAL TEST

UNIT 11 | 관계사

토익 기초 문법 OVERVIEW

A 관계대명사는 두 문장을 하나로 연결하는 접속사 역할을 하는 동시에 앞에 언급된 명사를 대신하는 대명사 역할을 한다. 관계대명사가 이끄는 절은 앞에 오는 명사(선행사)를 수식한다.

Mr. Brown hired a lawyer **and he** specializes in corporate law. Mr. Brown은 기업법을 전문으로 하는 변호사를 고용했다.

Mr. Brown hired **a lawyer** [**who** specializes in corporate law].
　　　　　　　　선행사　　　　　관계대명사절

B 관계대명사는 관계대명사절 안에서 주격, 목적격, 소유격의 역할을 할 수 있으며, 관계대명사의 수식을 받는 선행사가 사람이냐 사물/동물이냐에 따라 다르게 쓰인다.

선행사	주격	목적격	소유격
사람	who	who(m)	whose
사물, 동물	which	which	whose
사람, 사물, 동물	that	that	-

→ whom은 격식체로 쓰인다.

C 주격 관계대명사 who, which는 관계대명사절 안에서 주어 역할을 한다.

Library patrons [**who** fail to return a book by the due date] will be charged a fee.
　선행사　　　　　주격　동사　　　목적어　　　　　부사어
반납 기한을 어기는 도서관 이용자에게는 수수료가 부과됩니다.

The app suggests **the route** [**which** takes the least time].
　　　　　　　　선행사　　　주격　동사　　　목적어
그 앱은 시간이 가장 적게 걸리는 경로를 추천해 준다.

D 목적격 관계대명사 who(m), which는 관계대명사절 안에서 목적어 역할을 하며, 생략될 수 있다.

They hired **the candidate** [**(who/whom)** Mr. Baker recommended].
　　　　　선행사　　　　　(목적격)　　주어　　타동사
그들은 Mr. Baker가 추천한 지원자를 채용했다.

Mr. Brown carefully examined **the estimate** [**(which)** Millbrook Furniture provided].
　　　　　　　　　　　　선행사　　　(목적격)　　　　주어　　　　　타동사
Mr. Brown은 Millbrook Furniture에서 제공한 견적서를 꼼꼼히 검토했다.

E 앞에 언급된 선행사에 대한 부가적인 내용을 추가할 경우 [콤마(,) + 관계대명사]를 사용하며, 이를 관계대명사의 계속적 용법이라 한다.

Beginning April 1, Mr. Clark will succeed **Alfred Carlson, who** retired last week.
4월 1일부터 Mr. Clark는 Alfred Carlson의 뒤를 이을 것이며, Alfred Carlson은 지난주에 퇴임했다.

Visitors are encouraged to use **the shuttle bus service, which** will run every 15 minutes during the festival.
관람객들은 셔틀버스 서비스를 이용하도록 권장되며, 셔틀은 축제 동안 15분마다 운행될 것입니다.

F which, whom은 전치사의 목적어로 쓰여 [전치사 + which/whom]의 전치사구를 이룰 수 있다.

Expenses **for which** you cannot provide a receipt are not reimbursable.
영수증을 제공할 수 없는 비용은 환급받을 수 없습니다.

The video demonstrates **the various ways in which** the software can be used.
그 영상은 그 소프트웨어가 활용될 수 있는 다양한 방법을 보여 준다.

He has two children, **both of whom are accountants**. 그에게는 자식이 둘 있는데, 둘 다 회계사다.
of who (×) → 전치사 뒤에는 who, that을 쓸 수 없다.

G 소유격 관계대명사 whose는 앞에 오는 선행사(사람, 사물)의 소유격에 해당하며, 바로 뒤에 오는 명사를 한정한다.

= customers' lease
The e-mail reminders will be sent out to **customers whose lease** is about to expire.
임대가 곧 만료되는 고객에게는 알림 메일이 발송될 것이다.

= the OMC's target group
The OMC, **whose target group** is seniors, offers a variety of exercise programs.
OMC는 노년층을 주된 고객으로 하며, 다양한 운동 프로그램을 제공한다.

기초 문법 CHECK

정답 및 해설 p.37

1~6. 밑줄 친 부분 중 가장 적절한 것을 고르세요.

1. All customers who / which complete a survey will be offered a discount voucher.

2. Mr. Perez will be giving the opening keynote address at our conference, who / which will be held in Budapest next week.

3. Ms. Taylor will be sending conference participants a brochure who / that describes the new software.

4. Mr. Martin booked the hotel in which / for whom he stayed last summer.

5. He is known for designing the Victoria Art Museum, for which / for that he was awarded the 2020 World Design Award.

6. The last training session is for employees whose / of whom responsibilities include negotiating prices.

빈출 유형 공략 01　관계대명사

Passengers ------- would like to upgrade their tickets to first class may do so on the Web site.
(A) who　　　　(B) whose　　　　(C) whoever　　　　(D) to whom

쉬운 토익 공식　빈칸 앞에 사람 명사가 있고 뒤에는 동사가 바로 이어지면 주격 관계대명사 who가 정답이다.

풀이　빈칸 뒤의 관계사절에 주어가 없으므로 빈칸에는 주격 관계대명사가 들어가야 한다. 또한 선행사 Passengers는 사람이므로 (A) who가 정답이다.
해석　티켓을 1등석으로 업그레이드하길 원하는 승객은 웹사이트에서 그렇게 할 수 있습니다.

유형 돋보기

토익에서 관계대명사는 두세 달에 한 번 출제되는 편인데 기본적인 내용만 숙지하고 있으면 어렵지 않게 풀 수 있는 문제가 대부분이고, 주격 관계대명사가 가장 자주 나온다.

주격　The customer **who** rented the vehicle is usually liable for any damages incurred during rental.
차량을 대여했던 고객이 보통은 대여 기간 동안 발생된 손상에 책임을 진다.

목적격　Mr. Lance, **who(m)** we interviewed, was a former engineer at Techiro Inc.
우리는 Mr. Lance를 인터뷰했는데, 그는 Techiro Inc.의 전직 엔지니어였다.
Our funding comes from the support of foundations as well as readers, **for which** we are grateful.
우리는 독자뿐만 아니라 여러 재단에서 자금 지원을 받고 있으며, 그에 대해 감사하고 있습니다.
→ 주격/목적격 관계대명사는 선행사에 관계없이 that으로 바꿔 쓸 수 있다. 단, 콤마(,)와 전치사 바로 뒤에는 that을 쓸 수 없다는 점에 주의해야 한다.

소유격　Ms. Hayes booked the restaurant **whose** menus contain vegetarian dishes.
Ms. Hayes는 채식 메뉴가 있는 식당을 예약했다.

what　Excellent customer service is **what** sets us apart from our competitors.
훌륭한 고객 서비스가 우리를 경쟁사와 차별화하는 것이다.
→ 관계대명사 what(= the thing(s) which)은 '~ 것'이라고 해석하며, 이미 선행사를 포함하고 있기 때문에 what 앞에는 선행사가 올 수 없다. 또한 what 관계대명사절은 명사절로 쓰여 주어, 보어, 목적어 자리에 위치할 수 있다.

실전 감각 다지기

정답 및 해설 p.37

1. Mr. Jun is the manager ------- will be in charge of hiring new employees.
   (A) his　　　　(B) him
   (C) who　　　(D) whose

2. Private messages must only be seen by the person to ------- they are sent.
   (A) what　　　(B) whom
   (C) where　　 (D) whose

3. During yesterday's meeting, Maja Peterson took detailed notes, ------- she will print and distribute to everyone.
   (A) who　　　(B) what
   (C) which　　(D) that

4. Lamar Accessories, ------- handbags are popular among celebrities, will launch a new line of leather wallets.
   (A) how　　　(B) whose
   (C) most　　　(D) which

빈출 유형 공략 02 관계대명사의 생략

According to sales figures ------- by Jerome's Technologies, company profits rose 3% last quarter.

(A) to release (B) releasing (C) released (D) have released

쉬운 토익 공식 [주격 관계대명사 + be동사]가 생략된 구조라면 과거분사가 정답이다.

풀이 '------- by Jerome's Technologies'가 sales figures를 수식하는 구조이므로 빈칸 앞에 which were가 생략되어 있음을 알 수 있다. 이와 같이 [주격 관계대명사 + be동사]가 생략되면 관계사절은 분사구가 되어 앞 명사를 수식하는데, 수식 대상인 '판매 수치(sales figures)'가 Jerome's Technologies에 의해 발표되는 것이므로 빈칸과 수동 관계이다. 따라서 과거분사인 (C) released가 정답이다.

해석 Jerome's Technologies에서 발표한 판매 수치에 따르면 그 회사의 수익은 지난 분기에 3%가 증가했다.

유형 돋보기

1 [주격 관계대명사 + be동사]의 생략

[주격 관계대명사 + be동사]가 생략되면 선행사 뒤에 주로 분사가 이어진다. (Unit 09 빈출 유형 공략 02 참고)

Every purchase **priced** (which is) over $50 comes with a $5 discount coupon.
50달러 이상의 모든 구매에는 5달러 할인 쿠폰이 나갑니다.

2 목적격 관계대명사의 생략

목적격 관계대명사는 단독으로 생략할 수 있다. 토익에서는 목적격 관계대명사가 생략된 관계사절의 주어 자리에 들어갈 알맞은 인칭대명사를 묻는 문제나 동사 자리를 채우는 문제가 출제된다.

Professor Reid works with doctoral students (who(m)/that) **she** / ~~her~~ / ~~herself~~ advises.
Reid 교수는 자신이 지도하는 박사 과정생들과 작업하고 있다.

If you have a problem with the item you (which/that) ~~to order~~ / ~~ordering~~ / **ordered**, please contact us.
주문하신 제품에 문제가 있다면 저희에게 연락 주세요.

실전 감각 다지기

정답 및 해설 p.38

1. Ms. Gibson is looking for the contract file ------- left in the office yesterday.
   (A) she (B) her
   (C) hers (D) herself

2. In the event of inclement weather, the art festival ------- for April 20 will be postponed for one week.
   (A) scheduling (B) was scheduling
   (C) to schedule (D) scheduled

3. Prices ------- for our rotating special menu are subject to change depending on the ingredients used.
   (A) listed (B) have listed
   (C) listing (D) will list

4. The type of flooring we ------- is not available anymore.
   (A) usage (B) to use
   (C) using (D) were using

빈출 유형 공략 03 관계부사

Raw milk is sanitized in steel pipes, ------- it is heated until safe to drink.
(A) who   (B) which   (C) when   (D) where

풀이 빈칸 앞뒤에 완전한 절이 있으므로 빈칸에는 부사와 접속사 역할을 겸하는 관계부사가 들어가야 하며, 선행사가 스틸파이프 내부라는 장소를 나타내므로 (D) where가 정답이다.
해석 원유는 스틸파이프에서 살균 처리되는데, 그 파이프에서 원유가 섭취하기에 안전할 때까지 가열된다.

유형 돋보기

❶ 관계부사

- **시간** Mid-summer is the time **when(= at which)** we sell out of our bathing suits the fastest.
  여름 중순은 우리의 수영복이 가장 빨리 팔리는 시기이다.

- **장소** Conference Room C is the place **where(= in which)** they will hold the job interview today.
  C 회의실은 그들이 오늘 면접을 진행할 장소이다.

- **이유** Poor weather is probably the reason **why(= for which)** customers are not visiting our shop these days.
  아마도 굳은 날씨가 고객들이 요즘 우리 매장을 방문하지 않는 이유인 것 같다.

- **방법** The workshop will elaborate on **how[the way]** anyone can start their own business.
  그 워크숍에서 누구든 자신만의 사업을 시작할 수 있는 방법을 자세히 알려 줄 것이다.

→ 선행사가 명확하게 시간, 장소, 이유를 나타낼 때는 관계부사와 선행사 둘 중 하나를 생략할 수 있다. 단, 관계부사 how는 선행사 the way와 나란히 쓸 수 없으므로 항상 둘 중 하나만 쓴다.

❷ 관계부사 vs. 관계대명사

관계부사는 뒤에 문법적으로 완전한 절이 이어지고, 관계대명사는 뒤에 불완전한 절이 이어진다.

Mr. Wilson runs several businesses in London, **where / which** he grew up.
Mr. Wilson은 런던에서 사업체 몇 개를 운영하고 있는데, 그곳은 그가 성장기를 보낸 곳이다.
→ 뒤에 [주어(he) + 동사(grew up)] 구조로 완전한 절이 있으므로 관계부사 where가 알맞다.

실전 감각 다지기

정답 및 해설 p.38

1. Try shopping during times of the day ------- crowds are less likely to form.
   (A) what   (B) every
   (C) when   (D) how

2. A global economic recession is one major reason ------- the organic food market is having difficulty in sales.
   (A) what   (B) how
   (C) most   (D) why

3. Mr. Lowe received a full-time job offer from the firm ------- he did his summer internship.
   (A) where   (B) how
   (C) who   (D) which

4. If you're in the Lakefield Mall, you can visit our shop, ------- the latest wireless accessories are available for purchase.
   (A) such   (B) where
   (C) how   (D) which

빈출 유형 공략 04　복합관계사

The manager on duty should be notified ------- a customer makes a complaint.
(A) whenever　　(B) which　　(C) however　　(D) in spite of

풀이 빈칸 앞뒤에 완전한 절이 있으므로 빈칸에는 절을 연결할 수 있는 말이 들어가야 한다. 선택지 중 완전한 두 개의 절을 연결할 수 있는 것은 복합관계부사인 (A) whenever와 (C) however인데, 문맥상 '고객이 불만을 제기할 때마다'라는 내용이 되는 게 자연스러우므로 (A)가 정답이다.
해석 고객의 불만이 제기될 때마다 당직 관리자에게 알려야 한다.

유형 돋보기

1 복합관계대명사

복합관계대명사는 [관계대명사 + -ever] 형태이며, 관계대명사와 마찬가지로 뒤에 불완전한 절이 이어진다.

who(m)ever	whichever	whatever
명사절: ~하는 사람은 누구든지	명사절: ~인 것은 어느 것이든지	명사절: ~인 것은 무엇이든지
부사절: 누가[누구를] ~하든지	부사절: 어느 것이[어느 것을] ~하든지	부사절: 무엇이[무엇을] ~하든지

*whichever와 whatever는 [whichever/whatever + 명사 + 주어 + 동사] 구조로 쓰기도 한다.

Whoever leaves the office last is expected to turn off the lights.
사무실을 마지막으로 나가는 사람은 누구든지 불을 끄고 가야 한다.

2 복합관계부사

복합관계부사는 [관계부사 + -ever] 형태이며, 관계부사와 마찬가지로 뒤에 완전한 절이 이어진다.

however	wherever	whenever
~하는 것은 어떤 방식으로든; 아무리 ~하더라도	~하는 곳은 어디든지; 어디에서 ~하더라도	~할 때는 언제든지; 언제 ~하더라도

*however는 [however + 형용사/부사 + 주어 + 동사] 구조로 자주 쓴다.

New methods to improve customer satisfaction are always welcomed by management, **however insignificant** they may seem.　경영진은 아무리 사소해 보이더라도 고객 만족을 향상시킬 새로운 방식을 항상 환영한다.

실전 감각 다지기

정답 및 해설 p.38

1. Participants of the conference can join any of the events offered, ------- seems most relevant to their interests.
   (A) whichever　(B) however
   (C) everyone　　(D) much

2. Ms. Yamaguchi announced that ------- sells the most products by the end of the month will receive a special bonus.
   (A) this　　(B) whoever
   (C) whose　(D) which

3. ------- the department manager returns from a business trip, she brings souvenirs for her staff.
   (A) Whenever　(B) Whatever
   (C) Around　　(D) How

4. Thanks to the updated Internet service provider, shoppers can enjoy a strong WiFi signal ------- they go in the mall.
   (A) otherwise　(B) however
   (C) quickly　　(D) wherever

ACTUAL TEST

1. David Graham is a renowned writer ------- novels are famous for portraying modern economic crises.

   (A) another
   (B) who
   (C) whose
   (D) these

2. Enclosed with your purchase is a unique coupon code which ------- you to save 15% on your next order.

   (A) to allow
   (B) allowably
   (C) allowance
   (D) will allow

3. Go-Go Airlines flies daily from New York to Minneapolis—Saint Paul, ------- passengers can then connect to Honolulu.

   (A) sooner
   (B) when
   (C) where
   (D) then

4. Mr. Stevens works hard to be the best at ------- he does.

   (A) any
   (B) which
   (C) whoever
   (D) whatever

5. Customers ------- wish to do an exchange must present the item with its receipt and original packaging.

   (A) whose
   (B) who
   (C) which
   (D) whichever

6. The company is hosting a field day during ------- each participant gets a free T-shirt.

   (A) whose
   (B) while
   (C) whatever
   (D) which

7. The wait staff ------- in the main ballroom must maintain perfect etiquette and attire.

   (A) worked
   (B) have worked
   (C) will work
   (D) working

8. The new security product includes a sensor ------- detects any movement.

   (A) whichever
   (B) that
   (C) where
   (D) whose

9. Grandville Hotel organizes multicultural events, the list of ------- is updated on our Web site every Monday.

   (A) one
   (B) which
   (C) whose
   (D) another

10. Dano Properties signed a lease with Poli Insurance ------- offices are on the second floor.

    (A) which
    (B) who
    (C) what
    (D) whose

Questions 11-14 refer to the following letter.

Dear Mr. Kobayashi,

We appreciate your family's interest in our pumpkin picking activity. We hope that you and your family will have a great time ------- our farm and finding the perfect pumpkins. In this letter, I
    11.
have provided an informative brochure ------- explains all the special events available at our
                                        12.
farm. To participate in the pumpkin carving event, you must reserve a spot at least three days in advance. -------.
            13.
Please let us know if you would like ------- information or would like to book a reservation. For
                                     14.
convenience, you can call us at (201) 555-0127.

Sincerely,

Ms. Patty's Pumpkin Pickin' Farm Team

11. (A) exploring
(B) promoting
(C) requesting
(D) extending

12. (A) that
(B) there
(C) where
(D) what

13. (A) This small service charge includes a free pumpkin-flavored drink.
(B) We encourage you to bring your dog to help sniff out the best pumpkin.
(C) You can simply show up and participate on that day.
(D) This is a very popular event, so you might want to book early.

14. (A) factual
(B) temporary
(C) further
(D) ongoing

실전에서 바로 써먹는
쉬운 토익 공식 인강

toeic.eduwill.net

CHAPTER 2

PART 5 어휘

UNIT 01 명사 ❶ + TEST

UNIT 02 명사 ❷ + TEST

UNIT 03 형용사 ❶ + TEST

UNIT 04 형용사 ❷ + TEST

UNIT 05 동사 ❶ + TEST

UNIT 06 동사 ❷ + TEST

UNIT 07 부사 ❶ + TEST

UNIT 08 부사 ❷ + TEST

FINAL TEST

UNIT 01 빈출 어휘 [명사 ❶]

convenience
편의, 편리; 편의 시설

for the **convenience** of our customers 고객들의 편의를 위해
at your earliest **convenience** 가급적 빨리

---

revision
수정 (사항), 검토, 변경

revise ⑧ 수정하다, 변경하다
make a **revision** 수정하다
undergo a major **revision** 대폭 수정을 감행하다

---

recognition
인식; 인정

recognize ⑧ 알아보다, 인식하다; 인정하다
speech **recognition** software 음성 인식 소프트웨어
build brand **recognition** 브랜드 인지도를 쌓다
receive official **recognition** for their success 그들의 성공을 공식적으로 인정받다

---

supplier
공급자, 공급업체

supply ⑧ 공급하다 ⑲ 공급
contact the gas **supplier** 가스 공급업체에 연락하다
a leading[major] **supplier** of office equipment 사무기기의 주요 공급업체

> **연관 어휘**
> **supplies** (항상 복수형) 비품   medical **supplies** 의료용품들
> **supplementary** 추가의, 보충의   **supplementary** materials 추가 자료들
> **supplement** 보충(제); 부록; 추가 요금   dietary **supplements** 영양 보충제

---

destination
목적지

a tourist **destination** 관광지
a popular holiday **destination** 인기 있는 휴가지

---

location
지점; 장소, 위치

locate ⑧ 위치시키다, (특정 위치에) 두다; (위치를) 알아내다
open a second **location** on Wyoming Street 와이오밍가에 두 번째 지점을 열다
an appropriate choice of **location** 적절한 장소 선정

---

inventory
물품 목록; 재고(품)

make an **inventory** of all merchandise 모든 물품을 목록으로 만들다
take **inventory** 재고 조사를 하다
inventory management[control] 재고 관리

---

tendency
경향, 추세; 성향, 기질

tend ⑧ 경향이 있다
a general **tendency** 일반적인 경향
a **tendency** for farm sizes to decline 농장 규모가 축소되는 경향

---

panel
패널, 전문가 집단; 판; 계기판

a **panel** of experts 전문가 위원회
a control **panel** 제어판

---

demand
수요, 요구

meet the **demand** for a product 상품의 수요를 맞추다
increased[growing] **demand** 증가된[늘어난] 수요

policy 정책, 방침	a major change in hiring **policy** 채용 정책의 주요 변화 implement a new **policy** for vacation days 새로운 휴가 정책을 시행하다
estimate 견적(서); 추정(치)	submit an **estimate** for the work 그 작업의 견적서를 제출하다 a rough **estimate** 대략적인 추정치

> **연관 어휘**
> **estimated** 견적의; 추측의
> an **estimated** loss 손실 견적
> **estimated** production costs 예상 생산비

ability 능력, 재능, 기량	able ⓐ 재능 있는, 능력 있는 within their **ability** 그들의 능력 내에서 develop the **ability** to negotiate 교섭 능력을 기르다
area 지역; 구역; 부분; 분야	a residential **area** 주거 지역 cover a wider **area** 더 넓은 부분을 포함하다[다루다] an **area** of expertise 전문 분야
benefit 혜택, 이득	employee **benefits** plans 직원 복지 제도 provide mutual **benefit** 상호 이익을 제공하다
delegation 위임; 대표단	delegate ⓥ (일, 임무 등을) 위임하다; 대표[대리인]로 선정하다 **delegation** of tasks 업무 위임 a member of a **delegation** 대표단의 일원
strategy 전략, 계획	implement a **strategy** 전략을 실행하다 outline the marketing **strategy** 마케팅 전략을 간략하게 설명하다
charge 요금; 책임; 담당	free of **charge** 무료로 at no extra **charge** 추가 비용 없이 the person in **charge** of the contract 계약 담당자
strength 힘, 내구력; 강점	rely on the **strength** of the firm's name 그 회사 이름이 가진 힘에 기대다 **strengths** and weaknesses 장단점
element 요소, 성분	introduce basic **elements** of art 예술의 기본 요소를 소개하다 the key **element** in social media marketing 소셜 미디어 마케팅의 핵심 요소
purpose 목적, 의도	be used for training **purposes** 교육용으로 사용되다 adequate for our **purposes** 우리의 목적에 알맞은
history 역사; 이력	throughout **history** 역사를 통틀어서, 역사적으로 look over the candidate's career **history** 그 지원자의 이력을 검토하다 have a **history** of late payments 늦게 납부한 전력이 있다

maintenance (건물, 기계 등의) 유지	maintain ⑧ (관계, 상태, 수준 등을) 유지하다 regular[routine] **maintenance** 정기 유지 보수 **maintenance** expenses 유지비
investor 투자자	invest ⑧ 투자하다; (시간을) 쓰다 attract private **investors** 개인 투자자를 모으다 a potential[prospective] **investor** 잠재적 투자자
연관 어휘 **investment** 투자	make a risky **investment** 위험한 투자를 하다
license 면허(증), 자격(증)	a driver's[driving] **license** 운전면허증 renew an import **license** 수입 허가증을 갱신하다
period 기간; 시기, 시대	a registration **period** 등록 기간 a free trial **period** 무료 체험 기간
range 범위; 다양성	cover a limited **range** 한정된 범위를 다루다 deal with a broad **range** of issues 다양한 문제를 다루다
experience 경험	relevant[related] work **experience** 관련 업무 경험 previous work **experience** 이전 업무 경험 have extensive **experience** in the fashion industry 패션업계에서 폭넓은 경험이 있다
completion 완료, 완성	complete ⑧ 완료하다, 완성하다; (서식 등을) 빠짐없이 작성하다 ⑨ 완료된; 완전한 an expected **completion** date 예정 완료일 announce successful **completion** of the project 그 프로젝트의 성공적인 완료를 알리다
selection 선발, 선택(된 것들)	select ⑧ 선발하다, 선택하다 a wide **selection** of facilities 다양한 시설 sample a **selection** of Branson Vineyard's wines Branson Vineyard가 엄선한 와인을 시음해 보다
volume 용량; 음량	sales **volume** 매출량 a high **volume** of calls 많은 통화량

ACTUAL TEST

1. Birchwood Industries is the country's largest plastic manufacturer with 15 ------- nationwide.
   (A) locations
   (B) inclinations
   (C) regions
   (D) connections

2. During the interview, each candidate was asked to describe their previous work -------.
   (A) experience
   (B) guidance
   (C) drop
   (D) occasion

3. One ------- of working at Xymo Publishing is being able to take unlimited time off.
   (A) suggestion
   (B) benefit
   (C) replacement
   (D) improvement

4. Tonya Coats has become the leading ------- of medical uniforms and equipment in less than a year.
   (A) supplier
   (B) defect
   (C) inventory
   (D) feature

5. The winner of the logo design competition will be selected by a ------- of judges.
   (A) proof
   (B) crowd
   (C) panel
   (D) renewal

6. For the ------- of our guests, the Corvin Hotel offers early check-in and a waiting lounge with refreshments.
   (A) balance
   (B) purpose
   (C) convenience
   (D) consideration

7. The Apple Hill town committee announced plans to perform routine ------- at Kirsch Library next week.
   (A) management
   (B) alliance
   (C) maintenance
   (D) alignment

8. Next month, investors will have the opportunity to sample a ------- of our newest protein shakes.
   (A) nutrition
   (B) referral
   (C) selection
   (D) platform

9. Jerico Detailing doubled the size of its production to meet increased -------.
   (A) demand
   (B) shipping
   (C) awareness
   (D) costs

10. The new key cards will ensure that only authorized personnel can enter certain ------- of the building.
    (A) rewards
    (B) areas
    (C) portions
    (D) capacities

UNIT 02　빈출 어휘 [명사 ❷]

confirmation
확인

confirm ⑧ 확인하다; 확정하다
send a booking **confirmation** e-mail 예약 확인 이메일을 발송하다
provide a written **confirmation** 서면 확인서를 제공하다

production
생산(량)

product ⑱ 제품
mass **production** 대량 생산
a **production**[assembly] line 생산 라인

> **연관 어휘**
> **productive** 생산적인　　**productive** employees 생산성이 높은 직원들
> **productivity** 생산성　　enhance[improve] **productivity** 생산성을 높이다

connection
관련(성); 연결, 접속

connect ⑧ 연결하다, 잇다
make a strong **connection** between A and B A와 B를 밀접하게 연관시키다
have a bad **connection** 연결 상태가 좋지 않다

initiative
계획; 주도권; 진취성

initiate ⑧ 시작하다, 개시하다
a new marketing **initiative** 새로운 마케팅 계획
take the **initiative** 주도하다, 주도권을 행사하다

role
역할, 임무; 배역

hire an expert for a management **role** 관리 역할로 전문가를 고용하다
get the lead(ing) **role** in a film 영화의 주연을 맡다

approval
승인; 인정, 찬성

approve ⑧ 승인하다; ~을 좋게 생각하다(~ of)
obtain final **approval** 최종 승인을 받다
require prior **approval** by a supervisor 관리자의 사전 승인을 필요로 하다

amount
양; 총액

store huge **amounts** of data 막대한 양의 데이터를 저장하다
a substantial **amount** of money 상당한 액수의 돈

decline
감소, 하락

a significant **decline** in sales 현저한 판매 감소
lead to a sharp **decline** in revenue 수익의 급격한 하락으로 이어지다

proposal
제안(서), 제의

propose ⑧ 제안하다, 제의하다
submit a **proposal** 제안서를 제출하다
review a grant **proposal** 보조금 제안을 검토하다

attitude
태도, 자세

undergo a change in[of] **attitude** 마음가짐에 변화가 생기다
have a relaxed **attitude** towards their work 편안한 마음으로 업무에 임하다

approach 접근(법)	implement a different **approach** 다른 접근법을 취하다 need a fresh **approach** to financial planning 재정 계획에 신선한 접근법이 필요하다	
overview 개관, 개요	give an **overview** of the plan 계획을 개략적으로 설명하다 offer a brief **overview** 간략한 개요를 제공하다	
knowledge 지식; 이해	have a lot of expert **knowledge** 전문 지식이 많다 to our **knowledge** 우리가 알기로는	

연관 어휘
knowledgeable 많이 아는   be **knowledgeable** about art 예술에 대해 많이 알다

guidance 안내, 지도	guide ⑧ 안내하다, 인도하다 provide **guidance** on how to apply for a business loan 사업 대출을 신청하는 방법에 대해 안내하다 under expert **guidance** 전문가의 지도하에
service 서비스	be out of **service** 사용 불가하다 a **service** fee[charge] 서비스료, 수수료
promotion 승진, 진급; 홍보, 판촉	promote ⑧ 승진시키다; 홍보하다 approve a **promotion** 승진을 승인하다 the budget for **promotions** 홍보를 위한 예산
attention 주의, 주목; 관심, 배려	attend ⑧ 주의를 기울이다; 참석하다 require immediate **attention** 즉각적인 관심을 필요로 하다 give their entire **attention** to the project 그 프로젝트에 그들의 온 신경을 쏟다

연관 어휘
attend to ~을 처리하다   **attend to** an urgent business matter 급한 업무를 처리하다
attentive 주의를 기울이는; 배려하는, 신경 쓰는   stay **attentive** to major changes 주요 변화에 계속해서 주의를 기울이다

balance 균형, 조화; 잔고, 잔액	maintain a **balance** between work and their personal life 일과 개인 생활 사이에서 균형을 유지하다 an account **balance** 계좌 잔고
competition 경쟁(자); 대회	compete ⑧ 경쟁하다 price **competition** between enterprises 기업 간의 가격 경쟁 win a **competition** 우승하다

연관 어휘
competitive 경쟁력 있는; 경쟁을 하는   **competitive** rates 경쟁력 있는 이율

merchandise 물품, 상품	display **merchandise** 상품을 전시하다 sell a wide range of **merchandise** 다양한 상품을 판매하다
emphasis 강조, 역점	put **emphasis** on research and development 연구와 개발에 중점을 두다 speak with special **emphasis** on product quality 품질을 특히 강조하여 말하다
exception 예외, 이례	except 접 ~라는 점만 제외하면 전 ~을 제외하고 make an **exception** in this case 이 경우에는 예외로 하다 with the **exception** of express deliveries 속달은 제외하고
recommendation 추천(서); 권고	recommend 동 추천하다; 권고하다 a letter of **recommendation** 추천서 on the board's **recommendation** 이사회의 권고로
priority 우선 사항; 우선권	prior 형 우선하는; 사전의 give safety top **priority** 안전을 최우선으로 하다 take **priority** over everything else 다른 모든 것보다 우선시하다

> **연관 어휘**
> **prioritize** 우선순위를 매기다　　**prioritize** the tasks 업무의 우선순위를 정하다

reduction 축소, 삭감; 할인	reduce 동 줄이다; (가격을) 낮추다 a significant **reduction** in costs 상당한 비용 축소 make a 10% **reduction** 10% 할인해 주다
protection 보호; (보험) 보장	protect 동 보호하다, 지키다 consumer **protection** laws 소비자 보호법 offer complete **protection** against accidental damage 불의의 손상을 완벽하게 보장해 주다
standard 기준, 수준	a quality **standard** 품질 기준 meet necessary **standards** 필수 기준을 충족하다
awareness 인식, 의식, 관심	aware 형 자각하고 있는 raise **awareness** 인식을 높이다 convert customer **awareness** into purchases 고객의 관심을 구매로 전환시키다
delay 지연, 지체	cause a **delay** in shipment 배송 지연을 야기하다 apologize for a schedule **delay** 일정 지연을 사과하다
audit 회계 감사; (품질) 검사	an annual **audit** 연례 회계 감사 carry out a detailed **audit** 상세한 검사를 수행하다
confidence 신뢰; 자신감	have **confidence** in the CEO 그 CEO를 신뢰하다 restore consumer **confidence** 소비자 신뢰를 회복하다

ACTUAL TEST

1. All online ------- should include a coupon that can be used both online and offline to encourage sales.
   (A) contracts
   (B) policies
   (C) prices
   (D) promotions

2. To lower costs, Korkrin Auto Parts will outsource some of its ------- to a neighboring country.
   (A) information
   (B) production
   (C) volume
   (D) subject

3. The ATM on Fifth Avenue will be out of ------- until next Monday when the update is complete.
   (A) purpose
   (B) funds
   (C) service
   (D) practice

4. For a commercial to be effective, customers should be able to make a strong ------- between the song and the brand.
   (A) opinion
   (B) connection
   (C) profit
   (D) form

5. The research team cannot hire another researcher without the research department head's -------.
   (A) suggestion
   (B) approval
   (C) success
   (D) emphasis

6. For the ------- of confidential data, all staff should use the company intranet when sharing certain documents.
   (A) precision
   (B) maintenance
   (C) allocation
   (D) protection

7. The success of the latest park redevelopment project increased residents' ------- in the newly elected mayor.
   (A) associates
   (B) professions
   (C) confidence
   (D) guidance

8. The innovative marketing team at Hazco has put the automotive company far ahead of the -------.
   (A) audit
   (B) compliment
   (C) competition
   (D) assortment

9. The finished product must meet all quality ------- before being launched.
   (A) issues
   (B) readings
   (C) clauses
   (D) standards

10. The goal of the meeting was to discuss the company's regulations and offer ------- for improvement.
    (A) donations
    (B) reimbursements
    (C) customs
    (D) recommendations

UNIT 03 빈출 어휘 [형용사 ❶]

substantial
상당한

substance ⑲ 물질; 본질, 핵심
a **substantial** amount of time 상당한 시간
a **substantial** increase in production 생산량의 상당한 증가

additional
추가의

addition ⑲ 추가, 추가된 것
at no **additional** charge 추가 요금 없이
work **additional** hours 초과 근무를 하다

accurate
정확한, 정밀한

fairly **accurate** information 꽤 정확한 정보
accurate and timely advice 정확하고 시기적절한 충고

연관 어휘
accuracy 정확성, 정확도   measure with **accuracy** 정확히 재다

brief
(시간이) 짧은; 간단한

a **brief** time 짧은 시간
make a **brief** visit 잠깐 방문하다
to be **brief** 간단히 말하자면

tentative
잠정적인

contain a **tentative** schedule 잠정적인 일정이 포함되어 있다
reach a **tentative** conclusion 잠정적인 결론에 이르다

constructive
건설적인

construct ⑧ 건설하다
a **constructive** discussion 건설적인 토론
play a **constructive** role 건설적인 역할을 하다

reassuring
안심시키는, 걱정을 없애는

reassure ⑧ 안심시키다
a **reassuring** result 안심되는 결과
see some **reassuring** developments 일부 고무적인 진전을 보다

attractive
매력적인, 멋진

attract ⑧ 마음을 끌다, 끌어들이다
at **attractive** prices 적당한 가격으로
be **attractive** to the public 대중에게 매력적이다

dependent
좌우되는; 의존[의지]하는

depend on ⑧ ~에 달려 있다; ~에 의존[의지]하다
be **dependent** on the project 그 프로젝트에 달려 있다
be **dependent** on the income 수입에 의존하다

연관 어휘
independent 독립된, 독립적인   take on an **independent** project 독립된 프로젝트를 맡다

current 현재의, 지금의	**current** prices 현재 물가 the most **current** findings 가장 최근의 조사 결과
upcoming 다가오는, 곧 있을	an **upcoming** merger with Tandell Fixtures Ltd. 다가오는 Tandell Fixtures Ltd.와의 합병 an **upcoming** conference 곧 있을 콘퍼런스
joint 공동의, 합동의	put money into a **joint** account 공동 계좌에 돈을 넣다 establish a **joint** venture 합작 회사를 설립하다
final 마지막의, 최종적인	a **final** phase 마지막 단계 make a **final** decision 최종 결정을 내리다 changes made to the **final** draft 최종본에서 수정된 것들
favorable 호의적인; 유리한	favor ⑲ 호의, 친절 write a **favorable** review 호의적인 후기를 남기다 **favorable** terms 유리한 조건
improved 향상된, 개선된	improve ⑧ 향상하다, 개선하다 **improved** conditions 개선된 상태 provide **improved** services 개선된 서비스를 제공하다
optimistic 낙관적인, 낙관하는	optimist ⑲ 낙관론자 be **optimistic** about the future of the company 그 회사의 미래를 낙관하다 make **optimistic** projections 낙관적으로 예상하다
pleased 기쁜, 흡족한, 만족한	please ⑧ 기쁘게 하다 be **pleased** with the result 결과에 만족하다 be **pleased** to offer a discount 할인을 제공하게 되어 기쁘다
economical 경제적인, 실속 있는, 알뜰한	economic ⑲ 경제의 an **economical** manufacturing process 경제적인 제조 과정 be **economical** in time and resources 시간과 자원 측면에서 실속 있다
comfortable 편안한, 쾌적한	comfort ⑲ 안락, 편안; 위안 provide a **comfortable** work environment 편안한 근무 환경을 제공하다 make customers **comfortable** 고객들을 편안하게 하다
superior 우수한, 우월한	super ⑲ 최고의, 대단한 ⑼ 특히, 매우 **superior** analytical skills 우수한 분석 능력 be **superior** to competitor's products 경쟁사 제품들보다 우수하다
eligible 적격의, 적임의	be **eligible** for a promotion 승진할 자격이 되다 be **eligible** to apply for a membership 회원권을 신청할 자격이 되다

previous 이전의	show a slight decline in the **previous** quarter 이전 분기에서 약간의 감소세를 보이다 seek a chief technician with **previous** experience 경력이 있는 수석 기술자를 구하다	
limited 제한된, 한정된	be of **limited** use 사용이 제한적이다 on sale for a **limited** period only 한정된 기간에만 판매하는	
puzzled 어리둥절해하는, 얼떨떨한	puzzle ⑧ 어리둥절하게 하다 look **puzzled** 어리둥절해 보이다 be **puzzled** by the unexpected outcome 예상하지 못한 결과에 얼떨떨하다	
experienced 숙련된, 경험이 풍부한	experience ⑧ 경험하다, 겪다 ⑨ 경험 be **experienced** in dealing with difficult customers 어려운 고객을 상대하는 데 능숙하다 an **experienced** applicant 경험이 풍부한 지원자	
distinct 뚜렷한, 분명한; 확실한	have **distinct** characteristics 뚜렷한 특징이 있다 be **distinct** from other designs 다른 디자인들과 확연히 다르다	
연관 어휘 **distinction** 차이; 특별함 **distinctive** 독특한	a clear **distinction** 분명한 차이 a **distinctive** feature of a new model 새로운 모델의 독특한 특징	
extended 연장된	extend ⑧ 연장하다; (사업, 세력 등을) 확대하다 take **extended** leave 장기 휴가를 가다 offer **extended** weekend hours 주말 영업[운영] 시간을 연장하다	
mandatory 의무적인	include a **mandatory** clause 필수 조항을 포함하다 a **mandatory** training course[program] 필수 교육 과정	
specific 구체적인, 명확한; 특정한	make **specific** suggestions 구체적인 제안을 하다 for no **specific** reasons 특별한 이유 없이	
연관 어휘 **specification** (무언가를 만드는/행하는 방식에 관해 자세히 서술한) 설명서	make the product to the customer's **specifications** 고객의 요구 사항에 맞게 제품을 만들다	
core 핵심적인, 가장 중요한	**core** values 핵심 가치 concentrate on the **core** business 핵심 사업에 주력하다	
main 가장 중요한, 주된	be transferred to the **main** office 본사로 발령받다 close the **main** entrance for repairs 수리 작업 동안 정문을 폐쇄하다	

ACTUAL TEST

1. ------- accommodation expenses incurred during a business trip should be reimbursed.
   (A) Assertive
   (B) Eligible
   (C) Competent
   (D) Prominent

2. Aunt Patty's Restaurant will hire ------- workers if demand for its services continues to grow.
   (A) approximate
   (B) ambitious
   (C) additional
   (D) accountable

3. New recruits must take a ------- training program before being assigned their duties.
   (A) mandatory
   (B) determined
   (C) skeptical
   (D) considerate

4. After a ------- review by the famous food critic, profits rose 30% at the restaurant.
   (A) vivid
   (B) joint
   (C) favorable
   (D) growing

5. The ------- merger of Mount Telecom and Zenith Communications will be discussed at next week's meeting.
   (A) numerous
   (B) decisive
   (C) proper
   (D) upcoming

6. Mr. Payton's ------- editing skills will be a huge asset in his career.
   (A) superficial
   (B) nominal
   (C) external
   (D) superior

7. In order to predict the profitability of a company, its financial projection should be as ------- as possible.
   (A) lengthy
   (B) incidental
   (C) accurate
   (D) efficient

8. Even ------- accountants like Ms. Urso make mistakes.
   (A) frequent
   (B) preliminary
   (C) reserved
   (D) experienced

9. The company paid a ------- amount in royalties to the author.
   (A) substantial
   (B) costly
   (C) reputable
   (D) known

10. Employees' initial fears were calmed after a ------- announcement by Human Resources.
    (A) comparable
    (B) lucrative
    (C) reassuring
    (D) fortunate

UNIT 04 빈출 어휘 [형용사 ❷]

typical
전형적인, 대표적인
- a **typical** example of the marketing strategy 그 마케팅 전략의 전형적인 예
- be **typical** of Southern cooking 대표적인 남부식 요리이다

profitable
수익성이 있는; 유익한, 이득이 되는
- profit ⑲ 이익, 수익
- a **profitable** business 수익성이 있는 사업
- highly **profitable** investment 매우 이득이 되는 투자

severe
심각한, 극심한; 엄격한, 가혹한
- in the event of **severe** weather 날씨가 좋지 않을 경우에는
- come under **severe** criticism 혹평을 받다

extensive
광범위한; 대규모의
- extend ⑧ 연장하다; (사업, 세력 등을) 확대하다
- conduct **extensive** research 광범위한 연구를 하다
- have **extensive** experience in finance 재무에 많은 경험이 있다

> 연관 어휘
> **extent** 정도, 규모, 크기   to some **extent** 다소, 어느 정도까지
> **extension** 연장, 확대   a contract **extension** 계약 연장

certain
확실한, 틀림없는
- feel **certain** about a decision 결정에 관해 확신이 서다
- be **certain** of a positive outcome 긍정적 결과를 확신하다

ambitious
야심 있는, 야심 찬
- set an **ambitious** goal 야심 찬 목표를 세우다
- announce an **ambitious** plan 야심 찬 계획을 발표하다

exceptional
(이례적으로) 뛰어난; 예외적인
- exception ⑲ 이례, 예외
- an **exceptional** work of art 뛰어난 예술 작품
- only in **exceptional** circumstances 예외적인 상황에서만

frequent
잦은, 빈번한
- a **frequent** customer[visitor] 단골손님
- prepare for **frequent** inspections 잦은 검사에 대비하다

> 연관 어휘
> **frequency** 빈도   increase/decrease in **frequency** 빈도가 증가하다/줄다

multiple
다수의, 많은
- have **multiple** meanings 다양한 의미가 있다
- offer **multiple** features 다양한 기능을 제공하다

competitive
경쟁력 있는; 경쟁을 하는
- gain a **competitive** advantage over domestic rivals
  국내 경쟁사들 사이에서 경쟁 우위를 점하다
- a highly **competitive** market 매우 경쟁이 심한 시장

recent 최근의	**recent** policy updates 최근 정책 변화들 undergo many changes in **recent** years 최근 몇 년간 많은 변화를 겪다
attentive 주의를 기울이는; 배려하는, 신경 쓰는	attend ⑧ 주의를 기울이다; 참석하다 be **attentive** to the speech 그 연설을 경청하다 be **attentive** to customers' needs 고객 니즈에 신경 쓰다
연관 어휘 **attention** 주의, 주목; 관심, 배려	bring **attention** to major problems 주요 문제들에 관심을 불러 모으다
popular 유명한, 인기 있는; 일반적인	be **popular** among people 사람들에게 인기 있다 by **popular** demand 대중의 요구에 따라
연관 어휘 **popularity** 인기	the continuing **popularity** of the wireless speaker 그 무선 스피커의 계속되는 인기
preliminary 예비의, 사전의	a **preliminary** draft 초안 take **preliminary** actions 사전 조치를 취하다
advanced 진보된; 고급[상급]의	advance ⑲ 진전, 발전 ⑧ 앞으로 나아가다; 진보하다 have highly **advanced** technology 최첨단 기술을 보유하다 enroll in an **advanced** course in French 프랑스어 심화반에 등록하다
qualified 자격이 있는, 적임의	qualify ⑧ 자격을 얻다; 자격증을 취득하다 be fully **qualified** for the position 그 직책에 충분히 자격이 있다 recommend a **qualified** candidate 적임자를 추천하다
present 현재의; 참석한	a list of all clients, past and **present** 과거와 현재의 모든 의뢰인 명단 be **present** at the opening ceremony 개막식에 참석하다
reliable 믿을 만한, 신뢰할 만한	rely ⑧ 믿다, 신뢰하다 provide a **reliable** service 믿을 만한 서비스를 제공하다 based on **reliable** data 신뢰할 만한 자료를 기반으로 한
연관 어휘 **reliant** 의존하는	be **reliant** on exports 수출에 의존하다
valuable 소중한, 매우 중요한; 값비싼	value ⑲ 가치 ⑧ 소중하게 생각하다; (가치, 가격 등을) 평가하다 gain **valuable** experience 값진 경험을 하다 lock **valuable** items in a safe 값비싼 물품을 금고에 넣어 보관하다
stuck 꼼짝 못 하게 된	be[get] **stuck** in traffic 교통 체증에 갇혀 꼼짝 못 하다 be **stuck** with a financial problem 자금 문제로 곤란하다

available 이용할 수 있는; ~할 시간이 있는	be **available** to all hotel guests 모든 호텔 투숙객이 이용할 수 있다 be **available** to help with the show 그 공연을 도울 시간이 되다
possible 가능한; 있을 수 있는	do everything **possible** to meet the deadline 마감일을 맞추기 위해 가능한 모든 걸 하다 avoid any **possible** risks 발생할 수 있는 위험을 피하다
former 예전의; 전자의	be located in a **former** library 예전 도서관 자리에 위치해 있다 choose the **former** option 전자를 선택하다
direct 직접적인; 직행의	have **direct** access to the files 그 파일들에 직접 접근할 권한이 있다 a **direct** flight to New York 뉴욕 직항 항공편
leading 선두의, 주요한, 가장 중요한	a **leading** expert 선두적인 전문가 a **leading** provider of Internet services 주요 인터넷 서비스 공급업체
inactive 활동하지 않는, 소극적인; 사용되지 않는	active ⑧ 활동적인 an **inactive** market 침체된 시장 an **inactive** account 휴면 계좌
연관 어휘 **activate** 활성화하다, 작동시키다	**activate** a function 기능을 활성화하다
challenging (어렵지만) 도전적인, 도전 의식을 불러일으키는	a **challenging** and rewarding job 도전적이고 보람도 있는 일 go through a **challenging** time 어려운 시기를 겪다
numerous 많은	repeat **numerous** times 수차례 반복하다 perform **numerous** tasks 많은 업무를 처리하다
primary 가장 중요한, 주된	a **primary** goal 주된 목적 **primary** features of a product 제품의 주요 기능들
vacant 비어 있는	build a warehouse on the **vacant** lot 공터에 창고를 짓다 fall[become] **vacant** 결원이 생기다, 일자리에 공석이 생기다
exclusive 독점적인, 전용의; 고급의; ~을 제외하고	be **exclusive** to new subscribers 신규 구독자 전용이다 an **exclusive** restaurant (아무나 이용할 수 없는) 고급 레스토랑 **exclusive** of taxes 세금을 제외하고
연관 어휘 **inclusive** 포함된, 포괄적인	**inclusive** of meals and transportation 식사비와 교통비가 포함된

ACTUAL TEST

1. Monthly parking passes are ------- for purchase at the security office located by the front gate.
   (A) increasing
   (B) optional
   (C) available
   (D) anonymous

2. At Greenhorn Industries, our ------- concern for staff is workplace safety.
   (A) contrary
   (B) primary
   (C) perpetual
   (D) respectful

3. Because of rising production costs, it is no longer ------- for us to offer free shipping with every purchase.
   (A) profitable
   (B) eligible
   (C) questionable
   (D) durable

4. As a local artist, Ms. Nguyen has won several awards for her ------- work.
   (A) exclusive
   (B) lavish
   (C) abnormal
   (D) exceptional

5. Patients at Compass Medical now have ------- access to all of their medical files and laboratory reports.
   (A) reliable
   (B) deliberate
   (C) direct
   (D) eventual

6. Bunton Textiles is seeking a ------- accountant to look over their yearly budget.
   (A) repurposed
   (B) qualified
   (C) random
   (D) partial

7. Marketers must stay ------- of upcoming trends and evolving customer preferences.
   (A) vacant
   (B) attentive
   (C) attractive
   (D) reserved

8. Jerod's introduced a new membership program for ------- visitors to its stores.
   (A) coupled
   (B) structural
   (C) frequent
   (D) popular

9. Meeting the strict deadline for the shipment will be ------- but certainly possible.
   (A) challenging
   (B) fitting
   (C) encouraging
   (D) liveable

10. For years, Milton Charles has done ------- research on the history of mining in Cyprus.
    (A) considerate
    (B) extensive
    (C) temporary
    (D) probable

UNIT 05 빈출 어휘 [동사 ❶]

obtain
얻다, 획득하다

obtain free quotes 무료 견적을 받다
obtain information about a campaign 캠페인에 관한 정보를 얻다

anticipate
예상하다; 기대하다, 고대하다

anticipate the most likely problems 가장 발생 가능성이 있는 문제를 예측하다
anticipate pay increases 급여 인상을 기대하다

acquire
습득하다, 획득하다

acquire a reputation 명성을 얻다
acquire new premises 건물이 딸린 새 부지를 취득하다

attract
마음을 끌다, 끌어들이다

attract customers 고객을 모으다
attract the attention of the public 대중의 관심을 끌다

coincide with
~와 일치하다, ~와 동시에 일어나다

coincide with the plans 계획과 일치하다
coincide in opinion with the agency 그 에이전시와 의견이 일치하다
coincide with the completion of the project 프로젝트 완료와 동시에 일어나다

respond
대답하다; 반응을 보이다

respond promptly to customer complaints 고객 불만에 빠르게 대응하다
a smart speaker that responds to voice commands
음성 명령에 반응하는 스마트 스피커

연관 어휘

response 대답; 반응
responsive 즉각 반응하는; 호응하는

in response to customers' demands 고객 요구에 응하여
be responsive to guests' needs 투숙객의 요구에 즉각 반응하다
be highly responsive to consumer trends 소비자 트렌드에 민감하다

switch
바꾸다, 전환하다

switch the meeting from Monday to Wednesday
회의를 월요일에서 수요일로 바꾸다
switch the supplier because of frequent shipping delays
잦은 배송 지연 때문에 공급업체를 변경하다

complete
완료하다, 완성하다; (서식 등을) 빠짐없이 작성하다

complete a project report 프로젝트 보고서를 완료하다
complete an application form 지원서를 (빠진 데 없이) 작성하다

facilitate
가능하게 하다, 수월하게 하다

facilitate transportation 교통을 용이하게 하다
be designed to facilitate effective communication
효과적인 소통을 촉진하기 위해 고안되다

invite
초대하다; (정식으로) 요청하다

invite guests 손님을 초대하다
be invited to participate in the charity event 자선 행사에 참여하라고 요청받다

permit
허용하다, 허락하다

permit access to the laboratory 실험실 출입을 허용하다
only be **permitted** in a designated area 지정된 장소에서만 허락되다

연관 어휘
permission 허가 — seek **permission** for the development 그 개발을 위해 허가를 구하다

succeed
성공하다; 뒤를 잇다

succeed in business 사업에 성공하다
succeed the popular A21 model 인기 있는 A21 모델의 뒤를 잇다

연관 어휘
success 성공 — result in international **success** 국제적으로 성공하는 결과를 낳다
successful 성공적인, 성공한 — a **successful** candidate[applicant] 합격자

undergo
겪다, 경험하다

undergo repairs 수리를 받다
undergo a change 변화를 겪다

pass on
~을 넘겨주다, ~을 건네주다

pass on a task 업무를 넘겨주다
pass on a message 메시지를 전해 주다

withdraw
(돈을) 인출하다; 물러나다, 철회하다

withdraw money 돈을 인출하다
withdraw an offer 제안을 철회하다

submit
제출하다; 받아들이다, 따르다

submit an application 지원서를 제출하다
submit to a superior 상사의 지시에 따르다

establish
설립하다, 수립하다; (제도 등을) 확립하다

establish a company 회사를 설립하다
establish a refund policy 반품 정책을 확립하다

request
요구하다, 신청하다

request some information from the institute 기관에 정보를 요청하다
officially **request** an interview 공식적으로 인터뷰를 요청하다

recommend
추천하다, 권고하다

highly[strongly] **recommend** 강하게 권고하다
recommend a candidate for a position 직책에 맞는 후보를 추천하다

oversee
감독하다

oversee a construction site 건설 현장을 감독하다
oversee the staff members at work 근무 중인 직원을 감독하다

ensure
보장하다, 확실히 하다

a design to **ensure** safety 안전을 보장하는 디자인
ensure the quality of the new product 신제품의 품질을 보장하다

launch
출시하다; (새로운 일, 프로젝트 등을) 시작하다, 착수하다

launch the new model in June 6월에 새 모델을 출시하다
a newly **launched** engineering firm 최근에 출범된 엔지니어링 회사

place 놓다, 설치하다; (중요성, 가치 등을) 두다; (명령, 주문 등을) 하다	be **placed** alphabetically 알파벳순으로 배치되다 **place** a lot of emphasis on training 교육을 많이 강조하다 **place** an order 주문하다
recognize 알아보다, 인식하다; 인정하다	**recognize** the difference 차이를 인식하다 be **recognized** for his latest work 그의 최근 업무로 인정받다
pursue 추구하다, 밀고 나가다	**pursue** a goal 목표를 추구하다 **pursue** a degree in economics 경제학 학위를 따다
specialize 전공하다, 전문적으로 하다	**specialize** in trade 무역을 전문적으로 하다 **specialize** in Asian antiques 아시아 골동품을 전문적으로 팔다
demonstrate 보여 주다; 입증하다	**demonstrate** how to use the software 소프트웨어 사용법을 보여 주다 **demonstrate** their commitment to society 그들이 사회에 헌신하는 모습을 보이다
assign 맡기다, 배정하다	**assign** a key role 중요한 역할을 맡기다 be **assigned** to a task 업무를 배정받다 **assign** an employee to organize a meeting 회의를 주관할 직원을 배정하다
연관 어휘 **reassign** 다시 맡기다	be **reassigned** to a new position 새로운 직책으로 다시 배정받다
verify 확인하다, 입증하다	**verify** that the items are in stock 그 제품들이 재고가 있는 걸 확인하다 **verify** the contract's validity 계약서의 유효성을 확인하다
admit 인정하다; 입장[가입]을 허락하다	**admit** to a mistake 실수를 인정하다 be **admitted** to the reading club 그 독서 모임에 가입이 허가되다
연관 어휘 **admission** 입장 허가; 입장료	receive an **admission** pass 입장권을 받다

ACTUAL TEST

1. Employees can ------- replacement keys from security in the event they are lost.
   (A) obtain
   (B) select
   (C) apply
   (D) input

2. Ms. Sweeney ------- additional photos of the building site the company is planning to purchase.
   (A) intended
   (B) emphasized
   (C) informed
   (D) requested

3. At the community event, each volunteer will be ------- a different food stall.
   (A) corresponded
   (B) confronted
   (C) assigned
   (D) helped

4. Salespeople must ------- how their products work and answer questions with confidence.
   (A) demonstrate
   (B) fulfill
   (C) focus
   (D) conduct

5. Consumer comments and recommendations are ------- to the relevant departments for review.
   (A) filled in
   (B) passed on
   (C) let go
   (D) pushed aside

6. To ------- quality service, all product consultations are by appointment only.
   (A) warrant
   (B) confirm
   (C) ensure
   (D) justify

7. At Morgan Financial, we are proud to be ------- as a trusted member of Logan County's Account Council.
   (A) recognized
   (B) suited
   (C) allotted
   (D) achieved

8. Ms. Bolton will postpone her trip so it does not ------- with the annual inspection.
   (A) calibrate
   (B) collaborate
   (C) condense
   (D) coincide

9. All staff members are ------- to Mr. Vogel's retirement party next week.
   (A) celebrated
   (B) promised
   (C) invited
   (D) considered

10. Mr. Diaz noted that it is important to ------- safety policies regarding the use of company vehicles.
    (A) multiply
    (B) delegate
    (C) estimate
    (D) establish

UNIT 06 빈출 어휘 [동사 ❷]

apply
신청하다, 지원하다; 적용하다

apply for a management position 관리 직무에 지원하다
apply the new technology 신기술을 적용하다

---

expand
확대하다, 확장하다

expand a business overseas 사업을 해외로 확장하다
expand into new markets 새로운 시장으로 진출하다

---

develop
개발하다

develop a new line of cosmetics 새로운 계열의 화장품을 개발하다
develop a business plan 사업 계획을 구상하다

---

prove
입증하다, 증명하다; 드러나다, 판명되다

prove that the machine works perfectly 그 기계가 완벽하게 작동한다는 걸 입증하다
prove to be effective 효과적인 것으로 드러나다

> 연관 어휘
> **proof** 증명(서), 증거
> provide the receipt as **proof** of purchase 구매 증거로 영수증을 내다

---

staff
직원으로 일하다

be **staffed** by volunteers 자원봉사자들로 운영되다
be **staffed** with experienced employees 경력이 있는 직원들로 구성되다

> 연관 어휘
> **overstaffed** 인력 과잉의
> **understaffed** 인력이 부족한
> an **overstaffed** division 직원이 필요 이상으로 많은 부서
> be desperately **understaffed** 인력이 심각하게 부족하다, 인력난에 허덕이다

---

reach
도달하다, 이르다

reach a destination 목적지에 도달하다
reach an agreement 합의에 이르다

---

take down
~을 치우다; ~을 적다

take down an art piece from a wall 벽에 걸린 미술품을 떼다
take down the minutes 회의록을 작성하다

---

comply with
~을 지키다, ~을 따르다

comply with tax rules 세금 규정을 지키다
strictly **comply with** the instructions 그 지시 사항들을 철저하게 따르다

---

focus
집중하다

focus on the current issue 현 사안에 집중하다
focus its investments on projects with higher profitability
더 수익성이 높은 프로젝트에 투자를 집중하다

---

accept
받아들이다, 받아 주다

accept a job offer 일자리 제안을 받아들이다
blindly **accept** biased opinions 편향된 의견만 맹목적으로 받아들이다

---

authenticate
(진짜임을) 증명하다

authenticate the document 그 문서가 진짜임을 입증하다
be **authenticated** by experts 전문가에 의해 증명되다

grant 승인하다, 허락하다	**grant** a customer's request 고객의 요구를 들어주다 **grant** employees more paid vacation days 직원들에게 더 많은 유급 휴가를 허가하다
expect 예상하다, 기대하다	**expect** a rise in oil prices 유가가 오를 것으로 예상하다 **expect** the construction to be over next week 공사가 다음 주에 끝날 것으로 예상하다

> **연관 어휘**
> **expectation** 예상, 기대   exceed[surpass] all **expectations** 모든 기대를 뛰어넘다

reveal 드러내다, 밝히다; 폭로하다	**reveal** a development plan 개발 계획을 밝히다 **reveal** the company's latest high-tech gadget 그 회사의 최첨단 기기를 선보이다
enable 가능하게 하다	**enable** easier access to the station 그 역에 더 쉽게 접근할 수 있게 하다 **enable** employees to have meetings remotely 직원들이 원격으로 회의할 수 있게 하다
compare 비교하다	**compare** profit margins against industry averages 이윤을 업계 평균과 비교하다 **compare** favorably with competitors 경쟁사들에 비해 낫다[유리하다]
display 전시하다, 진열하다; 드러내다, 보이다	**display** decorations 장식물을 달다 **display** a remarkable ability to lead 뛰어난 지도력을 보이다
notice 알아채다, 인지하다, 주목하다	note ⓝ 메모, 기록 ⓥ 주목하다; 언급하다 **notice** an error in the form 그 양식에서 오류를 알아채다 fail to **notice** the change 변화를 인지하지 못하다

> **연관 어휘**
> **noticeable** 뚜렷한, 현저한, 분명한   make oneself **noticeable** 두각을 나타내다
> **notify** 알리다, 통지하다   **notify** the client of cancellation 고객에게 해약을 통지하다
> **notification** 알림, 통지   written **notification** of the new policy 새 정책에 대한 서면 통지

waive (권리, 요구 등을) 포기하다	**waive** objections to the plan 그 계획에 대한 반대 의견을 거두다 **waive** a registration fee 등록비를 면제해 주다
implement 시행하다, 실시하다	**implement** safety measures 안전 조치를 시행하다 **implement** a new system 새로운 시스템을 실시하다
distribute 나누어 주다, 배부하다; (상품을) 유통시키다	**distribute** the samples to prospective customers 잠재 고객들에게 샘플을 나누어 주다 **distribute** a film 영화를 배급하다

follow
따르다, 따라가다, 뒤따르다

follow proper procedures 적절한 절차를 따르다
follow simple instructions 간단한 지시 사항들을 따르다

announce
발표하다, 알리다

announce plans to hire new workers for its store
매장에 신규 직원을 채용할 계획을 발표하다
announce an increase in prices 가격 인상을 알리다

include
포함하다, 포함시키다

include tips on how to reduce energy use
에너지 절감 방법에 관한 팁을 포함시키다
include the information in the revised manual
그 정보를 개정된 설명서에 포함시키다

discount
할인하다

heavily **discount** unsold tickets 팔리지 않은 티켓을 대폭 할인하다
be **discounted** below retail prices 소매가 이하로 할인되다

divide
나누다, 가르다

equally **divide** the proceeds among local charities
그 수익금을 지역 자선 단체들이 똑같이 나누어 갖다
divide the company into two parts—automotive and electronics industries
그 회사를 두 부분, 즉 자동차 산업과 전자 산업으로 나누다

encourage
권장하다, 장려하다

encourage her to attend the conference
그녀에게 콘퍼런스에 참석할 것을 권장하다
encourage job creation 일자리 창출을 장려하다

[연관 어휘]
encouragement 격려

offer words of **encouragement** 격려의 말을 전하다

equip
장비를 갖추다, 준비를 갖춰 주다

be **equipped** with advanced software 첨단 소프트웨어가 갖춰져 있다
equip workers with the latest devices 작업자들에게 최신 장비를 갖춰 주다

require
필요하다, 요구하다

require excellent communication skills 뛰어난 소통 기술이 필요하다
be **required** to show their invitations 초대장을 보여 주도록 요구되다

[연관 어휘]
requirement 요건; 필요(한 것)

meet client's **requirements** 고객이 요구하는 것을 충족하다

ACTUAL TEST

1. Whalerton Foods recently ------- its fish products to feature more white fish options.
   (A) expanded
   (B) tasked
   (C) opened
   (D) included

2. Research by Restaurants for Tomorrow ------- that many restaurants did not follow the local regulations regarding the disposal of food waste.
   (A) compiled
   (B) composed
   (C) revealed
   (D) underwent

3. All users are required to ------- their account before using our cloud software.
   (A) authenticate
   (B) prioritize
   (C) deliver
   (D) develop

4. All freelance contractors must ------- with city regulations related to constructing and demolishing a building.
   (A) confirm
   (B) comply
   (C) convey
   (D) appoint

5. The Human Resource's office is looking for volunteers to ------- the food trucks for this year's Maxford Family Day.
   (A) employ
   (B) post
   (C) sign
   (D) staff

6. Usually, spectators leave Johnston Field after the winner of the game has been -------.
   (A) removed
   (B) announced
   (C) redeemed
   (D) returned

7. This presentation includes helpful tips on ------- anti-fraud techniques.
   (A) overcoming
   (B) yielding
   (C) implementing
   (D) withdrawing

8. Bricks Furniture is planning to ------- installation fees for customers who spend more than 500 dollars in July.
   (A) waive
   (B) forge
   (C) retreat
   (D) excuse

9. There are several event signs on the wall that should be ------- within this month.
   (A) used up
   (B) closed down
   (C) come across
   (D) taken down

10. Typically, last-minute plane fares to certain destinations are ------- by as much as 50%.
    (A) purchased
    (B) discounted
    (C) distributed
    (D) considered

UNIT 07　빈출 어휘 [부사 ❶]

increasingly
점점, 더욱 더

become **increasingly** important 점점 더 중요해지다
an **increasingly** competitive market 갈수록 경쟁이 치열해지는 시장

particularly
특히(= especially)

particular ⑱ 특정한
particularly helpful 특히 도움이 되는
be **particularly** popular with young people 젊은 사람들에게 특히 인기 있다

carefully
주의 깊게, 신중히

careful ⑱ 조심하는, 신중한
review all details **carefully** 모든 세부 사항을 주의 깊게 살펴보다
complete the form **carefully** 그 양식을 신중하게 작성하다

politely
정중하게, 예의 바르게

polite ⑱ 예의 바른, 공손한
politely ask 정중하게 묻다
politely decline the job offer 그 일자리 제안을 정중하게 거절하다

previously
이전에, 앞서

previous ⑱ 이전의
as mentioned **previously** 이전에 언급한 바와 같이
previously unavailable to the public 예전에는 대중이 이용할 수 없던

temporarily
일시적으로, 임시로

temporary ⑱ 일시적인, 임시의
temporarily out of stock 일시적으로 품절된
be **temporarily** closed 임시로 문을 닫다

correctly
정확하게, 제대로

correct ⑱ 맞는, 정확한
remember **correctly** 정확하게 기억하다
understand the plan **correctly** 그 계획을 제대로 이해하다

> **연관 어휘**
> **incorrect** 부정확한
> **correction** 정정, 수정
>
> **incorrect** data 부정확한 데이터
> make a **correction** 바로잡다, 고치다

highly
매우, 많이

a **highly** profitable business 매우 수익성 있는 사업
be **highly** regarded by fellow workers 동료 직원들에게 매우 인정받다

soon
곧, 머지않아

be expected to **soon** gain worldwide fame
곧 세계적인 명성을 얻을 것으로 예상되다
soon after returning from a business trip 출장에서 돌아오자마자

exclusively
독점적으로, 오로지

exclusive ⑱ 독점적인, 전용의; 고급의; ~을 제외하고
open **exclusively** to frequent customers 단골들에게만 개방된
exclusively produce milk products 오로지 유제품만 생산하다

significantly 상당히; 의미 있게, 중요하게	significant ⑱ 상당한; 중요한 at a **significantly** lower price 상당히 낮은 가격에 **significantly** increase productivity 생산성을 상당히 증가시키다
early 초기에, 빨리, 조기에	**early** next year 내년 초에 arrive/leave **early** 일찍 도착하다/떠나다
widely 널리, 폭넓게; 대단히, 크게	wide ⑱ 넓은; 폭이 ~인; 폭넓은, 광범위한 **widely** distributed 널리 분포된 be **widely** known for her expertise 그녀의 전문성으로 널리 알려져 있다
frequently 자주	frequent ⑱ 잦은, 빈번한 a **frequently** visited place 방문객들이 자주 찾는 장소 a **frequently** asked question 자주 받는 질문
properly 제대로, 적절히, 올바로	proper ⑱ 적절한, 올바른 work **properly** 일을 제대로 하다 be installed **properly** 제대로 설치되다
quickly 빠르게	quick ⑱ 빠른 ⑭ 재빨리, 신속히 sell out **quickly** 빨리 매진되다 react **quickly** to a change 변화에 빨리 반응하다
completely 완전히, 전적으로(= totally)	complete ⑱ 완료된; 완전한 ⑧ 완료하다, 완성하다; (서식 등을) 빠짐없이 작성하다 be **completely**[fully] booked 예약이 꽉 차다 fill out the form **completely** 양식을 빠진 데 없이 작성하다
regularly 정기적으로, 규칙적으로	regular ⑱ 정기적인, 규칙적인 a **regularly** scheduled meeting 정기 회의 **regularly** check the stock 재고를 정기적으로 확인하다
eventually 결국, 마침내	eventual ⑱ 궁극적인 **eventually** be promoted 결국 승진하다 **eventually** find a solution 결국 해결책을 찾다
moderately 적당히, 알맞게(= reasonably)	moderate ⑱ 적당한, 알맞은 **moderately** profitable 적당히 수익을 내는 a **moderately** successful artist 나름대로 성공한 예술가
promptly 지체 없이(= immediately); 정확히 제시간에(= on time)	prompt ⑱ 즉각적인 **promptly** respond to customer inquiries 고객 문의에 즉각 답변하다 arrive **promptly** at three o'clock 정확히 3시에 도착하다

diligently 부지런히, 열심히	diligent ⑱ 근면한, 성실한 perform her duties **diligently** 업무를 성실히 수행하다 **diligently** work on a project 열심히 프로젝트 관련 업무를 하다
thoroughly 완전히, 철저히	thorough ⑱ 빈틈없는, 철저한 **thoroughly** prepare in advance 사전에 철저히 준비하다 check **thoroughly** to avoid any errors 오류를 방지하기 위해 철저히 확인하다
randomly 무작위로	random ⑱ 무작위의 **randomly** assign a task 무작위로 업무를 배정하다 **randomly** chosen people 무작위로 선택된 사람들
enthusiastically 열광적으로, 열렬히	enthusiastic ⑱ 열광적인, 열렬한 **enthusiastically** applaud 열광적으로 갈채를 보내다 **enthusiastically** donate time and talent 시간과 재능을 열성적으로 기부하다
entirely 전적으로, 완전히	entire ⑱ 전체의 agree **entirely** 전적으로 동의하다 be **entirely** different from the original 원본과 완전히 다르다
rarely 거의 ~ 않는(= seldom)	rare ⑱ 희귀한, 드문 be **rarely** used 거의 사용되지 않다 **rarely** cause any problem 거의 문제를 일으키지 않다
occasionally 가끔	occasional ⑱ 가끔의 **occasionally** use public transportation 가끔가다 대중교통을 이용하다 **occasionally** reported complaints 가끔 보고되는 불만 사항들
definitely 분명히, 확실히	definite ⑱ 분명한, 확실한 **definitely** be worth the price 분명히 그만한 값어치가 있다 **definitely** the most outstanding person 확실히 가장 뛰어난 사람
fondly 애정을 담아서	fond ⑱ 애정을 느끼는, 좋아하는 be **fondly** remembered as a wonderful leader 훌륭한 리더로 좋게 기억되다 speak **fondly** of former CEO Thomas Turner 전 최고 경영자 Thomas Turner에 대해 매우 좋게 이야기하다

ACTUAL TEST

1. Review the attached images ------- before posting them on the company's Web site.
   (A) subjectively
   (B) carefully
   (C) lazily
   (D) ideally

2. An upgrade in equipment would ------- increase the convenience of our office staff.
   (A) privately
   (B) formally
   (C) significantly
   (D) faintly

3. All train tickets are ------- booked because of the national holiday this weekend.
   (A) completely
   (B) basically
   (C) casually
   (D) uncertainly

4. We promise that all customer inquiries will be answered -------.
   (A) promptly
   (B) rarely
   (C) resistantly
   (D) finally

5. Mr. Roberts assured the team that the new software update would run smoothly if everyone ------- follows the installation directions.
   (A) randomly
   (B) hastily
   (C) properly
   (D) frequently

6. The Leicester Art Show only accepts works from artists who have not ------- been shown.
   (A) previously
   (B) lastly
   (C) rapidly
   (D) shortly

7. The database is ------- unavailable due to the routine maintenance of the system.
   (A) temporarily
   (B) perfectly
   (C) evenly
   (D) securely

8. In the review, Ms. Hino spoke at length about the dish she ------- remembered.
   (A) equally
   (B) quietly
   (C) hopefully
   (D) fondly

9. Bethany Interior Design was ------- recommended by several people to carry out the renovations in the hotel.
   (A) highly
   (B) indefinitely
   (C) patiently
   (D) vibrantly

10. All transactions must be examined ------- to ensure they comply with tax regulations.
    (A) thoroughly
    (B) hardly
    (C) eagerly
    (D) wearily

UNIT 08 빈출 어휘 [부사 ❷]

finally
마침내; 마지막으로

final ⑱ 마지막의, 최종적인
finally conclude a speech 마침내 연설을 마무리하다
finally approve the application 마침내 그 신청서를 승인하다

currently
현재, 지금

current ⑱ 현재의, 지금의
currently under construction 현재 공사 중인
a topic that is **currently** being discussed 현재 논의 중인 주제

accidentally
우연히, 뜻하지 않게; 실수로

accidental ⑱ 우연한, 돌발적인
prevent the door from opening **accidentally** 문이 저절로 열리는 걸 방지하다
accidentally delete the file 그 파일을 실수로 지우다

strictly
엄격하게

strict ⑱ 엄격한
be **strictly** prohibited 엄격히 금지되다
strictly speaking 엄밀히 말하자면

mutually
서로, 상호 간에

mutual ⑱ 서로의, 상호 간의
a **mutually** convenient time 서로 편리한 시간
a **mutually** beneficial solution 서로 득이 되는 해결책

seriously
심각하게, 진지하게

serious ⑱ 심각한, 진지한
take the problem **seriously** 그 문제를 심각하게 여기다
be **seriously** concerned over high unemployment
높은 실업률을 심각하게 우려하다

clearly
분명히, 명확히

clear ⑱ 분명한, 확실한
be marked **clearly** on every product 모든 제품에 분명히 표시되다
explain everything **clearly** 모든 것을 명확하게 설명하다

considerably
상당히

considerable ⑱ (크기, 양, 정도가) 상당한
vary **considerably** in length 길이가 매우 다양하다
drop **considerably** in value 가치가 현저히 떨어지다

> **연관 어휘**
> **considerate** 사려 깊은, 배려하는   be **considerate** of a new employee 새로운 직원을 배려하다

unexpectedly
예기치 않게, 뜻밖에

unexpected ⑱ 예상 밖의, 뜻밖의
unexpectedly cancel the performance 예기치 않게 그 공연을 취소하다
be **unexpectedly** successful 뜻밖에 성공을 거두다

far
훨씬, 대단히; 멀리

fall **far** behind the competition 경쟁에서 한참 뒤처지다
far in advance 훨씬 전에

still 아직, 여전히; 그래도, 그런데도; 훨씬, 더욱	be **still** unavailable 아직 사용이 불가하다 a **still** more difficult problem 훨씬 더 어려운 문제
newly 최근에, 새로	new ⓗ 새로운 a **newly** hired employee 새로 채용된 직원 a **newly** renovated building 새로 단장한 건물
cautiously 조심스럽게, 신중하게	cautious ⓗ 조심스러운, 신중한 drive **cautiously** 조심해서 운전하다 be **cautiously** optimistic 조심스럽게 낙관하다
rapidly 빠르게, 급속히	rapid ⓗ 빠른 grow **rapidly** 빠르게 성장하다 **rapidly** expand a business 사업을 빠르게 확장하다
primarily 주로	primary ⓗ 주요한 be aimed **primarily** at young consumers 주로 젊은 소비자를 겨냥하다 a course intended **primarily** for designers 주로 디자이너를 대상으로 하는 강좌
seldom 거의 ~ 않는(= rarely)	**seldom** work overtime 거의 초과 근무를 하지 않다 be **seldom** longer than an hour 거의 한 시간이 걸리지 않다
unusually 유별나게; 대단히, 매우	unusual ⓗ 특이한, 색다른 **unusually** high demand (평소와 달리) 유별나게 높은 수요 an **unusually** large number of people 대단히 많은 사람들
closely 면밀히; 밀접하게	close ⓗ 가까운; 거의 ~할 것 같은 examine the paper **closely** 그 문서를 면밀히 검토하다 be **closely** connected 밀접하게 관련되다
patiently 참을성 있게	patient ⓗ 참을성 있는 **patiently** wait for a turn 참을성 있게 차례를 기다리다 **patiently** answer all questions 모든 질문에 끈기 있게 답변하다

연관 어휘

patience 참을성, 인내력	be out of **patience** 인내심이 바닥나다

generally 일반적으로, 대개; 개괄적으로	general ⓗ 일반적인, 보통의 a **generally** accepted view 일반적으로 받아들여지는 관점 be **generally** recognized as the best law firm 일반적으로 최고의 법률 회사로 인정받다

directly 직접, 바로	direct ⓗ 직접적인; 직행의 return **directly** to the office 사무실로 곧장 돌아오다 be **directly** affected by related policies 관련 정책들에 직접 영향을 받다

> **연관 어휘**
> **direction** 지시; 방향 — under the **direction** of the supervisor 그 관리자의 지휘하에
> **director** 임원; 책임자; 감독 — a marketing **director** 마케팅 책임자

shortly 얼마 안 되어, 곧	short ⓗ 짧은 **shortly** after/before 직후에/직전에 **shortly** be arriving at the station 그 역에 곧 도착하다
immediately 즉시, 즉각	immediate ⓗ 즉각적인 **immediately** after a meeting 회의 직후에 be implemented **immediately** 즉시 시행되다
sharply (비판 등을) 날카롭게, 신랄하게; 급격히	sharp ⓗ 날카로운, 신랄한; 급격한 be **sharply** critical of the decision 그 결정을 날카롭게 비판하다 rise/fall **sharply** 급격히 증가하다/떨어지다
effectively 효과적으로	effective ⓗ 효과적인 deal with the situation **effectively** 그 상황을 효과적으로 처리하다 **effectively** manage an organization 조직을 효과적으로 운영하다

> **연관 어휘**
> **effect** 영향, 결과, 효과 — go[come] into **effect** (법 등이) 발효되다, 시행되다

extremely 극도로, 매우	extreme ⓗ 극도의 **extremely** important/difficult/useful 극히 중요한/어려운/유용한 be **extremely** expensive to maintain 유지하기에는 지나치게 비싸다
alike 비슷하게; 둘 다, 똑같이	try to treat all customers **alike** 모든 손님을 동등하게 대하려고 노력하다 benefit employers and employees **alike** 노사 모두에게 똑같이 유익하다
conveniently 편리하게, 편의상	convenient ⓗ 편리한 be **conveniently** located 편리한 위치에 있다 **conveniently** packaged vegetables and fruits 간편하게 포장된 채소와 과일
approximately 대략, 약	take **approximately** 30 minutes 대략 30분이 걸리다 occupy **approximately** one-half of the property 그 부지의 절반 가까이를 차지하다

ACTUAL TEST

1. Kilton Technologies lost money in the third quarter but ------- managed to turn a profit by the end of the year.
   (A) anymore
   (B) seldom
   (C) still
   (D) closely

2. The city's safety commission urges drivers to drive ------- this holiday weekend.
   (A) rightfully
   (B) cautiously
   (C) nervously
   (D) solemnly

3. ------- hired employees must attend a one-month training program in Minneapolis.
   (A) Frequently
   (B) Partially
   (C) Newly
   (D) Highly

4. Due to a processing error, Martin Forwarders ------- shipped the office furniture to the other law firm.
   (A) accidentally
   (B) illegibly
   (C) correctly
   (D) extremely

5. The Winston Hills Hotel is ------- located in the center of downtown Knoxville.
   (A) conveniently
   (B) mildly
   (C) instantly
   (D) anonymously

6. Working after hours without prior approval is ------- prohibited.
   (A) constantly
   (B) strictly
   (C) quickly
   (D) sharply

7. Runway maintenance may cause the flight schedules to change ------- next month.
   (A) commonly
   (B) kindly
   (C) lightly
   (D) unexpectedly

8. ------- after the presentation, a short question-and-answer session with Mr. Omen will be held.
   (A) Effectively
   (B) Currently
   (C) Immediately
   (D) Rapidly

9. In regard to ensuring quality service, Mr. Portman takes his job -------.
   (A) seriously
   (B) frankly
   (C) significantly
   (D) lately

10. Hard hats and reflective gear will be available for construction site workers and visitors -------.
    (A) nearly
    (B) quite
    (C) far
    (D) alike

FINAL TEST

1. Owing to a shortage of materials, the renovations will not be finished by the original ------- date.
   (A) subscription
   (B) completion
   (C) option
   (D) delegation

2. Mr. Shull thought he would ------- be promoted because of his dedication to the company.
   (A) eventually
   (B) closely
   (C) frequently
   (D) effectively

3. The product development team is confident that their new cell phone will be ready to ------- next month.
   (A) launch
   (B) explore
   (C) facilitate
   (D) allow

4. Mayor Jenson has finally undertaken a local development ------- for the residents of Mountainview.
   (A) initiative
   (B) decision
   (C) lesson
   (D) preview

5. To our -------, Cloveman Shipping has never had a late delivery in their entire 10 year history.
   (A) credit
   (B) ability
   (C) knowledge
   (D) chance

6. Kingsley Corporation will ------- holiday bonuses to employees who have been with the company for over two years.
   (A) distribute
   (B) execute
   (C) surprise
   (D) demand

7. The general manager will step away from her duties for a ------- time to deal with a health issue.
   (A) remote
   (B) strict
   (C) remarkable
   (D) brief

8. Interns should ------- attend after-work events to get to know the rest of the staff better.
   (A) cautiously
   (B) exactly
   (C) definitely
   (D) predominantly

9. When signing in, employees must ------- their identities via a fingerprint scanner.
   (A) complete
   (B) announce
   (C) verify
   (D) display

10. A ------- schedule for next week's meeting has been set, but the details should be confirmed by the clients.
    (A) vacant
    (B) steady
    (C) direct
    (D) tentative

11. The candidate's ------- job involved customer analytics, so she has the relevant experience for the marketing manager role.
    (A) spacious
    (B) previous
    (C) absolute
    (D) entitled

12. Please ensure that customers input their addresses ------- on the form so their deliveries arrive at the right location.
    (A) quickly
    (B) secretly
    (C) correctly
    (D) originally

13. Bart Legal Firm's biggest ------- are customer satisfaction and its positive public image.
    (A) consequences
    (B) priorities
    (C) deals
    (D) responses

14. After submitting your application, you will be contacted by the Human Resources department -------.
    (A) lately
    (B) shortly
    (C) carefully
    (D) seemingly

15. Prospective investors were ------- concerned with the economic slowdown in the automotive industry.
    (A) randomly
    (B) proficiently
    (C) diligently
    (D) primarily

16. User accounts left ------- for more than three years will be deleted along with all personal information.
    (A) rigorous
    (B) perishable
    (C) inactive
    (D) unable

17. The company will ------- employees who exceed their sales goals an additional vacation day.
    (A) assume
    (B) donate
    (C) deliver
    (D) grant

18. The fire alarm on the third floor has a ------- to malfunction after a building renovation.
    (A) trend
    (B) revenue
    (C) tendency
    (D) pleasure

19. *Sunshine Morning Radio* will have an ------- interview with local sports star James Keaton.
    (A) able
    (B) exclusive
    (C) eligible
    (D) impulsive

20. Though the idea of a merger initially seemed lucrative, Electronix has decided to ------- the proposal.
    (A) destroy
    (B) classify
    (C) withdraw
    (D) admit

실전에서 바로 써먹는
쉬운 토익 공식 인강

toeic.eduwill.net

RC

CHAPTER 3

PART 6
장문 빈칸 채우기

UNIT 01 시제

UNIT 02 어휘

UNIT 03 접속부사

UNIT 04 문맥에 맞는 문장 고르기

ACTUAL TEST ❶

ACTUAL TEST ❷

CHAPTER 3

문제 유형 및 풀이 전략

지문 및 문제 구성

Part 6는 총 4개의 지문으로 구성되며, 각 지문당 4개의 빈칸 채우기 문제가 주어진다. 4문제 중 3문제는 주로 시제, 어휘, 접속부사, 품사, 대명사 등을 묻는 문제로 구성되며, 문맥에 맞는 문장 고르기 문제가 항상 한 문제씩 출제된다.

지문은 이메일, 편지, 기사, 회람, 공지, 안내 등이 주를 이룬다.

지문 미리보기

Questions 131-134 refer to the following notice.

해설 및 해석 p.49

Office-Wide Power Outage Scheduled

On Monday, January 27, the office ------- to all staff. The electricity in the building is
                                    131.
scheduled to be shut off at 9:30 A.M. and turned on again by the end of the day. An

emergency lighting system will be ------- during the outage. More specifically, prominent
                                  132.
exit signs and a backup generator will be added to meet the recent building codes.

Throughout the office, please unplug all desktops, Wi-Fi devices, and other electricity-

based equipment. -------, please remove any personal items you may have in the
                 133.
refrigerator. -------. If you have any questions, please direct them to the head of building
              134.
maintenance.

---

131. (A) closing
(B) was closed
(C) has closed
(D) will be closed

132. (A) removed
(B) installed
(C) retrieved
(D) discontinued

133. (A) Additionally
(B) However
(C) Meanwhile
(D) In other words

134. (A) The generator will prove useful in emergencies.
(B) Make sure to label food going into the refrigerator.
(C) Any items left in the refrigerator will be disposed of.
(D) Free snacks will be provided in the employee lounge.

문제 유형 및 풀이 전략

Part 6가 하나의 글을 읽어가며 문제를 풀어야 하는 파트이긴 하지만 상당수의 문제들은 Part 5와 마찬가지로 빈칸이 놓여 있는 문장만으로 답을 찾을 수 있다. 예를 들어, 품사 문제는 빈칸 문장의 문장 구조와 빈칸 앞뒤에 있는 단어들의 품사나 문장성분만 고려해도 답을 찾을 수 있다. 하지만 시제와 어휘 문제는 두 개 이상의 선택지가 정답 후보로 남을 경우 반드시 앞뒤 문맥을 고려해야만 정답을 찾을 수 있다. 특히 문장과 문장을 연결하는 접속부사나 문맥에 맞는 문장 고르기 문제는 예외 없이 문맥을 통해 해결해야 한다. 이번 챕터에서는 Part 6 문제 유형 중 문맥을 고려해서 답을 도출해야 하는 아래의 네 가지 유형만을 집중 학습해 보도록 하자.

시제

시제 문제는 Part 5와 마찬가지로 선택지에 동사원형, 분사, 동명사, to부정사 등이 섞여 동사 자리인지를 먼저 판별해야 하는 경우가 많으며, 태, 수 일치 등의 요소가 복합적으로 출제되기도 한다. 서로 다른 시제의 선택지가 최종 정답 후보로 남았을 경우에는, 일차적으로 빈칸이 속해 있는 문장 안의 시간 부사 또는 주절 및 종속절의 시제 등을 살펴본 뒤, 최종적으로는 앞뒤 문맥의 흐름을 통해 시제를 결정해야 한다. 또 이메일이나 기사, 공지 등의 경우, 해당 글이 작성된 날짜를 고려해 시제를 판단해야 하는 경우도 있다.

131. (A) closing
(B) was closed
(C) has closed
(D) will be closed

어휘

Part 5와 마찬가지로 어휘 문제는 항상 같은 품사의 단어가 선택지로 제시된다. 명사, 형용사, 동사, 부사가 골고루 출제되는 편이며, 빈칸의 앞뒤 단어와 잘 연결되는지를 일차적으로 고려하되 두 개 이상의 어휘가 모두 답이 될 수 있을 경우에는 앞뒤 문맥을 따져 판단해야 한다.

132. (A) removed
(B) installed
(C) retrieved
(D) discontinued

접속부사

접속부사는 항상 문장의 앞에 놓이며, 빈칸이 속한 문장과 바로 앞문장의 논리적 연결 관계(인과, 역접, 예시 등)가 판단의 기준이 된다. additionally(덧붙여), however(그러나) 등과 같이 한 단어로 된 접속부사뿐만 아니라 in other words(달리 말하면), in light of(~을 고려하여), if possible(가능하다면)과 같이 여러 단어로 이루어진 관용 표현들이 빈번하게 등장한다.

133. (A) Additionally
(B) However
(C) Meanwhile
(D) In other words

문맥에 맞는 문장 고르기

일반적으로 한 문단은 하나의 일관된 주제를 갖게 되므로 해당 문단이 다루는 중심 내용에서 빗나가는 선택지는 소거한다. 또한 문단의 시작 부분에 빈칸이 놓일 경우를 제외하고는 대부분의 빈칸은 바로 앞 문장과 얼마나 잘 연결되느냐가 우선적인 판단의 근거가 되므로, 빈칸 뒤에 오는 문장보다는 앞에 오는 문장을 항상 먼저 확인해야 한다.

134. (A) The generator will prove useful in emergencies.
(B) Make sure to label food going into the refrigerator.
(C) Any items left in the refrigerator will be disposed of.
(D) Free snacks will be provided in the employee lounge.

UNIT 01 시제

[notice (공지)]

Artist Alley Summer Painting Course

Artist Alley ------- a short painting course this summer from June 3 to July 27. The course will be
                1.
led by Cheryl Hicks, a local painter who ------- dozens of international awards for her work.
                                         2.
Though she focuses mostly on landscapes, she also has experience in portraits and still life paintings.

The course will take place every Saturday from 10 A.M. to 12 P.M. To sign up for the class, please register at www.artistalley.com/summercourse or call 555-0125 to speak directly to a representative.

1. (A) will host
   (B) hosting
   (C) hosted
   (D) has been hosting

2. (A) wins
   (B) has won
   (C) winning
   (D) will be winning

[e-mail (이메일)]

To: All Solar Solutions Staff
From: Riley Mendel
Date: August 18
Subject: Promotion

We would like to congratulate Josie Emerson on her promotion to Sales Manager, effective September 1. Ms. Emerson ------- her career with Twin Solar immediately after graduating from
                                              3.
Clifford University. She has worked here at Solar Solutions for the past eight years, making significant contributions to the team. Thanks to her strong leadership skills and years of experience, we are confident that Ms. Emerson ------- in her new role. Please congratulate her
                                                                        4.
when you get the chance.

Riley Mendel
Human Resources Director

3. (A) began
   (B) begins
   (C) will begin
   (D) beginning

4. (A) excels
   (B) has excelled
   (C) will excel
   (D) is excelling

[flyer (전단지)]

Burlington has made the list for Nation Magazine's "Top Ten Towns"! To acknowledge this special achievement, the town ------- a parade on Saturday, August 20. Local businesses, schools, and music groups ------- to join in the parade. Contact the event planner to find out how to sign up.
    5.   **6.**

You can visit the town's Web site to see the activities planned for the rest of the day as well. We hope that everyone in Burlington will come out and celebrate.

5. (A) held
(B) was held
(C) will hold
(D) to hold

6. (A) invite
(B) were invited
(C) had been invited
(D) are invited

[e-mail (이메일)]

To: Film crew
From: Leslie Kamara
Date: Wednesday, June 29
Subject: Animal shelter scene retake

Dear Crew,

This e-mail serves as a reminder that we ------- the animal shelter scene this Sunday. We were
    7.
unable to get the exact shots we needed because the animals were a bit unruly, but this time we will try hand-selecting the animals that will be featured. If possible, I would like to begin exactly at 7:00 A.M. so that we can film as many scenes as possible before lunch. Assuming everything goes to plan, we should be finished within a few hours. However, there is the possibility it may take longer.

I also want to emphasize the fact that this is a closed set. Only those directly involved in the scene ------- on set.
        8.

Leslie Kamara
Liberia Pictures

7. (A) reshooting
(B) reshot
(C) have reshot
(D) will be reshooting

8. (A) allow
(B) were allowed
(C) have been allowed
(D) will be allowed

UNIT 02　어휘

[notice (공지)]

> Starting from May 2, our store will be ------- self-checkout machines. Due to this, two out of six of our checkout lanes will be turned into self-checkout lanes. You can pay by cash or card at the machines, and receipts will be printed upon the transaction being completed.
>
> 1.

1. (A) closing
   (B) refurbishing
   (C) installing
   (D) replacing

[notice (공지)]

> Starting May 18, overnight parking will be ------- on all streets north of the Lowell Bridge from 12 A.M. to 6 A.M. This is due to upcoming construction of a new train station. Vehicles parked on these streets will be towed away without further notice.
>
> 2.

2. (A) permitted
   (B) prohibited
   (C) reserved
   (D) reviewed

[notice (공지)]

> Please note that the first time you choose to exchange tickets for a performance, you will not be charged a fee. However, any ------- exchanges will incur a $7 per ticket fee.
>
> 3.

3. (A) urgent
   (B) subsequent
   (C) frequent
   (D) upcoming

[e-mail (이메일)]

According to our records you have been a member of the National Society of Realtors for the past three years. Thank you for your ------- and we hope you're enjoying the benefits of being a part of this group.
                                  4.

4. (A) patience
 (B) expertise
 (C) patronage
 (D) referral

[e-mail (이메일)]

As we approach our peak season, it is important for employees to remember the vacation policy here at Toledo Inn. We ask that you request time off from your immediate supervisor at least two weeks in advance. The supervisor will decide whether or not to allow the time off based on the individual department's needs. Also, please note that taking off more than 10 consecutive business days may require ------- approval.
                                    5.

5. (A) widespread
 (B) prior
 (C) additional
 (D) strong

[information (정보)]

Legal Matters: The monthly magazine for lawyers

Our first issue of the year will highlight those who have recently ------- their careers in the law
                                                                6.
field. Working in the law business is no easy feat, and we want to feature those who are just getting started in their careers. Whether you're fresh out of law school or transitioning from another specialty, we want to hear your story.

Please send a ------- of no more than 1,000 words detailing why you chose this career path.
            7.
E-mail your work to features@legalmatters.com by November 10 for a chance to be published in our magazine.

6. (A) revived   **7.** (A) review
 (B) paused   (B) notice
 (C) begun   (C) letter
 (D) left   (D) submission

UNIT 03 접속부사

정답 및 해설 p.51

토익에 자주 등장하는 접속부사 또는 관용어구

인과	부가, 순서	요약
Accordingly 따라서 Consequently 따라서, 그 결과 Hence/Therefore/Thus 따라서 Then 그러니까, 그렇다면, 그 다음에 Now that 이제 ~이므로 As a result 결과적으로 For this reason 이러한 이유로	Additionally 추가적으로 In addition 게다가 Furthermore 게다가 Moreover 더구나 Besides 게다가 Subsequently 그 뒤에 Specifically 구체적으로 말하자면 More specifically 더 구체적으로 말하자면 First of all 우선	Briefly/In brief 간단히 말해 In conclusion 결론적으로 In summary 요약하자면 In other words 다시 말해서 All in all 대체로
시간, 빈도	**대조**	**비교**
Lately 최근에 Recently 최근에 Meanwhile 그 동안에, 한편 In the meantime 그 동안에 Occasionally 간혹 Before long 오래지 않아	But/However 하지만 Nevertheless 그럼에도 불구하고 Otherwise 그렇지 않으면 Rather 오히려 Instead 대신 With that said 그렇긴 하지만 Having said that 그렇긴 하지만 In contrast to ~과는 대조적으로	Likewise 마찬가지로 Similarly 마찬가지로, 유사하게 Equally 마찬가지로, 동시에
강조	**예시**	**기타 관용 표현**
Indeed 정말, 사실 Of course 물론 Certainly/Definitely 당연히, 분명 After all 결국 As a matter of fact 사실상	For example 예를 들어 For instance 예를 들어	In that case 그런 경우에는 In any case 어쨌든, 여하튼 In light of ~을 고려하여 If possible 가능하다면 On the other hand 한편, 반면

[article (기사)]

(18 October)—Fast food chain Burgers For Us announced that Robert Green has been appointed as the new vice president. Mr. Green has spent the last eight years as the chairperson of the board of directors at Tasty Tacos, a competing fast food chain. -------, he holds a wealth of information about how the industry works and how to manage large franchises.

1. (A) Therefore
   (B) Surprisingly
   (C) Instead
   (D) As a reminder

[notice (공지)]

We're asking for everyone's help on May 20 as we move to our new warehouse. On the moving day, one team will be loading trucks at the old site. -------, another team will be unloading trucks
                                                           2.
at the new site as they arrive. Everyone else should begin unpacking boxes and organizing our equipment. If you finish a task early, please assist other teams. After everything is moved, we invite employees to stay for a pizza party at the new site.

2. (A) Instead
   (B) Nevertheless
   (C) Meanwhile
   (D) Therefore

[memo (메모)]

Easton Inc. has recently taken on several high-profile clients, so security is more important than ever. ------- this, we are changing our visitor policy. From April 8, all visitors must sign in at the
         3.
security.

3. (A) Even if
   (B) On the contrary
   (C) In light of
   (D) Rather than

[announcement (발표)]

A recent study on market share revealed that the top two appliance brands in Nigeria are international companies. Bevin Appliances of Canada holds 23% of the market, and Lancelot Inc. of the U.S. holds 19%. Customers report that their number one reason for choosing Bevin Appliances is due to the products' durability. -------, Lancelot Inc. customers are more
                                                              4.
persuaded by that company's sleek designs. Representatives from both brands are looking for ways to appeal to more customers and expand their base.

4. (A) For example
   (B) As a matter of fact
   (C) In that case
   (D) On the other hand

UNIT 04 문맥에 맞는 문장 고르기

[instructions (지침)]

> Prinz Glassware
>
> **Preparing Goods for Packaging**
>
> As our glassware is very fragile, it is important that secure packaging is used for all orders. We endeavor to supply each customer with flawless items.
>
> The first step is to place the item in its specially designed box to minimize vibrations and impacts to the merchandise. Look for the box number for the item you are preparing. -------. **1.** Next, place the box in a larger box, filling the empty space with packing material. Finally, tape the box closed and attach the address label.
>
> If you have a shortage of supplies in your area, please notify a manager so that more can be brought to you.

1. (A) They are pleased with our high-quality finishes.
   (B) Assembly took longer than we had expected.
   (C) It can be found on the underside of the container.
   (D) The team leaders can assign you to groups.

[instructions (지침)]

> Employees must participate in all professional development workshops at Talmage Inc. This helps to ensure that everyone continues to build essential business skills. Sometimes, this requirement may be waived. In this case, the employee should complete a form to explain his or her absence. The employee should submit the form with details of the reason, along with the immediate supervisor's signature. If you miss a workshop, we ask that you still take the time to review the handouts that were distributed. -------. **2.**

2. (A) The theme has not been decided yet.
   (B) These materials will be informative no matter your role.
   (C) Nevertheless, the instructors have a lot of experience.
   (D) It is common for the front seats to fill up quickly.

[e-mail (이메일)]

From: Rina Honda <r.honda@sweepstakes.com>
To: Florence Dalton <florence_d@jmail.com>
Subject: Congratulations!

Dear Ms. Dalton,

I am writing to inform you that you are the lucky winner of this month's $500 Shopping Spree Sweepstakes! We will be sending your prize in the form of a gift certificate that is valid at any Grand Sphere Mall complex. -------3.-------.

Your gift certificate will be sent to the address you submitted when you registered for the contest. You can expect it to arrive in about three to four business days.

Congratulations again and happy spending!

Best,

Rina Honda
Sweepstakes.com Manager

3. (A) The contest rules can be found under the FAQ section of our Web site.
   (B) Submit your entry before the deadline to be considered.
   (C) The sweepstakes can be entered by anyone over 18 years old.
   (D) Please remember to register your gift certificate online before use.

[article (기사)]

LONDON (10 February)—In its annual report, Meyers Motors revealed that sales for its SuperBike 200 surpassed the company's expectations. According to CEO Madeline Meyers, two major factors have contributed to the new motorbike's success. First, its sleek design is available in a variety of colors. -------4.-------. Second, the reduced sale price is enticing for all customers. Despite being a high-quality vehicle, the motorbike is being offered at a surprisingly low cost. These characteristics are what sets the SuperBike 200 apart from similar vehicles on the market.

4. (A) The bike is about half the price of comparable vehicles.
   (B) This eye-catching look is popular with young motorists.
   (C) Meyers Motors was first founded in 1977.
   (D) Always wear a helmet when riding a motorbike.

ACTUAL TEST 1

Questions 1-4 refer to the following notice.

We are proud to announce that renovations to The Willow Theater have been completed. This historic site has been in operation for decades and is beloved by many. This Friday will be its grand re-opening. We ------- purchasing tickets in advance as we expect them to sell out early.
                                   1.
We always do our best to ensure an enjoyable and memorable theater experience. However, please understand ------- we are an outdoor theater, so we cannot always guarantee that a
                              2.
performance will go forward. ------- inclement weather, there may be a cancellation. Ticket-
                              3.
holders for canceled events may request a refund or exchange their tickets for another event. -------. This makes it easy for our staff to confirm your order.
4.

1. (A) recommends
   (B) recommend
   (C) will be recommended
   (D) are recommended

2. (A) whatever
   (B) which
   (C) that
   (D) those

3. (A) In case of
   (B) By all means
   (C) At least for
   (D) In addition to

4. (A) You can pick up a brochure about the performers.
   (B) When doing so, please have your confirmation number ready.
   (C) If you would like to share your feedback, we would love to hear from you.
   (D) For instance, the seats in the middle section tend to fill up quickly.

Questions 5-8 refer to the following e-mail.

To: Olivia Bowen <olivia.b@hmail.com>
From: Cook-Right <info@cook-right.com>
Date: April 30
Subject: Membership confirmation

Dear Ms. Bowen,

Thank you for choosing Cook-Right! With your one year membership, you can ------- thousands of recipes, making it easy to cook meals at home. We aim to ensure that all recipes are accurate, and we try to suggest alternative ingredients so that people can cook according to individual -------.

We value the feedback of our customers. -------, we encourage you to let us know how we can improve the site. If you notice an error on the Web site, please submit a report to the Cook-Right staff. -------.

We hope you enjoy cooking!

The Cook-Right Staff

5. (A) displace
   (B) inspire
   (C) access
   (D) predict

6. (A) preferring
   (B) preferred
   (C) preference
   (D) prefer

7. (A) Meanwhile
   (B) Additionally
   (C) Subsequently
   (D) Therefore

8. (A) It can be downloaded every Monday.
   (B) It will be corrected as quickly as possible.
   (C) It can be exchanged for gift certificates.
   (D) It has received excellent reviews.

Questions 9-12 refer to the following e-mail.

To: Chinua Alvarez <chinua.a@bonding.com>
From: The Fabulous Florist <info@thefabulousflorist.com>
Date: May 16
Subject: Grand Opening

Dear Ms. Alvarez,

We are ------- to announce that The Fabulous Florist is expanding its business to the midtown area and hope you will be able to join us for our grand opening next weekend. We are known for providing the freshest and best-smelling flowers on the market. We offer a wide variety of roses, daisies, carnations and more. -------.
For our grand opening, we are offering all ------- a 10% discount on purchases over $75. -------, all visitors will receive a free bag of white rose seeds upon entry. We hope to see you there!

Sincerely,

The Fabulous Florist Team

9. (A) happy
   (B) happily
   (C) happiness
   (D) happier

10. (A) Most of our flowers are artificially made.
    (B) We are sorry to close down our doors so soon.
    (C) This is our first time running a shop, so we are very excited.
    (D) We also carry flowers in an assortment of colors as well.

11. (A) clients
    (B) employees
    (C) customers
    (D) drivers

12. (A) However
    (B) Unfortunately
    (C) Additionally
    (D) Therefore

Questions 13-16 refer to the following advertisement.

Do you find it difficult to follow the ups and downs of the property market? Prices ------- monthly, so you should get your property valued regularly. This is not just recommended for those buying or selling a home. It is also useful when it comes to insurance. For example, you may need more coverage than expected.

That's where we, Home Helpers, come in. -------. Simply book an appointment for the low fee of just $95. After a visit from one of our staff members, you will receive a full report. It will have details about your home's value and ------- changes you can make to increase this figure. Call 555-4986 today to get started. We will ask you a few initial questions ------- your needs.

13. (A) measure
    (B) display
    (C) continue
    (D) fluctuate

14. (A) Most of them are surprised by the results.
    (B) Our valuation process is easy and affordable.
    (C) Your realtor will take photos of the home.
    (D) The mortgage process can be confusing.

15. (A) once
    (B) what
    (C) how
    (D) although

16. (A) having assessed
    (B) assessed
    (C) assessments
    (D) to assess

ACTUAL TEST 2

Questions 1-4 refer to the following e-mail.

To: Sharon Devi <sdevi@umail.net>
From: Justin Kumar <jkumar@bluestarair.com>
Date: March 8
Subject: Compensation for delays

Dear Ms. Devi,

We have received your complaint about Bluestar Air flight 754, which was scheduled to depart at 10:05 P.M. on 1 March. We apologize that the flight -------. Bluestar Air will compensate you
1.
for your trouble. We will ------- 50% of your original ticket price back into your account. If you
2.
are able to reply to this e-mail with a copy of a verifiable receipt ------- the hotel at which you
3.
were forced to stay because of the flight delay, we will also reimburse you the full price of your room. -------.
4.

Thank you for your understanding.

Justin Kumar
Bluestar Air Customer Service

1. (A) delays
   (B) is delaying
   (C) was delayed
   (D) had to delay

2. (A) refund
   (B) allocate
   (C) secure
   (D) offset

3. (A) from
   (B) above
   (C) besides
   (D) near

4. (A) We hope you have a great trip.
   (B) Please allow three business days for the refund to clear.
   (C) Your complaint has been sent to the executives.
   (D) We appreciate your suggestions for improvement.

Questions 5-8 refer to the following e-mail.

To: Sheri Tate <sheri@tastycafe.net>
From: Gloria Gibson <ggibson@lowriebank.com>
Date: May 21
Subject: Bank loan from Lowrie Bank

Dear Ms. Tate,

On behalf of Lowrie Bank, I would like to inform you that your request for a business loan for your café has been approved. You ------- the deposit in your business account within 3–5 business days.
                                                              5.

-------. This is due to the risky nature of the restaurant business in general. However, your
6.
business' ------- was well demonstrated through long-term financial records and the excellent
         7.
reputation of the establishment. -------, as you own the commercial building, you have a valuable
                                 8.
asset to make the loan more secure. The first loan payment is due on July 1.

Should you have any questions, please do not hesitate to contact me.

Gloria Gibson
Loan Officer, Lowrie Bank

5. (A) noticing
   (B) noticeable
   (C) should notice
   (D) had noticed

6. (A) Certainly, the food on the menu is healthy and delicious.
   (B) As we discussed, we usually do not issue such a high amount.
   (C) Bank employees must keep all records confidential.
   (D) Our customers can earn interest on their savings accounts.

7. (A) stable
   (B) stability
   (C) stabilize
   (D) stabilized

8. (A) As a result
   (B) Unfortunately
   (C) Conversely
   (D) In addition

Questions 9-12 refer to the following notice.

GameShop is looking for seasonal employees for the upcoming holidays. Anyone with a passion for and deep knowledge about video games ------- to apply. Duties ------- include greeting
                                                                                                  9.   **10.**
guests, explaining sales, and providing recommendations. -------. We are looking to hire warm
                                                                  11.
and punctual people to join our team. To apply, please check ------- Web site at
                                                                      12.
gameshop.com/apply. The deadline to apply is November 1.

9. (A) is encouraged
   (B) encouraging
   (C) will encourage
   (D) has been encouraged

10. (A) exceptionally
    (B) heavily
    (C) mainly
    (D) considerably

11. (A) You may also occasionally be asked to organize the merchandise.
    (B) Our store is open from 10 A.M. to 10 P.M.
    (C) GameShop can be found on the third floor of West Garden Mall.
    (D) We also sell figurines in addition to games.

12. (A) we
    (B) us
    (C) them
    (D) our

Questions 13-16 refer to the following article.

CAMERON COUNTY (September 9) — In the past year, Cameron County's ------- rate has gone
up by 4.7% with over 6,000 jobs being created. Retail jobs ------- the largest increase, and
service sector jobs had the second largest increase. Healthcare jobs came in third, which may
be due to the growing eldercare needs of the community. -------. "If the job market continues on
this positive trend, we will likely see more and more people ------- to Cameron County," said
market analyst Edward McKenzie.

13. (A) birth
(B) employment
(C) education
(D) turnover

14. (A) exhibited
(B) exhibiting
(C) will exhibit
(D) will be exhibited

15. (A) Residents think more money needs to be spent on infrastructure.
(B) Nevertheless, the labor market has not fully recovered.
(C) Average hourly earnings in the medical industry were flat last month.
(D) Office jobs came in last, though they did see a significant increase as well.

16. (A) advancing
(B) delegating
(C) migrating
(D) inspecting

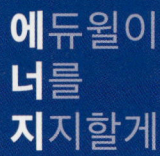

내를 건너서 숲으로
고개를 넘어서 마을로

어제도 가고 오늘도 갈
나의 길 새로운 길

– 윤동주, '새로운 길'

실전에서 바로 써먹는
쉬운 토익 공식 인강

toeic.eduwill.net

RC

CHAPTER 4

PART 7 독해

PART 7 질문 유형별 풀이 전략

문제 유형 및 풀이 전략

Part 7은 각 지문에 달린 문제들을 먼저 확인한 후 지문을 읽는 것이 효과적이다. 문제에 나온 질문을 염두에 두고 읽으면 질문과 관련된 부분에 보다 집중해서 지문을 읽어내려갈 수 있으며, 따라서 지문을 읽는 시간을 단축할 수 있기 때문이다. 문장 삽입 문제와 일부 NOT/True 문제를 제외한 대부분의 Part 7 문제의 단서는 지문에 순차적으로 제시되기 때문에 문제의 순서에 따라 답을 찾기 위한 단서의 위치도 짐작할 수 있다. 첫 번째 문제를 풀었다면, 두 번째 문제를 풀 때는 지문을 처음부터 검색할 필요 없이 첫 번째 문제의 단서가 나온 뒷부분만 검색해도 문제의 단서를 찾을 수 있다. 다음 예제의 문제 풀이 방법을 오른쪽 시뮬레이션 페이지에서 확인하자.

문제 미리보기

Questions 1-3 refer to the following notice.

해석 p.57

Addison Community Garage Sale

The city of Addison will host its biannual community garage sale this weekend at the Arbor Park Recreation Center, which is located next to the children's playground. The sale will take place on Saturday, August 13, from 9:00 A.M. to 6:00 P.M. and Sunday, August 14, from 11:00 A.M. to 6:00 P.M. All are welcome, even if they are not residents of Addison.

The garage sale will feature a wide array of goods such as grilling equipment, clothes, jewelry, plants, and more. Proceeds will go to free lunch programs for local schools.

Before the sale, we will accept donations of all kinds. We only ask that the objects be clean and in new or gently used condition. Donations will be accepted at the recreation center during the following times:

Monday to Wednesday: 9:00 A.M. to 4:00 P.M.
Thursday: 1:00 P.M. to 10:00 P.M.
Friday: 1:00 P.M. to 4:00 P.M.

---

1. What is true about the event?

   (A) It is held once a year.
   (B) It will focus on children.
   (C) Anyone can attend it.
   (D) Admission fees will be charged.

2. What is indicated about the proceeds from the garage sale?

   (A) They are expected to be high.
   (B) They are needed for a children's playground.
   (C) They will be spent on repairs at the center.
   (D) They will be used to provide meals.

3. When can donations be delivered in the evening?

   (A) On Monday
   (B) On Wednesday
   (C) On Thursday
   (D) On Friday

문제 풀이 시뮬레이션

Questions 1-3 refer to the following notice.

❶ 지문 종류 확인

Addison Community Garage Sale

The city of Addison will host its biannual community garage sale this weekend at the Arbor Park Recreation Center, which is located next to the children's playground. The sale will take place on Saturday, August 13, from 9:00 A.M. to 6:00 P.M. and Sunday, August 14, from 11:00 A.M. to 6:00 P.M. All are welcome, even if they are not residents of Addison.

The garage sale will feature a wide array of goods such as grilling equipment, clothes, jewelry, plants, and more. Proceeds will go to free lunch programs for local schools.

Before the sale, we will accept donations of all kinds. We only ask that the objects be clean and in new or gently used condition. Donations will be accepted at the recreation center during the following times:

Monday to Wednesday: 9:00 A.M. to 4:00 P.M.
Thursday: 1:00 P.M. to 10:00 P.M.
Friday: 1:00 P.M. to 4:00 P.M.

❷ 1번 문제 확인
1. What is true about the event?
첫 번째 문제의 단서는 지문의 앞부분에 나온다.

❸ 1번 문제의 단서 검색
❹ 선택지 확인
(✓) Anyone can attend it.

❺ 2번 문제 확인
2. What is indicated about the proceeds from the garage sale?
두 번째 문제를 풀 때는 첫 번째 문제의 단서가 나온 다음부터 검색한다.

❻ 2번 문제의 단서 검색
❼ 선택지 확인
(✓) They will be used to provide meals.

❽ 3번 문제 확인
3. When can donations be delivered in the evening?
세 번째 문제를 풀 때는 두 번째 문제의 단서가 나온 다음부터 검색한다.

❾ 3번 문제의 단서 검색
❿ 선택지 확인
(✓) On Thursday

209

❶ 주제/목적/대상 문제

특징

거의 모든 지문에서 첫 번째 문제로 자주 출제되며, 특히 이메일/편지, 기사, 공지 지문에서 출제 빈도가 높다. 반면 문자 메시지/온라인 채팅 지문에서는 거의 출제되지 않는다.

질문 유형

What is the article **mainly about**? 기사는 주로 무엇에 관한 것인가? [주제]
What is being **advertised**? 무엇이 광고되고 있는가? [주제]
What is the **purpose** of the e-mail? 이메일의 목적은 무엇인가? [목적]
For whom is the notice **intended**? 공지는 누구를 위한 것인가? [대상]

문제 풀이 전략

주제/목적/대상 문제라는 것을 확인했다면 선택지를 보지 말고 먼저 지문을 본다. 주제/목적/대상 문제는 거의 예외 없이 제목이나 지문의 앞부분에 단서가 나오는데, 그 내용을 정확히 파악한 후 가장 적절한 선택지를 선택한다.

문제 미리보기   [article (기사)]   해석 p.57

OTTAWA (September 3)—Tool manufacturer Cassidy Tools, which supplies power tools to hardware stores across the country, confirmed today that its current CEO is stepping down. Shannon Watson, who has been overseeing the company's operations for twelve years, plans to go into retirement next month. She will be replaced by Rick Saunders, the current CFO.

Mr. Saunders stated that he is "excited about taking the company in a new direction and showing off its amazing products." He is particularly interested in the company's new air compressor, the Hale-90, as it is powerful yet energy-efficient. He plans to conduct extensive ad campaigns for the product in hopes that it will become a bestseller. Mr. Saunders also aims to improve workplace conditions to help retain skilled employees.

> 기업의 동향을 알리는 기사의 경우 먼저 기업에 관한 짤막한 소개가 나온 후 기사에서 전달하고자 하는 내용이 이어진다. 첫 번째 문장의 Tool manufacturer ~ across the country가 기업에 관한 소개이고, 그 뒤에 이어지는 것이 기사가 전달하고자 하는 주제이다.

Q. Why was the article written?

   (A) To explain safety measures for some tools
   (B) To inform the public of a change in leadership
   (C) To announce the expansion of a store chain
   (D) To highlight a company's achievements

빈출 유형 공략

[letter (편지)]

> Dear Mr. Sigler,
>
> We are holding our annual Donor Appreciation Banquet on Saturday, December 4, and we hope that you can attend. During the five-course dinner, our director, Kimberly Elias, will give a speech about the facility's accomplishments so far and the plans for the new year.
>
> Fred Mullins
> Board Chairman, Patterson Museum of Architecture

1. What is the purpose of the letter?

    (A) To announce changes at a museum
    (B) To show appreciation for a suggestion
    (C) To extend an invitation to a meal
    (D) To request information about a building

[Web page (웹페이지)]

> Starting December 5, Pekka's Coat Factory will be having its annual Winter Coat Sale.
>
> Our annual sale is the talk of the town. The windbreakers, jackets, coats, and fleeces you've come to love from Pekka's will all be discounted during the sale. Nearly everything in our store will be at least 10% off, but some items will be as much as 50% off. Make sure you stop by and find the perfect coat for this winter before it's too late!

2. What is the purpose of the Web page?

    (A) To explain a product shortage
    (B) To advertise an upcoming event
    (C) To announce a store opening
    (D) To promote a new brand

❷ NOT / True 문제

특징

지문의 내용과 일치하거나 일치하지 않는 선택지를 찾는 문제로서, 문제를 풀기 위해 지문을 전반적으로 검색하여 선택지와 대조해야 하기 때문에 난이도가 가장 높은 편이다. 또한 단서가 순차적으로 제시되지 않는 경우가 종종 있다.

질문 유형

질문에 NOT, true나, 동사 indicate, mention, state 등이 포함되어 있는 것이 특징이다.

What is **NOT mentioned** as a feature of the program? 프로그램의 특징으로 언급되지 않은 것은 무엇인가?
What is **true** about the job? 일자리에 대해 사실인 것은 무엇인가?
What is **indicated** about the contest? 대회에 대해 나타난 것은 무엇인가?

문제 풀이 전략

NOT/True 문제는 '선택지 (A) → 지문 확인, 선택지 (B) → 지문 확인, 선택지 (C)..., 선택지 (D)...'와 같은 과정을 거쳐 각각의 선택지에 해당하는 부분을 지문에서 찾아 대조해가며 답을 찾아야 한다. NOT/True 문제를 풀기 위해서는 지문을 전반적으로 검색해야 하기 때문에 이 문제를 맨 처음에 풀게 되면 지문의 전반적인 내용과 문맥을 파악할 수 있어 다른 문제를 푸는 데 도움이 된다.

문제 미리보기 [article (기사)]

해석 p.58

MEXICO CITY (3 March)—Starting in early summer, residents of Mexico City will have a new way to travel around. Move It Inc. will be launching affordable rental bikes around various parts of the city. All you need is a smartphone and credit card to get started. Reserve one of the bikes on the Move It app, find the bike with the matching serial number, and off you go! Your card will be charged when you return the bike to an official Move It station. These Move It stations will be strategically placed around the city in heavily populated areas. "After our success in the United States, we decided to expand and give the people of Mexico a chance to enjoy our services as well," said Matthew Ortega, CEO of Move It Inc.

Q. 1 추론/암시 문제로서, Move It station을 키워드로 지문을 검색하면, will be strategically placed에서 아직 지어지지 않았다는 것을 추론할 수 있으므로 (C)가 정답이다.

Q. 2 NOT/True 문제로서 지문 내용과 선택지를 일일이 대조해야 한다. 미국에서 먼저 성공을 거두었다고 했으므로, 멕시코에서 처음 시작되었다는 내용의 (A)가 정답이다.

1. What is suggested about the Move It stations in Mexico City?

   (A) They are quite spacious.
   (B) They are in isolated areas.
   (C) They have not been built yet.
   (D) They are placed on each street.

2. What is NOT indicated about Move It Inc.?

   (A) It first started in Mexico City.
   (B) It allows users to borrow bikes.
   (C) It charges people after they use the service.
   (D) It offers reasonable prices.

[notice (공지)]

Redmond Gardens Film Festival

Redmond Gardens is pleased to announce its first-ever outdoor film festival
Thursday, August 8 - Sunday, August 11
6 P.M. to 9 P.M.

Tickets are $5 per person and include:
a soda or coffee and on-site parking

Local bands will perform from 6 P.M. to 7 P.M. and then the movie will be screened. Souvenir movie posters will be sold for $3 each at the ticket booth.

Visit www.redmondgardens.com for more information or to purchase tickets.

---

1. What is true about Redmond Gardens?

    (A) It is operated by the city.
    (B) It gives awards to filmmakers.
    (C) It has not held the festival before.
    (D) It closes at 7 P.M. every evening.

2. What is NOT included in the admission fee?

    (A) A poster
    (B) A beverage
    (C) Parking
    (D) Musical entertainment

[e-mail (이메일)]

Dear Mr. Sullivan,

I love reading your blog. I especially enjoy your homemade toy ideas. Though there is a Question-and-Answer page on your Web site, there are still times when I am left puzzled because I only have your advice. For example, I was trying to conduct one of your monthly science experiments, but I realized I was missing an ingredient. I was at a loss for what to do. Fortunately, I was able to find a good substitute by searching the comments of another Web site. So, it would be nice if there were a comments section on your Web page to let other people share ideas and solutions.

Wayne Hackett

---

3. What is the purpose of the e-mail?

    (A) To ask a specific question
    (B) To give a suggestion
    (C) To recommend a Web site
    (D) To offer a professional service

4. What is NOT indicated about Mr. Sullivan's blog?

    (A) It has science experiments.
    (B) It provides answers to some questions.
    (C) It displays a contact phone number.
    (D) It teaches people how to make toys.

❸ 추론/암시 문제

특징

지문에 언급된 내용을 바탕으로 그 안에 숨겨진 의미를 파악하여 이를 가장 잘 표현한 선택지를 고르는 문제이다. 선택지는 지문에 나온 표현이 그대로 나오거나 유사한 표현으로 패러프레이징되어 제시되는데, 패러프레이징의 난이도가 높은 경우에는 오답을 하나씩 소거해 가면서 정답을 찾는 것이 효율적이다.

질문 유형

질문에 most likely나 동사 suggest, imply 등이 포함되어 있는 것이 특징이다.

Who mostly likely is Mr. Martin? Martin 씨는 누구이겠는가?
What is **suggested** about Ms. Barrett? Barrett 씨에 대해 암시된 것은 무엇인가?
Where would the notice **most likely** appear? 공지는 어디에 나타나겠는가?

문제 풀이 전략

질문에 키워드가 있다면 지문에서 키워드를 검색하면 되지만, 그렇지 않은 경우 지문을 읽어 내려가며 선택지 내용을 하나하나 대조해야 한다. 지문이 길고 복잡한 경우 NOT/True 문제처럼 '선택지 (A) 확인 → 지문 확인 → 선택지 (B) 확인 → 지문 확인'과 같은 과정으로 문제를 푸는 것이 시간 절약에 효과적이다.

문제 미리보기 [report (보고서)] 해석 p.59

Smartphone Application Monetization Analysis
Prepared by DW Consulting

Company: **Cardack Development**
App Name: Fundamentalz

We have assessed the best way to monetize your smartphone application. In addition to the method recommended below, we also recommend creating a question-and-answer section in the app to increase engagement. The users could get answers from experts.

Primary Recommendation

Monthly Subscription: $4.99/month per user / **No change in fees as the collection of videos is expanded**

Q. What is suggested about Cardack Development?

(A) It receives one thousand views per day.
(B) It plans to add more videos to the application.
(C) It charges a fee to view each video.
(D) It has advertised the application heavily.

질문의 키워드인 Cardack Development로 지문을 검색한다. Cardack Development는 회사명이고 이 회사에 대한 컨설팅 내용임을 알 수 있으며, 지문을 읽어 내려가며 선택지 내용과 대조한다.

(A): one thousand views에 해당하는 내용을 지문에서 찾을 수 없으므로 오답이다.
(B): add more videos to the application이 지문의 the collection of videos is expanded와 내용이 일치하므로 정답이다.
(C): 월 4.99달러의 구독료를 제안하고 있으므로 오답이다.
(D): advertised the application heavily에 해당하는 내용이 없으므로 오답이다.

[article (기사)]

Intercity Bus Coming to Providence

(January 17)—New York City-based Transpo Co. has undertaken the job of creating bus routes between Providence and New York City. This decision has been made because of increasing public requests for the routes. Buses already stop at similarly popular destinations, such as New Haven and Old Saybrook, so "the decision was an easy one," said Transpo Co. CEO Marilyn Baskerville. "The new bus routes will be important for both tourism and commuting," she added. Construction on new bus stations to facilitate the change will begin this spring and is expected to be completed by the fall.

1. What is suggested about the new bus stations?

    (A) They still need to be funded.
    (B) They will be finished within a year.
    (C) Two companies are constructing them.
    (D) Local residents oppose their construction.

[notice (공지)]

Starting Your Own Business
17 June, 2:30 P.M. to 4:00 P.M.
Sydney Community Centre

Have you ever wanted to start your own business? If so, please join us for our workshop on how to do exactly that. This workshop will be led by Vincent Norton, founder and CEO of HJ VentureWorks. He will be sharing his expertise with the audience on how to start and run a successful business.

To register for the event, please visit www.sydneycc.co.au. The workshop is free, but prior registration is required. Light refreshments will be served.

2. Who most likely is Vincent Norton?

    (A) An event organizer
    (B) A government official
    (C) A business owner
    (D) A motivational speaker

4 세부 사항 문제

특징

Part 7에서 가장 많이 출제되는 질문 유형으로서, Who(누가), What(무엇을), Where(어디서), When(언제), How(어떻게), Why(왜)로 시작하여 세부적인 내용을 묻는다.

질문 유형

Who is Mr. McClellan? McClellan 씨는 누구인가?
What does Cregar sell? Cregar는 무엇을 판매하는가?
Why did Ms. Cairns send the memo? Cairns 씨는 왜 회람을 보냈는가?
How should Mr. Thurman respond to the request? Thurman 씨는 어떻게 요청에 답해야 하는가?

문제 풀이 전략

질문의 키워드로 지문을 검색한다. 주로 명사가 키워드가 되지만, 동사(구)도 키워드가 될 수 있다. 지문에서 키워드와 관련 있는 부분을 찾았다면 해당 문장이나 바로 앞뒤의 내용을 해석한 후 선택지를 확인한다.

문제 미리보기 [letter (편지)]   해석 p.60

Dear Ms. Reyes,

Thank you for contacting us about your Reppert 12-speed bicycle. You are correct that it is eligible for a refund because that model has been recalled for safety reasons. We've received the completed form with your banking details and proof of purchase. We will send the refund to the bank account that you have indicated on the form. We are collecting faulty bicycles at our retail stores. If this is inconvenient for you, you may take the item to your local recycling center or arrange a bulky waste collection for it. We apologize for any inconvenience caused.

Sincerely,

Bessie Maddux
Lambert Sports Customer Service

> 질문의 키워드는 Ms. Maddux와 Ms. Reyes인데, Ms. Reyes는 편지의 수신인이므로 지문에서 you로 나올 것이다. 또한 질문에서 Ms. Reyes가 할 수 있는 것이 무엇인지 물었으므로, 그에 관한 단서는 지문에서 you can[may] ~(당신은 ~할 수 있다)와 같은 형태로 나올 것임을 추론할 수 있다. you may로 시작하는 문장에서 자전거를 재활용 센터로 가져가거나 대형 쓰레기로 처리할 수 있다고 했으므로 '물품을 직접 폐기하기'라는 (B)가 정답이다.

Q. What does Ms. Maddux say that Ms. Reyes can do?

(A) Get another copy of the form
(B) Dispose of an item herself
(C) Call one of the business's stores
(D) Contact a repair center

빈출 유형 공략

해석 및 해설 p.61

[e-mail (이메일)]

From: John Charon
To: All Staff
Date: 10 April
Subject: New flooring

Dear all,

I just wanted to remind you that Bailey's Construction will be installing new flooring on the second floor of our office. They will be coming into the building on Wednesday morning to replace the flooring in the lounge and bathroom. We expect the work to last somewhere between seven to nine hours. There may be some minor disruptions, but please try to continue with business as usual.

John Charon

1. Who will be visiting the building on Wednesday?

    (A) New clients
    (B) An interior designer
    (C) A building remodeling crew
    (D) Cable electricians

[e-mail (이메일)]

To: All Determix Staff
From: Chan Mao
Date: July 31
Subject: Shipping Error

It seems that dozens of our customers had issues inputting their shipping information. Yesterday, our Web site only collected partial data from some customers who ordered online. As a result, we only have their e-mail addresses and phone numbers, but not their shipping addresses. If you are preparing a shipment and come across this issue, contact floor manager Kyle Stevenson. The IT department is working to fix the problem. Fortunately, they are upgrading the system next week, so we hope this won't happen again. We appreciate your cooperation until then.

2. When will the IT department upgrade a system?

    (A) In July
    (B) In August
    (C) In September
    (D) In October

❺ 문장 삽입 문제

특징
주어진 문장이 들어가기에 가장 적절한 위치를 찾는 문제로서, 해당 지문의 마지막 문제로 출제된다. 회람 지문에서 출제 빈도가 가장 높고, 웹페이지, 이메일/편지, 기사 지문에서도 많이 출제된다.

질문 유형
In which of the positions marked [1], [2], [3], and [4] does the following sentence best belong?
"It took a while for the concept to catch on."
[1], [2], [3], [4]로 표시된 위치 중 다음 문장이 들어가기에 가장 적절한 곳은?
"그 개념이 인기를 얻는 데는 다소의 시간이 걸렸다."

문제 풀이 전략
먼저 질문에서 따옴표로 묶인 문장을 정확히 해석한 후 문맥에 맞는 위치를 찾아야 한다. 그렇기 때문에 앞선 문제들을 풀면서 지문의 문맥을 파악하는 것이 유리하다. 또한 주어진 문장에 it, this와 같은 대명사가 있다면 그것이 가리키는 것이 나타난 문장의 뒤가 적절한 위치가 되며, additionally(또한), alternatively(그 대신에)와 같은 접속부사가 있다면 앞 문장과의 맥락을 파악하여 문제를 푼다.

문제 미리보기 [notice (공지)]
해석 p.61

Notice to Huerta Enterprises Employees

The management team is taking immediate steps to improve the safety of employees and the privacy of our company's operations. —[1]—. We aim to prevent unauthorized people from entering the building. —[2]—. Starting from Monday, March 15, employees can no longer use the rear entrance, which will be locked at all times. The only exception is maintenance workers who are loading materials into the building. —[3]—. Your supervisors will provide you with a new ID badge that can be scanned. We will be checking the badges manually the week of March 15, which will delay the time it takes for you to enter the office. —[4]—. The following week, the scanners will be fully functional. We appreciate your patience during this transition.

> 주어진 문장인 "Please arrive a bit earlier than usual during that time."을 해석하면 "그 기간 동안에는 평소보다 조금 일찍 도착해 주세요."이다. 따라서 바로 앞 문장에는 기간을 나타내는 단어가 나오고, 일찍 도착해야만 하는 이유가 제시된다는 것을 예상할 수 있다. [1], [2], [3], [4]의 바로 앞 문장을 살펴보면, [4]의 앞 문장에 the week of March 15라는 기간이 나왔고, We will be checking the badges manually라는 이유가 제시되었으므로 주어진 문장이 들어가기에 가장 적절한 위치는 [4]이다.

Q. In which of the positions marked [1], [2], [3], and [4] does the following sentence best belong?

"Please arrive a bit earlier than usual during that time."

(A) [1]　　(B) [2]　　(C) [3]　　**(D) [4]**

빈출 유형 공략

[memo (회람)]

To: All Staff
From: Rodney Kolar
Subject: New feature
Date: 21 February

As many of you have speculated, we are going to add a new feature to the weekend edition of our paper. —[1]—. Many townspeople have suddenly gained interest in the art form because of the introduction of the new photography museum downtown. —[2]—. A committee will be formed to choose the pictures, and Lisa Gould will be in charge of editing. —[3]—. We are still brainstorming names for this section of the paper, so please submit your ideas to me. —[4]—.

1. In which of the positions marked [1], [2], [3], and [4] does the following sentence best belong?

   "Its main goal will be to highlight photography from both local artists and residents."

   (A) [1]   (B) [2]   (C) [3]   (D) [4]

[letter (편지)]

Dear Mr. Ledbetter,

Our records indicate that your commercial business lease is due for renewal soon. —[1]—. Your rent will increase by two percent for the next period. Please visit our Web site to renew your lease. —[2]—.

The details of your current lease are as follows:
Location: 4615 Poplar Lane   Size: 4,000 square feet
Lease End: November 11   Amount: $7,500 per month
Status: Pending

We have an available property with a dining area and kitchen already installed. —[3]—. Contact us via e-mail or phone if you are interested in a tour. —[4]—.

Ashley Ramirez

2. In which of the positions marked [1], [2], [3], and [4] does the following sentence best belong?

   "Since your restaurant is doing so well, you might consider upgrading your space."

   (A) [1]   (B) [2]   (C) [3]   (D) [4]

⑥ 동의어 찾기 문제

특징

지문에 나온 특정 단어와 의미상 가장 유사한 단어를 찾는 질문 유형으로서, 단어의 사전적인 의미를 묻는 것이 아니라 문맥상 의미를 묻는다. 이메일/편지, 기사 지문에서 많이 출제된다.

질문 유형

질문 뒤에 물음표가 없는 것이 특징이며, 다중 지문의 경우 앞에 해당 지문의 종류가 명시된다.

[단일 지문] The word "measure" in paragraph 1, line 4, is **closest in meaning to**
첫 번째 단락 네 번째 줄의 'measure'와 의미상 가장 가까운 것은?

[다중 지문] **In the memo**, the word "courtesy" in paragraph 2, line 3, is **closest in meaning to**
회람에서 두 번째 단락 세 번째 줄의 'courtesy'와 의미상 가장 가까운 것은?

문제 풀이 전략

먼저 질문에서 따옴표로 묶인 단어를 지문에서 찾는다. 이메일의 수신인/발신인/날짜/제목과 기사나 광고의 제목 등은 단락(paragraph)으로 간주하지 않으므로 주의한다. 해당 단어가 지문에서 구동사나 콜로케이션의 일부라면 바로 앞뒤 단어만 확인해도 답을 찾을 수 있지만, 그렇지 않다면 단어가 속한 문장이나 절을 해석한 후 선택지를 확인하거나, 그마저도 어렵다면 선택지들을 문장에 하나씩 대입하여 해석해 본다.

문제 미리보기 [e-mail (이메일)]   해석 p.62

To: Undisclosed recipients
From: mail@rightcook.com
Date: September 1
Subject: A message from Rightcook

The Rightcook team would like to thank you for helping make our Web site a success. By signing up for our mailing list and checking out our new content daily, you have played a key part in the popularity of our business. We are thrilled to announce that we have **reached** our goal of one million monthly page views. As we grow, we will continue to work hard to bring you unique recipes developed by professional chefs to help you improve your cooking skills and put something delicious on the table for dinner.

해당 단어를 찾아 표시하고, 단어의 바로 앞뒤를 확인해 본다. reached our goal은 '우리의 목표를 달성했다'라는 의미의 콜로케이션이며, reached는 '달성하다'라는 뜻으로 쓰였다. 선택지에서 가장 비슷한 의미의 어휘는 achieved이므로 (C)를 정답으로 선택한다.

만약 reached our goal의 의미를 모른다면 "we have reached ~ page views"라는 절 해석, 전체 문장 해석, 선택지 대입과 같이 해석의 범위를 점차 확대하는 방법으로 문제 풀이를 시도한다.

Q. The word "reached" in paragraph 1, line 5, is closest in meaning to

(A) contacted (B) stretched
(C) achieved   (D) touched

[article (기사)]

STOCKHOLM (2 May)—Excite Unlimited recently announced its merger with HJ Gaming. The former competitors decided that the path to global expansion would best be forged through cooperation and teamwork. "Though we are former rivals, there is no doubt that we will be able to combine our team members' skills to create an organization capable of expanding into foreign markets," said Excite Unlimited CEO Lars Anderson.

Excite Unlimited is known mostly for its console video games, while HJ Gaming made a name for itself in the PC market. Anna Lindberg, CEO of HJ Gaming, is optimistic about the merger. "We are hoping that each company will be able to make up for the other's weak spot and develop the best video games on the market," Ms. Lindberg said.

1. The word "path" in paragraph 1, line 2, is closest in meaning to
   (A) street
   (B) boulevard
   (C) way
   (D) addition

[letter (편지)]

Dear Ms. Morelock,

My name is David Hallowell, and I am the superintendent of Albany's Public Works Department. I am writing to inform you that a traffic study will be taking place in your area in the coming months.

The city council has received countless complaints from residents in your area about increased traffic, especially during the morning and evening rush hours. Considering the large youth population in our town, this has led to safety concerns. As a way to mitigate this issue, the city has decided to implement directional changes to side streets to study their effects on traffic volume. Dye Street, Cornell Avenue, and Jameson Way will be converted to one-way streets, while Golden Ridge Road will remain a two-way street.

David Hallowell

2. The word "volume" in paragraph 2, line 5, is closest in meaning to
   (A) text
   (B) version
   (C) figure
   (D) amount

CHAPTER 4

PART 7
독해

UNIT 01

이메일, 편지

지문 미리보기

빈출 질문 유형

빈출 표현

빈출 유형 공략 01 이메일: 주제/목적 문제

빈출 유형 공략 02 편지: 문장 삽입 문제

ACTUAL TEST

UNIT 01

이메일, 편지

출제 경향
- Part 7에서 가장 많이 출제되는 지문 유형으로, 단일 지문은 회당 평균 2~3개가 출제되며, 다중 지문 중 하나의 지문으로 출제되는 빈도도 매우 높다. 이메일과 편지는 기본적으로 같은 형식의 지문이지만, 이메일이 편지보다 3배 이상 높은 빈도로 출제된다.
- 이메일에서는 주제/목적을 묻는 문제가 50%의 비율로 가장 많이 출제되는 반면, 편지는 문장 삽입 문제가 가장 많이 출제되므로 글의 흐름을 잘 파악하는 것이 중요하다.

지문 미리보기

To: Jennifer Park 〈j_park@nmail.com〉 **수신인 정보**
From: Customer Service 〈cs@fabfashion.com〉 **발신인 정보**
Date: 12 March **날짜**
Subject: RE: My order **제목**

Dear Ms. Park, **수신인**

❶ We would like to formally apologize for shipping you the wrong item for your order PX0067. As you mentioned in your previous e-mail, you ordered the shirt in beige, but we mistakenly sent you the item in black. We would like to apologize for our error.

❷ To show our sincerity, we would like to send the correct item via express shipping at no additional cost to you. Further, if you use the code "THXPX006" on your next order, you will receive a 10% discount on your purchase.

❸ Feel free to reply to this e-mail if you have any other questions or concerns. We hope you will return to us for all of your fabulous fashion needs.

FabFashion Customer Service Team **발신인 정보**

수신인, 발신인, 날짜, 제목
수신인과 발신인, 제목을 확인하고 이메일 주소도 확인한다. @ 오른쪽의 메일 주소가 같으면 동료간의 업무 관련 이메일이고, 주소가 다르면 고객과 기업/상점 간의 이메일일 가능성이 크다. RE:는 첫 번째 이메일에 대한 '회신'이라는 뜻이고, 제목 밑에 Attachment가 있다면 이메일에 첨부파일이 있다는 의미이다.

본문의 흐름
이메일/편지의 본문은 다음과 같이 글의 흐름이 이어지는 편이다.
❶ 인사말과 글의 목적
❷ 문제점에 대한 해결책 제시
❸ 요청 사항 및 맺음말

발신인 정보
발신인의 이름, 직위, 부서명, 회사명 등의 정보는 NOT/True나 세부 사항 문제의 단서가 될 수 있으므로 놓치지 말아야 한다.

|미리보기 해석|

수신: Jennifer Park 〈j_park@nmail.com〉
발신: 고객 서비스 〈cs@fabfashion.com〉
날짜: 3월 12일
제목: 회신: 저의 주문

Park 씨,
귀하의 주문인 PX0067에 잘못된 물품을 발송한 점에 대해 정식으로 사과드리고 싶습니다. 귀하가 전에 보내신 이메일에서 언급하셨던 것처럼, 귀하는 베이지색의 셔츠를 주문하셨는데, 저희가 실수로 검정색 물품을 보내드렸습니다. 저희 실수에 대해 사과를 드립니다.
저희의 진정성을 보여드리기 위해 추가 비용 없이 빠른 배송으로 올바른 물품을 보내드리고자 합니다. 또한 다음 주문 시 "THXPX006" 코드를 사용하시면 구매 시에 10% 할인을 받게 되실 겁니다.
다른 질문이나 우려 사항이 있으시면 언제든지 이 이메일에 회신해 주십시오. 최상의 패션에 대한 고객님의 니즈에 맞춰 저희를 다시 찾아주시기를 바랍니다.
FabFashion 고객 서비스 팀

빈출 질문 유형

주제/목적 질문 유형
What is the **purpose** of the **e-mail**? 이메일의 목적은 무엇인가?
Why was the **e-mail sent**? 왜 이메일이 발송되었는가?
Why did Mr. Lei **send** the **e-mail**? Lei 씨가 이메일을 보낸 이유는 무엇인가?

추론/암시 질문 유형
Who mostly likely is Ms. Adler? Adler 씨는 누구이겠는가?
What is **suggested about** Ms. Cassidy's apartment? Cassidy 씨의 아파트에 대해 무엇이 암시되었는가?
What is **implied about** Ms. Hamada? Hamada 씨에 대해 암시된 것은 무엇인가?
What most likely is the Crestview? Crestview는 무엇이겠는가?

NOT/True 질문 유형
What is **indicated about** Cardorama? Cardorama에 대해 나타난 것은 무엇인가?
What is **true about** Ms. White? White 씨에 대해 사실인 것은 무엇인가?
What is **NOT mentioned as** a service that EDW provides to its members?
EDW가 회원들에게 제공하는 서비스로 언급되지 않은 것은 무엇인가?

빈출 표현

이메일/편지를 보내는 목적을 알릴 때 쓰이는 표현
이메일이나 편지를 보내는 목적을 알리기 위해 자주 쓰이는 표현에는 I am writing to ~ (~하기 위해 글을 씁니다), This is to ~ (이것은 ~을 하기 위함입니다), This e-mail[letter] is to ~ (이 이메일[편지]은 ~하기 위함입니다) 등이 있다.

I am writing to let you know that the shipment will be late.
배송이 늦어질 것임을 알려 드리기 위해 글을 씁니다.
This is a reminder to submit your time sheets by Monday.
월요일까지 근무 시간표를 제출하셔야 한다는 것을 상기시켜 드립니다.
This e-mail is to confirm your stay with us at the Ipanema Hotel.
이 이메일은 귀하의 Ipanema 호텔 투숙을 확정하기 위함입니다.

제안할 때 쓰이는 표현
업체에서 고객에게 어떤 것을 제안할 때는 I would like to ~ (~하고 싶습니다), We are happy[delighted, pleased] to ~ (우리는 ~하게 되어 기쁩니다) 등의 표현을 자주 사용한다.

I would like to inform you of an exciting opportunity.
당신에게 흥미로운 기회에 대해 알려드리고 싶습니다.
We are delighted to be delivering your recent order to you.
귀하께서 최근에 주문하신 상품을 배송하게 되어 기쁘게 생각합니다.

빈출 유형 공략 01 이메일: 주제/목적 문제

해석 p.63

Question 1 refers to the following e-mail.

1. What is the purpose of the e-mail?

To: Erin Baldwin 〈e_baldwin@nmail.net〉
From: Kevin Villanueva 〈kevin.villanueva@gracetownhotel.com〉
Date: January 17
Subject: Room change

Dear Ms. Baldwin,

Thank you for choosing Gracetown Hotel for your stay here in Las Vegas. We successfully received your payment but regret to inform you that there was a mistake with hoteling.com, the Web site you used to make your reservation. It seems they promised you a room that has already been booked for the weekend of February 12 to 14.

In light of this situation, we would like to offer you an alternative room. Though you booked a standard suite with a queen-size bed, we have a deluxe suite with a king-size bed available for those same dates. Since you were not responsible for the booking error, we would be happy to offer you this room at no additional charge.

We appreciate your cooperation and look forward to meeting you soon!

Best,

Kevin Villanueva
Customer Service, Gracetown Hotel

(A) To inform people about a new hotel
(B) To apologize for a cancelled order
(C) ✓ To offer a room upgrade
(D) To suggest online sites to book hotels

STEP 1 질문 확인
이메일/편지의 주제 또는 목적은 보통 문두에 나오지만, 인사말이나 상황 설명이 끝난 후에 나오기도 하고, 목적이 둘 이상일 때 one purpose (목적 중 하나)를 묻는 문제는 뒷부분에 단서가 나오기도 한다는 것에 주의한다.

수신인, 발신인, 날짜, 제목
Gracetown이라는 호텔에 근무하는 Kevin Villanueva가 Erin Baldwin 에게 객실 교체와 관련하여 이메일을 보냈다는 정보를 얻을 수 있다.

STEP 2 지문에서 단서 찾기
첫 번째 단락에서는 문제점을 설명하고 있는데, 선택지 중에 첫 번째 단락 내용에 해당하는 것이 없으므로 두 번째 단락까지 읽는다.
두 번째 단락에서는 추가 비용 없이 standard suite를 deluxe suite로 바꿔 주겠다고 제안했다. 추가 비용이 없다는 것은 객실 등급이 상향 조정되었다는 것을 의미한다.

STEP 3 선택지 확인
객실 등급 상향 조정은 upgrade를 써서 표현하는 경우가 많다. 객실 상향 조정을 제안하는 (C)를 정답으로 선택한다.

빈출 유형 공략 02 편지: 문장 삽입 문제

Question 2 refers to the following letter.

2. In which of the positions marked [1], [2], [3], and [4] does the following sentence best belong?
"We can refine this figure after visiting the property."

> Meadow Realty
> 131 Sandoval Street
> Bloomington, IL 61704
>
> July 10
>
> Judy Calvin
> 2475 Ritter Avenue
> Bloomington, IL 61791

Dear Ms. Calvin,

Thank you for contacting the Meadow Realty office on July 9. We would be happy to assist you with the sale of your home. Our agency has been in business for over a decade, and we will work hard to get you the highest offer. —[1]—.

Our standard package includes having a professional photographer take pictures of your home for brochures and our Web site, drawing up a detailed floor plan, and arranging and conducting viewings with potential buyers. —[2]—. We will also manage the negotiations between you and the buyer. —[3]—.

I have done some research on properties in your area. Please find enclosed a rough calculation of how much your home would likely sell for. —[4]—.

Sincerely,

Clara Pardue
Senior Agent, Meadow Realty

(A) [1]
(B) [2]
(C) [3]
(D) [4] ✓

STEP 1 질문 확인
문장 삽입 문제의 경우 주어진 문장에 대명사나 지시형용사가 포함된 경우가 많으며, 그것이 문제 풀이의 단서가 된다. 이 문장에서는 this figure (이 수치)가 그에 해당한다.
"저희가 부동산을 방문한 후에 이 수치를 조정할 수 있습니다."

발신인 정보, 날짜, 수신인 정보
편지는 발신인 이름과 주소, 날짜, 수신인 이름과 주소의 순으로 발신인/수신인 정보가 제시되는 편이며, 이메일과 달리 제목이 명시되지 않는 경우가 대부분이다. 발신인 정보 없이 수신인의 이름과 주소만 제시되기도 한다. 이 지문에서 발신인은 Meadow Realty, 수신인은 Judy Calvin이다. 발신인/수신인 정보는 문장 삽입 문제와는 큰 관련이 없지만, 질문의 종류와 관계없이 이메일, 편지 지문에서는 가장 먼저 발신인/수신인/제목 정보를 확인하는 것이 좋다.

STEP 2 지문에서 단서 찾기
[4]의 앞 문장의 a rough calculation (대략적인 계산)이 this figure를 의미한다는 것을 확인한다.

STEP 3 선택지 확인
(D)를 정답으로 고른다.

ACTUAL TEST

Questions 1-2 refer to the following e-mail.

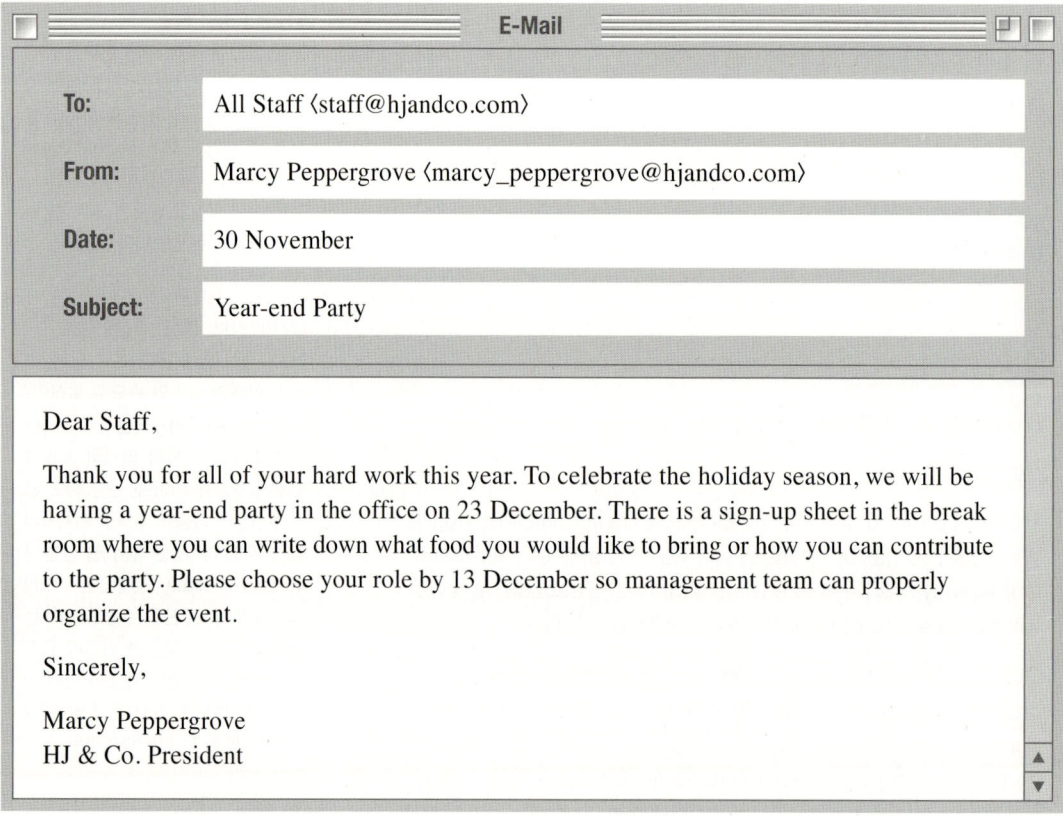

1. What is the purpose of the e-mail?

   (A) To tell employees about an event
   (B) To ask for donations for a charity
   (C) To report an incident at the office
   (D) To announce an extra vacation day

2. What is indicated about the year-end party?

   (A) It will be catered.
   (B) It will be coordinated by staff members.
   (C) It will take place at a hotel.
   (D) It will include employees and their families.

Questions 3-5 refer to the following letter.

Ms. Mariette Lampron
3132 Victoria Park Ave
Toronto, ON M2J 3T7

17 March

Dear Ms. Lampron,

Thank you for becoming a member of the Victoria City Bookstore. —[1]—. Your membership helps support small businesses and ensures that physical books remain in print. —[2]—. Though our storefront is modest, we offer a wide array of titles and express shipping for most books not currently on our shelves.

In addition to being a traditional bookseller, Victoria City Bookstore offers special programmes throughout the year. —[3]—. On Saturday mornings, we have reading events for children up to six years old. On Saturday evenings, we have open mic performances from 7:00 P.M. to 8:30 P.M. For more information on these programmes, visit our Web site at www.victoriacitybooks.ca and sign up to get text message alerts on your phone.

Finally, we are always looking for new staff, volunteers, and performers. If you are interested in any of these positions, we would love to get in contact with you! —[4]—.

Thank you again for your patronage.

Sincerely,

Charlie Beatham
Charlie Beatham
Owner of Victoria City Bookstore

3. What is the purpose of the letter?
   (A) To thank someone for joining a group
   (B) To promote a new store opening
   (C) To advertise a special promotion
   (D) To congratulate a new hire

4. How can patrons get updates about the bookstore's programmes?
   (A) By calling the store's number
   (B) By checking the local newspaper
   (C) By signing up for a text service
   (D) By visiting the store weekly

5. In which of the positions marked [1], [2], [3], and [4] does the following sentence best belong?
   "Please contact us at 555-0113 for further details."
   (A) [1]
   (B) [2]
   (C) [3]
   (D) [4]

Questions 6-9 refer to the following e-mail.

TO:	Lupita Medina
FROM:	Fernando Sibiya
DATE:	July 27
SUBJECT:	RE: Jackson Jewelry Fair

Dear Ms. Medina,

Thank you for expressing interest in selling your homemade earrings at the annual Jackson Jewelry Fair. There is a $30 application fee that everyone must submit by bank transfer. We also ask you to submit at least five photos of the items you wish to sell at the fair. —[1]—.

Additionally, we would like you to submit a sketch of how you want your work displayed. Each vendor will be given a stand, and we use these sketches to properly allocate which stand goes to which vendor. —[2]—.

Because September is the rainy season in Jackson, we must prepare for the possibility of inclement weather. The fair will be held even if conditions aren't favorable, so please make sure you have the appropriate equipment to handle the weather. —[3]—.

Lastly, the fair is becoming more and more popular as the years go by, so unfortunately, we cannot accept everyone who submits an application. There is particularly stiff competition with the items you plan to sell. We hope that you will be selected to be a vendor this year, but we encourage you to apply again next year with new designs if you are not. —[4]—.

Fernando Sibiya

6. What does Ms. Medina sell?

    (A) Necklaces
    (B) Bracelets
    (C) Earrings
    (D) Watches

7. What is NOT a requirement for selling at the jewelry fair?

    (A) Submitting several photos of one's goods
    (B) Sending samples of one's products to the judges
    (C) Drawing a sketch of one's potential stand
    (D) Transferring money from one's bank account

8. What is suggested about the jewelry fair?

    (A) This is the first time it is being held.
    (B) All applicants get a spot at the fair.
    (C) It may be held in the rain.
    (D) It is free to apply to be a vendor.

9. In which of the positions marked [1], [2], [3], and [4] does the following sentence best belong?

    "Do not worry about the quality of your drawing, because it is only used for planning purposes."

    (A) [1]
    (B) [2]
    (C) [3]
    (D) [4]

ACTUAL TEST

Questions 10-13 refer to the following e-mail.

E-Mail

TO:	customerservice@artemporium.com
FROM:	leena_agarwal@expressmail.com
DATE:	June 18
SUBJECT:	Art Competition Entry
ATTACHMENT:	Leena Agarwal Painting Entry

To Whom It May Concern:

As a frequent shopper at the Art Emporium, I was delighted to find out my favorite store is holding an art competition. I had already been working on a large modernist painting for a few months, so I thought this competition would be the perfect place to show my work.

Unfortunately, when I tried to upload a photo of my painting to your Web site, I kept getting an error message. I do not want to miss out on the chance to give my work some much-needed exposure and potentially win $2,000. The deadline for the competition is only three days away, and I really want to make sure my submission is considered. I have attached a photo of it to this e-mail. Could you help me ensure my painting is properly entered in the contest? If there is anything else I need to do, please let me know at your earliest convenience.

Thank you in advance!

Sincerely,

Leena Agarwal

---

10. The word "work" in paragraph 1, line 3, is closest in meaning to

(A) assignment
(B) responsibility
(C) painting
(D) performance

11. What problem does Ms. Agarwal mention?

(A) Her painting will not be finished in time.
(B) She does not think she will get enough votes.
(C) Her photo cannot be uploaded to the Web site.
(D) The Web site does not accept her credit card.

12. What is indicated about the competition?

(A) The winner receive a cash prize.
(B) Photography work is not accepted.
(C) There is a fee to submit artwork.
(D) Only professionals are allowed to enter.

13. What does Ms. Agarwal request from customer service?

(A) A complete list of competition rules
(B) Help with entering a contest
(C) Advice on her painting
(D) Assistance with the company Web site

CHAPTER 4
—
PART 7
독해

UNIT 02

문자 메시지, 온라인 채팅

지문 미리보기

빈출 질문 유형

빈출 구어체 표현

빈출 유형 공략 01 문자 메시지: 의도 파악 문제

빈출 유형 공략 02 온라인 채팅: 추론/암시 문제

ACTUAL TEST

UNIT 02

문자 메시지, 온라인 채팅

출제 경향
- 문자 메시지와 온라인 채팅 지문이 회당 1개씩 출제되며, 길이가 짧은 지문은 2문항, 길이가 긴 지문은 4문항으로 구성된다. 짧은 지문에는 2명의 화자가 등장하지만, 긴 지문에는 3명 이상의 화자가 등장하기 때문에 화자들의 관계를 정확히 파악해야 한다.
- 지문마다 의도 파악 문제가 1문제 나오고, 추론/암시 문제의 출제 비중도 70%를 넘는다. 한 지문에 여러 개의 추론/암시 문제가 나오는 경우도 많다. 그리고 나머지는 대부분 NOT/True와 세부 사항 문제로 구성된다.
- 지문의 특성상 구어체 표현이 종종 나오므로, 자주 나오는 구어체 표현을 익혀 두어야 한다.

지문 미리보기

Donna Koski (2:21 P.M.)
Grant, are you busy right now?

Grant Bowser (2:22 P.M.)
Not really. Why?

Donna Koski (2:23 P.M.)
Would you mind bringing some stamps from the storage closet to the first floor? Janice at the reception desk said they ran out.

Grant Bowser (2:24 P.M.)
No problem.

Donna Koski (2:25 P.M.)
Thanks! She's working alone, so she can't leave.

Grant Bowser (2:31 P.M.)
I found them, but everything's really disorganized in here. It seems people keep forgetting to put things back on the right shelves.

Donna Koski (2:33 P.M.)
Again? I'll post a notice about that.

질문, 문제 제기, 도움 요청
직원들이 업무상 문제점을 공유하고 해결책을 도출하는 내용이 대부분이다. 이 지문에서처럼 지금 시간이 있는지 묻거나 짧은 인사를 한 후 본론으로 들어가는 경우가 많다.

질문, 요청에 대한 답변
질문이나 요청을 받은 사람은 특정한 답변을 하거나, 요청을 수락하거나 거절한다. 요청에 대한 답변으로는 짧은 구어체 표현이 많이 쓰인다.

의도 파악 문제의 단서
의도 파악 문제의 단서는 주로 바로 앞의 문장에서 나온다. 예를 들어 지문의 맨 끝의 "I'll post a notice about that."이라는 문장의 의도를 파악하려면 바로 앞에 있는 2:31 P.M. 문장을 검색해야 한다.

| 미리보기 해석 |

Donna Koski (2:21 P.M.)
Grant, 지금 바빠요?
Grant Bowser (2:22 P.M.)
괜찮아요. 무슨 일이죠?
Donna Koski (2:23 P.M.)
비품 수납장에서 우표를 좀 꺼내서 1층으로 가져다 줄 수 있어요? 접수처에 있는 Janice가 우표가 다 떨어졌다고 하네요.
Grant Bowser (2:24 P.M.)
물론이죠.
Donna Koski (2:25 P.M.)
고마워요! 그녀는 혼자 일하고 있어서 자리를 비울 수 없거든요.
Grant Bowser (2:31 P.M.)
찾았어요. 그런데 여긴 모든 게 정말 정리가 안 되어 있네요. 사람들이 물건을 선반의 제자리에 갖다 놓는 것을 자꾸 잊어버리는 것 같아요.
Donna Koski (2:33 P.M.)
또요? 제가 그 점에 대해 공지할게요.

빈출 질문 유형

의도 파악 질문 유형

At 10:33 A.M., **what** does Mr. Perez **imply** when he writes, "That would make sense"?
오전 10시 33분에 Perez 씨가 "그건 말이 될 거예요"라고 쓸 때 그는 무엇을 암시하는가?

At 12:13 P.M., **what** does Ms. Wu **most likely mean** when she writes, "Now I feel better"?
오후 12시 13분에 Wu 씨가 "이제 기분이 좋아졌어요"라고 쓸 때 그녀가 의미하는 것은 무엇이겠는가?

At 10:04 A.M., **why** does Mr. Hunter **write**, "We'll get to it soon"?
오전 10시 4분에, Hunter 씨는 왜 "우리는 그곳에 곧 도착합니다"라고 쓰는가?

At 10:58 A.M., **what** does Ms. Meyer **indicate** she will do when she writes, "Let me check"?
오전 10시 58분에, Meyer 씨가 "제가 확인해 볼게요"라고 쓸 때 그녀는 무엇을 할 것임을 나타내는가?

추론/암시 질문 유형

What will Ms. Park most likely **do next**? Park 씨는 다음에 무엇을 하겠는가?	가장 많이 출제되는 유형으로서, 지문의 마지막 2~3행에 단서가 나오는 경우가 많다.
What is **suggested about** Mr. Jiang? Jiang 씨에 대해 암시된 것은 무엇인가?	지문에 나오는 사람의 직업, 한 일, 해야 할 일 등을 묻는 문제 유형으로서 지문의 전반적인 내용을 파악해야 한다.
Who most likely are the writers? 화자들은 누구이겠는가? In **what field/industry/department** do the writers most likely **work**? 화자들은 어느 분야/업계/부서에서 근무하겠는가?	직업, 부서, 업종을 묻는 문제 유형으로서, 지문에 나오는 특정 어휘나 지문에서 드러나는 화자들의 업무 내용을 파악하여 풀 수 있다.

빈출 구어체 표현

- Got it. 알았어요.
- Absolutely. 물론이죠.
- Definitely. 물론이죠.
- Exactly. 맞아요.
- I wish I could. (제가) 그럴 수 있으면 좋겠어요.
- I'm all for it. 전적으로 찬성해요.
- Possibly. 그럴 가능성이 있어요.
- Will do. 그렇게 할게요.
- Understood. 알았어요.
- Good to know. (정보를) 알려 줘서 고마워요.
- Indeed. 맞아요. / 정말 그래요.
- It happens. 그럴 수 있죠. / 세상사가 그런 거죠.
- No worries (at all). 괜찮아요. / 걱정 마세요.
- Sure thing. 〈〈제안에 대해〉〉 물론이죠.

- Sounds good. 그거 좋은데요.
- Correct. 맞아요.
- Let me check. 확인해 볼게요.
- I can't tell. 잘 모르겠어요. / 판단하기 어려워요.
- I'm all set. 저는 준비가 다 됐어요.
- I'll take care of it. 제가 처리할게요.
- Super! 아주 좋네요!
- Not at all. 괜찮아요. / 천만에요.
- Done. (당신이 말한 대로) 했어요.
- Hold on. 잠시만 기다리세요.
- My pleasure! 〈〈고맙다는 말에 대해〉〉 천만에요!
- No need. 〈〈제안에 대해〉〉 그럴 필요 없어요.
- One minute. 잠시만요.
- Fine by me. (그 제안이) 저는 좋아요.

빈출 유형 공략 01 문자 메시지: 의도 파악 문제

해석 p.67

Question 1 refers to the following text-message chain.

1. At 1:56 P.M., what does Ms. Copeland suggest when she writes, "Definitely"?

Noriya Yamauchi (1:52 P.M.)
Hi, Marie. I'm wondering how far along you are on the catalog design.

Marie Copeland (1:54 P.M.)
I finished it yesterday morning.

Noriya Yamauchi (1:55 P.M.)
Already? That was a lot faster than I expected. I guess our new procedure of having the interns work on the photos first helped a lot.

Marie Copeland (1:56 P.M.)
Definitely. I hope we can keep doing it that way.

Noriya Yamauchi (1:57 P.M.)
I don't see why not.

(A) She kept a copy of a catalog.
(B) She found a process helpful. ✓
(C) She wants to work as an intern.
(D) She was impressed with Mr. Yamauchi's work.

STEP 1 질문 확인
'At 시간'으로 시작하는 의도 파악 문제는 대개 주어진 문장의 바로 앞의 내용에 단서가 있다.

STEP 2 앞뒤 문맥 파악
질문에서 제시된 시간을 찾아가서 주어진 문장과 바로 앞뒤 문장을 연결하여 해석한다.

인턴 사원들에게 먼저 사진 작업을 시키는 우리의 새 절차가 도움이 많이 됐나 봐요.
물론이죠. 앞으로도 계속 그렇게 했으면 좋겠어요.

따라서 Marie Copeland는 새 절차가 도움이 많이 된다고 생각한다는 것을 알 수 있다.

STEP 3 선택지 확인
어떤 절차가 도움이 된다는 것을 알았다는 (B)를 정답으로 고른다.

빈출 유형 공략 02   온라인 채팅: 추론/암시 문제

해석 p.68

Question 2 refers to the following online chat discussion.

2. What kind of industry do the speakers most likely work in?

Adam Taylor (3:23 P.M.)
Hello. We need to get everything ready for the upcoming magazine release. How is everyone doing?

Eleanor Chamberlain (3:25 P.M.)
I've already completed the article on the new museum exhibit. Now I just need to write captions for the pictures.

Judy Brooks (3:26 P.M.)
I'm still undecided about the design for the cover. I wanted to get some advice.

Adam Taylor (3:27 P.M.)
Oh, I'm no good with that sort of thing. You should ask Eleanor for her opinion.

Eleanor Chamberlain (3:29 P.M.)
Judy, can you e-mail me the magazine cover?

Judy Brooks (3:30 P.M.)
Actually, can you just come to my desk right now? It's easier if we talk in person.

Eleanor Chamberlain (3:31 P.M.)
Not a problem. I can do that.

(A) Museum
(B) Real estate
(C) Publishing ✓
(D) Printing

STEP 1 질문 확인
화자들의 근무하는 업종을 묻는 추론/암시 문제. 지문에 나오는 단어가 선택지에 그대로 나오거나 그와 유사한 단어가 나올 경우 함정일 가능성이 높으므로 주의해야 한다.

STEP 2 지문에서 단서 찾기
단서 ①: 잡지 출간을 준비해야 한다
단서 ②: 박물관 전시회에 관한 기사를 완성했다
단서 ③: 표지 디자인을 아직 정하지 못했다

하나의 단서를 찾으면 그때그때 선택지를 확인하는 것이 좋다. 이 문제는 단서 ①을 통해 정답 후보를 (C)와 (D)로 압축한 후, 나머지 단서를 통해 정답을 골라야 한다. (A)는 지문에 나오는 단어를 이용한 함정이다.

STEP 3 선택지 확인
Publishing(출판업)이 적절한 선택지이므로 (C)를 정답으로 선택한다.

ACTUAL TEST

Questions 1-2 refer to the following text-message chain.

Clayton Balcom (10:37 A.M.)	Thanks for contacting Platinum Tech. How may I help you?
Esther Ross (10:38 A.M.)	Hello. I'm trying to connect my Ayala-7 wireless headphones to my laptop. I've turned on the Bluetooth on my laptop, but it can't find the signal from the headphones.
Clayton Balcom (10:39 A.M.)	Okay. Have you tried deleting the old wireless connections that appear in the Bluetooth list? Turning the headphones off and on again also works sometimes.
Esther Ross (10:40 A.M.)	I've done both of those things.
Clayton Balcom (10:41 A.M.)	They might need to be charged. But first, try turning off the Bluetooth and then turning it on again. Then click on the "Add Bluetooth or other device" button and see if the code from the side of your headphones appears in the Bluetooth list.
Esther Ross (10:42 A.M.)	There it is!
Clayton Balcom (10:43 A.M.)	Great! Now just click on that code and they should connect.
Esther Ross (10:44 A.M.)	They're working now. Thanks a lot!
Clayton Balcom (10:45 A.M.)	My pleasure.

1. What solution has Ms. Ross NOT tried?

   (A) Restarting the headphones
   (B) Requesting a new code
   (C) Turning on the Bluetooth
   (D) Deleting old connections

2. At 10:42 A.M., what does Ms. Ross probably mean when she writes, "There it is!"?

   (A) She clicked on a Web site link.
   (B) She has a user manual.
   (C) She sees a code.
   (D) She found a confirmation e-mail.

Questions 3-6 refer to the following online chat discussion.

Heidi Faulk (10:05 A.M.)
Just a reminder that we're meeting at 2 this afternoon to get ready for moving our office to the Derby Building.

Angela Phelps (10:06 A.M.)
Heidi, do you have time afterward to sort the old customer inquiry reports? We have to decide which should be kept and which should be shredded.

Heidi Faulk (10:07 A.M.)
Yes, today would work well for me.

Jerry Mullen (10:09 A.M.)
Beverly Conrad from the Abilene Branch has been through this process recently and will surely have some insights. She offered to join us remotely. Could you please set up a video conference?

Heidi Faulk (10:10 A.M.)
I'm on it.

Bernard Ledesma (10:11 A.M.)
I'll bring the quotes I've gathered from three different moving companies.

Angela Phelps (10:12 A.M.)
You've saved us a lot of time, Bernard.

Jerry Mullen (10:13 A.M.)
And don't forget that I have to leave after about forty-five minutes. I'm running the workshop for new salespeople at 3.

Heidi Faulk (10:14 A.M.)
That's fine, Jerry. I'll let you know what you missed later.

---

3. Why will Ms. Faulk hold a meeting today?
   (A) To sort some documents
   (B) To prepare for an office relocation
   (C) To sign a building lease
   (D) To tour the Derby Building

4. At 10:10 A.M., what does Ms. Faulk probably mean when she writes, "I'm on it"?
   (A) She will shred some documents.
   (B) She is in a meeting.
   (C) She is on the phone with Ms. Conrad.
   (D) She will arrange a video conference.

5. What does Mr. Ledesma plan to bring to the meeting?
   (A) A shopping list
   (B) Cost estimates
   (C) Work schedules
   (D) Inquiry reports

6. Why is Mr. Mullen unable to attend the entire meeting?
   (A) He needs to move his car.
   (B) He will give a presentation to a client.
   (C) He needs to lead a training session.
   (D) He has to prepare for a business trip.

Questions 7-10 refer to the following online chat discussion.

Justin Dube (10:35 A.M.)	Hi, Alphonso and Natalie. I just wanted to check in.
Alphonso Mantz (10:37 A.M.)	I'm taking measurements at various properties today. I'm at 901 Ella Street now and will be here until about 11:30.
Justin Dube (10:38 A.M.)	Okay. I've just heard from Joshua Caudill. We put up a wooden fence for him last month, but some of the boards are already coming loose. He is taking a flight to Dallas tomorrow, so he would like it fixed today so it doesn't get worse while he's gone.
Natalie Garrido (10:40 A.M.)	That means you'll arrive here at the George Avenue site late, right? How far away is Mr. Caudill's property?
Justin Dube (10:41 A.M.)	It's at 849 Mobile Street, so I'll head over to you as soon as I'm done. I don't think the job will take long. I can get there by 11:30 and have it done within about an hour.
Natalie Garrido (10:42 A.M.)	That's fine. We're ahead of schedule here anyway.
Justin Dube (10:44 A.M.)	Great. Do you need anything from the warehouse? I'm going to stop by the warehouse to pick up a few supplies.
Alphonso Mantz (10:45 A.M.)	I don't need anything. But today is Sunday.
Justin Dube (10:46 A.M.)	Don't worry. I've got keys.

7. What does the writers' company most likely specialize in?

(A) Real estate sales
(B) Vehicle repairs
(C) Fence installation
(D) Exterior painting

8. What does Mr. Caudill plan to do tomorrow?

(A) Sign a contract with Mr. Dube
(B) Have some measurements taken
(C) Take a trip out of town
(D) Entertain some visitors

9. When does Mr. Dube expect to complete a job at 849 Mobile Street?

(A) Around 11:00 A.M.
(B) Around 11:30 A.M.
(C) Around 12:30 P.M.
(D) Around 1:00 P.M.

10. At 10:45 A.M., what does Mr. Mantz most likely mean when he writes, "But today is Sunday"?

(A) He hopes to leave work early.
(B) The traffic to a worksite will not be heavy.
(C) Mr. Dube is eligible for an additional payment.
(D) Mr. Dube may have trouble accessing the warehouse.

Questions 11-14 refer to the following online chat discussion.

Renee Armstrong [2:01 P.M.]	Good afternoon. I'm wondering if you both had a chance to browse the online home furnishings catalog that I sent a link to. We need to decide whether to use curtains or blinds in the conference room, and which ones to get.
John Lugo [2:02 P.M.]	I like the vertical blinds with the wide slats. They look modern and would be easy to open and close.
Renee Armstrong [2:04 P.M.]	I thought those were nice, too. However, they seem rather thin, don't they?
Melvin Ochoa [2:07 P.M.]	I've been busy all morning. I can take a look now.
John Lugo [2:08 P.M.]	That's a good point, Renee. The conference room is always cold. It might be helpful to have thick curtains to help insulate the room a bit more.
Melvin Ochoa [2:09 P.M.]	Have you thought about colors? We could use green to complement our logo.
Renee Armstrong [2:10 P.M.]	I'm not sure which color would be best.
Melvin Ochoa [2:12 P.M.]	Maybe we could get some fabric samples from the supplier.
Renee Armstrong [2:13 P.M.]	Good idea.
Melvin Ochoa [2:14 P.M.]	I don't have the supplier's contact information.
Renee Armstrong [2:15 P.M.]	I can take care of that today. We just have to decide what colors we're interested in.

11. What is the discussion mainly about?
    (A) Options for window coverings
    (B) Layouts of a conference room
    (C) A budget for a renovation project
    (D) Topics for an upcoming meeting

12. At 2:07 P.M., what does Mr. Ochoa most likely mean when he writes, "I can take a look now"?
    (A) He will evaluate an employee.
    (B) He will review a contract.
    (C) He will visit a Web site.
    (D) He will tour a room.

13. What is most likely true about the conference room?
    (A) It is not at a comfortable temperature.
    (B) It has an outdated style.
    (C) It is too small for the business's needs.
    (D) It contains presentation equipment.

14. What will Ms. Armstrong do today?
    (A) Take some measurements
    (B) Contact a business representative
    (C) Return some fabric samples
    (D) Place an order online

CHAPTER 4

PART 7
독해

UNIT 03

기사, 안내문

지문 미리보기

빈출 질문 유형

빈출 표현

빈출 유형 공략 01 기사: 주제/목적 문제

빈출 유형 공략 02 안내문: 세부 사항 문제

ACTUAL TEST

UNIT 03

기사, 안내문

출제 경향
- 기사는 회당 1~2개의 지문이 출제되는 편이지만, 간혹 3개의 지문이 출제되기도 한다. 다중 지문에서는 이메일과 함께 출제되는 빈도가 높다.
- 주제/목적, 문장 삽입, 추론/암시, NOT/True, 동의어 찾기 문제가 비슷한 비중으로 출제된다.
- 안내문은 기사에 비해 출제 빈도가 낮으며, 기사, 광고, 공지 등의 다양한 성격을 띤다.

지문 미리보기

❶ BIRMINGHAM (13 February) — The Birmingham Botanical Gardens (BBG) has announced that its assistant director, Lawrence Osborn, will take over as director of the site from March 2.

❷ Mr. Osborn studied botany at Sutton University in Leicester. He worked at a flower shop in Wolverhampton after graduating but wanted to devote more time to growing plants. He went on to operate his own nursery in Coventry and cultivated many of the plants himself. He took further studies in business management at the Nature Institute in Kettering before accepting a job at the BBG six years ago.

❸ "I'm thrilled to continue my journey with the BBG," Osborn said. "I am dedicated to making the BBG a site for enjoying the beauty of nature and for teaching people about environmental issues. I hope to add more kid and youth activity classes to promote a love for nature and the environment at an early age."

기사의 주제/목적
대부분의 기사는 글의 앞부분에 주제가 드러나는 두괄식 구성을 취한다. 제목이 있다면 제목에서도 주제/목적을 추론할 수 있다.

인물 기사의 글의 흐름
인물 관련 기사는 다음과 같은 순서로 글의 흐름이 이어지는 편이다.
❶ 승진이나 임명 사실 발표
❷ 학력과 경력, 성공 배경
❸ 소감 및 앞으로의 포부

인용문
따옴표로 묶인 관련자의 인용문에서 NOT/True, 세부 사항 문제의 단서가 나올 가능성이 높다.

| 미리보기 해석 |

버밍엄 (2월 13일) — 버밍엄 식물원(BBG)은 부원장인 Lawrence Osborn 씨가 3월 2일부터 식물원의 원장으로 취임한다고 발표했다.

Osborn 씨는 레스터에 있는 서튼 대학에서 식물학을 공부했다. 그는 졸업 후 울버햄튼에 있는 화원에서 일했지만, 식물 재배에 더 많은 시간을 쏟기를 원했다. 그는 계속해서 코번트리에서 자신의 묘목장을 운영했고 많은 식물들을 직접 재배했다. 그는 6년 전 BBG의 입사 제의를 수락하기 전까지 케터링에 있는 자연 연구소에서 경영학을 추가로 공부했다.

"BBG와 함께 저의 여정을 계속할 수 있어 무척 기쁩니다."라고 Osborn 씨는 말했다. "저는 BBG를 자연의 아름다움을 만끽하고 사람들에게 환경 문제에 대해 교육하는 장으로 만드는 일에 전념하고 있습니다. 저는 어릴 적부터 자연과 환경에 대한 사랑을 고취시킬 수 있도록 더 많은 어린이, 그리고 청소년 활동 교실을 추가하고 싶습니다."

빈출 질문 유형

주제/목적 질문 유형
What is the **purpose** of the **article**? 기사의 목적은 무엇인가?
What is the **article** mainly **about**? 기사는 주로 무엇에 관한 것인가?
What is the **topic/subject** of the **article**? 기사의 주제는 무엇인가?

추론/암시 질문 유형
What is **suggested about** the shipyard? 조선소에 대해 암시된 것은 무엇인가?
What **most likely** will happen in August? 8월에는 무슨 일이 일어나겠는가?

세부 사항 질문 유형
How can a free lesson be obtained? 무료 레슨은 어떻게 받을 수 있는가?
What should vehicle owners do first? 차량 소유자들은 먼저 무엇을 해야 하는가?
Why should readers contact Ms. Cardona? 왜 독자들은 Cardona 씨에게 연락해야 하는가?

빈출 표현

문두에서 정보를 제공하는 표현

① '기업명, (보충 설명), said/announced ~'는 'XX기업이 ~라는 사실을 말했다/발표했다'라는 뜻이며, 기사의 주제, 목적, 대상 등의 단서가 포함된 경우가 많다.

- Kelsey Tech has **announced** a new cell phone that boasts a wider screen and faster Internet connectivity. Kelsey Tech는 보다 넓은 화면과 보다 빠른 인터넷 연결성을 자랑하는 새 휴대폰을 발표했다.

② 현재완료 시제의 문장은 인물이나 기업의 현황을 알리는 역할을 한다. 현재완료 시제 문장과 미래 시제 문장은 종종 시간의 부사구를 동반한다.

- Beijing's Chinese Literature Institute (CLI) **has been** a highly respected research organisation **for decades**. 베이징의 중국문학원(CLI)은 수십 년 동안 매우 존경받는 연구 기관이었다.

③ 미래 시제의 문장은 앞으로 일어날 일을 알리는 역할을 한다.

- **Beginning this spring**, all employees of the Glaspie Factory **will have** a new way to get around at work. 올봄부터 Glaspie Factory의 모든 직원들은 새로운 직장 내 이동 수단을 갖게 될 것이다.

추가 정보를 제시하는 표현

지문의 말미에서 다음과 같은 문장 형태로 추가적인 정보를 얻을 수 있는 방법을 제시하는 경우가 많다. 이러한 정보는 세부 사항 문제의 단서가 될 수 있으므로 소홀히 여기지 말아야 한다.

- A full list of this year's winners in all eleven categories is now available on Malaysia Dining's Web site at www.mydining.com.my.
  11개 부문 모두의 올해의 수상자 명단은 이제 Malaysia Dining의 웹 사이트인 www.mydining.com.my에서 확인할 수 있다.

- To book a tour, visit www.megatours.com/booking.
  투어를 예약하려면 www.megatours.com/booking을 방문해야 한다.

빈출 유형 공략 01 기사: 주제/목적 문제

Question 1 refers to the following article.

1. What is one purpose of the article?

STEP 1 질문 확인
기사의 목적은 제목이나 문두에 드러나는 편이지만, one purpose(목적 중 하나)를 묻는 문제는 후반부에 단서가 나올 수도 있다.

PhD Candidate Seeks to Restore Old Building

Many Jonestown residents know 44 Mirth Street as the old abandoned building at the end of the city line, but recent research has revealed that this decaying structure has quite the historical significance. While collecting data for her history dissertation, PhD candidate Sunny Norbert discovered the rich history behind the long-forgotten home.

"I was looking through newspapers from the mid-1800s and was shocked to see photos of 44 Mirth Street featured prominently in the local news," said Ms. Norbert. "It seems like this building was used as a safe house for many underprivileged groups such as African Americans, Native Americans, and Jewish Americans throughout the years."

As word about the building began to spread, Ms. Norbert decided to restore the building and have it designated as an official heritage site. To do so, she needs a group of dedicated volunteers, particularly those with home-building or restoration skills. Anyone looking to join her effort should e-mail her at s_norbert@fastmail.com.

STEP 2 지문에서 단서 찾기
이 지문은 초반부에서 다소 길게 배경 설명을 한 후 후반부에서 건물 복원을 위한 자원봉사자 모집이라는 주제/목적을 언급하고 있다.

(A) To recruit volunteers
(B) To search for history scholars
(C) To save a building from demolition
(D) To collect donations

STEP 3 선택지 확인
(A)를 정답으로 선택한다.

빈출 유형 공략 02 안내문: 세부 사항 문제

해석 p.72

Question 2 refers to the following information.

2. According to the information, how can employees get further details?

STEP 1 질문 확인
추가 정보를 얻을 수 있는 방법은 대개 지문의 말미에서 제시된다.

Information for Lexington Logistics Employees

The Lexington Logistics HR department will be conducting several training workshops for staff members. These events are optional, but they are an excellent way to develop your business skills. They will cover a variety of topics such as giving presentations in meetings, making a good impression with clients, and making your business writing more formal. To find out more, please come to the informational session on Thursday, June 7, at 2 P.M. in the break room.

STEP 2 지문에서 단서 찾기
직원들을 위한 교육 워크숍을 알리는 안내문이며, 더 많은 정보를 얻으려면 설명회에 오라고 했다. session은 교육, 워크숍, 발표 등의 어휘와 함께 자주 쓰이는 단어이다.

(A) By reading a document
(B) By attending a meeting ✓
(C) By visiting a Web site
(D) By e-mailing the HR department

STEP 3 선택지 확인
지문의 informational session과 come이 선택지에서 meeting과 attend로 각각 패러프레이징된 (B)를 정답으로 선택한다.

UNIT 03 기사, 안내문 **247**

ACTUAL TEST

Questions 1-2 refer to the following information.

Employee of the Month

Have you ever experienced exceptional service from any of our waitstaff at Rockin' Rogers? If so, now is your chance to show your appreciation. Starting next year, we will be announcing an Employee of the Month award on the first of each month. Customers and fellow waitstaff alike can vote for their favorite server at Rockin' Rodgers. Customers will be able to either write comments on the cards provided at our entrance or complete a survey online. Staff members can place their vote in an anonymous ballot box in the break room. The winner of the Employee of the Month award will win two free movie tickets to Moe's Theater, which is just next door. Thank you for your cooperation, and we look forward to counting your votes!

1. What is the purpose of the information?

    (A) To search for new waitstaff
    (B) To reward newly hired workers
    (C) To explain a voting system
    (D) To elect a new manager

2. How can servers most likely win the award?

    (A) By taking extra shifts
    (B) By impressing the boss
    (C) By staying late after work
    (D) By providing great service

Questions 3-5 refer to the following article.

Five Years of Foodwheels

(May 10)—Five years ago, Darren Hirsh had an idea for a food delivery company, Foodwheels, which delivered food from restaurants that lacked their own delivery service. —[1]—. But fortunately, Hirsh believed in his idea and stuck with it. He invested heavily in advertisements and made personal visits to every restaurant in town to convince the owners to join the platform. Within two years, Foodwheels had 200 restaurants in its network. Hirsh reinvested the profits to develop a smartphone app for customers to make ordering food even easier. —[2]—.

When companies with a similar business model, such as Fast Eatz, started gaining popularity, Hirsh thought of new ways to make Foodwheels stand out. —[3]—. He offered restaurants a discount on commissions if they listed their business exclusively on Foodwheels. —[4]—. This drove competitors out of the market, securing Foodwheels' place at the top.

3. Why was the article written?

   (A) To announce the merger of Foodwheels and Fast Eatz
   (B) To explain how Foodwheels rose to success
   (C) To advertise Foodwheels' new service
   (D) To inform people of an investment opportunity

4. What does the article indicate about Foodwheels?

   (A) Some businesses are eligible for a bulk discount.
   (B) Some customers use the service through their phones.
   (C) Restaurants are required to use Foodwheels exclusively.
   (D) Two hundred new customers have recently signed up.

5. In which of the positions marked [1], [2], [3], and [4] does the following sentence best belong?

   "It took a while for the concept to catch on."

   (A) [1]
   (B) [2]
   (C) [3]
   (D) [4]

Questions 6-9 refer to the following article.

Business Update: Perez Beverages

HOUSTON (June 18)—Beverage manufacturer Perez Beverages has announced that it will be changing the recipe for its signature drink, Zip Cola. The decision was made in an effort to deal with an unstable supply of certain ingredients, which has been an ongoing obstacle to meeting the growing demand. —[1]—.

The company posted on social media to reassure consumers that the difference in taste will be nearly impossible to detect. Despite this, the announcement led to a run on Zip Cola. —[2]—.

People are buying large quantities in hopes of reselling the soda on third-party Web sites at inflated prices once the original drink is no longer available.

Shelly Kellner, a representative of Perez Beverages, said that the company is dedicated to protecting the company's reputation for excellence. —[3]—. She added that after the new recipe hits the shelves, the company will release new versions of the drink such as Zip Berry Cola and Zip Vanilla Cola. "We're excited about reaching our customers in new ways," Kellner said. —[4]—.

6. What is the purpose of the article?
   (A) To announce a corporate merger
   (B) To summarize a company's success
   (C) To report on adjustments to a product
   (D) To highlight trends in the beverage industry

7. What is suggested about some Zip Cola customers?
   (A) They will spend less on a drink.
   (B) They hope to profit from a change.
   (C) They wanted healthier options.
   (D) They submitted suggestions to the company.

8. What did Ms. Kellner confirm?
   (A) The brand's packaging will be updated.
   (B) New flavors will be available.
   (C) Some factories will be hiring workers.
   (D) The business learned from past mistakes.

9. In which of the positions marked [1], [2], [3], and [4] does the following sentence best belong?

   "By solving this problem, the company expects a significant increase in production."

   (A) [1]
   (B) [2]
   (C) [3]
   (D) [4]

Questions 10-13 refer to the following article.

PLEASANTVILLE (September 21)—At the request of many townspeople, Pleasantville is finally getting its own holiday-themed store. Holiday Party will be open from the beginning of next month to help locals meet all their seasonal party needs. —[1]—. For each holiday season, customers can expect the entire store to be filled with decorations, costumes, arts and crafts, and other themed goods related to the appropriate season. —[2]—.

For its opening in October, Holiday Party will be embracing the Halloween spirit with a variety of scary costumes, delicious treats, and spooky decorations. From October 20 to 31, if visitors arrive to the store in their Halloween costumes, they will get 10% off their entire purchase for the Halloween Sale. —[3]—. Stop by Holiday Party regularly throughout the year to see what unexpected pleasures it has in store for you. —[4]—.

10. What is the purpose of the article?

(A) To promote a new business
(B) To advertise a Halloween party
(C) To review an arts and crafts store
(D) To announce a store closing

11. What is NOT mentioned about Holiday Party?

(A) It offers many seasonal items.
(B) It is open 24 hours a day.
(C) It sells both food and crafts.
(D) It has various costumes for sale.

12. What is stated about the Halloween Sale?

(A) It is only offered to certain customers.
(B) It is available all throughout October.
(C) It is only valid for one item.
(D) It can be combined with other discounts.

13. In which of the positions marked [1], [2], [3], and [4] does the following sentence best belong?

"There will even be eerie music to set the mood."

(A) [1]
(B) [2]
(C) [3]
(D) [4]

CHAPTER 4

PART 7
독해

UNIT 04

공지, 회람

지문 미리보기

빈출 질문 유형

빈출 표현

빈출 유형 공략 01   공지: 주제/목적 문제

빈출 유형 공략 02   회람: 세부 사항 문제

ACTUAL TEST

UNIT 04

공지, 회람

출제 경향
- 공지는 직원, 고객과 같은 불특정 다수에게 특정 사실을 알리는 글이고, 회람은 사내 직원들에게 보내는 글이다. 회람에서 주로 다루는 주제는 새로운 시스템의 도입, 사내 행사 공지, 문제점 공유 등이다.
- 매회 1~2개의 지문이 출제되며 공지의 출제 빈도가 회람보다 두 배 가량 높다.
- 공지는 주제/목적/대상을 묻는 문제와 추론/암시 문제의 출제 비율이 가장 높지만, 회람은 주제/목적과 문장 삽입 문제가 가장 많이 출세된다.

지문 미리보기

NOTICE TO HANOVER DEPARTMENT STORE CUSTOMERS

❶ Because of the severe storm on December 4, a section of our roof developed a leak. This resulted in water covering the floor and ruining some of the merchandise.

❷ We have closed off this section of the store and have temporarily moved some of the men's items near the footwear department. We are sorry for any inconvenience this may cause, but our patrons' safety is important to us.

❸ If you notice any other leaks or damage, please inform a sales associate or manager right away. Thank you for your cooperation.

공지의 주제/목적
공지와 회람은 정보 전달을 목적으로 하기 때문에 제목이나 지문 초반부에 주제/목적/대상이 드러나는 편이다. 이 글은 제목에서 백화점 고객이 공지의 대상이라는 것을 알 수 있다.

공지의 흐름
공지는 주로 다음과 같은 순서로 글의 흐름이 이어진다.
❶ 공지 사항 안내
❷ 부가 설명
❸ 당부 사항, 연락 방법

미리보기 해석

하노버 백화점 고객님께 드리는 공지

12월 4일의 맹렬한 폭풍우로 인해 백화점 지붕의 일부분에 누수가 발생했습니다. 이로 인해 바닥이 침수되어 일부 상품이 훼손되었습니다.
저희는 백화점의 이 구역을 폐쇄하고 남성용품 일부를 임시로 신발 매장 근처로 옮겼습니다. 이로 인해 불편을 끼쳐드려 죄송하지만, 고객님들의 안전은 저희에게 매우 중요한 문제입니다.
또 다른 누수나 손상이 발견되면 영업 담당자 또는 관리자에게 즉시 알려주십시오. 협조해 주셔서 감사합니다.

빈출 질문 유형

주제/목적/대상 질문 유형
What is the **purpose** of the **notice/memo**? 공지/회람의 목적은 무엇인가?
What is the **topic** of the **memo**? 회람의 주제는 무엇인가?
For whom is the **notice intended**? 공지는 누구를 위한 것인가?

추론/암시 질문 유형
What is **suggested about** Ms. Guerra? Guerra 씨에 대해 무엇이 암시되었는가?
Who most likely is Alex Kwon? Alex Kwon은 누구이겠는가?
What most likely is a part of Mr. Clist's job? Clist 씨의 업무에 포함되는 것은 무엇이겠는가?
Where would the **notice** most likely **appear**? 공지는 어디에 게시되겠는가?

빈출 표현

주제/목적을 알릴 때 쓰이는 표현
This is ~의 형태로 글의 주제와 목적을 알리거나, 미래 시제 문장으로 앞으로 일어날 일을 알리는 경우가 많다.

This is a reminder that all employees are required to attend this Thursday's staff meeting.
이번 주 목요일 직원 회의에 전 직원이 참석해야 한다는 것을 상기시켜 드립니다.
Kelsey's Clothing's annual winter coat sale **will soon begin**.
Kelsey's Clothing의 연례 겨울 코트 세일이 곧 시작될 것이다.
Our office printer **will be unavailable** from 2 P.M. to 4 P.M. on Friday as it is being serviced.
우리 사무실 프린터는 점검으로 인해 금요일 오후 2시부터 4시까지 사용할 수 없을 것입니다.

요청 사항을 전달할 때 쓰이는 표현
〈please + 동사원형〉으로 시작하는 명령문이나 must, should 등의 조동사를 사용하여 요청 사항을 전달하는 경우가 많다.

Sign up today for this year's annual Women in Tech conference!
오늘 올해의 연례 Women in Tech 컨퍼런스에 등록하세요!
Always inspect your ladder before climbing it.
사다리를 오르기 전에 항상 사다리를 점검하세요.
Please speak with the secretary to make an appointment with Ms. Smith.
Smith 씨와 약속을 잡으려면 비서에게 말씀하세요.
All restaurant employees **must** wash their hands before returning to work.
모든 식당 종업원은 업무에 복귀하기 전에 손을 씻어야 한다.

빈출 유형 공략 01　공지: 주제/목적 문제

해석 p.75

Question 1 refers to the following notice.

1. What is the topic of the notice?

NOTICE

To be in compliance with government regulations, employees must not operate any machinery without having the proper certification. In addition, gloves and goggles must be worn on the production floor at all times. These measures are in place to prevent injury. Please phone the HR department if you have questions.

(A) Performance reviews
(B) Employee benefits
(✓) Safety procedures
(D) Phone policies

STEP 1 질문 확인
공지/회람의 주제/목적은 문두에 드러나는 경우가 많지만 이 글처럼 길이가 짧은 지문은 지문 전반에 걸쳐 주제와 목적의 단서가 나오는 편이다.

STEP 2 지문에서 단서 찾기
조동사 must를 사용하여 요청 사항을 전달하고 있다.
① 직원들은 적절한 인증이 없으면 기계를 작동해서는 안 된다
② 생산 현장에서는 항상 장갑과 보안경을 착용해야 한다

STEP 3 선택지 확인
안전 절차에 관한 내용이므로 (C)를 정답으로 선택한다.

빈출 유형 공략 02   회람: 세부 사항 문제

해석 p.75

Question 2 refers to the following memo.

2. When will the technician visit the office?

STEP 1 질문 확인
technician이 사무실을 방문하는 시기를 묻는 질문. technician을 키워드로 지문을 검색한다.

MEMO

To: Staff
From: Kelly Oppenheimer
Date: 21 December
Subject: Broken printers

As you may have noticed, both of the office's color printers are out of order. Thankfully, the black-and-white printers are working just fine, so feel free to use those. Due to the upcoming holiday season, however, a technician is not able to assist us in person until next month. We ask for your patience until they can be serviced. If you absolutely require color printing, please send me an e-mail, and I will help send your documents to a printing facility.

STEP 2 지문에서 단서 찾기
회람은 이메일/편지처럼 수신인/발신인/날짜/제목 정보가 제시되는 경우가 많다. 이같은 정보는 세부 사항이나 NOT/True 문제의 단서가 될 수 있으므로 소홀히 하지 말고 확인해야 한다. technician이 다음 달이 될 때까지는 도움을 줄 수 없다는 정보를 확인했다면 상단의 날짜 정보를 확인해서 다음 달은 1월이라는 것을 파악한다.

(A) In December
(B) In January ✓
(C) In February
(D) In March

STEP 3 선택지 확인
(B)를 정답으로 선택한다. 상단의 Date: 21 December만 보고 (A)를 정답으로 고르지 않도록 주의한다.

ACTUAL TEST

Questions 1-2 refer to the following notice.

Free Tennis Lessons

Have you ever wanted to learn how to play tennis? If so, you'll be happy to know that members of the Scottsdale Tennis Club are offering free lessons.

Complimentary lessons for senior citizens will be held at the community recreation center. Group A will be on Saturdays from 3 to 5 P.M. starting in June. Group B will be on Sundays from 5 to 7 P.M. starting in July. Those who wish to participate should visit the recreation center and sign up at the front desk. Space is limited to eight people per group, so don't miss out!

These lessons are available for beginner learners and intermediate learners. Tennis rackets will be available for use during the course, free of charge.

1. For whom is the notice intended?
   (A) Elementary school students
   (B) Working professionals
   (C) Advanced tennis players
   (D) Elderly residents

2. According to the notice, what is true about the tennis lessons?
   (A) They are best suited for tennis club members.
   (B) They all take place at the same time.
   (C) Free rackets will be available during the lessons.
   (D) At least 10 participants are required per group.

Questions 3-5 refer to the following memo.

To: All Cottone Logistics Employees
From: Elise Gault
Date: October 6
Re: HQ Visit

This Friday, October 10, a representative from corporate headquarters, Lisa Finch, will be visiting our site. Several events have been planned to help Ms. Finch become more familiar with our operations and working environment. The schedule is as follows:

Time	Event	Who will attend	Room
9:30 A.M.	Branch status report	Management team	Conference Room 1
10:30 A.M.	Facility tour with branch manager	Elise Gault	—
12:30 P.M.	Lunch	Elise Gault & HR Team	Conference Room 1
1:30 P.M.	Presentation by Ms. Finch	All employees	Main hall
2:00 P.M.	Question-and-answer session, please submit your questions in advance	All employees	Main hall

Ms. Finch wants to see all the departments during the facility tour and may inquire about your role as well as company policies. I encourage you to review the employee handbook so that you feel confident in responding.

3. Who most likely is Ms. Gault?
   (A) A safety inspector
   (B) A headquarters representative
   (C) The branch manager
   (D) The business's owner

4. When will Ms. Finch answer some questions?
   (A) At 9:30 A.M.
   (B) At 10:30 A.M.
   (C) At 1:30 P.M.
   (D) At 2:00 P.M.

5. What does Ms. Gault suggest about Cottone Logistics employees?
   (A) They should attend all events on October 10.
   (B) They may have forgotten some company policies.
   (C) They will finish their shifts early on October 10.
   (D) They must confirm their attendance at a meeting.

Questions 6-8 refer to the following notice.

Attention Flyers:

The monorail at the Orlando Airport has officially begun reconstruction. Please be aware that from January 13 to April 10, the monorail will be closed and services will be suspended. —[1]—.

Orlando Airport's monorail is in need of repairs, refurbishing, and general updates. The updated monorail will boast faster travel times, extra seats, more luggage space, and a modern design. —[2]—.

A free bus service will be available for travelers who need to move between terminals. —[3]—. For more details, as well as concept photos and updates, please visit www.orlandoairport.com. We appreciate your cooperation and understanding. —[4]—.

6. What is scheduled to begin in January?

   (A) The construction of another airport wing
   (B) The creation of an updated transit system
   (C) An extended train service schedule
   (D) A change in airline routes

7. What is NOT indicated about Orlando Airport?

   (A) A bus service is available to downtown Orlando.
   (B) The current monorail is outdated.
   (C) It has an official Web site.
   (D) It has more than one terminal.

8. In which of the positions marked [1], [2], [3], and [4] does the following sentence best belong?

   "There will be increased service while monorail construction is underway."

   (A) [1]
   (B) [2]
   (C) [3]
   (D) [4]

Questions 9-12 refer to the following notice.

Youth Business Owners' Week

Morristown will be celebrating its eighth annual Youth Business Owners' Week from March 14 to 21. During that period, the Morristown community will be highlighting the entrepreneurial spirit of our local businesses. —[1]—.

Nearly all shops and restaurants run by small businesses will be offering a discount or promotion during this time. —[2]—. Muriel's Diner is joining the celebration for its fifth consecutive year with its Special Breakfast Sampler. Kathy's Jewelry Boutique will also be participating again this year, offering a 10% discount on all purchases. Yuna's Stationery will be participating in the event for the first time by offering a buy one, get one, following in the footsteps of Viola & Me Crafts' promotion last year. —[3]—.

For more details about the businesses involved and the unique discounts available, make sure to check www.morristown.com. —[4]—. Here's your chance to support local businesses and save some money while doing it!

9. What is the purpose of the notice?

   (A) To respond to a customer inquiry
   (B) To alert the public to an event
   (C) To advertise a restaurant opening
   (D) To promote female business owners

10. According to the notice, what business will be new to Youth Business Owners' Week?

    (A) Muriel's Diner
    (B) Kathy's Jewelry Boutique
    (C) Yuna's Stationary
    (D) Viola & Me Crafts

11. What is indicated about the event?

    (A) Businesses must pay to be featured.
    (B) All businesses with young owners join in.
    (C) It has been taking place for over a decade.
    (D) It only celebrates local businesses.

12. In which of the positions marked [1], [2], [3], and [4] does the following sentence best belong?

    "You can even find some printable coupons and vouchers for free gifts."

    (A) [1]
    (B) [2]
    (C) [3]
    (D) [4]

CHAPTER 4
—
PART 7
독해

UNIT 05

광고

지문 미리보기

빈출 질문 유형

빈출 표현

빈출 유형 공략 01   상품/서비스 광고: NOT/True 문제

빈출 유형 공략 02   구인 광고: 세부 사항 문제

ACTUAL TEST

UNIT 05

광고

출제 경향
- 매회 평균 1개의 지문이 나오는데, 주로 파트 7의 시작 부분에서 2~3문항짜리 지문으로 출제되는 경향이 있다.
- 크게 상품/서비스 광고(상품, 서비스, 업체, 행사, 부동산)와 구인 광고로 나뉘는데, 구인 광고의 출제 비중이 점점 증가하고 있다.
- 주제/목적/대상 문제, 추론/암시 문제, NOT/True 문제 등이 비슷한 비중으로 출제되며, 문장 삽입 문제와 동의어 찾기 문제도 간혹 출제된다.

지문 미리보기

Pete's Dry Cleaning
Affordable prices for all your dry-cleaning and alteration needs.

❶ Pete's Dry Cleaning has been offering dry-cleaning services in the East Haven neighborhood for the past twenty years. We are pleased to announce that we will now be doing alterations.

❷ Get your jackets, trousers, dresses, and skirts shortened or lengthened. Our employees can adjust the garment precisely for a perfect fit. The work is done on-site and can even be completed within a few hours with our express service.

❸ Visit our Web site at www.petesdrycleaning.com to see before-and-after pictures of our work. You'll be amazed at the quality! Alterations are available daily during our normal hours of operation.

광고의 목적/대상
상단의 제목, 업체명 등의 정보만으로도 무슨 광고인지, 대상이 누구인지 등을 알 수 있으므로 제목을 확인해야 한다.

광고의 흐름
광고는 다음과 같은 순서로 글의 흐름이 이어지는 편이다.
❶ 업체를 소개하는 인사말
❷ 광고하고자 하는 내용
❸ 상품/서비스 관련 추가 정보

| 미리보기 해석 |

Pete's Dry Cleaning
저렴한 가격에 고객님이 필요로 하는 모든 드라이클리닝 및 수선 서비스를 제공합니다.

Pete's Dry Cleaning은 지난 20년 동안 이스트 헤이븐 지역에서 드라이클리닝 서비스를 제공해 왔습니다. 저희가 이제 수선 서비스도 하게 된다는 기쁜 소식을 알려 드립니다.

재킷, 바지, 드레스, 그리고 치마의 줄임 및 늘임 작업을 맡겨 주세요. 완벽한 핏을 위해 저희 직원들이 정확하게 의류를 조절해 드립니다. 작업은 현장에서 이루어지며, 신속 서비스를 이용하면 몇 시간 안에 끝낼 수도 있습니다.

저희 웹 사이트인 www.petesdrycleaning.com을 방문하시어 저희 작업물의 전과 후 사진을 보시기 바랍니다. 그 품질에 놀라실 겁니다! 수선 업무는 매일 저희의 정상 영업시간 중에 가능합니다.

빈출 질문 유형

주제/목적/대상 질문 유형
What is the **purpose** of the **advertisement**? 광고의 목적은 무엇인가?
What is being **advertised**? 무엇이 광고되고 있는가?
Who is the intended **audience** of the **advertisement**? 광고가 목표로 하는 대상은 누구인가?

추론/암시 질문 유형
What is **suggested about** Canary Marketing? Canary Marketing에 대해 암시된 것은 무엇인가?
What does the **advertisement suggest about** the spring season?
광고는 봄 시즌에 대해 무엇을 암시하는가?
According to the advertisement, **why might** people want to arrive early?
광고에 의하면 사람들이 일찍 도착하기를 원하는 이유는 무엇이겠는가?

NOT/True 질문 유형
What is **NOT mentioned as** a feature of the program? 프로그램의 특징으로 언급되지 않은 것은 무엇인가?
What is **true about** the job? 일자리에 관해 사실인 것은 무엇인가?
What is **NOT listed as** a job responsibility? 직무로 나열되지 않은 것은 무엇인가?

빈출 표현

상품/서비스 광고 빈출 표현
상품과 서비스 광고는 명령문이나 의문문으로, 부동산 광고는 평서문으로 시작하는 경향이 있다. 첫 문장을 제대로 파악하면 업체의 업종 및 광고 목적 등을 파악할 수 있다.

Try a bright new paint job! 밝고 새로운 페인트칠을 시도해 보세요!
→ 페인트 제조업체 또는 페인트 공사 업체

Take advantage of the fall season to take care of your trees. 가을철을 이용해 당신의 수목을 가꾸세요.
→ 정원용품 또는 수목 관리 업체

Pineville is the ideal location for your start-up business. 파인빌은 당신의 창업에 이상적인 장소입니다.
→ 건물 임대업체, 부동산 중개업체

Conwell Street Apartments combine the amenities of a luxury hotel with the privacy of a residence. 콘웰 가 아파트는 고급 호텔의 편의 시설과 주택의 프라이버시를 결합했습니다.
→ 건물 임대업체, 부동산 중개업체

구인 광고 빈출 표현
구인 광고에서는 '기업명, (보충 설명), is seeking[looking for] ~ (XX기업이 ~을 찾고 있습니다)'와 같은 문장 형태로 구인 기업, 지원자의 자격 요건, 업무 영역 등을 보여준다.

Kiesel Video **is seeking** detail-oriented people to test our new software.
Kiesel Video는 당사의 새로운 소프트웨어를 테스트할 꼼꼼한 분들을 찾고 있습니다.

Nobu Marketing **is looking for** talented individuals who can join its expert team of researchers.
Nobu Marketing은 전문 연구원들로 구성된 팀에 합류할 재능 있는 사람들을 찾고 있습니다.

빈출 유형 공략 01   상품/서비스 광고: NOT/True 문제

해석 p.78

Question 1 refers to the following advertisement.

1. What quality does StarPoint Recruiters NOT promise in a candidate?

> **STEP 1 질문 확인**
> NOT/True 문제는 지문 내용과 선택지를 하나하나 대조해야 한다.

Searching for qualified candidates?

StarPoint Recruiters is exactly what you've been looking for. We have been in the recruiting business for over 20 years and have expertise in several fields such as marketing, finance, service, and management.

We are known for finding employees who:
✓ Are always on time
✓ Dress and behave in a professional manner
✓ Have verified experience in their field
✓ Are serious about advancing their careers

If you are interested in discovering more about our expert recruiters, come to our information session on April 8 at 2 P.M. During the session, our CEO will explain our selection process and how we ensure that we only recommend the best candidates for our clients.

> **STEP 2 지문에서 단서 찾기**
> 지문에 정보들이 나열되어 있다면 그곳에서 NOT/True 문제의 단서를 발견할 가능성이 크다.

(A) Punctuality
(B) Relevant qualifications
(C) ✓ Efficiency
(D) Appropriate attire

> **STEP 3 선택지 확인**
> 지문 내용과 선택지를 일일이 비교해가며 소거해야 한다.
> (A) on time – Punctuality: 소거
> (B) verified experience – qualifications: 소거
> (D) dress – attire: 소거
> 지문에 Efficiency에 해당하는 내용은 없으므로 (C)를 정답으로 선택한다.

빈출 유형 공략 02 　 구인 광고: 세부 사항 문제

해석 p.79

Question 2 refers to the following advertisement.

2. What kind of applicant is Superb Subs looking for?

Subtitlers Wanted!

Superb Subs is searching for spectacular workers to create subtitles for a variety of media including movies, television shows, Internet videos, and more. We offer free online training for those who pass our trial test. Superb Subs is currently looking for individuals who are native speakers of English and who have their own computer, reliable access to the Internet, and a headset.

When working for Superb Subs, you're in charge of your own schedule—you can work for 1 hour a day or 12 hours a day. You can also choose content that interests you. The average Superb Subs subtitler makes between $300 to $1,000 a week, depending on how much they work.

Sounds interesting? Check out www.superbsubs.com to apply today.

(A) Someone who is currently writing subtitles
(B) Someone who speaks multiple languages
(C) Someone with good Internet connectivity ✓
(D) Someone who can work full-time

STEP 1 질문 확인
세부 사항을 묻는 문제는 질문에서 키워드를 찾아 지문을 검색한다. 이 문제는 applicant가 키워드가 되며, 지원자의 자격 요건이 나열된 부분을 검색한다.

STEP 2 지문에서 단서 찾기
자격 요건이 나열된 곳을 찾았다면 지문의 내용과 선택지를 하나씩 대조해 가며 맞지 않는 것을 소거한다.

STEP 3 선택지 확인
(A) 언급 없음: 소거
(B) native speakers of English – speaks multiple languages: 소거
(C) reliable access to the Internet – good Internet connectivity: 정답
(D) you can work for one hour a day or 12 hours a day – work full-time: 소거

ACTUAL TEST

Questions 1-2 refer to the following online advertisement.

http://www.yummyveganfoods.com

Yummy Vegan Foods

Are you interested in removing animal products from your diet?
Are you looking for a healthier way of eating?
Do you like tasty food that's both good for you and the environment?

If this sounds like you, give Yummy Vegan Foods a try! You'll be surprised to see how many of your favorite dishes have healthier vegan alternatives. If you visit our Web site and use the code "vegancookies," you'll get six of our dairy-free chocolate chip cookies with any order!

This offer is valid until 31 December, so don't miss out!

1. What is the purpose of the advertisement?

   (A) To attract new customers
   (B) To promote a new line of product
   (C) To showcase a new menu
   (D) To advertise an updated Web site

2. What is available until the end of the year?

   (A) A discount on delivery fees
   (B) A weekly meal plan
   (C) A free dessert offer
   (D) A vegan cookbook

Questions 3-4 refer to the following advertisement.

LAWRENCE APARTMENT FOR RENT

One bedroom, sizeable windows overlooking the Pacific Ocean, bathroom with a spacious shower, recently renovated dining and kitchen areas. Minutes away from public transportation and the local beach. 110 square meters, $1,400 monthly, utilities included. One-year minimum lease required. Security deposit of two months' rent is due at signing. Available from August 1. Call 555-0124 for more details.

3. What does the advertisement NOT mention about the apartment?

(A) It has large windows.
(B) It is near public transit.
(C) It was recently renovated.
(D) It has a spacious bed.

4. What is mentioned in the advertisement?

(A) The utility bill is separate from the rent.
(B) A security deposit is required.
(C) The apartment is currently unoccupied.
(D) There is a tub in the bathroom.

Questions 5-7 refer to the following advertisement.

"Starting Your Own Business"
A presentation by
Debra Mitchell, Founder of Mitchell Consulting
Wednesday, November 10, 6:30 to 7:30 P.M.
Les Amis Restaurant, 2104 Poe Lane

Have you ever considered starting your own business? Do you know where to start? Where to find the best resources for small business owners? How to secure a loan? —[1]—.

Get answers to all your business-related questions at Mitchell Consulting's free seminar. —[2]—. Small business expert Debra Mitchell will be giving a presentation on how to get started in the business world and will answer all of your burning questions.

Though Ms. Mitchell is most known for Mitchell Consulting, she has a few other successful ventures, such as a coffee shop and a pet grooming salon. She is also the author of *Get It Right the First Time: A Guide to Success* and several other self-help books. She tours the country to give speeches and presentations to inspire people to follow their passions. —[3]—.

Register for this event at www.mitchellconsulting.com. —[4]—. Tickets do not include the cost of your meal, but a 50% off coupon will be offered for all Debra Mitchell books on sale during the seminar.

---

5. Why most likely is the event being organized?

(A) To attract business owners
(B) To celebrate a successful executive
(C) To help those new to business
(D) To encourage people to get loans

6. What do participants receive for attending the seminar?

(A) A discount
(B) A one-on-one meeting with Ms. Mitchell
(C) A free meal
(D) A personalized business plan

7. In which of the positions marked [1], [2], [3], and [4] does the following sentence best belong?

"With her wide array of talents and interests, she is sure to be of help to anyone looking to break into a new industry."

(A) [1]
(B) [2]
(C) [3]
(D) [4]

Questions 8-11 refer to the following advertisement.

RENT YOUR DREAM HOME IN ATLANTIC CITY

With summer coming in just a few months, now is the time to start planning your vacation. What better way to spend your days than in Atlantic City? You can experience beautiful ocean views, try your luck at one of the many casinos, or enjoy a delicious meal at some of the best restaurants in the area.

Instead of limiting your stay to a small hotel room, renting a spacious, private home is the best way to go. You can stay in a luxurious and well-maintained home while paying a fraction of what you would for a hotel.

Our rental program offers:
- Rentals for as short as one night or as long as several months
- Deep cleaning before every guest's arrival
- Fully stocked toiletries, bedding, and towels
- Discounts for larger groups and long stays
- Renters insurance

Take a virtual tour of your dream vacation home at www.rentalhomesac.com. To book a stay today, speak to one of our representatives at 555-1198.

---

8. Who is the target audience of the advertisement?

(A) Residents of Atlantic City
(B) Seasonal travelers
(C) Real estate agents
(D) Hotel managers

9. The word "fraction" in paragraph 2, line 3, is closest in meaning to

(A) part
(B) group
(C) crack
(D) end

10. What is NOT mentioned as a feature of the program?

(A) Cheaper rates for large parties
(B) Free cleaning services during a stay
(C) Rentals for various lengths of time
(D) Protection against accidental damage

11. How can people learn more information about the rental homes?

(A) By visiting a Web site
(B) By responding to the advertisement
(C) By stopping by the office
(D) By reading reviews online

CHAPTER 4

PART 7
독해

UNIT 06

웹페이지, 양식, 후기

지문 미리보기

빈출 질문 유형

빈출 표현

빈출 유형 공략 01 웹페이지: 추론/암시 문제

빈출 유형 공략 02 양식: 세부 사항 문제

ACTUAL TEST

UNIT 06

웹페이지, 양식, 후기

출제 경향
- 웹페이지는 인터넷 홈페이지 형식의 지문으로서 광고, 공지, 양식, 후기 등의 다양한 내용으로 출제된다.
- 목적/대상 문제, 문장 삽입 문제, NOT/True 문제, 추론/암시 문제가 거의 비슷한 비율로 출제되며, 동의어 찾기 문제의 출제 비율이 가장 낮다.
- 단일 지문으로 출제되는 빈도는 낮은 편이지만, 다중 지문 중 하나의 지문으로 출제되는 빈도는 매우 높으며, 주로 이메일과 함께 나온다.

지문 미리보기

| HOME | ABOUT US | CAREERS | CONTACT US |

MK Marketing is a major leader in the advertising field. We deal with clients both large and small and are known for our proven ability to increase sales within a variety of markets. We excel in print, digital, and physical advertising. With over 30 years of experience, we believe no project is too difficult for us to handle. Our key to success is cultivating several teams filled with experts dedicated to specific fields.

Don't know how to promote your new product line? Still trying to tap into the youth market? With MK Marketing, you don't have to worry about anything—simply tell us your goals, and we'll work with you to create a plan to reach them.

If this sounds interesting to you, please send us a message on our CONTACT US page, and we'll get back to you within one business day.

상단 탭, 인터넷 주소
지문 상단의 탭 또는 웹 사이트 주소는 지문의 목적/대상 및 앞으로 전개될 지문 내용까지 유추할 수 있는 단서가 된다. 이 지문은 ABOUT US 탭이 켜져 있으므로 업체를 소개하는 글이 나올 것을 유추할 수 있다.

웹페이지 내용
업체 소개 지문은 목적/대상이 언급되기 전에 업체에 대한 통상적인 홍보가 먼저 나오는 경우가 종종 있다. 홍보 내용으로는 창립 과정 및 배경, 개요와 연혁, 사업 영역 등이 소개되는 편이다.

추가 정보
마지막 단락에서는 추가적인 정보를 얻기 위한 전화번호, 웹 사이트 주소 등의 정보가 주로 제시된다.

미리보기 해석

| 홈 | 회사 소개 | 채용 정보 | 연락하기 |

MK Marketing은 광고 분야의 선두주자입니다. 크고 작은 규모의 업체 모두를 고객으로 두고 거래하고 있으며, 다양한 시장에서 매출을 증대시킬 수 있는 능력을 입증 받아 이름을 알리고 있습니다. 우리 회사는 인쇄, 디지털, 실물 광고에 뛰어납니다. 30년 이상의 경험을 기반으로 어떤 어려운 프로젝트도 우리가 처리하지 못하는 것은 없다고 자부합니다. 우리의 성공 비결은 특정 분야에 전념하는 전문가들로 구성된 여러 개의 팀을 양성하는 것입니다.

여러분의 신제품을 홍보하는 방법을 찾지 못하고 계신가요? 여전히 젊은층을 공략하려고 애쓰고 계신가요? MK Marketing과 함께라면 아무것도 걱정할 필요가 없습니다. 여러분이 목표로 하는 바를 말씀해 주시면 우리는 여러분과 협력하여 목표에 도달하기 위한 계획을 마련하겠습니다.

우리의 제안에 관심이 있으시다면, '연락하기' 페이지로 메시지를 보내주시면 영업일 기준으로 1일 이내에 회신을 드리겠습니다.

빈출 질문 유형

목적/대상 질문 유형
What is the **purpose** of the **Web page/form**? 웹페이지/양식의 목적은 무엇인가?
For whom is the **Web page intended**? 웹페이지는 누구를 대상으로 하는가?

추론/암시 질문 유형
What is **suggested about** the ingredients? 재료에 대해 암시되는 것은 무엇인가?
Who most likely is Ms. Wu? Wu 씨는 누구이겠는가?

세부 사항 질문 유형
What will happen on September 30? 9월 30일에 무슨 일이 일어날 것인가?
What does the hotel provide at no charge? 호텔은 무엇을 무료로 제공하는가?
What does the IAAF want to do? IAAF는 무엇을 하기를 원하는가?

빈출 표현

업체를 추천하는 표현
I would **definitely** use them **again**. 그들을 꼭 다시 이용하고 싶습니다.
We are **thrilled** that we chose them. 우리는 그들을 선택해서 매우 기쁩니다.
It is absolutely **worth the price**. 그것은 정말 값어치가 있습니다.
We plan to **use** them **in the years to come**. 우리는 앞으로 그들을 이용할 계획입니다.
I **give** this product **top ratings**. 저는 이 제품을 최고 등급으로 평가합니다.
I was **impressed with** the assistance we received. 저는 우리가 받은 도움에 감명을 받았습니다.
I **cannot** recommend this company **enough**. 이 회사를 아무리 추천해도 충분하지 않습니다.
I was so **pleased with** my experience with the company. 나는 그 회사와의 경험에 매우 만족했습니다.
I **highly recommend** the salmon at this restaurant. 이 음식점의 연어를 강력 추천합니다.

추가 정보를 얻을 수 있는 방법을 안내하는 표현
For more information, contact reservations@cityhotels.com.au.
보다 자세한 내용은 reservations@cityhotels.com.au로 연락 주시기 바랍니다.
Check out our Web site at www.eduwill.net for additional information.
저희 웹 사이트 www.eduwill.net을 확인해서 보다 많은 정보를 얻으세요.
Contact us today to see how you can get up to 20% off your next order.
오늘 저희에게 연락해서 다음 주문 시 최대 20%의 할인을 받을 수 있는 방법을 알아보세요.

당부할 때 사용하는 표현
Please note that the back entrance will be closed for repairs starting next week.
후문은 다음 주부터 수리를 위해 폐쇄된다는 것을 유념해 주세요.

빈출 유형 공략 01 　웹페이지: 추론/암시 문제

해석 p.81

Question 1 refers to the following Web page.

1. What is suggested about Trejo Bay Resort?

   https://www.trejobayresort.com/024836

   Thank you for your payment to Trejo Bay Resort. Please find the details below.

   Today's date: May 2

   Reservation dates: August 10–22
   Total: $2,580*
   Deposit received (May 2): $120, Credit Card XXXX-XXXX-XXXX-8774
   Outstanding balance: $2,460
   Customer: Robert Muntz

   *Reflects 10% discount for extended stay

   Should your travel plans change, please notify us as soon as possible. The cancellation fee is calculated based on how close to the reservation date the cancellation is made. Click here to read more about this policy.

   (A) It offers discounts on longer stays.
   (B) It allows free cancellations.
   (C) It has more than one location.
   (D) It changes its policies regularly.

STEP 1 질문 확인
Trejo Bay Resort에 대해 암시된 것을 묻는 문제. 추론/암시 문제는 단서가 명시적으로 드러나지 않으며, 지문 전체가 Trejo Bay Resort에 관한 내용이므로 키워드 검색이 아닌 지문을 읽어 내려가는 방식을 써야 한다.

STEP 2 지문에서 단서 찾기
양식, 혹은 양식 형태의 웹페이지에서는 별표(*) 또는 Note(유의 사항)가 정답의 단서로 연결되는 경우가 많다. 보통은 도표에 *가 나오고, 도표 밑에 그것이 의미하는 것이 무엇인지가 나오는데, 이 지문에서 *는 장기 투숙을 하면 할인을 해준다는 것을 강조하기 위해 사용되었다.

STEP 3 선택지 확인
장기 투숙에 할인을 해준다는 의미의 (A)가 정답이다. 지문의 extended stay가 선택지에서 longer stays로 패러프레이징되었다.

빈출 유형 공략 02   양식: 세부 사항 문제

해석 p.82

Question 2 refer to the following online form.

2. Why did Mr. Clevenger fill out the form?

STEP 1 질문 확인
양식을 작성한 이유를 묻는 질문. Clevenger를 키워드로 지문을 검색한다.

Motley Solutions
772 Coulter Lane
Dublin, Ireland

Customer Type:	Returning
Customer Name:	Earl Clevenger
E-mail Address:	e.clevenger@qmail.com
Phone Number:	555-0127
Number of Copies:	500
Color/Black and White:	Color

Attach specifications document here:
BEEFJERKY_AD

Additional information:

The Cheese and Meat Festival is coming to town, so I'd like to advertise the beef jerky stall I'm setting up for it. I need 500 color copies of the advertisement I've attached to this form. Last time I ordered, the flyers weren't glossy enough, so please use glossier paper when you print them. If you provide me with a price, I'll be happy to transfer you the money.

STEP 2 지문에서 단서 찾기
Clevenger가 양식의 작성자라는 것을 확인했다면, 작성된 정보를 종합하여 양식을 작성한 이유를 파악해야 한다. 이 지문은 인쇄업체에 복사를 요청하기 위해 작성하는 양식이다. 이처럼 작성해야 하는 빈칸이 많은 양식 지문은 이름, 연락처 등의 일반적인 정보와, 양식을 작성한 이유를 파악할 수 있는 정보를 빠르게 구분해야 한다. 빈칸 정보에서 단서를 찾고, 맨 밑의 추가 정보에서 그 단서를 확인하는 방식으로 문제를 풀어 나간다.

(A) To sign up for an event
(B) ✓ To request a service
(C) To file a complaint
(D) To offer feedback

STEP 3 선택지 확인
용역 또는 서비스를 요청하기 위한 것이라는 (B)를 정답으로 선택한다. Cheese and Meat Festival과 event를 연관 지어 (A)를 고르지 않도록 주의해야 한다.

UNIT 06 웹페이지, 양식, 후기   277

ACTUAL TEST

Questions 1-2 refer to the following Web page.

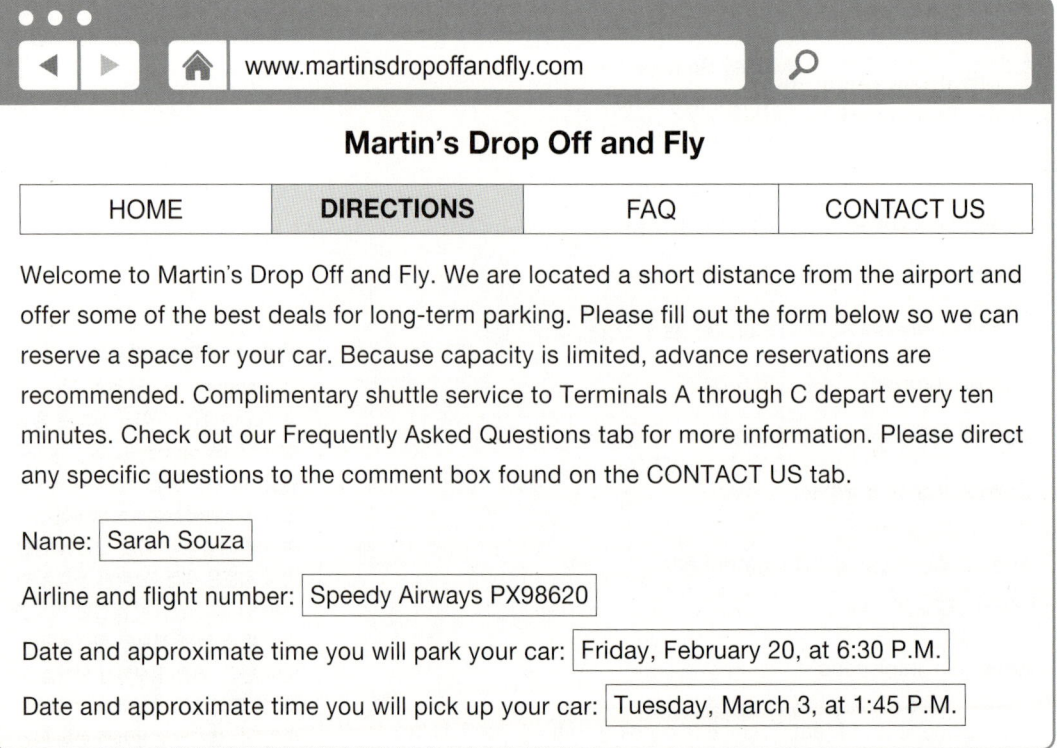

1. What is the form used for?

    (A) Issuing a formal complaint
    (B) Scheduling a taxi service
    (C) Securing a parking spot
    (D) Searching for plane tickets

2. What is indicated about the shuttle?

    (A) It does not have a fare.
    (B) It runs to two terminals.
    (C) It requires reservations.
    (D) It has an irregular schedule.

Questions 3-5 refer to the following review.

McKenzie Tailor Shop
Reviewed by Cheryl Wright
Rating (out of 5): 4.5

I recently used the services at McKenzie Tailor Shop in the Kenway Building for the first time. —[1]—. The owner, Antonio McKenzie, greeted me warmly and listened carefully to my needs. He and his two sons, who make up the staff, were very knowledgeable about dealing with old garments. —[2]—. I brought in a dress that I had purchased at a vintage shop. It needed one panel replaced because it had been stained with bleach. When the completed dress was returned to me, it looked as good as new. —[3]—. I was shocked that they were able to find an exact match for the fabric, even though it is nearly impossible to find.
I was very pleased with the service, but there is one thing that I should point out. The turnaround time for the work is two weeks, about double the average for the industry. —[4]—.

3. What is suggested about McKenzie Tailor Shop?
   (A) It recently moved to the Kenway Building.
   (B) It is a family-run business.
   (C) It has expanded its selection of services.
   (D) It offers vintage dresses for sale.

4. What was Ms. Wright surprised about?
   (A) The affordable cost of repairs
   (B) The sourcing of a rare fabric
   (C) The effectiveness of a cleaning product
   (D) The large size of the staff

5. In which of the positions marked [1], [2], [3], and [4] does the following sentence best belong?

   "Because of this, you should plan ahead for the service you need."

   (A) [1]
   (B) [2]
   (C) [3]
   (D) [4]

Questions 6-8 refer to the following Web page.

http://www.regalhotels.com/accommodations

The Auckland Regal Hotel is pleased to announce that construction of the Orange River Wing has officially been completed. —[1]—. This new area of the hotel has the most modern and luxurious design in New Zealand. —[2]—. There is a ballroom, a conference room, and even an event hall to cater to all of your special event needs. —[3]—.

In addition to our new rooms, we are proud to offer:
- An extensive room service menu
- Both indoor and outdoor pools with hot tubs
- 24-hour access to our gym facilities for a small fee
- A café with free, secure Internet access
- Complimentary tea and cookies in the lobby

The Auckland Regal Hotel is conveniently located near public transportation, tourist attractions, and shopping centres. Contact reservations@regalhotels.com for more information. —[4]—.

6. For whom is the information mainly intended?
   (A) Potential investors
   (B) City visitors
   (C) Hotel staff members
   (D) Local tour guides

7. What does the hotel provide for free to guests?
   (A) Light refreshments
   (B) Gym access
   (C) Room service
   (D) Conference equipment

8. In which of the positions marked [1], [2], [3], and [4] does the following sentence best belong?

   "In addition, guests who book more than two nights at the hotel will receive a discount for any large gatherings."

   (A) [1]
   (B) [2]
   (C) [3]
   (D) [4]

ACTUAL TEST

Questions 9-12 refer to the following review.

"Great service unless you have an issue."

Theresa Kirby

I promote the video games my company produces. —[1]—. One of my main duties is negotiating and securing advertising contracts. As we sell our goods around the world, it is essential for these contracts to be accurately translated, so that's why I use AGP Translation. I've always been impressed with how quickly their team can complete a translation project. They also sometimes ask questions before providing the final draft to ensure they completely understand my intended meaning. —[2]—. As they specialize in 20 different languages, I can use the same company for a variety of projects.

While that side of the service has always been excellent, I was surprised with how poorly my customer service issue was handled. I noticed an unexpected charge on my account for a project that I did not request. I contacted the customer service team by e-mail. I received an automated reply saying that the company would get in touch within three business days. —[3]—. After a week, I sent a follow-up e-mail and another one a few days after that. It was nearly a month later before someone at AGP Translation finally looked at my account and refunded the charge. —[4]—. This unfortunate experience has led me to look into other translation options.

9. Who most likely is Ms. Kirby?
   (A) A marketing manager
   (B) A product tester
   (C) A video game designer
   (D) An accountant

10. What is true about Ms. Kirby?
    (A) She asks the translation team a lot of questions.
    (B) She often has to travel for work.
    (C) She uses the service for legal documents.
    (D) She speaks more than one language.

11. What problem does Ms. Kirby mention?
    (A) The customer service team was not knowledgeable.
    (B) Her complaint was not addressed promptly.
    (C) Translation fees increased dramatically.
    (D) She was not informed about a policy change.

12. In which of the positions marked [1], [2], [3], and [4] does the following sentence best belong?

    "This was not the case at all."

    (A) [1]
    (B) [2]
    (C) [3]
    (D) [4]

CHAPTER 4
—
PART 7
독해

UNIT 07

다중 지문

문제 미리보기

연계 문제 풀이 전략

빈출 유형 공략 이메일을 포함하는 삼중 지문 문제

ACTUAL TEST

UNIT 07

다중 지문

출제 경향
- 이중 지문 문제는 10문항이 출제되며, 거의 언제나 이메일/편지 지문을 포함한다. 가장 자주 출제되는 유형은 이메일-이메일이고 웹페이지-이메일, 기사-이메일, 광고-이메일 지문도 자주 출제된다. 추론/암시 문제가 90% 가까이 출제되며, 동의어 찾기, 주제/목적, NOT/True 문제의 순으로 출제된다. 문장 삽입 문제는 출제되지 않는다.
- 삼중 지문 문제는 15문항이 출제되며, 웹페이지-이메일-이메일과 이메일-이메일-양식/목록 등의 출제 빈도가 높다. 추론/암시 문제가 가장 많이 출제되며, 주제/목적, NOT/True 문제가 뒤를 잇는다. 문장 삽입 문제와 동의어 찾기 문제는 출제되지 않는다.

지문 미리보기

Question 1 refers to the following e-mail and memo.

Dear Ms. Beck,

I am writing on behalf of Lacy Schulte, one of the temporary workers on my team. Her current contract is set to expire on October 13, and I think we should offer her a permanent position at Rosemead Enterprises. Lacy has been a tremendous asset to the team. Her work on our new presentation software released in early September was invaluable. Because this program was very complicated, our hotline was very busy with customers who had tech problems. I was impressed with how Lacy handled these calls. As demand for our products is growing, it is essential for us to retain high-performing employees like Lacy.

Douglas Parr

MEMO

I am pleased to announce that Lacy Schulte will be permanently joining the Rosemead Enterprises staff from October 15. Many of you already know Ms. Schulte from her work on the technology support team. Ms. Schulte graduated with a bachelor's degree in computer science and moved to Austin for a temporary position at our firm. Ms. Schulte's lack of experience was easily balanced by her hard-working attitude and desire to learn more about the industry. She already has an in-depth knowledge of our latest software program, Acrex, which was launched in September.

---

1. What most likely is Acrex used for?

(A) Monitoring databases
(B) Preparing presentations
(C) Keeping financial records
(D) Processing text documents

지문의 연관 관계 파악
이메일과 회람으로 이루어진 이중 지문 문제는 이메일에서 논의된 내용을 회람에서 다른 사람들과 공유하는 방식으로 글의 흐름이 이어질 가능성이 높다.

다중 지문 연계 문제 풀이 과정
① 질문 확인
What most likely is Acrex used for?
② 첫 번째 단서 찾기
질문의 키워드인 Acrex로 지문을 검색한다. 회람 하단의 our latest software program, Acrex를 통해 Acrex가 소프트웨어라는 단서를 확보한다.
③ 두 번째 단서 찾기
두 번째 단서는 다른 지문에 나온다. 이메일 중반부의 our new presentation software를 통해 Acrex가 프레젠테이션용 소프트웨어라는 것을 확인하고 선택지를 확인한다.

| 미리보기 해석 |

> Beck 씨,
> 저희 팀의 임시 직원 중 한 명인 Lacy Schulte 씨를 대신해서 글을 씁니다. 그녀의 현재 계약은 10월 13일에 만료될 예정이며, 저는 그녀에게 Rosemead Enterprises의 정규직을 제안해야 한다고 생각합니다. Lacy는 우리 팀에 엄청난 자산이었습니다. 9월 초에 출시된 새로운 프레젠테이션 소프트웨어에 있어서 그녀가 한 일은 매우 소중했습니다. 이 프로그램은 매우 복잡했기 때문에, 당사의 상담 전화는 기술적인 문제를 겪는 고객들로 쉴 틈이 없었습니다. 저는 Lacy가 이러한 전화들을 처리하는 방식에 감탄했습니다. 우리 제품에 대한 수요가 증가하고 있기 때문에, Lacy와 같이 성과가 우수한 직원을 놓치지 않는 것은 꼭 필요한 일입니다.
> Douglas Parr

> 회람
> Lacy Schulte 씨가 10월 15일부터 Rosemead Enterprises의 정직원으로 합류한다는 것을 알리게 되어 기쁩니다. Schulte 씨는 기술 지원팀에서 근무하기 때문에 많은 분들이 이미 그녀를 알고 있을 겁니다. Schulte 씨는 컴퓨터 공학 학사 학위를 취득했고 오스틴으로 이사를 와서 우리 회사의 임시직으로 근무했습니다. Schulte 씨의 경험 부족은 그녀의 근면한 태도와 업계에 대해 더 많은 것을 배우고자 하는 열망에 의해 쉽게 상쇄되었습니다. 그녀는 9월에 출시된 당사의 최신 소프트웨어 프로그램인 Acrex에 대해 이미 심도 있는 지식을 가지고 있습니다.

1. Acrex는 어떤 용도로 사용되겠는가?
   (A) 데이터베이스 감시용
   (B) 프레젠테이션 준비용
   (C) 재무 기록 보관용
   (D) 텍스트 문서 처리용

연계 문제 풀이 전략

연계 문제는 질문에 나온 특정 키워드 검색을 통해 하나의 지문에서 단서를 찾고, 다른 지문에서 그 단서를 뒷받침하는 정보를 찾는 방식으로 문제 풀이가 이루어진다. 첫 번째 단서는 첫 번째 지문에 나올 수도 있지만, 두 번째나 세 번째 지문에 나올 수도 있다는 점에 주의한다. 연계 문제를 가장 손쉽게 해결할 수 있는 방법은 동일한 숫자와 *과 같은 기호를 찾는 것이다. 아래 예시와 같이 첫 번째 지문과 두 번째 지문에 공통으로 나오는 숫자 $550이 정답의 단서가 될 가능성이 높다.

첫 번째 지문
Booth sizes and fees are as follows:
- 12-foot-by-12-foot booth for $300
- 12-foot-by-16-foot booth for $400
- 16-foot-by-20-foot booth for $550
- 20-foot-by-20-foot booth for $700

질문
What size booth will Ms. Montgomery most likely use?
(A) A 12-foot-by-12-foot booth
(B) A 12-foot-by-16-foot booth
(✓) A 16-foot-by-20-foot booth
(D) A 20-foot-by-20-foot booth

두 번째 지문
I have sent my $550 booth reservation fee.

빈출 유형 공략: 이메일을 포함하는 삼중 지문 문제

해석 p.85

Questions 1-2 refer to the following e-mails and form.

To: Oliver Gilbert 〈olivergilbert@gahaenterprises.net〉
From: Edinburg Stadium 〈service@edinburgstadium.com〉
Date: December 12
Subject: Private Viewing Box

Dear Mr. Gilbert,

Thank you for booking a private viewing box at Edinburg Stadium for the upcoming year. This e-mail is to confirm that you have been assigned Box #B12, which can accommodate up to 20 people. You are allowed to decorate the box however you wish, and you can use it even if there is no game or other event going on that day. You will have access to the box from January 2 through to December 31.

We provide a range of VIP activities for box holders. For example, you can participate in a meet-and-greet session with one of the athletes on the home team following the game. ¹⁻¹A 30% discount is provided on your first VIP activity as a way to welcome you to our stadium. Early booking is recommended.

Warmest regards,

Ronny Anderson
Guest Services, Edinburg Stadium

연계 문제 1

STEP 1 질문 확인
1. What is suggested about Mr. Gilbert?

STEP 2 단서 확인
단서 1-1: Gilbert를 키워드로 지문을 검색하며, 그가 스스로에 대해 언급했거나 상대방이 그에게 한 말을 찾아본다. 첫 번째 지문에서 첫 번째로 VIP 활동을 하면 30%의 할인을 받는다는 단서를 찾는다.
단서 1-2: 세 번째 지문에서 Oliver Gilbert가 30% 할인을 받았다는 단서를 찾는다.

STEP 3 선택지 확인
(A) He would like to renew the box for next year.
(B) He needs to change a guest list.
(C) ✓ He is booking a VIP activity for the first time.
(D) He had overpaid for a previous event.

286 CHAPTER 4 PART 7 독해

VIP Activity Request Form

Name: Oliver Gilbert
Box Number: B12
E-mail: olivergilbert@gahaenterprises.net
Date of Request: February 13
Event: Meet-and-Greet with [2-1]Edinburg Tigers Pitcher Joseph Pollard

Note: VIP activities have limited availability. Please list your desired dates in preferred order, and we will do our best to accommodate you.

[2-3]Choice 1	March 31, Home team vs. Hazelwood Knights
Choice 2	April 14, Home team vs. Grand Rapids Lions
Choice 3	April 6, Home team vs. Wakefield Tornadoes

We will send you an e-mail within two business days of the request.

To: Oliver Gilbert ⟨olivergilbert@gahaenterprises.net⟩
From: Edinburg Stadium ⟨service@edinburgstadium.com⟩
Date: February 14
Subject: Your VIP Activity Request
Attachment: VIP#02895

Dear Mr. Gilbert,

Thank you for requesting a VIP Activity at Edinburg Stadium. [2-2]For the session with Joseph Pollard, I am pleased to inform you that we are able to schedule you for your top choice among the dates you suggested. Your account has already been charged. Please find attached the receipt for this transaction. You will note that [1-2]you have been given a 30% discount through our special offer. During the event, you will be served light refreshments at no additional charge. Should you wish to order any food or drink beyond that, please let me know at least three days before the event.

Ronny Anderson
Guest Services, Edinburg Stadium

연계 문제 2

STEP 1 질문 확인
2. When will Mr. Gilbert most likely get to meet Joseph Pollard?

STEP 2 단서 확인
단서 2-1: Joseph Pollard를 키워드로 지문을 검색하여 두 번째 지문에서 그가 Edinburg Tigers의 투수라는 단서를 찾는다.
단서 2-2: Joseph Pollard를 키워드로 검색하여 세 번째 지문에서 Gilbert 씨가 선택한 1순위 날짜에 만남이 이루어진다는 단서를 찾는다.
단서 2-3: 단서 2-2에서 언급된 top choice를 키워드로 지문을 검색한다. 두 번째 지문에서 1순위 날짜가 3월 31일이라는 것을 확인한다.

STEP 3 선택지 확인
(A) March 31 ✗
(B) April 6
(C) April 14
(D) April 22

ACTUAL TEST

Questions 1-5 refer to the following article and e-mail.

SACRAMENTO (October 7)—Trucking company Marinello has announced the addition of eighty new trucks to its fleet. Domestically manufactured in Fremont, the Colchester features a hybrid engine, making it more environmentally friendly. The trucks will be sent to the company's headquarters for inspection before being put to use.

Marinello has been growing steadily for the past five years and is on pace to become an industry leader. "We were thrilled to invest in these new vehicles because they are good for the environment and will reduce our spending on gasoline," said company representative Leah Byrd. "It is our aim to equip thirty of the units with a refrigeration system. The rest will provide deliveries of goods that do not need to be kept at a certain temperature."

To:	Rahul Marwah ⟨r.marwah@swansonmetals.com⟩
From:	Walter Donovan ⟨donovan_wal@marinello.com⟩
Date:	October 30
Subject:	Deliveries

Dear Mr. Marwah,

Thank you for your ongoing patronage, and I hope you are fully satisfied with our delivery service. You are currently getting regular deliveries with our old delivery trucks. However, I think you should switch to our newest truck model. They are slightly larger, so they can fit more items in them, resulting in fewer deliveries.

The trucks have just finished their safety inspections in Portland. Therefore, as early as next week they could be used for the next delivery to your warehouse in Salem. You would need more time to unload the truck because of the additional goods. Please let me know if this is what you would like to do.

Sincerely,

Walter Donovan
Logistics Manager, Marinello

1. What is the Colchester?

   (A) A passenger van
   (B) A cargo ship
   (C) A truck model
   (D) A refrigerator brand

2. What is indicated about the Colchester?

   (A) It is sold internationally.
   (B) It was created by Marinello.
   (C) It is popular in the industry.
   (D) It will save on fuel costs.

3. In the article, the word "aim" in paragraph 2, line 4, is closest in meaning to

   (A) direction
   (B) intention
   (C) requirement
   (D) set

4. What is the purpose of the e-mail?

   (A) To recommend a change
   (B) To confirm a delivery time
   (C) To explain a delay
   (D) To modify an order

5. Where is Marinello's headquarters most likely located?

   (A) In Sacramento
   (B) In Fremont
   (C) In Portland
   (D) In Salem

Questions 6-10 refer to the following flyer and e-mails.

Carolina Cleaning
Serving Lexington for nearly 30 years!

Keep your buildings looking their best by having the main areas for tenants, such as hallways and lobbies, professionally cleaned. Regular cleaning not only helps to maintain the condition of your investment but also provides an enjoyable atmosphere for everyone living on site. You can select the service package that best suits your needs.

Economy Cleaning: Daily vacuuming and dusting of carpets in hallways and lobby
Standard Cleaning: All services included in Economy Cleaning as well as trash removal from shared areas and watering of plants
Standard Cleaning Plus: All services included in Standard Cleaning as well as cleaning the ground-floor windows, both inside and out
Comprehensive Cleaning: All services listed above as well as complete cleaning of a unit when someone moves out and steam-cleaning for carpets in public areas annually

To receive a quote based on your specific needs, please contact info@carolinacleaning.com.

E-Mail Message

From: richardatwood@whittingtonltd.com
To: info@carolinacleaning.com
Date: September 9
Subject: Need for cleaning services

To Whom It May Concern:

I own two apartment buildings in Lexington and am considering using your cleaning services. I saw your promotional flyer and was especially interested in hiring your company since you have been in business for a long time.

The work would be carried out at the Mallett Apartments in the Bedford neighborhood and the Valley Apartments in the Jackson neighborhood. Each building is five stories tall and has a lobby on the first floor. We would need your cleaning team to dust and vacuum the hallways and lobbies each day. We would also like you to collect our trash and take care of a few potted plants in the lobbies.

Please provide a cost estimate at your earliest convenience so that I can make a decision.

Sincerely,

Richard Atwood

From: info@carolinacleaning.com
To: richardatwood@whittingtonltd.com
Date: September 10
Subject: RE: Need for cleaning services
Attachment: Testimonial1

Dear Mr. Atwood,

Thank you for your interest in services from Carolina Cleaning. We would love the opportunity to provide you with a price quote for the work. Please let me know when you would be free for an in-person visit. One of our cleaners can assess the size of the areas needing cleaning and determine their condition.

In the meantime, please feel free to read the attached testimonial from Courtney Armstrong, one of our satisfied customers. She is the owner of the Gastonia Apartment Complex, which is right across the street from the Mallett Apartments.

I look forward to hearing from you.

Danielle Snyder

Business Manager, Carolina Cleaning

6. Who most likely is the intended audience of the flyer?

(A) Bankers
(B) Landlords
(C) Retail managers
(D) Job seekers

7. What does Mr. Atwood particularly like about Carolina Cleaning?

(A) It uses eco-friendly practices.
(B) It received good reviews.
(C) It is well-established.
(D) It is affordable.

8. Which service package will Mr. Atwood probably use?

(A) Economy Cleaning
(B) Standard Cleaning
(C) Standard Cleaning Plus
(D) Comprehensive Cleaning

9. What does Ms. Snyder ask Mr. Atwood to do?

(A) Sign a contract
(B) Send her the buildings' measurements
(C) Report on his availability
(D) Provide some photographs

10. What is suggested about Ms. Armstrong?

(A) She used to live in the Jackson neighborhood.
(B) She is interested in moving into Mallett Apartments.
(C) She owns a building in the Bedford neighborhood.
(D) She will schedule a visit with Mr. Atwood.

toeic.eduwill.net

RC

실전
모의고사

실전 모의고사 1회

실전 모의고사 2회

실전 모의고사 3회

ANSWER SHEET

실전 모의고사 1회

정답 및 해설 p.89

READING TEST

In the Reading test, you will read a variety of texts and answer several different types of reading comprehension questions. The entire Reading test will last 75 minutes. There are three parts, and directions are given for each part. You are encouraged to answer as many questions as possible within the time allowed.

You must mark your answers on the separate answer sheet. Do not write your answers in your test book.

PART 5

Directions: A word or phrase is missing in each of the sentences below. Four answer choices are given below each sentence. Select the best answer to complete the sentence. Then mark the letter (A), (B), (C), or (D) on your answer sheet.

101. Consumers should be aware of ------- impact on the environment.
    (A) their
    (B) them
    (C) they
    (D) theirs

102. The lecture begins at 6 P.M. sharp, so it is important for audience members to be -------.
    (A) urgent
    (B) punctual
    (C) brief
    (D) instant

103. Ms. Kelsey explained to the customer the ------- of overcharging his battery.
    (A) endanger
    (B) dangerous
    (C) dangers
    (D) endangered

104. The weather forecast predicted heavy rains ------- early morning until late at night.
    (A) at
    (B) from
    (C) on
    (D) between

105. If you recently ------- a vehicle from Kobayashi Motors, please visit our Web site to make sure it hasn't been recalled.
    (A) bought
    (B) buy
    (C) to buy
    (D) buying

106. The floor manager keeps ------- running smoothly at the factory.
    (A) operate
    (B) operationally
    (C) operations
    (D) operative

107. Pete's Paninis ------- changes its menu to keep diners interested in its offerings.
    (A) solidly
    (B) righteously
    (C) superficially
    (D) regularly

108. The Ichigawa Pet Store is famous for its collection of ------- iguanas.
    (A) spots
    (B) spot
    (C) spotting
    (D) spotted

109. The taxi fee from the hotel to the airport is ------- $15.
(A) approximation
(B) approximating
(C) approximately
(D) approximate

110. Even after months of planning for the building redesign, Mr. Lenape ------- isn't certain which direction to go in.
(A) still
(B) before
(C) later
(D) besides

111. After interviewing all the candidates, we will select the ------- that we feel will best fit the role.
(A) who
(B) some
(C) other
(D) one

112. User testing with the toy prototype resulted in the need for major -------.
(A) scales
(B) revisions
(C) deviations
(D) reminders

113. Our client had difficulty choosing ------- the modern design and the traditional design for their new advertising campaign.
(A) between
(B) as
(C) that
(D) whether

114. Curious customers often ------- how Real Recyclables is able to make such high-quality products from old materials.
(A) deliberate
(B) suggest
(C) wonder
(D) compete

115. Lola's Apparel is ------- one of the most successful retail chains in South America.
(A) argue
(B) arguably
(C) arguing
(D) arguable

116. Motorcycle riders are required to wear helmets ------- of skill level.
(A) therefore
(B) whenever
(C) despite
(D) regardless

117. The bank advises customers to keep track of all ------- while traveling abroad to avoid overspending.
(A) preventions
(B) precautions
(C) surroundings
(D) transactions

118. Because of a ------- of hiking boots, KLP Camping is holding a major sale.
(A) surplus
(B) type
(C) limitation
(D) centralization

119. MHG & Sons' CEO is always ------- to new ideas, even if they come from new recruits.
(A) openness
(B) openly
(C) open
(D) opening

120. It seems like Krazy Kola can be found -------, including remote parts of the world.
(A) everywhere
(B) sometimes
(C) consequently
(D) furthermore

GO ON TO THE NEXT PAGE

121. Tingley Travel has introduced ------- to Europe for groups of up to thirty people.
(A) excursions
(B) settlements
(C) institutions
(D) accomplishments

122. With our service, customers can now order fully ------- furniture for their living spaces.
(A) proposed
(B) discovered
(C) assembled
(D) listed

123. ------- the transaction is complete, the person who requested the transfer will receive a message confirming the deposit.
(A) Once
(B) Although
(C) Still
(D) While

124. The study proved that participants who practiced yoga ------- reported better flexibility than those who did not.
(A) consistently
(B) most consistent
(C) consistent
(D) consistency

125. When ------, employees stated flexible hours as one of the main reasons they enjoyed working for DFT International.
(A) to ask
(B) ask
(C) asked
(D) asking

126. Ms. Kay did well on her presentation ------- it was her first attempt at public speaking at her new job.
(A) considering
(B) however
(C) as if
(D) so that

127. All discarded confidential files are collected and shredded in a room -------.
(A) throughout
(B) anywhere
(C) upstairs
(D) near

128. There doesn't seem to be any arguments ------- changing the company policy to include three extra sick days.
(A) because
(B) against
(C) during
(D) as

129. Residents of Belleview are encouraged to -------- any old blankets or pillows to the local animal shelter.
(A) lease
(B) admit
(C) donate
(D) transfer

130. Since Mr. Choi had the best voice, he was in charge of ------- the project.
(A) maintaining
(B) exposing
(C) targeting
(D) narrating

PART 6

Directions: Read the texts that follow. A word, phrase, or sentence is missing in parts of each text. Four answer choices for each question are given below the text. Select the best answer to complete the text. Then mark the letter (A), (B), (C), or (D) on your answer sheet.

Questions 131-134 refer to the following e-mail.

To: Simone Onochie
From: customerservice@sportshere.com
Date: 29 March
Subject: Your recent order (No. 8744463628)

Dear Ms. Onochie,

Thank you for ordering from Sports Here! Your nylon shorts in the color caramel have been shipped. -------. To check the status of your delivery, head over to
                    131.
www.sportshere.com/myorder/track and input your order number.

We are sure you'll love our products, but in order to guarantee customer satisfaction, we -------
                                                                                              132.
that you fill out a short survey at www.sportshere.com/survey. Thanks to valuable feedback from our customers, we are ------- to provide excellent service. After you ------- the survey, a
                                   133.   **134.**
coupon for 10% off your next order will be sent to your e-mail. Happy spending!

Sports Here! Customer Service

---

131. (A) You can expect your package within 3-4 business days.
(B) We're sorry, but exchanges are not available.
(C) Bring your receipt to any Sports Here! store for a refund.
(D) We will e-mail you when your replacement item is sent.

132. (A) requested
(B) request
(C) had requested
(D) were requesting

133. (A) careful
(B) manageable
(C) able
(D) allowed

134. (A) complete
(B) demonstrate
(C) explain
(D) publish

GO ON TO THE NEXT PAGE

Questions 135-138 refer to the following information.

The private room in Riley's Café can be booked for all your personal meeting needs. Have a study session, after-hours work party, or any other kind of celebration with the ------- of Riley's
                                                                                                                                                                135.
coffee and treats only a few steps away. Visit www.rileyscafe.com/reservation ------- a time slot.
                                                                                                          136.
If your preferred time slot is open, your reservation will be confirmed. A $10 deposit is required. If you have a specific event you are planning, it is highly ------- that you reserve the room well in
                                                                                                          137.
advance to avoid missing your chance. -------.
                                               138.
We look forward to having you!

135. (A) surprise
(B) rescue
(C) convenience
(D) determination

136. (A) to request
(B) requesting
(C) is requesting
(D) requested

137. (A) guaranteed
(B) encouraged
(C) implied
(D) denied

138. (A) Additionally, please note that guests are responsible for their own cleanup.
(B) Therefore, you should anticipate spending a lot of money.
(C) Thank you for coming to today's grand opening.
(D) Prizes will be available for contestants who answer questions correctly.

Questions 139-142 refer to the following notice.

Attention, Markswell Employees:

This is a reminder that next Thursday, June 27, we will be moving to the ninth floor of our current building. All large items such as desks, computers, printers, and chairs ------- by the movers. Personal items, however, must be moved on an individual basis. ------- moving to your new space, we recommend cleaning it first before reorganizing your things. -------, please pay attention to the movements of others so as to avoid any accidents. -------. Thank you for your cooperation.

139. (A) handle
(B) handled
(C) will handle
(D) will be handled

140. (A) When
(B) As
(C) Plus
(D) Where

141. (A) However
(B) Therefore
(C) Additionally
(D) Similarly

142. (A) Let's make this transition as smooth as possible.
(B) Don't forget to submit your vacation request.
(C) Leave your suggestions in the box at the front desk.
(D) The move was a great success thanks to your hard work.

Questions 143-146 refer to the following memo.

To: All employees
From: Mai Hoan, Owner of Central Records
Subject: Open Mic Coordinator
Date: April 17

To All Staff,

This announcement will be featured in tomorrow's paper, but I wanted to make you all aware first. Following the ------- of the Open Mic last Saturday, Central Records has decided to host a monthly Open Mic series. As such, we are looking for an Open Mic Coordinator to organize and carry out the monthly events. The selected candidate ------- working for June's Open Mic, continuing for all subsequent Open Mic events.

-------. Previous on-the-job experience working with bands is essential. ------- Central Records staff are highly encouraged to apply. Please contact me for more details about the position.

Sincerely,

Mai Hoan

143. (A) pressure
(B) success
(C) dissatisfaction
(D) surprise

144. (A) will begin
(B) begin
(C) has begun
(D) was beginning

145. (A) We are still deciding how often to hold the events.
(B) The interview panel was impressed with the candidates.
(C) Please note that this is not an entry-level position.
(D) Most people seemed to enjoy the Open Mic performances.

146. (A) Interested
(B) Suspected
(C) Prestigious
(D) Observed

PART 7
Directions: In this part you will read a selection of texts, such as magazine and newspaper articles, e-mails, and instant messages. Each text or set of texts is followed by several questions. Select the best answer for each question and mark the letter (A), (B), (C), or (D) on your answer sheet.

Questions 147-148 refer to the following notice.

Attention, Moncrieff Suitcase Customers!

As part of our effort to reduce waste, Moncrieff Suitcase will now offer repairs on any items in our product line. For example, we can replace damaged handles, broken zippers, and missing wheels. Get your suitcase fixed at a fraction of the cost of buying a new one. Our specialist, Joseph Osburne, will be on site from Tuesday through Saturday. He can inspect your bag and give you a free quote before any work begins.

147. Why was the notice written?
(A) To announce a new service
(B) To promote a warranty offer
(C) To give advice on suitcase shopping
(D) To introduce a popular product

148. What will Mr. Osburne provide to customers?
(A) A store voucher code
(B) A product demonstration
(C) A free cost estimate
(D) A sales receipt

Questions 149-150 refer to the following e-mail.

═══════════════════════ E-Mail Message ═══════════════════════

To: Lori Carmona <lcarmona@duncanfashions.com>
From: Howard Monroe <howard@gloryincorporated.com>
Date: January 8
Subject: Glory Incorporated

Dear Ms. Carmona,

Every year, Glory Incorporated holds a brief phone meeting with each of our clients to check that our service is satisfactory and identify possible ways that we can assist in supporting their business. We understand that hiring staff for international branches can be difficult. That's why we thoroughly investigate the career background and skills of anyone we put forward for your open positions, only connecting you with the most experienced people.

Please let me know when would be a convenient time to call you.

All the best,

Howard Monroe

149. Why does Mr. Monroe want to arrange a phone call with Ms. Carmona?

(A) To identify investment opportunities
(B) To assess her company's needs
(C) To introduce a new service
(D) To arrange some branch visits

150. How does Mr. Monroe's business most likely help Ms. Carmona business?

(A) By investigating fashion trends
(B) By providing tax advice for international branches
(C) By recruiting qualified staff members for positions
(D) By finding properties for new offices

Questions 151-152 refer to the following article.

LAKEWOOD (March 3)—The city of Lakewood has announced that motorists crossing Westbury Bridge will soon have to pay a toll. Following vigorous debate at a recent city council meeting, the decision was made to impose the fee, with a vote of 11 to 3. Work to install tollbooths will begin on March 20, and the charges will begin from March 31. Cars and motorcycles will pay $4 to cross the bridge. Larger vehicles will be charged according to their size, with oversized freight trucks paying up to $20 to cross.

Ever since it was built by the city more than 40 years ago, the Westbury Bridge has been free to all drivers. However, the heavy use of the bridge has contributed to the need for increasingly frequent repairs. With these rising costs, the council had no choice but to find a way to fund the bridge.

A "Fast Pass" system is being considered, and locals are encouraged to share their opinions about this at the April 20 council meeting.

151. When will a new regulation go into effect?

(A) On March 3
(B) On March 20
(C) On March 31
(D) On April 20

152. According to the article, what prompted officials to make a change?

(A) Overloaded freight trucks
(B) Increasing repair costs
(C) A lack of business taxes
(D) Pressure from environmental groups

GO ON TO THE NEXT PAGE

Questions 153-154 refer to the following text-message chain.

Victoria Melrose (9:05 A.M.)
Hi, Ethan and Oscar. I know we were supposed to have our team meeting today at 11, but are you free at 2 instead?

Oscar Prentice (9:06 A.M.)
Sure. I can be there.

Ethan Clayborn (9:08 A.M.)
Me too. Was there a problem reserving the conference room?

Victoria Melrose (9:09 A.M.)
No, but Jamie has a medical appointment. I don't want anyone to miss the meeting.

Oscar Prentice (9:10 A.M.)
That makes sense. I've already printed the agendas, though, and they say eleven o'clock. I can reprint them if you'd like.

Victoria Melrose (9:11 A.M.)
Thanks, but that's not necessary.

153. Why does Ms. Melrose want to change a meeting time?
(A) She has not prepared the materials.
(B) A staff member cannot attend at that time.
(C) A meeting room has been double-booked.
(D) A client has requested the change.

154. At 9:11 A.M., what does Ms. Melrose probably mean when she writes, "that's not necessary"?
(A) She can change her medical appointment.
(B) She has already selected a meeting site.
(C) The current documents can be used.
(D) The printer does not need to be replaced.

Questions 155-157 refer to the following instructions.

Macon Footwear
Caring for your Macon Sheepskin Slippers

Thank you for your purchase. With the correct care, your Macon Sheepskin Slippers will last for many years.

Before wearing the slippers, we recommend using a protective spray for the suede exterior of the slippers. This will create a barrier to prevent water from getting in. Follow the instructions on the spray can, and reapply the spray as necessary. When you are not wearing the slippers, use the cardboard wedges provided. Place one inside each slipper to help them maintain their shape.

To remove dirt, brush the outside of the slippers gently with a wire brush. Do not brush over any embroidered sections of the slipper, as this could spoil the design. For tough stains, dip a soft cotton cloth in white vinegar and dab the area. As natural sheepskin has a tendency to absorb odors, air out the slippers frequently. This is especially effective outdoors, but it must be done in the shade. Otherwise, prolonged exposure to sunlight may cause fading.

155. Why does the company recommend using a spray?

(A) To make the surface easy to clean
(B) To reduce odors
(C) To keep moisture out
(D) To reduce color fading

156. What is NOT mentioned as a tip in the instructions?

(A) Airing out the slippers regularly
(B) Brushing the embroidery gently
(C) Keeping the slippers out of direct sunlight
(D) Putting an insert in after use

157. The word "spoil" in paragraph 3, line 2, is closest in meaning to

(A) indulge
(B) damage
(C) disappoint
(D) decay

GO ON TO THE NEXT PAGE

Questions 158-160 refer to the following notice.

Attention All Speakers for the Titan Annual Tech Conference:

Upon arrival, you should report to Alana Sheppard, the event planner. The staff at the registration desk will be able to tell you where to find her. Ms. Sheppard will collect your presentation materials to be distributed later. She will also direct you to the stage, where you can do a sound check and make sure your slideshow is working properly. If you have any special requests, such as the placement of the podium, please let her know. Please note that a photographer from the *Bloomfield Herald* will be taking photos during the event, as the newspaper will carry an article about it the following day.

All presenters will remain offstage until their turn, but they may watch other presentations from backstage. Following the presentations, all participants will be served dinner in the banquet hall. There will be a special table and seat reserved for you. Simply look for your name card.

Should you have any issues or concerns, please call Ms. Sheppard at 555-3019. Thank you.

158. Why was the notice written?
 (A) To recruit volunteers for an event
 (B) To assign tasks to conference staff
 (C) To inform presenters about a procedure
 (D) To remind participants about regulations

159. The word "carry" in paragraph 1, line 7, is closest in meaning to
 (A) publish
 (B) hold
 (C) transport
 (D) accept

160. What is indicated about the Titan Annual Tech Conference?
 (A) It is exclusively designed for business owners.
 (B) It is held at the same site every year.
 (C) It includes a meal for attendees.
 (D) It does not require advance registration.

Questions 161-163 refer to the following article.

AUGUSTA (February 10)—The city of Augusta has been working hard to attract new businesses to the area to support the local economy. —[1]—. One such business, interior design firm Chic Choices, has announced plans to move from its current offices in Waynesboro to a commercial unit in the Highland Office Complex here in Augusta. —[2]—. The firm is expecting to have a full-time staff of at least fifteen people, and additional temporary workers will be hired during the peak season. The company's owner, Angela Strom, is dedicated to using local suppliers for as many goods as possible, which means that most of the revenue generated by the business will stay in Augusta.

Chic Choices currently specializes in home renovations, but it has plans to expand to commercial projects as well, which could mean even more job creation. —[3]—. The renovation process is made easy through the firm's unique software, a program called Wave-360. Photos of a room can be uploaded into the program. Then the room can be "decorated" virtually, letting the customer view what the room would look like before beginning the project. However, the firm does not just work virtually. It will have a 2,500-square-foot showroom for customers to browse carpet, tiles, paint, and more. Its current showroom is less than half that size. —[4]—.

161. What is the article mainly about?

(A) The history of a business founder
(B) Trends in the interior design industry
(C) The benefits of a company relocation
(D) Changes to local business policies

162. What does the Wave-360 program allow users to do?

(A) Calculate the cost of home renovations
(B) Take accurate photos of a room
(C) Receive recommendations for color combinations
(D) See potential changes to a room

163. In which of the positions marked [1], [2], [3], and [4] does the following sentence best belong?

"Now people can check out a greater number of samples than ever."

(A) [1]
(B) [2]
(C) [3]
(D) [4]

GO ON TO THE NEXT PAGE

Questions 164-167 refer to the following e-mail.

From:	Sebastian Dwyer
To:	Gabrielle Redmond
Date:	April 8
Subject:	Ainsley Manor
Attachment:	Ainsley Manor Photos

Dear Gabrielle,

I've finally had a chance to visit Ainsley Manor, and I think it may be a great site for shooting our commercial. The historic building looks impressive from the outside. The fountain in front of the house is operational, and it creates a peaceful mood. Using the rear of the building would also be an option. There is a large rock garden as well as a few bronze statues. The flowerbeds were covered because frost is expected tonight, but I'm sure they would look fine as well.

Because the house is located so close to a major highway, I was concerned that there would be too much noise from the traffic passing by. Fortunately, there is a long line of bushes, so this isn't an issue. Some of the trees on the property, however, do not look very healthy. I spoke to a staff member about this, and he said they could be trimmed to remove any discolored parts.

To contain the cost of using this site, we should try to get all of our shots done in half a day. It would take a lot of planning, but that would help us stay within our budget. Let's discuss this further at our next meeting.

Sincerely,

Sebastian Dwyer

164. What is the purpose of the e-mail?
(A) To recommend an attraction for a tour
(B) To suggest a company outing
(C) To oppose the purchase of a commercial property
(D) To express support for a filming site

165. What is NOT something that Mr. Dwyer viewed in person?
(A) Some flowerbeds
(B) Some statues
(C) A fountain
(D) A rock garden

166. What problem did Mr. Dwyer raise with an employee?
(A) The cost of renting a property is too high.
(B) The trees are in poor condition.
(C) The traffic noise is very disruptive.
(D) The building should be painted.

167. The word "contain" in paragraph 3, line 1, is closest in meaning to
(A) consist of
(B) keep down
(C) retain
(D) enclose

Questions 168-171 refer to the following online chat discussion.

Caroline Ingram (5:12 P.M.)	Thanks for the help in rewriting the employee handbook. I know it's late on a Friday, but I wanted to check in to make sure everyone's tasks are still on track because the new employees are coming on Wednesday next week. I've finished the text for the company history, so I could help with something else, if needed.
Eric Hale (5:14 P.M.)	I've made sure all of the policy information is current, especially since we've changed the way that internal committees work. I still need to proofread it, but I can send it before I leave today.
Andre Silva (5:15 P.M.)	Most of the facility's information is also completed, but I need some help. I can't draw a map of the building because I don't have any design programs installed on my computer.
Caroline Ingram (5:16 P.M.)	That's fine, Andre. You can use the map from the company's Web site since I just updated it yesterday.
Eric Hale (5:17 P.M.)	This will be a big print job. Someone should call the print shop to ensure we can get overnight service when we submit the final draft on Monday afternoon.
Andre Silva (5:18 P.M.)	I'm on it.

168. What has Ms. Ingram written about?

(A) The business's background
(B) Workplace policies
(C) Facility information
(D) Employee benefits

169. Why does Mr. Silva need some assistance?

(A) He has not been trained for a task.
(B) He does not have the right software.
(C) He has another urgent project to finish.
(D) He lost some important files.

170. When did Ms. Ingram update a map online?

(A) On Monday
(B) On Wednesday
(C) On Thursday
(D) On Friday

171. At 5:18 P.M., what does Mr. Silva most likely mean when he writes, "I'm on it"?

(A) He will proofread a draft.
(B) He will repair a printer.
(C) He will attend an orientation.
(D) He will contact a business.

GO ON TO THE NEXT PAGE

Questions 172-175 refer to the following article.

IFSA Taking On Global Challenges
By Jeremiah Roark

SAN DIEGO (March 20)—The International Food Safety Association (IFSA) will hold its annual conference August 3–5, bringing together specialists, policymakers, and business owners from over 40 countries. —[1]—. The conference will teach people how to enact and follow practices that help to ensure safe food for everyone worldwide. The IFSA hopes to give people in the field a chance to meet and share their knowledge, fostering partnerships in both the public and private sectors. A series of presentations and workshops will showcase cutting-edge technology, allowing participants to prepare for the future and make the industry more trustworthy for consumers.

To ensure widespread participation, and to reduce pollution from unnecessary traveling, the conference will be held entirely through videoconferencing. Participants only need a stable Internet connection. —[2]—. There will also be an opportunity to rewatch some parts of the conference on the IFSA Web site later.

"I'm looking forward to this year's event," said Uta Holzman, owner of Arbor Supermarket. "The insights from last year were invaluable, and I've already applied them to my business. —[3]—. But I am just an individual. With the world population growing so quickly, we need a coordinated effort to solve the problem of food safety, so I'm glad that a conference like this exists."

The IFSA is also looking ahead to next year's event, and those who would like to contribute their expertise are encouraged to contact Angelica Lucchesi at a.lucchesi@ifsa.org. —[4]—.

172. What is the purpose of the article?

(A) To announce the winners of an industry award
(B) To emphasize the need for new regulations
(C) To promote an educational business event
(D) To highlight safety issues in the food supply

173. What is NOT indicated as a goal of the IFSA?

(A) Introducing new technology
(B) Building consumer trust
(C) Increasing jobs in the sector
(D) Creating networking opportunities

174. What is true about Ms. Holzman?

(A) Her expertise is in food-handling procedures.
(B) Her business has been growing steadily.
(C) She thinks people should focus on working together.
(D) She wants to work in the public sector.

175. In which of the positions marked [1], [2], [3], and [4] does the following sentence best belong?

"They will be able to view the activities live and comment in real time."

(A) [1]
(B) [2]
(C) [3]
(D) [4]

Questions 176-180 refer to the following memo and form.

MEMO

To: Planning Committee Members
From: Hilda Geiger
Subject: Reimbursement procedures
Date: April 19

I would like to remind you about Acosta Finance's reimbursement policy as we prepare for the arrival of our visitors from the Tokyo branch on May 10. As we make arrangements for the welcome reception for these important company representatives, please keep the company's reimbursement policy in mind. Because company credit cards are only issued to department directors, other employees will need to pay for the items themselves first and request reimbursement. Small transactions of less than $10.00 will be reimbursed in cash when you submit your form. Anything over that amount will be deposited to your bank account on the same day as your next paycheck.

Please be sure to keep the budget in mind. The reception should not make up more than 10% of our annual event budget. Otherwise, we may have to cancel some employee appreciation events later in the year. If you are unsure about any of the tasks you have been assigned, please contact me directly or feel free to bring them up in the next event planning meeting.

I appreciate your hard work on this committee.

Acosta Finance Employee Expense Form

Name: Sheila Hale
Submission Date: May 3
Reason for Purchase(s): Welcome reception
Approved by: Hilda Geiger

Date of Purchase	Amount	Business Name	Description
May 1	$238.50	Diaz Catering	Food order
May 1	$5.95	Party Palace	Balloons
May 2	$34.99	Ace Printing	Welcome banner
May 2	$55.00	Lena Electronics	Portable speakers
May 2	$11.25	A2B Taxis	Ride to shopping center
May 2	$12.85	A2B Taxis	Return trip to office

Please include all receipts for the above purchases.

176. What does Ms. Geiger say will happen on May 10?
(A) A new company policy will go into effect.
(B) A new staff member will be introduced.
(C) Some job candidates will be interviewed.
(D) Some VIP guests will visit the office.

177. What is mentioned about company credit cards?
(A) They do not require the user to keep a receipt.
(B) They are only issued to department heads.
(C) They will be given to committee members soon.
(D) They can be picked up in Ms. Geiger's office.

178. In the memo, the phrase "make up" in paragraph 2, line 1, is closest in meaning to
(A) prepare
(B) invent
(C) agree
(D) comprise

179. Which business's charge will NOT be included in Ms. Hale's next paycheck?
(A) Diaz Catering
(B) Party Palace
(C) Ace Printing
(D) Lena Electronics

180. What did Ms. Hale most likely do on May 3?
(A) Made a copy of a credit card statement
(B) Submitted receipts for transportation
(C) Contacted another committee member
(D) Traveled to a shopping center

Questions 181-185 refer to the following Web page and e-mail.

http://www.ryriesupplies.com

The food industry is highly competitive, and the best way to build brand loyalty for the products you make is to provide consistency. With silicone baking mats from Ryrie Supplies, you can ensure even heat distribution, giving you the same results every time. Our mats can be frozen to -40°F or baked up to 480°F, so you can rest assured that there will be no cracking or melting, no matter what your project may require. Our mats are available in a variety of sizes, as below.

Model Name	Gaffney	Jimna	Marloo	Quinton
Width	35 cm	30 cm	42 cm	40 cm
Length	20 cm	42 cm	62 cm	55 cm
Thickness	0.75 mm	0.65 mm	0.95 mm	0.80 mm

To:	Erma Shahan <ermashahan@ryriesupplies.com>
From:	Walter Davila <w_davila@miramarinc.com>
Date:	June 19
Subject:	Miramar Inc. order

Dear Ms. Shahan,

I'd like to let you know that we will not be submitting an order at this time as we usually do. We have a new manager joining the company next month, so all of our ordering is currently on hold. We have been using your thinnest mat for about six months, and we are very pleased with it. However, we are currently developing a new product to be released next year, and we think a thicker one might be better. Would you be able to send a few samples of the Quinton model? Of course, I will experiment with options from a few different companies to see which one is most suitable.

Kindest regards,

Walter Davila

181. Where most likely would Ryrie Supplies' products be used?

(A) In storage facilities
(B) In pharmaceutical factories
(C) In commercial kitchens
(D) In financial institutions

182. What is indicated about the Ryrie Supplies' products?

(A) They can be rolled up to save storage space.
(B) They should be handled with special gloves.
(C) They are made from recycled materials.
(D) They can withstand a wide range of temperatures.

183. According to Mr. Davila, when will a new manager start working at Miramar Inc.?

(A) In June
(B) In July
(C) In six months
(D) Next year

184. Which model is Miramar Inc. currently using?

(A) Gaffney
(B) Jimna
(C) Marloo
(D) Quinton

185. What is suggested about Mr. Davila?

(A) He needs to use a new shipping address.
(B) He will leave the company soon.
(C) He plans to try different brands.
(D) He is dissatisfied with the current product.

GO ON TO THE NEXT PAGE

Questions 186-190 refer to the following e-mails and schedule.

To:	All Derosa Inc. Staff
From:	Priya Kapil
Date:	June 8
Subject:	Free workshops

Dear Staff,

Next month, our company will hold a series of professional development workshops. They will take place in the evenings, so there will be no interruptions to your regular work duties. A catered meal will be provided. For each session, there are some articles and information packets that you should look over in advance to save time. Your attendance will have a positive effect on your annual performance evaluation.

If you are interested in the workshops, please e-mail Masaru Akita at m.akita@derosa.com, as he is in charge of registering participants.

Thank you,

Priya Kapil

\multicolumn{4}{	c	}{Professional Development Opportunities for Derosa Inc. Staff}
Date	Presenter	Title	Notes
July 6	Brandon Thomas, Marketing Director	How to Influence Others	Build professional relationships and lead teams with these techniques.
July 13	Masaru Akita, Assistant Manager	Navigating Changes in the Workplace	Improve your skills in adapting to new situations quickly.
July 20	Priya Kapil, HR Director	Time Management Tips	Make the most of your schedule, no matter what your role is.
July 26	Veronica Shapiro, General Manager	Creative Problem-Solving	Learn to "think outside the box" when problems arise.

E-Mail Message

To: Priya Kapil
From: Aurora Reutter
Date: July 27
Subject: Workshop

Dear Ms. Kapil,

I'd like to thank you and the other people who planned the company's professional development opportunities. I learned a lot at yesterday's session. I liked the examples the instructor used from the book *Business Blast*. In fact, the members of my discussion group plan to meet at lunchtime on the first Tuesday of every month to work through the rest of the activities in the book. Would it be possible for you to announce these temporary meetings on the company's online calendar so that other employees can join in if they wish?

Thank you!

Aurora Reutter

---

186. What does the first e-mail suggest about the workshops?
(A) Their sessions will last for approximately one hour.
(B) Their participants will complete an evaluation at the end.
(C) They will take place outside of business hours.
(D) They are mainly aimed at the management team.

187. What should participants do prior to the workshops?
(A) Send questions to presenters
(B) Submit dietary restrictions
(C) Get a supervisor's approval
(D) Review some reading materials

188. Who is responsible for registration?
(A) The general manager
(B) The assistant manager
(C) The HR director
(D) The marketing director

189. Which workshop did Ms. Reutter attend?
(A) How to Influence Others
(B) Navigating Changes in the Workplace
(C) Time Management Tips
(D) Creative Problem-Solving

190. What does Ms. Reutter ask Ms. Kapil to do?
(A) Provide a list of group members
(B) Reserve a meeting space
(C) Post some information online
(D) Suggest a workshop topic

GO ON TO THE NEXT PAGE

Questions 191-195 refer to the following e-mail, Web page, and advertisement.

To:	Design Team ⟨design@orono.net⟩
From:	Joan Elliot ⟨jelliot@orono.net⟩
Date:	October 30
Subject:	New staff member

Dear Design Team,

We are pleased to welcome a new employee to our team, Ms. Marianne Noland. She will be working on graphic designs to help Jerome Perez keep up with the increased demand for our O700 line. Marianne has her own freelance graphic design business, so she will only be working part-time for Orono. She will occasionally work in the office, but the majority of her projects for Orono will be done from home.

We are excited about Marianne's potential contributions to our company. She has an impressive portfolio of work for commercial projects as well as nonprofit organizations, including the Prima Group, which she founded with two of her friends.

We will hold a small welcome reception on November 4, at 9:30 A.M., in the break room. Tea, coffee, and doughnuts will be served, and Marianne will briefly introduce herself. We hope you will all take the opportunity to meet Marianne. There is no need to RSVP. Simply come to the break room at the appointed time.

Thank you,

Joan Elliot

---

http://www.nolanddesign.com/about

Noland Design
Custom graphic designs to suit your business and your budget!

About: Marianne Noland received a bachelor's degree in graphic design from Cranford University. She has been working as a freelancer for three years, receiving excellent reviews from her customers. She recently started working part-time for a major producer of appliances to design instruction manuals for the popular O700 line. Should you need help with a project, please get in touch for a free consultation and price estimate.

The Prima Group Volunteer Recruitment Drive

Sunday, December 8, 3 P.M.

McCormack Hall, Room 103

Three years ago, three friends who were born and raised in Greenville wanted to find a way to make art accessible to the children in their town. They created the Prima Group to help raise money for art programs in schools. The Prima Group is now looking for more volunteers. The founders as well as the volunteer coordinators will be at the recruitment event to answer your questions and find a role that best suits your skills and interests. We hope to see you there!

191. What is indicated in the e-mail about Ms. Noland?
    (A) She previously only worked for nonprofit organizations.
    (B) She was hired by a family-run business.
    (C) She will replace Mr. Perez.
    (D) She will mainly work remotely for Orono.

192. What will happen at the event on November 4?
    (A) Ms. Noland will give a brief talk.
    (B) Ms. Noland will receive an award.
    (C) A meal will be served.
    (D) An employee will be promoted.

193. What kind of business is Orono?
    (A) A magazine publisher
    (B) An appliance manufacturer
    (C) A construction firm
    (D) A retail clothing store

194. According to the advertisement, what does the Prima Group aim to do?
    (A) Open an art museum in the town
    (B) Provide funding for art education
    (C) Support artists through exhibitions
    (D) Host art classes for elderly people

195. What most likely is true about Ms. Noland?
    (A) She volunteers as an instructor.
    (B) She is the Prima Group's volunteer coordinator.
    (C) Her hometown is Greenville.
    (D) Her business donated to the Prima Group.

GO ON TO THE NEXT PAGE

Questions 196-200 refer to the following brochure and e-mails.

Sunshine Tours

Sunshine Tours has been sharing the adventurist spirit of Lochmere Island with tourists for decades. Our exciting tours for ages 18 and up are led by experienced guides, most of whom are local to the island. Tours operate daily, excluding some public holidays, and all include a packed lunch, drinks, and snacks.

Sightseeing by Water (B039)
Relax and take in the gorgeous scenery of Lochmere Island from a unique perspective—the water! We'll visit several sites on the island where you can get excellent photos of the shore from the boat. Standard Price: $70 / With a framed group photo: $75

Under the Sea (S013)
This snorkeling tour allows you to get a close look at local ocean wildlife. We'll visit Ashby Cove, Sandy Bay, and Sol Bay. We can also provide all participants with an underwater digital camera to capture their own unique images as they swim. Standard price: $85 / With digital camera rental: $90

Trailblazers (T074)
Take a scenic bike ride through the forest to discover the amazing plants and animals that live on the island. Standard price: $55 / With zipline experience: $80

Ascent Adventure (A085)
Enjoy breathtaking views of the sea on this rock-climbing tour. This tour is hard work but well worth it! Standard price: $125 / With additional safety training (required for beginners): $145

E-Mail Message

To: Darlene Amos; Glenn Roth
From: Maurice Stotler
Date: August 3
Subject: Tour

Hi, Darlene and Glenn!

Regarding tomorrow's tour, I know that you usually go to Ashby Cove first, but the client has asked to visit Sandy Bay first instead. Some of the group members are inexperienced and would like to swim in shallower water first to get used to the equipment, so I've agreed to this. Darlene, be sure to check off the name of each person on the participant list when they arrive, as we'll need this record for insurance purposes. Also, Glenn, I know you're renewing your boating license soon, so please send me a copy once you get that. Thank you!

Maurice Stotler

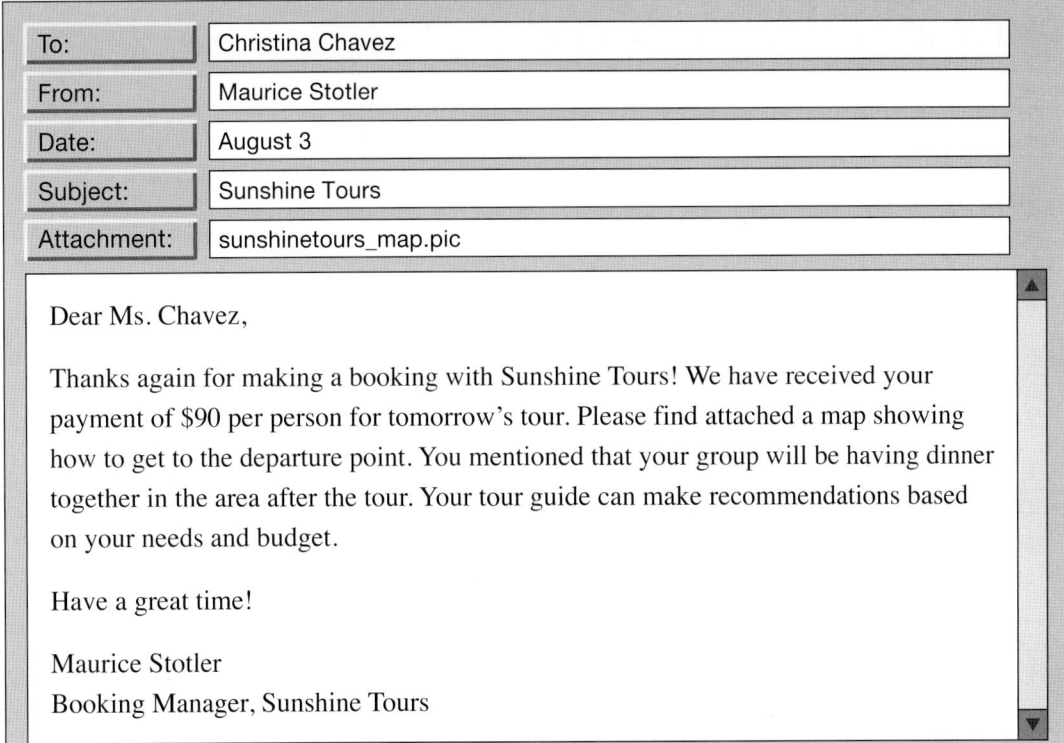

196. What is mentioned about Sunshine Tours?

(A) Its tours are intended for adults only.
(B) It was founded ten years ago.
(C) It mainly leads boat trips.
(D) It offers discounts for large groups.

197. What is indicated about all tours from Sunshine Tours?

(A) They have the same departure point.
(B) They include a meal.
(C) They last for a full day.
(D) They are always run by two employees.

198. Why did Mr. Stotler send the first e-mail?

(A) To send a copy of Mr. Roth's boating license
(B) To inform employees of a change
(C) To provide Ms. Amos with a list of participants
(D) To show appreciation to tour guides for working extra hours

199. To which tour have Ms. Amos and Mr. Roth been assigned for August 4?

(A) B039
(B) S013
(C) T074
(D) A085

200. What is suggested about Ms. Chavez's group?

(A) They will arrive later than usual.
(B) They recommended the tour to others.
(C) They would like to use special cameras.
(D) They want to take a group photo.

Stop! This is the end of the test. If you finish before time is called, you may go back to Parts 5, 6, and 7 and check your work.

READING TEST

In the Reading test, you will read a variety of texts and answer several different types of reading comprehension questions. The entire Reading test will last 75 minutes. There are three parts, and directions are given for each part. You are encouraged to answer as many questions as possible within the time allowed.

You must mark your answers on the separate answer sheet. Do not write your answers in your test book.

PART 5
Directions: A word or phrase is missing in each of the sentences below. Four answer choices are given below each sentence. Select the best answer to complete the sentence. Then mark the letter (A), (B), (C), or (D) on your answer sheet.

101. Mr. Cardwell happily ------- the position of vice president at BNH Incorporated.
    (A) to accept
    (B) accepting
    (C) accept
    (D) accepted

102. The weather forecast says it will rain this weekend, ------- the county fair will continue as scheduled.
    (A) but
    (B) or
    (C) for
    (D) so

103. The company needs to find a new distributor if AX Shipping cannot fulfill ------- orders.
    (A) we
    (B) ours
    (C) our
    (D) us

104. This restaurant's cosmopolitan menu has dishes ------- over 20 different countries.
    (A) until
    (B) from
    (C) as
    (D) into

105. The marketing team's goal is to leave a lasting ------- on the audience's mind.
    (A) impressing
    (B) impressive
    (C) impression
    (D) impressed

106. Ms. Herzberg was surprised that ------- a small change in packaging could make a big impact on her company's sales.
    (A) since
    (B) such
    (C) so
    (D) as

107. The ------- of Everlasting Pillows is what makes the brand so popular.
    (A) softness
    (B) soft
    (C) softly
    (D) softening

108. ------- our yearly goals have been decided, the company can finally move forward.
    (A) As well as
    (B) Now that
    (C) Above all
    (D) Because of

109. Chef Charles Pinto is joining forces with his biggest ------- to open a high-class restaurant by the end of the year.
    (A) competitor
    (B) competing
    (C) competitive
    (D) competitively

110. After more than five years of construction, the Westbury Mall will finally be opening -------.
    (A) after
    (B) then
    (C) soon
    (D) right

111. ------- could stop Mr. Charles's entrepreneurial spirit, which is why he has opened three businesses before turning 30.
    (A) Nor
    (B) Not
    (C) Neither
    (D) Nothing

112. Only people with highly specialized ------- should apply for this position.
    (A) knowledge
    (B) activity
    (C) provision
    (D) relocation

113. Our new intern is talented but sometimes lacks confidence in ------- ideas.
    (A) ours
    (B) his
    (C) its
    (D) those

114. Workers at P&K Realtors wanted to ------- their boss to let them have an extra day off for winter break.
    (A) incorporate
    (B) tolerate
    (C) surprise
    (D) convince

115. If you have ------- comments or concerns, please leave them in the suggestion box.
    (A) any
    (B) that
    (C) those
    (D) all

116. The post office is the building ------- the old bank on the corner.
    (A) into
    (B) about
    (C) beside
    (D) among

117. Newman Fashion uses a special ------- that ensures the best quality for its suits and ties.
    (A) materialize
    (B) material
    (C) materialistic
    (D) materially

118. When creating her custom cakes, Ms. Carmen always aligns her designs and letters -------.
    (A) perfect
    (B) perfectly
    (C) perfection
    (D) perfecting

119. If the temperature is ------- 40 degrees Fahrenheit, the cement will not cure properly.
    (A) below
    (B) next to
    (C) during
    (D) alongside

120. Travelers should purchase insurance to protect ------- from financial losses due to cancellations or delays.
    (A) they
    (B) themselves
    (C) them
    (D) their

GO ON TO THE NEXT PAGE

121. Ms. Lawson's goal is for the average person ------- her company's logo without a second thought.
    (A) recognizable
    (B) recognition
    (C) recognize
    (D) to recognize

122. Attendees were reminded to pick up the package of handouts ------- useful information before the lecture.
    (A) containing
    (B) contain
    (C) containable
    (D) contained

123. Customers with ------- for their items will be able to exchange or refund them easily.
    (A) options
    (B) receipts
    (C) ports
    (D) potential

124. Publishers must check to see if information is ------- before it is released to the public.
    (A) equal
    (B) factual
    (C) domestic
    (D) relative

125. Mr. Royal hoped his new hotel key card would work ------- because his last one was malfunctioning.
    (A) newly
    (B) properly
    (C) happily
    (D) quickly

126. Developers at Perfume Palace modified their formulas for the new scent until the majority of the testers gave ------- reviews.
    (A) eligible
    (B) permanent
    (C) favorable
    (D) practical

127. Ms. Higgins is concerned about the specifics of the ------- merger with JN Electronics.
    (A) proposed
    (B) proposal
    (C) proposition
    (D) proposing

128. The ------- between Cedarville and Pleasant Town is marked by a beautiful row of daisies.
    (A) boundary
    (B) difference
    (C) benefits
    (D) regulation

129. Mr. Flomo prefers ------- designs for advertisements that promote his company's products.
    (A) simply
    (B) simplification
    (C) simplify
    (D) simplistic

130. Please measure the ------- of your home precisely before ordering furniture.
    (A) insurance
    (B) depth
    (C) dimensions
    (D) privacy

PART 6

Directions: Read the texts that follow. A word, phrase, or sentence is missing in parts of each text. Four answer choices for each question are given below the text. Select the best answer to complete the text. Then mark the letter (A), (B), (C), or (D) on your answer sheet.

Questions 131-134 refer to the following information.

Thank you for choosing Channing's Sporting Goods for all your athletic needs. Our quality-control team quadruple-checks our products to ensure perfection just ------- any abnormalities slipped through our first three checks. -------. Because of this, Channing's Sporting Goods rarely has any customer complaints, but when we do, we make sure to handle them as quickly as possible. If you are dissatisfied with your order for any reason, contact our customer service team and your request ------- right away. We are happy to provide free return shipping for refunds and exchanges because we prefer to go ------- what is necessary to provide exemplary service to our valued consumers.

131. (A) because
(B) in case
(C) through
(D) as soon as

132. (A) Factory positions are often posted in the local paper.
(B) We are currently offering 20% off all sneakers.
(C) This attention to detail sets us apart from other sellers.
(D) Our brand is famous for its eye-catching styles.

133. (A) will be handled
(B) will handle
(C) is handled
(D) to be handled

134. (A) next
(B) around
(C) near
(D) above

Questions 135-138 refer to the following e-mail.

From: Adorlee Lambert <a.lambert@fashionnow.net>
To: Russell Fluet <russell_fluet@ragstorussell.com>
Date: 20 November
Subject: Rags to Russell Feature

Dear Mr. Fluet,

I am pleased to inform you that your fashion boutique, Rags to Russell, has been selected as one of this year's Top 20 Emerging Fashion Brands in Paris by *Fine Fashion Magazine*. We will be ------- your business in our upcoming January issue. Our list only includes the finest ------- in the fashion industry, so this is a once-in-a-lifetime opportunity.
135. **136.**

To really bring your feature to life, we would like to include a photo of both you and your store in our magazine. -------. We would need to receive it ------- 10 December at the latest. Please let
137. **138.**
us know if you have any issues with taking the photo, and we would be happy to help.

Thank you and congratulations!

Adorlee Lambert
Fine Fashion Magazine Editor-in-Chief

---

135. (A) featured
(B) features
(C) featuring
(D) feature

136. (A) ventures
(B) democracies
(C) delicacies
(D) monopolies

137. (A) Do not forget to send a sample of your best clothing items.
(B) The grand prize is worth over $5,000.
(C) We are seeking a high-resolution image in full color.
(D) We will send several copies to your business.

138. (A) through
(B) in
(C) at
(D) by

Questions 139-142 refer to the following e-mail.

From: Muhammed Sayid <m_sayid@ncf.org>
To: All Staff <stafflist@ncf.org>
Subject: NCF's New Director
Date: 14 August

To the NCF team and partners:

I am happy to inform you all that the board of directors ------- (139.) to hire Thomas Silva as the new National Children's Fund director. Mr. Silva is well known in the nonprofit field for his work in administration and community organizing.

Mr. Silva most recently worked at Saint Mark's Cancer Research Center and helped raise millions of dollars for the organization. At Saint Mark's, he was in charge of hundreds of volunteers and workers and made sure ------- (140.) ran smoothly. ------- (141.).

Mr. Silva has just finished setting up his new office, so please take a minute out of your day to introduce ------- (142.) to him.

All the best,

Muhammed Sayid
National Children's Fund CEO

139. (A) decides
(B) has decided
(C) to decide
(D) be deciding

140. (A) renovations
(B) operations
(C) announcement
(D) experiences

141. (A) Congratulations on passing the second round of interviews.
(B) We are sure his expertise will contribute positively to our team as well.
(C) We are pleased to announce that renovations are complete.
(D) I am writing to request a special favor.

142. (A) your
(B) yours
(C) you
(D) yourself

Questions 143-146 refer to the following flyer.

Samoa National Tourist Organization's Free Visitor Passes

The Samoa National Tourist Organization (SNTO) has a special announcement to make. The SNTO, ------- the businesses listed on the back of this flyer, has collaborated to sponsor a new
143.
program that allows tourists to gain free entry to a number of culturally significant attractions.

We ------- to make Samoa an inviting travel destination for those on a budget and for those
144.
looking to explore our country's deep history. ------- attractions include the Tafua Peninsula
145.
Rainforest Preserve, the Museum of Samoa, and a tour of famed writer Robert Louis Stevenson's former home.

To claim a pass, check out our Web site at www.snto.org/culturepass or visit our booth at the airport. -------.
146.

143. (A) unlike
(B) throughout
(C) along with
(D) in spite of

144. (A) aim
(B) to aim
(C) aiming
(D) aims

145. (A) Retired
(B) Discovered
(C) Luxury
(D) Featured

146. (A) We appreciate your consistent patronage.
(B) We look forward to checking you into our hotel.
(C) The pass can be used for up to one week.
(D) Both cash and card are acceptable forms of payment.

PART 7

Directions: In this part you will read a selection of texts, such as magazine and newspaper articles, e-mails, and instant messages. Each text or set of texts is followed by several questions. Select the best answer for each question and mark the letter (A), (B), (C), or (D) on your answer sheet.

Questions 147-148 refer to the following contract.

Kennewick Communications
Network Services Provider Agreement

Customer Name: Lily Cronin
Address: 1406 Fieldcrest Lane, Omaha, NE 68102
Package Type: Fiber Broadband   Start Date: March 15
Setup Fee: $35   Monthly Fee: $85
Contract Term: 1 year   Payment Type: Bank transfer

Thank you for becoming a Kennewick Communications customer. We are pleased to bring you the fastest and most reliable Internet service in the region. A technician will visit your property to bring the necessary equipment and set up the service. The monthly fee for the first three months is $68, which is 20% off the regular fee. And after this period, no further discounts will be applied to the payment unless we offer a special promotion. You can cancel your contract without penalty during the first 3 months. Should you experience any technical issues with the service, please call us at 555-4331.

Signed: *Lily Cronin*
Date: March 10

147. What is mentioned about customers who cancel a contract?

(A) They must return all equipment.
(B) They will be charged a 20% fee.
(C) They can cancel for free in the first three months.
(D) They can only cancel if there is a technical issue.

148. Why would Ms. Cronin call the number provided?

(A) To change an address
(B) To terminate her contract
(C) To report a problem
(D) To inquire about new deals

GO ON TO THE NEXT PAGE

Questions 149-150 refer to the following text-message chain.

Belle Chauvet [4:18 P.M.]
Hi, Ernest. Do you have the list of participants for the trip to Paris?

Ernest Lessard [4:20 P.M.]
Are you talking about the one taking place on June 3?

Belle Chauvet [4:21 P.M.]
Yes, that's it.

Ernest Lessard [4:22 P.M.]
Yes, there are twenty-three people in total. We may have some last-minute bookings like we did last time, so I've already informed the hotel. I'm planning to send the itineraries to everyone on Friday.

Belle Chauvet [4:24 P.M.]
Great! Could you please forward me the list and let me know later if there are any changes?

149. What kind of business do the writers most likely work for?

(A) An educational institute
(B) A tour operator
(C) A bank
(D) A hotel

150. At 4:21 P.M., why does Ms. Chauvet write, "Yes, that's it"?

(A) She is expressing her interest in visiting Paris.
(B) She is saying that Mr. Lessard is correct.
(C) She promises to finish a task on time.
(D) She agrees with Mr. Lessard's business plan.

Questions 151-152 refer to the following notecard.

Overall, I was pleased with the features of the coffee grinder you sent for our monthly review process. The ground coffee beans had a consistent size, meaning that the extraction rate will be the same from cup to cup. I liked the clear assembly instructions. Because of the shape of the collection chamber, it was hard to get my cleaning sponge in there, though. I think this could be improved. I did like the large size of it, though, and I think a lot of customers will appreciate that. One more component that concerned me was the handle. It seemed to be made from very thin plastic, so it could easily break off when grinding the coffee beans.

Mona Yang

151. What is implied about Ms. Yang?
(A) She wants to return a coffee grinder.
(B) She owns a coffee shop.
(C) She regularly provides feedback.
(D) She is missing one of the device's components.

152. What does Ms. Yang mention about the collection chamber?
(A) It is not large enough.
(B) It was difficult to clean.
(C) It should be made of plastic.
(D) It could break easily.

Questions 153-154 refer to the following letter.

Dear Mr. Thurman,

The National Association of Environmental Responsibility (NAER) is the country's leading advocate of eco-friendly practices in the construction industry. Every year, through our Sustainable Engineering Award, we recognize companies that use innovative methods to make the best use of our earth's resources. As you are an expert in the field, we would love to hear your opinion about the buildings that represent the best of sustainable design and construction.

In a few days, you will receive a paper ballot to nominate up to three buildings that you believe deserve recognition. Should you wish to participate in the nomination process, please complete the form and send it back to us in the envelope provided.

I am available by phone at 555-8205 if you have any questions.

Sincerely,

Vivian Demott

153. What does Ms. Demott request from Mr. Thurman?

(A) A letter of recommendation
(B) A list of innovative buildings
(C) A summary of his accomplishments
(D) Confirmation of event attendance

154. How should Mr. Thurman respond to the request?

(A) By completing a phone survey
(B) By meeting Ms. Demott
(C) By visiting a Web site
(D) By returning a form by mail

Questions 155-157 refer to the following product description.

Paintstop is a paint additive that is specially designed to stop mold from growing on walls. It is perfect for areas prone to dampness, such as bathrooms and kitchens. To use Paintstop, simply mix the 50-milliliter container into any 2.5-liter can of paint, including acrylic and oil paint.

Paintstop kills mold spores and ensures that they will not return. Its effectiveness lasts for the life of the paint. And, unlike our competitors' products, which make the paint color slightly lighter, Paintstop preserves the true color.

Say goodbye to unsightly and unhealthy mold with Paintstop!

155. What is Paintstop designed to do?

(A) Reduce moisture levels in rooms
(B) Remove stains caused by mold
(C) Make paint last longer
(D) Prevent the growth of mold

156. According to the product description, what is true about Paintstop?

(A) It should be reapplied regularly.
(B) It can be used with different types of paint.
(C) It slows down the paint's drying time.
(D) It is sold in 2.5-liter containers.

157. How does Paintstop differ from other products on the market?

(A) It is easier to apply to a wall.
(B) It is not damaged by light.
(C) It does not alter paint colors.
(D) It does not contain harmful ingredients.

Questions 158-160 refer to the following instructions.

Thank you for your purchase of the Z-880 electric drill from Zamora Manufacturing. —[1]—. Keeping your drill in proper working order can maintain the drill's performance as well as the safety of the drill while in operation. —[2]—. After use, the drill should be wiped down with a dry cloth and stored in its original case. This will protect it from unnecessary dust, which can block important air vents. The battery should be removed if you plan to store it for a long time.

When charging the device, make sure the battery is fully charged before removing it from the charger. —[3]—. At least every six months, you should let the battery run out completely. This will help to extend the life of the battery. —[4]—.

Check out www.zamora.com/z-880 for tips and tricks to get the most out of your drill.

158. For whom most likely are the instructions intended?

(A) Shop employees
(B) Safety inspectors
(C) Manufacturing employees
(D) Owners of a power tool

159. What is recommended for storing the item?

(A) Checking for dust in air vents
(B) Cleaning it with a damp cloth first
(C) Taking out the battery every time
(D) Using the container that came with it

160. In which of the positions marked [1], [2], [3], and [4] does the following sentence best belong?

"This will be indicated by a green light."

(A) [1]
(B) [2]
(C) [3]
(D) [4]

Questions 161-163 refer to the following e-mail.

E-Mail

To: Complete Customer List
From: Soltero Spa
Date: April 10
Subject: Cancellations

Dear Soltero Spa Clients,

At Soltero Spa, we want to ensure that all customers can get their desired treatments at their convenience. From May 1, we will begin charging a fee of 30% of the treatment cost for any cancellations made within 24 hours of the appointment. We hope this will encourage guests to let us know about schedule changes early so that we can offer the appointment to someone else. This is critical for helping us keep up with the high demand for our services. Adding five new treatment rooms to our building has reduced the long wait times for scheduling treatments, but we hope this new rule will help even more.

Warmest regards,

William Soltero
Owner, Soltero Spa

161. Why was the e-mail written?

(A) To apologize for a cancellation
(B) To reschedule an appointment
(C) To announce a policy change
(D) To introduce a new treatment

162. The word "critical" in paragraph 1, line 5, is closest in meaning to

(A) urgent
(B) problematic
(C) negative
(D) important

163. What is suggested about Soltero Spa?

(A) It completed a building expansion project.
(B) It will extend its business hours.
(C) It regularly trains staff members.
(D) It accepts appointments by phone.

Questions 164-167 refer to the following article.

Funding the Home Office Environment

OAKLAND (January 8)—With more people than ever working from home, businesses are making adjustments not only to the way they communicate with remote workers but also to the way they support them. A new trend followed by many businesses is offering a home office budget to employees. Many roles within a company can be performed away from the office. —[1]—. Therefore, companies are starting to provide funding for purchases such as desks, office chairs, and even coffee machines—all tools that employees can use to maintain their productivity. —[2]—.

"I was pleased that I didn't have to use my own funds to create my home office," said Albert Steiner, a sales representative at Conifer Enterprises. "Since I often have video calls with clients, it's important for me to have a professional-looking space in my background." —[3]—.

"This is another way that we can support our employees," explained Patricia Miller, HR Director of Elysian. "We started offering a home office budget last year to show our employees that we value them and that we want to build a comfortable working environment for them, wherever that may be. It is an important part of making sure the most skilled and experienced staff members stay with our company for a long time. —[4]—."

---

164. Why was the article written?

(A) To recommend funding employee outings
(B) To explain the advantages of working remotely
(C) To explain a recently introduced employee benefit
(D) To give advice on productivity issues

165. What is true about Mr. Steiner?

(A) He helps people set up workspaces.
(B) He speaks with clients online.
(C) He prefers to work in the office.
(D) He is a new Conifer Enterprises employee.

166. Why did Ms. Miller's company make a change last year?

(A) To move to a smaller office
(B) To increase a stock's value
(C) To reduce operating costs
(D) To retain talented staff

167. In which of the positions marked [1], [2], [3], and [4] does the following sentence best belong?

"But not everyone has the right setup."

(A) [1]
(B) [2]
(C) [3]
(D) [4]

Questions 168-171 refer to the following Web page.

Updated January 2

Showcase your items at the Nashville Festival! Attendance has been growing steadily over the past few years, and it is the largest exhibition event for items made by hand such as pottery, knitted clothing, household decorations, and more. The festival is held three times a year. Applications for booth rental must be received by February 15 (for the spring festival), May 15 (summer), or July 15 (autumn). Businesses that have exhibited at the festival before will be given priority for booth selection. Fees for booth rental vary and are calculated based on the booth size.

When planning your booth, please note that it should be well-organized and attractive. We encourage table coverings and decorations. Heavy-duty and sturdy tents only will be accepted, as anything else can become dangerous in high winds. Prices should be clearly marked on items, and all signs must be professionally printed.

All booths must be ready to open at 8 A.M. and stay open until 7 P.M. (in the rear courtyard) or 8 P.M. (inside the building) on the festival day. There must be at least one person working at the booth during the festival hours.

Click here for the booth rental application.

168. What most likely is sold at the Nashville Festival?

(A) Locally grown produce
(B) Handmade crafts
(C) Gardening supplies
(D) Used equipment

169. What is the deadline for applying for a booth at the summer festival?

(A) January 2
(B) February 15
(C) May 15
(D) July 15

170. What is implied about the Nashville Festival?

(A) It has both indoor and outdoor exhibition spaces.
(B) It will be launched this year for the first time.
(C) Its staff works on a volunteer basis.
(D) Its proceeds will be donated to charity.

171. What is NOT true about booths at the festival?

(A) They must be staffed at all times.
(B) Lightweight tents are not allowed.
(C) The cost depends on the size of the booth.
(D) Signs should be approved in advance.

Questions 172-175 refer to the following online chat discussion.

Sam Aubry (10:03 A.M.)		Mary and Daniel, are you busy today? I need someone to add graphics to my presentation. I have to go to an off-site workshop, and the deadline for the project is coming up.
Mary Shin (10:04 A.M.)		I can do that.
Sam Aubry (10:05 A.M.)		Thanks! It's an outline of our services, explaining how we recruit and screen job candidates on behalf of our clients.
Daniel Bingham (10:06 A.M.)		But you're usually so organized, Sam. How did you run out of time?
Sam Aubry (10:07 A.M.)		The deadline was suddenly moved forward.
Mary Shin (10:08 A.M.)		I see. If you have a certain photo style in mind, just let me know.
Daniel Bingham (10:09 A.M.)		Got it.
Sam Aubry (10:10 A.M.)		Whatever you think looks best, Mary.
Mary Shin (10:11 A.M.)		Alright. For the presentation, I know you had planned to get an endorsement from one of our current clients. Did you have time to do that?
Sam Aubry (10:12 A.M.)		Unfortunately, no.
Daniel Bingham (10:13 A.M.)		I'm going to meet with Ms. Lowe after lunch. I'll ask her to write a testimonial for us. She's really happy with our services, so I'm sure she wouldn't mind helping us out.

172. Where do the speakers most likely work?

(A) At a rental car office
(B) At an employment agency
(C) At a research laboratory
(D) At a financial consulting firm

173. What is suggested about Mr. Aubry?

(A) He is a new member of the team.
(B) He plans to switch jobs soon.
(C) He usually works with a detailed plan.
(D) He was not able to complete a sale.

174. At 10:12 A.M., what does Mr. Aubry suggest when he writes, "Unfortunately, no"?

(A) He doesn't understand the conversation.
(B) He cannot meet with Ms. Lowe after lunch.
(C) He cannot send the report to his coworkers.
(D) He was too busy to complete a task.

175. What does Mr. Bingham plan to do this afternoon?

(A) Attend a workshop
(B) Search for some photos
(C) Ask a client for a favor
(D) Practice a presentation

GO ON TO THE NEXT PAGE

Questions 176-180 refer to the following e-mail and article.

E-Mail

To:	Callum Baxter
From:	Phoebe Hagai
Date:	May 8
Subject:	Proposal discussion

Dear Mr. Baxter,

I would like to set up a meeting so we can discuss removing the video screens from our taxis. Most passengers report being very irritated by the noisy videos, and even though there is a mute button, it often doesn't work. We get comments about this a few times a week. I understand that the videos generate revenue through advertising, but it's time to use a different approach for making a profit, as complaints about the video screens are the most common issue mentioned on our Web site.

As these screens are also used for payments, I think they should be replaced with basic credit card readers. We should also consider buying some passenger vans so that we can accommodate larger groups of people. In addition, it's time to start investing in electric vehicles. I'm looking forward to discussing all of the above parts of my proposal with you.

Sincerely,

Phoebe Hagai

Clover Taxis to Take a New Turn

By Georgina Willis

(May 27)—Clover Taxis has announced plans to remove the highly criticized screens in the back seats of its vehicles and replace them with credit card readers. In addition, the company has secured funding to purchase twenty new regular-sized taxis for its fleet: four-door electric cars. These will have the same green and white painting on the outside to make them easily recognizable. Clover Taxis will also hire more drivers to cover peak times. The changes will result in a small increase in fares, but this still puts the company slightly below its competitors in terms of pricing.

176. According to the e-mail, what has Ms. Hagai's company received frequent complaints about?

(A) The company's high fares for taxi rides
(B) The sound of the video screens
(C) The lack of air conditioning
(D) The issues with processing credit cards

177. In the e-mail, the word "approach" in paragraph 1, line 5, is closest in meaning to

(A) movement
(B) passage
(C) arrival
(D) method

178. What is suggested about Clover Taxis customers?

(A) They are invited to a meeting.
(B) They can enroll in a loyalty program.
(C) They have shared feedback online.
(D) They mainly learned of the company through ads.

179. According to the article, what does Clover Taxis plan to keep the same?

(A) The number of taxi drivers
(B) The vehicle's exterior appearance
(C) The price of using its services
(D) The television technology

180. What is implied about Ms. Hagai?

(A) She had part of her proposal rejected.
(B) She used to be a taxi driver.
(C) She will research the company's competitors.
(D) She inspected some vehicles with Mr. Baxter.

GO ON TO THE NEXT PAGE

Questions 181-185 refer to the following e-mails.

To:	Houghton Bank Staff
From:	Fen Lang
Date:	October 4
Subject:	Staff uniforms

Dear Staff:

On November 1, Houghton Bank will be changing from the current light gray uniforms to navy blue ones, though they'll still be made from the lightweight cotton you're used to. We have made arrangements with Uniworld Supplies to have employees directly order the items they need. To do so, visit www.uniworldsupplies.com, input the six-digit code for our bank, which is 856227, and it will bring you to the ordering page. There are four options available:

Set 1: Long-sleeved shirt, trousers
Set 2: Short-sleeved shirt, trousers, cardigan
Set 3: Long-sleeved shirt, skirt
Set 4: Short-sleeved shirt, skirt, cardigan

The price of each set is $100 dollars, and $100 will be credited to your account by the bank. You can order uniforms above this limit at your own expense. Be sure to order them by October 26, as they can take up to five days for delivery.

Sincerely,

Fen Lang

TO:	Chelsea Moss ⟨moss.c@houghtonbank.com⟩
FROM:	Uniworld Supplies ⟨orders@uniworldsupplies.com⟩
DATE:	October 20
SUBJECT:	Order #045935

Dear Ms. Moss,

Thank you for your business! Unfortunately, at this time, we are unable to send you two complete sets, as you requested. We have sent part of the complete set, which includes two short-sleeved shirts and two pairs of trousers. The remainder of your order will be shipped as soon as the items are back in stock. We are sorry for any inconvenience this may cause.

The Uniworld Supplies Team

181. According to Mr. Lang, what should employees do when ordering staff uniforms?

(A) Use the bank's mailing address
(B) Save a receipt for reimbursement
(C) Input a company code
(D) Get a supervisor's approval

182. What is NOT true about the Houghton Bank uniforms?

(A) They will be a different color than before.
(B) They consist of at least three pieces.
(C) They may take five days to arrive.
(D) They are made from a lightweight fabric.

183. Which option did Ms. Moss most likely order?

(A) Set 1
(B) Set 2
(C) Set 3
(D) Set 4

184. What is the purpose of the second e-mail?

(A) To report a delay
(B) To introduce a new item
(C) To confirm a payment
(D) To provide a refund

185. What is suggested about Ms. Moss?

(A) She found damage to an item.
(B) She ordered the wrong size.
(C) She will pay for part of her order.
(D) She should request a refund.

GO ON TO THE NEXT PAGE

Questions 186-190 refer to the following article, Web page, and e-mail.

EDMONTON (16 January)—The Hartland Design Institute (HDI), based in Edmonton, is now under new ownership. The institute was sold to Albright International. Luan Melo, a spokesperson for the company, confirmed this at a press briefing yesterday. "We are excited to have the opportunity to operate courses that help students achieve their career goals. Competition within the design industry has increased significantly over the past few years, so it is essential for designers to equip themselves with the skills that will make them stand out from the crowd," Mr. Melo said.

Despite the change, there will be no interruptions to the teaching schedule, and the faculty will remain largely the same. One improvement, which students are looking forward to, is the plan to add online classes in June.

Visit www.hartlanddesign.ca for the latest information.

---

http://www.hartlanddesign.ca

| HOME | REGISTER | FACULTY | CONTACT |

Hartland Design Institute (HDI)

Enrollment for our spring term, starting March 10, is now open! Courses are available on a first-come, first-served basis, so early enrollment is recommended. Please see below for the complete list of classes. Click on MORE DETAILS to read a class description and view class times. A deposit of 10% of the course fee must be paid at the time of enrollment. The remainder is due by the first day of class.

B048 Product Packaging	Instructor: Lucio Napolitano	MORE DETAILS
G051 Advanced Advertising Design*	Instructor: Oliva Baldwin	MORE DETAILS
G052 Advanced Advertising Design*	Instructor: Saita Heida	MORE DETAILS
P115 Logo Design (certification received)	Instructor: Wyatt Dobson	MORE DETAILS
T236 Skyrock Illustrator (certification received)	Instructor: Antoine Yates	MORE DETAILS
T237 Skyrock Illustrator (certification received)	Instructor: Delmina Greco	MORE DETAILS

*Online course

To: <contact@hartlanddesign.ca>
From: <rcuomo@bealsmail.ca>
Subject: Message
Date: March 26

Dear Hartland Design Institute,

I would like to report an error with your e-mail system. I am currently taking a class at your institute, but I will not be in attendance on March 30 due to a work conflict. I tried to e-mail my instructor, Wyatt Dobson, but I received an automated message saying that my e-mail could not be delivered. Could you please make sure Mr. Dobson knows that I will not be in class and also that other students may be having the same difficulty in contacting him?

Thank you,

Rosa Cuomo

---

186. What is the article mainly about?
(A) Current trends in an industry
(B) Business opportunities in Edmonton
(C) The sale of an educational institution
(D) The relocation of an institute

187. What does Mr. Melo indicate in the article?
(A) A field is becoming more competitive.
(B) Wages in the area are rising.
(C) Classes are increasing in popularity.
(D) Businesses are changing their requirements.

188. What is implied about HDI?
(A) It is offering online classes sooner than expected.
(B) It experienced a delay in its grand opening.
(C) It provides discounts to students who register early.
(D) It may add more classes to the spring term.

189. According to the Web page, what is true about HDI's courses?
(A) They all provide a certificate at the end.
(B) They do not have space for new students.
(C) Some are taught by the same instructors.
(D) Some are offered more than once in a term.

190. What is suggested about Ms. Cuomo?
(A) She has completed other courses at HDI.
(B) She is taking classes remotely.
(C) She would like a job at HDI.
(D) She is interested in designing logos.

GO ON TO THE NEXT PAGE

Questions 191-195 refer to the following invoice and e-mails.

Emerald Landscaping
2478 Goodwin Road
Ft. Lauderdale, FL 33311
www.emeraldlandscaping.net

Date: September 1
Client: Ridenour Consulting
Phone: 555-5781

Invoice No: 06581
Representative: Shirley Lusk
E-mail: luskshirley@ridenourconsulting.com

Date	Description of Services	Fee
August 3	Lawn mowing (Clarksville Branch)	$850
	Lawn mowing (Simpson Branch)	$600
	Fertilizer treatment (Clarksville Branch)	$200
August 13	Lawn mowing (Clarksville Branch)	$850
	Lawn mowing (Simpson Branch)	$600
	Planting lilac bushes (Clarksville Branch)	$550
August 23	Lawn mowing (Clarksville Branch)	$850
	Lawn mowing (Simpson Branch)	$600
	Tree trimming (Simpson Branch)	$1200

Subtotal: $6300
Previous balance in account: $350
Balance due: **$5950**

From:	Shirley Lusk ⟨luskshirley@ridenourconsulting.com⟩
To:	Emerald Landscaping ⟨contact@emeraldlandscaping.net⟩
Date:	September 3
Subject:	August services

Dear Emerald Landscaping,

I would like to report an error in the most recent invoice you sent for Ridenour Consulting. We had arranged to have lilac bushes planted last month, but this task was never carried out. But, when looking over the invoice we received yesterday, I noticed that a charge for this service was listed. Please remove this charge from the bill and send an updated invoice at your earliest convenience. We will be able to make the payment promptly after that.

Thank you,

Shirley Lusk
Ridenour Consulting

From:	Alan Gilliam ⟨agilliam@emeraldlandscapting.net⟩
To:	Shirley Lusk ⟨luskshirley@ridenourconsulting.com⟩
Date:	September 4
Subject:	Your Emerald Landscaping inquiry
Attachment:	Invoice_06581_revised

Dear Ms. Lusk,

Thank you for e-mailing us yesterday regarding the issue with your most recent bill. On behalf of the accounting department, I would like to say that I'm sorry for this error. I've confirmed with our crew leader that the bushes you requested were never planted because our usual supplier of lilac bushes suddenly went out of business. Should you wish to rebook the service in the future, we can do so anytime thanks to our new supplier.

Please find attached an amended invoice. By way of apology, we would like to offer you a free fertilizer treatment like the one you received in August. As this is recommended once every three months, it will be scheduled for November.

Thank you for your understanding and your patronage.

Sincerely,

Alan Gilliam

191. What is indicated about Ridenour Consulting in the invoice?
    (A) It used a coupon in August.
    (B) It has more than one location.
    (C) It uses lawn-mowing services once a week.
    (D) It requested the removal of a tree.

192. How much does Ms. Lusk think she has been overcharged?
    (A) $350
    (B) $550
    (C) $600
    (D) $850

193. What most likely is Mr. Gilliam's job?
    (A) Repair technician
    (B) Crew leader
    (C) Accountant
    (D) Driver

194. According to Mr. Gilliam, what caused a problem with a service?
    (A) Adverse weather conditions
    (B) A broken piece of equipment
    (C) An unexpected business closure
    (D) A problem with staff scheduling

195. What is suggested about Ms. Lusk?
    (A) She received a reply to her e-mail on the same day.
    (B) She was advised to have the lawn fertilized more often.
    (C) Her contract with Emerald Landscaping will expire in November.
    (D) Her business will receive a free service worth 200 dollars.

GO ON TO THE NEXT PAGE

Questions 196-200 refer to the following listing, e-mail, and review.

Property Listing: Lakeside Cabins, construction in progress
Location: Swan Estates (North side of Bassell Lake)
Contact: Frank Clements, 555-4701

Relax and enjoy lakeside living in Swan Estates! Our luxury cabins are perfect for vacations year-round, as you can enjoy lake activities in the summer and ski at nearby Hickory Hills Resort in the winter.

The Violet and Sage models include a private dock for your boat. The Marigold model features oak flooring and granite countertops. The Lily model has a spacious backyard with space for playground equipment. The Iris model, the smallest of the options, is energy efficient and cozy.

Completed Cabins: Ready for Sale

Cabin Number	Model Type	Bedrooms	Bathrooms
4A	Violet	Four	Two
8B	Sage	Three	Two
15A	Marigold	Two	Two
18D	Iris	Two	One

To: Karl Reynolds <karl@swanestates.com>
From: Hannah Baek <baekh@barrington1.com>
Date: April 4
Subject: Lakeside Cabin

Dear Mr. Reynolds,

My brother recently bought a Swan Estates cabin and said that it was fantastic, so I am interested in buying one as well. I live quite far from the area, so I would like to ensure availability before I come for a tour. I plan to use the cabin just for vacations, so two bedrooms would be enough. I would prefer to have two bathrooms, though, as I think that would be more convenient. I can take a cabin tour this Friday or Saturday, April 8 or 9, or the following weekend on Saturday or Sunday, April 16 or 17. You can reach me at this e-mail address.

Many thanks,

Hannah Baek

Property Review: Swan Estates

I purchased a cabin in Swan Estates, and I was pleased with the process from start to finish. Karl Reynolds gave us a tour of a few different cabins and answered all of the questions we had. The cabin itself is well built and is situated in a beautiful setting. The only thing that buyers should note is that tours are only available on weekdays. This may be difficult for people who do not want to take time off work to visit the cabins.

Hannah Baek

196. What is true about Swan Estates?
    (A) It includes boat rentals for residents.
    (B) It is not open to visitors yet.
    (C) It overlooks a public park.
    (D) It is near a ski resort.

197. Which Swan Estates cabin type is still being constructed?
    (A) Sage
    (B) Marigold
    (C) Lily
    (D) Iris

198. What is indicated about Ms. Baek in the e-mail?
    (A) Her family member recommended Swan Estates.
    (B) Her brother will invest in a cabin with her.
    (C) She plans to use the cabin year-round.
    (D) She lives near a different part of Bassell Lake.

199. Which Swan Estates cabin would best suit Ms. Baek?
    (A) 4A
    (B) 8B
    (C) 15A
    (D) 18D

200. When did Ms. Baek most likely tour some cabins?
    (A) On April 8
    (B) On April 9
    (C) On April 16
    (D) On April 17

Stop! This is the end of the test. If you finish before time is called, you may go back to Parts 5, 6, and 7 and check your work.

READING TEST

In the Reading test, you will read a variety of texts and answer several different types of reading comprehension questions. The entire Reading test will last 75 minutes. There are three parts, and directions are given for each part. You are encouraged to answer as many questions as possible within the time allowed.

You must mark your answers on the separate answer sheet. Do not write your answers in your test book.

PART 5

Directions: A word or phrase is missing in each of the sentences below. Four answer choices are given below each sentence. Select the best answer to complete the sentence. Then mark the letter (A), (B), (C), or (D) on your answer sheet.

101. Mr. Peacock was unable to find ------- parking spots outside of the stadium.
    (A) others
    (B) its
    (C) any
    (D) none

102. Billboards are a great way to ------- restaurants located near major highways.
    (A) promote
    (B) celebrate
    (C) diminish
    (D) discount

103. The average Forest Ville resident ------- three books from the library each year.
    (A) borrows
    (B) to borrow
    (C) borrowing
    (D) borrower

104. Lawrence Inc.'s stock analysis report is the ------- of a short novel.
    (A) lengthily
    (B) lengthen
    (C) lengthy
    (D) length

105. Great politicians ------- listen to their voters and try to do what's best for them.
    (A) next
    (B) always
    (C) while
    (D) including

106. Only the most ------- candidates will have the chance to be interviewed.
    (A) frequent
    (B) experienced
    (C) closed
    (D) maintained

107. The red battery icon is an ------- that your phone needs to be charged.
    (A) allowance
    (B) accessibility
    (C) indication
    (D) example

108. The project will be a success if ------- team completes the assigned tasks on time.
    (A) each
    (B) both
    (C) someone
    (D) everything

109. Employees having issues with the new software should speak ------- the IT department.
    (A) near
    (B) beside
    (C) to
    (D) at

110. Molly's Candles sells products with ------- scents that set it apart from other candle makers.
    (A) distinct
    (B) distinctness
    (C) distinctly
    (D) distinction

111. The deans at the university will be at the orientation to ------- students as best they can.
    (A) envision
    (B) interact
    (C) support
    (D) discuss

112. PK Realtors has ------- cheaper commission rates than other realtors in the area.
    (A) comparatively
    (B) compare
    (C) comparison
    (D) comparable

113. The Greenville City Council will host a free ------- for small businesses looking to expand.
    (A) workshop
    (B) ticket
    (C) policy
    (D) announcement

114. Hermes's Restaurant is known for its ------- service and delectable cuisine.
    (A) excellently
    (B) excel
    (C) excellent
    (D) excellence

115. The Thanksgiving Day parade will ------- around the whole town twice next Thursday.
    (A) jump
    (B) stroll
    (C) limp
    (D) circle

116. Even though it was only 10 A.M., Hardy Bakery had ------- sold out of fresh bread for the day.
    (A) soon
    (B) already
    (C) frequently
    (D) never

117. The apartment building has been abandoned since it ------- two years ago.
    (A) had demolished
    (B) was demolished
    (C) was demolishing
    (D) demolished

118. For some ------- reason, customers seemed to prefer the mini purse to the standard-sized purse.
    (A) exact
    (B) unknown
    (C) incorrect
    (D) exciting

119. The temperature settings of the heater can be adjusted ------- using buttons on the front of the unit.
    (A) easily
    (B) easy
    (C) easier
    (D) easiest

120. This limited edition vinyl record comes with both a signed poster ------- a photo book.
    (A) next
    (B) and
    (C) since
    (D) with

GO ON TO THE NEXT PAGE

121. For the project manager, properly addressing customer complaints is of ------- importance.
(A) critique
(B) critic
(C) critical
(D) critically

122. Mr. Bennett's team members spoke ------- of him when they shared pleasant memories at his retirement dinner.
(A) rarely
(B) vaguely
(C) fondly
(D) firmly

123. Groover Tech's new smartphone is the ------- project the company has worked on so far.
(A) secretiveness of
(B) as secretive as
(C) most secretive
(D) more secretive than

124. Most buyers seem ------- in SuperSwim's bathing suit options this year.
(A) interesting
(B) interested
(C) interest
(D) interests

125. ------- locals enjoyed Pete's Coffee, it had trouble competing with the major franchises that kept opening nearby.
(A) Therefore
(B) Because of
(C) Since
(D) Although

126. ------- his interview, Mr. Delgado appeared to be the ideal candidate to the hiring committee.
(A) As soon as
(B) Before
(C) Just as
(D) Nearly

127. After a careful inspection, the mechanic realized everything in the car was working properly ------- the taillights.
(A) although
(B) among
(C) except for
(D) because

128. Roller coaster operators must ensure that all passengers are secured ------- to their seats.
(A) tightening
(B) tightness
(C) tightly
(D) tightened

129. This car boasts unparalleled ------- that outperforms any other car on the market.
(A) speeding
(B) speedily
(C) speedy
(D) speed

130. ------- taking a course on business, Ms. Alfaro had no idea how to get her company started.
(A) Next
(B) Due to
(C) Yet
(D) Prior to

PART 6

Directions: Read the texts that follow. A word, phrase, or sentence is missing in parts of each text. Four answer choices for each question are given below the text. Select the best answer to complete the text. Then mark the letter (A), (B), (C), or (D) on your answer sheet.

Questions 131-134 refer to the following e-mail.

To: Multiple Recipients
From: Lovely Closet <information@lovelycloset.com>
Subject: Mobile App Issues
Date: 28 April

Dear Valued Customer:

We at Lovely Closet pride ourselves on our dedicated service to our customers. We are the #1 clothes shopping app in the country ------- we are committed to offering the highest quality
131.
garments for the best prices. Unfortunately, we ------- with an issue with our mobile app at the
132.
moment. -------. We have discussed this problem with our IT department, and they are trying to
133.
fix it. -------, feel free to use our Web site to find great fashion and place your orders. We apologize
134.
for the inconvenience and promise to have the application running as soon as possible.

Sincerely,

Pavel Lee

CEO of Lovely Closet

131. (A) because
(B) as if
(C) yet
(D) in spite of

132. (A) dealing
(B) had been dealing
(C) are dealing
(D) to deal

133. (A) We cannot seem to find the source of the issue.
(B) Users cannot use the app despite having stable Internet.
(C) Users reported preferring the design of a competitor's app.
(D) We have been working on this app for five years now.

134. (A) Otherwise
(B) For now
(C) Similarly
(D) Eventually

GO ON TO THE NEXT PAGE

Questions 135-138 refer to the following information.

Gizo Technology now guarantees that its electronics will work as good as ------- for at least
                                                                          135.
three years after the date of purchase. -------. This warranty applies to all products sold at Gizo
                                         136.
Technology stores, authorized -------, and on our Web site. Any malfunctioning products under
                               137.
warranty can be shipped directly to one of our factories for repair or exchange. If possible,
please ship the item to us in its ------- packaging with a valid receipt included.
                                  138.

135. (A) new
(B) newly
(C) newness
(D) renew

136. (A) All products have a lifetime warranty.
(B) Please speak to a representative for product samples.
(C) This new guarantee adds two years to our previous warranty.
(D) Our new batteries are more energy efficient than ever.

137. (A) distribution
(B) distributing
(C) distributors
(D) distributes

138. (A) originating
(B) originates
(C) originated
(D) original

Questions 139-142 refer to the following notice.

Pricilla's Home Garden Supplier has something new for our valued consumers. We will be renovating certain parts of the store, which will be temporarily closed to shoppers. Starting from May 17, the potted plants department ------- to be under construction. -------, seeds and
                                                                      139.   **140.**
fertilizer from this section of the store will not be available during renovations. Remodeling is scheduled to be finished by May 26. Our interior design staff and managers believe a -------
                                                                                                                                                             141.
days of disruption will be worth the effort in the end.

-------. During this time, customers will be able to win free plant starter kits and seeds. They can
142.
also enter a prize raffle for a rare Venus flytrap plant.

139. (A) slating
     (B) slates
     (C) is slated
     (D) to be slated

140. (A) Consequently
     (B) Because
     (C) Afterwards
     (D) Surprisingly

141. (A) never
     (B) small
     (C) little
     (D) few

142. (A) Customers are encouraged to bring coupons.
     (B) The entire store will close for two days.
     (C) After renovations, there will be a special celebration.
     (D) Artificial turf is available upon request.

Questions 143-146 refer to the following article.

BRISBANE (20 October)—Fast Co. revealed its annual Sports Car Showcase today. According to Elizabeth Hawkins, spokesperson for Fast Co., the company's ------- event is dedicated to highlighting the best and fastest cars in the industry. Some familiar corporations, as well as some new vendors, will be joining this year. One car of particular interest is the brand-new Manfrin 6000, which runs entirely on solar energy. -------. "Visitors can expect to see an environmental focus during the auto show," said Hawkins. "------- will be pleased to know that all of the cars featured are exceptionally eco-friendly. Each manufacturer has followed global ------- on how to make vehicles that have a reduced impact on the environment, and we hope buyers will appreciate that."

143. (A) frequent
 (B) occasional
 (C) monthly
 (D) yearly

144. (A) Most vehicles on the road are not sports cars.
 (B) This car reflects changing industry standards.
 (C) Hydroelectric energy is popular among some industries.
 (D) Prices are available on the Web site.

145. (A) It
 (B) She
 (C) They
 (D) He

146. (A) regulations
 (B) regulatory
 (C) regulate
 (D) regulating

PART 7
Directions: In this part you will read a selection of texts, such as magazine and newspaper articles, e-mails, and instant messages. Each text or set of texts is followed by several questions. Select the best answer for each question and mark the letter (A), (B), (C), or (D) on your answer sheet.

Questions 147-148 refer to the following advertisement.

JACKSONTOWN GRACE COUNTRY CLUB
Grand Opening 14 May

We at Grace Country Club would like to invite all interested leisure enthusiasts to join us for our grand opening at our newest site, located at 84 Belle Parkway. Experience our first-class facilities, exceptional service, and unique international cuisine for yourself.

Special Offer: Enjoy 10% off your first two months of membership! This is only available for new members and cannot be combined with any other offer. Offer is valid for any of the Grace Country Club franchises from the grand opening until 15 July.

For more information, please visit www.gracecountryclub.com/jacksontown or come see our premises yourself during a guided tour.

147. What is indicated about Jacksontown Grace Country Club?

(A) It is the first franchise.
(B) It is open five days a week.
(C) It offers exotic dishes.
(D) A membership is not required.

148. What is NOT mentioned about the special offer?

(A) It only applies to the Jacksontown branch.
(B) It is not valid for returning members.
(C) It lasts for two months.
(D) It cannot be used with other coupons.

GO ON TO THE NEXT PAGE

Questions 149-150 refer to the following note.

Dear Guest,

We hope you enjoy your stay in both Los Angeles and at the Murray Hotel. We are glad to have you as a guest. From 6:00 A.M. to 11:00 A.M., a complimentary breakfast is served in the dining area adjacent to the lobby. Our daily breakfast includes an assortment of pastries, scrambled eggs, toast, fruit, and sausage. Coffee and tea are also available. Please be advised that on June 18, breakfast will not be served in order to prepare for a conference being held later that day. However, guests are welcome to place a free room service order during breakfast time to receive their meal.

Gwen Alton
Murray Hotel Manager

149. What is one purpose of the note?

(A) To inform guests about a renovation
(B) To explain a change in meal services
(C) To announce a public event
(D) To send private invitations

150. What is true about the breakfast?

(A) It is available until noon.
(B) It is not available on June 18.
(C) It is offered for free.
(D) It is constantly updated.

Questions 151-152 refer to the following e-mail.

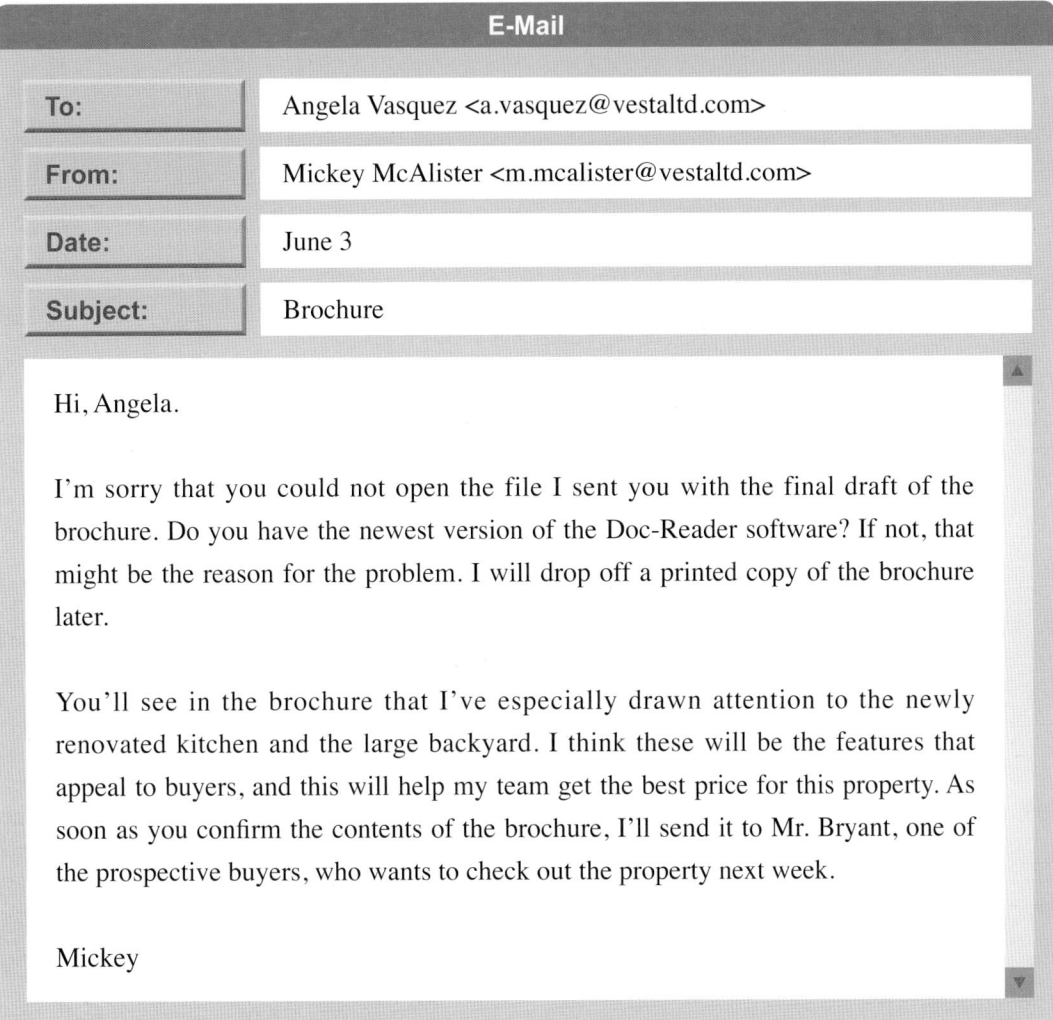

E-Mail	
To:	Angela Vasquez <a.vasquez@vestaltd.com>
From:	Mickey McAlister <m.mcalister@vestaltd.com>
Date:	June 3
Subject:	Brochure

Hi, Angela.

I'm sorry that you could not open the file I sent you with the final draft of the brochure. Do you have the newest version of the Doc-Reader software? If not, that might be the reason for the problem. I will drop off a printed copy of the brochure later.

You'll see in the brochure that I've especially drawn attention to the newly renovated kitchen and the large backyard. I think these will be the features that appeal to buyers, and this will help my team get the best price for this property. As soon as you confirm the contents of the brochure, I'll send it to Mr. Bryant, one of the prospective buyers, who wants to check out the property next week.

Mickey

151. Why does Mr. McAlister think Ms. Vasquez had an issue with the file?
(A) It contained a computer virus.
(B) It was redirected to another folder.
(C) She used the wrong file name.
(D) Her software may be outdated.

152. What most likely is Mr. McAlister's job?
(A) Construction worker
(B) Architect
(C) Real estate agent
(D) Landlord

Questions 153-154 refer to the following text-message chain.

Angelica Robinson (11:49 A.M.):
Hey, James. I'm at the butcher shop looking for flank steak, but I don't like any of the cuts available. Can you check to see if we have any left over from last night? If not, I might have to get a different cut of beef.

James Gorski (11:56 A.M.):
Looks like we're all out. I'll speak to the head chef.

Angelica Robinson (11:57 A.M.):
Thanks a bunch.

James Gorski (12:01 P.M.):
She said that flat iron steaks or chuck steaks would be fine substitutes. We'd just have to inform customers when they place their orders.

Angelica Robinson (12:03 P.M.):
No problem. Thanks!

153. For what business does Mr. Gorski most likely work?

(A) A grocery store
(B) An event planner
(C) A clothing store
(D) A restaurant

154. At 11:56 A.M., what does Mr. Gorski mean when he writes, "Looks like we're all out"?

(A) No one else is available to work.
(B) Some supplies have run out.
(C) A deadline has passed.
(D) There are no customers.

Questions 155-157 refer to the following notice.

Attention, Members of the Tarry Town Tea Society:

Next Saturday, the Tarry Town Tea Society will introduce a new tea flavor: Saffron Tea. —[1]—. This highly sought-after spice makes a delicious tea that offers a myriad of health benefits. —[2]—. As a way to show our appreciation for your continued support, we decided that Tea Society members will be able to try the tea at our club meeting a month before the general public. —[3]—.

In addition, you can show your Tarry Town Tea Society ID at any of the participating coffee shops in town and receive a cup of Saffron Tea at a reduced rate. Gold and Diamond level members will also get a free dessert of their choice with their order. —[4]—.

This Tea Society event starts today. For more details about special event dates, please visit our Web site at www.tarrytowntea.com/members.

---

155. What is available for all Tarry Town Tea Society members?

(A) An exclusive drink
(B) A private party
(C) New types of desserts
(D) Some rare spices

156. According to the notice, what is available on the Web site?

(A) A discount code
(B) A schedule
(C) A recipe
(D) A printable flyer

157. In which of the positions marked [1], [2], [3], and [4] does the following sentence best belong?

"Platinum members will get a small bag of authentic saffron to take home for tea or cooking purposes."

(A) [1]
(B) [2]
(C) [3]
(D) [4]

Questions 158-159 refer to the following article.

Onio Factory Gets a New Look

March 26—The Onio Factory, once known for its pasta-making capabilities, is getting a huge makeover this spring. The city council is working to turn the abandoned factory into a pedestrian mall with restaurants, stores selling clothing and other goods, and two stages for live shows.

The factory was almost demolished to make space for a new corporate office, but local residents protested the proposal. Community members view the factory as a historical landmark, as it had been in operation for over 50 years. After such strong opposition, city officials decided to go with their current plan.

"Onio was once one of the nation's largest pasta plants," noted Mayor Aurora Larsen. "When people opted for more office jobs, Onio eventually shut down. Thankfully, this new project will breathe life back into the building. We hope the updated space will be a safe area for residents to enjoy good food, shopping, and performances."

158. What is NOT mentioned in the current plans for the factory?

(A) Performance spaces
(B) Dining establishments
(C) Corporate offices
(D) Retail shops

159. What is suggested about the Onio Factory?

(A) It is the largest pasta factory in operation.
(B) It has been open for over a century.
(C) It was replaced by modern technology.
(D) It is significant to the city residents.

Questions 160-163 refer to the following memo.

MEMO

To: Customer Service Team
From: Adriano Fonti, Customer Service Manager
Date: October 13

Next week will be the first Customer Service Appreciation Week at Mike's Hardware. — [1] —. Throughout the week, we have special events planned for you. We do this to thank each of you for your commitment to excellence and quality service this year. Management has heard great things about each of the customer service representatives, and we couldn't be more proud. — [2] —. Even though the collaboration with Kevin's Woodworks was a bit difficult, our staff still pulled together and provided the amazing service our customers have come to expect. Management was highly impressed by everyone's dedication and professionalism.

On Monday morning, we will be taking personalized delivery orders from Henry's Café for everyone. On Tuesday, a fruit platter and an assortment of pastries will be available for breakfast. For Wednesday, we're getting pizza delivered for lunch. — [3] —. On Thursday, we're having an optional dinner at El Quesadilla. And finally, on Friday, we'll be going to the local bar for an after-work happy hour. — [4] —.

I hope you all get excited about what we have in store for you!

160. Why did Mr. Fonti write this memo?

(A) To ask for employee opinions
(B) To discuss a future training session
(C) To give details about a series of events
(D) To scold his employees

161. What is suggested about Mike's Hardware?

(A) It has Employee of the Month awards.
(B) Its business is not doing well.
(C) Its owner is considering selling the business.
(D) It appreciates its staff members.

162. When will an event take place in the morning?

(A) On Tuesday
(B) On Wednesday
(C) On Thursday
(D) On Friday

163. In which of the positions marked [1], [2], [3], and [4] does the following sentence best belong?

"Two drinks each will be paid for by the company."

(A) [1]
(B) [2]
(C) [3]
(D) [4]

Questions 164-167 refer to the following instructions.

Cregar

Cregar customers value quality and style, and they look forward to seeing the new items we introduce every season. To maximize sales, it is important to show what our store has to offer and help customers imagine a lifestyle that includes our leather handbags, belts, and more. When creating store displays, you need to tell a story. The merchandise should be eye-catching and arranged in an attractive way. Any signs included with the items should be brief, and their colors should complement the products. Limit the number of items placed on the display. Otherwise, you run the risk of making customers too distracted to pay attention to what we are trying to show them. Place the most important products near the entrance, and make sure the area around the shelving unit is kept clear.

164. For whom most likely were the instructions written?

(A) Salespeople who contact Cregar customers
(B) Employees who set up Cregar displays
(C) Customers who purchased Cregar products
(D) Developers of Cregar merchandise

165. What does Cregar most likely sell?

(A) Appliances
(B) Cosmetics
(C) Accessories
(D) Software

166. Why do the instructions advise using a small number of items?

(A) It reduces the time spent on a task.
(B) It requires much less space.
(C) It can help focus customers' attention.
(D) It reduces the overall cost of the project.

167. The word "clear" in paragraph 1, line 10, is closest in meaning to

(A) pure
(B) understandable
(C) empty
(D) obvious

Questions 168-171 refer to the following online chat discussion.

Beatrice Iden (4:14 P.M.)	Hi, everyone. I wanted to check in with you all before the weekend. Eric, how did your meeting with Kloud Department Store go?
Eric Neely (4:16 P.M.)	It went well! They agreed to purchase five hundred of our two-person tents as an initial order. I've got the signed contract right in front of me.
Beatrice Iden (4:17 P.M.)	Amazing! Great job out there today.
Kenneth Wolf (4:21 P.M.)	Congrats! I think this means you're the top salesperson for the second month in a row.
Susan Kuzma (4:22 P.M.)	I'm happy for you, Eric. If you get all your receipts back to me when you get to the office, I can put in the request for your travel reimbursement.
Eric Neely (4:23 P.M.)	Are you sure about that, Kenneth? I heard Jamie Hill just landed a huge sale.
Beatrice Iden (4:25 P.M.)	Jamie's customers changed their minds at the last minute. They decided to go with another company because it was offering a better discount.
Eric Neely (4:26 P.M.)	That's too bad. Oh, thanks for helping me out, Susan.
Susan Kuzma (4:27 P.M.)	No problem!

168. In what type of business are the writers most likely involved?

(A) Travel planning
(B) Programming
(C) Employee training
(D) Camping equipment

169. What most likely is Ms. Iden's job title?

(A) Sales manager
(B) Secretary
(C) Head of human resources
(D) Marketing director

170. What is indicated about Ms. Hill?

(A) She recently joined the company.
(B) She is an executive board member.
(C) She did not complete her sale.
(D) She is switching companies soon.

171. At 4:27 P.M., what does Ms. Kuzma most likely mean when she writes, "No problem!"?

(A) Negotiations with a supplier went well.
(B) Her computer is functioning normally.
(C) She is happy that it is the end of the day.
(D) She doesn't mind helping Mr. Neely.

Questions 172-175 refer to the following e-mail.

To: stafflist@milton-data.com
From: williamsc@milton-data.com
Date: September 6
Subject: Company Retreat

Dear Staff,

Thank you for your active participation in last month's company retreat. We hope you all had a great time. This annual event is an important part of building cooperative relationships with staff in different departments. It also gives us a chance to focus on the company's mission for the future.

I have reviewed your responses on the employee comment cards, but I would like you to elaborate on your answers. These answers will help with planning next year's retreat. Please respond by e-mail to the following questions:

- What were the advantages and disadvantages of the selected venue?
- Which session did you like best and why?
- What activities or topics would you like to see added to next year's agenda?
- Would you be interested in presenting on a topic? If so, what is your area of expertise?

I am already looking into booking a venue for next year, as it's difficult to find a venue offering the range of spaces we need at an affordable price during the peak season. However, I would like to hear your responses first. Therefore, I ask that you reply as quickly as possible. Thank you in advance for your responses. They will help me in making the necessary plans for next year's retreat.

Sincerely,

Clara Williams

172. What is indicated about the company retreat?

(A) It was longer than usual this year.
(B) It is held every year in July.
(C) It facilitates teamwork among departments.
(D) It brings together several company branches.

173. What is suggested about the employee comment cards?

(A) They have not been read by Ms. Williams yet.
(B) They contained some incorrect information.
(C) They were only sent to the company's managers.
(D) They did not include long answers from participants.

174. Why does Ms. Williams ask for prompt feedback?

(A) She plans to make a reservation soon.
(B) She will meet with some board members.
(C) She wants to take advantage of a discount.
(D) She is waiting for a promotion.

175. Who most likely is Ms. Williams?

(A) A Web site developer
(B) An event coordinator
(C) A building owner
(D) A company investor

Questions 176-180 refer to the following advertisement and e-mail.

Custom-Made Business Cards

Sakai Printers is happy to announce its new Web site: www.sakaiprinters.com. In addition to coming to our shop in person or sending an e-mail, customers can now visit us online to make their orders. With our new system, you can upload photos, design your own business cards, and order them to your doorstep with a few simple clicks.

Here are our different options:

Type	Description	Minimum Order
Basic	Simple, lightweight paper	50 cards
Standard	Standard quality paper, smooth texture	50 cards
Premium	High-quality paper, multiple colors available	100 cards
Luxury	Highest possible quality, multiple colors and gold trim	150 cards

If you would like to receive a sample of each option, please contact us via e-mail before placing your order.

To: customerservice@sakaiprinters.com
From: deon_hogg@perfectpetgoods.com
Date: 19 January
Subject: RE: Order 6754
Attachment: NewLogo_PerfectPetGoods

To Whom It May Concern:

Thank you so much for pausing my order and allowing me to change the design before the business cards went off to print. Even though I placed an order for the minimum amount, it would have been unfortunate to have 100 cards that I could not use.

As mentioned in my previous e-mail, I accidentally uploaded the old version of my company's logo on the Web site. I have attached the updated version to this e-mail, so please continue with my order using the new image. Please let me know if there are any issues with the new file.

Thank you again!

Deon Hogg

176. What is mentioned about Sakai Printers?

(A) It offers five types of business cards.
(B) It does not have a physical location.
(C) It accepts orders via e-mail.
(D) It is a newly opened business.

177. According to the advertisement, what can customers do through e-mail?

(A) Submit feedback on their experiences
(B) Ask questions about the service
(C) Request sample cards
(D) Ask for a refund or exchange

178. What type of business card did Mr. Hogg most likely order?

(A) Basic
(B) Standard
(C) Premium
(D) Luxury

179. Why does Mr. Hogg want to replace the logo on his business cards?

(A) Its colors did not match well.
(B) Its design was outdated.
(C) Its size was too large.
(D) Its placement was misaligned.

180. In the e-mail, the word "issues" in paragraph 2, line 4, is closest in meaning to

(A) problems
(B) papers
(C) notebooks
(D) records

GO ON TO THE NEXT PAGE

Questions 181-185 refer to the following Web page and e-mail.

http://www.allentownpoets.org/workshop

Allentown Poetry Workshop

Have you always wanted to publish your poetry? Do you have a stack of poems waiting to be appreciated by the public? If so, consider applying for the Allentown Poetry Workshop (APW).

APW is an opportunity for both aspiring and practicing poets to gather, exchange ideas, and emerge as better writers. For the past 12 years, APW has helped writers from all over the country develop their creative voice. Please consider applying for the next workshop if you would enjoy peer workshops, public poetry readings, and having your work published in the *Allentown Quarterly*.

- The workshop will be held on weekdays from June 13 to June 30.
- Each class will meet from 10 A.M. to 4 P.M. with an hour and a half break for lunch at noon.
- Tuition is $1,299 and must be paid in full by June 1.
- Financial aid is available to those who have a demonstrated need.
- Each class is capped at eight students.

To apply:
Please send five to ten pages worth of poetry and an autobiographical statement of no more than 300 words to apply@allentownpoets.org by April 1. Due to the volume of applications, only those who have been accepted will receive a response.

From:	Marie Owen ⟨m.owen@allentownpoets.org⟩
To:	Jasper Fultz ⟨jasper_fultz@jmail.com⟩
Date:	May 3
Subject:	Congratulations! You've been selected
Attachment:	Student Form

Dear Mr. Fultz,

My name is Marie Owen, and I am one of the instructors at the Allentown Poetry Workshop. I am pleased to inform you that you have been accepted into this year's poetry workshop. Our committee was particularly impressed with the imagery in your writing samples.

As for myself, I have been teaching at the APW since it began. I have written three collections of poetry, and several of my poems have been featured in internationally distributed publications.

Please complete the Student Form attached to this e-mail and send it back to me or drop it off at the Allentown Arts Academy by June 1. I look forward to meeting you for our first day of class on June 13. In the next few days, keep an eye out for your first assignment, which I will send by e-mail and expect to be completed by the first day of class.

Marie Owen

181. According to the Web page, what is true about the poetry classes?
    (A) The deadline to apply is June 1.
    (B) Classes are three times a week.
    (C) Tuition is due on the first day of class.
    (D) Classes have a maximum of eight students.

182. What must be included in the application?
    (A) A short self-description
    (B) A résumé
    (C) A professional photo
    (D) A published poem

183. What is the purpose of Ms. Owen's e-mail?
    (A) To convince a friend to apply for an activity
    (B) To outline her numerous awards
    (C) To invite an applicant to an interview
    (D) To congratulate a successful applicant

184. What is suggested about Ms. Owen?
    (A) She has taught at APW for 12 years.
    (B) She is the only person who read Mr. Fultz's work.
    (C) She has written dozens of poetry collections.
    (D) She has a close relationship with Mr. Fultz.

185. What is Mr. Fultz asked to do?
    (A) Send another writing sample
    (B) Prepare for a class assignment
    (C) Seek financial aid
    (D) Pay the tuition immediately

Questions 186-190 refer to the following Web page, online form, and search results.

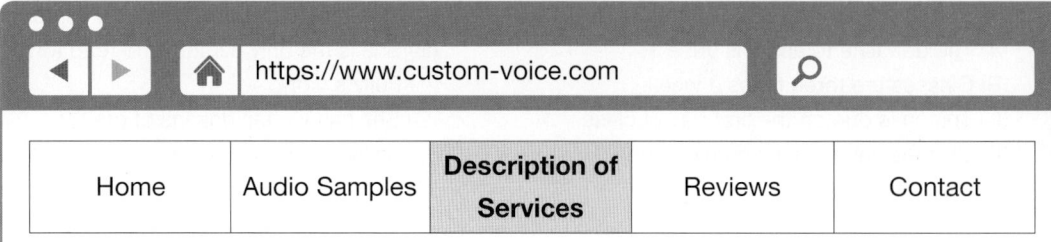

| Home | Audio Samples | **Description of Services** | Reviews | Contact |

With over 5,000 voice actors speaking more than 40 languages, Custom Voice is ready to help you with your project. We only hire native speakers with voice acting experience, and they can record your text in our studio or on location at the site of your choice. For decades, we have been providing high-quality recordings of speaking and singing. And now our sound technicians can put in additional recorded sounds such as nature sounds, traffic noise, and weather sounds.

Service A: Voice recording of spoken word with a single speaker. Perfect for corporate narration, audiobooks, and telephone prompts.
Service B: Voice recording of spoken word with two or more speakers. Our most popular service, used for commercials and e-learning materials.
Service C: Voice recording of singing with a single singer. Popular for advertising jingles and educational songs.
Service D: Voice recording of singing with two or more singers, which can include soprano, alto, tenor, and bass. Can include backup vocals for commercial music albums.

Please note that lyrics and sheet music must be provided at least 48 hours in advance for all musical recordings. For a cost estimate, please complete our Project Overview Form with the details of your project.

Custom Voice: Project Overview Form

Name: Gavin Barrett
Date: March 16

Please provide an overview of your project and its needs:
I've created some nonstick pots and pans, and I'd like a voiceover with one speaker for a video that gives instructions on how to clean them. The script is approximately 350 words long. I'd like the speaker to be male, and I prefer a UK accent for my target audience. I would like to have this project completed within one week, if possible.

Custom Voice: Performers available for the Barrett, Gavin project:

Name	Age Bracket	Male/Female	Details
Trisha Blanchard	20–29	Female	An American singer and voice actress with three years' experience.
Salvador Campanella	40–49	Male	A British voice actor and singer who has performed in many animated films.
Kirby Garrison	30–39	Male	An American voice actor with ten years of experience.
Bonnie Walsh	40–49	Female	A British voice actress known for her audiobooks and corporate voiceovers.

All actors are native speakers of the target language.

186. What is implied about Custom Voice?

(A) Its employees can travel for work.
(B) Its recordings are for personal use only.
(C) It can write scripts for clients.
(D) It was founded a few years ago.

187. What new service is now available at Custom Voice?

(A) Writing original music
(B) Adding sound effects
(C) Supplying different accents
(D) Providing an express service

188. What is true about Mr. Barrett?

(A) He needs the work finished overnight.
(B) He has used Custom Voice before.
(C) He designed some cookware.
(D) He wants to shorten his script.

189. Which Custom Voice service would be best for Mr. Barrett?

(A) Service A
(B) Service B
(C) Service C
(D) Service D

190. Who would be most suitable for Mr. Barrett's project?

(A) Trisha Blanchard
(B) Salvador Campanella
(C) Kirby Garrison
(D) Bonnie Walsh

GO ON TO THE NEXT PAGE

Questions 191-195 refer to the following Web page and e-mails.

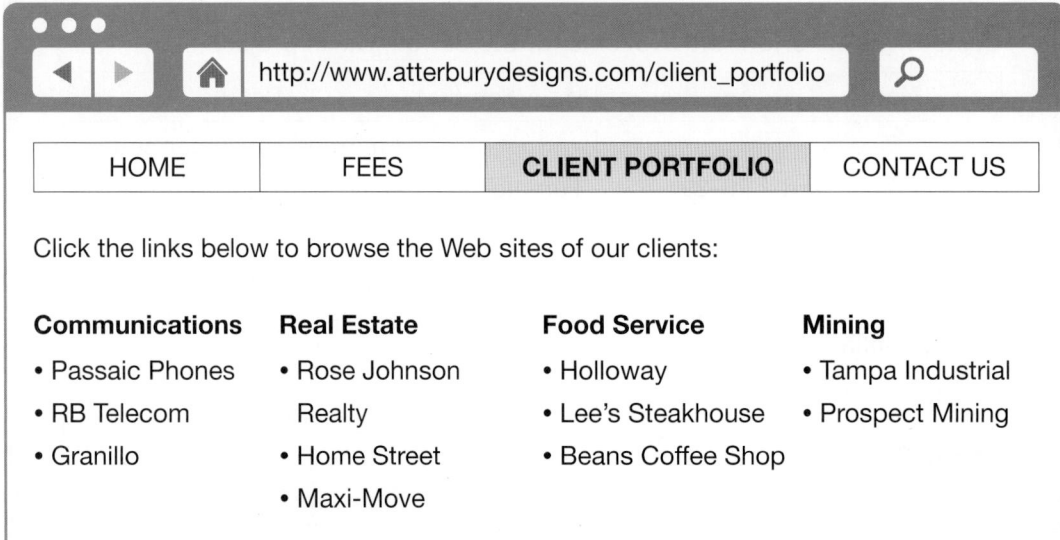

http://www.atterburydesigns.com/client_portfolio

| HOME | FEES | **CLIENT PORTFOLIO** | CONTACT US |

Click the links below to browse the Web sites of our clients:

Communications
- Passaic Phones
- RB Telecom
- Granillo

Real Estate
- Rose Johnson Realty
- Home Street
- Maxi-Move

Food Service
- Holloway
- Lee's Steakhouse
- Beans Coffee Shop

Mining
- Tampa Industrial
- Prospect Mining

To: Daniel McClellan <dmcclellan@mail-storage.net>
From: Leah Atterbury <leah@atterburydesigns.com>
Date: September 18
Subject: Greetings from Austin

Dear Mr. McClellan,

How are you? I hope you are doing well. After completing my studies at Cartwright Design Institute, I worked at Howarth Services for about a year. It was a great opportunity to put my new design skills to use and to learn how to communicate well with clients. However, when the company relocated to San Diego, I decided to stay in Austin.

After I quit my job, I launched my own company, starting by building a Web site for Granillo. From there, I have slowly taken on more clients, and I'm fortunate to be busier than ever. That is why I am writing to you. I'm sure you know a lot of Web designers because of your work. I'm wondering if you could recommend someone who could work for me on a freelance basis. This would help me to keep up with the workload. I would really appreciate any help you can give.

Thank you so much,

Leah

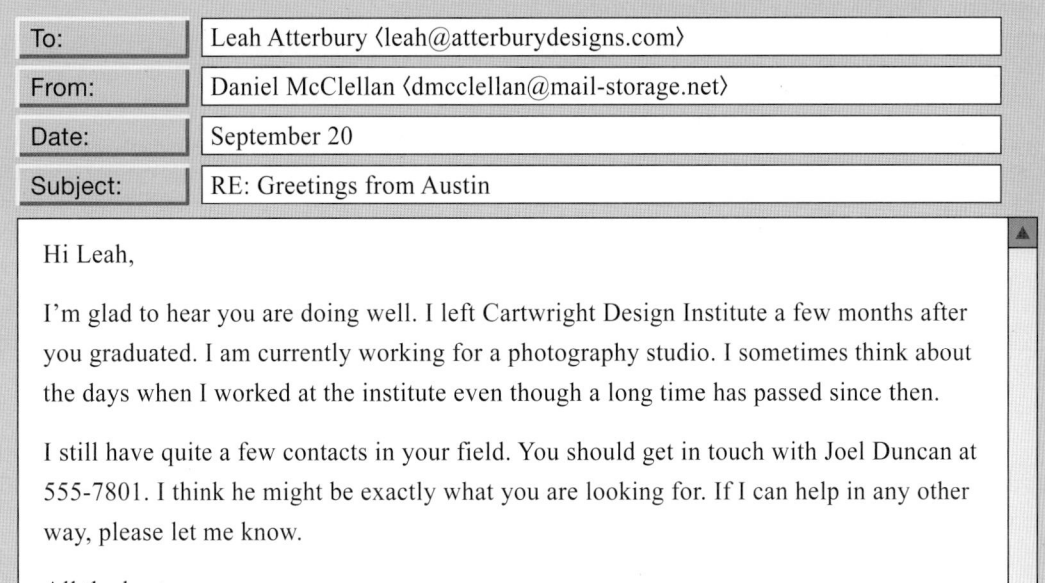

Hi Leah,

I'm glad to hear you are doing well. I left Cartwright Design Institute a few months after you graduated. I am currently working for a photography studio. I sometimes think about the days when I worked at the institute even though a long time has passed since then.

I still have quite a few contacts in your field. You should get in touch with Joel Duncan at 555-7801. I think he might be exactly what you are looking for. If I can help in any other way, please let me know.

All the best,

Daniel

191. What is true about Atterbury Designs?
(A) It recently started working in real estate.
(B) It specializes in small businesses.
(C) It was launched about one year ago.
(D) It has clients in different industries.

192. What kind of business was the first client of Atterbury Designs?
(A) A communications company
(B) A real estate company
(C) A food service company
(D) A mining company

193. What does Ms. Atterbury indicate about Howarth Services?
(A) It was founded in San Diego.
(B) It offers employees one-year contracts.
(C) It no longer operates in Austin.
(D) It allows staff members to work remotely.

194. Who most likely is Mr. McClellan?
(A) Ms. Atterbury's former coworker
(B) The owner of the Cartwright Institute
(C) Ms. Atterbury's former teacher
(D) An employee at Howarth Services

195. Why will Ms. Atterbury most likely call Mr. Duncan?
(A) To design a Web page for his business
(B) To offer him a job opportunity
(C) To ask for a reference letter
(D) To inquire about an office space

Questions 196-200 refer to the following e-mails and schedule.

TO:	All Staff
FROM:	Richard Rhodes
DATE:	December 2
SUBJECT:	Updates

Dear All,

I have some exciting news on behalf of Belfour Inc. Our company has seen outstanding growth over the past year with no sign of stopping. Just last month, we were able to conduct over 10 sales strategies workshops in the New Rotom area alone.

Due to this positive trend, we have decided to hire two new workshop presenters for our team. Robin Niva is an expert in digital marketing and has over six years' worth of experience. Tai Tsuda will be our medical sales authority, and he brings over 15 years of medical training with him. These two will begin holding workshops sometime next month.

Please welcome them to the Belfour Inc. family!

Richard Rhodes, CEO

Belfour Inc.
Proposed Training Schedule
The Second Week of January

Course Title	Date	Length	Location	Presenter
Effective E-mail Advertising	January 6	Full Day	New Rotom Convention Center	Robin Niva
Creating Interesting Ad Copy	January 7	Half Day	New Rotom Convention Center	Joseph Bronston
Selling Your Experimental Products	January 8	Full Day	New Rotom Research Hospital	Tai Tsuda
How to Appeal to Family Doctors	January 9	Half Day	New Rotom Family Hospital	To Be Announced

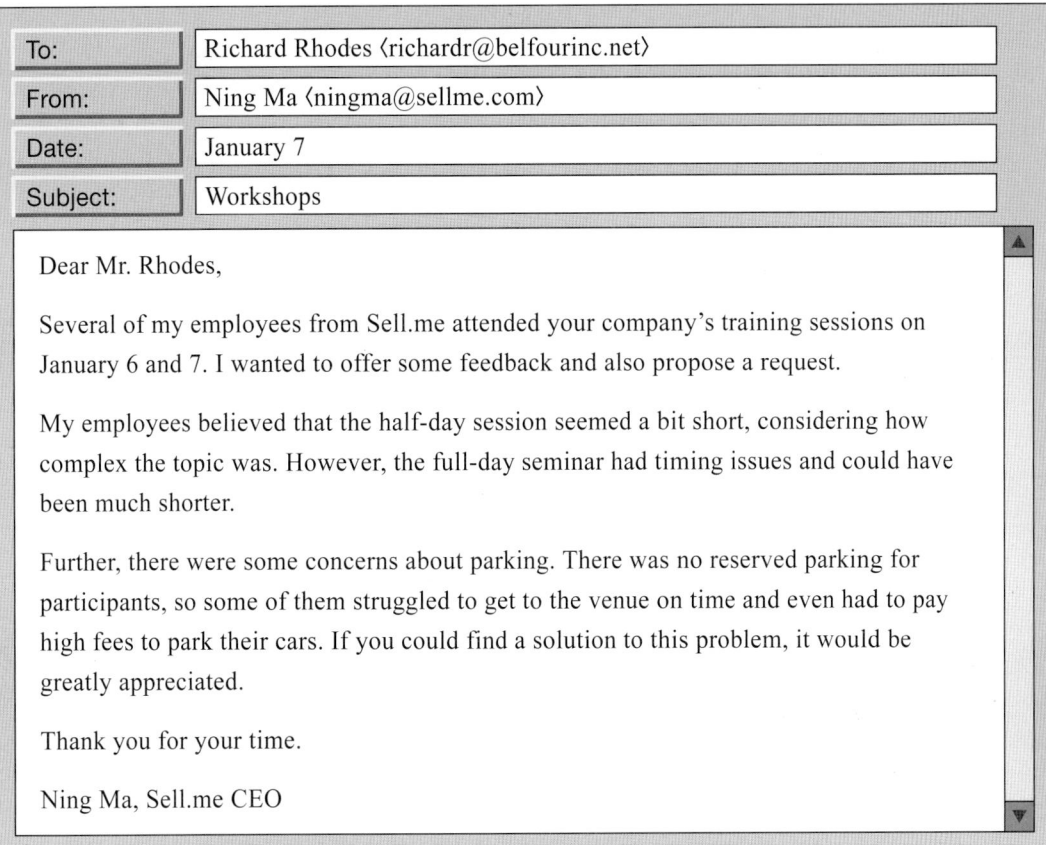

To: Richard Rhodes ⟨richardr@belfourinc.net⟩
From: Ning Ma ⟨ningma@sellme.com⟩
Date: January 7
Subject: Workshops

Dear Mr. Rhodes,

Several of my employees from Sell.me attended your company's training sessions on January 6 and 7. I wanted to offer some feedback and also propose a request.

My employees believed that the half-day session seemed a bit short, considering how complex the topic was. However, the full-day seminar had timing issues and could have been much shorter.

Further, there were some concerns about parking. There was no reserved parking for participants, so some of them struggled to get to the venue on time and even had to pay high fees to park their cars. If you could find a solution to this problem, it would be greatly appreciated.

Thank you for your time.

Ning Ma, Sell.me CEO

196. What is the purpose of the first e-mail?
(A) To invite employees to a conference
(B) To plan a company's future growth
(C) To introduce new staff members
(D) To announce a new branch opening

197. In what area does Belfour Inc. most likely specialize?
(A) Telemarketing
(B) Sales Training
(C) Medical technology
(D) Digital training

198. What does the schedule indicate about the workshops?
(A) Some are held at the same place.
(B) There are several breaks throughout the day.
(C) They are all led by the same person.
(D) They usually last a full day.

199. Who will most likely lead the workshop on January 9?
(A) Mr. Rhodes
(B) Ms. Niva
(C) Mr. Bronston
(D) Mr. Tsuda

200. What does Ms. Ma suggest about her employees' training experience?
(A) They were completely satisfied.
(B) The January 6 workshop was too long.
(C) Parking was readily available.
(D) The topics were uninteresting.

Stop! This is the end of the test. If you finish before time is called, you may go back to Parts 5, 6, and 7 and check your work.

ANSWER SHEET

TOEIC 실전 모의고사

응시일자	20 . .
이름	
맞은 개수	/100

ANSWER SHEET

TOEIC 실전 모의고사

응시일자	20 . . .
이름	
맞은 개수	/100

READING (Part V ~ VII)									
101	ⓐ ⓑ ⓒ ⓓ	121	ⓐ ⓑ ⓒ ⓓ	141	ⓐ ⓑ ⓒ ⓓ	161	ⓐ ⓑ ⓒ ⓓ	181	ⓐ ⓑ ⓒ ⓓ
102	ⓐ ⓑ ⓒ ⓓ	122	ⓐ ⓑ ⓒ ⓓ	142	ⓐ ⓑ ⓒ ⓓ	162	ⓐ ⓑ ⓒ ⓓ	182	ⓐ ⓑ ⓒ ⓓ
103	ⓐ ⓑ ⓒ ⓓ	123	ⓐ ⓑ ⓒ ⓓ	143	ⓐ ⓑ ⓒ ⓓ	163	ⓐ ⓑ ⓒ ⓓ	183	ⓐ ⓑ ⓒ ⓓ
104	ⓐ ⓑ ⓒ ⓓ	124	ⓐ ⓑ ⓒ ⓓ	144	ⓐ ⓑ ⓒ ⓓ	164	ⓐ ⓑ ⓒ ⓓ	184	ⓐ ⓑ ⓒ ⓓ
105	ⓐ ⓑ ⓒ ⓓ	125	ⓐ ⓑ ⓒ ⓓ	145	ⓐ ⓑ ⓒ ⓓ	165	ⓐ ⓑ ⓒ ⓓ	185	ⓐ ⓑ ⓒ ⓓ
106	ⓐ ⓑ ⓒ ⓓ	126	ⓐ ⓑ ⓒ ⓓ	146	ⓐ ⓑ ⓒ ⓓ	166	ⓐ ⓑ ⓒ ⓓ	186	ⓐ ⓑ ⓒ ⓓ
107	ⓐ ⓑ ⓒ ⓓ	127	ⓐ ⓑ ⓒ ⓓ	147	ⓐ ⓑ ⓒ ⓓ	167	ⓐ ⓑ ⓒ ⓓ	187	ⓐ ⓑ ⓒ ⓓ
108	ⓐ ⓑ ⓒ ⓓ	128	ⓐ ⓑ ⓒ ⓓ	148	ⓐ ⓑ ⓒ ⓓ	168	ⓐ ⓑ ⓒ ⓓ	188	ⓐ ⓑ ⓒ ⓓ
109	ⓐ ⓑ ⓒ ⓓ	129	ⓐ ⓑ ⓒ ⓓ	149	ⓐ ⓑ ⓒ ⓓ	169	ⓐ ⓑ ⓒ ⓓ	189	ⓐ ⓑ ⓒ ⓓ
110	ⓐ ⓑ ⓒ ⓓ	130	ⓐ ⓑ ⓒ ⓓ	150	ⓐ ⓑ ⓒ ⓓ	170	ⓐ ⓑ ⓒ ⓓ	190	ⓐ ⓑ ⓒ ⓓ
111	ⓐ ⓑ ⓒ ⓓ	131	ⓐ ⓑ ⓒ ⓓ	151	ⓐ ⓑ ⓒ ⓓ	171	ⓐ ⓑ ⓒ ⓓ	191	ⓐ ⓑ ⓒ ⓓ
112	ⓐ ⓑ ⓒ ⓓ	132	ⓐ ⓑ ⓒ ⓓ	152	ⓐ ⓑ ⓒ ⓓ	172	ⓐ ⓑ ⓒ ⓓ	192	ⓐ ⓑ ⓒ ⓓ
113	ⓐ ⓑ ⓒ ⓓ	133	ⓐ ⓑ ⓒ ⓓ	153	ⓐ ⓑ ⓒ ⓓ	173	ⓐ ⓑ ⓒ ⓓ	193	ⓐ ⓑ ⓒ ⓓ
114	ⓐ ⓑ ⓒ ⓓ	134	ⓐ ⓑ ⓒ ⓓ	154	ⓐ ⓑ ⓒ ⓓ	174	ⓐ ⓑ ⓒ ⓓ	194	ⓐ ⓑ ⓒ ⓓ
115	ⓐ ⓑ ⓒ ⓓ	135	ⓐ ⓑ ⓒ ⓓ	155	ⓐ ⓑ ⓒ ⓓ	175	ⓐ ⓑ ⓒ ⓓ	195	ⓐ ⓑ ⓒ ⓓ
116	ⓐ ⓑ ⓒ ⓓ	136	ⓐ ⓑ ⓒ ⓓ	156	ⓐ ⓑ ⓒ ⓓ	176	ⓐ ⓑ ⓒ ⓓ	196	ⓐ ⓑ ⓒ ⓓ
117	ⓐ ⓑ ⓒ ⓓ	137	ⓐ ⓑ ⓒ ⓓ	157	ⓐ ⓑ ⓒ ⓓ	177	ⓐ ⓑ ⓒ ⓓ	197	ⓐ ⓑ ⓒ ⓓ
118	ⓐ ⓑ ⓒ ⓓ	138	ⓐ ⓑ ⓒ ⓓ	158	ⓐ ⓑ ⓒ ⓓ	178	ⓐ ⓑ ⓒ ⓓ	198	ⓐ ⓑ ⓒ ⓓ
119	ⓐ ⓑ ⓒ ⓓ	139	ⓐ ⓑ ⓒ ⓓ	159	ⓐ ⓑ ⓒ ⓓ	179	ⓐ ⓑ ⓒ ⓓ	199	ⓐ ⓑ ⓒ ⓓ
120	ⓐ ⓑ ⓒ ⓓ	140	ⓐ ⓑ ⓒ ⓓ	160	ⓐ ⓑ ⓒ ⓓ	180	ⓐ ⓑ ⓒ ⓓ	200	ⓐ ⓑ ⓒ ⓓ

READING (Part V ~ VII)									
101	ⓐ ⓑ ⓒ ⓓ	121	ⓐ ⓑ ⓒ ⓓ	141	ⓐ ⓑ ⓒ ⓓ	161	ⓐ ⓑ ⓒ ⓓ	181	ⓐ ⓑ ⓒ ⓓ
102	ⓐ ⓑ ⓒ ⓓ	122	ⓐ ⓑ ⓒ ⓓ	142	ⓐ ⓑ ⓒ ⓓ	162	ⓐ ⓑ ⓒ ⓓ	182	ⓐ ⓑ ⓒ ⓓ
103	ⓐ ⓑ ⓒ ⓓ	123	ⓐ ⓑ ⓒ ⓓ	143	ⓐ ⓑ ⓒ ⓓ	163	ⓐ ⓑ ⓒ ⓓ	183	ⓐ ⓑ ⓒ ⓓ
104	ⓐ ⓑ ⓒ ⓓ	124	ⓐ ⓑ ⓒ ⓓ	144	ⓐ ⓑ ⓒ ⓓ	164	ⓐ ⓑ ⓒ ⓓ	184	ⓐ ⓑ ⓒ ⓓ
105	ⓐ ⓑ ⓒ ⓓ	125	ⓐ ⓑ ⓒ ⓓ	145	ⓐ ⓑ ⓒ ⓓ	165	ⓐ ⓑ ⓒ ⓓ	185	ⓐ ⓑ ⓒ ⓓ
106	ⓐ ⓑ ⓒ ⓓ	126	ⓐ ⓑ ⓒ ⓓ	146	ⓐ ⓑ ⓒ ⓓ	166	ⓐ ⓑ ⓒ ⓓ	186	ⓐ ⓑ ⓒ ⓓ
107	ⓐ ⓑ ⓒ ⓓ	127	ⓐ ⓑ ⓒ ⓓ	147	ⓐ ⓑ ⓒ ⓓ	167	ⓐ ⓑ ⓒ ⓓ	187	ⓐ ⓑ ⓒ ⓓ
108	ⓐ ⓑ ⓒ ⓓ	128	ⓐ ⓑ ⓒ ⓓ	148	ⓐ ⓑ ⓒ ⓓ	168	ⓐ ⓑ ⓒ ⓓ	188	ⓐ ⓑ ⓒ ⓓ
109	ⓐ ⓑ ⓒ ⓓ	129	ⓐ ⓑ ⓒ ⓓ	149	ⓐ ⓑ ⓒ ⓓ	169	ⓐ ⓑ ⓒ ⓓ	189	ⓐ ⓑ ⓒ ⓓ
110	ⓐ ⓑ ⓒ ⓓ	130	ⓐ ⓑ ⓒ ⓓ	150	ⓐ ⓑ ⓒ ⓓ	170	ⓐ ⓑ ⓒ ⓓ	190	ⓐ ⓑ ⓒ ⓓ
111	ⓐ ⓑ ⓒ ⓓ	131	ⓐ ⓑ ⓒ ⓓ	151	ⓐ ⓑ ⓒ ⓓ	171	ⓐ ⓑ ⓒ ⓓ	191	ⓐ ⓑ ⓒ ⓓ
112	ⓐ ⓑ ⓒ ⓓ	132	ⓐ ⓑ ⓒ ⓓ	152	ⓐ ⓑ ⓒ ⓓ	172	ⓐ ⓑ ⓒ ⓓ	192	ⓐ ⓑ ⓒ ⓓ
113	ⓐ ⓑ ⓒ ⓓ	133	ⓐ ⓑ ⓒ ⓓ	153	ⓐ ⓑ ⓒ ⓓ	173	ⓐ ⓑ ⓒ ⓓ	193	ⓐ ⓑ ⓒ ⓓ
114	ⓐ ⓑ ⓒ ⓓ	134	ⓐ ⓑ ⓒ ⓓ	154	ⓐ ⓑ ⓒ ⓓ	174	ⓐ ⓑ ⓒ ⓓ	194	ⓐ ⓑ ⓒ ⓓ
115	ⓐ ⓑ ⓒ ⓓ	135	ⓐ ⓑ ⓒ ⓓ	155	ⓐ ⓑ ⓒ ⓓ	175	ⓐ ⓑ ⓒ ⓓ	195	ⓐ ⓑ ⓒ ⓓ
116	ⓐ ⓑ ⓒ ⓓ	136	ⓐ ⓑ ⓒ ⓓ	156	ⓐ ⓑ ⓒ ⓓ	176	ⓐ ⓑ ⓒ ⓓ	196	ⓐ ⓑ ⓒ ⓓ
117	ⓐ ⓑ ⓒ ⓓ	137	ⓐ ⓑ ⓒ ⓓ	157	ⓐ ⓑ ⓒ ⓓ	177	ⓐ ⓑ ⓒ ⓓ	197	ⓐ ⓑ ⓒ ⓓ
118	ⓐ ⓑ ⓒ ⓓ	138	ⓐ ⓑ ⓒ ⓓ	158	ⓐ ⓑ ⓒ ⓓ	178	ⓐ ⓑ ⓒ ⓓ	198	ⓐ ⓑ ⓒ ⓓ
119	ⓐ ⓑ ⓒ ⓓ	139	ⓐ ⓑ ⓒ ⓓ	159	ⓐ ⓑ ⓒ ⓓ	179	ⓐ ⓑ ⓒ ⓓ	199	ⓐ ⓑ ⓒ ⓓ
120	ⓐ ⓑ ⓒ ⓓ	140	ⓐ ⓑ ⓒ ⓓ	160	ⓐ ⓑ ⓒ ⓓ	180	ⓐ ⓑ ⓒ ⓓ	200	ⓐ ⓑ ⓒ ⓓ

에듀윌이 너를 지지할게

ENERGY

삶의 순간순간이
아름다운 마무리이며
새로운 시작이어야 한다.

– 법정 스님

에듀윌 토익 READING RC (리딩 종합서)

발 행 일	2022년 9월 1일 초판 ǀ 2023년 4월 6일 2쇄 ǀ 2023년 12월 13일 3쇄
편 저 자	에듀윌 어학연구소
펴 낸 이	양형남
펴 낸 곳	(주)에듀윌
등록번호	제25100-2002-000052호
주　　소	08378 서울특별시 구로구 디지털로34길 55 코오롱싸이언스밸리 2차 3층

* 이 책의 무단 인용 · 전재 · 복제를 금합니다.

www.eduwill.net
대표전화 1600-6700

여러분의 작은 소리
에듀윌은 크게 듣겠습니다.

본 교재에 대한 여러분의 목소리를 들려주세요.
공부하시면서 어려웠던 점, 궁금한 점,
칭찬하고 싶은 점, 개선할 점, 어떤 것이라도 좋습니다.

에듀윌은 여러분께서 나누어 주신 의견을
통해 끊임없이 발전하고 있습니다.

에듀윌 도서몰 book.eduwill.net
- 부가학습자료 및 정오표: 에듀윌 도서몰 → 도서자료실
- 교재 문의: 에듀윌 도서몰 → 문의하기 → 교재(내용,출간) / 주문 및 배송

꿈을 현실로 만드는
에듀윌

DREAM

공무원 교육
- 선호도 1위, 신뢰도 1위!
  브랜드만족도 1위!
- 합격자 수 2,100% 폭등시킨
  독한 커리큘럼

자격증 교육
- 9년간 아무도 깨지 못한 기록
  합격자 수 1위
- 가장 많은 합격자를 배출한
  최고의 합격 시스템

직영학원
- 검증된 합격 프로그램과 강의
- 1:1 밀착 관리 및 컨설팅
- 호텔 수준의 학습 환경

종합출판
- 온라인서점 베스트셀러 1위!
- 출제위원급 전문 교수진이
  직접 집필한 합격 교재

어학 교육
- 토익 베스트셀러 1위
- 토익 동영상 강의 무료 제공

콘텐츠 제휴 · B2B 교육
- 고객 맞춤형 위탁 교육 서비스 제공
- 기업, 기관, 대학 등 각 단체에 최적화된
  고객 맞춤형 교육 및 제휴 서비스

부동산 아카데미
- 부동산 실무 교육 1위!
- 상위 1% 고수익 창업/취업 비법
- 부동산 실전 재테크 성공 비법

학점은행제
- 99%의 과목이수율
- 17년 연속 교육부 평가 인정 기관 선정

대학 편입
- 편입 교육 1위!
- 최대 200% 환급 상품 서비스

국비무료 교육
- '5년우수훈련기관' 선정
- K-디지털, 산대특 등 특화 훈련과정
- 원격국비교육원 오픈

에듀윌 교육서비스 **AI 교육** AI 프롬프트 연구소/AI CLASS(ChatGPT/AICE/노션 AI/중개업 AI 등) **공무원 교육** 9급공무원/소방공무원/계리직공무원 **자격증 교육** 공인중개사/주택관리사/손해평가사/감정평가사/노무사/전기기사/경비지도사/검정고시/소방설비기사/소방시설관리사/사회복지사1급/대기환경기사/수질환경기사/건축기사/토목기사/직업상담사/청소년상담사/전기기능사/산업안전기사/산업위생관리기사/건설안전기사/위험물산업기사/위험물기능사/설비보전기사/에너지관리기사/유통관리사/물류관리사/행정사/한국사능력검정/한경TESAT/매경TEST/KBS한국어능력시험·실용글쓰기/국제무역사/무역영어 **어학 교육** 토익 교재/토익 동영상 강의 **금융/IT/비즈니스** 전산세무회계/ERP정보관리사/재경관리사/정보처리기사/컴퓨터활용능력/SQLD/ADsP **대학 편입** 편입영어·수학/연고대/의약대/경찰대/논술/면접 **직영학원** 공무원학원/소방학원/공인중개사 학원/주택관리사 학원/전기기사 학원/편입학원 **종합출판** 공무원·자격증 수험교재 및 단행본 **학점은행제** 교육부평가인정기관 원격평생교육원(사회복지사2급/경영학/CPA) **콘텐츠 제휴·B2B 교육** 교육 콘텐츠 제휴/기업 맞춤 자격증 교육/대학취업역량 강화 교육 **부동산 아카데미** 부동산 창업CEO/부동산 경매 마스터/부동산 컨설팅 **주택취업센터** 실무 특강/실무 아카데미 **국비무료 교육(국비교육원)** 전기기능사/전기(산업)기사/소방설비(산업)기사/IT(빅데이터/자바프로그램/파이썬)/게임그래픽/3D프린터/실내건축디자인/웹퍼블리셔/그래픽디자인/영상편집(유튜브) 디자인/온라인 쇼핑몰광고 및 제작(쿠팡, 스마트스토어)/전산세무회계/컴퓨터활용능력/ITQ/GTQ/직업상담사

교육문의 **1600-6700** www.eduwill.net

· 2022 소비자가 선택한 최고의 브랜드 공무원·자격증 교육 1위 (조선일보) · 2023 대한민국 브랜드만족도 공무원·자격증·취업·학원·편입·부동산 실무 교육 1위 (한경비즈니스)
· 2017/2022 에듀윌 공무원 과정 최종 환급자 수 기준 · 2023년 성인 자격증, 공무원 직영학원 기준 · YES24 공인중개사 부문, 2025 에듀윌 공인중개사 이영방 필살키 부동산학개론 (2025년 9월 월별 베스트) 그 외 다수 · YES24 한국산업인력공단 부문, 2025 에듀윌 산업안전기사 필기 한권끝장 (2025년 7월 월별 베스트) 그 외 다수 · 교보문고 취업/수험서 부문, 2025 에듀윌 공기업 코레일 한국철도공사 실전모의고사 9+2+4회(2025년 2월 1일~2월 28일, 인터넷 월간 베스트) 그 외 다수 · 알라딘 시사/상식 부문, 2025 최신판 에듀윌 취업 공기업 기출 일반상식 (2025년 6월 5주 주별 베스트) 그 외 다수 · YES24 컴퓨터활용능력 부문, 2024 컴퓨터활용능력 1급 필기 초단기끝장(2023년 10월 3~4주 주별 베스트) 그 외 다수 · YES24 신규자격증 부문, 2025 에듀윌 SQL 개발자 SQLD 2주끝장+무료특강(2025년 7월 월별 베스트) 그 외 다수 · YES24 eBook 부문, 2025 에듀윌 취업 SKCT SK그룹 종합역량 통합기본서 (2025년 4월 2주 주별 베스트) 그 외 다수 · YES24 국어 외국어사전영어 토익/TOEIC 기출문제/모의고사 분야 베스트셀러 1위 (에듀윌 토익 READING RC 4주끝장 리딩 종합서, 2022년 9월 4주 베스트) · 에듀윌 토익 교재 입문~실전 인강 무료 제공 (2022년 최신 강좌 기준/109강) · 2024년 종강반 중 모든 평가항목 정상 참여자 기준, 99% (평생교육원 기준) · 2008년~2024년까지 234만 누적수강학점으로 과목 운영 (평생교육원 기준) · 에듀윌 국비교육원 구로센터 고용노동부 지정 "5년우수훈련기관" 선정 (2023~2027)
· KRI 한국기록원 2016, 2017, 2019년 공인중개사 최다 합격자 배출 공식 인증 (2025년 현재까지 업계 최고 기록)

에듀윌 토익 READING RC
4주끝장

정답 및 해설

에듀윌 토익 READING RC
정답 및 해설

에듀윌 토익
READING RC
정답 및 해설

CHAPTER 1   PART 5&6 문법

UNIT 01 명사

기초 문법 CHECK
본문 p.31

1. information   2. support   3. equipment
4. instructions   5. payment   6. attendees

1.
해설 information은 불가산명사이므로 복수형으로 쓸 수 없다.
해석 두 자동차 임대 회사에 대한 정보를 첨부했습니다.

2.
해설 support가 '지원, 지지'를 뜻할 때는 불가산명사이므로 복수형으로 쓸 수 없다.
해석 귀하의 지지에 감사드리며 앞으로도 저희 서비스[업체]를 이용해 주시기 바랍니다.

3.
해설 equipment는 불가산명사이므로 복수형으로 쓸 수 없다.
해석 유효한 면허를 가진 사람만 중장비를 조작할 수 있다.

4.
해설 instruction이 '설명서'를 뜻할 때는 복수형으로 쓴다.
해석 설치할 때는 항상 설명서에 명시된 공구를 사용하십시오.

5.
해설 문맥상 지불이 늦으면 수수료가 발생한다는 내용이 되는 게 자연스러우므로 '지불'을 뜻하는 payment가 정답이다.
해석 연체 시 50달러의 수수료가 발생한다.

6.
해설 문맥상 콘퍼런스에 참석하는 사람들에게 객실을 특가로 제공한다는 내용이 되는 게 자연스러우므로 '참석자'를 뜻하는 attendees가 정답이다.
해석 Hudson Hotel은 콘퍼런스 참석자들에게 객실을 특가로 제공한다.

빈출 유형 공략 01
본문 p.32

1. (D)   2. (C)   3. (A)   4. (D)

1.
해설 빈칸 앞에 관사가 있고 뒤에는 전치사구가 있으므로 빈칸은 명사 자리이다. 따라서 선택지 중 명사인 (D) collection이 정답이다.
해석 Hawkins Library의 북관에는 희귀 서적들이 소장되어 있다.
어휘 house 보관하다, 소장하다; 거처를 제공하다   rare 희귀한, 드문

2.
해설 빈칸 앞에 형용사가 있고 뒤에는 복수 동사가 있으므로 빈칸은 복수 명사 자리이다. 따라서 선택지 중 복수 명사인 (C) defects가 정답이다.
해석 그 박물관은 구조적 결함이 수리될 때까지 대중에게 개방될 수 없습니다.
어휘 public 대중; 대중의, 공공의   structural 구조적인   defect 결함

3.
해설 빈칸 앞에 동사가 있고 뒤에는 to부정사구가 있으므로 빈칸은 명사 자리이다. 선택지 중 명사인 (A) permission과 (D) permit가 정답 후보인데, 빈칸 앞에 부정관사가 없으므로 빈칸에는 가산명사 복수형이나 불가산명사가 들어가야 한다. 따라서 불가산명사인 (A)가 정답이다.
해석 Harriet's Home Goods의 직원들만 창고 출입이 허가된다.
어휘 access 접근하다; 접속하다

4.
해설 빈칸 앞에 소유한정사가 있으므로 빈칸은 명사 자리이다. 따라서 선택지 중 명사인 (D) profits가 정답이다.
해석 Nicholas&Son과 Johnston Co.는 이익을 늘리기 위해 상호 이득이 되는 파트너십을 맺었다.
어휘 mutually 서로, 상호 간에   beneficial 유익한   profit 이익

빈출 유형 공략 02
본문 p.33

1. (B)   2. (C)   3. (D)   4. (C)

1.
해설 빈칸 뒤에 전치사구가 있고 그 뒤에 동사(depends)가 이어지므로 빈칸은 주어 역할을 하는 명사 자리이다. 따라서 선택지 중 명사인 (B) Acceptance가 정답이다.
해석 그 로펌의 인턴십 합격 여부는 대학교 성적 증명서와 인터뷰 기량, 그리고 추천서에 달려 있다.
어휘 depend on ~에 달려 있다; ~에 의존[의지]하다   transcript 성적 증명서   recommendation 추천(서); 권고

2.
해설 빈칸에는 menu와 결합하여 동사 make의 목적어 역할을 할 수 있는 말이 들어가야 한다. 따라서 선택지 중 명사인 (C) substitutions가 정답이다.
해석 O'Brian's는 대체 메뉴를 원하는 식당 손님들을 받는 데 전혀 문제가 없다.
어휘 make a substitution 대체하다

3.

해설 빈칸 앞에 전치사가 있으므로 빈칸은 전치사의 목적어 자리이다. 따라서 선택지 중 명사인 (D) success가 정답이다.

해석 새로운 로고와 마케팅 전략으로 Sistema Inc.는 성공을 향해 나아가고 있다.

어휘 strategy 전략   head (특정 방향으로) 가다, 향하다   direction 방향; 지시

4.

해설 동사 offer는 [offer+간접목적어+직접목적어] 구조로 목적어를 두 개 취하는 동사이다. 빈칸 앞에 간접목적어(her workers)가 있는 것으로 보아 빈칸은 직접목적어 자리이므로 선택지 중 명사인 (C) flexibility가 정답이다.

해석 Ms. Nolan은 여직원과 남직원에게 출산 휴가를 탄력적으로 부여한다.

어휘 maternity leave 출산 휴가   paternity leave 배우자의 출산 휴가   flexibility 유연성

빈출 유형 공략 03 본문 p.34

1. (A)   **2.** (C)   **3.** (D)   **4.** (C)

1.

해설 빈칸은 동사 form의 목적어 자리이며, 문맥상 위원회를 구성했다는 내용이 되는 게 자연스러우므로 '위원회'를 뜻하는 (A) committee가 정답이다.

해석 시 정부는 시민들의 불만을 처리하는 걸 돕기 위해 위원회를 구성했다.

어휘 deal with complaints 불만을 처리하다   citizen 시민

2.

해설 빈칸은 주어 자리이며, 문맥상 신청서가 제출되었다고 하는 게 자연스러우므로 '신청서'를 뜻하는 (C) application이 정답이다.

해석 Kingsdale High School에서 영화 장면을 촬영하기 위한 신청서가 교장에게 제출되었다.

어휘 submit 제출하다   principal 교장, 학장

3.

해설 빈칸은 전치사의 목적어 자리이며, 문맥상 이 출판물에 실린 사진이 가장 뛰어난 것으로 여겨진다고 하는 게 자연스러우므로 '출판물'을 뜻하는 (D) publication이 정답이다.

해석 이 출판물에 실린 사진들은 잡지계에서 가장 뛰어난 것으로 여겨진다.

어휘 consider 여기다, 간주하다   industry 산업

4.

해설 빈칸은 동사 inform의 목적어 자리이며, 문맥상 통지를 받는 대상이 사람이 되는 게 자연스러우므로 '예금주'를 뜻하는 (C) depositors가 정답이다.

해석 Trust Bank는 예금주들에게 새로운 예금 계좌 이율과 이용 가능한 신용 카드를 알려 준다.

어휘 inform 알리다, 통지하다   savings account 예금 계좌   rate 이율; 비율; 요금

빈출 유형 공략 04 본문 p.35

1. (C)   **2.** (D)   **3.** (A)   **4.** (C)

1.

해설 빈칸 뒤의 dates와 어울려 '유통 기한'을 의미하는 게 문맥상 자연스러우므로 (C) expiration이 정답이다.

해석 식당 매니저들은 주방에 재고를 채울 때 항상 유통 기한을 확인해야 한다.

어휘 restock (사용하거나 팔린 물건들 자리에 새로운 것들을) 다시 채우다, 보충하다

2.

해설 빈칸 뒤의 regulations와 어울려 '안전 규정'을 의미하는 게 문맥상 자연스러우므로 (D) Safety가 정답이다.

해석 현지 공장의 안전 규정은 많은 부상을 예방해 왔다.

어휘 prevent 예방하다, 방지하다   countless 셀 수 없이 많은   injury 부상

3.

해설 빈칸 앞의 service와 어울려 '서비스 요금'을 의미하는 게 문맥상 자연스럽다. (A) charge와 (B) charges가 정답 후보인데, 빈칸 앞에 부정관사 a가 있으므로 (A)가 정답이다.

해석 위탁 수하물이 25킬로그램 이상이면 상당한 서비스 요금이 부과됩니다.

어휘 significant 상당한; 중요한

4.

해설 빈칸 앞의 job과 어울려 '일자리 창출'을 의미하는 게 문맥상 자연스러우므로 (C) creation이 정답이다.

해석 블리스필드의 새로운 세금 우대 조치는 소기업 사이에서 일자리 창출을 장려할 것으로 예상된다.

어휘 incentive 우대 조치, 장려책

ACTUAL TEST
본문 p.36

1. (B)	2. (B)	3. (B)	4. (B)	5. (D)
6. (A)	7. (C)	8. (C)	9. (B)	10. (D)
11. (C)	12. (A)	13. (C)	14. (D)	

1. 명사 자리 [과거분사 뒤]
해설 빈칸 앞에 과거분사가 있으므로 빈칸은 명사 자리이다. 따라서 선택지 중 명사인 (B) agreement가 정답이다.

해석 HC Media와 그 밴드 사이의 서면 합의에는 음반 판권 조건들이 명확하게 설명되어 있었다.

어휘 written agreement 서면 합의 outline 설명하다 terms (항상 복수형) 조건 license 허가하다

2. 복합 명사
해설 빈칸 뒤의 policy와 어울려 '보안 정책'을 의미하는 게 문맥상 자연스러우므로 (B) security가 정답이다.

해석 그 회사의 보안 정책은 데이터를 보호하기 위해 직원들이 강력한 암호를 생성하도록 한다.

어휘 mandate (공식적으로) 명령하다; 권한을 주다

3. 명사 자리 [관사 뒤]
해설 빈칸 앞에 관사가 있고 뒤에는 전치사구가 있으므로 빈칸은 명사 자리이다. 따라서 선택지 중 명사인 (B) excess가 정답이다.

해석 예상치 못한 경쟁으로 인해 그 가게에는 재고로 남은 텔레비전이 아직도 100대 이상 있었다.

어휘 unexpected 예상 밖의, 뜻밖의 in stock 재고로 excess 초과량, 과잉

4. 사람 명사 vs. 사물/추상 명사
해설 빈칸은 전치사의 목적어 자리이며, 문맥상 Norbert 거래처 일을 잘 처리했다는 내용이 되는 게 자연스러우므로 '거래처; 거래'를 뜻하는 (B) account가 정답이다.

해석 Ms. Kent가 Norbert 거래처 일을 잘 처리한 걸 축하하고 싶습니다.

어휘 account 거래처; 거래; 계좌 accountant 회계사

5. 가산명사 단수형 vs. 복수형
해설 빈칸에는 dentist와 결합하여 주어 역할을 하는 동시에 한정사 all의 수식을 받을 수 있는 말이 들어가야 한다. 선택지 중 명사인 (C) appointment와 (D) appointments가 정답 후보인데, appointment가 '약속, 예약'을 뜻할 때는 가산명사로 쓰므로 복수 명사인 (D)가 정답이다.

해석 치과용 드릴이 고장 나서 오늘 자 예약은 모두 일정을 다시 잡아야 합니다.

어휘 reschedule 일정을 다시 잡다

6. 사람 명사 vs. 사물/추상 명사
해설 빈칸 앞에 한정사가 있고 뒤에는 전치사구가 있으므로 빈칸은 명사 자리이다. 문맥상 선택하는 주체는 사람이어야 하므로 '구독자'를 뜻하는 (A) subscribers가 정답이다.

해석 EcoFriendly Magazine의 많은 구독자는 환경에 미치는 영향을 줄이기 위해 디지털 책자를 받겠다고 선택했다.

어휘 opt to do ~하기로 선택하다 environmental 환경의

7. 복합 명사
해설 빈칸 앞의 building과 어울려 '건물 관리'를 의미하는 게 문맥상 자연스러우므로 (C) management가 정답이다.

해석 건물 관리 책임자인 Mr. Kumar는 직원들에게 다음 주 공사로 인해 소음이 발생할 수도 있음을 알리는 이메일을 보냈다.

어휘 potential 가능성이 있는; 잠재력 construction 공사

8. 가산명사 단수형 vs. 복수형
해설 빈칸에는 Housekeeping과 결합하여 주어 역할을 할 수 있는 말이 들어가야 한다. 선택지 중 명사인 (A) service와 (C) services가 정답 후보인데, 빈칸 뒤에 are가 있으므로 복수 명사인 (C)가 정답이다.

해석 객실 관리 서비스는 모든 투숙객에게 무료이며 하루에 한 번 실시됩니다.

9. 명사의 역할 [목적어]
해설 동사 give는 [give+간접목적어+직접목적어] 구조로 목적어를 두 개 취하는 동사이다. 빈칸 앞에 간접목적어(its clients)가 있는 것으로 보아 빈칸은 직접목적어 자리이므로 선택지 중 명사인 (B) predictions가 정답이다.

해석 Murphy Co.의 광범위한 시장 조사는 고객들에게 그들의 사업에 영향을 미칠 수 있는 동향에 대한 예측을 제공한다.

어휘 extensive 광범위한; 대규모의 prediction 예측, 예견

10. 사람 명사 vs. 사물/추상 명사
해설 빈칸 앞에 형용사가 있고 뒤에는 전치사구가 있으므로 빈칸은 명사 자리이며, 문맥상 그 나라의 최대 생산업체라고 하는 게 자연스러우므로 '생산자, 제작자'를 뜻하는 (D) producer가 정답이다.

해석 Grenadine's Fabrics는 그 나라에서 가장 큰 직물 생산업체임에도 불구하고 수익이 지속적으로 감소하고 있다.

어휘 textile 직물 steady 꾸준한, 지속적인 decline 감소, 하락

Cordova Realty는 록스베리 지사의 전임 행정 보조를 [11]채용하고 있습니다. 행정 보조의 역할은 표준 계약서에 설명된 바와 같이 주로 서류 정리와 자산 데이터베이스 업데이트, [12]그리고 걸려 오는 전화 응대로 구성되어 있습니다. [13]직원에게는 유급 휴가와 분기별 성과급도 보장됩니다. 최소 2년의 사무 경험이 있는 분을 우대합니다. 당사는 전문 소프트웨어 사용법에 대한 교육을 제공할 것입니다. [14]게다가 전문성 개발 워크숍이 일 년 내내 열립니다. 지원서는 늦어도 10월 3일까지 hr@cordova-realty.com으로 보내야 합니다.

어휘 administrative 행정의 assistant 보조원, 비서 consist of ~로 구성되다 file (문서 등을 정리하여) 보관하다 property 재산, 소유물; 부동산; 건물; 속성 quarterly 분기의; 분기별로 no later than 늦어도 ~까지

11. 동사 어휘

어휘 suggest 제안하다 apply 신청하다, 지원하다 offer 제공하다

12. 접속사 어휘

어휘 so 그래서 yet 그렇지만, 그런데도 once 일단 ~하면; ~하자마자

13. 사람 명사 vs. 사물/추상 명사

해설 빈칸 앞에 관사가 있으므로 빈칸은 명사 자리이며, 문맥상 유급 휴가와 성과급이 보장되는 대상은 사람이어야 하므로 '직원'을 뜻하는 (C) employee가 정답이다.

14. 알맞은 문장 고르기

해설 빈칸 앞에서 회사가 직원에게 전문 소프트웨어 사용 방법에 관한 교육을 제공한다고 했다. 따라서 빈칸에는 그 밖에 어떤 교육을 제공하는지 언급하는 게 가장 자연스러우므로 (D)가 정답이다.

해석 (A) 팀장이 그 일에 가장 적합한 사람을 뽑았습니다.
(B) 마찬가지로 우리 직원 대부분은 대중교통을 이용해 통근합니다.
(C) 새 정책은 다음 달 1일부터 시행될 것입니다.
(D) 게다가 전문성 개발 워크숍이 일 년 내내 열립니다.

어휘 qualified 자격이 있는, 적임의 commute 통근하다 public transportation 대중교통 go into effect 시행되다, 실시되다 furthermore 게다가, 뿐만 아니라

UNIT 02 대명사와 한정사

기초 문법 CHECK 본문 p.41

1. theirs 2. it 3. its
4. those 5. every 6. all

1.

해설 주어 역할을 할 수 있는 소유대명사 theirs가 정답이다.

해석 영업 팀은 프린터가 교체되는 동안 회계 팀의 프린터를 사용하셔야 합니다.

2.

해설 Lillard Ltd.를 지칭하는 대명사 it이 정답이다.

해석 Lillard Ltd.는 Quester Inc.와 합병할 것이라고 오늘 발표했다.

3.

해설 Kadiri Hotel을 지칭하는 동시에 명사를 수식해야 하므로 소유한정사 its가 정답이다.

해석 Kadiri Hotel은 중심지에 위치해 있으며 자체 레스토랑이 있습니다.

4.

해설 분사구의 수식을 받을 수 있는 those가 정답이다.

해석 그 과정은 의료업에 관심 있는 사람들을 위한 것이다.

5.

해설 단수 명사(order)를 수식할 수 있는 every가 정답이다.

해석 Yellow Coffee는 1주일 동안만 30달러 이상 주문 시 커피 머그잔을 무료로 드립니다.

6.

해설 복수 명사(restaurants)를 수식할 수 있는 all이 정답이다.

해석 Burpee는 모든 그의 식당에 독점 납품하고 있다.

빈출 유형 공략 01 본문 p.42

1. (B) 2. (A) 3. (D) 4. (B)

1.

해설 동사 give는 [give+간접목적어+직접목적어] 구조로 목적어를 두 개 취하는 동사이다. 빈칸 뒤에 직접목적어(the new schedule)가 있는 것으로 보아 빈칸은 간접목적어 자리이므로 목적격 대명사인 (B) us가 정답이다.

해석 그 부장이 여름 시즌을 위한 새 스케줄을 우리에게 줄 겁니다.

2.

해설 빈칸 앞에 접속사가 있고 뒤에는 명사가 있으므로 빈칸에는 명사를 수식하는 말이 들어가야 한다. 따라서 소유한정사인 (A) their가 정답이다.

해석 발표자들은 그들의 슬라이드가 컬러가 아닌 흑백으로 되어 있어서 놀랐다.

어휘 presenter 발표자 instead of ~ 대신에

3.

해설 빈칸 앞에 전치사가 있고 뒤에는 동사가 있으므로 빈칸은 전치사의 목적어 자리이다. 따라서 소유대명사인 (D) mine이 정답이다.

해석 제 동료가 몇 주 후에 울란바토르로 출장을 갑니다.

어휘 coworker (함께 일하는) 동료 take a business trip 출장을 가다

4.

해설 빈칸은 주어 자리인데, 문맥상 빈칸에 들어갈 대명사는 경기장 허가가 승인된 상황을 가리키므로 주격 대명사인 (B) it이 정답이다.

해석 경기장 허가가 승인되자마자 주민들은 그것이 지역 사회에 어떤 영향을 미칠지 궁금해하기 시작했다.

어휘 permit 허가(증) approve 승인하다; ~을 좋게 생각하다(~ of) resident 주민 wonder 궁금해하다

빈출 유형 공략 02 본문 p.43

1. (C) 2. (C) 3. (B) 4. (B)

1.

해설 빈칸은 동사 organize의 목적어 자리이다. 선택지 중 목적어

자리에 쓸 수 있는 것은 (B) them과 (C) themselves인데, 문맥상 빈칸에 들어갈 말이 주어 workers와 동일한 대상이므로 재귀대명사인 (C)가 정답이다.

해석 팀 단합 활동에서 직원들은 4인 1조로 편성하도록 요청받았다.

어휘 organize 조직하다, 구성하다; 준비하다, 정리하다

2.
해설 빈칸 앞에 [주어(Ms. Shaw)+동사(finished)+목적어(the assignment)] 구조의 완전한 문장이 있으므로 빈칸에는 생략해도 문장이 성립할 수 있는 말이 들어가야 한다. 따라서 재귀대명사인 (C) herself가 정답이다.

해석 Ms. Shaw는 근무 시간 후에도 남아서 직접 업무를 마쳤다.

어휘 work hours 근무 시간 assignment 과제, 업무

3.
해설 빈칸이 없어도 [주어(the article)+동사(was)+주격 보어(only ~ long)] 구조의 완전한 문장이므로 빈칸에는 생략해도 문장이 성립할 수 있는 말이 들어가야 한다. 따라서 재귀대명사인 (B) itself가 정답이다.

해석 기사 자체는 한 단락에 불과했지만 그 주제에 대한 댓글은 수천 개가 달렸다.

어휘 post 게시하다 article 기사 paragraph 단락

4.
해설 빈칸 앞의 전치사 by와 함께 쓸 수 있는 말을 골라야 한다. by oneself는 '혼자서, 다른 사람의 도움 없이'를 뜻하므로 (B) himself가 정답이다.

해석 Mr. Wilson은 혼자서 이 일을 맡기로 결심했지만 약간의 도움이 필요하다는 것을 깨달았다.

어휘 be determined to do ~하기로 결심하다 take on a task 업무를 맡다 realize 깨닫다 assistance 도움, 지원

빈출 유형 공략 03   본문 p.44
1. (B)   2. (C)   3. (B)   4. (C)

1.
해설 빈칸은 주격 관계대명사절(who ~ demonstration)의 수식을 받는 자리이다. 따라서 선택지 중 관계대명사절의 수식을 받을 수 있는 (B) those가 정답이다. (D) everyone은 who 뒤에 단수 동사가 이어지므로 답이 될 수 없다.

해석 Mr. Kroll이 제품 시연회에 참석하고자 하는 사람들은 자신에게 직접 연락해 달라고 요청했다.

어휘 attend 참석하다 product demonstration 제품 시연

2.
해설 빈칸은 주격 관계대명사절(that did not)의 수식을 받는 자리이다. 따라서 선택지 중 관계대명사절의 수식을 받을 수 있는 (C) those가 정답이다.

해석 그 조사는 보상 프로그램이 있는 가게가 그렇지 않은 가게보다 단골 고객이 더 많다는 것을 보여 줬다.

어휘 rewards program 재구매 고객에게 포인트 등의 보상을 주는 프로그램 repeat customer 단골 고객

3.
해설 빈칸 뒤에 복수 명사가 있으므로 빈칸에는 복수 명사를 수식할 수 있는 말이 들어가야 한다. 따라서 this의 복수형인 (B) these가 정답이다.

해석 이 꽃병들은 매우 깨지기 쉬우니 추가 포장재로 포장해 주세요.

어휘 wrap 포장하다, 싸다 packaging 포장 extremely 극도로, 매우 fragile 깨지기 쉬운, 취약한

4.
해설 빈칸에는 전치사구의 수식을 받는 동시에 앞에 나온 복수 명사(The commercial real estate prices)를 대신할 수 있는 말이 들어가야 하므로 복수 지시대명사인 (C) those가 정답이다.

해석 사우스필드의 상업용 부동산 가격은 셔우드보다 현저히 낮다.

어휘 commercial 상업의; 광고 real estate 부동산 significantly 상당히

빈출 유형 공략 04   본문 p.45
1. (D)   2. (A)   3. (B)   4. (A)

1.
해설 빈칸에는 동사 formulate의 목적어 역할을 하면서 앞에 언급된 coffee blend를 지칭하는 말이 들어가야 한다. 문맥상 긍정적인 평가를 받은 커피 블렌드 외에 또 다른 커피 블렌드를 만들어 내기로 결정했다는 내용이 되는 게 자연스러우므로 '또 하나, 또 다른 것[사람]'을 의미하는 (D) another가 정답이다.

해석 새로운 커피 블렌드에 긍정적인 평가를 받고 나서 Ms. Darden은 커피 블렌드를 하나 더 만들어 내기로 결정했다.

어휘 positive 긍정적인 formulate (다른 것들을 합쳐서 새로운 것을) 만들어 내다

2.
해설 빈칸 뒤에 복수 명사가 있으므로 빈칸에는 복수 명사를 수식할 수 있는 말이 들어가야 한다. 따라서 (A) other가 정답이다.

해석 다른 회사들과 차별화하기 위해 Lance's Electronics는 독특한 로고와 색 배합을 사용한다.

어휘 distinguish 구별하다; 차이를 보이다 unique 독특한 scheme (정보, 아이디어 등의) 구성, 조직

3.
해설 빈칸에는 동사 help의 목적어 역할을 할 수 있는 말이 들어가야 한다. 문맥상 서로 돕는다는 내용이 되는 게 자연스러우므로 (B) each other가 정답이다.

해석 영업 팀 직원들은 거래를 성사시키고 회사의 전반적인 수익을 증대시킬 수 있도록 최선을 다해 서로 돕는다.

어휘 do one's best 최선을 다하다 close a deal 계약을 체결하다 overall 전반적인 revenue 수익

4.
해설 빈칸에는 관사(the)와 주격 관계대명사절(who ~ designer)의 수식을 받으면서 앞에 언급된 candidates를 지칭하는 말이 들어가야 한다. 관계사절에 단수 동사 is가 있으므로 단수 명사인 (A) one이 정답이다.
해석 모든 후보를 고려하여 총괄 디자이너 역할에 가장 적합한 후보 한 명을 선정할 것이다.
어휘 candidate 후보, 지원자 be suited for ~에 적합하다 role 역할, 임무; 배역

빈출 유형 공략 05   본문 p.46
1. (B)   2. (D)   3. (C)   4. (C)

1.
해설 빈칸에는 동사 reveal의 목적어 역할을 하는 동시에 형용사 뒤에 위치할 수 있는 말이 들어가야 한다. 문맥상 부정적인 그 어느 것도 부각하지 않았다는 내용이 되는 게 자연스러우므로 (B) anything이 정답이다.
해석 연례 업무 평가에는 우리 부서에서 일하는 사람들에 대한 부정적인 점이 드러나지 않았다.
어휘 reveal 드러내다, 밝히다; 폭로하다 negative 부정적인

2.
해설 빈칸은 주어 자리이며, 문맥상 주방 감독을 행하는 주체는 사람이어야 하므로 '누군가'를 뜻하는 (D) Someone이 정답이다.
해석 총주방장이 자리를 비운 동안 누군가는 Bistrona의 주방을 감독해야 할 것이다.
어휘 supervise 감독하다

3.
해설 문맥상 영업 능력을 보여 주는 주체는 사람이어야 하므로 불명확한 인원을 나타내는 부정대명사인 (C) some이 정답이다. (A) everyone은 주격 관계대명사절의 동사(demonstrate)가 복수형이므로 답이 될 수 없다.
해석 경영진은 우수한 영업 능력을 분명히 보여 주는 일부 직원들에게 특별 혜택을 제공할 것이다.
어휘 perk 혜택, 특전 demonstrate 보여 주다; 입증하다 capability 능력

4.
해설 빈칸 뒤에 복수 명사가 있으므로 빈칸에는 복수 명사를 수식할 수 있는 말이 들어가야 한다. 따라서 (C) any가 정답이다. (A) another와 (B) each는 단수 명사를 수식하기 때문에 답이 될 수 없다.
해석 어린이 사고를 예방하기 위해 그 제품에는 안전 라벨이 부착되어 있다.

어휘 safety label 안전 라벨 be attached to ~에 붙어 있다 prevent 예방하다, 방지하다

빈출 유형 공략 06   본문 p.47
1. (B)   2. (C)   3. (C)   4. (D)

1.
해설 빈칸 뒤에 복수 명사가 있으므로 빈칸에는 복수 명사를 수식할 수 있는 말이 들어가야 한다. 따라서 (B) several이 정답이다. (A) another는 단수 명사를 수식하기 때문에 답이 될 수 없다.
해석 인사부가 먼저 심사를 하고 나서 경영진은 대표와 인터뷰할 후보자를 몇 명 선택할 것이다.
어휘 initial 처음의, 초기의 screening 심사, 검사

2.
해설 빈칸 뒤에 단수 명사가 있으므로 빈칸에는 단수 명사를 수식할 수 있는 말이 들어가야 한다. 따라서 (C) every가 정답이다. (B) all은 복수 명사를 수식하기 때문에 답이 될 수 없다. (D) entire는 단수 명사를 수식할 수 있지만 앞에 관사나 소유한정사가 있어야 하며, 의미상으로도 자연스럽지 않으므로 오답이다.
해석 우리 관리자들은 모든 제품이 최고의 품질을 갖추고 있다는 걸 보장합니다.
어휘 ensure 보장하다, 확실히 하다

3.
해설 빈칸에는 of his coworkers와 결합하여 that이 이끄는 명사절의 주어 역할을 할 수 있는 말이 들어가야 한다. 선택지 중 대명사인 (B) anyone과 (C) all이 정답 후보인데, of 뒤에 복수 명사(coworkers)가 있으므로 (C)가 정답이다.
해석 Mr. Lambert는 은퇴식에서 동료 모두가 자신에게 편지를 쓴 것에 놀랐다.
어휘 retirement 은퇴

4.
해설 빈칸 뒤에 복수 명사가 있으므로 빈칸에는 복수 명사를 수식할 수 있는 말이 들어가야 한다. 따라서 (D) many가 정답이다. (A) another와 (C) every는 단수 명사를 수식하고 (B) much는 불가산명사를 수식하기 때문에 답이 될 수 없다.
해석 Dove Hotel은 여러 괜찮은 쇼핑몰과 식당을 걸어서 갈 수 있는 거리 내에 있다.
어휘 walking distance 걸어서 갈 수 있는 거리 fine 질 좋은, 괜찮은

ACTUAL TEST   본문 p.48
1. (A)   2. (D)   3. (C)   4. (C)   5. (C)
6. (B)   7. (D)   8. (A)   9. (B)   10. (D)
11. (C) 12. (D) 13. (C) 14. (B)

1. 한정사 any

해설 빈칸 뒤에 복수 명사가 있으므로 빈칸에는 복수 명사를 수식할 수 있는 말이 들어가야 한다. 따라서 (A) any가 정답이다. (B) each 와 (D) every는 단수 명사를 수식하기 때문에 답이 될 수 없다.

해석 투어 참가자는 버스에 귀중품을 두어서는 안 됩니다.

어휘 of value 값비싼, 귀중한

2. 재귀대명사 [강조 용법]

해설 빈칸 앞에 [주어(The CEO)+동사(gives)+간접목적어(new employees)+직접목적어(a building tour)] 구조의 완전한 문장이 있으므로 빈칸에는 생략해도 문장이 성립할 수 있는 말이 들어가야 한다. 따라서 재귀대명사인 (D) himself가 정답이다.

해석 Stockton Tech의 대표는 보통 신규 입사자들에게 직접 건물 이곳저곳을 보여 준다.

어휘 give ~ a tour ~에게 구경을 시켜 주다

3. 한정사 each

해설 빈칸 뒤에 단수 명사가 있으므로 빈칸에는 단수 명사를 수식할 수 있는 말이 들어가야 한다. 따라서 (C) each가 정답이다. 나머지 선택지는 모두 복수 명사를 수식하기 때문에 답이 될 수 없다.

해석 생산 라인에서 품질 관리 책임자는 각 제품이 필수 안전 기준을 충족하는지 확인한다.

어휘 quality control 품질 관리   standard 기준, 수준

4. 인칭대명사 [주격]

해설 빈칸은 생략된 that이 이끄는 명사절의 주어 자리이다. 선택지 중 주격 대명사인 (A) it과 (C) they가 정답 후보인데, 문맥상 지칭하는 대상이 복수 명사(electrical issues)이고 빈칸 뒤에 be동사 복수형인 were가 있으므로 (C)가 정답이다.

해석 사무실에 전기 문제가 있었는데, 전기 기술자는 그것이 어젯밤의 폭풍우 때문이라고 생각했다.

어휘 electrical 전기의

5. 부정대명사 the other

해설 빈칸에는 관사(the)의 수식을 받으면서 앞에 언급된 한 명의 지원자 외에 나머지 한 명을 나타낼 수 있는 말이 들어가야 한다. 따라서 (C) other가 정답이다.

해석 지원자 중 한 명은 이력서가 탄탄했지만 다른 한 명은 대인 관계 능력이 더 뛰어났다.

어휘 candidate 후보, 지원자   résumé 이력서   interpersonal skills 대인 관계 능력

6. 소유한정사

해설 빈칸 앞에 접속사가 있고 뒤에는 명사가 있으므로 빈칸에는 명사를 수식하는 말이 들어가야 한다. 따라서 소유한정사인 (B) her가 정답이다.

해석 Ms. Duda는 자신의 팀이 준비될 때까지 제품 출시를 미뤄 달라고 경영진을 설득하고 있다.

어휘 persuade 설득하다   postpone 연기하다, 미루다

7. 한정사 all

해설 빈칸 뒤에 복수 명사가 있으므로 빈칸에는 복수 명사를 수식할 수 있는 말이 들어가야 한다. 따라서 (D) all이 정답이다. (A) every 와 (C) each는 단수 명사를 수식하기 때문에 답이 될 수 없다.

해석 Whitetail은 이번 달에만 모든 주방 가전제품을 무료로 배송하고 설치해 준다.

어휘 installation 설치   appliance 가전제품

8. 지시대명사 these

해설 빈칸은 주어 자리이며, be동사 복수형인 are와 수 일치되는 말이 들어가야 한다. 따라서 this의 복수형인 (A) These가 정답이다.

해석 이것들은 우리가 이번 달 말까지 달성해야 하는 올 중반 목표들이다.

어휘 reach 도달하다, 이르다

9. 소유대명사

해설 빈칸 앞에 be동사가 있으므로 빈칸은 주격 보어 자리이다. 따라서 소유대명사인 (B) theirs가 정답이다.

해석 공사장 인부들은 자신들의 장비에 라벨을 붙이는 걸 깜빡해서 어느 것이 자신들의 것인지 잘 모른다.

어휘 construction site 공사장   label 라벨을 붙이다; 분류하다

10. 지시대명사 those

해설 빈칸은 주격 관계대명사절(who ~ event)의 수식을 받는 자리이다. 따라서 선택지 중 관계대명사절의 수식을 받을 수 있는 (D) those가 정답이다.

해석 지금은 셔틀버스가 운행하지 않아서 그 행사장까지 셔틀버스를 타고 가길 원하는 분들은 그렇게 하실 수 없습니다.

어휘 unavailable 이용할 수 없는; 획득할 수 없는   get a ride (차 등을) 타다

Graystone Publishing House는 매년 Graystone Creative Writing Competition을 개최하고 있습니다. 이 공모전은 아마추어 작가들에게 열려 있습니다. 과거에 우리 회사는 이 행사를 통해 많은 재능 있는 신인 작가들을 ¹¹발굴했습니다. 그 작가들 중 일부는 현재 전문 작가로 전업하여 일하고 있습니다. 출품작은 4월 1일부터 15일까지 저희 웹사이트 www.graystonepublishing.com을 통해 접수될 예정입니다. 작가들이 ¹²스스로를 충분히 표현할 수 있도록 세 가지 분야(단편 소설과 시, 그리고 수필)를 모집합니다. 분야별로 ¹³요구 사항이 다르므로 단어 수와 기타 세부 정보를 주의 깊게 확인해 주십시오. 작가들은 심사를 위해 최대 세 편을 제출할 수 있습니다. 다른 많은 글쓰기 공모전과 달리 참가비는 없습니다. ¹⁴여러분의 글을 평가받을 수 있는 절호의 기회입니다.

어휘 hold (행사 등을) 열다, 개최하다   annual 연례의   submission (결정권자에게 제출하는) 서류; 제출, 접수   poetry 시   express 표현하다   fully 완전히, 충분히   piece (작품) 한 점   consideration 고려 사항; 숙고

11. 동사 어휘
어휘 occupy 차지하다; 점유하다   preserve 지키다, 보전하다
enter 입장하다, 들어가다

12. 재귀대명사 [재귀 용법]
해설 빈칸은 동사 express의 목적어 자리이다. 문맥상 빈칸에 들어갈 말이 주어 writers와 동일한 대상이므로 재귀대명사인 (D) themselves가 정답이다.

13. 명사 어휘
어휘 identification 신분 증명(서); 식별   location 장소; 지점
warranty 품질 보증

14. 알맞은 문장 고르기
해설 빈칸 앞에서 글쓰기 공모전에 대해 전반적으로 소개했으므로 빈칸에는 공모전 참여를 독려하는 내용이 들어가는 게 가장 자연스럽다. 따라서 이번 공모전이 글을 평가받을 기회라고 한 (B)가 정답이다.
해석 (A) 이 작가는 또 다른 소설 출간을 앞두고 있습니다.
(B) 여러분의 글을 평가받을 수 있는 절호의 기회입니다.
(C) 여러분의 열정은 심사위원들에게 깊은 인상을 남겼습니다.
(D) 출판업계에는 몇몇 시장 선두 주자가 있습니다.
어휘 put ~ to the test ~을 시험해 보다   enthusiasm 열정
judging panel 심사위원   publishing industry 출판업계

UNIT 03 형용사와 부사

기초 문법 CHECK   본문 p.53
1. Successful   2. open   3. suitable
4. restless   5. accomplished   6. aspiring
7. easily   8. unlikely

1.
해설 명사를 수식할 수 있는 품사는 형용사이다.
해석 합격자는 메릴랜드주나 뉴저지주에 배치될 것이다.

2.
해설 연결동사의 보어 역할은 형용사가 한다.
해석 그 피트니스 센터는 월요일부터 금요일까지 3시간 연장 운영할 것이다.

3.
해설 -one으로 끝나는 단어는 형용사가 뒤에서 수식한다.
해석 적당한 사람을 찾는 데 시간이 좀 걸릴 겁니다.

4.
해설 make의 목적격 보어 역할은 형용사가 한다.
해석 긴 발표는 청중을 따분하게 할 것이다.

5.
해설 accomplished author는 '뛰어난 작가'를 뜻한다.
해석 그 서점은 뛰어난 작가 Jonathan Bate의 책 사인회를 개최할 것이다.

6.
해설 aspiring architect는 '건축가 지망생'을 뜻한다.
해석 그 웹사이트는 건축가 지망생에게 굉장히 유용한 자료원이다.

7.
해설 형용사를 수식할 수 있는 품사는 부사이다.
해석 Vien Art Museum의 새로운 위치는 자동차나 버스로 쉽게 갈 수 있다.

8.
해설 명사를 수식할 수 있는 품사는 형용사이다.
해석 혹시라도 배송 물품이 만족스럽지 않다면 구매 후 14일 이내에 반품할 수 있습니다.

빈출 유형 공략 01   본문 p.54
1. (C)   **2.** (D)   **3.** (A)   **4.** (A)

1.
해설 빈칸 앞에 관사가 있고 뒤에는 명사(video)가 있으므로 빈칸은 명사를 수식하는 형용사 자리이다. 따라서 선택지 중 형용사인 (C) instructional이 정답이다.
해석 신입 직원들은 그 장치를 조립하는 방법에 관한 교육 비디오를 시청할 것이다.
어휘 assemble 조립하다; 모으다, 집합시키다   device 장비, 장치
instructional 교육의

2.
해설 빈칸은 [keep+목적어+목적격 보어] 구조에서 목적격 보어 자리이다. 따라서 선택지 중 형용사인 (D) secure가 정답이다.
해석 호텔 방의 금고는 귀하의 귀중품을 안전하게 보관하도록 설계되었습니다.
어휘 safe 금고   be designed to do ~하도록 설계[고안]되다
valuables (항상 복수형) 귀중품   secure 안전한, 안심하는

3.
해설 빈칸은 be동사 are 뒤의 주격 보어 자리로 주어인 The LED lights의 상태나 상황을 나타낼 수 있는 말이 들어가야 한다. 따라서 선택지 중 형용사인 (A) bright가 정답이다. 명사인 (D) brightness는 주어와 동격 관계일 때만 주격 보어 자리에 위치할 수 있을 뿐만 아니라 부사의 수식을 받을 수도 없기 때문에 오답이다.
해석 길을 가던 사람이 가게 안으로 들어오도록 하기 위해 이 부티크 밖에 있는 LED 등은 매우 밝은 빛을 낸다.
어휘 persuade 설득하다   pedestrian 보행자

4.
해설 빈칸 앞에 한정사(several)가 있고 뒤에는 명사구(advertising campaigns)가 있으므로 빈칸은 명사를 수식하는 형용사 자리이다. 따라서 선택지 중 형용사인 (A) successful이 정답이다.

해석 우리 회사의 말레이시아 지사는 몇 차례의 성공적인 광고 활동 덕분에 지속적으로 성장해 왔다.

어휘 continuous 지속적인, 계속되는 growth 성장

빈출 유형 공략 02 본문 p.55
1. (C) **2.** (B) **3.** (D) **4.** (A)

1.
해설 빈칸 앞에 소유한정사가 있고 뒤에는 명사(part)가 있으므로 빈칸은 명사를 수식하는 형용사 자리이다. 선택지 중 형용사인 (B) favorable(호의적인; 유리한)과 (C) favorite(가장 좋아하는) 중에서 의미상 part를 수식하기에 가장 적절한 것은 (C)이다.

해석 최근 조사에 따르면 그 리조트에서 투숙객 대부분이 좋아하는 부분은 옥상 정원이다.

어휘 survey 설문 조사

2.
해설 빈칸 앞에 전치사가 있고 뒤에는 명사(information)가 있으므로 빈칸은 명사를 수식하는 형용사 자리이다. 선택지 중 형용사인 (B) reliable(믿을 수 있는)과 (C) reliant(의존적인) 중에서 의미상 information을 수식하기에 가장 적절한 것은 (B)이다.

해석 신뢰할 수 있는 정보가 없다면 증권 거래인은 고객의 투자금을 책임감 있게 처리할 수 없을 것이다.

어휘 stock trader 증권 거래인 handle 다루다, 처리하다

3.
해설 빈칸은 be동사 is 뒤의 주격 보어 자리로 주어인 The success의 상태나 상황을 나타낼 수 있는 말이 들어가야 한다. 선택지 중 형용사인 (C) dependable(믿을 만한)과 (D) dependent(의존하는) 중에서 의미상 The success의 상태를 나타내기에 가장 적절한 것은 (D)이다.

해석 우리 신제품의 성공 여부는 마케팅 팀의 전략에 달려 있다.

어휘 strategy 전략, 계획

4.
해설 빈칸 앞에 관사가 있고 뒤에는 명사(turnout)가 있으므로 빈칸은 명사를 수식하는 형용사 자리이다. 선택지 중 형용사인 (A) considerable(상당한)과 (B) considerate(사려 깊은) 중에서 의미상 turnout을 수식하기에 가장 적절한 것은 (A)이다.

해석 KL Sneakers는 새로운 운동화 출시 행사에 상당한 인파를 예상하고 있다.

어휘 turnout (행사 등의) 참석자 수 launch 출시

빈출 유형 공략 03 본문 p.56
1. (C) **2.** (B) **3.** (C) **4.** (D)

1.
해설 빈칸은 형용사(difficult)를 수식하는 자리이므로 선택지 중 부사인 (C) increasingly가 정답이다.

해석 관리자들은 비정규직 근로자 고용과 관련하여 점점 더 어려운 결정에 직면해 왔다.

어휘 face 직면하다 regarding ~에 관하여 temporary worker 비정규직[임시직] 근로자

2.
해설 빈칸은 동사(work)를 수식하는 자리이므로 선택지 중 부사인 (B) collaboratively가 정답이다.

해석 이 프로젝트는 팀 리더가 모든 사람이 협력하여 일하게 해야만 성공할 수 있다.

어휘 collaboratively 협력하여

3.
해설 빈칸은 조동사(will)와 동사(sign) 사이의 부사 자리이므로 선택지 중 부사인 (C) personally가 정답이다.

해석 낭독이 끝나고 나서 작가는 팬들을 위해 자신의 새 소설에 직접 사인해 줄 것이다.

어휘 personally 직접, 개인적으로

4.
해설 빈칸은 be동사(is)와 과거분사(stated) 사이의 부사 자리이므로 선택지 중 부사인 (D) clearly가 정답이다.

해석 그 가게의 환불 정책은 웹사이트에 분명하게 명시되어 있다.

어휘 refund policy 환불 정책 state 명시하다

빈출 유형 공략 04 본문 p.57
1. (C) **2.** (D) **3.** (A) **4.** (D)

1.
해설 선택지 중 (C) quite와 (D) enough가 문맥에 가장 어울리는데 형용사를 앞에서 수식해야 하므로 (C)가 정답이다.

해석 전사 규모의 회의 준비는 비교적 신입인 직원이 하기에는 꽤 어렵다.

어휘 organize 준비하다, 정리하다 company-wide 전사적인 relatively 비교적, 상대적으로

2.
해설 선택지 중 (B) yet과 (D) still이 문맥에 가장 어울리는데 빈칸 뒤에 not이 있으므로 (D)가 정답이다.

해석 재료의 가격이 오르긴 했지만 Mike's Pizzeria는 그래도 메뉴 가격을 인상하지 않을 것이다.

어휘 ingredient 재료, 성분   raise (양, 수준 등을) 올리다

3.
해설 선택지 중 (A) so와 (C) very가 문맥에 가장 어울리는데 빈칸 뒤에 that절이 이어지므로 (A)가 정답이다.
해석 그 광고 캠페인은 매우 성공적이어서 판매 목표가 예상보다 빠르게 달성되었다.
어휘 achieve 달성하다, 성취하다   anticipate 예상하다; 기대하다, 고대하다

4.
해설 빈칸은 be organized를 뒤에서 수식하는 부사 자리이다. 따라서 선택지 중 동사를 뒤에서 수식할 수 있는 (D) enough가 정답이다.
해석 홍보 팀 직원들은 근무하는 내내 여러 프로젝트를 진행할 수 있을 만큼 충분히 조직적이어야 한다.
어휘 publicity 홍보   organize 조직하다, 구성하다   multiple 다수의, 많은   workday 업무 시간, 근무일

빈출 유형 공략 05   본문 p.58
1. (A)   2. (B)   3. (D)   4. (D)

1.
해설 빈칸은 be동사 are의 주격 보어 자리이며 빈칸 뒤에 비교 대상을 나타내는 전치사 than이 있으므로 형용사의 비교급이 들어가야 한다. 따라서 high의 비교급인 (A) higher가 정답이다.
해석 이곳 직원들은 자존감이 높아서 생산 수준이 평균보다 높다.
어휘 productivity 생산성

2.
해설 as와 as 사이에는 형용사나 부사의 원급이 들어가야 한다. 여기서는 동사 advertise를 수식하는 부사가 들어가야 하므로 (B) efficiently가 정답이다.
해석 PW Marketing Firm만큼 제품을 효율적으로 광고할 수 있는 회사는 거의 없다.
어휘 advertise 광고하다   efficiently 효율적으로

3.
해설 빈칸은 [make + 목적어 + 목적격 보어] 구조에서 목적격 보어 자리이다. 따라서 빈칸에는 형용사가 들어가야 하는데 빈칸 앞에 비교급 강조 부사 even이 있으므로 bold의 비교급인 (D) bolder가 정답이다.
해석 그 포스터가 더 주목받게 하기 위해 디자이너들은 색을 훨씬 더 선명하게 하기로 결정했다.
어휘 draw attention 관심을 끌다   bold 선명한; 용감한

4.
해설 빈칸 앞에 be동사 is가 있고 뒤에는 비교급이 있으므로 빈칸에는 비교급을 수식하는 부사가 들어가야 한다. 따라서 비교급을 강조하여 '훨씬'의 뜻을 나타내는 (D) much가 정답이다.
해석 최근에 출시된 Voyager Prime Phone은 5년 된 동종 기기보다 훨씬 더 크다.
어휘 newly 최근에, 새로   release 출시하다   counterpart (동일한 지위의) 상대편, 대응물

빈출 유형 공략 06   본문 p.59
1. (B)   2. (A)   3. (D)   4. (B)

1.
해설 빈칸 앞에 정관사가 있고 뒤에는 명사구(health benefit)가 있으므로 빈칸은 명사구를 수식하는 형용사 자리이다. 문맥상 '가장 큰 건강상 이점'이라고 하는 게 자연스러우며, 이때 최상급 표현을 위해 정관사와 함께 쓸 수 있어야 하므로 (B) greatest가 정답이다.
해석 이 보충제의 가장 큰 효능은 지방 분해 능력이다.
어휘 benefit 혜택, 이득   supplement 보충(제); 부록; 추가 요금

2.
해설 빈칸 앞에 최상급이 있고 뒤에는 to부정사구가 이어지므로 빈칸에는 최상급을 수식하는 부사가 들어가야 한다. 선택지 중 최상급을 수식할 수 있는 부사인 (A) ever와 (B) very, 그리고 (C) quite가 정답 후보인데, 이 문장에서는 최상급을 뒤에서 수식해야 하므로 (A)가 정답이다.
해석 그 광고는 Glit의 신형 노트북이 역대 출시된 노트북 중 가장 얇다는 사실을 강조했다.
어휘 emphasize 강조하다   release 출시하다

3.
해설 빈칸 뒤에 최상급이 있으므로 빈칸에는 최상급을 수식하는 부사가 들어가야 한다. 따라서 최상급을 강조하여 '단연 가장 ~한'의 뜻을 나타내는 (D) Even이 정답이다.
해석 가장 최근에 입사한 인턴도 중요한 프로젝트에 참여할 기회가 있습니다.
어휘 opportunity 기회   take part in ~에 참여하다   significant 상당한; 중요한

4.
해설 빈칸 앞에 정관사가 있고 뒤에는 명사(element)가 있으므로 빈칸은 명사를 수식하는 형용사 자리이다. 문맥상 '가장 필수적인 요소'라고 하는 게 자연스러우며, 이때 최상급 표현을 위해 정관사 the와 함께 쓸 수 있어야 하므로 (B) most essential이 정답이다.
해석 어떤 식당이든 고객 만족도가 중요하긴 하지만 실제로는 식품 안전성이 성공적인 사업장의 가장 필수적인 요소이다.
어휘 customer satisfaction 고객 만족(도)   crucial 중요한, 결정적인   food safety 식품 안전(성)   essential 필수적인

ACTUAL TEST

본문 p.60

1. (B)	2. (C)	3. (A)	4. (D)	5. (C)
6. (D)	7. (C)	8. (A)	9. (B)	10. (D)
11. (D)	12. (B)	13. (D)	14. (B)	

1. 부사 자리 [동사 뒤]

해설 빈칸은 동사(advertises)를 수식하는 자리이므로 선택지 중 부사인 (B) heavily가 정답이다.

해석 BT News는 소셜 미디어에 대대적으로 광고를 하기 때문에 웹사이트 통신량이 많다.

어휘 traffic 전산망에서 전송되는 정보의 양[흐름]; 교통(량)
advertise 광고하다

2. 형용사 자리 [주격 보어]

해설 빈칸은 연결동사 seem 뒤의 주격 보어 자리로 주어인 The recruits의 상태나 상황을 나타낼 수 있는 말이 들어가야 한다. 따라서 선택지 중 형용사인 (C) eager가 정답이다.

해석 신입 사원들은 하루 빨리 업무 첫날이 시작되길 바라는 것 같다.

어휘 recruit 신입 사원   eager to do ~하기를 간절히 바라는, ~하기를 몹시 고대하는

3. 최상급 비교

해설 빈칸 앞에 정관사가 있고 뒤에는 명사구(sales numbers)가 있으므로 빈칸은 명사구를 수식하는 형용사 자리이다. 문맥상 '가장 높은 매출액'이 되는 게 자연스러우며, 이때 최상급 표현을 위해 정관사 the와 함께 쓸 수 있어야 하므로 (A) highest가 정답이다.

해석 뭄바이 지점은 전체 글로벌 영업 팀 중에서 매출액이 가장 높았다.

어휘 sales numbers 판매 실적, 매출액   out of ~ 중에서

4. 부사 자리 [동사 앞]

해설 빈칸은 동사(printed)를 수식하는 자리이므로 선택지 중 부사인 (D) accidentally가 정답이다.

해석 교육생 중 한 명은 그 소프트웨어에 익숙하지 않아서 Traylyn Inc.의 배너를 실수로 열 개나 더 인쇄하고 말았다.

어휘 unfamiliar 익숙하지 않은   extra 추가의, 여분의

5. 혼동하기 쉬운 형용사 [confidential vs. confident]

해설 빈칸은 감각동사 feel 뒤의 주격 보어 자리로 주어인 customers의 상태나 상황을 나타낼 수 있는 말이 들어가야 한다. 선택지 중 형용사인 (B) confidential(기밀의)과 (C) confident(자신감 있는) 중에서 의미상 customers를 수식하기에 가장 적절한 것은 (C)이다.

해석 Tony's Electronics는 항상 할인을 많이 하기 때문에 고객들은 자신들이 구입한 물건이 과하게 비싼 게 아닐 거라고 확신할 수 있다.

어휘 generous 후한, 관대한   feel confident 자신하다, 확신하다
overcharge 과다 청구하다

6. 부사 자리 [형용사 앞]

해설 빈칸은 형용사(understanding)를 수식하는 자리이므로 선택지 중 부사인 (D) remarkably가 정답이다.

해석 그 CEO는 성격이 거칠 것 같지만 놀라울 정도로 이해심이 많은 리더이다.

어휘 intimidate 겁을 주다, 겁먹게 하다   understanding 이해심 많은   remarkably 놀라울 정도로

7. 형용사 자리 [명사 앞]

해설 빈칸 앞에 소유한정사가 있고 뒤에는 명사가 있으므로 빈칸은 명사를 수식하는 형용사 자리이다. 따라서 선택지 중 형용사인 (C) economical이 정답이다.

해석 Gracie's Fashions는 경제적인 제조 과정 덕분에 직원에게는 임금을 넉넉하게 지불하고 소비자에게는 저렴한 가격에 판매할 수 있다.

어휘 manufacturing 제조   fairly 꽤, 상당히; 공정하게   pass A on to B B에게 A만큼의 값을 지불하게 하다; B에게 A를 전달하다

8. quite vs. enough

해설 빈칸은 형용사(different)를 수식하는 자리이므로 부사가 들어가야 한다. 선택지 중 부사인 (A) quite와 (C) enough가 정답 후보인데, 형용사를 앞에서 수식해야 하므로 (A)가 정답이다.

해석 그 회사의 사장과 부사장은 스타일이 꽤 다르긴 했지만 둘 다 훌륭한 연설을 했다.

어휘 vice president 부사장   give a speech 연설을 하다

9. 형용사 자리 [명사 앞]

해설 빈칸 앞에 동사가 있고 뒤에는 명사가 있으므로 빈칸은 명사를 수식하는 형용사 자리이다. 따라서 선택지 중 형용사인 (B) noticeable이 정답이다.

해석 Investgain의 새로운 CEO인 Rachel Fendley가 현재의 역할을 맡은 이후로 눈에 띄는 발전을 이루어 냈다.

어휘 improvement 개선, 향상   noticeable 눈에 띄는, 뚜렷한

10. 부사 자리 [비교급 강조]

해설 빈칸 앞에 be동사 is가 있고 뒤에는 비교급이 있으므로 빈칸에는 비교급을 수식하는 부사가 들어가야 한다. 따라서 비교급을 강조하여 '훨씬'의 뜻을 나타내는 (D) considerably가 정답이다.

해석 보통의 구매자에게 미니 태블릿은 초대형 태블릿보다 훨씬 더 매력적이다.

어휘 average 보통의, 평범한; 평균의   attractive 매력적인, 멋진   considerably 상당히

수신인: 전 직원
발신인: Jin Baek
날짜: 3월 24일
제목: 긴급

3월 28일에 Avery Investments는 사무실을 Murphy Building으로 옮길 예정입니다. 이번 ¹¹이전으로 사업이 성장

함에 따라 더 많은 직원을 수용할 수 있는 충분한 공간이 확보될 것입니다. 직원 여러분은 건물 1층에 있는 카페를 편리하게 이용할 수 있습니다. 저희 호실 내에 있는 ¹²별도의 회의실도 마음껏 이용하실 수 있습니다. 필요한 준비를 할 시간이 ¹³거의 없다는 점은 미안하게 생각합니다. 3월 27일에는 모든 직원이 일상적인 업무보다는 사무실을 정리하게 될 겁니다. ¹⁴따라서 편한 옷을 입는 걸 추천합니다.

Jin Baek
지원 서비스 관리자

어휘 take on ~을 채용[고용]하다 convenient 편리한 ground floor 1층 unit (건물의) 한 공간; 구성단위; 한 개 preparation 준비, 대비 pack up (짐을) 싸다 business duty 업무

11. 명사 어휘
어휘 addition 추가, 추가된 것 supplement 보충(제); 부록; 추가 요금 treatment 대우; 치료, 처치

12. 형용사 자리 [명사 앞]
해설 빈칸 앞에 관사가 있고 뒤에는 명사구(meeting rooms)가 있으므로 빈칸은 명사구를 수식하는 형용사 자리이다. 따라서 선택지 중 형용사인 (B) private가 정답이다.
어휘 private 사유의, 전용의

13. 한정사
해설 빈칸 뒤에 불가산명사가 있으므로 빈칸에는 불가산명사를 수식할 수 있는 말이 들어가야 한다. 따라서 (D) little이 정답이다.

14. 알맞은 문장 고르기
해설 빈칸 앞에서 3월 27일에는 사무실을 정리할 거라고 했으므로 빈칸에는 활동에 편한 옷을 입고 오라는 내용이 들어가는 게 가장 자연스럽다. 따라서 편한 옷을 입는 걸 추천한다고 한 (B)가 정답이다.
해석 (A) 첨부된 휴가 일정을 확인해 주세요.
(B) 따라서 편한 옷을 입는 걸 추천합니다.
(C) 매년 우리는 열심히 일한 직원들에게 포상을 합니다.
(D) 일부 지점에서는 자체 교육을 실시할 수도 있습니다.
어휘 be encouraged to do ~하도록 권장[권고]받다 casual 편한, 격식을 차리지 않는

UNIT 04 전치사

기초 문법 CHECK 본문 p.65

1. operation   2. us   3. attending
4. on   5. at   6. in

1.
해설 전치사 뒤에는 명사가 위치하므로 operation이 정답이다.
해석 새 지점은 7월 1일이 되어야 운영될 것이다.

2.
해설 전치사 뒤에는 목적격 대명사가 위치하므로 us가 정답이다.
해석 Mr. Scott은 이번 주 금요일에 우리와 최종 계약을 체결할 것이다.

3.
해설 전치사 뒤에는 동명사가 위치하므로 attending이 정답이다.
해석 많은 직원이 콘퍼런스 참석에 관심이 있다.

4.
해설 요일을 나타낼 때는 on을 쓴다.
해석 Lotus Restaurant는 토요일마다 특별 저녁 메뉴를 제공한다.

5.
해설 구체적인 시점을 딱 집어서 나타낼 때는 at을 쓴다. on은 at보다 넓은 범위의 시간 개념을 이를 때 쓰는데 뒤에 날짜, 요일, 특정일을 나타내는 말이 이어진다.
해석 직원들은 매달 말에 월급을 받는다.

6.
해설 넓은 지역이나 장소, 무언가의 내부를 나타낼 때는 in을 쓴다.
해석 그 상점은 레이크뷰 대로의 모퉁이에 있는 쇼핑센터에 있다.

빈출 유형 공략 01 본문 p.66
1. (C)   2. (A)

1.
해설 빈칸 뒤에 요일(Saturday)이 있으므로 (C) on이 정답이다.
해석 토요일에 La Tortilla를 방문한 사람들은 Super Salsa Special에 만족했다.
어휘 be pleased with ~에 만족하다, ~에 기뻐하다

2.
해설 문맥상 특정 시점까지 '계속' 가게를 운영하지 않을 거라는 내용이 되어야 한다. 따라서 '지속'의 의미가 있는 (A) until이 정답이다. (C) by는 특정 시점까지 행위나 동작이 '완료'되는 것을 강조하는 전치사이므로 이 문장에는 적절하지 않다.
해석 겨울철에는 장사가 잘되지 않아서 Polly's Ice Cream Parlor는 5월이 되어야 문을 열 것이다.
어휘 slow business 영업 부진

빈출 유형 공략 02 본문 p.67
1. (A)   2. (B)

1.
해설 문맥상 공항에서부터 4마일 떨어진 거리에 있다는 내용이 되는 게 자연스러우므로 '~로부터'를 뜻하는 (A) from이 정답이다.

해석 Highland Tower는 유명 관광지로, 공항에서 4마일 밖에 떨어져 있지 않다.
어휘 well-known 잘 알려진, 유명한   tourist spot 관광지

2.
해설 문맥상 걸어서 갈 수 있는 거리 내에 있다는 내용이 되는 게 자연스러우므로 '~ 내에'를 뜻하는 (B) within이 정답이다.
해석 이 아파트는 많은 인기 명소에 도보로 갈 수 있는 거리에 있어서 최상급 주택이다.
어휘 attraction 명소; 매력   prime 최상의   real estate 부동산

빈출 유형 공략 03 본문 p.68
1. (A)   **2.** (C)

1.
해설 문맥상 고객 비밀 유지에 관한 문제점들을 알려 준다는 내용이 되는 게 자연스러우므로 '~에 대하여'를 뜻하는 (A) concerning이 정답이다.
해석 다음 주에 매니저가 고객 비밀 유지에 관한 문제점들을 알려 줄 계획입니다.
어휘 inform A of B A에게 B를 알리다   confidentiality 비밀(을 지켜야 하는 상황)

2.
해설 문맥상 기업 트레이너로서의 뛰어난 기량 덕분에 승진 제안을 받았다는 내용이 되는 게 자연스러우므로 '~로서'를 뜻하는 (C) as가 정답이다.
해석 Ms. Almaraz가 승진을 제안받은 주된 이유는 기업 트레이너로서의 뛰어난 기량 때문이었다.
어휘 promotion 승진, 진급; 홍보, 판촉   mainly 주로, 대개   remarkable 뛰어난, 주목할 만한   corporate 기업의

빈출 유형 공략 04 본문 p.69
1. (A)   **2.** (C)

1.
해설 문맥상 디자이너의 반대에도 불구하고 개점 날짜를 고수하기로 했다는 내용이 되는 게 자연스러우므로 '~에도 불구하고'를 뜻하는 (A) in spite of가 정답이다.
해석 Mr. Benton은 인테리어 디자이너의 반대에도 불구하고 새 레스토랑의 개점 날짜를 그대로 유지하기로 결정했다.
어휘 opposition 반대

2.
해설 문맥상 문을 잠그기 전에 경보 장치가 설정되어 있는지 확인하라는 내용이 되는 게 자연스러우므로 '~ 전에'를 뜻하는 (C) prior to가 정답이다.

해석 마지막으로 퇴근하는 사람은 문을 잠그기 전에 보안 경보 장치가 설정되어 있는지 확인해야 한다.
어휘 security alarm 보안 경보 장치

빈출 유형 공략 05 본문 p.70
1. (A)   **2.** (B)

1.
해설 형용사 eligible과 함께 쓰이는 (A) for가 정답이다.
해석 회사에서 6개월 이상 근무한 사람은 누구나 상여금을 받을 수 있다.
어휘 holiday bonus 상여금, (명절, 휴가, 연말 등에 받는) 보너스

2.
해설 명사 increase와 함께 쓰이는 (B) in이 정답이다.
해석 CoolBeats Tech는 유명 블로거로부터 무료 홍보를 받은 후 매출이 크게 증가했다.
어휘 promotion 홍보, 판촉; 승진, 진급

빈출 유형 공략 06 본문 p.71
1. (B)   **2.** (B)

1.
해설 빈칸 뒤의 our expectations와 함께 쓰여 기대 이상으로 업무를 잘했다는 내용이 되는 게 자연스러우므로 (B) beyond가 정답이다.
해석 예전에 인턴이었던 직원은 우리의 기대 이상으로 일을 잘해서 지금은 정규직이다.
어휘 excel 뛰어나다   expectation 예상, 기대   permanent employee 정규직

2.
해설 빈칸 뒤의 Ms. Keaton's supervision과 함께 쓰여 Ms. Keaton의 지휘하에 영업 팀이 목표치를 달성했다는 내용이 되는 게 자연스러우므로 (B) Under가 정답이다.
해석 Ms. Keaton의 지휘하에 그 영업 팀은 목표치를 달성할 수 있었다.
어휘 supervision 감독, 지도   reach 도달하다, 이르다

ACTUAL TEST 본문 p.72
1. (C)	**2.** (B)	**3.** (C)	**4.** (C)	**5.** (C)
6. (C)	**7.** (B)	**8.** (A)	**9.** (C)	**10.** (A)
11. (A)	**12.** (C)	**13.** (A)	**14.** (B)	

1. 동사+전치사 [move A to B]
해설 빈칸 앞의 has been moved와 함께 쓰여 오후 2시 30분으로 회의 시간이 변경되었다는 내용이 되는 게 자연스러우므로 (C) to가 정답이다.
해석 오늘 거래처와의 미팅이 오후 2시 30분으로 변경되었다.

2. 도구/방법/수단을 나타내는 전치사
해설 문맥상 비디오 게임 출시로 수익성이 높은 회사가 되었다는 내용이 되는 게 자연스러우므로 '~을 가지고'를 뜻하는 (B) With가 정답이다.
해석 가상 자동차 경주 비디오 게임 출시로 Popka Inc.는 그 나라에서 가장 수익성이 높은 게임 회사가 되었다.
어휘 release 출시 profitable 수익성이 있는; 유익한

3. 도구/방법/수단을 나타내는 전치사
해설 문맥상 신용 카드로 지불할 수 있다는 내용이 되는 게 자연스러우므로 '(방법, 수단 등)으로'를 뜻하는 (C) by가 정답이다.
해석 매주 열리는 농산물 직판장의 판매자들은 현금을 선호하긴 하지만 고객은 신용 카드로도 지불할 수 있다.
어휘 farmer's market 농산물 직판장 prefer 선호하다

4. 추가를 나타내는 전치사
해설 문맥상 일찍 출근하는 것 외에 주말 근무도 한다는 내용이 되는 게 자연스러우므로 '~ 외에도'를 뜻하는 (C) In addition to가 정답이다.
해석 Mr. Earl은 일찍 출근하는 것 외에 마감일을 맞추기 위해 가끔 주말에 일을 하기도 한다.
어휘 meet a deadline 마감일을 지키다

5. 시간을 나타내는 전치사 [on vs. in]
해설 빈칸 뒤에 구체적인 기간(three weeks)이 있으므로 (C) in이 정답이다. in 뒤에 숫자가 포함된 시간 표현이 오면 '~ 후에'를 의미할 수 있다.
해석 이번 겨울의 새로운 부츠 컬렉션은 3주 후에 출시될 예정이다.

6. 추가를 나타내는 전치사
해설 문맥상 오케스트라에서 지휘하는 것 외에 피아노 레슨도 하고 있다는 내용이 되는 게 자연스러우므로 '~ 외에도'를 뜻하는 (C) Besides가 정답이다.
해석 Mr. Graham은 Philadelphia Orchestra를 지휘하는 것 외에 대학생들과 다른 성인들에게 피아노 레슨도 한다.
어휘 conduct 지휘하다; (특정 활동을) 수행하다

7. 제외를 나타내는 전치사
해설 문맥상 업무를 마무리해야 하는 사람들을 제외하고 나머지 직원들은 일찍 퇴근했다는 내용이 되는 게 자연스러우므로 '~을 제외하고'를 뜻하는 (B) except for가 정답이다.
해석 급한 업무를 마무리해야 하는 사람들을 제외한 직원 대부분은 휴가를 위해 일찍 퇴근했다.
어휘 last-minute 막바지의, 임박한

8. 동사+전치사 [adapt to]
해설 동사 adapt와 함께 쓰여 새로운 트렌드에 빠르게 적응한다는 내용이 되는 게 자연스러우므로 (A) to가 정답이다.
해석 Pearl Cosmetics는 새로운 트렌드에 빠르게 적응하기 때문에 성공을 거두고 있다.

9. 기간을 나타내는 전치사
해설 빈칸 뒤에 two months라는 기간이 제시되었으며 문맥상 '대략 2달 동안'이라고 해석되어야 하므로 (C) for가 정답이다.
해석 Alex's Diamonds는 수리가 완료될 동안 약 두 달 정도 문을 닫을 예정이다.
어휘 shut down 닫다, 폐쇄되다 renovation 개조, 리모델링

10. 전치사 관용 표현
해설 빈칸 뒤의 time과 함께 쓰여 케이크를 제때 배달하겠다고 약속했다는 내용이 되는 게 자연스러우므로 (A) on이 정답이다.
해석 바쁜 결혼 시즌에도 불구하고 Marcy's Cakes는 제때 케이크를 배달하겠다고 약속했다.
어휘 despite ~에도 불구하고 deliver 배달하다 confection 케이크, (사탕이나 과자와 같은) 당과

공지
Jamestown Hotel의 높은 [11]수준을 유지하기 위해 이번 주 월요일인 6월 7일에 옥상 수영장을 대대적으로 청소할 예정입니다. 그날[12]에는 투숙객들이 옥상에 접근할 수 없으니 수영하기를 원하는 분들은 호텔 바로 옆에 있는 야외 수영장을 이용하시기를 권합니다.
[13]이로 인해 발생할 수 있는 문제에 대해 진심으로 사과드립니다. [14]궁금한 사항이 있으면 프런트 직원에게 문의해 주십시오.
Jamestown Hotel 관리부

어휘 maintain (관계, 상태, 수준 등) 유지하다 access 접근; 접속 take advantage of ~을 이용하다 direct a question to ~에게 질문[문의]하다

11. 명사 자리 [형용사 뒤]
해설 빈칸 앞에 형용사가 있고 뒤에는 부사가 있으므로 빈칸은 명사 자리이다. 선택지 중 명사인 (A) standards와 (B) standardization이 정답 후보인데, 문맥상 높은 수준을 유지하기 위해 수영장을 대청소한다는 내용이 되는 게 자연스러우므로 '기준, 수준'을 뜻하는 (A)가 정답이다.
어휘 standardization 표준화, 규격화

12. 시간을 나타내는 전치사 [on vs. in]
해설 빈칸 뒤에 날짜(that date)가 있으므로 (C) On이 정답이다. (D) In은 연도, 계절, 월, 오전/오후 등을 나타낼 때 쓴다.

13. 알맞은 문장 고르기
해설 빈칸 앞에서 대청소 때문에 옥상 수영장을 사용할 수 없다고 했으므로 빈칸에는 수영장을 사용하지 못하는 문제에 따른 사과를 하는 게 가장 자연스럽다. 따라서 (A)가 정답이다.

해석 (A) 이로 인해 발생할 수 있는 문제에 대해 진심으로 사과드립니다.
(B) 옥상 수영장은 투숙하는 동안 언제든 즐기십시오.
(C) 저희 호텔은 150년 이상 운영되어 왔습니다.
(D) 만약 귀하가 수영 수업을 할 자격이 된다면 오늘 저희에게 연락 주세요.
어휘 sincerely 진심으로 at any time 언제든지, 아무 때나 qualified 자격이 있는, 적임의

14. 명사 어휘
어휘 recommendation 추천(서); 권고 application 적용; 지원(서), 신청(서) dispute 논쟁

UNIT 05 수 일치

기초 문법 CHECK
본문 p.77

1. is   2. specifies   3. has
4. is   5. are   6. are
7. is

1.
해설 주어 The company가 단수이므로 단수 동사 is가 정답이다.
해석 그 회사는 주 전역에 유통을 확대할 계획이다.

2.
해설 주어 The employment contract가 단수이므로 단수 동사 specifies가 정답이다.
해석 고용 계약서에는 근로자가 퇴사를 원하면 한 달 전에 통지해야 한다고 명시되어 있다.

3.
해설 기업 이름은 -s가 붙어도 단수 취급하므로 단수 동사 has가 정답이다.
해석 Chowlan Pharmaceuticals는 예방약 재고를 늘렸다.

4.
해설 접속사 and 뒤에 생략된 말이 Ms. Walters이므로 단수 동사 is가 정답이다.
해석 Ms. Walters는 지난 5년간 Phoenix의 부사장으로 재직해 왔으며 다음 달에 은퇴할 예정이다.

5.
해설 주어 Several properties가 복수이므로 복수 동사 are가 정답이다.
해석 이 거리의 몇몇 부지는 팔려고 내놓은 것이다.

6.
해설 주어 Prices가 복수이므로 복수 동사 are가 정답이다.
해석 당사 웹사이트에 나열된 주방 물품의 가격은 예고 없이 변경될 수 있습니다.

7.
해설 주어 The schedule이 단수이므로 단수 동사 is가 정답이다.
해석 내일 있을 개막식 일정이 첨부되어 있습니다.

빈출 유형 공략 01
본문 p.78

1. (C)   2. (C)   3. (A)   4. (A)

1.
해설 The number of 뒤에는 복수 명사가 이어지므로 (C) producers가 정답이다.
해석 커피 원두 생산자의 수는 지난 몇 년간 꾸준히 증가했다.
어휘 steadily 점차, 꾸준히 producer 생산자, 제작자

2.
해설 주어가 [숫자+퍼센트]이므로 of 뒤의 명사 KLP&Co.'s business에 동사를 수 일치해야 한다. 따라서 단수 동사인 (C) comes가 정답이다.
해석 KLP&Co.의 사업 실적 중 약 40%는 해외 고객에게서 나오는 것이다.
어휘 roughly 대략, 약 business 사업 (실적) overseas 해외의, 국외의 come from ~에서 나오다, ~에서 기인하다

3.
해설 주어 Several managers가 복수이므로 복수 동사인 (A) are having이 정답이다.
해석 지금 부장 몇 명이 회의실에서 중요한 회의를 하고 있다.

4.
해설 주어가 [a number of+복수 명사]이므로 복수 동사인 (A) believe가 정답이다.
해석 설문 조사 데이터에 따르면 상당수의 재방문 고객은 새로운 메뉴가 개선되었다고 생각한다.
어휘 according to ~에 따르면 significant 상당한; 중요한 returning guest 재방문 손님 improvement 개선, 향상

빈출 유형 공략 02
본문 p.79

1. (C)   2. (A)   3. (D)   4. (A)

1.
해설 [not only A but also B]는 B에 수 일치한다. 이 문장에서는 its competitors가 B에 해당하므로 복수 동사인 (C) distribute가 정답이다.
해석 Procon Company뿐만 아니라 경쟁사들도 소비자에게 직접 제품을 유통한다.

어휘 competitor 경쟁자, 경쟁사   directly 직접, 바로   distribute (상품을) 유통시키다; 나누어 주다, 배부하다

2.
해설 and로 연결된 주어는 복수 동사로 수 일치하므로 (A) have separated가 정답이다.
해석 혁신과 위험을 감수하는 자세는 Yonder Technologies를 전통적인 전자 회사들과 구분 짓는다.
어휘 innovation 혁신   risk-taking 위험을 감수하는   separate A from B A를 B와 구분 짓다

3.
해설 nor로 연결된 주어는 nor 뒤의 명사에 동사를 수 일치한다. 빈칸 뒤에 복수 동사 were가 있는 것으로 보아 빈칸에는 복수 명사가 들어가는 게 적절하므로 (D) employees가 정답이다.
해석 Mr. Herbert와 그의 직원들 모두 놀이공원의 안전 문제를 인지하지 못했다.
어휘 be aware of ~을 자각[인지]하다   safety issue 안전 문제

4.
해설 [A of B] 주어는 A에 동사를 수 일치한다. 이 문장에서는 Many projects가 A에 해당하므로 (A) are being conducted가 정답이다.
해석 고객층을 파악하기 위해 많은 시장 조사 프로젝트가 진행되고 있다.
어휘 identify 확인하다, 알아보다

빈출 유형 공략 03   본문 p.80
1. (A)   **2.** (B)   **3.** (A)   **4.** (C)

1.
해설 주어 Clothes가 과거분사구(made by Vincenzo)의 수식을 받는 구조이다. 따라서 빈칸에는 복수 동사가 들어가야 하므로 (A) are designed가 정답이다.
해석 Vincenzo가 만든 옷은 젊은 소비자들에게 어필할 수 있도록 디자인되었다.
어휘 appeal to ~의 관심을 끌다   consumer 소비자

2.
해설 주어 All the sculptures가 전치사구(at Central Museum)의 수식을 받는 구조이다. 따라서 빈칸에는 복수 동사가 들어가야 하므로 (B) are scheduled가 정답이다.
해석 Central Museum에 있는 모든 조각상은 이달 내에 정원에 전시될 예정이다.
어휘 sculpture 조각상   display 전시하다, 진열하다; 드러내다, 보이다   be scheduled to do ~하기로 예정되다

3.
해설 'that ------ for five years'는 a quality guarantee를 수식하는 주격 관계대명사절로 빈칸은 동사 자리이다. 주격 관계대명사절의 동사는 선행사에 수 일치하므로 단수 동사인 (A) lasts가 정답이다.
해석 Walencia의 시계는 5년 품질 보증서가 딸려 온다.
어휘 quality guarantee 품질 보증서   last 계속되다, 지속되다

4.
해설 주어 Many painters가 주격 관계대명사절(who visit the city hall for the first time)의 수식을 받는 구조이다. 따라서 빈칸에는 복수 동사가 들어가야 하므로 (C) are inspired가 정답이다.
해석 그 시청을 처음 방문하는 많은 화가는 영감을 받아 그곳을 예술품으로 재현한다.
어휘 recreate 재탄생시키다

빈출 유형 공략 04   본문 p.81
1. (B)   **2.** (B)   **3.** (A)   **4.** (D)

1.
해설 주어가 [half of+명사]이므로 of 뒤의 명사 the country's luxury hotels에 동사를 수 일치해야 한다. 선택지 중 복수 동사인 (B) are situated와 (C) have situated가 정답 후보인데, 빈칸 뒤에 목적어가 없으므로 수동태인 (B)가 정답이다.
해석 그 나라에 있는 고급 호텔의 거의 절반이 해안을 따라 위치해 있다.
어휘 coast 해안   situate (특정 위치에) 두다

2.
해설 'that ------ on the screen'은 the proposed budget changes를 수식하는 주격 관계대명사절로 빈칸은 동사 자리이다. 주격 관계대명사절의 동사는 선행사에 수 일치하므로 복수 동사인 (A) were displaying과 (B) are displayed가 정답 후보인데, 빈칸 뒤에 목적어가 없으므로 수동태인 (B)가 정답이다.
해석 화면에 나와 있는 제안된 예산 변경안을 살펴봐 주시기 바랍니다.
어휘 look over ~을 (대강) 살펴보다   budget 예산   display 드러내다, 보이다; 전시하다, 진열하다

3.
해설 주어 An increase가 전치사구(in profits)의 수식을 받는 구조이다. 따라서 빈칸에는 단수 동사가 들어가야 하므로 (A) has allowed와 (D) was allowed가 정답 후보인데, 빈칸 뒤에 목적어(Warren Industries)가 있으므로 능동태인 (A)가 정답이다.
해석 수익 증가로 Warren Industries는 더 많은 직원을 고용할 수 있게 되었다.
어휘 profit 이익   hire 채용하다, 고용하다

4.

해설 'who ------- for Melon Technologies for over 30 years'는 Mr. Schmidt를 수식하는 주격 관계대명사절로 빈칸은 동사 자리이다. 주격 관계대명사절의 동사는 선행사에 수 일치하므로 단수 동사가 정답 후보인데, 뒤에 현재완료 시제와 어울려 쓰이는 표현(for over 30 years)이 있으므로 현재완료 시제인 (D)가 정답이다.

해석 Mr. Schmidt의 은퇴 파티가 다음 주에 열리는데, 그는 Melon Technologies에서 30년 넘게 일해 왔다.

어휘 retirement 은퇴

ACTUAL TEST
본문 p.82

1. (A)   2. (B)   3. (B)   4. (C)   5. (D)
6. (C)   7. (A)   8. (A)   9. (B)   10. (D)
11. (C) 12. (B) 13. (D) 14. (D)

1. 전치사구의 수식을 받는 주어와 동사의 수 일치

해설 주어 The customers가 전치사구(in line)의 수식을 받는 구조이다. 따라서 빈칸에는 복수 동사가 들어가야 하므로 (A) are starting이 정답이다.

해석 줄을 서 있는 손님들이 너무 오래 기다려서 안달을 내기 시작했다.

어휘 in line 줄을 선   restless 초조해하는, 안절부절못하는, 안달 내는

2. 수 일치와 태 복합

해설 주어 Those가 주격 관계대명사절(who ~ festival)의 수식을 받는 구조이다. 따라서 빈칸에는 복수 동사가 들어가야 하므로 (A) encourage와 (B) are encouraged가 정답 후보인데, 빈칸 뒤에 목적어가 없으므로 수동태인 (B)가 정답이다.

해석 다음 달 Open Slate 축제에 참가하고자 하는 분들은 일찍 신청할 것을 권합니다.

어휘 participate in ~에 참여하다   sign up 신청하다, 등록하다   be encouraged to do ~하도록 권장[권고]받다

3. 전치사구의 수식을 받는 주어와 동사의 수 일치

해설 주어 The robots가 전치사구(on this assembly line)의 수식을 받는 구조이다. 따라서 빈칸에는 복수 동사가 들어가야 하므로 (B) are controlled가 정답이다.

해석 이 조립 라인의 로봇들은 원격으로 제어되어 작업자의 부상을 방지한다.

어휘 assembly line (공장의) 조립 라인   remotely 원격으로, 멀리서   prevent 예방하다, 방지하다   injury 부상

4. 수 일치와 시제 복합

해설 주어가 [the number of+복수 명사]이므로 단수 동사인 (B) increases와 (C) has increased가 정답 후보이다. 이제 시제를 따져 봐야 하는데 앞에 현재완료와 어울려 쓰이는 부사절(Since ~ window)이 있으므로 현재완료 시제인 (C)가 정답이다.

해석 Henry's Café가 드라이브스루 창을 만든 이후 커피숍을 찾는 사람들의 수가 증가했다.

어휘 drive-through (카페, 패스트푸드점 등에서) 차에 탄 채로 물건을 구매할 수 있는

5. 수량 표현이 쓰인 주어와 동사의 수 일치

해설 주어가 [half of+명사]이므로 of 뒤의 명사 the employees에 동사를 수 일치해야 한다. 따라서 복수 동사인 (D) drive가 정답이다.

해석 Tuscana 직원 중 약 절반이 출퇴근을 위해 매일 차를 몰고 다닌다.

6. 수 일치와 시제 복합

해설 주어 Customers가 복수 명사인 것으로 보아 빈칸에는 복수 동사가 들어가야 한다. 따라서 복수 동사인 (C) have trusted와 (D) trust가 정답 후보인데, 뒤에 현재완료 시제와 어울려 쓰이는 표현(for decades)이 있으므로 현재완료 시제인 (C)가 정답이다.

해석 Mantique Furniture의 품질에 대한 고집 때문에 고객들은 수십 년간 이 업체를 신뢰해 왔다.

어휘 decade 10년   commitment 헌신, 전념; 약속

7. 주격 관계대명절의 동사 수 일치

해설 'that ------- to older consumers'는 an ideal marketing format을 수식하는 주격 관계대명사절로 빈칸은 동사 자리이다. 주격 관계대명사절의 동사는 선행사에 수 일치하므로 단수 동사인 (A) appeals가 정답이다.

해석 Koolie Co.는 나이 든 소비자들의 관심을 끌 수 있는 이상적인 마케팅 방식을 찾고 있다.

어휘 search for ~을 찾다   ideal 이상적인   appeal to ~의 관심을 끌다

8. 수 일치와 시제 복합

해설 주어 the buses가 복수 명사인 것으로 보아 빈칸에는 단수 동사가 들어갈 수 없으므로 (C)와 (D)는 오답으로 소거한다. 또한 시간 부사절에서는 미래 시제 대신 현재 시제를 쓰므로 (A) arrive가 정답이다.

해석 버스가 도착하자마자 청소부들이 다음 승객들을 위해 버스를 채비하기 시작한다.

어휘 passenger 승객

9. 전치사구의 수식을 받는 주어와 동사의 수 일치

해설 주어 Feedback이 전치사구(from employees)의 수식을 받는 구조이다. 따라서 빈칸에는 단수 동사가 들어가야 하므로 (B) allows가 정답이다.

해석 직원들의 피드백을 통해 관리 팀은 사무실에 필요한 개선을 할 수 있다.

어휘 necessary 필수적인, 필요한

10. 수 일치와 태 복합

해설 'that ------- to my e-mail'은 the presentation files를 수식하는 주격 관계대명사절로 빈칸은 동사 자리이다. 주격 관계

대명사절의 동사는 선행사에 수 일치하므로 복수 동사인 (A) were attaching과 (D) are attached가 정답 후보인데, 빈칸 뒤에 목적어가 없으므로 수동태인 (D)가 정답이다.

해석 제 이메일에 첨부되어 있는 발표 파일들의 핵심 사항을 참고해 주세요.

어휘 note 주목하다; 언급하다 attach 첨부하다; 붙이다

> 우스터 (1월 28일)—Sparkle Dance Studio는 이번 주말에 설립 3주년을 ¹¹맞는다. Rachel Chapman 원장은 그렇게 작은 마을에 스튜디오를 여는 것에 대해 걱정했다. 다행히도 1학기 수업은 정원이 거의 꽉 차서 안심할 수 있었다. 학기 말에는 학생들의 진척을 보여 주는 댄스 공연이 열렸다. ¹²그것은 관객들에게 스튜디오를 알리는 데에도 도움이 되었다. Ms. Chapman은 그 후 온라인에 ¹³입소문이 난 댄스 강의 비디오를 게시했다. 그 비디오 홍보로 인해 그녀의 사업에 대한 관심이 갑자기 급증했다. Ms. Chapman은 그 기회를 이용하여 더 많은 강사를 고용했다. 그녀는 또한 사업 ¹⁴성장에 맞춰 더 큰 곳으로 이사했다.

어휘 concern 걱정, 우려; 관심사 semester 학기 be at full capacity 정원이 꽉 차다 relieve 안심시키다 recital 연주회, 발표회 progress 진행, 진척 instructional 교육의 go viral (영상, 이야기 등이) 빠르게 퍼져 나가다, 입소문이 나다 publicity 홍보 result in 결과적으로 ~가 되다 surge 급증, 급등 take advantage of ~을 이용하다 accommodate 수용하다, 받아들이다

11. 주어와 동사의 수 일치
해설 주어 Sparkle Dance Studio가 단수이므로 단수 동사인 (C) is celebrating이 정답이다. 미래완료 시제인 (D) will have celebrated는 과거나 미래에 시작된 일이 미래의 특정 시점에 완료됨을 나타낼 때 쓰는 표현이므로 문맥상 답이 될 수 없다.

12. 알맞은 문장 고르기
해설 빈칸 앞에서 학기 말에 댄스 공연이 열렸다고 했으므로 빈칸에는 그로 인해 댄스 스튜디오가 더 알려졌다는 내용이 들어가는 게 가장 자연스럽다. 따라서 (B)가 정답이다.
해석 (A) 그것의 티켓은 다음 주에 스튜디오 웹사이트에서 판매된다.
(B) 그것은 관객들에게 스튜디오를 알리는 데에도 도움이 되었다.
(C) 그녀는 자신의 진로를 완전히 바꾸기로 결심했다.
(D) 그녀는 소프트웨어 프로그램으로 그것들을 직접 디자인했다.

어휘 go on sale 판매에 들어가다, 시판되다 career path 진로 dramatically 급격하게

13. 주격 관계대명사
해설 빈칸 앞에 완전한 절이 있고 뒤에는 주어가 없는 불완전한 문장이 이어지므로 빈칸은 주격 관계대명사 자리이다. 따라서 (D) which가 정답이다.

14. 명사 어휘
어휘 innovation 혁신 vacancy (호텔 등의) 빈방, 빈 객실 supervision 관리, 감독

UNIT 06 수동태

기초 문법 CHECK
본문 p.87

1. run
2. being considered
3. be charged
4. had been delivered
5. encouraged
6. priced
7. be given

1.
해설 주어 The Tokyo store는 타동사 run의 행위를 받는 대상이고 뒤에 [by+행위 주체]인 by Ms. Saito도 있으므로 동사는 [be+과거분사] 형태의 수동태가 적절하다. 따라서 run이 정답이다.
해석 도쿄 매장은 Ms. Saito가 운영하고 있다.

2.
해설 주어 Ms. Allen은 타동사 consider의 행위를 받는 대상이므로 밑줄에는 [be+과거분사] 형태의 수동태가 적절하다. 따라서 being considered가 정답이다.
해석 Ms. Allen은 관리직으로 고려되고 있다.

3.
해설 주어 A 10% cancellation fee는 타동사 charge의 행위를 받는 대상이므로 밑줄에는 [be+과거분사] 형태의 수동태가 적절하다. 따라서 be charged가 정답이다.
해석 예약이 취소될 경우 10%의 취소 수수료가 부과된다.

4.
해설 주어 the package는 타동사 deliver의 행위를 받는 대상이므로 밑줄에는 [be+과거분사] 형태의 수동태가 적절하다. 따라서 had been delivered가 정답이다.
해석 Ms. Hall이 어제 보낸 소포가 배송되었는지 확인하기 위해 오늘 아침에 전화했다.

5.
해설 주어 Every employee는 타동사 encourage의 행위를 받는 대상이므로 동사는 [be+과거분사] 형태의 수동태가 적절하다. 따라서 encouraged가 정답이다.
해석 모든 직원은 AI 콘퍼런스에 참석하도록 권장된다.

6.
해설 주어 The new apartment complex는 타동사 price의 행위를 받는 대상이므로 동사는 [be+과거분사] 형태의 수동태가 적절하다. 따라서 priced가 정답이다.
해석 새 아파트 단지는 가격이 적당하게 책정되었다.

7.
해설 주어 Ticket-holders는 타동사 give의 행위를 받는 대상이므로 밑줄에는 [be+과거분사] 형태의 수동태가 적절하다. 따라서 be given이 정답이다. 참고로 이 문장은 능동태 문장에서 간접목적어였던 ticket-holders for the performances가 수동태의 주어가 되고 직접목적어였던 a refund가 동사 뒤에 남은 구조이다.
해석 공연 티켓 소지자는 환불을 받게 될 것이다.

빈출 유형 공략 01 본문 p.88

1. (B) **2.** (D) **3.** (D) **4.** (C)

1.
해설 빈칸 뒤에 목적어가 없고 선행사 employees는 행위를 받는 대상이므로 빈칸에는 [be+과거분사] 형태의 수동태가 적절하다. 따라서 (B) are involved가 정답이다.
해석 고객과 화상 회의를 하는 데 관련 있는 직원들을 위한 특별 교육 과정이 열릴 것이다.
어휘 conduct (특정 활동을) 수행하다; 지휘하다 involve 포함하다, 관련시키다

2.
해설 빈칸 앞에 전치사 from이 있으므로 빈칸은 동명사 자리이다. (C) damaging과 (D) being damaged가 정답 후보인데, 빈칸 뒤에 목적어가 없고 대명사 it이 가리키는 Each vase는 행위를 받는 대상이므로 빈칸에는 수동태가 적절하다. 따라서 (D)가 정답이다.
해석 각 꽃병은 운송 중에 손상되지 않도록 조심스럽게 포장되고 고정된다.
어휘 secure 고정하다 prevent 예방하다, 방지하다 transit 수송

3.
해설 빈칸 뒤에 목적어가 없고 주어 Ms. Delacruz's bronze statue는 행위를 받는 대상이므로 빈칸에는 [be+과거분사] 형태의 수동태가 적절하다. 따라서 (D) was praised가 정답이다.
해석 그 전시회에서 Ms. Delacruz의 동상은 중요한 현대 미술 작품으로 높이 평가받았다.
어휘 piece (작품) 한 점 contemporary 현대의 praise 칭찬하다

4.
해설 빈칸 뒤에 목적어가 없고 주어 All merchandise는 행위를 받는 대상이므로 빈칸에는 [be+과거분사] 형태의 수동태가 적절하다. 따라서 (C) is inspected가 정답이다.
해석 모든 상품은 우리의 품질 기준에 부합한다는 걸 확실히 하기 위해 점검된다.
어휘 merchandise 물품, 상품 guarantee 보장하다, 보증하다

빈출 유형 공략 02 본문 p.89

1. (B) **2.** (D) **3.** (C) **4.** (D)

1.
해설 빈칸 뒤에 목적어가 없고 주어 An employment offer는 타동사 send의 행위를 받는 대상이므로 빈칸에는 [be+과거분사] 형태의 수동태가 적절하다. 따라서 (B) will be sent가 정답이다. 참고로 이 문장은 능동태 문장에서 직접목적어였던 an employment offer가 수동태의 주어가 되면서 간접목적어였던 you 앞에 전치사 to가 붙은 것이다.

해석 계약 세부 사항이 확정되면 채용 제안서가 발송됩니다.
어휘 employment 고용, 채용 detail 세부 사항 contract 계약(서) finalize 결론짓다

2.
해설 주어 Account holders는 타동사 charge의 행위를 받는 대상이므로 빈칸에는 [be+과거분사] 형태의 수동태가 적절하다. 따라서 (D) will be charged가 정답이다. 참고로 이 문장은 능동태 문장에서 간접목적어였던 account holders가 수동태의 주어가 되고 직접목적어였던 an overdraft fee가 동사 뒤에 남은 구조이다.
해석 자신의 계좌에서 사용 가능한 금액보다 더 많은 돈을 쓰는 계좌 소유자에게 초과 사용분에 대한 수수료가 부과될 것이다.
어휘 account holder 계좌 소유자 overdraft 당좌 대월, 계좌에서 잔고 이상의 돈을 인출하면 수수료를 부과하는 제도 charge (요금 등을) 부과하다

3.
해설 주어 any changes는 타동사 make의 행위를 받는 대상이므로 빈칸에는 [be+과거분사] 형태의 수동태가 적절하다. 따라서 (C) should be made가 정답이다. 참고로 이 문장은 능동태 문장에서 목적어였던 any changes to our formula가 수동태의 주어가 되고 목적격 보어였던 public이 동사 뒤에 남은 구조이다.
해석 투명성을 유지하기 위해 당사 제조법의 변경 사항은 회사 웹사이트에 공개하고 발표해야 한다.
어휘 maintain (관계, 상태, 수준 등을) 유지하다 transparency 투명성 formula 제조법; 공식, 방식 make ~ public ~을 공표하다

4.
해설 주어 Newman Tech는 타동사 consider의 행위를 받는 대상이므로 빈칸에는 [be+과거분사] 형태의 수동태가 적절하다. 따라서 (D) was considered가 정답이다. 참고로 이 문장은 능동태 문장에서 목적어였던 Newman Tech가 수동태의 주어가 되고 목적격 보어였던 innovative가 동사 뒤에 남은 구조이다.
해석 Newman Tech가 반도체에 새로운 표준 규격을 개발한 이후 많은 사람에게 혁신적이라고 여겨졌다.
어휘 standard 표준 규격; 기준, 수준 semiconductor 반도체 innovative 혁신적인, 획기적인

빈출 유형 공략 03 본문 p.90

1. (B) **2.** (B) **3.** (D) **4.** (C)

1.
해설 선택지가 permit의 활용형으로 구성되어 있고 빈칸 뒤에 to부정사가 있는 것으로 보아 빈칸에는 뒤에 to부정사를 취할 수 있는 permit의 활용형이 들어가야 한다. 따라서 (B) permitted가 정답이다.
해석 보안 데스크에 체크인하고 나서 방문자들은 공장의 일부 구역을 방문할 수 있다.

어휘 select 엄선된, 정선된

2.
해설 선택지가 ask의 활용형으로 구성되어 있고 빈칸 뒤에 to부정사가 있는 것으로 보아 빈칸에는 뒤에 to부정사를 취할 수 있는 ask의 활용형이 들어가야 한다. 수동태인 (B) are asked와 능동태인 (C) ask, (D) have asked가 정답 후보인데, 문맥상 주어가 요청을 받는 대상이 되는 게 자연스러우므로 (B)가 정답이다.

해석 연말맞이 푸드 드라이브에 기부하고 싶은 분들은 이번 월요일에 음식을 가지고 출근해야 합니다.

어휘 donate 기부하다 food drive 푸드 드라이브, 형편이 어려운 사람들에게 음식을 기부하는 활동

3.
해설 선택지가 equip의 활용형으로 구성되어 있고 빈칸 뒤에 전치사 with가 있는 것으로 보아 빈칸에는 뒤에 with를 취할 수 있는 equip의 활용형이 들어가야 한다. 따라서 (D) is equipped가 정답이다.

해석 이 고급 차량에는 열선 핸들과 마사지 시트, 그리고 빌트인 우산 홀더가 갖춰져 있다.

어휘 vehicle 차량 steering wheel 운전대, 핸들 built-in 내장된, 붙박이의

4.
해설 선택지가 please의 활용형으로 구성되어 있고 빈칸 뒤에 전치사 with가 있는 것으로 보아 빈칸에는 뒤에 with를 취할 수 있는 please의 활용형이 들어가야 한다. 따라서 (C) pleased가 정답이다.

해석 그 CEO는 지난 몇 년간 회사가 꾸준히 성장해 온 것에 매우 만족하고 있다.

어휘 steady 꾸준한, 지속적인 growth 성장

빈출 유형 공략 04 본문 p.91
1. (C) 2. (B) 3. (B) 4. (D)

1.
해설 빈칸 뒤에 목적어가 있으므로 빈칸에는 능동태가 들어가야 한다. (B) will be outperforming과 (C) have been outperforming이 정답 후보인데, 빈칸 앞에 현재완료 시제와 어울려 쓰이는 표현(For the past few weeks)이 있으므로 현재완료 시제인 (C)가 정답이다.

해석 지난 몇 주 동안 Shoe Emporium에서 하이힐의 판매가 운동화를 능가하고 있다.

어휘 outperform 더 나은 결과를 내다, 능가하다

2.
해설 빈칸 뒤에 목적어가 없고 주어 her flight는 행위를 받는 대상이므로 빈칸에는 [be+과거분사] 형태의 수동태가 적절하다. (B) has been delayed와 (D) would have been delayed가 정답 후보인데, 문맥상 안 좋은 날씨가 현재 시점에도 계속 영향을 주고 있으므로 현재완료 시제인 (B)가 정답이다. 참고로 would have p.p.는 '아마도 ~했을 것이다'를 뜻하며 일어날 수도 있었던 과거의 일을 약하게 추측할 때 쓴다.

해석 Ms. Lai는 오늘 도착하기로 되어 있었지만 위험한 기상 상태 때문에 비행기가 연착되었다.

어휘 be supposed to do ~하기로 되어 있다 weather condition 기상 상태

3.
해설 빈칸 뒤에 목적어가 있으므로 빈칸에는 능동태가 들어가야 한다. (B) had not overseen과 (D) will not oversee가 정답 후보인데, 문맥상 과거의 일을 표현하고 있으므로 미래 시제는 적절하지 않다. 따라서 과거완료 시제인 (B)가 정답이다.

해석 Mr. Cameron이 그 과정의 모든 단계를 감독하지는 않았지만 그는 개발 팀의 새로운 프로토타입에 만족했다.

어휘 process 과정 be pleased with ~에 기뻐하다 prototype 프로토타입, 시제품

4.
해설 빈칸 뒤에 목적어처럼 보이는 명사구(the newest director of quality control)가 있으나 문맥상 주어 Former floor manager Mr. Nyman은 행위를 받는 대상이 되는 게 자연스럽다. (B) will be appointed와 (D) was appointed가 정답 후보인데, 빈칸 뒤에 과거 시제와 어울려 쓰이는 표현(last week)이 있으므로 과거 시제인 (D)가 정답이다.

해석 전 매장 관리인 Mr. Nyman이 지난주에 새로운 품질 관리 책임자로 임명되었다.

어휘 quality control 품질 관리 appoint 임명하다

ACTUAL TEST 본문 p.92
1. (B) 2. (D) 3. (B) 4. (D) 5. (D)
6. (A) 7. (A) 8. (B) 9. (C) 10. (C)
11. (C) 12. (B) 13. (D) 14. (B)

1. 태와 시제 복합
해설 빈칸 뒤에 목적어가 있으므로 빈칸에는 능동태가 들어가야 한다. 또한 '지난달'을 뜻하는 last month가 있으므로 과거 시제인 (B) established가 정답이다.

해석 Mongoose LTC는 지난달 동남아 시장에 진출하기 위해 방콕에 지점을 신설했다.

어휘 branch 지점 cover 다루다, 포함시키다 establish 설립하다, 수립하다

2. 수동태 vs. 능동태
해설 빈칸은 The latest sculpture by Daniel Kirkpatrick을 주어로 하는 동사 자리이다. (A) regards와 (D) is regarded가 정답 후보인데, 빈칸 뒤에 목적어가 없고 주어는 행위를 받는 대상이므로 빈칸에는 [be+과거분사] 형태의 수동태가 적절하다. 따라서

(D)가 정답이다.

해설 Daniel Kirkpatrick의 최근 조각상은 그의 최대 야심작으로 여겨진다.

어휘 latest 최신의, 가장 최근의 sculpture 조각상 ambitious 야심 찬 piece (작품) 한 점 regard 여기다, 간주하다

3. 수동태 vs. 능동태
해설 빈칸 뒤에 목적어가 있고 주어 A maintenance worker는 행위를 하는 주체이므로 빈칸에는 능동태가 적절하다. 따라서 (B) emptied가 정답이다.

해설 관리 직원은 3층에 있는 쓰레기통과 재활용 통을 비웠다.

어휘 maintenance (건물, 기계 등의) 유지 empty 비우다

4. be p.p.+to부정사
해설 빈칸은 each branch를 주어로 하는 동사 자리이다. 선택지가 invite의 활용형으로 구성되어 있고 빈칸 뒤에 to부정사가 있는 것으로 보아 빈칸에는 뒤에 to부정사를 취할 수 있는 invite의 활용형이 들어가야 한다. 따라서 (D) is invited가 정답이다.

해설 Marsh&Sons는 새로운 로고 디자인 공모전을 개최하고 있으며, 각 지사는 최고의 아이디어를 제출하도록 요청받았다.

어휘 submit 제출하다 concept (새로운 것에 대한) 생각, 아이디어; 개념

5. 수동태 vs. 능동태
해설 빈칸 뒤에 목적어가 없고 주어 Further studies는 행위를 받는 대상이므로 빈칸에는 [be+과거분사] 형태의 수동태가 적절하다. 따라서 (D) will be performed가 정답이다.

해설 그 약의 부작용을 더 잘 이해하기 위해 추가 연구가 진행될 것이다.

어휘 study 연구 medication 약물 side effect 부작용

6. 수동태 vs. 능동태
해설 선행사 The tasks는 타동사 assign의 행위를 받는 대상이므로 빈칸에는 [be+과거분사] 형태의 수동태가 적절하다. 따라서 (A) were assigned가 정답이다. 참고로 이 문장은 능동태 문장에서 직접목적어였던 the tasks가 수동태의 주어가 되면서 간접목적어였던 the marketing team 앞에 전치사 to가 붙은 것이다.

해설 새 인턴들의 능력을 평가하기 위해 그들에게 마케팅 팀에 배정된 업무들이 주어졌다.

어휘 assess 평가하다 assign 맡기다, 배정하다

7. be p.p.+to부정사
해설 선택지가 expect의 활용형으로 구성되어 있고 빈칸 뒤에 to부정사가 있는 것으로 보아 빈칸에는 뒤에 to부정사를 취할 수 있는 expect의 활용형이 들어가야 한다. 수동태인 (A) is expected와 능동태인 (C) had expected, (D) expects가 정답 후보인데, 문맥상 주어가 예측되는 대상이 되는 게 자연스러우므로 (A)가 정답이다.

해설 새 시청 건물의 최종 청사진은 9월 말까지 완성될 것으로 예상된다.

어휘 blueprint 청사진 city hall 시청 complete 완료하다, 완성하다

8. be p.p.+전치사
해설 선택지가 direct의 활용형으로 구성되어 있고 빈칸 뒤에 전치사 to가 있는 것으로 보아 빈칸에는 뒤에 to를 취할 수 있는 direct의 활용형이 들어가야 한다. 따라서 (B) be directed가 정답이다.

해설 개선을 위한 제안은 Ms. Loggia에게 전달되어야 하며, 그녀가 의견을 정리해 인사부에 보낼 겁니다.

어휘 suggestion 제안, 제의 improvement 개선, 향상 organize 준비하다, 정리하다

9. 수동태 vs. 능동태
해설 빈칸 뒤에 목적어가 없고 주어 Robin Kelton은 행위를 받는 대상이므로 빈칸에는 [be+과거분사] 형태의 수동태가 적절하다. 따라서 (C) was recognized가 정답이다.

해설 시상식에서 Robin Kelton은 McEvoy Engineering에서 20년간 일한 공로를 인정받았다.

어휘 awards ceremony 시상식 recognize 인정하다; 알아보다, 인식하다

10. 태와 시제 복합
해설 빈칸 뒤에 목적어가 없으므로 빈칸에는 수동태가 들어가야 한다. (B) will have been selected와 (C) had been selected가 정답 후보인데, 문맥상 과거의 일을 표현하고 있으므로 미래 시제는 적절하지 않다. 따라서 과거완료 시제인 (C)가 정답이다.

해설 Mr. Dixon은 Ms. Parson이 출산 휴가를 간 동안 팀장 역할을 하도록 선정되었다.

어휘 maternity leave 출산 휴가 select 선발하다, 선택하다

수신인: Camden Inc. 전 직원
발신인: Jeremy Schubert
제목: 웹사이트
날짜: 1월 8일

친애하는 직원 여러분,

회사 웹사이트 업그레이드는 다음 주에 완료될 예정입니다. 업그레이드된 웹사이트에는 예전과 같이 고객을 위한 일반 카탈로그와 온라인 쇼핑 포털이 있을 것입니다. [11]그러나 직원만을 위해 새로 추가된 부분이 있을 것입니다.

직원 포털을 통해 여러분은 근무 시간을 보고하거나 휴가를 신청하고 최신 회사 소식을 얻을 수 있습니다. 일반 회원은 웹사이트의 이 부분에 접근할 수 없습니다.

시스템에 의해 고유한 사용자 이름과 암호가 [12]생성될 겁니다. 프롬프트에 따라 여러분이 직접 암호를 쉽게 변경할 수 있습니다. 여러분은 사용자 이름을 변경할 수도 있지만 그러려면 부서장의 [13]허가를 받아야 합니다.

Camden Inc.의 임원들은 직원들에게 충분한 정보를 제공하는 걸 항상 최우선으로 해 왔기에 새로운 직원 포털을 개발하는 데 이르렀습니다. [14]이 변화가 그 목표에 기여하기를 바랍니다.

부사장 Jeremy Schubert

어휘 complete 완료하다, 완성하다 portal 포털 (사이트) newly 최근에, 새로 access 접근하다, 접속하다 unique 고유한,

독특한 prompt 컴퓨터 시스템이 사용자에게 보내는 메시지 department head 부서장 place importance 중요시하다, 중점을 두다 utmost 최고의 keep ~ informed ~에게 정보를 계속 알려 주다

11. 접속부사 어휘
해설 for example 예를 들어 in fact 사실은, 실제로는 even though 비록 ~일지라도

12. 태와 시제 복합
해설 빈칸 뒤에 목적어가 없으므로 빈칸에는 수동태가 들어가야 한다. (C) had been generated와 (D) will be generated가 정답 후보인데, 문맥상 웹사이트 개발이 완료된 상황이 아니므로 과거완료 시제는 적절하지 않다. 따라서 미래 시제인 (D)가 정답이다.

13. 명사 어휘
해설 failure 실패 creation 창조(물) resistance 저항, 반대

14. 알맞은 문장 고르기
해설 빈칸 앞에서 회사가 직원들에게 충분한 정보를 제공하는 걸 가장 중요하게 생각하기 때문에 새 직원 포털을 개발하게 되었다고 했다. 따라서 빈칸에는 이것이 잘 이루어졌으면 하는 바람에 대한 내용이 들어가는 게 가장 자연스러우므로 (B)가 정답이다.
해석 (A) 즉각적인 피드백을 주셔서 감사합니다.
(B) 이 변화가 그 목표에 기여하기를 바랍니다.
(C) 그곳에서 뵙기를 고대합니다.
(D) 그것이 누락되면 저에게 알려 주시기 바랍니다.
어휘 immediate 즉각적인 contribute 기여하다 look forward to ~하는 것을 고대하다

UNIT 07 시제

기초 문법 CHECK 본문 p.97

1. open
2. relocated
3. will be running
4. has grown
5. has been increasing
6. had been left

1.
해설 현재 시제와 어울려 쓰이는 표현(usually)이 있으므로 open이 정답이다.
해석 Main Street에 있는 식당들은 보통 금요일에 일찍 문을 연다.

2.
해설 과거 시제와 어울려 쓰이는 표현(last year)이 있으므로 relocated가 정답이다.
해석 Sedwick Electronics는 작년에 주 공장을 더블린으로 이전했다.

3.
해설 미래 시제와 어울려 쓰이는 표현(next month)이 있으므로 will be running이 정답이다.
해석 White Fox는 5주년을 기념하기 위해 다음 달에 특별 세일을 할 것이다.

4.
해설 현재완료 시제와 어울려 쓰이는 표현(for the past three years)이 있으므로 has grown이 정답이다.
해석 미니밴 시장은 지난 3년간 폭발적으로 성장했다.

5.
해설 현재완료 시제와 어울려 쓰이는 표현(since 2019)이 있으므로 has been increasing이 정답이다.
해석 킹햄의 관광객 수는 2019년 이래로 꾸준히 증가하고 있다.

6.
해설 과거의 특정 시점(건물이 매입됨)보다 앞선 때에 발생한 일(건물이 비어 있었음)은 과거완료로 나타내므로 had been left가 정답이다.
해석 이 건물은 2년 전 Steffan Young에 의해 매입되기 전까지 거의 20년 동안 비어 있었다.

빈출 유형 공략 01 본문 p.98

1. (D) **2.** (C) **3.** (B) **4.** (A)

1.
해설 빈칸 뒤에 미래 시제와 어울려 쓰이는 표현(tomorrow)이 있으므로 (D) will attend가 정답이다.
해석 내일 연회에는 직원과 그들의 가족 모두 참석하기 때문에 총 146인분이 필요합니다.
어휘 banquet 연회 serving 1인분 altogether 모두 합쳐

2.
해설 빈칸 뒤에 과거 시제와 어울려 쓰이는 표현(last month)이 있으므로 (C) expected가 정답이다.
해석 Diesel Motors는 지난달 콜로라도에 새 공장을 열 것으로 예상했으나 인력난에 직면했다.
어휘 face 직면하다 labor 인력, 노동 shortage 부족

3.
해설 빈칸 뒤에 현재 시제와 어울려 쓰이는 표현(every Thursday)이 있으므로 (B) orders가 정답이다.
해석 비서가 매주 목요일에 사무용품을 주문하니 그 전에 요청 사항이 있으면 그에게 이메일을 보내세요.
어휘 secretary 비서 office supplies 사무용품

4.
해설 빈칸 뒤에 미래 시제와 어울려 쓰이는 표현(next Friday)이 있으므로 (A) will air가 정답이다.

해석 Eva Santiago 셰프와 함께 하는 텔레비전 쇼는 다음 주 금요일에 4번 채널에서 방송될 것이다.

어휘 air 방송하다

빈출 유형 공략 02
본문 p.99
1. (B) 2. (B) 3. (D) 4. (A)

1.
해설 빈칸 뒤에 현재 시제와 어울려 쓰이는 표현(right now)이 있으므로 (B) is gaining이 정답이다.
해석 Cup of Joe의 커피는 흔치 않은 블렌드와 독특한 향으로 지금 인기를 얻고 있다.
어휘 popularity 인기 rare 희귀한, 드문 unique 독특한, 고유한

2.
해설 빈칸 뒤에 미래 시제와 어울려 쓰이는 표현(soon)이 있으므로 (B) will be calling이 정답이다.
해석 상하이 지사에서 곧 온라인 회의를 소집할 테니 회의실로 모이세요.
어휘 gather 모이다

3.
해설 빈칸 앞에 미래 시제와 어울려 쓰이는 표현(Next Saturday)이 있는데 현재진행 시제가 가까운 미래를 나타내는 표현과 함께 쓰이면 예정된 미래의 일을 나타낼 수 있으므로 (D) is giving이 정답이다.
해석 다음 주 토요일에 Kenny's Sporting Goods는 Gibson 배트를 구입하는 고객들에게 무료로 야구공을 증정할 예정이다.
어휘 purchase 구매[구입]하다

4.
해설 빈칸 뒤에 미래 시제와 어울려 쓰이는 표현(next week)이 있으므로 (A) will be sending이 정답이다.
해석 본사는 다음 주에 뉴욕에서 열리는 전사적인 연말 파티를 위한 초대장을 이메일로 보낼 예정이다.
어휘 invitation 초대(장)

빈출 유형 공략 03
본문 p.100
1. (B) 2. (B) 3. (C) 4. (A)

1.
해설 빈칸 뒤에 현재완료 시제와 어울려 쓰이는 표현(in recent weeks)이 있으므로 (B) has made가 정답이다.
해석 VitaMint는 최근 몇 주간 그들의 새로운 보충제 제조법에 주요한 개선을 했다.
어휘 improvement 개선, 향상 supplement 보충(제); 부록; 추가 요금 formula 제조법; 공식; 방식

2.
해설 빈칸 앞에 과거완료 시제와 어울려 쓰이는 표현(by the time+주어+동사의 과거형)이 있으므로 (B) had managed가 정답이다.
해석 Ms. Coleman이 우리 부서의 재무 책임자로 합류했을 무렵에 그녀는 수년간 고객 회계를 관리했었다.
어휘 join 합류하다, 함께 하다; 가입하다 finance 금융, 재무

3.
해설 빈칸 앞에 미래완료 시제와 어울려 쓰이는 표현(By the end of this month)이 있으므로 (C) will have sold가 정답이다.
해석 이번 달 말까지 우리 가게는 50만 달러 상당의 보석을 팔게 될 것이다.
어휘 worth ~의 가치가 있는

4.
해설 빈칸 앞에 현재완료 시제와 어울려 쓰이는 표현(Since)이 있으므로 (A) has increased가 정답이다.
해석 Calvin's Coffee가 프리퀀시 리워드를 제공하기 시작한 이래로 재방문 고객의 수가 증가했다.
어휘 frequency rewards 고객이 상품을 구매하거나 이용할 때마다 제공하는 포인트 등의 보상 returning customer 재방문 고객

빈출 유형 공략 04
본문 p.101
1. (C) 2. (A) 3. (B) 4. (D)

1.
해설 주절의 시제가 과거 시제(understood)이므로 종속절도 과거 시제로 써야 한다. 따라서 (C) gave가 정답이다.
해석 Mr. Han이 발표를 하고 나서 직원들은 새로운 소프트웨어를 더 명확하게 이해했다.

2.
해설 종속절의 시제가 현재완료 시제(has still not been fixed)이지만 주절에 미래 시제와 어울려 쓰이는 표현(tomorrow)이 있으므로 빈칸에는 미래 시제가 적절하다. 따라서 (A) will be allowed가 정답이다.
해석 에어컨이 아직 고쳐지지 않았기 때문에 직원들은 내일 재택근무를 할 수 있을 것이다.
어휘 air conditioning 에어컨 work from home 재택근무를 하다

3.
해설 주절의 시제가 미래 시제(will choose)이고 문맥상 캠페인에 가장 잘 어울리는 포스터를 고를 것이라는 내용이 되는 게 자연스러우므로 종속절은 현재 시제로 써야 한다. 따라서 (B) suits가 정답이다.
해석 Eco-Green은 회사 마케팅 캠페인에 어느 포스터 제안서가 가장 잘 어울릴지 선택할 것이다.
어휘 proposal 제안(서), 제의 suit 잘 맞다, (잘 맞아서) 편리하다

4.
해설 주절의 시제가 과거 시제(was closed)이므로 종속절도 과거 시제로 써야 한다. 따라서 과거완료 시제인 (D) had celebrated가 정답이다.

해석 멕시코가 독립 기념일을 맞았기 때문에 멕시코시티 지점은 어제 문을 닫았다.

어휘 branch 지점 celebrate 기념하다

빈출 유형 공략 05 본문 p.102
1. (B)   2. (C)   3. (D)   4. (D)

1.
해설 빈칸 뒤에 미래 시제와 어울려 쓰이는 표현(next week)이 있지만 시간 부사절에서는 미래 시제 대신 현재 시제를 쓰므로 (B) return이 정답이다.

해석 Mr. Grantham은 직원들이 다음 주에 겨울 휴가에서 돌아오면 좋은 소식을 발표할 예정이다.

어휘 announce 발표하다, 알리다 break 휴가, 휴식

2.
해설 조건 부사절의 시제가 현재 시제(includes)이므로 주절은 현재나 미래 시제로 써야 한다. 따라서 (C) will be canceled가 정답이다. 참고로 주절을 현재 시제로 쓰면 보편적이고 일반적인 현재 사실을 나타내고, 미래 시제로 쓰면 if절에 제시된 조건이 맞을 경우 일어날 가능성이 높은 일을 나타낼 수 있다.

해석 수채화 수업은 등록 인원이 열 명 미만이면 취소될 것이다.

어휘 registration 등록

3.
해설 주절의 시제가 미래 시제(will be carried over)이지만 조건 부사절에서는 미래 시제 대신 현재 시제를 쓰므로 (D) are transferred가 정답이다.

해석 신용 카드 잔금에 대한 지불은 납기일 이후에 이체된다면 다음 청구 주기로 이월됩니다.

어휘 payment 지불 credit card 신용 카드 balance 잔금; 잔고, 잔액 carry over (다음 상황으로 계속) ~가 이어지다 payment due date 지불 기한, 납기일 transfer 이체하다; 이동하다

4.
해설 문맥상 미래의 일을 나타내고 있지만 시간 부사절에서는 미래 시제 대신 현재 시제를 쓰므로 (D) perfects가 정답이다.

해석 마케팅 팀이 현재의 광고 캠페인을 완성하면 몇 주 안에 대중에게 공개될 것이다.

어휘 public 공개되는; 대중의, 공공의 perfect 완벽하게 하다

빈출 유형 공략 06 본문 p.103
1. (D)   2. (A)   3. (C)   4. (B)

1.
해설 주절의 동사(would not have)가 [would+동사원형]인 것으로 보아 가정법 과거 문장임을 알 수 있다. 따라서 if절의 동사는 과거형이 되어야 하므로 (D) were reduced가 정답이다.

해석 소금 함량이 더 줄어들면 Haier의 칩은 같은 맛이 나지 않을 것이다.

어휘 content 함량; 내용물 reduce 줄이다

2.
해설 Had가 문장 앞으로 도치된 것으로 보아 원래는 'If a sudden miscommunication had not interrupted ~'였던 가정법 과거완료 문장임을 알 수 있다. 따라서 주절의 동사는 [would/could/might+have p.p.]가 되어야 하므로 (A) would have merged가 정답이다.

해석 갑작스런 의사소통 오류가 협상을 방해하지 않았다면 그 두 회사는 평화롭게 합병했을 것이다.

어휘 sudden 갑작스러운 miscommunication 의사소통 오류 interrupt 방해하다 negotiation 협상, 거래 merge 합병하다

3.
해설 주절의 동사(would not have been)가 [would+have p.p.]인 것으로 보아 가정법 과거완료 문장임을 알 수 있다. 따라서 if절의 동사는 [had p.p.]가 되어야 하므로 (C) had arrived가 정답이다.

해석 비행기가 예정대로 도착했다면 Ms. Ferebee는 콘퍼런스에 늦지 않았을 것이다.

4.
해설 if절의 동사(had followed)가 [had p.p.]인 것으로 보아 가정법 과거완료 문장임을 알 수 있다. 따라서 주절의 동사는 [would/could/might+have p.p.]가 되어야 하므로 (B) would not have been confronted가 정답이다.

해석 유통업자가 모든 필수 보건 수칙을 제대로 지켰다면 그만큼의 비판에 직면하지 않았을 것이다.

어휘 distributor 유통업자 criticism 비난, 비판 regulation 규정; 규제, 통제 confront (문제, 곤란한 상황 등에) 맞서다, 직면하다

ACTUAL TEST 본문 p.104
1. (C)   2. (B)   3. (D)   4. (D)   5. (A)
6. (D)   7. (C)   8. (B)   9. (B)   10. (B)
11. (B) 12. (C) 13. (D) 14. (A)

1. 주절―종속절의 시제
해설 빈칸은 Ms. Bax를 주어로 하는 동사 자리이다. (C) will be leading과 (D) had led가 정답 후보인데, 종속절의 시제가 현재 시제(is)이고 문맥상 동료가 자리를 비워서 대신 회의를 진행하는 것이므로 주절은 미래 시제로 써야 한다. 따라서 (C)가 정답이다.

해설 Mr. Gonzalez가 International Marketing Conference 때문에 출장 중이어서 Ms. Bax가 오늘 있을 이사회를 진행할 것이다.

2. 시간 부사절의 시제

해설 문맥상 미래의 일을 나타내고 있지만 시간 부사절에서는 미래 시제 대신 현재 시제를 쓰므로 (B) opens가 정답이다.

해석 Brentwood Mills가 마을에 새로운 벌목 공장을 열면 거의 40개의 새로운 일자리가 창출될 것이다.

어휘 nearly 거의 logging 벌목

3. 현재완료 시제

해설 빈칸 뒤에 현재완료 시제와 어울려 쓰이는 표현(in just one year)이 있으므로 (D) has won이 정답이다.

해석 LP Law Firm은 1년 만에 30건이 넘는 소송에서 승소했다.

어휘 case 소송

4. 과거완료 시제

해설 과거의 특정 시점(프로젝트를 완료함)보다 앞선 때에 발생한 일(프로젝트 작업을 시작함)은 과거완료로 나타내므로 (D) had started가 정답이다.

해석 IT 부서는 지난주에 작업을 시작했음에도 불구하고 그 프로젝트를 완료했다.

어휘 complete 완료하다, 끝내다 even though 비록 ~일지라도 work on ~에 착수하다, ~에 노력을 들이다

5. 조건 부사절의 시제

해설 조건 부사절의 시제가 현재 시제(continues)이므로 주절은 현재나 미래 시제로 써야 한다. 따라서 (A) will affect가 정답이다. 참고로 주절을 현재 시제로 쓰면 보편적이고 일반적인 현재 사실을 나타내고, 미래 시제로 쓰면 if절에 제시된 조건이 맞을 경우 일어날 가능성이 높은 일을 나타낼 수 있다.

해석 백설탕 부족이 계속되면 우리 식당의 레모네이드 판매에 영향을 미칠 것이다.

어휘 granulated sugar (알갱이 형태의) 백설탕 shortage 부족 continue 계속되다 affect 영향을 미치다

6. 현재완료 시제

해설 빈칸 앞에 현재완료 시제와 어울려 쓰이는 표현(So far)이 있으므로 (D) has partnered가 정답이다.

해석 지금까지 Alliance Foods는 두 개의 운송 회사와 제휴하여 제품 유통을 관리해 왔다.

어휘 shipping company 운송 회사 distribution 유통; 분배, 배급

7. 시간 부사절의 시제

해설 문맥상 미래의 일을 나타내고 있지만 시간 부사절에서는 미래 시제 대신 현재 시제를 쓰므로 (C) is reestablished가 정답이다.

해석 사무실의 와이파이 연결이 복구될 때까지 이더넷 케이블을 사용하여 인터넷에 접속하세요.

어휘 connection 연결, 접속; 관련(성) access 접속하다; 접근하다

8. 미래 시제

해설 빈칸 앞에 미래 시제와 어울려 쓰이는 표현(Later this week)이 있으므로 (D) will be interviewing이 정답이다.

해석 이번 주 후반에 Ms. Harden은 필기 시험에 합격한 입사 지원자들을 인터뷰할 것이다.

어휘 applicant 지원자

9. 가정법 과거완료

해설 주절의 동사(would not have been)가 [would+have p.p.]인 것으로 보아 가정법 과거완료 문장임을 알 수 있다. 따라서 if절의 동사는 [had p.p.]가 되어야 하므로 (B) had not focused가 정답이다.

해석 BND Technology가 혁신에 집중하지 않았다면 그만큼 수익이 나지 않았을 것이다.

어휘 innovation 혁신 profitable 수익성이 있는; 유익한, 이득이 되는

10. 미래완료 시제

해설 빈칸 앞에 미래완료 시제와 어울려 쓰이는 표현(At the end of the month)이 있으므로 (B) will have served가 정답이다.

해석 이달 말이면 야간 근무조 관리자 Rolan Mojica가 La Suprema Tacos에서 근무한 지 20년이 된다.

어휘 night shift 야간 근무조

Zielo Tours 가이드 구인

Zielo Tours는 바르셀로나와 마드리드 단체 관광에 [11]신청한 사람들을 위한 여행 가이드를 고용하고 있습니다. 여행 가이드는 각 명소에서 관광객들이 적절한 시간을 보낼 수 있도록 관광 속도를 [12]관리할 것입니다. 가이드는 영어와 스페인어 둘 다 유창해야 합니다. [13]현지에 대한 지식 또한 상당히 필요합니다. 근무 혜택으로 무료 혹은 할인된 가격으로 여행을 할 수 있을 뿐만 아니라 경쟁력 있는 임금을 받을 수도 있습니다. 지원하려면 이력서를 zielotours.com에 업로드해 주세요. 또한 초기 심사 단계를 통과하게 되면 두 명의 예전 고용주로부터 [14]추천서를 받아 제출할 것을 요청합니다.

어휘 sign up 신청하다, 등록하다 pace 속도 ensure 보장하다, 확실히 하다 appropriate 적절한 fluent 유창한 benefit 혜택, 이득 competitive 경쟁력 있는; 경쟁을 하는 B as well as A A뿐만 아니라 B도 professional 직업의, 전문적인 initial 처음의, 초기의 screening 심사, 검사 phase 단계, 시기

11. 주격 관계대명사

해설 빈칸 앞에 완전한 절이 있고 뒤에는 주어가 없는 불완전한 문장이 이어지므로 빈칸은 주격 관계대명사 자리이다. 따라서 (B) who가 정답이다.

12. 미래 시제

해설 문맥상 가이드가 하게 될 업무에 대한 설명을 하고 있으므로 빈칸에는 미래 시제가 들어가야 한다. 따라서 (C) will manage가 정답이다.

13. 알맞은 문장 고르기

해설 빈칸 앞에서 가이드가 갖춰야 하는 조건에 대해 설명했으므로 빈칸에는 추가적인 조건을 언급하는 내용이 들어가는 게 가장 자연스럽다. 따라서 (D)가 정답이다.

해석 (A) 우리는 오픈 이후 꾸준히 성장하고 있습니다.
(B) 그 과정에서 이 단계는 건너뛸 수 없습니다.
(C) 호텔 방의 크기를 선택할 수 있습니다.
(D) 현지에 대한 지식 또한 상당히 필요합니다.

어휘 steadily 점차, 꾸준히 process 과정 knowledge 지식; 이해

14. 명사 어휘

어휘 question 질문 negotiation 협상, 거래 characteristic 특징

UNIT 08 to부정사와 동명사

기초 문법 CHECK 본문 p.111

1. to hold   2. to replace   3. to cancel
4. to access 5. to create   6. improving
7. drawing

1.
해설 the perfect place를 수식해야 하므로 to부정사인 to hold가 정답이다.
해석 Cavendish Conference Centre는 기업 행사를 개최하기에 완벽한 장소입니다.

2.
해설 동사 plan의 목적어 역할을 해야 하므로 to부정사인 to replace가 정답이다.
해석 금요일에 귀하의 사무실 카펫을 교체할 계획입니다.

3.
해설 동사 would like의 목적어 역할을 해야 하므로 to부정사인 to cancel이 정답이다.
해석 제품 D12의 주문을 취소하고 싶습니다.

4.
해설 동사 allow는 [동사+목적어+to부정사] 형태로 쓸 수 있으므로 to부정사인 to access가 정답이다.
해석 이 소프트웨어를 사용하면 필요한 모든 장소에서 파일에 접근할 수 있다.

5.
해설 [expect+목적어+to부정사]는 수동태로 전환될 때 [be expected to부정사] 형태로 쓰므로 to부정사인 to create가 정답이다.
해석 이 프로젝트는 200개 이상의 새로운 일자리를 창출할 것으로 기대된다.

6.
해설 전치사 at의 목적어 역할을 할 수 있는 동명사 improving이 정답이다.
해석 새로운 시스템은 회사 보안을 향상시키는 것을 목표로 한다.

7.
해설 동사 finish의 목적어 역할을 할 수 있는 동명사 drawing이 정답이다.
해석 Ms. Lopez는 예산 편성을 끝내기 위해 늦게까지 일해야 했다.

빈출 유형 공략 01 본문 p.112

1. (C) 2. (A) 3. (B) 4. (B)

1.
해설 빈칸 앞이 완전한 절이므로 빈칸 이하가 명사구 new ways를 수식하는 구조가 되어야 한다. 그러므로 빈칸 뒤의 명사(packages)를 목적어로 취하면서 new ways를 뒤에서 수식할 수 있는 (C) to deliver가 정답이다.
해석 Ichihara Solutions는 고객에게 택배를 훨씬 더 빨리 배달할 수 있는 새로운 방법을 모색하고 있다.
어휘 search for ~을 찾다

2.
해설 빈칸은 be동사 is의 주격 보어 자리이다. to부정사가 명사 역할을 할 때는 보어 자리에 올 수 있으므로 (A) to sell이 정답이다.
해석 이번 달 목표는 지난달보다 5% 더 많이 판매하는 것이다.
어휘 objective 목표, 목적

3.
해설 [invite+목적어+to부정사]는 수동태로 전환될 때 [be invited to부정사] 형태로 쓰므로 (B) to visit가 정답이다.
해석 그 마을 최고의 명소들에 대해 더 많이 알기 위해 관광객들은 안내 센터를 방문하도록 요청받는다.
어휘 attraction 명소; 매력

4.
해설 빈칸은 동사 plan의 목적어 자리이며, plan은 to부정사를 목적어로 취하므로 (B) to broaden이 정답이다.
해석 Moussa TV는 케냐에서 호평을 받은 후 동아프리카 전역으로 방송 범위를 넓힐 계획이다.
어휘 critical acclaim 비평가의 호평 coverage 범위, 서비스 구역 broaden 넓히다, 확장하다

빈출 유형 공략 02 본문 p.113

1. (C) 2. (A) 3. (B) 4. (B)

1.
해설 빈칸 앞에 전치사 of가 있으므로 빈칸에는 전치사의 목적어 역할을 할 수 있는 동명사가 들어가야 한다. 따라서 (C) overseeing이 정답이다.

해석 Ms. Kirk는 조립 라인에서 일어나는 모든 일을 감독하는 일을 맡고 있다.

어휘 be in charge of ~을 담당하다   assembly line (공장의) 조립 라인

2.
해설 빈칸 앞에 전치사 Before가 있으므로 빈칸에는 전치사의 목적어 역할을 할 수 있는 동명사가 들어가야 한다. 따라서 (A) leaving이 정답이다.

해석 사무실을 떠나기 전에 모든 전등과 컴퓨터가 꺼져 있는지 확인해 주세요.

어휘 shut off (전원 등을) 끄다

3.
해설 빈칸은 동사 consider의 목적어 자리이며, consider는 동명사를 목적어로 취하므로 (B) expanding이 정답이다.

해석 계속 높은 수익이 유지된다면 이사회는 그 사업을 다른 모험적인 사업으로 확장하는 걸 고려할 것이다.

어휘 board of trustees 이사회   consider 고려하다; 여기다, 간주하다   venture (다소 위험이 따르는) 새로운 사업   profit 이익   remain 계속 ~이다, 남아 있다

4.
해설 빈칸 뒤에 본동사 will help가 있으므로 빈칸에는 명사구 an impressive portfolio를 목적어로 취하면서 문장의 주어 역할을 할 수 있는 말이 들어가야 한다. 따라서 동명사인 (B) Creating이 정답이다.

해석 전문성을 보여 주는 인상적인 포트폴리오를 만드는 것은 그래픽 디자인 분야에서 직업을 얻는 데 도움이 될 것이다.

어휘 impressive 인상적인   technical 전문적인

빈출 유형 공략 03   본문 p.114

1. (C)   **2.** (A)   **3.** (A)   **4.** (C)

1.
해설 빈칸은 wording을 수식하는 자리인데 wording은 -ing형 명사로 일반 명사처럼 형용사의 수식을 받을 수 있다. 따라서 (C) descriptive가 정답이다.

해석 이 마케팅 조사는 서술적인 표현이 청중의 관심을 끄는 데 큰 역할을 한다는 것을 보여 준다.

어휘 attract attention 관심을 끌다   audience 청중   descriptive 서술적인

2.
해설 빈칸 앞에 관사 the가 있고 뒤에는 전치사 of가 있으므로 빈칸은 명사 자리이다. (A) opening과 (B) openness가 정답 후보인데, 문맥상 새 커피숍 개점을 준비한다는 내용이 되는 게 자연스럽고 -ing형 명사는 일반 명사처럼 관사의 수식을 받을 수 있으므로 (A)가 정답이다.

해석 직원들이 새 커피숍 개점 준비를 서두르고 있다.

어휘 hurriedly 급하게   openness (솔직하여) 숨김이 없음; 개방적임

3.
해설 빈칸 앞에 관사와 형용사가 있으므로 빈칸은 명사 자리이다. 따라서 (A) exception이 정답이다.

해석 Lucier Theater의 주인은 극장에서 사적인 파티를 여는 걸 예외적으로 특별히 허락했다.

어휘 make an exception 예외로 하다   rare 희귀한, 드문   host 주최하다

4.
해설 빈칸 앞에 전치사 After가 있고 뒤에는 명사구 the downtown area가 이어지므로 빈칸에는 동명사가 들어가야 한다. 따라서 (C) evaluating이 정답이다.

해석 그 시내 지역을 평가하고 난 후에 Mr. Tait는 식당을 클리프턴으로 옮기지 않기로 결정했다.

어휘 evaluate 평가하다

빈출 유형 공략 04   본문 p.115

1. (C)   **2.** (B)   **3.** (D)   **4.** (C)

1.
해설 be willing to 뒤에는 동사원형이 이어져야 하므로 (C) supervise가 정답이다.

해석 Ms. Presley는 Mr. Morgan이 없을 때 보스턴 지사의 운영을 감독할 용의가 있었다.

어휘 operation 운영; 작업   in one's absence ~가 부재 시에

2.
해설 have trouble 뒤에는 동명사가 이어져야 하므로 (B) accessing이 정답이다.

해석 고객들이 우리 웹사이트에서 계정에 접속하는 데 문제가 있는 것 같다.

어휘 account 계정; 계좌

3.
해설 be advisable to 뒤에는 동사원형이 이어져야 하므로 (D) communicate가 정답이다.

해석 가장 좋은 기회를 찾는 방법에 대한 조언을 구하기 위해 채용 담당자들과 소통하는 것을 권합니다.

어휘 recruiter 채용 담당자   opportunity 기회

4.

해설 be accustomed to 뒤에는 동명사가 이어져야 하므로 (C) listening이 정답이다.

해석 Fresh Park의 록 발라드를 듣는 데 익숙한 팬들은 새 앨범에 놀랄 것이다.

ACTUAL TEST
본문 p.116

1. (B)	2. (C)	3. (D)	4. (B)	5. (D)
6. (B)	7. (B)	8. (D)	9. (D)	10. (C)
11. (A)	12. (C)	13. (A)	14. (D)	

1. to부정사의 역할 [형용사]

해설 빈칸 앞이 완전한 절이므로 빈칸 이하가 명사 ways를 수식하는 구조가 되어야 한다. 그러므로 빈칸 뒤의 명사구(their ideas)를 목적어로 취하면서 ways를 뒤에서 수식할 수 있는 (B) to communicate가 정답이다.

해석 Business Writing Workshop은 참가자들에게 아이디어를 명확하고 효과적으로 전달하는 방법을 알려줄 것이다.

어휘 participant 참가자 clearly 분명히, 명확히 effectively 효과적으로

2. 동명사 자리 [전치사 뒤]

해설 빈칸 앞에 전치사 from이 있으므로 빈칸에는 전치사의 목적어 역할을 할 수 있는 동명사가 들어가야 한다. (C) being lost와 (D) losing이 정답 후보인데, 빈칸 뒤에 목적어가 없으므로 수동태인 (C)가 정답이다.

해석 중요한 정보가 유실되지 않도록 문서 작업을 할 때 주기적으로 저장하시기 바랍니다.

어휘 document 문서 regularly 정기적으로, 규칙적으로 prevent A from -ing A가 ~하는 것을 예방[방지]하다

3. to부정사 자리

해설 빈칸 앞에 완전한 절이 있고 뒤에는 동사원형이 있으므로 빈칸에는 동사원형 앞에 위치할 수 있는 말이 들어가야 한다. 따라서 (D) in order to가 정답이다.

해석 MaryAnn's Coffee는 고객들이 개인 컵을 가져오도록 장려하기 위해 종이컵으로 받는 음료의 가격을 인상했다.

어휘 encourage 권장하다, 장려하다

4. 동명사 자리 [목적어 자리]

해설 빈칸은 동사 suggest의 목적어 자리이며, suggest는 동명사를 목적어로 취하므로 (B) contacting이 정답이다.

해석 제품에 기계와 관련된 문제가 있으면 먼저 제조업체에 직접 문의하여 지원받을 것을 권장합니다.

어휘 mechanical 기계와 관련된 manufacturer 제조업체 directly 직접, 바로

5. to부정사 관용 표현

해설 be available to 뒤에는 동사원형이 이어져야 하므로 (D) purchase가 정답이다.

해석 Paris Museum Tour의 티켓은 온라인 또는 참여하는 박물관에서 구입할 수 있습니다.

어휘 participate 참여하다

6. 동명사 관용 표현

해설 have trouble 뒤에는 동명사가 이어져야 하므로 (B) managing이 정답이다.

해석 Mr. Rangel은 지도력이 뛰어나서 그 팀을 관리하는 데 문제가 없을 것이다.

7. be p.p.+to부정사

해설 [expect+목적어+to부정사]는 수동태로 전환될 때 [be expected to부정사] 형태로 쓰므로 (B) to increase가 정답이다.

해석 공급망 문제로 인해 이번 달에 원자재 가격이 인상될 것으로 예상된다.

어휘 supply chain 공급망 issue 문제, 사안; 쟁점 expect 예상하다, 기대하다

8. to부정사의 역할 [부사]

해설 빈칸 앞이 완전한 절이므로 빈칸 이하는 부사 역할을 해야 한다. 선택지에서 부사 역할을 할 수 있는 것은 to부정사인 (D) to repair뿐이다.

해석 작업자들이 도로에 생긴 균열을 보수하기 위해 작업할 때 약간의 소음이 있을 겁니다.

어휘 disruption 지장, 방해 crew (특별한 기술을 가지고 공동으로 작업하는) 팀, 조; 승무원 crack 갈라지다, 금이 가다

9. 동명사 vs. 명사

해설 빈칸 앞에 전치사 Since가 있으므로 빈칸에는 전치사의 목적어 역할을 할 수 있는 동명사가 들어가야 한다. 따라서 (D) performing이 정답이다. 명사인 (A) performers와 (B) performance도 전치사의 목적어 역할을 할 수 있지만 빈칸에 들어가기에는 문맥상 어색할뿐더러 빈칸 앞에 명사의 의미를 한정해 주는 관사도 없기 때문에 답이 될 수 없다.

해석 Nori Shibutani는 텔레비전의 오디션 프로그램에서 공연한 이후 가수로 큰 인기를 끌고 있다.

어휘 take off 갑자기 인기를 얻다, 뜻밖의 성공을 거두다 perform 공연하다

10. to부정사 관용 표현

해설 make sure 뒤에는 to부정사가 이어져야 하므로 (C) to address가 정답이다.

해석 환자의 건강 문제는 반드시 비밀을 유지하여 다루어야 합니다.

어휘 in confidence 비밀리에, 조용히 address (문제 등을) 다루다

퀸스타운은 새로운 공공 도서관의 건설이 완료되었다는 것을 발표하게 되어 기쁩니다. 주민 여러분은 6월 18일 개관식을 위해 3번가에 위치한 도서관에 ¹¹방문해 주시기 바랍니다. 그날 내내 사서들은 새로 ¹²설비된 시설들을 안내할 것입니다. 도서관에는

컴퓨터실과 어린이 놀이방, 그리고 인쇄실이 있습니다. ¹³게다가 도서관 카드를 신청하는 퀸스타운 주민은 우리 도서관이 소장하고 있는 전자책에 접속할 수도 있게 됩니다. ¹⁴여기에는 전자책으로 대여할 수 있는 만 권 이상의 책이 포함되어 있습니다. 분명 여러분이 재미있게 읽을 만한 걸 발견하게 될 겁니다.
그곳에서 뵙기를 바랍니다!

어휘 announce 발표하다, 알리다 construction 건설, 공사 resident 주민 be encouraged to do ~하도록 권장[권고]받다 throughout ~ 내내 facility (보통 복수형) 시설 feature 특징으로 하다, 특별히 선보이다 sign up 신청하다, 등록하다 access 접근; 접속 certain 확실한, 틀림없는

11. be p.p.+to부정사
해설 [encourage+목적어+to부정사]는 수동태로 전환될 때 [be encouraged to부정사] 형태로 쓰므로 (A) to visit이 정답이다.

12. 분사 자리 [과거분사]
해설 빈칸 앞에 부사 newly가 있고 뒤에는 명사 facilities가 있으므로 빈칸에는 명사를 수식할 수 있는 말이 들어가야 한다. 과거분사인 (C) developed와 현재분사인 (D) developing이 정답 후보인데, 시설은 '개발하는' 주체가 아니라 '개발되는' 대상이므로 수동의 의미를 나타내는 (C)가 정답이다.

13. 접속부사 어휘
어휘 however 하지만 therefore 그러므로 unfortunately 안타깝게도, 유감스럽게도

14. 알맞은 문장 고르기
해설 빈칸 앞에서 전자책 컬렉션에 대한 내용을 언급했으므로 빈칸에는 전자책을 얼마나 많이 소장하고 있는지 언급하는 내용이 들어가는 게 가장 자연스럽다. 따라서 (D)가 정답이다.
해석 (A) 안내 데스크에 문의해 주십시오.
(B) 그 로비는 유명한 건축가에 의해 디자인되었습니다.
(C) 도서관 직원들은 매우 친절합니다.
(D) 여기에는 전자책으로 대여할 수 있는 만 권 이상의 책이 포함되어 있습니다.

어휘 architect 건축가 incredibly (믿을 수 없을 정도로) 매우, 엄청나게

UNIT 09 분사

기초 문법 CHECK
본문 p.121

1. enclosed 2. Rising 3. accomplished
4. wishing 5. containing 6. Founded
7. satisfied

1.
해설 수식 대상인 spaces와 수동 관계이므로 과거분사인 enclosed가 정답이다.
해석 그 환기 시스템은 외부 공기를 안으로 들임으로써 폐쇄된 공간을 환기하는 데 도움이 된다.

2.
해설 수식 대상인 labor costs와 능동 관계이므로 현재분사인 Rising이 정답이다.
해석 상승하는 인건비로 인해 어쩔 수 없이 가격을 5% 인상했습니다.

3.
해설 문맥상 '뛰어난 임원'이 자연스러우므로 accomplished가 정답이다.
해석 Senior Planning Committee는 매우 우수한 임원들로 구성되어 있다.

4.
해설 수식 대상인 All employees와 능동 관계이므로 현재분사인 wishing이 정답이다.
해석 휴가를 원하는 모든 직원은 일주일 전에 요청서를 제출해야 한다.

5.
해설 e-mails를 수식하는 동시에 뒤에 있는 명사 errors를 목적어로 취할 수 있어야 하므로 현재분사인 containing이 정답이다.
해석 오류가 있는 이메일을 받은 고객 목록이 첨부되어 있습니다.

6.
해설 수식 대상인 the cookware company와 수동 관계이므로 과거분사인 Founded가 정답이다.
해석 벨기에에 설립되고 본사가 있는 이 조리용품 회사는 현재 아시아에서 사업을 시작하는 과정에 있다.

7.
해설 주어인 you는 만족시키는 주체가 아니라 만족을 느끼는 대상이므로 과거분사인 satisfied가 정답이다.
해석 상품이 만족스럽지 않다면 구매 후 10일 이내에 반품하여 전액 환불 받으시기 바랍니다.

빈출 유형 공략 01
본문 p.122

1. (B) 2. (B) 3. (C) 4. (B)

1.
해설 빈칸 앞에 관사가 있고 뒤에는 명사가 있으므로 빈칸은 명사를 수식하는 자리이다. 선택지 중 명사를 수식할 수 있는 것은 과거분사 (B) proposed와 현재분사 (C) proposing인데, 수식 대상인 100-foot sculpture는 행위자에 의해 '제안되는' 대상이기 때문에 빈칸과 수동 관계이므로 (B)가 정답이다.
해석 시장은 제안받은 100피트짜리 조각상이 그 도시에 관광객들을 끌어들일 거라고 믿는다.

어휘 mayor 시장 sculpture 조각상 attract 끌어들이다

2.

해설 빈칸 앞에 관사가 있고 뒤에는 명사가 있으므로 빈칸은 명사를 수식하는 자리이다. 선택지 중 명사를 수식할 수 있는 것은 과거분사 (B) corrected와 현재분사 (C) correcting인데, 수식 대상인 agreement는 행위자에 의해 '수정되는' 대상이기 때문에 빈칸과 수동 관계이므로 (B)가 정답이다.

해석 즉시 Mr. Jones에게 연락해서 수정된 동의서를 이메일로 보내 주십시오.

어휘 contact 연락하다 agreement 동의, 합의 correct 바로 잡다, 수정하다; 맞는, 정확한

3.

해설 빈칸 뒤에 명사가 있으므로 빈칸은 명사를 수식하는 자리이다. 선택지 중 명사를 수식할 수 있는 것은 과거분사 (B) Departed와 현재분사 (C) Departing인데, 수식 대상인 passengers는 '출발하는' 주체이기 때문에 빈칸과 능동 관계이므로 (C)가 정답이다.

해석 출발하는 승객들은 비행을 하기 위해 보안 검사를 완료해야 한다.

어휘 passenger 승객 security check 보안 검사

4.

해설 빈칸 앞에 소유한정사가 있고 뒤에는 명사가 있으므로 빈칸은 명사를 수식하는 자리이다. 선택지 중 명사를 수식할 수 있는 것은 과거분사 (B) allotted와 현재분사 (C) allotting인데, 수식 대상인 budget은 행위자에 의해 '할당되는' 대상이기 때문에 빈칸과 수동 관계이므로 (B)가 정답이다.

해석 영업 부서는 할당된 예산보다 더 많은 돈을 이미 써 버렸다.

어휘 budget 예산 allot (시간, 돈, 공간 등을) 할당하다

빈출 유형 공략 02 본문 p.123

1. (C)　2. (C)　3. (D)　4. (C)

1.

해설 빈칸에는 several of the conditions를 뒤에서 수식할 수 있는 말이 들어가야 한다. 선택지 중 현재분사인 (B) listing과 과거분사인 (C) listed가 정답 후보인데, 수식 대상이 행위자에 의해 '나열되는' 것이기 때문에 빈칸과 수동 관계이므로 (C)가 정답이다.

해석 회사 변호사들조차 제안된 합병안에 열거된 몇 가지 조건에 대해 혼란스러워했다.

어휘 condition (요구) 조건; 상태 merger 합병

2.

해설 빈칸에는 damages를 뒤에서 수식할 수 있는 말이 들어가야 한다. 선택지 중 과거분사인 (B) resulted와 현재분사인 (C) resulting이 정답 후보인데, 수식 대상이 '결과를 초래하는' 주체이기 때문에 빈칸과 능동 관계이므로 (C)가 정답이다. 또한 result는 자동사이므로 수동을 나타내는 과거분사로는 쓸 수 없다.

해석 이 보증에는 의료 장비의 부적절한 사용으로 인한 손상이 포함되어 있지 않다.

어휘 warranty 품질 보증(서) cover 다루다, 포함시키다

improper 부적절한 medical equipment 의료 장비

3.

해설 빈칸에는 several new deals를 수식하는 동시에 뒤에 있는 명사구 16 million pounds를 목적어로 취할 수 있는 말이 들어가야 한다. 따라서 현재분사인 (D) totaling이 정답이다.

해석 올해 Louis and Son Contracting은 다 합쳐서 1,600만 파운드에 달하는 몇몇 새로운 계약을 맺었다.

어휘 sign a deal 계약을 체결하다 total 합계[총액]가 ~가 되다

4.

해설 빈칸에는 an e-mail을 수식하는 동시에 뒤에 있는 대명사 them을 목적어로 취할 수 있는 말이 들어가야 한다. 따라서 현재분사인 (C) informing이 정답이다.

해석 경영진은 모든 직원에게 새 회사 방침을 알리는 이메일을 보냈다.

어휘 policy 정책, 방침 inform A of B A에게 B를 알리다

빈출 유형 공략 03 본문 p.124

1. (A)　2. (C)　3. (D)　4. (D)

1.

해설 빈칸이 포함된 접속사절에 주어와 동사가 없으므로 [접속사+분사] 구조의 분사구문임을 알 수 있다. 과거분사인 (A) polled와 현재분사인 (B) polling이 정답 후보인데, 생략된 주어(residents of Pleasantville)는 행위자에 의해 '여론 조사를 받는' 대상이기 때문에 빈칸과 수동 관계이므로 (A)가 정답이다.

해석 최근 여론 조사에서 플레전트빌 주민들은 공립 학교를 개선하는 것이 그들의 최대 관심사라고 말했다.

어휘 public school 공립 학교 poll 여론 조사를 하다

2.

해설 빈칸이 포함된 접속사절에 주어와 동사가 없으므로 [접속사+분사] 구조의 분사구문임을 알 수 있다. 현재분사인 (C) remaining과 과거분사인 (D) remained가 정답 후보인데, 빈칸 뒤에 있는 형용사구 faithful to the founder's original goal을 보어로 취할 수 있어야 하므로 (C)가 정답이다.

해석 창업자의 원래 목표에 충실하면서 새로운 대표 이사는 회사에 큰 변화를 줄 계획이다.

어휘 faithful 충실한 founder 창업자 remain 계속 ~이다, 남아 있다

3.

해설 빈칸이 포함된 접속사절에 주어와 동사가 없으므로 [접속사+분사] 구조의 분사구문임을 알 수 있다. 또한 빈칸 앞에 As가 있는 것으로 보아 [as+과거분사] 관용 표현이므로 (D) discussed가 정답이다.

해석 논의된 바와 같이 Paul Young의 은퇴 파티는 5월 10일 금요일 오후 2시에 열릴 예정입니다.

어휘 retirement 은퇴

4.
해설 빈칸이 포함된 접속사절에 주어와 동사가 없으므로 [접속사 + 분사] 구조의 분사구문임을 알 수 있다. 또한 빈칸 앞에 as가 있는 것으로 보아 [as + 과거분사] 관용 표현이므로 (D) intended가 정답이다.
해석 다행스럽게도 새로운 시제품은 의도한 대로 작동하는 것 같다.
어휘 thankfully 고맙게도, 다행스럽게도 prototype 프로토타입, 시제품 intend 의도하다

빈출 유형 공략 04 본문 p.125
1. (B) 2. (B) 3. (B) 4. (D)

1.
해설 특정 분사구문은 형태나 의미가 굳어져 관용적으로 쓰인다. starting은 주로 문장의 앞에 사용되며, 어떤 일의 시작 시점을 나타내는 표현으로 항상 현재분사로 사용하므로 (B)가 정답이다.
해석 이번 4월부터 Greenwood Retails는 사무실 책상을 더 이상 팔지 않을 것이다.

2.
해설 특정 분사구문은 형태나 의미가 굳어져 관용적으로 쓰인다. depending on은 의존성을 나타내는 표현으로 항상 현재분사로 사용하므로 (B)가 정답이다.
해석 Lacy's Cosmetics는 재방문 고객에게 결제 금액에 따라 상당한 할인을 제공한다.
어휘 returning customer 재방문 고객 generous 후한, 관대한 spend 소비하다, (돈을) 쓰다

3.
해설 특정 분사구문은 형태나 의미가 굳어져 관용적으로 쓰인다. based on은 무언가의 근거를 나타내는 표현으로 항상 과거분사로 사용하므로 (B)가 정답이다.
해석 Ms. Keenan은 자신의 경험을 바탕으로 사업 계획 수립에 대한 전문적인 지침을 제공한다.
어휘 expert 전문적인, 전문가의 guidance 안내, 지도

4.
해설 특정 분사구문은 형태나 의미가 굳어져 관용적으로 쓰인다. thus -ing는 결과를 나타내는 표현으로 항상 현재분사로 사용하므로 (D)가 정답이다.
해석 그 지역 슈퍼마켓은 계산대를 하나 더 추가해서 고객들이 장보기를 더 빨리 끝낼 수 있도록 했다.
어휘 checkout 계산대 grocery 식료품 및 잡화

ACTUAL TEST 본문 p.126
1. (C) 2. (C) 3. (A) 4. (D) 5. (C)
6. (A) 7. (C) 8. (C) 9. (A) 10. (C)
11. (C) 12. (C) 13. (A) 14. (B)

1. 명사 + 현재분사
해설 빈칸에는 many factors를 뒤에서 수식할 수 있는 말이 들어가야 한다. 선택지 중 현재분사인 (C) contributing과 과거분사인 (D) contributed가 정답 후보인데, 수식 대상이 감소에 '기여하는' 주체이기 때문에 빈칸과 능동 관계이므로 (C)가 정답이다.
해석 종이 신문에 대한 관심 감소에 기여하는 많은 요인이 있다.
어휘 factor 요인 contribute to ~에 기여하다

2. 관용적 분사구문
해설 특정 분사구문은 형태나 의미가 굳어져 관용적으로 쓰인다. depending on은 의존성을 나타내는 표현으로 항상 현재분사로 사용하므로 (C)가 정답이다.
해석 Noble Gardener의 판매량은 날씨에 따라 변동한다.
어휘 fluctuate 오르락내리락하다, 요동치다

3. 명사 + 과거분사
해설 빈칸에는 the delicious cookies를 뒤에서 수식할 수 있는 말이 들어가야 한다. 선택지 중 과거분사인 (A) offered와 현재분사인 (C) offering이 정답 후보인데, 수식 대상이 행위자에 의해 '제공되는' 것이기 때문에 빈칸과 수동 관계이므로 (A)가 정답이다.
해석 Bizmark Hotel에서 즐거운 시간 보내시고 특별 라운지에서 제공되는 맛있는 쿠키를 꼭 드셔 보세요.

4. 현재분사 + 명사
해설 빈칸 앞에 관사가 있고 뒤에는 명사가 있으므로 빈칸은 명사를 수식하는 자리이다. 선택지 중 명사를 수식할 수 있는 것은 과거분사 (B) remained와 현재분사 (D) remaining인데, 수식 대상인 applications는 '남아 있는' 주체이기 때문에 빈칸과 능동 관계이므로 (D)가 정답이다. 참고로 remaining은 하나의 형용사로 굳어져 '남아 있는, 남은'을 뜻한다.
해석 편집장직으로 들어온 나머지 지원서는 월요일에 검토될 것이다.
어휘 application 지원(서), 신청(서) managing editor 편집장 remain 계속 ~이다, 남아 있다

5. 현재분사 + 명사
해설 빈칸 앞에 관사가 있고 뒤에는 명사가 있으므로 빈칸은 명사를 수식하는 자리이다. 선택지 중 명사를 수식할 수 있는 것은 과거분사 (B) led와 현재분사 (D) leading인데, 수식 대상인 publisher는 '이끄는' 주체이기 때문에 빈칸과 능동 관계이므로 (D)가 정답이다. 참고로 leading은 하나의 형용사로 굳어져 '선두의, 주요한, 가장 중요한'을 뜻한다.
해석 Tesmi House는 지난 5년 동안 자서전 출판사로 선두 자리에 있었습니다.
어휘 publisher 출판사

6. 과거분사 + 명사
해설 빈칸 앞에 전치사가 있고 뒤에는 명사가 있으므로 빈칸은 명사를 수식하는 자리이다. 따라서 과거분사인 (A) increased가 정답이다.
해석 스타트업 회사들에 투자하는 것은 높은 위험이 따르지만 수백만 달러를 벌 수도 있는 가능성을 동반한다.

어휘 risk 위험   potential 잠재력; 가능성이 있는

7. 접속사가 생략된 분사구문
해설 빈칸 뒤에 전치사구가 있고 콤마로 완전한 절이 연결된 것을 보아 '------- in France for over 10 years'는 분사구문임을 알 수 있다. 선택지 중 분사는 (A) Lived와 (C) Having lived인데, 분사구문의 생략된 주어인 Mr. Barreto는 프랑스에서 '사는' 주체이기 때문에 빈칸과 능동 관계이므로 (C)가 정답이다.

해석 Mr. Barreto는 프랑스에서 10년 이상 살아서 그에게 프랑스 고객과의 상담 업무가 맡겨졌다.

어휘 in charge of ~을 담당하는   consult 상담하다

8. [접속사+분사] 구문
해설 빈칸이 포함된 접속사절에 주어와 동사가 없으므로 [접속사+분사] 구조의 분사구문임을 알 수 있다. 현재분사인 (B) accompanying과 과거분사인 (C) accompanied가 정답 후보인데, 생략된 주어(Visitors)는 행위자에 의해 '동반되는' 대상이기 때문에 빈칸과 수동 관계이므로 (C)가 정답이다.

해석 12세 미만의 관람객은 성인을 동반한 경우에만 박물관에 입장할 수 있습니다.

어휘 accompany 동반하다, 동행하다

9. 과거분사 + 명사
해설 빈칸 앞에 전치사가 있고 뒤에는 명사가 있으므로 빈칸은 명사를 수식하는 자리이다. 선택지 중 명사를 수식할 수 있는 것은 과거분사 (A) limited와 현재분사 (B) limiting인데, 수식 대상인 hours는 행위자에 의해 '제한되는' 대상이기 때문에 빈칸과 수동 관계이므로 (A)가 정답이다. 참고로 limited는 하나의 형용사로 굳어져 '제한된, 한정된'을 뜻한다.

해석 그 대학의 중앙 도서관은 겨울 방학에 제한된 시간 동안 문을 열 것이다.

10. 과거분사 + 명사
해설 빈칸 앞에 관사가 있고 뒤에는 명사가 있으므로 빈칸은 명사를 수식하는 자리이다. 선택지 중 명사를 수식할 수 있는 것은 현재분사 (B) paying과 과거분사 (C) paid인데, 수식 대상인 internship은 행위자에 의해 '보수를 받는' 대상이기 때문에 빈칸과 수동 관계이므로 (C)가 정답이다. 참고로 paid는 하나의 형용사로 굳어져 '유급의, 보수를 받는'을 뜻한다.

해석 HM Technology에 지원한 사람들은 대부분 본사에서 유급 인턴십을 마쳤다.

어휘 applicant 지원자   complete 완료하다, 완성하다; (서식 등을) 빠짐없이 작성하다   headquarters (항상 복수형) 본사

수신인: Katie Kitson 〈katiekitson@sunshinefabrics.net〉
발신인: Estevan Oliveira 〈e.oliveira@caval-inc.com〉
날짜: 9월 30일
제목: Caval Inc.

Ms. Kitson에게

지난주 International Textiles Expo에서 귀하를 만나서 반가웠습니다. 귀하가 사업을 시작한 지 [11]비교적 얼마 안 된 것을 알고 있습니다. 그래서 저희 회사가 브라질로 상품을 수출하는 걸 도울 수 있는 훌륭한 자산이 될 것이라고 믿습니다.

[12]저희 회사는 귀하가 신뢰할 수 있는 높은 수준의 전문 지식을 가지고 있습니다. 동종 업계 중 가장 오래되었고 직원들은 대부분 이 분야에서 적어도 5년 이상 근무해 왔습니다. [13]엄격한 수출입 규정을 잘 다루고 큰 손실을 낼 수 있는 실수를 방지하도록 저희가 도와 드릴 수 있습니다. 또한 저희는 정부가 [14]금지한 물품들을 보내는 데 시간을 낭비하지 않도록 하기 위해 최신 정책 변화를 계속 확인하고 있습니다. 저희가 제공하는 서비스에 대해 더 자세히 논의할 수 있는 기회를 주시면 감사하겠습니다.

Estevan Oliveira

어휘 asset 자산, 재산; (가장 중요한) 장점, 이점   export 수출하다   goods (항상 복수형) 상품, 제품   navigate (복잡한 상황을) 처리하다, 다루다   regulation 규정; 규제, 통제   costly 대가가 큰; 많은 돈이 드는   keep up on ~에 대한 최신 정보를 계속 파악하다   government 정부

11. 부사 어휘
어휘 diligently 부지런히, 열심히   thoroughly 완전히, 철저히   incidentally 부수적으로

12. 알맞은 문장 고르기
해설 빈칸 앞 문단에서 수출 사업에 대한 도움을 제공하겠다고 했으며, 빈칸 뒤에는 직원의 경력을 강조하는 내용이 이어진다. 따라서 빈칸에는 회사의 전문성을 강조하는 내용이 들어가는 게 가장 자연스러우므로 (C)가 정답이다.

해석 (A) 변경 사항은 언제든지 제 사무실로 문의해 주십시오.
(B) 내년 행사 때 다시 뵙기를 바랍니다.
(C) 저희 회사는 귀하가 신뢰할 수 있는 높은 수준의 전문 지식을 가지고 있습니다.
(D) 견적 수수료는 협상이 가능한 비용입니다.

어휘 expertise 전문 지식, 전문성   quote 견적을 내다   estimate 견적(서); 추정(치)   negotiate 협상하다

13. 형용사 어휘
어휘 identical 동일한   emerged 드러난, 알려진   optional 선택적인

14. 분사 자리 [과거분사]
해설 빈칸에는 items를 뒤에서 수식할 수 있는 말이 들어가야 한다. 선택지 중 과거분사인 (B) prohibited와 현재분사인 (C) prohibiting이 정답 후보인데, 수식 대상이 행위자에 의해 '금지되는' 것이기 때문에 빈칸과 수동 관계이므로 (B)가 정답이다.

UNIT 10 접속사

기초 문법 CHECK 본문 p.131

1. to schedule 2. and 3. so
4. Although 5. that

1.
해설 등위접속사 or는 구와 구를 대등하게 이어 주므로 앞에 있는 to receive와 같은 to부정사인 to schedule이 정답이다.
해석 자세한 정보를 원하거나 예약을 하려면 555-1230으로 전화하십시오.

2.
해설 접속사를 기준으로 앞에서는 요청을 처리했다는 내용이, 뒤에서는 멤버십이 1년 더 지속될 거라는 내용이 병렬 연결되어 있으므로 '그리고'를 뜻하는 and가 정답이다.
해석 귀하의 요청을 처리했으며 멤버십은 1년 더 지속될 것입니다.

3.
해설 접속사를 기준으로 앞 문장이 뒤 문장의 이유가 되므로 '그래서'를 뜻하는 so가 정답이다.
해석 수하물은 매우 비슷해 보이는 경우가 많으니 수하물 ID 태그를 확인하세요.

4.
해설 문맥상 접속사절과 주절이 서로 반대되는 내용이므로 '비록 ~일지라도'를 뜻하는 Although가 정답이다.
해석 그 골프 클럽의 등록비는 비싸지만 월 요금이 저렴하다.

5.
해설 앞에 타동사 note가 있고 뒤에는 완전한 절이 이어지므로 note의 목적어인 명사절을 이끌 수 있는 접속사 that이 정답이다.
해석 예약은 선착순이라는 점에 주의해 주십시오.

빈출 유형 공략 01 본문 p.132

1. (A) 2. (C) 3. (C) 4. (C)

1.
해설 빈칸을 기준으로 명사 patent와 copyright law가 대등하게 연결되어 있으므로 '그리고'를 뜻하는 (A) and가 정답이다.
해석 HF Law Firm은 현재 특허법과 저작권법에 해박한 변호사를 찾고 있다.
어휘 look for ~을 찾다 have deep knowledge of ~에 해박한 지식이 있다 patent 특허권 copyright 저작권, 판권

2.
해설 빈칸 뒤에 and로 fashion과 interior design이 연결되어 있으므로 빈칸에는 and와 짝을 이루는 상관 접속사가 들어가야 한다. 따라서 (C) both가 정답이다.

해석 Girvan Tran은 패션과 인테리어 디자인 모두에서 독특한 아이디어를 개발하는 능력을 분명히 보여 주었다.
어휘 demonstrate 보여 주다; 입증하다 ability 능력, 재능, 기량 unique 독특한, 고유한 concept (새로운 것에 대한) 생각, 아이디어; 개념

3.
해설 빈칸 뒤에 nor로 CFG&Son과 Hardknocks Co.가 연결되어 있으므로 빈칸에는 nor와 짝을 이루는 상관 접속사가 들어가야 한다. 따라서 (C) Neither가 정답이다.
해석 CFG&Son과 Hardknocks Co. 둘 다 두 회사를 합병하기 위해 공정한 계약을 맺는 방법을 알지 못했다.
어휘 figure out ~을 알아내다 fair 공정한, 공평한 contract 계약(서) merge 합병하다

4.
해설 빈칸 뒤에 or로 두 가지 제안 방식이 연결되어 있으므로 빈칸에는 or와 짝을 이루는 상관 접속사가 들어가야 한다. 따라서 (C) either가 정답이다.
해석 개선을 위한 제안은 회사 이메일로 보내거나 건의함에 익명으로 넣을 수 있습니다.
어휘 suggestion 제안, 제의 improvement 개선, 향상 anonymously 익명으로

빈출 유형 공략 02 본문 p.133

1. (C) 2. (A) 3. (D) 4. (A)

1.
해설 문맥상 정문이 수리되는 동안 뒷문을 이용하라는 내용이 되는 게 자연스러우므로 '~하는 동안'을 뜻하는 (C) While이 정답이다.
해석 정문이 보수되는 동안 모든 사람은 뒷문으로 출근해야 한다.
어휘 main entrance 정문 renovate 개조하다, 보수하다; 혁신하다 report to work 출근하다

2.
해설 문맥상 허가가 없으면 로비를 떠나서는 안 된다는 내용이 되는 게 자연스러우므로 '만약 ~가 아니라면'을 뜻하는 (A) unless가 정답이다.
해석 방문객들은 특정한 허가를 받지 않는 이상 로비를 떠나서는 안 됩니다.
어휘 specific 구체적인, 명확한, 특정한

3.
해설 문맥상 만장일치로 결정이 날 때까지 문제 해결 방안을 고민할 거라는 내용이 되는 게 자연스러우므로 '~할 때까지'를 뜻하는 (D) Until이 정답이다.
해석 임원들은 만장일치로 결정을 내릴 때까지 앞으로 몇 시간 동안 그 문제의 해결 방안을 고민할 것이다.

어휘 come to a decision 결정하다 unanimous 만장일치의
figure out ~을 알아내다

4.
해설 문맥상 생산 공정을 간소화할 때 상품이 효율적으로 만들어진다는 내용이 되는 게 자연스러우므로 '~할 때'를 뜻하는 (A) When이 정답이다.
해석 생산 공정을 간소화하면 상품을 더 효율적으로 만들 수 있다.
어휘 streamline 간소화하다 efficiently 효율적으로

빈출 유형 공략 03 본문 p.134
1. (B) **2.** (A) **3.** (C) **4.** (D)

1.
해설 빈칸은 specify의 목적어인 명사절을 이끄는 접속사가 들어갈 자리이며, 문맥상 종이 영수증을 원하는지 전자 영수증을 원하는지 명시하라는 내용이 되는 게 자연스러우므로 '~인지 아닌지'를 뜻하는 (B) whether가 정답이다.
해석 종이 영수증을 원하는지 전자 영수증을 원하는지 명시하십시오.
어휘 specify (구체적으로) 명시하다 physical 물질의, 물질적인 electronic 전자의 receipt 영수증

2.
해설 빈칸 앞에 타동사 believe가 있고 뒤에는 완전한 절이 이어지므로 빈칸에는 believe의 목적어인 명사절을 이끌 수 있는 말이 들어가야 한다. 따라서 명사절 접속사인 (A) that이 정답이다.
해석 소비자들은 자신들이 직접 기구를 설치하는 것보다 기술자를 쓰는 게 더 쉽다고 생각한다.
어휘 install 설치하다

3.
해설 빈칸 앞에 타동사 require가 있고 뒤에는 완전한 절이 이어지므로 빈칸에는 require의 목적어인 명사절을 이끌 수 있는 말이 들어가야 한다. 따라서 명사절 접속사인 (C) that이 정답이다.
해석 Nard LTE는 신입 사원들이 회사 기밀을 공유하지 않도록 비밀 유지 서약서에 서명할 것을 요구한다.
어휘 confidentiality agreement 기밀 유지 서약서

4.
해설 [명사절 접속사(that)+주어(their print advertisements)+-------+전치사구(to ~ newspapers)] 구조이므로 빈칸은 동사 자리이다. 이 문장에서는 that절이 동사 request의 목적어 역할을 하는데, request가 요구나 요청을 의미할 때는 that절의 동사를 '(should) 동사원형'으로 써야 하므로 (D) be sent가 정답이다.
해석 고객이 인쇄 광고를 유명 신문사 몇 군데에 보내 달라고 요청했다.
어휘 prominent 중요한, 유명한; 눈에 띄는

빈출 유형 공략 04 본문 p.135
1. (C) **2.** (C) **3.** (D) **4.** (B)

1.
해설 빈칸 뒤에 완전한 절이 있으므로 빈칸은 절을 이끌 수 있는 접속사 자리이다. 문맥상 강사의 지시가 있지 않으면 다음 단계로 진행하지 말라는 내용이 되는 게 자연스러우므로 '만약 ~가 아니라면'을 뜻하는 (C) unless가 정답이다.
해석 강사가 괜찮다고 말하지 않으면 다음 단계로 진행하지 마십시오.
어휘 process 과정 instructor 강사

2.
해설 빈칸 뒤에 완전한 절이 있으므로 빈칸은 절을 이끌 수 있는 접속사 자리이다. 문맥상 장비가 교체된 이후에 조립 라인이 다시 가동됐다는 내용이 되는 게 자연스러우므로 '~한 후에'를 뜻하는 (C) after가 정답이다.
해석 그 조립 라인은 결함이 있는 장비가 발견되고 교체된 후 약 1시간 만에 가동을 재개했다.
어휘 assembly line (공장의) 조립 라인 resume 재개하다 operation 운용, 작동; 작업 faulty 결함이 있는

3.
해설 빈칸 뒤에 명사구 the online meeting이 있으므로 빈칸은 전치사 자리이다. 따라서 (D) during이 정답이다.
해석 온라인 회의를 하는 동안에 기술적인 문제가 발생하면 IT 부서에 연락하세요.
어휘 encounter 맞닥뜨리다, 부딪히다 technical 기술적인; 전문적인

4.
해설 빈칸 뒤에 완전한 절이 있으므로 빈칸은 절을 이끌 수 있는 접속사 자리이다. 문맥상 큰 문제가 되기 전에 적절한 관리로 작은 문제를 미리 발견할 수 있다는 내용이 되는 게 자연스러우므로 '~하기 전에'를 뜻하는 (B) before가 정답이다.
해석 수영장 장비를 제대로 관리하면 사소한 문제가 큰 문제가 되기 전에 반드시 발견할 수 있다.
어휘 maintenance (건물, 기계 등의) 유지 equipment 도구, 장비 ensure 보장하다, 확실히 하다 major 주요한, 중대한

ACTUAL TEST 본문 p.136
1. (A) **2.** (D) **3.** (A) **4.** (C) **5.** (C)
6. (C) **7.** (A) **8.** (A) **9.** (D) **10.** (D)
11. (C) **12.** (A) **13.** (A) **14.** (C)

1. 부사절 접속사
해설 빈칸 뒤에 완전한 절이 있으므로 빈칸은 절을 이끌 수 있는 접속사 자리이다. 문맥상 눈이 치워지는 대로 버스가 운행할 것이라는 내용이 되는 게 자연스러우므로 '~하자마자'를 뜻하는 (A) as soon

as가 정답이다.

해석 간밤에 내린 눈이 치워지는 대로 시외버스 운행을 재개할 예정입니다.

어휘 intercity bus 시외버스 resume 재개하다 blizzard 눈보라

2. 부사절 접속사

해설 빈칸 뒤에 완전한 절이 있으므로 빈칸은 절을 이끌 수 있는 접속사 자리이다. 문맥상 시장 조사 후에 새로운 캠페인을 시작할 것이라는 내용이 되는 게 자연스러우므로 '~한 후에'를 뜻하는 (D) after가 정답이다.

해석 광고 팀은 시장 조사를 마치고 나서 새로운 캠페인을 시작할 것이다.

어휘 get started 시작하다 conduct research 조사하다

3. 부사절 접속사

해설 빈칸 뒤에 주어와 동사를 갖춘 완전한 절이 있고, 콤마로 새로운 절이 연결되어 있으므로 빈칸에는 부사절 접속사가 들어가야 한다. 문맥상 잉크가 부족할 때마다 보고하라는 내용이 되는 게 자연스러우므로 '~할 때마다'를 뜻하는 (A) Whenever가 정답이다.

해석 프린터 잉크가 부족할 때마다 관리 부서에 보고하면 사람을 보내 줄 겁니다.

어휘 be out of ~가 (남은 게) 전혀 없다 maintenance (건물, 기계 등의) 유지

4. 명사절 접속사

해설 빈칸 앞에 타동사 request가 있고 뒤에는 완전한 절이 이어지므로 빈칸에는 request의 목적어인 명사절을 이끌 수 있는 말이 들어가야 한다. 따라서 명사절 접속사인 (C) that이 정답이다.

해석 Pulaski Theater는 공연장에 들어가기 전에 관객들이 모든 모바일 기기의 전원을 끌 것을 요청한다.

어휘 auditorium 강당

5. 등위 접속사

해설 빈칸을 기준으로 앞 문장이 뒤 문장의 이유가 되므로 '그래서'를 뜻하는 (C) so가 정답이다.

해석 B 카페테리아는 대청소를 위해 수요일에 문을 닫을 예정이니 A 카페테리아를 이용하시거나 점심을 직접 챙겨 오시기 바랍니다.

어휘 deep cleaning 대청소

6. 상관 접속사

해설 빈칸 뒤에 and로 the design team과 the marketing team이 연결되어 있으므로 빈칸에는 and와 짝을 이루는 상관 접속사가 들어가야 한다. 따라서 (C) Both가 정답이다.

해석 디자인 팀과 마케팅 팀 모두 가장 눈길을 끄는 책 표지를 만들기 위해 협업한다.

어휘 eye-catching 눈길을 끄는

7. 부사절 접속사

해설 빈칸 뒤에 주어와 동사를 갖춘 완전한 절이 있고, 콤마로 새로운 절이 연결되어 있으므로 빈칸에는 부사절 접속사가 들어가야 한다. 문맥상 신제품이 성공하든 실패하든 계속 모험을 하는 것이 중요하다는 내용이 되는 게 자연스러우므로 (A) Whether가 정답이다.

해석 신제품 출시가 성공하든 실패하든 계속 실험적인 디자인을 해보는 것이 중요하다.

어휘 take a risk 모험을 하다, 도전하다

8. 상관 접속사

해설 빈칸은 앞에 있는 either와 짝을 이루는 말이 들어갈 자리이므로 (A) or가 정답이다.

해석 Carol's Cabinets는 뛰어난 품질로 알려져 있으며 경재 또는 합판으로 된 제품을 제공합니다.

어휘 outstanding 뛰어난 hardwood 경재, 단단한 목재 plywood 합판

9. 접속사 vs. 전치사

해설 빈칸 뒤에 완전한 절이 있으므로 빈칸은 절을 이끌 수 있는 접속사 자리이다. 문맥상 금고가 수리되는 동안 은행을 닫을 것이라는 내용이 되는 게 자연스러우므로 '~하는 동안'을 뜻하는 (D) while이 정답이다.

해석 내일 점심 이후에 금고가 수리되는 동안에는 은행이 문을 닫을 것이다.

어휘 vault (특히 은행) 금고

10. 부사절 접속사

해설 빈칸 뒤에 완전한 절이 있으므로 빈칸은 절을 이끌 수 있는 접속사 자리이다. 문맥상 대조되는 내용이 되는 게 자연스러우므로 '~한 반면에'를 뜻하는 (D) whereas가 정답이다.

해석 매장 적립금 지급은 고객이 다시 방문하도록 유도하지만 단순 환불로는 다시 방문할 이유가 생기지 않는다.

어휘 issue store credit (환불하는 대신) 물건 가격만큼 포인트를 지급하다 encourage 장려하다

아내와 저는 최근에 결혼식을 올리기로 결정했습니다. 날씨가 너무 추워지기 전에 식을 올리고 싶었기 때문에 우리는 모든 걸 [11]급하게 준비해야 했습니다. 저는 웨딩 케이크를 찾는 일을 맡게 되었는데, 리뷰 웹사이트에서 Grace's Baking Company를 우연히 발견하게 되어 기뻤습니다. 온라인 리뷰에는 다소 회의적[12]이긴 하지만 저는 사진들을 보고 감명받았습니다. 저는 큰 행사를 2주 앞두고 Grace를 방문했고, 그녀는 제 결혼식 날까지 작업을 끝낼 수 있을 거라고 장담했습니다. [13]그녀는 전체적인 케이크 디자인까지 혼자서 생각해 냈습니다.

Grace는 제빵 기술의 [14]달인입니다. 결혼식에서 케이크가 얼마나 아름다웠는지 믿을 수가 없었죠. 언제라도 또 케이크가 필요하다면 저는 그녀의 전문가적인 조언만 받을 겁니다.

Adio Clarke, Jamestown

어휘 task 업무[임무]를 주다 stumble upon ~을 우연히 만나다 skeptical 회의적인, 의심이 많은 assure A that + 주어 + 동사 A에게 ~라는 걸 확신[확인]시켜 주다 craft 기술, 기교; 수공예

11. 부사 자리

해설 빈칸은 동사(prepare)를 수식하는 자리이므로 선택지 중 부사인 (C) hastily가 정답이다.

12. 접속사 vs. 전치사

해설 빈칸 뒤에 주어와 동사를 갖춘 완전한 절이 있고, 콤마로 새로운 절이 연결되어 있으므로 빈칸에는 부사절 접속사가 들어가야 한다. 문맥상 온라인 리뷰는 잘 믿지 않지만 사진을 보고 감명받았다는 내용이 되는 게 자연스러우므로 (A) Although가 정답이다.

어휘 in case ~한 경우에 대비하여 despite ~에도 불구하고 now that 이제 ~이므로

13. 알맞은 문장 고르기

해설 빈칸 앞에 Grace가 2주 만에 케이크를 준비할 수 있다고 장담했다는 내용이 있으므로 빈칸에는 Grace의 실력이 얼마나 대단한지 추가로 언급하는 내용이 들어가는 게 가장 자연스럽다. 따라서 (A)가 정답이다.

해석 (A) 그녀는 전체적인 케이크 디자인까지 혼자서 생각해 냈습니다.
(B) 초콜릿 케이크는 제가 가장 좋아하는 디저트입니다.
(C) 제 불평을 들어줄 사람을 찾기가 어려웠습니다.
(D) 다른 케이크들을 맛보기 위해 기꺼이 다시 갈 겁니다.

14. 명사 어휘

어휘 competitor 경쟁자, 경쟁사 novice 초보자 pupil (특히 어린) 학생

UNIT 11 관계사

기초 문법 CHECK 본문 p.141

1. who   2. which   3. that
4. in which   5. for which   6. whose

1.

해설 앞에 사람을 나타내는 명사가 있으므로 who가 정답이다.

해석 설문 조사를 완료한 모든 고객에게는 할인권이 제공됩니다.

2.

해설 앞에 사물을 나타내는 명사가 있으므로 which가 정답이다.

해석 Mr. Perez가 우리 학회에서 개회 기조연설을 할 예정인데, 그 학회는 다음 주에 부다페스트에서 열립니다.

3.

해설 앞에 사물을 나타내는 명사가 있으므로 that이 정답이다.

해석 Ms. Taylor는 컨퍼런스 참석자들에게 새 소프트웨어에 대한 설명을 담은 브로슈어를 발송할 것입니다.

4.

해설 앞에 사물을 나타내는 명사가 있으므로 in which가 정답이다.

해석 Mr. Martin은 지난여름에 묵었던 호텔을 예약했다.

5.

해설 전치사의 목적어 역할을 할 수 있는 것은 which이므로 for which가 정답이다.

해석 그는 Victoria Art Museum을 디자인한 것으로 잘 알려져 있으며, 이것으로 그는 2020년 World Design Award를 수상했다.

6.

해설 employees와 responsibilities는 '직원들의 업무'로 소유 관계가 성립하므로 whose가 정답이다.

해석 마지막 교육은 업무 내용에 가격 협상이 포함되어 있는 직원들을 위한 것이다.

빈출 유형 공략 01 본문 p.142

1. (C)   2. (B)   3. (C)   4. (B)

1.

해설 빈칸 앞에 사람을 나타내는 명사가 있고 뒤에는 동사가 바로 이어지므로 빈칸은 주격 관계대명사 자리이다. 따라서 (C) who가 정답이다.

해석 Mr. Jun은 신입 사원 채용을 담당할 부장입니다.

어휘 be in charge of ~을 담당하다

2.

해설 빈칸 앞에 전치사 to가 있으므로 빈칸에는 전치사의 목적어 역할을 할 수 있는 말이 들어가야 한다. 따라서 목적격 관계대명사인 (B) whom이 정답이다. 원래는 'the person whom they are sent to'였으나 관계대명사절 끝에 남은 전치사가 관계대명사 앞으로 이동한 것이다.

해석 개인 메시지는 전달받은 사람만 볼 수 있습니다.

어휘 private 사유의, 전용의

3.

해설 빈칸 앞에 사물을 나타내는 명사가 있고 뒤에는 목적어가 없는 절이 이어지므로 빈칸은 목적격 관계대명사 자리이다. (C) which와 (D) that이 정답 후보인데, 콤마 뒤에는 that을 쓸 수 없기 때문에 (C)가 정답이다.

해석 어제 회의에서 Maja Peterson은 회의 내용을 꼼꼼하게 기록했는데, 그녀는 그것을 인쇄해서 모두에게 나눠 줄 것이다.

어휘 take a note 적어 두다, 메모를 남기다 distribute 나누어 주다, 배부하다; (상품을) 유통시키다

4.

해설 '------- ~ celebrities'는 Lamar Accessories를 수식하는 관계대명사절이다. 선택지 중 소유격 관계대명사인 (B) whose와 목적격 관계대명사인 (D) which가 정답 후보인데, 빈칸 앞의 Lamar Accessories와 빈칸 뒤의 handbags는 'Lamar Accessories의 핸드백'으로 소유 관계가 성립하므로 (B)가 정답이다.

해석 Lamar Accessories는 핸드백이 유명인들 사이에서 인기

를 끌고 있는데, 가죽 지갑 신제품을 출시할 것이다.

어휘 popular 유명한, 인기 있는   launch 출시하다

빈출 유형 공략 02   본문 p.143
1. (A)   2. (D)   3. (A)   4. (D)

1.
해설 빈칸 앞에 완전한 절이 있으므로 '------ left in the office yesterday'는 the contract file을 수식하는 관계대명사절이다. 또한 left(leave의 과거형)의 목적어가 없으므로 the contract file과 빈칸 사이에 목적격 관계대명사가 생략되어 있음을 알 수 있다. 따라서 빈칸에는 동사의 주어 역할을 할 수 있는 명사가 들어가야 하므로 주격 인칭대명사인 (A) she가 정답이다.

해석 Ms. Gibson은 어제 사무실에 두고 간 계약서 파일을 찾고 있다.

어휘 look for ~을 찾다   contract 계약(서)

2.
해설 '------ for April 20'가 the art festival을 수식하는 구조이므로 빈칸 앞에 which is가 생략되어 있음을 알 수 있다. 선택지 중 현재분사인 (A) scheduling과 과거분사인 (D) scheduled가 정답 후보인데, 수식 대상이 행위자에 의해 '일정이 잡히는' 것이기 때문에 빈칸과 수동 관계이므로 (D)가 정답이다.

해석 날씨가 좋지 않을 경우에는 4월 20일로 예정된 예술제가 1주일 연기될 것입니다.

어휘 inclement weather 악천후   postpone 연기하다, 미루다

3.
해설 '------ for our rotating special menu'가 Prices를 수식하는 구조이므로 빈칸 앞에 which are가 생략되어 있음을 알 수 있다. 선택지 중 과거분사인 (A) listed와 현재분사인 (C) listing이 정답 후보인데, 수식 대상이 행위자에 의해 '나열되는' 것이기 때문에 빈칸과 수동 관계이므로 (A)가 정답이다.

해석 스페셜 순환 메뉴의 가격은 사용하는 재료에 따라 달라질 수 있습니다.

어휘 rotating menu 월이나 계절의 일정한 주기에 따라 반복되는 메뉴   be subject to ~의 대상이다

4.
해설 'we ------'이 The type of flooring을 수식하는 구조이므로 we 앞에 목적격 관계대명사 which나 that이 생략되어 있음을 알 수 있다. 따라서 빈칸에는 주어 we의 동사 역할을 할 수 있는 말이 들어가야 하므로 (D) were using이 정답이다.

해석 우리가 사용하던 바닥 타입은 더 이상 사용할 수 없습니다.

어휘 flooring 바닥재   available 이용할 수 있는; ~할 시간이 있는

빈출 유형 공략 03   본문 p.144
1. (C)   2. (D)   3. (A)   4. (B)

1.
해설 빈칸 앞뒤에 완전한 절이 있으므로 빈칸에는 부사와 접속사 역할을 겸하는 관계부사가 들어가야 하며, 선행사가 times of the day라는 시간을 나타내므로 (C) when이 정답이다.

해석 인파가 몰릴 가능성이 낮은 시간대에 쇼핑을 해 보십시오.

어휘 crowd 무리, 군중   form 구성하다, 형성하다

2.
해설 빈칸 앞뒤에 완전한 절이 있으므로 빈칸에는 부사와 접속사 역할을 겸하는 관계부사가 들어가야 하며, 선행사가 one major reason이라는 이유를 나타내므로 (D) why가 정답이다.

해석 세계적인 경기 불황이 유기농 식품 시장이 판매에 어려움을 겪는 한 가지 주요 원인이다.

어휘 economic recession 경기 불황   major 주요한, 중대한   organic food 유기농 식품   have difficulty in ~에 어려움을 겪다

3.
해설 빈칸 앞뒤에 완전한 절이 있으므로 빈칸에는 부사와 접속사 역할을 겸하는 관계부사가 들어가야 하며, 선행사가 the firm이라는 장소를 나타내므로 (A) where가 정답이다.

해석 Mr. Lowe는 여름 인턴십을 했던 회사로부터 정규직 제안을 받았다.

어휘 full-time job 정규직

4.
해설 빈칸 앞뒤에 완전한 절이 있으므로 빈칸에는 부사와 접속사 역할을 겸하는 관계부사가 들어가야 하며, 선행사가 our shop이라는 장소를 나타내므로 (B) where가 정답이다.

해석 여러분이 Lakefield Mall에 있다면 저희 가게를 방문해 보세요. 최신 무선 기기를 구입할 수 있습니다.

어휘 wireless 무선의   available 이용할 수 있는; ~할 시간이 있는

빈출 유형 공략 04   본문 p.145
1. (A)   2. (B)   3. (A)   4. (D)

1.
해설 '------ ~ interests'가 앞에 있는 절을 수식하는 부사 역할을 하고 있으므로 빈칸에는 부사절을 이끌 수 있는 말이 들어가야 한다. 따라서 선택지 중 주어가 없는 불완전한 절을 이끌 수 있는 복합관계대명사인 (A) whichever가 정답이다.

해석 콘퍼런스 참가자는 어떤 이벤트가 자신의 관심사와 가장 관련 있어 보이는지 간에 제공되는 어느 이벤트든 참여할 수 있습니다.

어휘 relevant 관련된, 연관된

2.

해설 '------ ~ the month'가 that절의 주어 역할을 하고 있으므로 빈칸에는 명사절을 이끌 수 있는 말이 들어가야 한다. 따라서 선택지 중 주어가 없는 불완전한 절을 이끌 수 있는 복합관계대명사인 (B) whoever가 정답이다.

해석 Ms. Yamaguchi는 이달 말까지 가장 많은 제품을 판매하는 사람은 누구든지 특별 보너스를 받게 될 거라고 발표했다.

어휘 announce 발표하다, 알리다

3.

해설 빈칸 뒤에 주어와 동사를 갖춘 완전한 절이 있고, 콤마로 새로운 절이 연결되어 있으므로 빈칸에는 완전한 두 개의 절을 연결할 수 있는 접속사가 들어가야 한다. 따라서 복합관계부사인 (A) Whenever가 정답이다.

해석 그 부서장은 출장에서 돌아올 때마다 직원들에게 줄 기념품을 가져온다.

어휘 business trip 출장 souvenir 기념품

4.

해설 빈칸 앞뒤에 완전한 절이 있으므로 빈칸에는 절을 연결할 수 있는 말이 들어가야 한다. 선택지 중 완전한 두 개의 절을 연결할 수 있는 것은 복합관계부사인 (B) however와 (D) wherever인데, 문맥상 '쇼핑몰에서 어디를 가든'이라는 내용이 되는 게 자연스러우므로 (D)가 정답이다.

해석 최신 인터넷 서비스 제공업체 덕분에 쇼핑객들은 쇼핑몰에서 어디를 가든 강력한 와이파이 신호를 즐길 수 있다.

어휘 thanks to ~ 덕분에

ACTUAL TEST   본문 p.146

1. (C)	2. (D)	3. (C)	4. (D)	5. (B)
6. (D)	7. (D)	8. (B)	9. (B)	10. (D)
11. (A)	12. (A)	13. (D)	14. (C)	

---

1. 소유격 관계대명사

해설 '------ novels ~ crises'는 a renowned writer를 수식하는 관계대명사절이다. 선택지 중 목적격 관계대명사인 (B) who와 소유격 관계대명사 (C) whose가 정답 후보인데, 빈칸 앞의 a renowned writer와 빈칸 뒤의 novels는 '저명한 작가의 소설들'로 소유 관계가 성립하므로 (C)가 정답이다.

해석 David Graham은 근대 경제 위기를 묘사한 것으로 잘 알려져 있는 소설들을 쓴 저명 작가이다.

어휘 renowned 저명한, 명성 있는 portray 묘사하다, 그리다 crisis 위기

2. 관계대명사절의 동사 자리

해설 빈칸 앞에 which가 있고 뒤에는 목적어 you가 이어지므로 빈칸은 주격 관계대명사절의 동사 자리이다. 따라서 (D) will allow가 정답이다.

해석 구매품에는 다음 주문 때 15%를 할인받을 수 있는 고유 쿠폰 코드가 들어 있습니다.

어휘 enclose 동봉하다 purchase 구매[구입]한 것 unique 독특한, 고유한

3. 관계부사

해설 빈칸 앞뒤에 완전한 절이 있으므로 빈칸에는 부사와 접속사 역할을 겸하는 관계부사가 들어가야 하며, 선행사가 Minneapolis—Saint Paul이라는 장소를 나타내므로 (C) where가 정답이다.

해석 Go-Go Airlines는 매일 뉴욕에서 미니애폴리스—세인트폴로 비행을 하는데 그곳에서 승객들은 호놀룰루로 환승할 수 있다.

어휘 connect (다른 노선이나 교통수단으로 갈아탈 수 있도록 교통편이) 연결되다

4. 복합관계대명사

해설 '------ he does'가 전치사 at의 목적어 역할을 하고 있으므로 빈칸에는 명사절을 이끌 수 있는 말이 들어가야 한다. 선택지 중 목적어가 없는 불완전한 절을 이끌 수 있는 것은 (C) whoever와 (D) whatever인데, 문맥상 무슨 일이든 최선을 다한다는 내용이 되는 게 자연스러우므로 (D)가 정답이다.

해석 Mr. Stevens는 자기가 하는 일이 무엇이든 최고가 되기 위해 열심히 한다.

5. 주격 관계대명사

해설 빈칸 앞에 사람을 나타내는 명사가 있고 뒤에는 동사가 바로 이어지므로 빈칸은 주격 관계대명사 자리이다. 따라서 (B) who가 정답이다.

해석 교환을 원하는 고객은 상품을 영수증 및 원래의 포장지와 함께 주셔야 합니다.

어휘 exchange 교환 present 제시하다, 제출하다 packaging 포장

6. 전치사 + 관계대명사

해설 빈칸 앞에 전치사 during이 있으므로 빈칸에는 전치사의 목적어 역할을 할 수 있는 말이 들어가야 한다. 따라서 목적격 관계대명사인 (D) which가 정답이다. 원래는 'a field day which each participant gets a free T-shirt during'이었으나 관계대명사절 끝에 남은 전치사가 관계대명사 앞으로 이동한 것이다.

해석 그 회사는 모든 참가자가 무료 티셔츠를 받는 체육 대회를 개최할 것이다.

어휘 field day 체육 대회, 운동회 participant 참가자

7. 관계대명사의 생략

해설 '------ ~ ballroom'은 축약된 관계사절로 The wait staff를 뒤에서 수식하는 구조이다. 선택지 중 과거분사인 (A) worked와 현재분사인 (D) working이 정답 후보인데, 수식 대상이 '근무하는' 주체이기 때문에 빈칸과 능동 관계이므로 (D)가 정답이다.

해석 주 연회장에서 근무하는 직원들은 완벽한 에티켓과 복장을 유지해야 한다.

어휘 wait staff (식당 등에서 손님 시중을 드는) 종업원 maintain (관계, 상태, 수준 등을) 유지하다 attire 복장

8. 주격 관계대명사
해설 빈칸 앞에 사물을 나타내는 명사가 있고 뒤에는 동사가 바로 이어지므로 빈칸은 주격 관계대명사 자리이다. 따라서 (B) that이 정답이다.

해석 새 보안 제품에는 어떤 움직임도 감지하는 센서가 있다.

어휘 security 보안 include 포함하다, 포함시키다 detect 발견하다, 감지하다

9. 목적격 관계대명사
해설 콤마 앞에 있는 절은 완전한 절이고 뒤에 있는 절은 전치사 of의 목적어가 없는 불완전한 절이다. 또한 두 개의 절을 하나로 연결하려면 접속사가 있어야 하므로 빈칸에는 접속사 역할을 하는 동시에 전치사의 목적어 역할을 할 수 있는 말이 들어가야 한다. 따라서 선택지 중 목적격 관계대명사인 (B) which가 정답이다.

해석 Grandville Hotel은 다문화 행사를 기획하는데, 행사 리스트는 매주 월요일에 저희 웹사이트에 업데이트됩니다.

어휘 organize 조직하다, 구성하다 multicultural 다문화의

10. 소유격 관계대명사
해설 빈칸 앞에 사물을 나타내는 명사가 있고 뒤에는 주어와 동사가 이어진다. 따라서 목적격 관계대명사인 (A) which와 소유격 관계대명사인 (D) whose가 정답 후보인데, 빈칸 앞의 Poli Insurance와 빈칸 뒤의 offices는 'Poli Insurance의 사무실들'로 소유 관계가 성립하므로 소유격 관계대명사인 (D)가 정답이다.

해석 Dano Properties는 사무실이 2층에 위치한 Poli Insurance와 임대 계약을 체결했다.

어휘 sign a lease 임대 계약을 하다

Mr. Kobayashi에게

저희 호박 따기 활동에 관심을 가져 주셔서 감사합니다. 귀하와 가족들이 농장을 ¹¹탐험하고 완벽한 호박을 찾으며 즐거운 시간을 보내기를 바랍니다. 이 편지에 저희 농장에서 이용할 수 있는 모든 특별한 행사를 ¹²설명하는 안내 책자를 넣었습니다. 호박 조각 행사에 참가하시려면 적어도 3일 전에 장소를 예약해야 합니다. ¹³매우 인기 있는 행사이니 일찍 예약해 두는 게 좋을 겁니다.

¹⁴추가 정보나 예약을 원하신다면 알려 주시기 바랍니다. 편의를 위해 (201) 555-0127로 전화하시면 됩니다.

Ms. Patty's Pumpkin Pickin' Farm Team

어휘 appreciate 고마워하다; 인정하다; 감상하다 informative (도움이 되는) 정보를 주는 available 이용할 수 있는; ~할 시간이 있는 participate in ~에 참여하다 reserve 예약하다; (자리 등을) 따로 잡아 두다 in advance 사전에, 미리 book a reservation 예약하다 convenience 편의, 편리; 편의 시설

11. 동사 어휘
어휘 promote 승진시키다; 홍보하다 request 요구하다, 신청하다 extend 연장하다; (사업, 세력 등을) 확대하다

12. 주격 관계대명사
해설 빈칸 앞에 명사 brochure가 있고 뒤에는 동사 explains가 바로 이어지므로 빈칸은 주격 관계대명사 자리이다. 따라서 (A) that이 정답이다.

13. 알맞은 문장 고르기
해설 빈칸 앞에서 호박 조각 행사를 안내하며 미리 장소를 예약해야 한다고 했으므로 빈칸에는 예약 관련 내용이 이어지는 게 자연스럽다. 따라서 (D)가 정답이다.

해석 (A) 이 얼마 안 되는 서비스 요금에는 무료 호박 맛 음료가 포함되어 있습니다.
(B) 냄새로 최고의 호박을 찾기 위해 귀하의 개를 데려오기를 권장합니다.
(C) 그냥 그날 와서 참여하셔도 됩니다.
(D) 매우 인기 있는 행사이니 일찍 예약해 두는 게 좋을 겁니다.

어휘 service charge 서비스 요금 include 포함하다, 포함시키다 encourage 권장하다, 장려하다 sniff out 냄새로 ~을 찾다 show up (예정된 곳에) 나타나다 book 예약하다

14. 형용사 어휘
어휘 factual 사실에 입각한 temporary 일시적인, 임시의 ongoing 진행 중인

CHAPTER 2　　PART 5 어휘

UNIT 01 명사 ❶

ACTUAL TEST　　본문 p.153

1. (A)　2. (A)　3. (B)　4. (A)　5. (C)
6. (C)　7. (C)　8. (C)　9. (A)　10. (B)

1.
해석　Birchwood Industries는 그 나라에서 가장 큰 플라스틱 제조사로 전국에 열다섯 개의 지점이 있다.
어휘　manufacturer 제조사　nationwide 전국적으로　inclination 성향, 경향　region 지역　connection 관련(성); 연결, 접속

2.
해석　인터뷰 동안 각 지원자는 자신들의 이전 경력을 설명하도록 요청받았다.
어휘　candidate 후보, 지원자　describe 설명하다, 묘사하다　guidance 안내, 지도　drop 하락, 감소　occasion 때, 경우; 행사

3.
해석　Xymo Publishing에서 일하는 것의 한 가지 이점은 원하는 만큼 휴가를 낼 수 있다는 것이다.
어휘　take time off 휴가를 내다　unlimited 제한 없는, 무한한　suggestion 제안, 제의　replacement 교체(품); 후임자　improvement 개선, 향상

4.
해석　Tonya Coats는 일 년도 안 되어 의료복과 장비의 주요 공급업체가 되었다.
어휘　leading 주요한, 가장 중요한　less than ~보다 적은　defect 결함　inventory 물품 목록; 재고(품)　feature 특징; 특징으로 하다

5.
해석　로고 디자인 대회의 우승자는 심사 위원단에 의해 선정될 것이다.
어휘　competition 경쟁(자); 대회　select 선발하다, 선택하다　judge 심사위원; 심판; 판사　proof 증명(서), 증거　crowd 무리, 군중　renewal 갱신, 재개

6.
해석　투숙객의 편의를 위해 Corvin Hotel은 얼리 체크인과 다과가 있는 대기실을 제공합니다.
어휘　waiting lounge 대기실　refreshments (항상 복수형) 다과　balance 균형, 조화; 잔고, 잔액　purpose 목적, 의도　consideration 고려 사항; 숙고

7.
해석　Apple Hill 자치 위원회는 다음 주에 Kirsch Library에서 정기적인 유지 보수를 수행할 계획을 발표했다.
어휘　routine 정기적인; 일상적인　management 경영(진)　alliance 동맹, 연합　alignment 정렬, 가지런함; (정치적) 지지

8.
해석　다음 달에 투자자들은 우리의 신상 단백질 셰이크를 시음할 기회를 갖게 될 것이다.
어휘　opportunity 기회　sample 맛보다, 시음[시식]하다　nutrition 영양　referral 위탁, 소개(서), 추천(서)　platform 플랫폼; 연단, 강단

9.
해석　Jerico Detailing은 증가된 수요를 맞추기 위해 제품 생산 규모를 두 배로 늘렸다.
어휘　double 두 배가 되다　shipping (특히 배를 이용한) 배송, 운송　awareness 인식, 의식, 관심　costs (항상 복수형) 경비, 비용

10.
해석　새로운 키 카드는 허가받은 직원만 그 건물의 특정 구역에 출입할 수 있게 할 것이다.
어휘　ensure 보장하다, 확실히 하다　authorized 권한을 부여받은　personnel 인원, 직원들　reward 보상(금)　portion 부분, 일부　capacity 용량, 수용력; 능력

UNIT 02 명사 ❷

ACTUAL TEST　　본문 p.157

1. (D)　2. (B)　3. (C)　4. (B)　5. (B)
6. (D)　7. (C)　8. (C)　9. (D)　10. (D)

1.
해석　모든 온라인 프로모션에는 판매를 장려하기 위해 온라인과 오프라인에서 모두 사용할 수 있는 쿠폰이 포함되어야 한다.
어휘　include 포함하다, 포함시키다　encourage 격려하다, 권장하다, 부추기다　contract 계약　policy 정책, 방침　price 가격

2.
해석　Korkrin Auto Parts는 비용을 낮추기 위해 생산량 일부를 이웃 나라에 위탁할 것이다.
어휘　lower 낮추다, 내리다; 낮은, 아래쪽의　outsource 외부에 위탁하다　neighboring 근처의, 인접한; 이웃의　information 정보　volume 용량; 음량　subject 주제; 과목

3.
해석 5번가에 있는 현금 자동 지급기는 업데이트가 완료될 다음 주 월요일까지 사용할 수 없습니다.
어휘 complete 완료된; 완전한　purpose 목적, 의도　funds (항상 복수형) 자금, 기금　practice 실행; 관행

4.
해석 광고가 효과적이려면 고객들이 광고 음악과 브랜드를 바로 연결 지을 수 있어야 한다.
어휘 commercial 광고; 상업의　effective 효과적인　opinion 의견, 견해　profit 이익　form 양식

5.
해석 그 연구 팀은 연구부장의 승인 없이 다른 연구원을 채용할 수 없다.
어휘 head (단체, 조직 등의) 책임자　suggestion 제안, 제의　success 성공　emphasis 강조, 역점

6.
해석 기밀 데이터 보호를 위해 모든 직원은 특정 문서를 공유할 때 회사 인트라넷을 사용해야 합니다.
어휘 confidential 기밀의　precision 정확(성), 정밀(성)　maintenance (건물, 기계 등의) 유지　allocation 할당(량)

7.
해석 최근 공원 재개발 사업의 성공으로 얼마 전 선출된 시장에 대한 주민들의 신뢰가 높아졌다.
어휘 redevelopment 재개발　newly 최근에, 새로　associate (직장) 동료, 직원　profession 전문직; (특정 직종) 종사자들　guidance 안내, 지도

8.
해석 Hazco의 혁신적인 마케팅 팀은 그 자동차 회사가 경쟁에서 압도적인 우위를 점하게 했다.
어휘 innovative 혁신적인, 획기적인　put A ahead of B A를 B보다 앞에 두다　audit 회계 감사; (품질) 검사　compliment 칭찬　assortment (여러 가지의) 종합, 모음

9.
해석 완제품은 출시되기 전에 모든 품질 기준을 충족해야 한다.
어휘 quality 질; 우수함　launch 출시하다　issue 주제, 안건; 쟁점　reading 독서, 읽기　clause 조항, 조목

10.
해석 그 회의의 목적은 회사의 규정에 대해 논의하고 개선에 대한 권고안을 제시하는 것이었다.
어휘 regulation 규정; 규제, 통제　offer 제공하다　improvement 개선, 향상　donation 기부, 기증　reimbursement 상환, 환급, 배상　customs (항상 복수형) 세관; 관세

UNIT 03 형용사 ❶

ACTUAL TEST　　본문 p.161

| 1. (B) | 2. (C) | 3. (A) | 4. (C) | 5. (D) |
| 6. (D) | 7. (C) | 8. (D) | 9. (A) | 10. (C) |

1.
해석 출장 중에 발생된 적법한 숙박비는 환급될 것입니다.
어휘 accommodation 숙소, 숙박 시설　expense (보통 복수형) 경비, 비용　incur (손해 등을) 입다, (비용을) 발생시키다　reimburse 환급하다　assertive 적극적인, 확신에 찬　competent 유능한; (그럭저럭) 괜찮은　prominent 중요한, 유명한; 눈에 띄는

2.
해석 Aunt Patty's Restaurant는 서비스에 대한 수요가 계속 증가하면 직원을 추가로 고용할 것이다.
어휘 demand 수요, 요구　continue 계속되다　approximate 근사치의; 대강의　ambitious 야심 있는, 야심 찬　accountable (해명할) 책임이 있는

3.
해석 신입 사원들은 업무 배정을 받기 전에 교육 프로그램을 의무로 이수해야 한다.
어휘 recruit 신입 사원　assign 맡기다, 배정하다, 선임하다　duty 업무; 직무, 임무　determined 단호한, 완강한　skeptical 회의적인, 의심이 많은　considerate 사려 깊은, 배려하는

4.
해석 유명 음식 평론가의 호평을 받은 후에 그 식당은 수익이 30% 증가했다.
어휘 critic 비평가, 평론가　rise (높은 위치, 수준 등으로) 오르다　vivid 선명한, 생생한　joint 공동의, 합동의　growing 증가하는

5.
해석 곧 있을 Mount Telecom과 Zenith Communications의 합병은 다음 주 회의에서 논의될 것이다.
어휘 merger 합병　numerous 많은　decisive 결정적인, 결단력 있는　proper 적절한

6.
해석 Mr. Payton의 뛰어난 편집 실력은 그의 경력에 큰 자산이 될 것이다.
어휘 asset (가장 중요한) 장점, 이점; 자산, 재산　superficial 깊이 없는, 피상적인　nominal 명목상의, 이름뿐인　external 외부의

7.
해석 회사의 수익성을 예상하려면 재무 예측이 가능한 한 정확해야 한다.
어휘 projection 추정, 추산　lengthy 장황한, 지루한　incidental 부수적인　efficient 능률적인, 효율적인

8.

해석 Ms. Urso와 같은 경험 많은 회계사들조차도 실수를 한다.

어휘 accountant 회계사　make a mistake 실수를 하다　frequent 잦은, 빈번한　preliminary 예비의, 사전의　reserved 내성적인, 말을 잘 하지 않는

9.

해석 그 회사는 저자에게 상당한 인세를 지불했다.

어휘 amount 총액, 액수　royalty (책의) 인세, (음악 등의) 저작권 사용료　costly 많은 돈이 드는; 대가가 큰　reputable 평판이 좋은　known 알려진

10.

해석 직원들의 당초 우려는 인사부가 입장 발표로 달래고 나서 사그라들었다.

어휘 initial 처음의, 초기의　calm 진정시키다　comparable 비교할 만한　lucrative 수익성이 좋은　fortunate 운 좋은

UNIT 04 형용사 ❷

ACTUAL TEST　　　　　　본문 p.165

| 1. (C) | 2. (B) | 3. (A) | 4. (D) | 5. (C) |
| 6. (B) | 7. (B) | 8. (C) | 9. (A) | 10. (B) |

1.

해석 월 주차 이용권은 정문 옆에 있는 경비실에서 구입할 수 있습니다.

어휘 parking pass 주차권　purchase 구매, 구입; 구매[구입]한 것; 구매[구입]하다　security office 경비실　locate 위치시키다, (특정 위치에) 두다; (위치를) 알아내다　increasing 증가하는　optional 선택적인　anonymous 익명의

2.

해석 Greenhorn Industries에서 직원들에 대한 우리의 주된 관심사는 작업장 안전입니다.

어휘 concern 관심사; 걱정, 우려　workplace 직장, 업무 현장　contrary 상반되는, 적합하지 않은　perpetual 빈번한　respectful 존경심을 보이는, 공손한

3.

해석 생산비 상승으로 인해 모든 구매에 무료 배송을 제공하는 것은 우리에게 더 이상 이익이 되지 않는다.

어휘 rise (높은 위치, 수준 등으로) 오르다　production 생산(량)　costs (항상 복수형) 경비, 비용　no longer 더 이상 ~ 않는　shipping (특히 배를 이용한) 배송, 운송　eligible 자격이 있는　questionable 의심스러운　durable 내구성이 있는; 오래가는

4.

해석 Ms. Nguyen은 지역 예술가로서 뛰어난 작품으로 여러 상을 받았다.

어휘 win an award 수상하다　exclusive 독점적인, 전용의; 고급의; ~을 제외하고　lavish 호화로운　abnormal 비정상적인

5.

해석 Compass Medical의 환자들은 이제 모든 자신의 의료 기록과 실험실 보고서에 직접 접근할 수 있습니다.

어휘 access 접근; 접속　laboratory 실험실, 연구실　reliable 믿을 만한, 신뢰할 만한　deliberate 고의의, 의도적인　eventual 궁극적인

6.

해석 Bunton Textiles는 연간 예산을 검토해 줄 만한 자격 있는 회계사를 찾고 있다.

어휘 seek 찾다, 구하다　accountant 회계사　look over ~을 (대강) 살펴보다　budget 예산　repurposed 다른 목적에 맞게 만든　random 무작위의　partial 부분적인, 불완전한

7.

해석 마케터들은 다가올 트렌드와 진화하는 고객 선호도에 계속 관심을 가져야 한다.

어휘 upcoming 다가오는, 곧 있을　evolve (점차) 달라지다, 발전하다; 진화하다　preference 선호(도), 선호하는 것　vacant 비어 있는　attractive 매력적인, 멋진　reserved 내성적인, 말을 잘 하지 않는

8.

해석 Jerod's는 매장의 단골손님들을 위해 새로운 회원제 프로그램을 도입했다.

어휘 introduce 도입하다, 들여오다; 소개하다　coupled 연결된, 결합된　structural 구조적인　popular 유명한, 인기 있는; 일반적인

9.

해석 배송 날짜를 철저하게 지키는 건 어렵긴 하지만 확실히 가능하긴 합니다.

어휘 meet deadline 마감일을 지키다　strict 엄격한　shipment 배송(물), 수송(물)　certainly 틀림없이, 분명히　possible 가능한; 있을 수 있는　fitting (특정 상황에) 어울리는　encouraging 격려의　liveable 살 만한, 살기에 적합한

10.

해석 Milton Charles는 수년 동안 사이프러스의 광산 역사에 대해 광범위한 연구를 해 왔다.

어휘 research 연구, 조사　mining 광산(업)　considerate 사려 깊은, 배려하는　temporary 일시적인, 임시의　probable 있을 것 같은, 개연성 있는

UNIT 05 동사 ❶

ACTUAL TEST 본문 p.169
1. (A) 2. (D) 3. (C) 4. (A) 5. (B)
6. (C) 7. (A) 8. (D) 9. (C) 10. (D)

1.
해석 열쇠를 분실한 경우에 직원들은 경비실에서 예비 열쇠를 받을 수 있다.
어휘 replacement 교체(품); 후임자 in the event (that) ~할 경우에 select 선발하다, 선택하다 apply 신청하다, 지원하다; 적용하다 input 입력하다

2.
해석 Ms. Sweeney는 그 회사가 매입할 예정인 건축 부지 사진을 추가로 요청했다.
어휘 additional 추가의 intend 의도하다 emphasize 강조하다 inform 알리다, 통지하다

3.
해석 지역 사회 행사에서 자원봉사자는 각기 다른 음식 노점을 배정받을 것이다.
어휘 stall 노점, 진열대 correspond 일치하다, 부합하다 confront (문제, 곤란한 상황 등에) 맞서다, 직면하다 help 돕다, 도움이 되다

4.
해석 판매원들은 자신이 판매하는 제품이 작동하는 방식을 설명하고 질문에 자신감 있게 답해야 한다.
어휘 fulfill (요구 조건을) 충족시키다, (목표나 의무를) 달성하다 focus 집중하다 conduct 지휘하다; (특정 활동을) 수행하다

5.
해석 소비자 의견과 건의 사항은 검토를 위해 관련 부서들에 전달된다.
어휘 recommendation 권고; 추천(서) relevant 관련된, 연관된 fill in (서식 등을) 빠짐없이 작성하다 let go ~을 놓아 주다(~ of); ~을 해고하다 push aside (자리, 직위 등을 차지하기 위해) ~을 밀어내다; (특히 안 좋은 것을) 생각하지 않으려 하다

6.
해석 양질의 서비스를 보장하기 위해 모든 제품 상담은 예약제로만 이루어진다.
어휘 quality 질 좋은; 우수함 consultation 상담 appointment 약속, 예약 warrant 정당화하다; (사실임을) 약속하다 confirm 확인하다; 확정하다 justify 합리화하다, (남들이 잘못되었다고 하는 걸) 옳다고 하다

7.
해석 Morgan Financial에서 우리는 Logan County's Account Council의 신뢰할 수 있는 멤버로 인정받은 것을 자랑스럽게 생각한다.
어휘 be proud to do ~해서 자랑스럽다 suit 잘 맞다, (잘 맞아서) 편리하다 allot (시간, 돈, 공간 등을) 할당하다 achieve 달성하다, 성취하다

8.
해석 Ms. Bolton은 연례 감사와 겹치지 않도록 출장을 연기할 것이다.
어휘 postpone 연기하다, 미루다 annual 연례의 inspection 검사, 점검 calibrate 눈금을 매기다 collaborate 협력하다 condense (글 등을) 줄이다; 응축하다

9.
해석 다음 주에 있을 Mr. Vogel의 은퇴식에 전 직원이 초대된다.
어휘 retirement 은퇴 celebrate 기념하다 promise 약속하다 consider 여기다, 간주하다

10.
해석 Mr. Diaz는 회사 차량 사용에 관한 안전 정책을 수립하는 것이 중요하다고 언급했다.
어휘 note 주목하다, 언급하다 regarding ~에 관하여 multiply 곱하다; (양이) 크게 증가하다 delegate (일, 임무 등을) 위임하다; 대표[대리인]로 선정하다 estimate 견적을 내다; 견적(서); 추정(치)

UNIT 06 동사 ❷

ACTUAL TEST 본문 p.173
1. (A) 2. (C) 3. (A) 4. (B) 5. (D)
6. (B) 7. (C) 8. (A) 9. (D) 10. (B)

1.
해석 Whalerton Foods는 더 많은 흰 살 생선 옵션에 주력하기 위해 최근에 생선 제품을 확장했다.
어휘 feature 특징으로 하다, 특별히 선보이다 task 업무[임무]를 주다 open 열다, 열리다 include 포함하다, 포함시키다

2.
해석 Restaurants for Tomorrow의 조사는 많은 식당이 음식물 쓰레기 배출에 관한 지역의 법규를 따르지 않았다는 걸 드러냈다.
어휘 regulation 규정; 규제, 통제 regarding ~에 관하여 disposal 처분, 폐기 compile 편집하다, 엮다 compose 작곡하다; 작성하다, 쓰다; 구성하다 undergo 겪다, 경험하다

3.
해석 모든 사용자는 우리의 클라우드 소프트웨어를 사용하기 전에 자신의 계정을 인증해야 한다.
어휘 be required to do ~하도록 요구받다 account 계정; 계좌 prioritize 우선순위를 매기다 deliver 배달하다 develop 성장하다, 개발하다

4.

해석 모든 프리랜서 계약자는 건물 시공 및 철거와 관련된 시 규정을 준수해야 한다.

어휘 regulation 규정; 규제, 통제 related to ~와 관련된 construct 건설하다 demolish (건물을) 철거하다 confirm 확인하다; 확정하다 convey (생각, 감정 등을) 전달하다; 나르다 appoint 임명하다; (시간, 장소 등을) 정하다

5.

해석 인사부는 올해 Maxford Family Day에 푸드 트럭 근무를 자원할 사람을 구하고 있다.

어휘 look for ~을 찾다 employ 고용하다 post 게시하다 sign 서명하다, 계약하다

6.

해석 관중들은 대개 경기의 승자가 발표되고 나서 Johnston Field를 떠난다.

어휘 spectator 관중 remove 제거하다 redeem (상품권/쿠폰 등을) 현금/상품으로 바꾸다; 빚을 상환하다 return (물건 등을) 되돌려 주다, 반환하다; 돌아가다

7.

해석 이 발표에는 사기 행위 방지 기법을 실행하는 것에 관해 도움이 되는 팁이 포함되어 있다.

어휘 anti-fraud 사기 행위를 방지하는 overcome 극복하다, 이겨내다 yield 도출하다, 산출하다 withdraw (돈을) 인출하다; 물러나다, 철회하다

8.

해석 Bricks Furniture는 7월에 500달러 이상 결제하는 고객들에게 설치비를 면제해 줄 계획이다.

어휘 installation fee 설치비 forge (관계를) 구축하다; (문서, 돈 등을) 위조하다 retreat 후퇴하다; (하려던 일에서) 물러서다 excuse 용서하다; 변명하다

9.

해석 이번 달 내에 철거되어야 하는 행사 간판 몇 개가 벽에 있다.

어휘 use up ~을 다 써버리다 close down 폐업하다, 문을 닫다 come across ~을 우연히 마주치다

10.

해석 대개 특정 목적지로 가는 땡처리 항공권 요금은 많게는 50%까지 할인된다.

어휘 typically 대개; 전형적으로 last-minute 막바지의, 임박한 fare (교통) 요금 destination 목적지 purchase 구매[구입]하다 distribute 나누어 주다, 배부하다; (상품을) 유통시키다 consider 여기다, 간주하다

UNIT 07 부사 ❶

ACTUAL TEST 본문 p.177

| 1. (B) | 2. (C) | 3. (A) | 4. (A) | 5. (C) |
| 6. (A) | 7. (A) | 8. (D) | 9. (A) | 10. (A) |

1.

해석 회사 웹사이트에 게시하기 전에 첨부된 이미지를 꼼꼼하게 검토하십시오.

어휘 post 게시하다 subjectively 주관적으로 lazily 게으르게; 느긋하게, 여유롭게 ideally 이상적으로

2.

해석 장비를 업그레이드하면 우리 사무실 직원들의 편의가 크게 증진될 것이다.

어휘 equipment 도구, 장비 convenience 편의, 편리; 편의 시설 privately 개인적으로, 사적으로; 따로, 은밀히 formally 공식적으로; 정중하게; 형식적으로 faintly 희미하게

3.

해석 이번 주말은 공휴일이어서 기차표가 매진되었다.

어휘 book 예약하다 basically 기본적으로 casually (격식 없이) 가볍게; 무심하게; 우연히; (정규직이 아닌) 임시로 uncertainly 불확실하게, 애매모호하게

4.

해석 모든 고객 문의에 신속하게 답변해 드릴 것을 약속합니다.

어휘 inquiry 문의, 질문 rarely 거의 ~ 않는 resistantly 저항하여 finally 마침내; 마지막으로

5.

해석 Mr. Roberts는 그 팀에게 설치 지시만 잘 따르면 새로운 소프트웨어 업데이트는 순조롭게 진행될 거라고 장담했다.

어휘 assure A that + 주어 + 동사 A에게 ~라는 걸 확신[확인]시켜 주다 smoothly 순조롭게; 부드럽게 installation 설치 direction 지시; 방향 randomly 무작위로 hastily 급하게 frequently 자주

6.

해석 Leicester Art Show는 이전에 선보인 적 없었던 예술가들의 작품만 받는다.

어휘 accept 받아들이다, 받아 주다 work 작품 lastly 마지막으로, 끝으로 rapidly 빠르게, 급속히 shortly 얼마 안 되어, 곧

7.

해석 시스템 정기 점검 때문에 그 데이터베이스는 일시적으로 사용할 수 없다.

어휘 unavailable 이용할 수 없는; 획득할 수 없는 due to ~ 때문에 routine 정기적인; 일상적인 maintenance (건물, 기계 등의) 유지 perfectly 완벽하게 evenly 공평하게; 고르게, 골고루 securely (안전하도록) 단단하게, 확실하게; 안정적으로

8.
해석 그 후기에서 Ms. Hino는 자신에게 좋은 기억으로 남아 있는 그 요리에 대해 자세히 말했다.
어휘 at length 길게, 상세히; 한참 후에 dish 요리 equally 똑같이, 동일[동등]하게 quietly 조용하게 hopefully 바라건대

9.
해석 그 호텔의 보수 공사 시행을 위해 Bethany Interior Design이 몇몇 사람에 의해 적극 추천되었다.
어휘 recommend 추천하다; 권고하다 carry out ~을 수행[실행]하다 renovation 개조, 리모델링 indefinitely 무기한으로 patiently 참을성 있게 vibrantly 활기차게; (빛, 색 등이) 밝게

10.
해석 모든 거래는 세금 규정을 지키는지 확인하기 위해 철저히 조사되어야 한다.
어휘 transaction 거래 examine 조사하다, 살펴보다 ensure 보장하다, 확실히 하다 comply with ~을 지키다 regulation 규정; 규제, 통제 hardly 거의 ~않는 eagerly 간절하게, 몹시 고대하여 wearily 지쳐서; 싫증나서

UNIX O8 부사 ❷

ACTUAL TEST 본문 p.181

| 1. (C) | 2. (B) | 3. (C) | 4. (A) | 5. (A) |
| 6. (B) | 7. (D) | 8. (C) | 9. (A) | 10. (D) |

1.
해석 Kilton Technologies는 3분기에 손실을 봤지만 그래도 연말에는 간신히 흑자를 냈다.
어휘 manage to do 간신히 ~하다 turn a profit 수익을 내다 anymore 더 이상 seldom 거의 ~않는 closely 면밀히; 밀접하게

2.
해석 시 안전 위원회는 운전자들에게 이번 공휴일이 낀 주말에는 조심해서 운전할 것을 촉구한다.
어휘 urge 촉구하다, 거듭 권유하다 holiday weekend 공휴일이 낀 주말 rightfully 정당하게 nervously 초조하게, 불안하게 solemnly 엄숙하게

3.
해석 새로 고용된 직원들은 미니애폴리스에서 한 달 교육 프로그램에 참석해야 한다.
어휘 attend 참석하다; 주의를 기울이다 frequently 자주 partially 부분적으로 highly 매우, 많이

4.
해석 처리 오류로 인해 Martin Forwarders는 사무용 가구를 실수로 다른 로펌으로 운송했다.
어휘 processing 처리 ship (상품을) 배송하다 illegibly (글자 등을) 알아보기 어렵게 correctly 정확하게, 제대로 extremely 극도로, 매우

5.
해석 Winston Hills Hotel은 녹스빌 번화가의 중심지에 있어 편리한 위치에 있다.
어휘 locate 위치시키다, (특정 위치에) 두다; (위치를) 알아내다 mildly 가볍게; 온화하게 instantly 즉시 anonymously 익명으로

6.
해석 사전 승인 없이 시간 외 근무를 하는 것은 엄격히 금지된다.
어휘 prior approval 사전 승인 prohibit 금지하다 constantly 끊임없이 quickly 빠르게 sharply (비판 등을) 날카롭게, 신랄하게; 급격히

7.
해석 활주로 정비로 인해 다음 달 비행 일정이 예기치 않게 변경될 수 있습니다.
어휘 maintenance (건물, 기계 등의) 유지 commonly 흔히, 보통 kindly 친절하게 lightly 가볍게

8.
해석 발표 직후에 Mr. Omen과의 짧은 질의응답 시간이 있을 겁니다.
어휘 session (특정한 활동을 위한) 시간 effectively 효과적으로 currently 현재, 지금 rapidly 빠르게, 급속히

9.
해석 Mr. Portman은 양질의 서비스 보장에 관해서는 직업의식이 투철하다.
어휘 in regard to ~에 관하여 quality 질 좋은 frankly 솔직하게 significantly 상당히; 의미 있게, 중요하게 lately 최근에

10.
해석 건설 현장 근로자와 방문객 모두에게 안전모와 반사 작업복이 제공될 것이다.
어휘 hard hat 안전모 reflective gear (빛을 반사하는 띠가 있어 어두운 곳에서도 눈에 잘 띄도록 만든) 반사 작업복 construction site 공사장 nearly 거의 quite 꽤, 상당히 far 멀리

FINAL TEST

본문 p.182

1. (B)	2. (A)	3. (A)	4. (A)	5. (C)
6. (A)	7. (D)	8. (C)	9. (C)	10. (D)
11. (B)	12. (C)	13. (B)	14. (B)	15. (D)
16. (C)	17. (D)	18. (C)	19. (B)	20. (C)

1.
해석 자재 부족 때문에 그 보수 공사는 원래 완공 날짜까지 끝나지 못할 것이다.
어휘 owing to ~ 때문에 shortage 부족 renovation 개조, 리모델링 subscription 구독(료) option 선택(권) delegation 위임; 대표단

2.
해석 Mr. Shull은 자신이 회사에 전념했기 때문에 결국 승진할 것이라고 생각했다.
어휘 promote 승진시키다; 홍보하다 dedication 헌신, 전념 closely 면밀히; 밀접하게 frequently 자주 effectively 효과적으로

3.
해석 제품 개발팀은 새 휴대폰이 다음 달에 출시될 준비가 될 것이라고 자신하고 있다.
어휘 confident 자신하는, 확신하는 explore 탐구하다, 탐색하다 facilitate 가능하게 하다, 수월하게 하다 allow 허락하다, 가능하게 하다

4.
해석 Jenson 시장은 마침내 마운틴뷰 주민들을 위한 지역 개발 계획에 착수했다.
어휘 undertake (일을 맡아서) 착수하다 development 개발, 발달 decision 결정 lesson 수업; 교훈 preview 시사회

5.
해석 우리가 알기로 Cloveman Shipping은 10년 역사를 통틀어서 한 번도 배송이 늦은 적이 없습니다.
어휘 entire 전체의 credit 신용 거래; 칭찬, 인정 ability 능력, 재능, 기량 chance 기회

6.
해석 Kingsley Corporation은 회사에서 2년 이상 근무한 직원들에게 상여금을 지급할 것이다.
어휘 holiday bonus 상여금, (명절, 휴가, 연말 등에 받는) 보너스 execute 연주하다; 실행하다, 수행하다 surprise 놀라게 하다 demand 요구하다

7.
해석 총지배인은 건강 문제를 해결하기 위해 잠시 동안 일선에서 물러날 것이다.
어휘 step away from ~에서 물러나다 deal with ~을 처리하다, ~을 다루다 remote (거리가) 먼, 멀리 떨어진; (시간상으로) 먼; (가능성이) 희박한 strict 엄격한 remarkable 뛰어난, 주목할 만한

8.
해석 인턴들은 나머지 직원들에 대해 더 잘 알기 위해 반드시 퇴근 후 행사에 참석해야 합니다.
어휘 cautiously 조심스럽게, 신중하게 exactly 정확하게 predominantly 주로, 대개

9.
해석 출근 등록을 할 때 직원들은 지문 스캐너를 통해 신분을 입증해야 한다.
어휘 sign in (서명하여) 도착했음을 기록하다 fingerprint scanner 지문 스캐너 complete 완료하다, 완성하다; (서식 등을) 빠짐없이 작성하다 announce 발표하다, 알리다 display 전시하다, 진열하다; 드러내다, 보이다

10.
해석 다음 주 회의 일정은 잠정적으로 잡혀 있지만 자세한 사항은 고객에게 확인받아야 합니다.
어휘 detail 세부 사항 confirm 확인하다; 확정하다 vacant 비어 있는 steady 꾸준한, 지속적인 direct 직접적인; 직행의

11.
해석 그 지원자의 이전 직업은 고객 분석을 포함하고 있어서 마케팅 매니저 직무와 관련 있는 경력을 가지고 있습니다.
어휘 involve 포함하다, 관련시키다 relevant 관련된, 연관된 spacious 넓은 absolute 완전한, 철저한; 확실한, 확고한; 절대적인 entitled 자격이 되는

12.
해석 배달물이 올바른 장소에 도착할 수 있도록 고객들이 양식에 주소를 제대로 기입했는지 확인하십시오.
어휘 ensure 보장하다, 확실히 하다 input 입력하다 quickly 빠르게 secretly 비밀리에, 남모르게 originally 원래, 애초에

13.
해석 Bart Legal Firm의 최우선 사항은 고객 만족과 긍정적인 대외 이미지이다.
어휘 customer satisfaction 고객 만족(도) public 대중의, 공공의 consequence 결과 deal 거래, 합의; 취급, 대우 response 대답; 반응

14.
해석 지원서를 제출하고 나면 인사 부서에서 곧 연락이 갈 겁니다.
어휘 submit 제출하다 application 지원(서), 신청(서) lately 최근에 carefully 주의 깊게, 신중히 seemingly 겉보기에는; 보아하니

15.
해석 예비 투자자들은 주로 자동차 산업의 경기 침체를 우려했다.

어휘 **prospective** 장래의, 예비의; 기대되는, 가망 있는 **slowdown** 침체, 둔화 **automotive** 자동차의 **randomly** 무작위로 **proficiently** 숙련되게, 능숙하게 **diligently** 부지런히, 열심히

16.
해석 3년 이상 활동 내역이 없는 사용자 계정은 모든 개인 정보와 함께 삭제될 것입니다.

어휘 **rigorous** 철저한, 엄격한 **perishable** (음식이) 금방 상하는 **unable** ~할 수 없는

17.
해석 그 회사는 매출 목표를 초과한 직원 누구에게나 추가 휴가를 줄 것이다.

어휘 **exceed** 초과하다 **additional** 추가의 **assume** 가정[추측]하다; (직책을) 맡다 **donate** 기부하다 **deliver** 배달하다

18.
해석 3층에 있는 화재경보기는 건물 보수 후에 오작동하는 경향이 있다.

어휘 **fire alarm** 화재경보기 **malfunction** 오작동하다; 오작동 **renovation** 개조, 리모델링 **trend** 추세, 동향 **revenue** 수익 **pleasure** 기쁨, 즐거움

19.
해석 Sunshine Morning Radio에서는 지역 스포츠 스타 James Keaton과 단독 인터뷰를 할 것입니다.

어휘 **able** ~을 할 수 있는, 능력 있는 **eligible** 자격이 있는, 적임의 **impulsive** 충동적인

20.
해석 합병 아이디어가 처음에는 수익성이 있어 보였지만 Electronix는 그 제안을 철회하기로 결정했다.

어휘 **merger** 합병 **initially** 처음에 **lucrative** 수익성이 좋은 **proposal** 제안(서), 제의 **destroy** 파괴하다 **classify** 분류하다 **admit** 인정하다; 입장[가입]을 허락하다

CHAPTER 3   PART 6 장문 빈칸 채우기

문제 유형 및 풀이 전략

사무실 전체 정전 일정

1월 27일 월요일은 전 직원 131휴무입니다. 건물 내 전기는 오전 9시 30분에 차단되고 그날 저녁 중으로 다시 복구될 예정입니다. 정전 중에는 비상 조명 시스템이 132설치될 것입니다. 좀 더 구체적으로 말하면, 건물이 최신 규정에 충족되도록 눈에 띄는 출구 표지판과 예비 발전기가 추가될 예정입니다.

사무실 전체에서 모든 데스크톱, Wi-Fi 장치 및 기타 전기 기반 장치의 플러그를 뽑아 주십시오. 133또한, 냉장고에 있을 수 있는 개인 물품은 모두 치워 주시기 바랍니다. 134냉장고에 남은 식품은 모두 폐기됩니다. 궁금하신 점이 있으시면 건물 관리 책임자에게 문의해 주시기 바랍니다.

어휘 outage 정전 shut off (가스·수돗물·전기 등을) 차단하다 turn on 켜다 specifically 구체적으로 prominent 눈에 띄는 generator 발전기 meet the codes 규정을 충족하다 throughout 도처에 unplug (플러그를) 뽑다 equipment 장비, 장치 building maintenance 건물 관리

131. 태+시제
해설 빈칸 앞에 주어진 office는 닫는 행동을 할 수 있는 능동적인 주체가 아니므로 빈칸은 수동태여야 한다. 또한 바로 뒤 문장의 is scheduled to be shut off에서 미래에 예정된 일임을 알 수 있으므로 미래 시제를 사용한 (D)가 정답이다.

132. 동사 어휘
해설 바로 뒤의 문장에서 앞 문장의 내용을 구체화하고 있으며, 출구 표지판과 예비 발전기가 추가될(will be added) 것이라고 했으므로 빈칸에는 '설치'된다는 뜻의 단어가 알맞다.
(A) removed 제거될
(B) installed 설치될
(C) retrieved 회수될
(D) discontinued 중단될

133. 접속부사
해설 빈칸 앞의 내용을 보면 '전기 기반 장치의 플러그'의 연결 해제에 대한 내용이며, 빈칸 뒤에는 '냉장고에 있을 수 있는 개인 식품' 처리에 대한 내용이 이어진다. 따라서 첫 번째 행동 지침에 추가적인 행동 지침을 알리는 것이므로 '또한'이라는 뜻의 (A)가 정답이다.

134. 문맥에 맞는 문장 고르기
(A) 그 발전기는 비상시에 유용하게 쓰일 것입니다.
(B) 냉장고에 들어가는 음식에 라벨을 꼭 붙이세요.
(C) 냉장고에 남은 식품은 모두 폐기됩니다.
(D) 무료 간식은 직원 휴게실에서 제공될 것입니다.

어휘 prove 증명하다 label 라벨[꼬리표]을 붙이다 dispose of ~을 처리하다, ~을 없애다

UNIT 01 시제

본문 p.188

1. (A) **2.** (B) **3.** (A) **4.** (C) **5.** (C)
6. (D) **7.** (D) **8.** (D)

[1-2]

Artist Alley 여름 회화 강좌

Artist Alley는 이번 여름, 6월 3일부터 7월 27일까지 짧은 그림 강좌를 1개최할 예정입니다. 이 강좌는 작품으로 많은 국제적인 2상을 받은 지역 화가인 Cheryl Hicks가 이끌 것입니다. 그녀는 주로 풍경화에 초점을 맞추지만, 초상화나 정물화에도 경험이 있습니다.

이 과정은 매주 토요일 오전 10시부터 오후 12시까지 열릴 것입니다. 강좌에 등록하시려면, www.artistalley.com/summercourse로 등록하시거나 555-0125로 전화하셔서 담당자에게 직접 말씀하시기 바랍니다.

어휘 host 개최하다 dozens of 많은 landscape 풍경화 portrait 초상화 still life 정물화 take place 열리다 sign up 등록하다 register 등록하다 representative 담당자

1. 미래 시제
해설 바로 뒤에 이어지는 문장에서 The course will be led by...라고 하였으므로 미래에 있을 행사에 대한 내용임을 알 수 있다. 따라서 (A)가 정답이다.

2. 현재완료 시제
해설 강사의 이력을 소개하는 내용이므로 현재까지 많은 국제적인 상을 수상해 왔다는 의미의 현재완료 시제가 알맞다. 따라서 (B)가 정답이다.

[3-4]

수신인: Solar Solutions 전 직원
발신인: Riley Mendel
날짜: 8월 18일
제목: 승진

9월 1일자로 영업부장으로 승진하게 된 Josie Emerson에게 축하를 보냅니다. Ms. Emerson은 클리포드 대학을 졸업한 후 곧바로 Twin Solar에서 경력을 3쌓기 시작했습니다. 그녀는 지난 8년 동안 이곳 Solar Solutions에서 일하며 팀에 중요한 기여를 했습니다. 그녀의 강한 리더십 스킬과 다년간의 경험 덕분에, 우리는 Ms. Emerson이 그녀의 새로운 역할에서 4뛰어난 기량을 발휘할 것이라고 확신합니다. 기회가 되면 축하해 주세요.

Riley Mendel
인사부장

어휘 congratulate A on ~에 대해 A를 축하하다 immediately after ~한 후 바로 make a contribution to ~에 기여하다

3. 과거 시제
해설 Ms. Emerson이 현 직장에 다니기 전의 과거 이력을 이야기하고 있으므로 과거 시제가 알맞다. 따라서 (A)가 정답이다.

4. 미래 시제
해설 새로운 직위로 승진한 후 맡은 역할을 잘 해낼 것이라는 내용이므로 미래 시제가 알맞다. 따라서 (C)가 정답이다.

[5-6]

> 벌링턴은 Nation Magazine의 "Top Ten Towns"의 순위에 올랐습니다! 이 특별한 업적을 기념하기 위해, 8월 20일 토요일에 퍼레이드를 ⁵열 것입니다. 퍼레이드에 참여할 지역 기업, 학교, 음악 단체들을 ⁶초대합니다. 이벤트 기획자에게 문의하여 가입 방법을 알아보세요.
> 더불어 마을의 웹사이트를 방문해서 그날 계획된 활동들을 확인할 수 있습니다. 우리는 벌링턴의 모든 사람들이 나와서 함께 기념하기를 바랍니다.

어휘 make a list 순위에 오르다 acknowledge 인정하다, 감사를 표하다 achievement 업적, 성취 sign up 신청하다, 가입하다 rest 나머지 (the rest of the day 퍼레이드가 끝난 이후의 시간)

5. 미래 시제
해설 두 번째 문단 마지막 줄에서 벌링턴의 모든 사람들이 나와서 축하해 주기를 바란다고 했으므로 퍼레이드 개최는 미래의 일임을 알 수 있다. 따라서 미래 시제인 (C)가 정답이다.

6. 태 + 시제
해설 빈칸 앞의 주어는 초대되는 대상이므로 빈칸은 수동태이다. 또한 앞으로 진행될 퍼레이드에 대한 초대이므로 현재 시제인 (D)가 정답이다.

[7-8]

> 받는 사람: 영화 제작진
> 보낸 사람: Leslie Kamara
> 날짜: 6월 29일 수요일
> 제목: 동물보호소 장면 재촬영
>
> 제작진에게,
>
> 이 이메일은 이번 주 일요일 동물보호소 장면을 다시 ⁷촬영할 것임을 알려드리기 위함입니다. 동물들이 좀 제멋대로여서 우리가 필요한 정확한 장면을 찍을 수 없었으니, 이번에는 출연할 동물들을 직접 선택해 보도록 하겠습니다. 가능하면 정확히 오전 7시에 시작해서 점심시간 전에 최대한 많은 장면을 찍을 수 있었으면 좋겠습니다. 모든 것이 계획대로 된다면, 몇 시간 안에 끝날 것입니다. 하지만 시간이 더 걸릴 가능성도 있습니다.
> 또한 이건 제한된 촬영이라는 사실을 강조하고 싶네요. 촬영 장면과 직접 관련된 제작진들만 촬영장에 ⁸들어올 수 있습니다.
>
> Leslie Kamara
> Liberia Pictures

어휘 film crew 영화 제작진 reminder 다시 상기시키는 것 reshoot 재촬영하다 exact 정확한 unruly 제멋대로인, 다루기 힘든 go to plan 계획대로 되다

7. 미래 시제
해설 첫 번째 문단 두 번째 줄에서 but this time we will try...라고 했으므로 이번 일요일에 재촬영할 예정임을 알 수 있다. 따라서 미래 시제인 (D)가 정답이다.

8. 미래 시제
해설 빈칸 앞에 주어진 '관련된 제작진'은 참여에 대한 허락을 받는 대상이므로 빈칸은 수동태이며, 앞으로 있을 촬영에 대한 것이므로 미래 시제를 사용한 (D)가 정답이다.

UNIT 02 어휘

본문 p.190

1. (C)	2. (B)	3. (B)	4. (B)	5. (C)
6. (C)	7. (D)			

1. 동사 어휘

> 5월 2일부터 저희 가게는 셀프 계산기를 ¹설치할 예정입니다. 이로 인해, 계산대 6개 중 2개는 셀프 계산대로 바뀔 것입니다. 기계에서 현금이나 카드로 결제가 가능하며, 영수증은 거래가 완료되는 대로 출력됩니다.

어휘 self-checkout machine 셀프 계산대 cash 현금 receipt 영수증 transaction 거래

(A) closing 닫을
(B) refurbishing 새로 꾸밀
(C) installing 설치할
(D) replacing 교체할

2. 동사 어휘

> 5월 18일부터 Lowell Bridge 북쪽의 모든 도로에서 오전 12시부터 6시까지 야간 주차가 ²금지될 것입니다. 이것은 다가오는 새로운 기차역 건설로 인한 것입니다. 이 거리에 주차된 차량은 경고 없이 즉각 견인될 것입니다.

어휘 overnight 야간 upcoming 다가오는, 곧 있을 construction 공사 vehicle 차량 tow away ~을 견인하다 without further notice 추가인 공지 없이

(A) permitted 허용될
(B) prohibited 금지될
(C) reserved 보존될
(D) reviewed 검토될

3. 형용사 어휘

> 공연 티켓을 처음 교환할 때는 수수료가 부과되지 않습니다. 그러나 ³이후 교환 시 티켓당 7달러의 수수료가 부과됩니다.

어휘 exchange 교환하다 performance 공연 charge 청구하다 incur 발생하다, 초래하다

(A) urgent 급박한, 긴급한
(B) subsequent 그 다음의, 차후의
(C) frequent 빈번한, 잦은
(D) upcoming 다가오는

4. 명사 어휘

> 기록에 따르면 귀하는 지난 3년간 National Society of Realtors의 회원이었습니다. ⁴후원에 감사드리며 이 그룹의 일원이 됨으로써 얻게 되는 혜택을 누리고 계시기를 바랍니다.

어휘 according to ~에 따르면 benefit 혜택

(A) patience 인내심
(B) expertise 전문 지식
(C) patronage 후원
(D) referral 소개, 추천

5. 형용사 어휘

> 성수기가 다가옴에 따라 직원들이 Toledo Inn의 휴가 정책을 기억하는 것이 중요합니다. 우리는 직원들이 최소 2주 전에 자신의 직속 상사에게 휴가를 신청해 줄 것을 요청합니다. 상사는 개별 부서의 필요에 따라 휴무 허용 여부를 결정할 것입니다. 또한 10일 이상 연속 휴무는 ⁵추가 승인이 필요할 수 있습니다.

어휘 approach 다가오다 time off 휴가 immediate supervisor 직속 상사 in advance 미리 consecutive 연속의 approval 승인

(A) widespread 광범위한
(B) prior 사전의
(C) additional 추가의
(D) strong 강한

[6-7]

> Legal Matters: 법조인들을 위한 월간 잡지
>
> 올해의 첫 호는 최근에 법조계에서 경력을 ⁶시작한 사람들을 조명할 것입니다. 법조계에서 일하는 것은 쉬운 일이 아니며, 우리는 이제 막 그 직업에 뛰어든 사람들을 특집으로 하고 싶습니다. 로스쿨을 갓 졸업했든 아니면 다른 분야에서 전환을 하였건 간에, 저희는 당신의 이야기를 듣고 싶습니다.
>
> 이 진로를 선택한 이유를 1,000자 내외로 상세히 기술하여 ⁷제출해 주십시오. 11월 10일까지 features@legalmatters.com으로 원고를 보내주시면 저희 잡지에 실릴 기회를 얻을 수 있습니다.

어휘 highlight 강조하다 be no easy feat 쉬운 일이 아니다 feature 특별히 포함하다 transition 옮기다 specialty 전문 분야, 전공 detail 상세히 알리다

6. 동사 어휘

(A) revived 부활시켰다
(B) paused 잠시 멈췄다
(C) begun 시작했다
(D) left 떠났다

7. 명사 어휘

(A) review 논평, 보고서
(B) notice 공지, 공고문
(C) letter 편지
(D) submission 제출 원고[서류], (서류나 제안서 등의) 제출

UNIT 03 접속부사

본문 p.192

1. (A)   **2.** (C)   **3.** (C)   **4.** (D)

1. 인과

> (10월 18일)—패스트푸드 체인 Burgers For Us는 Robert Green이 새로운 부사장으로 임명되었다고 발표했다. Mr. Green은 지난 8년 동안 경쟁 패스트푸드 체인인 Tasty Tacos의 이사회 의장으로 일했었다. ¹따라서, 그는 패스트푸드 산업이 어떻게 돌아가고 대형 프랜차이즈를 어떻게 운영해야 하는지에 대한 풍부한 정보를 가지고 있다.

어휘 appoint 임명하다 vice president 부사장 chairperson 의장 compete 경쟁하다 (a competing company 경쟁사) a wealth of information 풍부한 정보

(A) Therefore 따라서
(B) Surprisingly 뜻밖에
(C) Instead 대신
(D) As a reminder 다시 일러드리지만

2. 시간

> 5월 20일에 새 창고로 이전하면서 우리는 모두의 도움을 필요로 합니다. 이삿날에는 한 팀이 옛 부지에서 트럭에 적재할 것입니다. ²한편, 다른 팀은 새로운 부지에서 트럭들이 도착하면 하역할 것입니다. 다른 분들은 박스를 풀고 장비들을 정리해야 합니다. 만약 여러분이 주어진 일을 일찍 끝내면, 다른 팀들을 도와주세요. 모든 것이 옮겨진 후, 새로운 부지에서 피자 파티가 있으며 직원 모두 초대됩니다.

어휘 load a truck 트럭에 적재하다 assist 돕다

(A) Instead 대신
(B) Nevertheless 그럼에도 불구하고
(C) Meanwhile 한편
(D) Therefore 따라서

3. 관용 표현

> Easton Inc.는 최근 몇몇 유명 고객들을 유치하였으며, 이로 인해 보안이 그 어느 때보다도 중요해졌습니다. ³이를 고려하여 우리는 방문자 정책을 수정할 것입니다. 4월 8일부터 모든 방문객들은 보안 데스크에 등록해야 합니다.

어휘 take on 떠맡다, ~을 갖기 시작하다　high-profile 세간의 이목을 끄는

(A) Even if ~일지라도
(B) On the contrary 반대로
(C) In light of ~을 고려하여, ~에 비추어
(D) Rather than ~보다는

4. 관용 표현

> 최근 시장 점유율에 대한 연구는 나이지리아에서 상위 2개 가전 브랜드가 국제적인 회사라는 것을 밝혔냈습니다. 캐나다의 Bevin Appliances는 시장의 23퍼센트를, 미국의 Lancelot Inc.는 19퍼센트를 보유하고 있다. 고객들은 Bevin Appliances를 선택하는 가장 큰 이유가 제품의 내구성 때문이라고 말한다. ⁴한편, Lancelot Inc.의 고객들은 그 회사의 날렵한 디자인에 더 많이 매료된다. 두 브랜드 대표는 더 많은 고객에게 어필하고 저변을 넓힐 수 있는 방안을 모색하고 있다.

어휘 reveal 드러내다　appliance (가정용) 기기　hold 보유하다　durability 내구성　sleek (모양이) 날렵한　base 기반

(A) For example 예를 들어
(B) As a matter of fact 사실상
(C) In that case 그런 경우에
(D) On the other hand 한편, 반면

UNIT 04 문맥에 맞는 문장 고르기

본문 p.194

1. (C)　**2.** (B)　**3.** (D)　**4.** (B)

1.

> **Prinz Glassware**
> 포장을 위한 상품 준비
>
> 유리제품은 매우 깨지기 쉬우므로 모든 주문에 안전한 포장 자재를 사용하는 것이 중요합니다. 우리는 모든 고객에게 완벽한 제품을 공급하기 위해 노력합니다.
>
> 첫 번째 단계는 제품을 특수 설계된 상자에 넣어 제품에 대한 진동과 충격을 최소화하는 것입니다. 준비 중인 물품의 해당 상자 번호를 찾습니다. ¹이것은 용기의 밑면에서 찾을 수 있습니다. 다음으로, 상자를 더 큰 상자에 넣고, 빈 공간을 포장재로 채웁니다. 마지막으로 테이프를 붙여 상자를 봉하고 주소 라벨을 부착합니다.

> 만약 당신이 일하는 구역에 물자가 부족하다면, 매니저에게 알려서 더 많은 물자를 가져다 줄 수 있도록 하세요.

어휘 fragile 깨지기 쉬운　secure 안전한　endeavor 노력하다　flawless 흠 없는　minimize 최소화하다　vibration 진동　impact 충격　merchandise 물품, 상품　attach 부착하다　shortage 부족　supplies 용품

(A) 그들은 고품질 마감에 만족합니다.
(B) 조립하는 데 예상보다 시간이 더 걸렸습니다.
(C) 이것은 용기의 밑면에서 찾을 수 있습니다.
(D) 팀 리더가 당신을 그룹에 배치할 수 있습니다.

어휘 assembly 조립, 집회　underside 밑면　container 그릇, 용기

2.

> 직원들은 Talmage Inc.의 모든 전문성 개발 워크숍에 참여해야 합니다. 이를 통해 모든 직원들은 계속해서 필수적인 비즈니스 기술을 습득할 수 있습니다. 때로는 참석 의무에서 면제될 수 있습니다. 이 경우, 자신의 결석을 설명하는 양식을 작성해야 합니다. 해당 직원은 직속 상사의 서명과 함께 사유를 상세히 기재한 양식을 제출해야 합니다. 워크숍을 참석하지 못하더라도 배포된 유인물을 검토하는 데 시간을 할애해 주시기 바랍니다. ²이 자료들은 여러분의 역할에 상관없이 유익할 것입니다.

어휘 participate 참가하다, 참여하다　essential 필수적인　requirement 필요, 요건　waive 철회하다, 포기하다　absence 결석　immediate supervisor 직속 상사　handout 유인물

(A) 주제는 아직 정해지지 않았습니다.
(B) 이 자료들은 여러분의 역할에 상관없이 유익할 것입니다.
(C) 그럼에도 불구하고, 강사들은 많은 경험을 가지고 있습니다.
(D) 앞자리가 빨리 차는 것이 일반적입니다.

어휘 informative 유익한　nevertheless 그럼에도 불구하고　instructor 강사

3.

> 보낸 사람: Rina Honda 〈r.honda@sweepstakes.com〉
> 받는 사람: Florence Dalton 〈florence_d@jmail.com〉
> 제목: 축하합니다!
>
> Ms. Dalton께,
>
> 귀하께서 이번 달 500달러 Shopping Spree Sweepstakes 당첨자임을 알려드리기 위해 이 메일을 씁니다! Grand Sphere Mall의 모든 단지에서 사용 가능한 상품권을 상품으로 보내드리겠습니다. ³사용 전에 상품권을 온라인으로 등록하는 것을 잊지 마십시오.
>
> 경품에 등록할 때 제출한 주소로 상품권이 발송됩니다. 영업일 기준 3~4일 정도면 도착할 것으로 예상됩니다.
>
> 다시 한 번 축하드리고 즐거운 쇼핑하시기 바랍니다!
>
> Rina Honda
> Sweepstakes.com 관리자

어휘 shopping spree 물건을 왕창[흥청망청] 사는 것   sweepstakes (건 돈을 승자에게 모두 주는) 복권   gift certificate 상품권   valid 유효한   register 등록하다

(A) 대회 규칙은 당사 웹사이트의 FAQ 섹션에서 확인할 수 있습니다.
(B) 심사받기 위해서는 마감일 전에 출품작을 제출하세요.
(C) 경품 행사는 18세 이상이면 누구나 참가할 수 있습니다.
(D) 사용 전에 상품권을 온라인으로 등록하는 것을 잊지 마십시오.

4.

> 런던 (2월 10일)—Meyers Motors는 연례 보고서에서 SuperBike 200의 판매량이 회사의 예상을 뛰어넘었다고 밝혔다. CEO Madeline Meyers에 따르면, 이 새로운 오토바이의 성공에 두 가지 주요 요인이 기여했다. 첫째, 매끈한 디자인이 다양한 색상으로 제공된다. ⁴이 눈길을 끄는 디자인은 젊은 오토바이 운전자들에게 인기 있다. 둘째, 할인된 판매가격이 모든 고객에게 매력적이다. 고품질의 차량임에도 불구하고, 이 오토바이는 놀라울 정도로 저렴한 가격에 제공되고 있다. 이러한 특성들이 SuperBike 200을 시중에 나와 있는 유사한 오토바이와 차별화하는 요인이다.

어휘 annual 연간의   sales 판매량   surpass 능가하다   expectation 기대, 예상   major 중요한   contribute to ~에 기여하다   sleek (모양이) 날렵한   high-quality 고품질의   set A apart from ~로부터 A를 차별화하다

(A) 그 오토바이는 동급 오토바이의 약 절반 가격이다.
(B) 이 눈길을 끄는 디자인은 젊은 오토바이 운전자들에게 인기 있다.
(C) Meyers Motors는 1977년에 설립되었다.
(D) 오토바이를 탈 때는 항상 헬멧을 착용하세요.

어휘 eye-catching 눈길을 끄는   be popular with ~에게 인기가 있다

ACTUAL TEST ❶   본문 p.196

1. (B)	2. (C)	3. (A)	4. (B)
5. (C)	6. (C)	7. (D)	8. (B)
9. (A)	10. (D)	11. (C)	12. (C)
13. (D)	14. (B)	15. (B)	16. (D)

[1-4]

> The Willow Theater의 보수 공사가 완료되었음을 알려드리게 되어 자랑스럽게 생각합니다. 이 역사적인 장소는 수십 년 동안 운영되어 왔고 많은 사람들에게 사랑 받고 있습니다. 이번 주 금요일, 극장이 다시 성대한 개장을 맞이합니다. 표가 조기에 매진될 것으로 예상하므로 표를 미리 구매하는 것을 ¹권합니다.
>
> 즐겁고 기억에 남는 극장 경험을 할 수 있도록 저희는 항상 최선을 다합니다. 하지만 이 극장은 야외극장이기 때문에 공연이 항상 예정대로 진행된다고 장담할 수는 없다는 ²것을 이해해 주시기 바랍니다. 악천후인 ³경우 관람이 취소될 수 있습니다. 취소된 행사의 티켓 소유자는 환불을 요청하거나 다른 이벤트 티켓으로 교환할 수 있습니다. ⁴그렇게 할 때, 확인 번호를 준비해 주시기 바랍니다. 이를 통해 우리 직원이 주문 확인을 쉽게 할 수 있을 겁니다.

어휘 historic 역사적인   in operation 운영되는   ensure 보장하다   go forward 진전되다   inclement (날씨가) 궂은   ticket-holder 표 구매자

1. 수 일치+태
해설 빈칸 앞에는 복수 주어 We가 제시되어 있고, 뒤에는 목적어로 동명사가 있으므로 빈칸에는 복수 동사 능동태가 들어가야 한다. 따라서 (B)가 정답이다.

2. 명사절 접속사 that
해설 빈칸 앞에는 명령문의 형태로 목적어가 없는 불완전한 문장이 제시되어 있으므로 빈칸은 뒤에 이어지는 완전한 문장을 목적어절로 연결할 수 있는 접속사 자리이다. 따라서 (C)가 정답이다.

3. 전치사
해설 빈칸 뒤에 [형용사+명사]가 오므로 선택지 중 전치사로 끝나는 (A), (C), (D)가 정답 후보이며, 맥락상 '악천후인 경우'에 대한 내용을 언급해야 하므로 정답은 (A)이다.

4. 문맥에 맞는 문장 고르기
(A) 공연자들에 대한 안내 책자를 가져갈 수 있습니다.
(B) 그렇게 할 때, 확인 번호를 준비해 주시기 바랍니다.
(C) 피드백을 공유하고자 한다면 귀하의 의견을 듣고 싶습니다.
(D) 예를 들어, 가운데 부분의 좌석은 빠르게 채워지는 경향이 있습니다.

[5-8]

> 받는 사람: Olivia Bowen
> 보낸 사람: Cook-Right
> 날짜: 4월 30일
> 제목: 멤버십 확인
>
> Ms. Bowen께,
>
> Cook-Right를 선택해 주셔서 감사합니다! 당신의 1년 회원권으로 수천 가지 요리법에 ⁵접근할 수 있어 집에서 간편하게 식사를 만들 수 있습니다. 우리는 모든 조리법을 정확하게 하는 것을 목표로 하고 있으며, 사람들이 개인 ⁶취향에 따라 요리할 수 있도록 대체 재료를 제안하고자 노력합니다.
>
> Cook-Right는 저희 고객들의 피드백을 소중하게 생각합니다. ⁷따라서 사이트를 개선할 수 있는 방법을 알려주시길 권장하고 있습니다. 웹사이트에서 오류가 발견되면 Cook-Right 직원에게 제보해 주세요. ⁸그것은 가능한 한 빨리 수정될 것입니다.
>
> 요리를 즐기시길 바랍니다!
>
> Cook-Right 직원 일동

어휘 confirmation 확인   recipe 요리법   alternative 대안이 되는, 대체 가능한

5. 동사 어휘
(A) displace 대신하다
(B) inspire 영감을 주다
(C) access 접근하다
(D) predict 예견하다

6. 명사 자리
해설 빈칸 앞에는 형용사 individual이 있으며, 빈칸은 전치사 to 의 목적어 자리에 위치한 명사 자리이다. 따라서 (C)가 정답이다.

7. 접속부사
(A) Meanwhile 한편
(B) Additionally 추가적으로
(C) Subsequently 그 뒤에
(D) Therefore 따라서

8. 문맥에 맞는 문장 고르기
(A) 그것은 매주 월요일에 다운로드 받을 수 있습니다.
(B) 그것은 가능한 한 빨리 수정될 것입니다.
(C) 그것은 상품권으로 교환될 수 있습니다.
(D) 그것은 좋은 평가를 받았습니다.

[9-12]

수신인: Chinua Alvarez
발신인: The Fabulous Florist
날짜: 5월 16일
제목: 개장

Ms. Alvarez께,

저희는 The Fabulous Florist가 중심가 지역으로 사업을 확장한다는 것을 알려드리게 되어 ⁹기쁘며, 다음 주말에 열리는 그랜드 오픈에 함께해 주시기를 바랍니다. 우리는 가장 신선하고 향기로운 꽃을 판매하는 것으로 유명합니다. 저희는 다양한 종류의 장미, 데이지, 카네이션 등을 제공합니다. ¹⁰우리는 또한 다양한 색깔의 꽃들을 판매합니다.

개장 기념으로 모든 ¹¹고객에게 75달러 이상 구매 시 10%를 할인해 드리고 있습니다. ¹²게다가, 모든 방문객들은 입장할 때 흰 장미 씨앗이 든 봉지를 무료로 받게 됩니다. 거기서 뵙기를 바랍니다!

The Fabulous Florist 팀

어휘 announce 발표하다 expand 확장하다 midtown (도심지와 시 외곽 사이의) 중간 지대 be known for ~으로 유명하다 a wide variety of 다양한 carry (가게에서 품목을) 취급하다 seed 씨앗 upon entry 입장할 때

9. 형용사 자리
해설 'be happy to 동사원형'은 '~하게 되어 기쁩니다'라는 뜻이다. 따라서 (A)가 정답이다.

10. 문맥에 맞는 문장 고르기
(A) 우리 가게의 대부분의 꽃은 조화입니다.
(B) 이렇게 빨리 문을 닫게 되어 죄송합니다.
(C) 저희가 가게를 운영하는 게 처음이라 굉장히 기대됩니다.
(D) 우리는 또한 다양한 색깔의 꽃들을 판매합니다.

11. 명사 어휘
(A) clients 의뢰인들
(B) employees 직원들
(C) customers 손님들
(D) drivers 운전자들

12. 접속부사
(A) However 하지만
(B) Unfortunately 불행히도
(C) Additionally 추가적으로, 게다가
(D) Therefore 따라서

[13-16]

부동산 시장의 기복을 따라가기가 어렵다고 생각하시나요? 가격이 매달 ¹³변동하기 때문에 정기적으로 부동산 가격을 확인해야 합니다. 이것은 집을 사거나 파는 사람들에게만 권장되는 것이 아닙니다. 보험에 있어서도 유용하죠. 예를 들어, 예상보다 넓은 보험 혜택 범위가 필요할 수 있습니다.

저희 Home Helpers에 맡겨 주세요. ¹⁴저희가 제공하는 평가 과정은 쉽고 저렴합니다. 단지 95달러의 저렴한 요금으로 예약을 하세요. 저희 직원 중 한 명이 방문한 후, 전체 보고서를 받으실 수 있습니다. 이 보고서는 여러분의 집의 가치와 그 가치를 증가시키기 위해 여러분이 ¹⁵어떤 변화를 줄 수 있는지에 대한 세부 정보를 제공할 것입니다. 지금 바로 555-4986으로 전화하시면 시작할 수 있습니다. 여러분의 필요 사항을 ¹⁶파악하기 위해 몇 가지 초기 질문을 드리겠습니다.

어휘 ups and downs 기복 property 부동산, 소유 value 평가하다 insurance 보험 coverage 보상 범위 appointment 예약, 약속 figure 수치 initial 초기의, 처음의

13. 동사 어휘
(A) measure 측정하다
(B) display 진열하다
(C) continue 계속하다
(D) fluctuate 변동하다

14. 문맥에 맞는 문장 고르기
(A) 그들 대부분은 그 결과에 놀랍니다.
(B) 저희가 제공하는 평가 과정은 쉽고 저렴합니다.
(C) 부동산 중개인이 주택 사진을 찍을 것입니다.
(D) 대출 절차는 혼란스러울 수 있습니다.

15. 한정사
해설 빈칸 앞의 내용을 확인하면 등위접속사 and에 이어서 전치사 about의 목적어로 올 명사 자리라는 것을 알 수 있으며, 명사 changes를 수식하는 한정사 역할을 하는 동시에 명사절을 이끌 수 있는 것은 what밖에 없으므로 (B)가 정답이다.

16. to부정사 (부사 역할)
해설 빈칸 앞에서는 완전한 문장이 제시되므로 빈칸은 부사 역할이

라는 것을 알 수 있다. 따라서 부사 역할을 하는 to부정사인 (D)가 정답이다.

ACTUAL TEST ②
본문 p.200

1. (C) 2. (A) 3. (A) 4. (B)
5. (C) 6. (B) 7. (B) 8. (D)
9. (A) 10. (C) 11. (A) 12. (D)
13. (B) 14. (A) 15. (D) 16. (C)

[1-4]

받는 사람: Sharon Devi
보낸 사람: Justin Kumar
날짜: 3월 8일
제목: 지연에 대한 보상

Ms. Devi께,

3월 1일 오후 10시 5분 출발 예정이었던 Bluestar Air 754편에 대한 귀하의 불만을 접수했습니다. 비행기가 [1]연착된 것에 대해 사과드립니다. Bluestar Air가 이로 인해 발생한 문제에 대해 보상해 드릴 것입니다. 원래 티켓 가격의 50%를 귀하의 계좌로 [2]환불해 드리겠습니다. 비행기 연착으로 인해 어쩔 수 없이 묵어야 했던 호텔[3]로부터 받은 확인 가능한 영수증 사본을 첨부하여 이 이메일로 답장해 주신다면, 호텔 방의 전체 가격 또한 환급해 드리겠습니다. [4]환불이 완료되기까지 영업일 기준 3일을 기다려 주십시오.

이해해 주셔서 감사합니다.

Justin Kumar
Bluestar Air 고객 서비스

어휘 complaint 불만 depart 출발하다 apologize 사과하다 compensate 보상하다 verifiable 입증할 수 있는 be forced to do 어쩔 수 없이 ~하다 reimburse 환급하다

1. 수동태
해설 빈칸 앞에 위치한 주어 flight는 연착되는 대상이므로 빈칸은 수동태가 되어야 한다. 따라서 정답은 (C)이다.

2. 동사 어휘
(A) refund 환불하다
(B) allocate 할당하다
(C) secure 확보하다
(D) offset 상쇄하다

3. 전치사
해설 빈칸은 명사 앞 전치사 자리이다. 문맥상 호텔에서 받은 영수증을 요청하고 있으므로 (A)가 정답이다.

4. 문맥에 맞는 문장 고르기
(A) 즐거운 여행이 되길 바랍니다.
(B) 환불이 완료되기까지 영업일 기준 3일을 기다려 주십시오.
(C) 귀하의 불만 사항이 경영진에게 전달되었습니다.

(D) 귀하의 개선 제안에 감사드립니다.

[5-8]

받는 사람: Sheri Tate
보낸 사람: Gloria Gibson
날짜: 5월 21일
제목: Lowrie Bank로부터의 은행 대출

Ms. Tate에게,

Lowrie Bank를 대표하여 귀하의 카페 사업 대출 요청이 승인되었음을 알려드립니다. 영업일 기준 3-5일 이내에 귀하의 거래 계좌에 착수금이 입금된 것을 [5]확인하실 수 있을 것입니다.

[6]논의한 것처럼, 보통 그렇게 많은 대출을 승인하지는 않습니다. 이는 외식업이 전반적으로 사업 위험성이 높기 때문입니다. 그러나 귀사의 사업 [7]안정성은 장기적인 재무 기록과 회사의 훌륭한 평판을 통해 잘 입증되었습니다. [8]게다가, 귀하가 상업용 빌딩을 소유하고 있기 때문에, 이 귀중한 자산을 통해 대출의 안전성을 한층 더 높일 수 있었습니다. 첫 번째 대출금 상환일은 7월 1일입니다.

질문이 있으시면 주저하지 마시고 제게 연락 주십시오.

Gloria Gibson
대출 담당자, Lowrie Bank

어휘 on behalf of ~을 대신하여 business loan 사업 대출 deposit 착수금, 보증금, 예치금 business day 영업일 in general 보통, 대개 demonstrate 보여주다 reputation 평판 establishment 기관, 설립 loan payment 대출[융자] 상환금 hesitate 망설이다, 주저하다

5. 동사 자리
해설 빈칸 앞에 주격 대명사 You가 있고 빈칸 뒤에는 목적어가 있으므로 빈칸은 동사 자리임을 알 수 있다. 내용상 입금이 완료된 상태가 아니므로 (C)가 정답이다.

6. 문맥에 맞는 문장 고르기
(A) 확실히, 메뉴에 있는 음식은 건강하고 맛있습니다.
(B) 논의한 것처럼, 보통 그렇게 많은 대출을 승인하지는 않습니다.
(C) 은행 직원은 모든 기록을 기밀로 유지해야 합니다.
(D) 고객들은 그들의 예금 계좌에서 이자를 받을 수 있습니다.

7. 명사 자리
해설 빈칸 앞에는 소유격 business'가 있고 빈칸 뒤에는 be동사가 있으므로, 빈칸은 주어 역할을 하는 명사 자리이다. 따라서 명사인 (B)가 정답이다.

8. 접속부사 (부가)
(A) As a result 결과적으로
(B) Unfortunately 유감스럽게도
(C) Conversely 정반대로, 역으로
(D) In addition 게다가

[9-12]

> GameShop이 다가오는 연휴를 맞아 단기 직원을 모집합니다. 비디오 게임에 대한 열정과 깊은 지식을 가진 사람이라면 누구나 지원하기 [9]바랍니다. 업무는 [10]주로 손님맞이, 제품 설명, 추천 등이 포함됩니다. [11]또한 때때로 상품을 정리하라는 요청을 받을 수도 있습니다. 저희는 마음이 따뜻하고 시간을 엄수하는 사람들을 팀에 채용하려고 합니다. 신청하려면 [12]당사 웹사이트 gameshop.com/apply를 확인하십시오. 신청 마감일은 11월 1일입니다.

어휘 upcoming 다가오는 duty 업무 deadline 마감일

9. 태+시제
해설 빈칸은 동사 자리이며, 주어는 Anyone이므로 지원하도록 권고되는 대상이다. 따라서 encourage(권고하다)의 수동태이며 현재 시제인 (A)가 정답이다.

10. 부사 어휘
(A) exceptionally 유난히, 특별히
(B) heavily 심하게, 아주 많이
(C) mainly 주로
(D) considerably 상당히

11. 문맥에 맞는 문장 고르기
(A) 또한 때때로 상품을 정리하라는 요청을 받을 수도 있습니다.
(B) 저희 가게는 오전 10시부터 오후 10시까지 영업합니다.
(C) GameShop은 West Garden Mall 3층에 있습니다.
(D) 우리는 게임 외에 피규어도 판매합니다.

어휘 occasionally 가끔 figurine 작은 조각상, 피규어

12. 소유한정사 자리
해설 명령문에서 동사 뒤 목적어로 웹사이트가 제시되고, 빈칸이 그 앞에 제시되므로 빈칸은 소유한정사 자리이다. 따라서 소유한정사인 (D)가 정답이다.

[13-16]

> 캐머런 카운티 (9월 9일)—지난 1년 동안 캐머런 카운티의 [13]고용률이 4.7% 증가하면서 6,000개 이상의 일자리가 창출되었다. 소매업이 가장 큰 증가폭을 [14]보였고, 서비스업 일자리가 두 번째로 큰 증가폭을 보였다. 의료 직업은 3위를 차지했는데, 이것은 지역사회의 증가하는 노인 의료 수요 때문일 수 있다. [15]사무직이 꼴찌이긴 하지만 역시나 큰 폭의 증가율을 보였다. 시장 분석가 Edward McKenzie는 "고용시장이 이런 긍정적인 흐름을 이어간다면 캐머런 카운티로 [16]이주하는 사람들이 점점 늘어날 것"이라고 전망했다.

어휘 sector 부문 healthcare 의료 eldercare 노인 의료 community 공동체 market analyst 시장 분석가

13. 명사 어휘
(A) birth 출생, 출산
(B) employment 고용
(C) education 교육
(D) turnover 매출량, 총 매상고, 이직률

14. 과거 시제
해설 빈칸의 앞에 주어인 명사가 있고, 뒤에는 목적어인 명사가 있으므로 빈칸은 동사 자리이다. 앞서 고용률이 증가했다는 것에 대한 부가적인 설명이므로 과거 시제인 (A)가 정답이다.

15. 문맥에 맞는 문장 고르기
(A) 주민들은 인프라에 더 많은 돈이 쓰여야 한다고 생각한다.
(B) 그럼에도 불구하고 고용 시장은 완전히 회복되지 못했다.
(C) 지난달에 의료계의 평균 시급은 제자리걸음을 했다.
(D) 사무직이 꼴찌이긴 하지만 역시나 큰 폭의 증가율을 보였다.

어휘 infrastructure 공공 기반 시설 earnings 소득, 수입 significant 중요한

16. 동사 어휘
(A) advancing 진전하는
(B) delegating 위임하는
(C) migrating 이주하는
(D) inspecting 점검하는

CHAPTER 4   PART 7 독해

PART 7 질문 유형별 풀이 전략

[notice (공지)]   본문 p.208

> 애디슨 커뮤니티 벼룩 시장
>
> 애디슨시는 이번 주말에 어린이 놀이터 옆에 위치한 아버 파크 레크리에이션 센터에서 반 년에 한 번 열리는 지역사회 벼룩 시장을 개최할 예정입니다. 벼룩 시장은 8월 13일 토요일 오전 9시부터 오후 6시까지, 그리고 8월 14일 일요일 오전 11시부터 오후 6시까지 열립니다. 애디슨 주민이 아니더라도 모두 환영합니다.
>
> 벼룩 시장은 바비큐 장비, 의류, 보석류, 식물 등과 같은 다수의 물건들을 선보일 것입니다. 수익금은 지역 학교의 무료 점심 급식 프로그램에 쓰일 것입니다.
>
> 판매에 앞서, 우리는 모든 종류의 기증품을 접수할 것입니다. 물건은 상태가 깨끗하거나, 새것이거나 사용감이 별로 없으면 됩니다. 기증품은 다음의 기간 동안 레크리에이션 센터에서 접수됩니다:
>
> 월요일부터 수요일: 오전 9시부터 오후 4시
> 목요일: 오후 1시부터 10시
> 금요일: 오후 1시부터 4시

어휘 community 지역사회 garage sale 벼룩 시장, 중고 물품 판매 biannual 연 2회의 next to 바로 옆의 take place 열리다, 발생하다 feature 특징으로 하다 a wide array of 다수의 goods 물품, 상품 grill 그릴에 굽다 jewelry 보석류 plant 식물 proceeds 수익금, 돈 donation 기부, 기증 object 물건

1.
행사에 대한 사실은 무엇인가?
(A) 1년에 한 번 열린다.
(B) 어린이들에게 초점을 맞출 것이다.
(C) 누구나 참여할 수 있다.
(D) 참가비가 부과될 것이다.

2.
벼룩 시장의 수익금에 대해 시사된 것은 무엇인가?
(A) 금액이 많을 것으로 예상된다.
(B) 어린이 놀이터에 필요하다.
(C) 센터 수리에 사용될 것이다.
(D) 음식을 제공하는 데 쓰일 것이다.

3.
저녁에 기증품을 전달할 수 있는 요일은 언제인가?
(A) 월요일
(B) 수요일
(C) 목요일
(D) 금요일

❶ 주제/목적/대상 문제

[문제 미리보기]   본문 p.210

> 오타와 (9월 3일)—전국에 있는 철물점에 전동 공구를 공급하는 공구 제조업체인 Cassidy Tools가 현 최고경영자가 물러난다는 사실을 오늘 확인해 주었다. 12년 동안 회사의 운영을 총괄해 온 Shannon Watson 씨는 다음 달에 은퇴할 계획이다. 그녀는 현 최고재무책임자인 Rick Saunders 씨로 교체될 것이다.
>
> Saunders 씨는 "회사를 새로운 방향으로 이끌고 회사의 놀라운 제품을 선보이는 것에 대해 흥분됩니다."라고 말했다. 그는 특히 회사의 새로운 공기 압축기인 Hale-90에 관심이 있는데, 그것은 강력하면서도 에너지 효율이 좋기 때문이다. 그는 그 제품에 대한 대대적인 광고 캠페인을 벌일 계획으로, 그것이 베스트셀러 제품이 되기를 기대하고 있다. Saunders 씨는 또한 숙련된 직원들의 이탈을 막기 위해 직장 환경을 개선하는 것도 목표로 하고 있다.

어휘 manufacturer 제조업체 supply 공급하다 hardware store 철물점 confirm 공식화하다, 확정하다 step down 물러나다, 사임하다 oversee 감독하다 operation 운영 go into retirement 은퇴하다 replace 대체하다, 교체하다 CFO 최고재무책임자(= chief financial officer) state 말하다, 진술하다 show off 뽐내다, 자랑하다 compressor 압축기 energy-efficient 에너지 효율적인 extensive 광범위한 aim 목표로 하다 workplace 직장, 작업장 retain 보유하다, 유지하다

Q.
기사는 왜 작성되었는가?
(A) 일부 공구에 대한 안전 조치를 설명하려고
(B) 사람들에게 지도부의 교체를 알리려고
(C) 체인점의 확장을 알리려고
(D) 회사의 성과를 강조하려고

패러프레이징 CEO, CFO → leadership

어휘 safety measures 안전 조치 inform A of B A에게 B를 알리다 leadership 지도부, 지도력 expansion 확대, 확장 highlight 강조하다 achievement 성과

빈출 유형 공략   본문 p.211

1. (C)   **2.** (B)

[letter (편지)]

> Sigler 씨,
>
> 우리는 12월 4일 토요일에 연례 기증자 감사 연회를 개최할 예정이며, 귀하께서 참석해 주시기를 바랍니다. 5가지 코스 요리로

이루어진 만찬에서 Kimberly Elias 관장이 지금까지 우리 박물관이 거둔 성과와 내년 계획에 대해 연설할 예정입니다.

Fred Mullins
Patterson 건축박물관 이사장

어휘 hold 열다, 개최하다 annual 연례의 donor 기부자, 기증자 appreciation 감사 banquet 만찬 director 책임자, 임원 give a speech 연설하다 facility 시설 accomplishment 업적 so far 지금까지 board 이사회

1.
편지의 목적은 무엇인가?
(A) 박물관의 변화를 알리기 위해
(B) 제안에 대해 감사를 표하기 위해
(C) 식사 초대를 하기 위해
(D) 건물에 대한 정보를 요청하기 위해

해설 주제/목적
Donor Appreciation Banquet에 참석해 달라는 목적을 말하고 있으므로 (C)가 정답이다. 그 다음 문장에 나오는 the five-course dinner도 단서가 된다.

패러프레이징 banquet → meal

어휘 extend an invitation 초대하다, 초대장을 보내다

[Web page (웹페이지)]

12월 5일부터 Pekka's Coat Factory에서 연례 겨울 코트 세일을 합니다.

저희의 연례 세일이 장안의 화제입니다. Pekka's의 제품들 중 여러분이 사랑해 주신 바람막이, 재킷, 코트, 그리고 플리스가 모두 세일 기간 동안 할인됩니다. 저희 매장의 거의 모든 품목이 최소 10% 할인되고, 일부 품목은 50%까지 할인됩니다. 너무 늦기 전에 매장에 들러 이번 겨울에 입을 완벽한 코트를 찾아보세요!

어휘 sale (할인) 판매, 세일 windbreaker 바람막이 fleece 플리스, 양털처럼 생긴 직물 discount 할인하다 at least 적어도, 최소한 item 물품, 품목 as much as ~ 정도까지 많이 make sure 확실히 하다 stop by 잠깐 들르다

2.
웹페이지의 목적은 무엇인가?
(A) 제품 부족을 설명하기 위해
(B) 곧 있을 행사를 광고하기 위해
(C) 상점의 개장을 알리기 위해
(D) 새로운 브랜드를 홍보하기 위해

해설 주제/목적
제목에 Winter Coat Sale이라는 행사가 나오고, 이어지는 내용에서 그 행사에 대해 언급하고 있으므로 (B)가 정답이다.

어휘 shortage 부족 upcoming 다가오는, 곧 있을

❷ NOT/True 문제

[문제 미리보기]

멕시코시티 (3월 3일)—이른 여름부터 멕시코시티의 주민들은 새로운 이동 수단을 갖게 된다. [2B] [2D] Move It 사는 시의 다양한 지역에서 저렴한 가격의 렌탈 자전거 서비스를 개시할 것이다. 스마트폰과 신용카드만 있으면 서비스를 시작할 수 있다. Move It 앱에서 자전거 한 대를 예약하고 일련번호가 일치하는 자전거를 찾은 후 출발하면 된다! [2C]공식 Move It 스테이션에 자전거를 반납하면 카드에 요금이 부과된다. [1]이러한 Move It 스테이션들은 시에서 인구가 많은 지역 주변에 전략적으로 배치될 것이다. "[2A]미국에서 성공을 거둔 후, 우리는 서비스를 확장하여 멕시코 사람들에게도 우리의 서비스를 즐길 수 있는 기회를 주기로 결정했습니다."라고 Move It 사의 최고경영자인 Matthew Ortega 씨가 말했다.

어휘 launch 출시하다, 개시하다 affordable 저렴한, (가격이) 알맞은 get started 시작하다 reserve 예약하다 app 애플리케이션 match 일치하다 serial number 일련번호 charge (비용을) 부과하다 station 정거장, 정류장 strategically 전략적으로 place 놓다, 두다 heavily populated 인구가 밀집한 expand 확장하다

1.
멕시코시티의 Move It 스테이션에 대해 암시된 것은 무엇인가?
(A) 상당히 넓다.
(B) 외딴 지역에 있다.
(C) 아직 지어지지 않았다.
(D) 각 거리에 위치해 있다.

어휘 spacious 넓은, 널찍한 isolated 외딴, 고립된

2.
Move It 사에 대해 나타나지 않는 것은 무엇인가?
(A) 멕시코시티에서 처음 시작했다.
(B) 사용자들이 자전거를 빌릴 수 있도록 해준다.
(C) 사람들이 서비스를 이용한 후에 요금을 부과한다.
(D) 합리적인 가격을 제공한다.

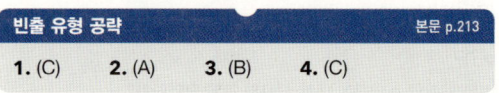

[notice (공지)]

Redmond Gardens 영화제

Redmond Gardens는 [1]최초의 야외 영화제를 기쁜 마음으로 발표합니다.

8월 8일 목요일 ~ 8월 11일 일요일

오후 6시부터 9시까지

[2B] [2C] 티켓은 1인당 5달러이며, 다음을 포함합니다:

탄산수 또는 커피와 현장 주차

> ²ᴰ지역 밴드들이 오후 6시부터 7시까지 공연을 한 뒤 영화가 상영될 것입니다.
> 기념품 영화 포스터는 매표소에서 개당 3달러에 판매됩니다.
> 더 많은 정보를 얻거나 티켓을 구입하려면
> www.redmondgardens.com을 방문하세요.

어휘 film festival 영화제 outdoor 야외의 include 포함하다 soda 탄산수 on-site 현지의, 현장의 perform 공연하다, 연주하다 screen 상영하다

1.
Redmond Gardens에 대해 사실은 무엇인가?
(A) 시에 의해 운영된다.
(B) 영화 제작자들에게 상을 준다.
(C) 전에 축제를 개최한 적이 없다.
(D) 매일 저녁 7시에 문을 닫는다.

해설 NOT/True
지문의 first-ever outdoor film festival에서 영화제가 처음으로 열린다는 것을 알 수 있으므로 (C)가 정답이다.

어휘 operate 운영하다 award 상 filmmaker 영화 제작자

2.
입장료에 포함되지 않은 것은 무엇인가?
(A) 포스터
(B) 음료
(C) 주차
(D) 음악 공연

해설 NOT/True
admission fee를 키워드로 지문을 검색한다. 지문의 Tickets are $5 per person이 admission fee에 해당하는데, 그 문장과 주변을 살펴보면 단서를 찾을 수 있다. Souvenir movie posters는 3달러에 유료 판매되므로 포스터는 입장료에 포함되지 않는다. 따라서 (A)가 정답이다.

패러프레이징 soda or coffee → beverage / Local bands will perform → Musical entertainment

어휘 beverage 음료 entertainment 오락, 연예

[e-mail (이메일)]

> Sullivan 씨,
> 저는 당신의 블로그를 읽는 것을 좋아합니다. ⁴ᴰ특히 당신이 직접 만든 장난감 아이디어가 마음에 들어요. ⁴ᴮ당신의 웹 사이트에 질의응답 페이지가 있기는 하지만, 당신의 조언만으로는 여전히 난감할 때가 있습니다. 예를 들어, ⁴ᴬ제가 당신의 월간 과학 실험 중 하나를 시도해 보고 있었는데, 재료 하나를 빠뜨렸다는 것을 깨달았어요. 저는 어찌할 바를 몰랐어요. 다행히도 다른 웹 사이트의 댓글들을 검색해서 좋은 대체물을 찾을 수 있었습니다. ³그렇기 때문에 당신의 웹페이지에 다른 사람들이 아이디어와 해결책을 공유하도록 하는 의견란이 있으면 좋을 것 같습니다.
> Wayne Hackett

어휘 homemade 손수 만든 puzzled 어리둥절한 conduct (특정 활동을) 하다 experiment 실험 miss 놓치다, 빠뜨리다 ingredient 재료 be at a loss 어찌할 바를 모르다 substitute 대체물, 대체자 comment 의견, 논평 section 부분 solution 해결책

3.
이메일의 목적은 무엇인가?
(A) 특정한 질문을 하려고
(B) 제안을 하려고
(C) 웹 사이트를 추천하려고
(D) 전문적인 서비스를 제공하려고

해설 주제/목적
주제 또는 목적은 보통은 문두에 나오지만, 짧은 지문의 경우 지문 전반에 걸쳐 나오기도 한다. 지문의 후반부에서 웹 사이트에 comments section을 추가할 것을 제안하고 있으므로 (B)가 정답이다.

어휘 specific 특정한, 구체적인 give a suggestion 제안하다 professional 전문적인

4.
Sullivan 씨의 블로그에 대해 시사되지 않은 것은 무엇인가?
(A) 과학 실험이 게시되어 있다.
(B) 질문에 답변을 해 준다.
(C) 연락 가능한 전화번호가 나와 있다.
(D) 사람들에게 장난감 만드는 법을 가르친다.

해설 NOT/True
웹페이지에 contact phone number(연락처 전화번호)가 있다는 내용은 없으므로 (C)가 정답이다.

패러프레이징 homemade toy ideas → how to make toys

어휘 display 보여 주다

❸ 추론/암시 문제

[문제 미리보기]   본문 p.214

> 스마트폰 애플리케이션 수익화 분석
> DW 컨설팅 작성
>
> **회사: Cardack Development**
> 앱 명칭: Fundamentalz
>
> 우리는 귀사의 스마트폰 애플리케이션의 수익을 낼 수 있는 가장 좋은 방법을 판단해 보았습니다. 아래 권장되는 방법 외에도, 참여를 늘리기 위해 앱에 질의응답 코너를 만드는 방법도 추천합니다. 사용자들은 전문가들로부터 해답을 얻을 수 있을 것입니다.
>
> 주요 권고 사항
>
> 월 구독료: 사용자 1인당 월 4.99달러 / 동영상 콘텐츠 숫자가 늘어도 요금에 변동 없음

어휘 application 애플리케이션, 앱 monetization 수익화, 이익 창출 analysis 분석 assess 평가하다, 가늠하다 in addition

to ~에 더하여, ~뿐만 아니라 method 방법 section 부분
engagement 참여 expert 전문가 primary 주요한, 주된
subscription 구독 expand 확대하다, 확장하다

Q.
Cardack Development에 대해 암시된 것은 무엇인가?
(A) 일일 1천 건의 조회 수를 받는다.
(B) 애플리케이션에 더 많은 동영상을 추가할 계획이다.
(C) 각각의 동영상을 보는 데 요금을 부과한다.
(D) 애플리케이션을 대대적으로 광고하고 있다.

어휘 view 보기, 조회 charge 부과하다 heavily 상당히, 과하게

빈출 유형 공략   본문 p.215
1. (B)   **2.** (C)

[article (기사)]

시외버스가 프로비던스에 오다

(1월 17일)—뉴욕시에 본사를 둔 Transpo 사는 프로비던스와 뉴욕시를 오가는 버스 노선을 개발하는 업무에 착수했다. 이 결정은 해당 노선에 대한 사람들의 요구가 증가함으로 인해 이루어졌다. 버스는 이미 뉴헤이븐과 올드 세이브룩 등 비슷하게 인기 있는 목적지에 정차하기 때문에 "그 결정은 쉬운 것이었습니다."라고 Transpo 사의 최고경영자인 Marilyn Baskerville 씨가 말했다. "새로운 버스 노선은 관광산업과 통근에 모두 중요할 것입니다."라고 그녀는 덧붙였다. 이같은 변화를 촉진하기 위한 새로운 버스 정류장 건설 공사는 올 봄 시작되어 가을까지 완공될 것으로 예상된다.

어휘 intercity 도시와 도시를 이동하는 undertake 하다, 착수하다 route 노선 make a decision 결정을 내리다 increasing 증가하는 public 대중의, 일반인의 similarly 비슷한 destination 목적지 tourism 관광산업 commute 통근하다 add 덧붙이다

1.
새로운 버스 정류장에 대해 암시된 것은 무엇인가?
(A) 여전히 자금 지원이 필요하다.
(B) 1년 내에 완성될 것이다.
(C) 두 개의 회사가 그것들을 건설하고 있다.
(D) 지역 주민들은 정류장 건설에 반대한다.

해설 추론/암시
마지막 문장에서 공사가 봄에 시작하여 가을에 끝난다고 했으므로 1년 내에 완성된다는 것을 알 수 있으므로 (B)가 정답이다.

어휘 fund 자금을 대다

[notice (공지)]

창업하기
6월 17일, 오후 2시 30분에서 오후 4시까지
시드니 커뮤니티 센터
창업을 원했던 적이 있나요? 그렇다면 정확히 어떻게 창업을 해야 하는지에 대한 워크숍에 참석해 보시기 바랍니다. 이번 워크숍은 HJ VentureWorks의 설립자 겸 최고경영자인 Vincent Norton 씨가 이끌 것입니다. 그는 성공적인 사업을 시작하고 운영하는 방법에 대한 자신의 전문 지식을 청중들과 공유할 것입니다.

행사에 등록하려면 www.sydneycc.co.au를 방문하세요. 워크숍은 무료이지만 사전 등록이 필요합니다. 간단한 다과가 제공될 것입니다.

어휘 business 사업, 업체 exactly 정확히 founder 설립자 share 공유하다, 나누다 expertise 전문 지식 audience 청중 register for ~에 등록하다 prior 사전의 registration 등록 refreshments 다과, 간식

2.
Vincent Norton은 누구이겠는가?
(A) 행사 주최자
(B) 정부 관리
(C) 사업주
(D) 동기 부여 연설자

해설 추론/암시
HJ VentureWorks라는 업체를 설립하고 경영하는 사람이라고 했으므로 (C)가 정답이다.

패러프레이징 founder, CEO → business owner

어휘 organizer 주최자, 조직자 motivational 동기 부여의

---

❹ 세부 사항 문제

[문제 미리보기]   본문 p.216

Reyes 씨,

귀하의 Reppert 12단 자전거에 관해 저희에게 연락 주셔서 감사합니다. 그 모델은 안전상의 이유로 리콜되었기 때문에 환불이 가능하다는 귀하의 말씀이 맞습니다. 저희는 귀하의 은행 거래 세부 정보와 구매 증명이 포함된 완성된 양식을 받았습니다. 저희는 귀하가 양식에 표시해 주신 은행 계좌로 환불 금액을 보내 드릴 것입니다. 저희 소매점에서 결함이 있는 자전거를 수거하고 있습니다. 만약 이것이 불편하시다면, 물품을 지역 재활용 센터로 가져가시거나, 대형 쓰레기 수거 처리를 하셔도 됩니다. 불편을 끼쳐 드려 죄송합니다.

Bessie Maddux
Lambert Sports 고객 서비스

어휘 correct 맞는, 정확한 be eligible for ~의 자격이 있다 refund 환불 recall 리콜하다, 회수하다 safety 안전 form 양식 proof 증거 purchase 구매 bank account 은행 계좌 indicate 나타내다, 표시하다 collect 모으다, 수거하다 faulty 결점이 있는, 불량한 retail store 소매점 item 물품, 품목 arrange 마련하다, 준비하다 bulky 부피가 큰 waste 쓰레기 inconvenience 불편 cause 야기하다, 일으키다

Q.
Maddux 씨는 Reyes 씨가 무엇을 할 수 있다고 말하는가?

(A) 양식의 다른 복사본 구하기
(B) 물품을 직접 폐기하기
(C) 업체의 매장 한 곳에 전화하기
(D) 수리 센터에 연락하기

어휘 dispose of ~을 처리하다, 처분하다

빈출 유형 공략 본문 p.217

1. (C)   **2.** (B)

[e-mail (이메일)]

발신: John Charon
수신: 전 직원
날짜: 4월 10일
제목: 새 바닥재

여러분,

여러분에게 Bailey's Construction이 우리 사무실의 2층에 새로운 바닥재를 설치할 거라는 사실을 상기시켜 드리고자 합니다. 그들은 라운지와 화장실의 바닥재를 교체하기 위해 수요일 아침에 건물 안으로 들어올 것입니다. 작업은 7시간에서 9시간 정도 계속될 것으로 예상됩니다. 약간의 차질이 있을 수도 있지만, 평소처럼 업무를 계속해 주시기 바랍니다.

John Charon

어휘 flooring 바닥재   remind 상기시키다   install 설치하다   last 지속되다, 계속되다   somewhere 대략, ~쯤   minor 사소한   disruption 방해, 장애   as usual 늘 그렇듯이, 평소대로

1.
수요일에 누가 건물을 방문할 것인가?

(A) 신규 고객
(B) 인테리어 디자이너
(C) 건물 리모델링 작업자들
(D) 케이블 전기 기사

해설 세부 사항
visit, Wednesday 등을 키워드로 지문을 검색하면 두 번째 문장에서 "They will be coming into the building on Wednesday morning ~"이라는 문장을 찾을 수 있다. 문장의 주어인 They는 바닥재를 설치하러 오는 Bailey's Construction의 직원들을 가리키므로 (C)가 정답이다.

어휘 client 고객   crew 팀, 반, 무리   electrician 전기 기사

[e-mail (이메일)]

수신: Determix 전 직원
발신: Chan Mao
날짜: 7월 31일
제목: 배송 오류

우리 고객 수십 명이 배송 정보를 입력할 때 문제를 겪었던 것 같습니다. 어제 우리 웹 사이트는 온라인으로 주문한 일부 고객들로부터 부분적인 데이터만 수집했습니다. 결과적으로, 그 고객들의 이메일 주소와 전화번호만 있고, 배송 주소가 없습니다. 여러분이 발송을 준비하다가 이 문제를 마주치게 되면 현장 관리자인 Kyle Stevenson 씨에게 연락하세요. IT 부서에서 문제를 해결하기 위해 노력하고 있습니다. 다행히도 그들이 다음 주에 시스템을 업그레이드한다고 하니, 다시는 이런 일이 발생하지 않기를 바라 봅니다. 그때까지 여러분의 협조에 감사드립니다.

어휘 shipping 발송, 배송   dozens of 수십의   issue 문제   input 입력하다   partial 부분적인   as a result 결과적으로, 그 결과   shipment 발송, 선적   come across 우연히 만나다   fix 고치다   appreciate 감사하다   cooperation 협조

2.
IT 부서는 언제 시스템을 업그레이드할 것인가?

(A) 7월
(B) 8월
(C) 9월
(D) 10월

해설 세부 사항
IT department, upgrade a system 등을 키워드로 지문을 검색하면 다음 주에 시스템을 업그레이드할 것이라는 내용이 나온다. 이메일의 날짜를 찾아보면 7월 31일이므로 다음 주는 8월이라는 것을 알 수 있다. 따라서 (B)가 정답이다.

---

❺ 문장 삽입 문제

[문제 미리보기] 본문 p.218

Huerta Enterprises 직원에게 알리는 공지

관리팀은 직원들의 안전과 우리 회사 운영의 보안을 개선하기 위해 즉각적인 조치를 취하고 있습니다. 우리는 인가를 받지 않은 사람들이 건물로 들어오는 것을 막는 것을 목표로 하고 있습니다. 3월 15일 월요일부터 직원들은 더 이상 후문을 이용할 수 없는데, 그 문은 항상 잠겨 있게 될 것입니다. 유일한 예외는 건물 안으로 자재를 나르는 유지보수 근로자들뿐입니다.

여러분의 관리자가 스캔이 되는 새로운 신분증을 제공할 것입니다. 우리는 3월 15일이 있는 그 주에 신분증을 수작업으로 확인하는데, 그것이 여러분이 사무실에 들어가는 데 걸리는 시간을 지연시킬 것입니다. 그 기간 동안에는 평소보다 조금 일찍 도착해 주세요. 그 다음 주에는 스캐너가 완전히 작동할 것입니다. 이같은 전환 기간 동안 인내해 주셔서 여러분께 감사드립니다.

어휘 take steps 조치를 취하다   immediate 즉각적인   privacy 프라이버시, 비밀   operation 운영   aim 목표로 하다   unauthorized 허가받지 않은   rear entrance 후문   at all times 항상   exception 예외   maintenance 유지, 보수   load 싣다   material 자재   supervisor 관리자, 감독   provide A

with B A에게 B를 제공하다　ID badge 신분증　scan 스캔하다
manually 손으로, 수동으로　delay 지연시키다　functional 작동
하는, 기능하는　appreciate 감사하다　patience 인내
transition 전환, 이전

Q.
[1], [2], [3], [4]로 표시된 위치 중 다음 문장이 들어가기에 가장 적절한 곳은?
"그 기간 동안에는 평소보다 조금 일찍 도착해 주세요."
(A) [1]
(B) [2]
(C) [3]
(D) [4]

빈출 유형 공략

본문 p.219

1. (A)　　**2.** (C)

[memo (회람)]

수신: 모든 직원
발신: Rodney Kolar
제목: 새 특집 기사
날짜: 2월 21일

많은 분들이 예상하셨듯이, 우리는 우리 신문의 주말판에 새로운 특집을 추가할 것입니다. 그것의 주된 목적은 지역 예술가들과 주민들의 사진을 집중적으로 다루는 것이 될 것입니다. 시내에 새로운 사진 박물관이 들어서게 되어 많은 주민들이 갑자기 그 예술 형태에 관심을 갖게 되었습니다. 위원회가 구성되어 사진을 선별할 것이며, Lisa Gould 씨가 편집을 담당할 것입니다. 우리는 여전히 신문의 이 섹션의 이름을 브레인스토밍하고 있으니, 여러분의 아이디어를 제게 제출해 주세요.

어휘 feature 특집 (기사)　speculate 추측하다, 짐작하다　edition (신문의) 판　townspeople 도시 주민　gain interest 관심을 갖다　introduction 도입, 소개　photography 사진 (촬영)　downtown 시내에　committee 위원회　edit 편집하다　brainstorm 브레인스토밍을 하다, 아이디어를 짜내다　section 부분, 난　submit 제출하다

1.
[1], [2], [3], [4]로 표시된 위치 중 다음 문장이 들어가기에 가장 적절한 곳은?
"그것의 주된 목적은 지역 예술가들과 주민들의 사진을 집중적으로 다루는 것이 될 것입니다."
(A) [1]
(B) [2]
(C) [3]
(D) [4]

해설 문장 삽입
주어진 문장의 주어인 Its main goal에서 it이 가리키는 것을 찾아야 한다. it은 신문 주말판의 특집이고, 주어진 문장의 '지역 예술가들과 주민들의 사진을 집중적으로 다루는 것'은 그것의 목적이므로

주어진 문장은 신문의 주말판이 언급된 다음인 [1]에 오는 것이 자연스럽다. 따라서 (A)가 정답이다.

어휘 main 주된, 주요한　goal 목표, 목적　highlight 강조하다

[letter (편지)]

Ledbetter 씨,

저희 기록에 따르면 귀하의 상업용 부동산 임대차 계약의 갱신 시기가 곧 다가옵니다. 다음 기간 동안 귀하의 임대료가 2% 인상됩니다. 임대차 계약을 갱신하려면 저희 웹 사이트를 방문하세요.

귀하의 현 임대차 계약의 세부 정보는 다음과 같습니다.
위치: 포플러 레인 4615번지　　규모: 4,000 평방피트
임대차 계약 종료: 11월 11일　　금액: 월 7,500달러
상태: 계약 갱신 여부 미정

저희는 식당 공간과 주방이 이미 설치된 가용 부동산이 있습니다. 귀하의 음식점이 아주 잘 되고 있으므로, 공간을 상향 조정하는 것을 고려해 보시는 게 어떨까요. 부동산을 둘러보고 싶으시다면 이메일이나 전화로 저희에게 연락하십시오.

Ashley Ramirez

어휘 record 기록　indicate 나타내다, 보여 주다　commercial 상업의　lease 임대차 계약　due ~하기로 되어 있는　renewal 갱신　rent 임대료　period 기간　detail 세부 사항　current 현재의　status 상태, 지위　pending 미정의, 계류 중인　available 이용 가능한　property 부동산　install 설치하다　contact 연락하다

2.
[1], [2], [3], [4]로 표시된 위치 중 다음 문장이 들어가기에 가장 적절한 곳은?
"귀하의 음식점이 아주 잘 되고 있으므로, 공간을 상향 조정하는 것을 고려해 보시는 게 어떨까요."
(A) [1]
(B) [2]
(C) [3]
(D) [4]

해설 문장 삽입
주어진 문장의 음식점, 공간 상향 조정 등과 관련 있는 문장이 앞이나 뒤에 나와야 한다. 따라서 이미 특정 조건들이 갖추어진 부동산이 있다고 말하는 문장의 뒤인 [3]에 오는 것이 적절하다.

❻ 동의어 찾기 문제

[문제 미리보기]

본문 p.220

수신: 미공개 수신인들
발신: mail@rightcook.com
날짜: 9월 1일
제목: Rightcook의 메시지

Rightcook 팀은 우리 웹 사이트가 성공하도록 도움을 준 여러분들께 감사를 드리고 싶습니다. 당사의 메일링 리스트에 등록하고 매일 우리의 새로운 콘텐츠를 확인함으로써, 여러분은 당

사의 사업이 인기를 얻는 데 중요한 역할을 해주셨습니다. 우리는 월간 페이지 조회수 목표인 100만 건을 달성했음을 알리게 되어 매우 기쁩니다. 우리는 앞으로 성장해 나가는 동안, 전문 요리사들에 의해 개발된 이색 요리법들을 여러분께 소개함으로써 여러분이 요리 실력을 향상시키고 저녁 식탁에 맛있는 것들을 올릴 수 있도록 돕기 위해 계속해서 열심히 노력하겠습니다.

Q.
첫 번째 단락, 다섯 번째 줄의 "reached"와 의미상 가장 가까운 것은?
(A) 연락하다
(B) 늘리다
(C) 달성하다
(D) 감동시키다

빈출 유형 공략
본문 p.221
1. (C)   **2.** (D)

[article (기사)]

스톡홀름 (5월 2일)—Excite Unlimited는 최근에 HJ Gaming과의 합병을 발표했다. 이전의 경쟁자들은 세계 확장으로 가는 길은 협력과 팀워크를 통해 가장 잘 만들어질 것으로 판단했다. "우리는 과거의 라이벌이지만, 우리 팀들의 역량을 결집하여 해외 시장 진출이 가능한 조직을 만들 수 있을 것이라는 데는 의심의 여지가 없습니다."라고 Excite Unlimited의 최고경영자인 Lars Anderson 씨가 말했다.
Excite Unlimited는 주로 콘솔 비디오 게임으로 알려진 반면, HJ Gaming은 PC 시장에서 이름을 알렸다. HJ Gaming의 최고경영자인 Anna Lindberg 씨는 합병에 대해 낙관적이다. "우리는 각각의 회사가 상대방의 약점을 보완하고 시장에서 최고의 비디오 게임을 개발할 수 있기를 희망합니다."라고 Lindberg 씨가 말했다.

어휘 recently 최근에 merger 합병 former 이전의, 예전의 competitor 경쟁자 path 길 expansion 확장 forge 만들다, 구축하다 there is no doubt that ~라는 것에 의심의 여지가 없다 combine 합치다, 결합하다 capable of ~할 수 있는 mostly 주로 make a name 유명해지다 optimistic 낙관적인 weak spot 약점

1.
첫 번째 단락, 두 번째 줄의 "path"와 의미상 가장 가까운 것은?
(A) 도로
(B) 대로
(C) 길, 방법
(D) 덧셈

해설 동의어 찾기
해당 단어를 찾아 표시하고, 그 단어의 바로 앞뒤를 확인해 본다. the path to global expansion은 '세계 확장으로 가는 길'이며, 여기서 path는 추상적인 의미의 '길' 또는 '방법'이라는 의미로 쓰였

다. 선택지에서 그러한 의미로 쓰이는 것은 way이므로 (C)를 정답으로 선택한다.

[letter (편지)]

Morelock 씨,
제 이름은 David Hallowell이고 올버니 공공사업부서의 감독관입니다. 앞으로 몇 달 동안 귀하가 계시는 지역에서 교통 조사가 실시될 예정임을 알려드리기 위해 글을 씁니다.
시의회는 귀하가 거주하는 지역의 주민들로부터 특히 아침과 저녁의 혼잡 시간대의 교통량 증가에 관해 수없이 많은 불만을 접수하고 있습니다. 우리 도시의 많은 청소년 인구를 고려했을 때, 이것은 안전에 대한 우려로 이어졌습니다. 이 문제를 완화하기 위한 방안으로, 시는 이면도로의 교통 방향을 바꾸는 정책을 시행하여 교통량에 미치는 영향을 조사하기로 결정했습니다. Dye Street, Cornell Avenue, 그리고 Jameson Way는 일방통행로로 전환될 것이지만, Golden Ridge Road는 양방향 도로를 유지하게 될 것입니다.
David Hallowell

어휘 superintendent 관리자, 감독관 public works 공공사업 inform 알리다 take place 발생하다, 일어나다 in the coming months 다음 몇 달 동안 city council 시의회 countless 수없이 많은, 무수한 rush hour 혼잡 시간대, 러시아워 population 인구 lead to ~로 이어지다 concern 걱정, 우려 mitigate 완화하다, 경감하다 implement 시행하다 directional 방향의 side street 이면도로 effect 영향 convert 전환하다 one-way street 일방통행로

2.
두 번째 단락, 다섯 번째 줄의 "volume"과 의미상 가장 가까운 것은?
(A) 글, 텍스트
(B) 판, 버전
(C) 수치
(D) 분량

해설 동의어 찾기
해당 단어를 찾아 표시하고, 그 단어의 바로 앞뒤를 확인해 본다. traffic volume은 '교통량'이라는 의미로서 volume은 '수량, 분량'이라는 의미로 쓰였다. 선택지에서 그러한 의미로 쓰이는 것은 amount이므로 (D)를 정답으로 선택한다.

UNIT 01 이메일, 편지

빈출 유형 공략 01
본문 p.226

수신: Erin Baldwin 〈e_baldwin@nmail.net〉
발신: Kevin Villanueva 〈kevin.villanueva@gracetownhotel.com〉
날짜: 1월 17일

제목: 객실 교체

Baldwin 씨,

이곳 라스베이거스에서 머물기 위해 Gracetown 호텔을 선택해 주셔서 감사합니다. 저희는 귀하의 대금 지불을 성공적으로 받았지만, 유감스럽게도 귀하께서 예약에 사용하신 웹 사이트인 hoteling.com에 오류가 있었다는 것을 알려드립니다. 그쪽에서 귀하께 2월 12일부터 14일까지 주말 동안 예약이 이미 완료된 객실을 약속했던 것으로 보입니다.

이러한 상황을 고려하여, 저희는 귀하께 다른 객실을 제공하고 싶습니다. 귀하께서는 퀸 사이즈의 침대가 있는 스탠더드 스위트룸을 예약하셨지만, 같은 날짜에 킹 사이즈의 침대가 있는 디럭스 스위트룸이 이용 가능합니다. 귀하는 예약 오류에 대한 책임이 없었으므로, 추가 비용 없이 귀하께 기꺼이 이 객실을 제공해 드리겠습니다.

귀하의 협조에 감사드리며 곧 뵙기를 기대합니다!

Kevin Villanueva
Gracetown 호텔, 고객 서비스

어휘 payment (비용) 지불 inform 알리다 make a reservation 예약하다 book 예약하다 in light of ~을 고려하여, ~에 비추어 alternative 대체의, 대안의 suite 스위트룸 available 이용 가능한, 구할 수 있는 offer 제공하다 additional charge 추가 비용 appreciate 감사하다 cooperation 협조 look forward to ~을 고대하다

1.
이메일의 목적은 무엇인가?
(A) 사람들에게 새로운 호텔을 알리기 위해
(B) 취소된 주문에 대해 사과하기 위해
(C) 객실 상향 조정을 제공하기 위해
(D) 호텔을 예약하기 위한 온라인 사이트를 제안하기 위해

어휘 apologize for ~을 사과하다 upgrade 상향 조정, 업그레이드

빈출 유형 공략 02
본문 p.227

Meadow 부동산
산도발 로 131번지
블루밍턴, 일리노이 61704

7월 10일

Judy Calvin
리터 가 2475번지
블루밍턴, 일리노이 61791

Calvin 씨,

7월 9일에 Meadow 부동산 사무실에 연락 주셔서 감사합니다. 저희는 기꺼이 귀하의 주택 매매를 도와 드리겠습니다. 저희 중개소는 10년 이상 영업해왔으며, 귀하에게 최고의 가격을 안겨 드리기 위해 노력할 것입니다.

저희 표준 패키지 상품에는 전문 사진작가가 브로슈어와 저희 웹 사이트에 올릴 목적으로 귀하의 주택을 촬영하는 것, 상세한 평면도를 작성하는 것, 잠재 구매자들에게 주택을 보여주는 것을 준비하고 실시하는 것이 포함됩니다. 저희는 또한 귀하와 구매자 간의 협상도 처리할 것입니다.

제가 귀하가 계신 지역에 있는 부동산에 대해 몇 가지 조사를 했습니다. 귀하의 주택이 얼마에 매매될 수 있을지에 대한 대략적인 계산을 동봉했습니다. <u>저희가 부동산을 방문한 후에 이 수치를 조정할 수 있습니다.</u>

Clara Pardue
Meadow 부동산, 선임 중개사

어휘 realty 부동산 contact 연락하다 assist A with B A가 B하는 것을 돕다 agency 소개소, 대리점 be in business 영업하다, 장사를 하다 decade 10년 offer 호가, 제안 standard 표준의 package 패키지 상품, 일괄 계약 photographer 사진작가 draw up 작성하다 detailed 상세한 floor plan 평면도 arrange 마련하다, 준비하다 conduct 수행하다 viewing 보기, 조망 potential buyer 잠재 구매자 negotiation 협상 property 부동산 enclose 동봉하다 rough 개략적인 calculation 계산

2.
[1], [2], [3], [4]로 표시된 위치 중 다음 문장이 들어가기에 가장 적절한 곳은?
"저희가 부동산을 방문한 후에 이 수치를 조정할 수 있습니다."
(A) [1]
(B) [2]
(C) [3]
(D) [4]

어휘 refine 다듬다, 정제하다 figure 수치, 숫자

ACTUAL TEST
본문 p.228

1. (A)	**2.** (B)	**3.** (A)	**4.** (C)	**5.** (D)
6. (C)	**7.** (B)	**8.** (C)	**9.** (B)	**10.** (C)
11. (C)	**12.** (A)	**13.** (B)		

[1-2] 이메일

수신: 전 직원 〈staff@hjandco.com〉
발신: Marcy Peppergrove 〈marcy_peppergrove@hjandco.com〉
날짜: 11월 30일
제목: 송년회

직원 여러분,

올 한해 여러분 모두의 노고에 감사드립니다. [1]휴가 시즌을 기념하기 위해 12월 23일에 사무실에서 송년회를 열 예정입니다. [2]휴게실에 신청서가 있으므로 여러분이 파티에 어떤 음식을 가져오고 싶은지, 아니면 파티에 어떻게 기여할 수 있는지를 적을 수 있습니다. 경영팀이 행사를 적절히 준비할 수 있도록 12월 13일까지 여러분이 맡을 역할을 선택해 주십시오.

Marcy Peppergrove
HJ & Co. 대표

어휘 celebrate 축하하다, 기념하다 holiday season 휴가철, 축제 시즌 sign-up sheet 신청서 break room 휴게실 contribute 기여하다, 이바지하다 management 경영(진) properly 적절히, 제대로 organize 준비하다, 마련하다

1.
이메일의 목적은 무엇인가?
(A) 직원들에게 행사에 대해 말하기 위해
(B) 자선 단체에 기부를 요청하기 위해
(C) 사무실에서 발생한 사건을 보고하기 위해
(D) 추가 휴일을 알리기 위해

해설 주제/목적
글의 목적은 문두에 확인한다. 회사에서 송년회를 열 것이라고 했으므로 (A)가 정답이다.

패러프레이징 party → event

어휘 ask for ~을 요청하다 donation 기부 charity 자선 (단체) incident 사건 extra 추가의

2.
송년회에 대해 나타난 것은 무엇인가?
(A) 출장 뷔페가 차려질 것이다.
(B) 직원들에 의해 마련될 것이다.
(C) 호텔에서 열릴 것이다.
(D) 직원들과 그들의 가족을 포함할 것이다.

해설 NOT/True
직원들이 파티 준비를 할 것이라고 했으므로 (B)가 정답이다.

어휘 cater 출장 뷔페를 제공하다 coordinate 조직하다, 편성하다 take place 일어나다, 열리다 include 포함하다

[3-5] 편지

Mariette Lampron 씨
빅토리아 파크 애비뉴 3132번지
토론토, 온타리오, M2J 3T7

3월 17일

Lampron 씨,

³빅토리아 시티 서점의 회원이 되어 주셔서 감사합니다. 귀하의 회원 가입은 소기업들을 지원하는 데 도움이 되고, 종이책들이 계속 출간되도록 해 줍니다. 우리 매장은 규모는 크지 않지만, 다양한 종류의 책들을 구비하고 있으며, 현재 우리 매장 선반에 진열되어 있지 않은 대부분의 책들에 대해 빠른 배송을 제공합니다.

빅토리아 시티 서점은 기본적으로 책을 판매하는 것 외에도 일년 내내 특별한 프로그램들을 제공합니다. 토요일 아침에는 6세 이하의 어린이들을 위한 책읽기 행사가 있습니다. 토요일 저녁에는 7시부터 8시 30분까지 오픈 마이크 공연이 있습니다. ⁴이 프로그램들에 대한 보다 자세한 정보를 원하시면 저희 웹 사이트 www.victoriacitybooks.ca를 방문하셔서 휴대폰 문자 알림을 신청하십시오.

⁵마지막으로, 우리는 항상 새로운 직원, 자원봉사자, 그리고 공연자들을 찾고 있습니다. 이런 자리에 관심이 있는 분께는 기꺼이 연락을 드리고 싶습니다! 자세한 사항은 555-0113으로 저희에게 연락해 주시기 바랍니다.

귀하의 성원에 감사드립니다.

Charlie Beatham
빅토리아 시티 서점주

어휘 membership 회원 (자격) ensure 보장하다 physical 물질적인, 물리적인 in print 출간되는 storefront 점두, 가게의 앞쪽 modest 소박한 a wide array of 다양한 title 서적, 출판물 express 속달의, 급행의 shipping 배송 currently 현재 shelf 선반 in addition to ~에 더하여 up to ~까지 open mic 오픈 마이크의, 누구나 참여할 수 있는 performance 공연 sign up 신청하다 alert 알림, 알람 performer 공연자 get in contact with ~와 연락하다 patronage 후원

3.
편지의 목적은 무엇인가?
(A) 단체에 가입한 사람에게 감사를 표하기 위해
(B) 새 상점의 개업을 홍보하기 위해
(C) 특별 판촉을 광고하기 위해
(D) 신입 사원을 축하하기 위해

해설 주제/목적
글의 목적은 문두에 나온다. 서점의 회원이 되어 준 것에 감사하다고 했으므로 (A)가 정답이다.

패러프레이징 becoming a member → joining a group

어휘 promote 홍보하다 congratulate 축하하다 new hire 신입 사원

4.
고객들은 어떻게 서점의 프로그램에 대한 새로운 소식을 얻을 수 있는가?
(A) 매장의 전화번호로 전화함으로써
(B) 지역 신문을 확인함으로써
(C) 문자 서비스를 신청함으로써
(D) 매주 매장을 방문함으로써

해설 세부 사항
질문의 get updates는 '새로운 소식을 얻다'라는 뜻이므로, 지문에서 새로운 소식을 얻을 수 있는 방법을 검색한다. 휴대폰 문자 알림을 신청하면 보다 자세한 정보를 얻을 수 있다고 했으므로 (C)가 정답이다.

어휘 patron 고객 update 최신 정보 check 확인하다 local 지역의 weekly 매주, 주마다

5.
[1], [2], [3], [4]로 표시된 위치 중 다음 문장이 들어가기에 가장 적절한 곳은?
"자세한 사항은 555-0113으로 저희에게 연락해 주시기 바랍니다."
(A) [1]
(B) [2]
(C) [3]
(D) [4]

해설 **문장 삽입**

주어진 문장은 맺음말에 자주 사용되는 표현이다. further details(자세한 사항)가 의미하는 것은 서점의 직원이나 자원봉사자, 혹은 공연자가 되는 방법을 의미하므로 주어진 문장은 [4]에 들어가는 것이 가장 알맞다.

어휘 contact 연락하다 further 추가의 details 세부 정보

[6-9] 이메일

> 수신: Lupita Medina
> 발신: Fernando Sibiya
> 날짜: 7월 27일
> 제목: 회신: 잭슨 보석 박람회
>
> Medina 씨,
>
> [6]연례 잭슨 보석 박람회에서 귀하가 직접 만든 귀걸이를 판매하는 데 관심을 보여 주셔서 감사합니다. [7D 8D]모든 사람이 은행 송금으로 내야 하는 30달러의 신청 수수료가 있습니다. [7A]또한 박람회에서 판매하고자 하는 물품의 사진을 최소 5장 이상 제출해 주실 것을 요청 드립니다.
> [7C]또한, 귀하의 작품을 어떻게 전시하고 싶은지에 대한 스케치를 제출해 주실 것을 요청 드립니다. [9]각각의 판매자에게는 하나의 판매대가 주어지는데, 우리는 이 스케치를 이용해서 어느 판매대가 어느 판매자에게 갈 것인지를 적절히 배분합니다. 귀하의 그림은 기획의 목적으로만 사용되므로 그 수준에 대해서는 걱정하지 마십시오.
> [8C]9월은 잭슨에서 우기이기 때문에 우리는 악천후의 가능성에 대비해야 합니다. 기상 상태가 좋지 않더라도 박람회는 열릴 것이므로 날씨에 대비한 적절한 장비를 갖추어 주시기 바랍니다.
> 마지막으로, [8A]해가 갈수록 박람회가 점점 더 인기를 끌고 있어서 [8B]안타깝게도 신청서를 제출하는 모든 분들을 수용할 수가 없습니다. 특히 귀하가 판매하고자 하는 물품은 경쟁이 치열합니다. 귀하가 올해 판매자로 선정되기를 바라지만, 만약 그렇지 않더라도 내년에 새로운 디자인으로 다시 신청해 주셨으면 합니다.
>
> Fernando Sibiya

어휘 jewelry 보석류 fair 박람회, 전시회 express 나타내다, 표시하다 homemade 수제의, 집에서 만든 annual 연례의 application 신청(서) fee 비용, 요금 submit 제출하다, 내다 bank transfer 은행 계좌 이체 at least 적어도, 최소한 item 물품, 품목 additionally 또한, 게다가 display 진열하다, 전시하다 vendor 판매자, 행상인 allocate 배정하다, 배분하다 rainy season 우기 possibility 가능성 inclement weather 악천후 appropriate 적절한 equipment 장비 handle 다루다, 처리하다 stiff 치열한 competition 경쟁 encourage 권하다, 장려하다 apply 신청하다, 지원하다

6.
Medina 씨는 무엇을 판매하는가?
(A) 목걸이
(B) 팔찌
(C) 귀걸이
(D) 시계

해설 **세부 사항**

Dear Ms. Medina라고 호칭하면서 첫 번째 문장에서 'selling your homemade earrings(귀하가 직접 만든 귀걸이를 판매하는 것)'라고 했으므로 Medina 씨의 판매 품목은 귀걸이라는 것을 알 수 있다. 따라서 (C)가 정답이다.

7.
보석 박람회에서 판매를 위한 필요조건이 아닌 것은 무엇인가?
(A) 여러 장의 상품 사진을 제출하기
(B) 심사위원들에게 제품 샘플을 보내기
(C) 잠재적인 판매대의 스케치를 그리기
(D) 은행 계좌에서 돈을 이체하기

해설 **NOT/True**

첫 번째에서 세 번째 단락에 걸쳐 박람회 참가에 필요한 요구사항들이 나오는데, 심사위원들에게 제품 샘플을 보내라는 언급은 없으므로 (B)가 정답이다.

어휘 requirement 필요조건 judge 심사위원, 심판 draw 그리다 potential 잠재적인 transfer 이체하다

8.
보석 박람회에 대해 암시된 것은 무엇인가?
(A) 이번에 처음으로 열린다.
(B) 모든 신청자가 박람회에서 자리를 얻는다.
(C) 빗속에서 열릴지도 모른다.
(D) 판매자로 지원하는 것은 무료이다.

해설 **추론/암시**

우기와 악천후에 대비해야 한다고 말했고, 기상 상태가 좋지 않더라도 전시회는 열릴 것이라고 했으므로 (C)가 정답이다. 박람회는 해가 갈수록 인기를 끌고 있다고 했으므로 (A)는 오답이고, 신청서를 제출하는 사람 모두를 박람회에 수용할 수 없다고 했으므로 (B)도 오답, 그리고 30달러의 신청 수수료가 있다고 했으므로 (D)도 오답이다.

어휘 applicant 신청자, 지원자 spot 자리

9.
[1], [2], [3], [4]로 표시된 위치 중 다음 문장이 들어가기에 가장 적절한 곳은?
"귀하의 그림은 기획의 목적으로만 사용되므로 그 수준에 대해서는 걱정하지 마십시오."
(A) [1]
(B) [2]
(C) [3]
(D) [4]

해설 **문장 삽입**

주어진 문장의 drawing이 가리키는 것을 찾아야 한다. 두 번째 단락에 나오는 sketch가 drawing이라는 것을 파악했다면 [2]에 들어가는 것이 가장 적절함을 알 수 있다.

어휘 quality 품질 planning 기획

[10-13] 이메일

수신: customerservice@artemporium.com
발신: leena_agarwal@expressmail.com
날짜: 6월 18일
제목: 미술 공모전 참가
첨부파일: Leena Agarwal 미술 출품작

담당자 귀하:

Art Emporium에서 자주 쇼핑하는 사람으로서, 저는 제가 좋아하는 상점이 미술 대회를 열고 있다는 사실을 알고 기뻤습니다. 저는 이미 몇 달 동안 규모가 큰 모더니즘 그림을 그려왔기 때문에, 이번 대회가 제 ¹⁰작품을 보여줄 수 있는 완벽한 곳이라고 생각했습니다.

¹¹유감스럽게도, 제가 귀사의 웹 사이트에 제 그림의 사진을 올리려고 했을 때, 계속해서 오류 메시지를 받았습니다. 저는 몹시도 원했던 바인, ¹²제 작품을 외부에 선보일 기회이자 2천 달러를 받을 가능성도 있는 기회를 놓치고 싶지 않습니다. 대회 마감일이 3일밖에 남지 않았고, 제가 제출한 것이 꼭 심사를 받도록 하고 싶습니다. ¹³이 이메일에 제 작품의 사진을 첨부했습니다. 제 그림이 공모전에 제대로 출품되었는지 확인해 주시겠습니까? 제가 해야 하는 것이 있다면 되도록 빨리 제게 알려 주시기 바랍니다.

미리 감사드립니다!

Leena Agarwal

어휘 competition 대회, 시합   entry 참가, 출품작   attachment 첨부 파일   to whom it may concern ≪정확한 수신인을 모를 때 사용하는 인사말≫ 담당자 귀하   frequent shopper 단골 고객   upload 업로드하다   error message (컴퓨터의) 오류 메시지   miss out on ~을 놓치다   exposure 노출   potentially 잠재적으로   deadline 마감   make sure 확실히 하다   submission 제출(물)   consider 심사하다, 고려하다   attach 첨부하다   properly 제대로, 적절히   at one's earliest convenience 되도록 일찍   in advance 미리, 사전에

10.
첫 번째 단락 세 번째 줄의 'work'와 의미상 가장 가까운 것은?
(A) 할당
(B) 책임
(C) 그림
(D) 성과, 공연

해설 동의어 찾기
지문에서 work는 art competition에 제출할 미술 작품이라는 뜻이다. 선택지 중에서 의미가 가장 비슷한 것은 (C)이다.

11.
Agarwal 씨는 어떤 문제를 말하는가?
(A) 그녀의 그림은 제시간에 완성되지 않을 것이다.
(B) 그녀는 충분한 표를 얻지 못할 것이라고 생각한다.
(C) 그녀의 사진은 웹 사이트에 업로드되지 않는다.
(D) 웹 사이트에서 그녀의 신용카드를 받지 않는다.

해설 세부 사항
웹 사이트에 사진을 업로드하려고 했는데 계속해서 오류 메시지를 받았다는 것은 결국 업로드하지 못했다는 의미이다. 따라서 (C)가 정답이다.

어휘 in time 제시간에, 시간 내에   vote 표, 투표

12.
대회에 대해 시사된 것은 무엇인가?
(A) 수상자는 상금을 받는다.
(B) 사진 작품은 접수되지 않는다.
(C) 미술품 제출에 수수료가 있다.
(D) 전문가만 참가가 허용된다.

해설 NOT/True
지문의 potentially win $2,000에서 상금이 2천 달러라는 것을 알 수 있다. 따라서 (A)가 정답이다.

어휘 cash 현금   prize 상품   artwork 미술품, 예술 작품   professional 전문가   enter 참가하다

13.
Agarwal 씨는 고객 서비스에 무엇을 요청하는가?
(A) 대회 규정의 전체 목록
(B) 대회 참가에 대한 도움
(C) 그녀의 그림에 대한 조언
(D) 회사 웹 사이트에 대한 지원

해설 세부 사항
customer service는 이메일의 수신이다. Ms. Agarwal은 자신의 그림 사진을 Art Emporium의 웹 사이트에 업로드하지 못해 고객 서비스에 도움을 요청하고 있으므로 (B)가 정답이다.

어휘 complete 완전한   list 목록   assistance 도움, 지원

UNIT 02 문자 메시지, 온라인 채팅

빈출 유형 공략 01   본문 p.236

Noriya Yamauchi (오후 1시 52분)
안녕하세요, Marie. 카탈로그 디자인을 어디까지 진행했는지 궁금해서요.

Marie Copeland (오후 1시 54분)
어제 오전에 끝냈어요.

Noriya Yamauchi (오후 1시 55분)
벌써요? 제가 예상했던 것보다 훨씬 빠르네요. 인턴 사원들에게 먼저 사진 작업을 시키는 우리의 새 절차가 도움이 많이 됐나 봐요.

Marie Copeland (오후 1시 56분)
물론이죠. 앞으로도 계속 그렇게 했으면 좋겠어요.

Noriya Yamauchi (오후 1시 57분)
안 할 이유가 없죠.

어휘 wonder 궁금하다   along 진척되어   expect 예상하다, 기대

하다 procedure 절차 intern 인턴

1.
오후 1시 56분에, Copeland 씨가 "물론이죠"라고 쓸 때 그녀는 무엇을 암시하는가?
(A) 그녀는 카탈로그 사본을 보관했다.
(B) 그녀는 어떤 과정이 도움이 된다는 것을 알았다.
(C) 그녀는 인턴 사원으로 일하고 싶어 한다.
(D) 그녀는 Yamauchi 씨의 업무에 깊은 인상을 받았다.

어휘 copy 사본 process 과정 helpful 도움이 되는 impress 깊은 인상을 주다

빈출 유형 공략 02
본문 p.237

Adam Taylor (3:23 P.M.)
여러분, 우리는 곧 있을 잡지 출간을 위해 모든 것을 준비해 놓아야 합니다. 다들 어떻게 진행되고 있나요?

Eleanor Chamberlain (3:25 P.M.)
저는 새로운 박물관 전시회에 관한 기사를 이미 완성했어요. 이제 사진에 캡션만 달면 돼요.

Judy Brooks (3:26 P.M.)
표지 디자인은 아직 정하지 못했어요. 조언이 필요했어요.

Adam Taylor (3:27 P.M.)
아, 저는 그런 걸 잘 못해요. Eleanor의 의견을 물어보세요.

Eleanor Chamberlain (3:29 P.M.)
Judy, 잡지 표지를 이메일로 제게 보내줄 수 있나요?

Judy Brooks (3:30 P.M.)
실은 지금 제 책상으로 와줄 수 있어요? 우리가 직접 이야기하면 더 쉬울 거예요.

Eleanor Chamberlain (3:31 P.M.)
문제 없어요. 그렇게 할게요.

어휘 upcoming 곧 있을, 다가오는 release 출시, 발간 article 기사 exhibit 전시회 caption 캡션 undecided 결정하지 못한 cover 표지 sort 종류 in person 직접

2.
화자들은 어떤 업종에서 근무하겠는가?
(A) 박물관
(B) 부동산
(C) 출판
(D) 인쇄

ACTUAL TEST
본문 p.238

1. (B) **2.** (C) **3.** (B) **4.** (D) **5.** (B)
6. (C) **7.** (C) **8.** (C) **9.** (C) **10.** (D)
11. (A) **12.** (C) **13.** (A) **14.** (B)

[1-2] 문자 메시지

Clayton Balcom (오전 10:37)
Platinum Tech에 연락 주셔서 감사합니다. 무엇을 도와드릴까요?

Esther Ross (오전 10:38)
안녕하세요. 제 Ayala-7 무선 헤드폰을 노트북 컴퓨터에 연결하려고 하는데요. [1C]제 노트북의 블루투스를 켰는데 헤드폰에서 나오는 신호를 잡지 못하네요.

Clayton Balcom (오전 10:39)
알겠습니다. [1D]블루투스 목록에 나오는 예전 무선 연결을 삭제해 보셨나요? [1A]헤드폰을 껐다가 다시 켜는 것도 때로는 효과가 있습니다.

Esther Ross (오전 10시 40분)
[1A] [1D]두 가지를 모두 해봤어요.

Clayton Balcom (오전 10시 41분)
헤드폰이 충전되어야 할 수도 있습니다. 하지만 먼저 블루투스를 껐다가 다시 켜 보세요. 그런 다음 "블루투스 또는 기타 장치 추가" 버튼을 클릭해서 [2]헤드폰의 측면에 있는 코드가 블루투스 목록에 나타나는지 보세요.

Esther Ross (오전 10시 42분)
있어요!

Clayton Balcom (오전 10시 43분)
좋아요! 이제 그 코드를 클릭하면 연결될 겁니다.

Esther Ross (오전 10:44)
이제 작동하네요. 정말 고맙습니다!

Clayton Balcom (오전 10:45)
별 말씀을요.

어휘 contact 연락하다 connect 연결하다 wireless 무선의 turn on ~을 켜다 signal 신호 delete 삭제하다 work 효과가 있다 charge 충전하다

1.
Ross 씨가 시도하지 않은 해결책은 무엇인가?
(A) 헤드폰을 다시 시작하기
(B) 새로운 코드를 요청하기
(C) 블루투스를 켜기
(D) 예전 연결을 삭제하기

해설 NOT/True
NOT/True 문제는 지문을 전반적으로 확인하면서 선택지를 소거해야 한다. 지문과 선택지를 대조해 보면, 지문의 I've turned on the Bluetooth on my laptop이 Turning on the Bluetooth로, Turning the headphones off and on again이 선택지에서 Restarting the headphones로, deleting the old wireless connections가 Deleting old connections로 패러프레이징되었다. 새로운 코드를 요청했다는 내용은 나오지 않았으므로 (B)가 정답이다.

어휘 solution 해결책, 해법

2.
오전 10시 42분에, Ross 씨가 "있어요!"라고 쓸 때 그녀는 무엇을 의미하는가?
(A) 그녀는 웹 사이트의 링크를 클릭했다.
(B) 그녀는 사용 설명서를 가지고 있다.
(C) 그녀에게 코드가 보인다.
(D) 그녀는 확정 이메일을 찾았다.

해설 의도 파악
의도 파악 문제는 바로 앞에 나오는 내용을 확인해야 한다. 오전 10:41에 "블루투스 또는 기타 장치 추가" 버튼을 클릭해서 헤드폰 측면에 있는 코드가 블루투스 목록에 나타나는지 보라는 Clayton Balcom의 말에 이처럼 말했으므로 코드가 보인다는 것을 알 수 있다. 따라서 (C)가 정답이다.

어휘 user manual 사용 설명서

[3-6] 온라인 채팅

> **Heidi Faulk** (오전 10:05)
> ³우리 사무실을 Derby 빌딩으로 옮길 준비를 하기 위해 우리가 오늘 오후 2시에 만나기로 했다는 것을 상기시켜 드릴게요.
>
> **Angela Phelps** (오전 10:06)
> Heidi, 그 이후에 오래된 고객 문의 보고서를 정리할 시간이 있어요? 우리는 어떤 것을 보관하고 어떤 것을 파기해야 할지 결정해야 해요.
>
> **Heidi Faulk** (오전 10:07)
> 네, 저는 오늘 괜찮을 것 같아요.
>
> **Jerry Mullen** (오전 10:09)
> 애빌린 지사의 Beverly Conrad 씨가 최근에 이 과정을 겪었기 때문에 분명히 알고 있는 것이 꽤 있을 거예요. 그녀가 원격으로 우리와 함께하겠다고 제안해 왔습니다. ⁴화상 회의 준비를 해주실 수 있나요?
>
> **Heidi Faulk** (오전 10:10)
> 제가 할게요.
>
> **Bernard Ledesma** (오전 10:11)
> ⁵저는 이삿짐 업체 세 군데에서 받은 견적서를 가져올게요.
>
> **Angela Phelps** (오전 10:12)
> 덕분에 우리의 시간이 많이 절약됐어요, Bernard.
>
> **Jerry Mullen** (오전 10:13)
> ⁶그리고 제가 45분 정도 후에 자리를 떠야 한다는 것도 잊지 마세요. 3시에 신입 영업사원들을 위한 워크숍을 운영해야 하거든요.
>
> **Heidi Faulk** (오전 10:14)
> 괜찮아요, Jerry. 당신이 놓친 부분은 제가 나중에 알려줄게요.

어휘 reminder 상기시키는 것 get ready for ~을 준비하다 afterward 나중에, 후에 sort 분류하다 inquiry 문의, 질문 shred (문서를) 잘게 자르다, 파쇄하다 work well for ~에게 좋다 branch 지사, 지점 recently 최근에 surely 분명히 insight 통찰력, 이해 remotely 원격으로, 멀리서 set up 설치하다, 준비하다 video conference 화상 회의 quote 견적 moving company 이삿짐 회사 run a workshop 워크숍을 진행하다

miss 놓치다

3.
Faulk 씨가 오늘 회의를 하는 이유는 무엇인가?
(A) 몇 가지 문서를 정리하기 위해
(B) 사무실 이전을 준비하기 위해
(C) 건물 임대차 계약서에 서명하기 위해
(D) Derby 빌딩을 둘러보기 위해

해설 주제/목적
지문의 목적은 보통 문두에서 제시되며, Ms. Faulk라는 이름이 제시되었으므로 지문에서 Heidi Faulk의 말을 확인한다. 사무실 이전 준비를 하기 위해 2시에 회의를 한다고 했으므로 (B)가 정답이다.

패러프레이징 get ready for moving our office → prepare for an office relocation

어휘 relocation 이전 lease 임대차 계약 tour 돌아보다, 견학하다

4.
오전 10시 10분에, Faulk 씨가 "제가 할게요"라고 쓸 때 그녀는 무엇을 의미하는가?
(A) 그녀는 문서 몇 장을 파쇄할 것이다.
(B) 그녀는 회의 중이다.
(C) 그녀는 Conrad 씨와 전화를 하고 있다.
(D) 그녀는 화상 회의를 준비할 것이다.

해설 의도 파악
의도 파악 문제는 바로 앞에 나오는 내용을 확인해야 한다. "Could you please set up a video conference?"라는 질문에 대한 답변이므로, 자신이 화상 회의를 준비하겠다고 답한 것이다. 따라서 (D)가 정답이다.

어휘 arrange 준비하다, 마련하다

5.
Ledesma 씨는 회의에 무엇을 가져올 계획인가?
(A) 쇼핑 목록
(B) 비용 견적
(C) 작업 일정
(D) 문의 보고서

해설 세부 사항
지문에서 Bernard Ledesma가 한 말을 확인한다. quotes를 가져온다고 했으므로 (B)가 정답이다.

패러프레이징 quotes → cost estimates

어휘 estimate 견적, 예상치

6.
Mullen 씨는 왜 회의에 끝까지 참석하지 못하는가?
(A) 차를 이동시켜야 한다.
(B) 고객에게 발표를 할 것이다.
(C) 교육을 진행해야 한다.
(D) 출장 준비를 해야 한다.

해설 세부 사항
지문에서 Jerry Mullen이 한 말을 확인한다. 워크숍을 진행하러 떠나야 한다고 했으므로 (C)가 정답이다.

패러프레이징 running the workshop → lead a training session

어휘 give a presentation 발표하다 client 고객 lead 이끌다 training session 교육 business trip 출장

[7-10] 온라인 채팅

> Justin Dube (오전 10:35)
> 안녕하세요, Alphonso와 Natalie. 진행 상황을 좀 확인할게요.
>
> Alphonso Mantz (오전 10:37)
> 저는 오늘 여러 부지에서 치수를 재고 있어요. 저는 지금 엘라가 901번지에 있는데, 대략 11시 30분까지는 여기 있을 거예요.
>
> Justin Dube (오전 10시 38분)
> 알았어요. [8]방금 Joshua Caudill 씨로부터 연락이 왔어요. [7]우리가 지난달에 목재 울타리를 쳐드렸는데 벌써 널빤지의 일부가 헐거워지고 있다네요. [8]그분은 내일 댈러스행 항공기에 탑승하시는데, 여기 안 계시는 동안 상태가 더 나빠지지 않게 오늘 고쳐 주었으면 좋겠대요.
>
> Natalie Garrido (오전 10시 40분)
> 그럼 당신은 이곳 조지 가의 현장에 늦게 도착하시겠네요. Caudill 씨의 부지는 얼마나 멀리 떨어져 있나요?
>
> Justin Dube (오전 10시 41분)
> [9]모빌 가 849번지에 있으니 제가 끝나는 대로 당신이 있는 곳으로 바로 갈게요. 일은 오래 걸리지 않을 것 같아요. [9]11시 30분까지는 도착해서 약 1시간 내에 일을 끝낼 수 있어요.
>
> Natalie Garrido (오전 10시 42분)
> 괜찮아요. 어쨌든 여긴 예정보다 빨리 진행되고 있으니까요.
>
> Justin Dube (오전 10:44)
> 잘됐네요. 창고에서 뭐 필요한 거 있으세요? [10]비품 몇 개를 가지러 창고에 들를 거라서요.
>
> Alphonso Mantz (오전 10:45)
> 저는 아무것도 필요 없어요. 그런데 오늘은 일요일이잖아요.
>
> Justin Dube (오전 10:46)
> 걱정 마세요. 저에게 열쇠가 있어요.

어휘 take a measurement 치수를 재다 property 부동산 board 널빤지 come loose 헐거워지다 fix 고치다 warehouse 창고 stop by 잠깐 들르다 supplies 물품

7.
화자들의 회사는 무엇을 전문으로 하겠는가?
(A) 부동산 판매
(B) 차량 수리
(C) 울타리 설치
(D) 외부 도색

해설 추론/암시
We put up a wooden fence for him last month에서 울타리를 설치하는 회사라는 것을 알 수 있다. 따라서 (C)가 정답이다.

패러프레이징 put up a wooden fence → fence installation

어휘 specialize in ~을 전문으로 하다 real estate 부동산

vehicle 차량 installation 설치 exterior 외부

8.
Caudill 씨는 내일 무엇을 할 계획인가?
(A) Dube 씨와 계약하기
(B) 몇 가지 측정을 하기
(C) 타지로 여행하기
(D) 몇몇 방문객을 접대하기

해설 세부 사항
화자 중에는 Caudill이라는 사람이 없으므로, 대화 내용에서 Caudill을 검색해야 한다. Justin Dube의 말에서 Joshua Caudill은 회사의 고객이며, 내일 댈러스로 떠난다는 것을 알 수 있으므로 (C)가 정답이다.

패러프레이징 taking a flight to Dallas → Take a trip out of town

어휘 entertain 접대하다, 즐겁게 하다

9.
Dube 씨는 모빌 가 849번지에서 언제 일을 마칠 것으로 예상하는가?
(A) 오전 11시경
(B) 오전 11시 30분경
(C) 오후 12시 30분경
(D) 오후 1시경

해설 세부 사항
Justin Dube가 한 말을 확인해야 한다. 그는 11시 30분까지 모빌 가 849번지에 도착한 뒤 1시간 내에 작업을 끝낸다고 했으므로 (C)가 정답이다.

10.
오전 10시 45분에 Mantz 씨가 "그런데 오늘은 일요일이잖아요"라고 쓸 때 그가 의미하는 것은 무엇이겠는가?
(A) 그는 일찍 퇴근하기를 희망한다.
(B) 작업장으로 가는 교통량이 많지 않을 것이다.
(C) Dube 씨는 추가 급여를 받을 자격이 있다.
(D) Dube 씨가 창고에 들어가는 데 문제가 있을 수 있다.

해설 의도 파악
의도 파악 문제는 바로 앞에 나오는 내용을 확인해야 한다. 창고에 들를 거라는 Justin Dube의 말에 이와 같이 말했으므로, 직원이 근무하지 않는 휴일이기 때문에 창고에 들어가지 못할 수도 있음을 암시한 것이다. 따라서 (D)가 정답이다.

어휘 leave work 퇴근하다 worksite 직업장 eligible for ~을 받을 자격이 있는 additional 추가적인 access 접근하다, 출입하다

[11-14] 온라인 채팅

> Renee Armstrong [오후 2:01]
> 안녕하세요. [12]두 분 모두 제가 링크를 보내 드린 온라인 가정용 가구 카탈로그를 보실 기회가 있었는지 궁금해서요. [11]우리는 회의실에 커튼을 할지 블라인드를 할지, 그리고 어떤 것을 구입할지 결정해야 해요.

John Lugo [오후 2:02]
저는 넓은 나무 널이 있는 버티컬 블라인드가 마음에 듭니다. 모던하게 보이고, 쉽게 열고 닫을 수 있을 거예요.

Renee Armstrong [오후 2:04]
저도 그게 좋다고 생각했어요. 하지만 좀 얇은 것 같네요.

Melvin Ochoa [오후 2:07]
저는 오전 내내 바빴습니다. 이제야 그걸 볼 수 있겠네요.

John Lugo [오후 2:08]
좋은 지적이에요, Renee. 13 회의실은 항상 추워요. 사무실을 조금이라도 더 단열하려면 두꺼운 커튼을 다는 것이 도움이 될지도 몰라요.

Melvin Ochoa [오후 2:09]
색깔은 생각해 보셨어요? 우리 로고와 어울리도록 녹색을 써도 될 것 같아요.

Renee Armstrong [오후 2:10]
어떤 색이 가장 좋을지 모르겠어요.

Melvin Ochoa [오후 2:12]
공급업체로부터 원단 샘플 몇 가지를 받을 수 있을 거예요.

Renee Armstrong [오후 2:13]
좋은 생각이에요.

Melvin Ochoa [오후 2:14]
14 저에게는 공급업체의 연락처가 없어요.

Renee Armstrong [오후 2:15]
14 그건 제가 오늘 처리할게요. 우리가 어떤 색깔에 관심이 있는지 정하기만 하면 돼요.

어휘 browse 훑어보다 vertical 수직의 slat 널, 조각 thin 얇은 take a look 한번 보다 thick 두꺼운 insulate 단열하다 complement 보완하다 fabric 직물, 천 supplier 공급업체

11.
주로 무엇에 관한 논의인가?
(A) 창문 가리개 선택
(B) 회의실의 배치
(C) 보수 공사 예산
(D) 곧 있을 회의의 주제

해설 주제/목적
문자 메시지나 온라인 채팅의 주제 또는 목적은 문두에 드러날 가능성이 크다. 회의실에 커튼과 블라인드 중에서 어느 것을 달지 결정하기 위한 채팅이므로 (A)가 정답이다.

패러프레이징 curtains or blinds → window coverings

어휘 option 선택권, 옵션 covering 덮개, 가리개 layout 배치 budget 예산 renovation 수리, 보수 topic 주제, 화제 upcoming 곧 있을, 다가오는

12.
오후 2시 7분에, Ochoa 씨가 "이제야 그걸 볼 수 있겠네요"라고 쓸 때 그가 의미하는 것은 무엇이겠는가?
(A) 그는 직원을 평가할 것이다.
(B) 그는 계약서를 검토할 것이다.
(C) 그는 웹 사이트를 방문할 것이다.
(D) 그는 방을 둘러볼 것이다.

해설 의도 파악
의도 파악 문제는 바로 앞에 나오는 내용을 확인해야 한다. 하지만 이 지문에서는 바로 앞의 Renee Armstrong과 John Lugo의 말에 단서가 나오지 않으므로 맨 위의 Renee Armstrong의 말까지 확인해야 한다. Melvin Ochoa의 말은 자신이 보낸 온라인 카탈로그를 봤는지 물어 보는 Renee Armstrong의 질문에 대한 답변이므로 이제 해당 링크를 방문해서 카탈로그를 보겠다는 의미이다. 따라서 (C)가 정답이다.

어휘 evaluate 평가하다 review 검토하다 tour 둘러보다, 견학하다

13.
회의실에 관해 가장 사실일 것 같은 것은 무엇인가?
(A) 온도가 쾌적하지 않다.
(B) 스타일이 구식이다.
(C) 업체의 필요성에 비해 너무 작다.
(D) 발표 장비를 갖추고 있다.

해설 추론/암시
회의실의 상태에 관해 언급된 것은 "The conference room is always cold."라는 문장 하나뿐이다. 회의실은 춥다고 했으므로 온도가 쾌적하지 않다고 볼 수 있다. 따라서 (A)가 정답이다.

어휘 temperature 온도 outdated 구식의, 시대에 뒤진 contain 들어 있다, 포함하다 presentation 발표 equipment 장비

14.
Armstrong 씨는 오늘 무엇을 할 것인가?
(A) 몇 가지 측정을 하기
(B) 업체 대표에게 연락하기
(C) 일부 원단 샘플을 반송하기
(D) 온라인으로 주문하기

해설 세부 사항
Armstrong을 키워드로 지문을 검색한다. Renee Armstrong은 "I can take care of that today."라고 말했는데, 이 말은 공급업체의 연락처가 없다는 Melvin Ochoa의 말에 대한 답변이므로 자신이 공급업체에게 연락하겠다는 의미이다. 따라서 (B)가 정답이다.

어휘 take a measurement 치수를 재다 contact 연락하다 representative 대표자 place an order 주문하다

UNIT 03 기사, 안내문

빈출 유형 공략 01
본문 p.246

박사 과정생이 오래된 건물 복원을 모색하다

많은 존스타운 주민들은 머쓰가 44번지 건물을 시의 경계선 끝에 있는 오래된 버려진 건물로 알고 있지만, 최근의 연구는 이 퇴락해 가는 건축물이 상당한 역사적인 중요성을 가지고 있다는 것을 밝혀냈다. 박사 과정생인 Sunny Norbert 씨는 자신의 역사 학위 논문 자료를 수집하던 중 오랫동안 잊혀진 이 집에 숨겨진 풍부한 역사를 발견했다.

"저는 1800년대 중반의 신문을 훑어보던 중에 머쓰가 44번지 건물이 지역 뉴스에서 대서특필된 사진들을 보고 깜짝 놀랐습니다."라고 Norbert 씨는 말했다. "이 건물은 아프리카계 미국인, 아메리카 원주민, 그리고 유대계 미국인들과 같은 많은 소외 계층들의 안전 가옥으로 오랫동안 사용되었던 것 같습니다."

건물에 대한 소문이 퍼지기 시작하자 Norbert 씨는 건물을 복원해서 그것을 공식적인 문화유산으로 지정받도록 하기로 결심했다. 그렇게 하기 위해서 그녀에게는 일단의 헌신적인 자원봉사자들, 특히 집을 짓거나 복원하는 기술을 가진 사람들이 필요하다. 그녀의 노력에 동참하고 싶은 사람은 s_norbert@fastmail.com으로 이메일을 보내면 된다.

어휘 PhD 박사(= Doctor of Philosophy) seek 찾다 restore 복원하다 abandoned 버려진 city line 시의 경계 reveal 밝히다, 드러내다 decay 퇴락하다, 부패하다 structure 건축물, 구조 significance 중요성 dissertation 논문 feature 특집 기사로 다루다 prominently 두드러지게 safe house 안전 가옥 underprivileged 혜택을 못 받는 designate 지정하다 heritage 문화유산 dedicated 헌신적인 volunteer 지원자, 자원봉사자 restoration 복원

1.
기사의 목적 중 하나는 무엇인가?
(A) 자원봉사자를 모집하기 위해
(B) 역사학자들을 찾기 위해
(C) 건물을 철거로부터 보존하기 위해
(D) 기부금을 모으기 위해

어휘 recruit 모집하다 scholar 학자 save A from B A를 B로부터 구하다 demolition 파괴 donation 기부, 기증

빈출 유형 공략 02
본문 p.247

Lexington Logistics 직원들을 위한 안내문

Lexington Logistics 인사과에서 직원들을 위해 몇 가지 교육 워크숍을 진행할 예정입니다. 이러한 행사는 선택 사항이지만 여러분의 비즈니스 역량을 개발하는 데 매우 훌륭한 방법입니다. 워크숍은 회의에서 발표하기, 고객들에게 좋은 인상을 심어 주기, 비즈니스 글쓰기를 보다 격식 있게 만들기와 같은 다양한 주제를 다룰 것입니다. 보다 자세한 내용은 6월 7일 목요일 오후 2시 휴게실에서 열리는 설명회에 참석해 주시기 바랍니다.

어휘 HR department 인사과 conduct 하다, 수행하다 optional 선택적인 cover 다루다, 포함하다 a variety of 다양한 topic 주제 give a presentation 발표하다 make a good impression 좋은 인상을 주다 formal 공식적인, 정식의 session (특정 활동을 위한) 시간

2.
안내문에 따르면, 직원들은 어떻게 더 많은 정보를 얻을 수 있는가?
(A) 문서를 읽음으로써
(B) 회의에 참석함으로써
(C) 웹 사이트를 방문함으로써
(D) 인사과에 이메일을 보냄으로써

어휘 further 추가의 detail 세부 정보 attend 참석하다, 참가하다

ACTUAL TEST
본문 p.248

1. (C)	2. (D)	3. (B)	4. (B)	5. (A)
6. (C)	7. (B)	8. (B)	9. (A)	10. (A)
11. (B)	12. (A)	13. (B)		

[1-2] 안내문

이달의 직원

[2]Rockin' Rogers의 우리 서빙 직원들 중 어떤 사람으로부터 특별한 서비스를 받은 경험이 있나요? 그렇다면, 지금이 당신의 고마움을 보여줄 기회입니다. [1]내년부터 우리는 매월 1일에 이달의 직원상을 발표할 예정입니다. [2]고객들과 동료 서빙 직원들 모두 Rockin' Rogers에서 자신이 가장 좋아하는 서빙 직원에게 투표를 할 수 있습니다. 고객들은 입구에 비치된 카드에 의견을 쓰거나 온라인으로 설문조사를 완료할 수 있습니다. 직원들은 휴게실에 있는 익명으로 참여하는 투표함에 자신의 표를 넣을 수 있습니다. 이달의 직원상 수상자는 바로 옆에 있는 Moe's Theater의 무료 영화표 두 장을 받게 될 것입니다. 협조해 주셔서 감사드리며, 우리는 여러분의 표를 집계하는 순간을 고대합니다!

어휘 exceptional 뛰어난, 특별한 waitstaff 웨이터, 서빙 직원 appreciation 감사, 고마움 fellow 동료 alike 모두 server 웨이터, 종업원 comment 의견 survey 설문조사 vote 표, 투표 anonymous 익명의 ballot box 투표함 break room 휴게실 next door 옆 건물에 cooperation 협조 count (숫자를) 세다

1.
안내문의 목적은 무엇인가?
(A) 새로운 서빙 직원을 찾기 위해
(B) 신입 사원들을 포상하기 위해
(C) 투표 제도를 설명하기 위해
(D) 새 관리자를 선발하기 위해

해설 주제/목적
주제와 목적은 대개 지문의 첫머리에 나온다. 첫 문장을 의문문으로 제시하여 궁금증을 고조시킨 후 투표를 통해 이달의 직원을 뽑을 수 있다고 안내하고 있으므로 (C)가 정답이다.

어휘 reward 상을 주다   voting 투표   elect 선출하다

2.
서빙 직원들이 상을 받을 수 있는 방법은 무엇이겠는가?
(A) 추가 근무를 함으로써
(B) 상사를 감동시킴으로써
(C) 퇴근 후 늦게까지 남음으로써
(D) 좋은 서비스를 제공함으로써

해설 추론/암시
고객은 exceptional service(특별한 서비스)를 제공한 서빙 직원에게 투표할 수 있다고 했으므로 (D)가 정답이다.

패러프레이징 exceptional service → great service

어휘 extra 추가적인   shift 교대근무   impress 깊은 인상을 주다
provide 주다, 제공하다

[3-5] 기사

Foodwheels의 5년

(5월 10일)—³5년 전, Darren Hirsh 씨는 Foodwheels라는 음식 배달 회사에 대한 아이디어를 떠올렸는데, 그것은 자체 배달 서비스가 없는 음식점들에서 음식을 배달하는 것이었다. 그 개념이 인기를 얻는 데는 다소의 시간이 걸렸다. 하지만 다행히도 Hirsh 씨는 자신의 아이디어를 믿었고 그것을 고수했다. 그는 광고에 많은 투자를 했고, 시내의 모든 음식점을 직접 방문해서 점주들에게 플랫폼에 가입할 것을 설득했다. 2년 내에 Foodwheels는 자사의 네트워크에 200개의 음식점을 포섭했다. ⁴Hirsh 씨는 고객들이 음식을 보다 쉽게 주문할 수 있도록 스마트폰 앱을 개발하기 위해 수익을 재투자했다.

유사한 비즈니스 모델을 가진 Fast Eatz와 같은 업체가 인기를 얻기 시작했을 때 Hirsh 씨는 Foodwheels를 차별화시킬 새로운 방법을 생각해냈다. 그는 음식점들이 Foodwheels에만 업체를 등록할 경우 수수료를 할인해 주겠다고 제안했다. 이 방법은 경쟁자들을 시장에서 몰아냈고, Foodwheels의 정상의 지위를 공고히 하였다.

어휘 lack 부족하다, 없다   stick with ~을 계속하다   heavily 아주 많이, 심하게   advertisement 광고   make a visit 방문하다
convince 설득하다   platform 플랫폼   reinvest 재투자하다
profit 수익   stand out 두드러지다, 눈에 띄다   offer a discount 할인을 해주다   commission 수수료   exclusively 독점적으로, 배타적으로   competitor 경쟁자   secure 확보하다, 고정시키다

3.
기사가 작성된 이유는 무엇인가?
(A) Foodwheels와 Fast Eatz의 합병을 발표하기 위해
(B) Foodwheels가 어떻게 성공하게 되었는지를 설명하기 위해
(C) Foodwheels의 새로운 서비스를 광고하기 위해
(D) 사람들에게 투자 기회를 알리기 위해

해설 주제/목적
주제 또는 목적 문제의 단서는 문두에 나오는 경우가 많은데, 이 지문의 경우 기사 전반에 걸쳐 단서가 제시되어 있다. Foodwheels가 처음에 어떻게 생겨났는지부터 시작하여 어떤 방법으로 사업에 성공하고 경쟁자들을 따돌렸는지를 서술하고 있으므로 (B)가 정답이다.

어휘 merger 합병   rise to success 성공하다   inform A of B A에게 B를 알리다   investment 투자   opportunity 기회

4.
기사는 Foodwheels에 대해 무엇을 나타내는가?
(A) 어떤 업체들은 대량 구입에 따른 할인을 받을 자격이 있다.
(B) 어떤 고객들은 그들의 전화기를 통해 서비스를 이용한다.
(C) 음식점들은 Foodwheels를 독점적으로 이용해야 한다.
(D) 2백 명의 새로운 고객이 최근에 가입했다.

해설 추론/암시
고객들은 스마트폰 앱을 통해 음식을 쉽게 주문할 수 있다는 것을 추론할 수 있으므로 (B)가 정답이다.

패러프레이징 smartphone → phone

어휘 business 업체   eligible for ~을 받을 자격이 있는
bulk discount 대량 구입에 따른 할인   sign up 등록하다

5.
[1], [2], [3], [4]로 표시된 위치 중 다음 문장이 들어가기에 가장 적절한 곳은?
"그 개념이 인기를 얻는 데는 다소의 시간이 걸렸다."
(A) [1]
(B) [2]
(C) [3]
(D) [4]

해설 문장 삽입
주어진 문장의 the concept가 가리키는 것을 찾아야 한다. 그러한 개념이 인기를 얻는 데 시간이 오래 걸렸다고 했으므로 사업 초기라는 것을 짐작할 수 있고, 첫 번째 문장의 an idea가 the concept로 다르게 표현되었다는 것을 확인했다면 (A)를 정답으로 고를 수 있다.

어휘 take a while 시간이 다소 걸리다   concept 콘셉트, 개념, 아이디어   catch on 인기를 얻다, 유행하다

[6-9] 기사

비즈니스 최신 뉴스: Perez Beverages

휴스턴 (6월 18일)—⁶음료 제조업체인 Perez Beverages는 자사의 대표 음료인 Zip Cola의 제조법을 바꿀 것이라고 발표했다. ⁹그 결정은 특정 재료의 불안정한 수급 문제를 처리하기 위한 노력의 일환으로 내려졌는데, 그 문제는 증가하는 수요를 충족시키는데 지속적인 장애물이 되고 있었다. 이 문제를 해결함으로써, 회사는 생산량이 상당히 증가할 것으로 기대하고 있다.

회사는 맛의 차이를 발견하는 것이 거의 불가능할 것이라고 소비자들을 안심시키기 위해 SNS에 글을 올렸다. 그럼에도 불구하고, 그 발표는 Zip Cola에 대한 수요 폭증으로 이어졌다. ⁷사람들은 원래 음료가 더 이상 판매되지 않으면 제3의 웹 사이트에서 부풀려진 가격으로 탄산음료를 재판매하기를 희망하며 대량으로 구입하고 있다.

Perez Beverages의 대표자인 Shelly Kellner 씨는 회사가 탁월함에 대한 회사의 평판을 지키기 위해 헌신하고 있다고 말

했다. [8]그녀는 새로운 제조법으로 만든 음료가 출시되고 나면 Zip Berry Cola와 Zip Vanilla Cola와 같은 새로운 버전의 음료를 출시할 것이라고 덧붙였다. "우리는 새로운 방식으로 고객에게 다가갈 수 있어 기쁩니다."라고 Kellner 씨는 말했다.

어휘 update 최신 뉴스 beverage 음료 signature 대표적인 in an effort to ~하기 위한 노력의 일환으로 deal with ~을 다루다 unstable 불안정한 supply 공급 ingredient 재료 ongoing 계속 진행 중인 obstacle 장애물 meet demand 수요를 충족시키다 post 게시하다 social media 소셜 미디어, SNS reassure 안심시키다 detect 감지하다, 발견하다 lead to ~으로 이어지다 run 대량 구매 quantity 수량, 분량 inflated 부당하게 인상된, 팽창한 once 일단 ~하고 나면 representative 대표자 reputation 평판, 명성 hit the shelf 매장에 진열되다 release 발매하다, 공개하다

6.

기사의 목적은 무엇인가?
(A) 기업 합병을 발표하기 위해
(B) 회사의 성공을 요약하기 위해
(C) 제품에 대한 조정 사항을 알리기 위해
(D) 음료 산업의 동향을 강조하기 위해

해설 주제/목적
주제 또는 목적 문제는 문두에 나오는 경우가 많다. 첫 번째 문장에서 음료 회사가 자사의 음료 제조법을 바꿀 것이라고 했으므로 (C)가 정답이다.

패러프레이징 changing the recipe for its signature drink → adjustments to a product

어휘 corporate 기업의, 회사의 merger 합병 summarize 요약하다 adjustment 조정, 수정 highlight 강조하다 trend 경향, 트렌드 industry 산업

7.

일부 Zip Cola 고객에 대해 무엇이 암시되었는가?
(A) 그들은 음료에 돈을 덜 쓸 것이다.
(B) 그들은 변화로부터 이익을 얻기를 희망한다.
(C) 그들은 보다 건강한 선택권을 원했다.
(D) 그들은 회사에 제안을 했다.

해설 추론/암시
일부 고객들이 Zip Cola를 부풀려진 가격으로 재판매하기 위해 대량 구매하고 있다고 했으므로 (B)가 정답이다. Zip Cola의 제조법 변경을 변화(change)로 표현했다.

어휘 profit from ~로부터 이득을 얻다 submit 제출하다 suggestion 제안

8.

Kellner 씨는 무엇을 확인해 주었는가?
(A) 상표의 포장이 새로워질 것이다.
(B) 새로운 맛을 구입할 수 있을 것이다.
(C) 몇몇 공장들이 직원들을 채용할 것이다.
(D) 기업은 과거의 실수로부터 교훈을 얻었다.

해설 세부 사항
문제에서 Kellner라는 이름이 나왔으므로 지문에서 Kellner를 키워드로 검색해야 한다. Zip Berry Cola와 Zip Vanilla Cola와 같은 새로운 버전의 음료를 출시할 것이라고 했으므로 (B)가 정답이다.

어휘 confirm 확인하다, 확정하다 packaging 포장 update (현대적으로) 갱신하다 flavor 풍미 available 이용 가능한 factory 공장

9.

[1], [2], [3], [4]로 표시된 위치 중 다음 문장이 들어가기에 가장 적절한 곳은?
"이 문제를 해결함으로써, 회사는 생산량이 상당히 증가할 것으로 기대하고 있다."
(A) [1]
(B) [2]
(C) [3]
(D) [4]

해설 문장 삽입
주어진 문장을 정확히 해석하는 것이 중요하다. this problem은 앞에서 언급된 문제점이며, 생산량의 증가를 막고 있다는 것을 알 수 있다. 지문을 확인하면 this problem은 특정 재료의 불안정한 수급 문제를 의미하므로 [1]에 들어가는 것이 가장 적절하다.

어휘 solve 풀다, 해결하다 significant 상당한

[10-13] 기사

플레전트빌(9월 21일)—[10]많은 시민들의 요청에 따라 마침내 플레전트빌에 휴일을 테마로 한 상점이 생길 예정이다. Holiday Party는 다음 달 초에 문을 열어 지역 주민들이 시즌별 파티에 필요한 요구 사항을 충족시키는 데 일조할 것이다. [11A 11C 13]각각의 휴가철마다 고객들은 매장 전체가 그 시즌과 관련된 장식, 의상, 미술품과 공예품, 그리고 기타 테마에 맞춘 상품으로 채워질 것으로 기대할 수 있다. 분위기를 살리기 위한 으스스한 음악도 있을 것이다.
10월 개장을 위해 [11C 11D]Holiday Party는 다양한 종류의 무시무시한 의상, 맛있는 간식, 그리고 으스스한 장식품들로 핼러윈의 정신을 품을 것이다. [12]10월 20일부터 31일까지 방문객들은 핼러윈 복장을 입고 매장에 도착하면 핼러윈 세일을 위해 구매하는 모든 구매품에 대해 10% 할인을 받게 된다. 일 년 내내 정기적으로 Holiday Party에 들러서 어떤 예상치 못한 즐거움이 매장에 준비되어 있는지 확인해 보기 바란다.

어휘 at the request of ~의 요청으로 townspeople 읍민, 시민 local 주민, 현지인 meet one's needs ~의 요구를 충족시키다 entire 전체의 decoration 장식 costume 의상, 옷 arts and crafts 공예 appropriate 적절한 embrace 끌어안다 spirit 정신 scary 무서운 treat 대접, 한턱 spooky 무시무시한 stop by 잠깐 들르다 regularly 정기적으로, 주기적으로 throughout the year 일 년 내내 unexpected 예상치 못한

10.

기사의 목적은 무엇인가?

(A) 새로운 업체를 홍보하기 위해
(B) 핼러윈 파티를 광고하기 위해
(C) 미술 공예품 매장에 대한 후기를 쓰기 위해
(D) 폐점을 알리기 위해

해설 **주제/목적**
문두에서 Pleasantville is finally getting its own holiday-themed store라고 하면서 상점의 개장을 알리고 있으므로 (A)가 정답이다.

어휘 promote 홍보하다   business 업체   review 논평하다, 검토하다

11.
Holiday Party에 대해 언급되지 않은 것은 무엇인가?
(A) 많은 계절적인 물품을 제공한다.
(B) 하루 24시간 운영된다.
(C) 음식과 공예품을 모두 판매한다.
(D) 다양한 판매용 의상을 보유하고 있다.

해설 **NOT/True**
Holiday Party를 키워드로 지문을 검색한다. goods related to the appropriate season은 (A), arts and crafts와 delicious treats는 (C), 그리고 a variety of scary costumes에서 (D)에 대한 단서를 찾을 수 있지만 (B)에 대한 내용은 찾을 수 없으므로 (B)가 정답이다.

어휘 24 hours a day 하루 종일   various 다양한   for sale 판매용의

12.
핼러윈 세일에 대해 무엇이 언급되었는가?
(A) 특정 고객들에게만 제공된다.
(B) 10월 내내 이용할 수 있다.
(C) 한 개의 품목에 대해서만 유효하다.
(D) 다른 할인 혜택과 결합해서 이용할 수 있다.

해설 **NOT/True**
Halloween Sale을 키워드로 지문을 검색한다. 핼러윈 복장을 입고 매장을 찾은 고객들은 10% 할인을 받을 것이라고 했으므로 (A)가 정답이다.

어휘 certain 어떤, 특정한   available 이용 가능한   valid 유효한   combine 결합하다   discount 할인

13.
[1], [2], [3], [4]로 표시된 위치 중 다음 문장이 들어가기에 가장 적절한 곳은?
"분위기를 살리기 위한 으스스한 음악도 있을 것이다."
(A) [1]
(B) [2]
(C) [3]
(D) [4]

해설 **문장 삽입**
주어진 문장에 부사 even(~조차)과 매장의 분위기를 묘사하는 eerie music(음악)이 있으므로, 주어진 문장의 앞에는 매장의 특징이나 분위기를 묘사하는 내용이 나와야 한다. 따라서 (B) [2]가 정답이다.

어휘 eerie 으스스한   mood 분위기

UNIT 04 공지, 회람

빈출 유형 공략 01 본문 p.256

공지
정부 규정을 준수하기 위해 직원들은 적절한 인증이 없으면 기계를 작동해서는 안 됩니다. 또한 생산 현장에서는 항상 장갑과 보안경을 착용해야 합니다. 이 조치들은 부상을 예방하기 위해 시행되고 있습니다. 문의 사항이 있으면 인사과에 전화하세요.

어휘 in compliance with ~에 따라   regulation 규제, 통제   operate 운영하다, 작동시키다   machinery 기계류   proper 적당한, 적절한   certification 증명, 인증   in addition 또한, 게다가   goggles 보안경   at all times 항상   measures 조치   in place 가동 중인   prevent 막다, 방지하다   injury 부상   phone 전화하다

1.
공지의 주제는 무엇인가?
(A) 성과 평가
(B) 직원 복리후생
(C) 안전 절차
(D) 전화 응대 방침

빈출 유형 공략 02 본문 p.257

회람
수신: 직원들
발신: Kelly Oppenheimer
날짜: 12월 21일
제목: 프린터 고장

여러분도 알아차리셨겠지만 우리의 컬러 프린터 두 대가 모두 고장 났습니다. 다행히 흑백 프린터들은 정상 작동하고 있기 때문에, 그것들은 자유롭게 사용하셔도 됩니다. 하지만 곧 있을 휴가 시즌 때문에 다음 달이 될 때까지는 기술자가 우리를 직접 도울 수 없을 겁니다. 프린터가 점검을 받을 수 있을 때까지 여러분의 인내를 부탁드립니다. 컬러 출력이 반드시 필요하다면, 제게 이메일을 주시면 여러분이 보낸 문서를 인쇄 시설로 보내는 것을 도와 드리겠습니다.

어휘 notice 알아차리다   out of order 고장 난   thankfully 다행스럽게도   black-and-white 흑백의   upcoming 다가오는, 곧 있을   service 점검하다   absolutely 무조건, 절대적으로   facility 시설

2.
기술자는 언제 사무실을 방문하는가?

(A) 12월
(B) 1월
(C) 2월
(D) 3월

ACTUAL TEST   본문 p.258

1. (D)	2. (C)	3. (C)	4. (D)	5. (B)
6. (B)	7. (A)	8. (C)	9. (B)	10. (C)
11. (D)	12. (D)			

[1-2] 공지

무료 테니스 레슨

테니스 치는 법을 배우고 싶었던 적이 있으셨나요? 만약 그렇다면, ²ᴬScottsdale 테니스 클럽의 회원들이 무료 레슨을 제공한다는 기쁜 소식을 알려 드립니다.

¹어르신들을 위한 무료 레슨이 지역 레크리에이션 센터에서 열립니다. ²ᴮA그룹은 6월부터 시작해서 매주 토요일 오후 3시부터 5시까지 있을 것입니다. B그룹은 7월부터 시작해서 매주 일요일 오후 5시부터 7시까지 있을 것입니다. 참가를 희망하는 사람은 레크리에이션 센터를 방문하여 프런트에서 등록해야 합니다. ²ᴰ그룹당 8명까지로 자리가 한정되어 있으니 놓치지 마세요! 이 레슨은 초급 교습생과 중급 교습생을 대상으로 합니다. ²ᶜ테니스 라켓은 강습 동안 무료로 이용할 수 있습니다.

어휘 offer 제공하다 complimentary 무료의 senior citizen 노인, 어르신 sign up 신청하다 front desk 프런트 (데스크) limited 제한된 miss out (기회를) 놓치다 available 이용 가능한 intermediate 중급의 racket 라켓 free of charge 무료의

1.
누구를 위한 공지인가?
(A) 초등학생
(B) 전문직 종사자
(C) 숙련된 테니스 선수
(D) 고령의 주민

해설 대상
두 번째 단락에서 senior citizens를 대상으로 한다고 했으므로 (D)가 정답이다.

패러프레이징 senior citizens → Elderly residents

어휘 intend 의도하다 professional 전문가 advanced 고급의, 상급의 elderly 나이가 든 resident 주민

2.
공지에 따르면 테니스 레슨에 관해 사실인 것은 무엇인가?
(A) 레슨은 테니스 동호회 회원들에게 가장 적합하다.
(B) 레슨은 모두 같은 시간에 열린다.
(C) 레슨 도중 무료 라켓을 이용할 수 있다.
(D) 그룹당 10명 이상의 참가자가 필요하다.

해설 NOT/True
마지막 단락에서 테니스 라켓을 무료로 이용할 수 있다고 했으므로 (C)가 정답이다.

어휘 suited for ~에 적당한 take place 일어나다, 발생하다 at least 적어도 participant 참가자 per ~당

[3-5] 회람

수신: Cottone Logistics 전 직원
³발신: Elise Gault
날짜: 10월 6일
회신: 본사 방문

이번 주 금요일인 10월 10일에 본사의 대표이신 Lisa Finch 씨가 우리 현장을 방문할 예정입니다. 핀치 씨가 우리 업무와 작업 환경에 보다 익숙해지도록 돕기 위해 여러 행사가 기획되었습니다. 일정은 다음과 같습니다.

시간	행사	참석 예정자	호실
오전 9:30	지점 현황 보고	경영팀	1번 회의실
오전 10:30	³지점장 동행 시설 견학	³Elise Gault	—
오후 12:30	중식	Elise Gault & 인사팀	1번 회의실
오후 1:30	Finch 씨의 발표	전 직원	본관
⁴오후 2:00	⁴질의응답 시간, 질문은 사전에 제출하세요	전 직원	본관

⁵Finch 씨는 시설 투어 도중 모든 부서를 보고 싶어 하시며 회사의 정책뿐만 아니라 여러분의 역할에 대해 문의할 수 있습니다. 자신 있게 답변할 수 있도록 직원 안내서를 검토할 것을 권합니다.

어휘 HQ 본사(= headquarters) representative 대표, 대리인 corporate 기업의, 회사의 site 현장, 장소 operation 활동, 운영 environment 환경 branch 지점, 지사 status 현황 conference room 회의실 facility 시설 presentation 발표 question-and-answer session 질의응답 시간 submit 제출하다 in advance 미리, 사전에 role 역할 as well as ~뿐만 아니라 policy 정책, 방침 encourage 장려하다 handbook 안내서

3.
Gault 씨는 누구이겠는가?
(A) 안전 조사관
(B) 본사 대표
(C) 지점장
(D) 사업주

해설 추론/암시
Gault를 키워드로 지문을 검색한다. Elise Gault는 회람의 발신인으로서, 가운데 도표를 보면 Lisa Finch를 동행해서 지점을 견학하게 될 지점장으로 나오므로 (C)가 정답이다.

어휘 safety 안전 inspector 조사관, 감독관

4.
Finch 씨가 질문에 답변할 시간은 언제인가?
(A) 오전 9시 30분
(B) 오전 10시 30분
(C) 오후 1시 30분
(D) 오후 2시

해설 세부 사항
answer some questions를 키워드로 지문을 검색한다. 도표에서 질의응답 시간은 오후 2시로 나오므로 (D)가 정답이다.

5.
Gault 씨가 Cottone Logistics의 직원들에 대해 암시하는 것은 무엇인가?
(A) 10월 10일에 모든 행사에 참석해야 한다.
(B) 몇 가지 회사 방침을 잊어버렸을 수 있다.
(C) 10월 10일에는 교대 근무를 일찍 끝낼 것이다.
(D) 회의 참석을 확정해야 한다.

해설 추론/암시
Elise Gault는 회람의 발신인이므로 지문에서 대명사 I로 나온다는 것을 파악해야 한다. Lisa Finch가 직원들에게 회사의 정책과 직원들의 역할에 대해 질문을 할 수 있으므로 미리 직원 안내서를 검토하라고 했다. 직원 안내서에 나오는 회사 방침을 미리 숙지하라는 것이므로 (B)가 정답이다.

어휘 attend 참석하다 shift 교대 근무 confirm 확인하다, 확정하다

[6-8] 공지

> 항공기 승객들은 주목해 주십시오:
> ⁶올랜도 공항의 모노레일이 공식적으로 재건축에 들어갔습니다. 1월 13일부터 4월 10일까지 모노레일이 폐쇄되고 운행이 중단된다는 점을 유념하시기 바랍니다.
> ⁷ᴮ올랜도 공항의 모노레일은 수리, 재단장 및 전반적인 기능 향상이 필요합니다. 새로워진 모노레일은 더 빠른 이동 시간, 추가 좌석, 더 많은 수하물 공간, 그리고 현대적인 디자인을 자랑할 것입니다.
> ⁷ᴰ ⁸터미널 사이를 이동해야 하는 여행객들은 무료 버스 서비스를 이용할 수 있을 것입니다. 모노레일 공사 진행 중에는 운행이 증편될 것입니다. ⁷ᶜ조감도와 최신 정보를 비롯한 상세한 사항은 www.orlandoairport.com을 방문하시기 바랍니다. 여러분의 협조와 양해에 감사드립니다.

어휘 flyer 비행기 승객 monorail 모노레일, 단궤 열차 reconstruction 재건축 be aware that ~라는 것을 알다 suspend (서비스를) 중단하다 refurbish 재단장하다 update 갱신, 최신 정보; 갱신하다 boast 자랑하다 extra 추가의, 여분의 luggage 수하물 available 이용 가능한 underway 진행 중인 concept photo 조감도

6.
1월에 무엇이 시작될 예정인가?
(A) 또 다른 공항 부속 건물의 건설
(B) 최신 운송 시스템의 제작
(C) 열차 운행 일정 연장
(D) 항공 노선의 변경

해설 세부 사항
January를 키워드로 지문을 검색한다. 1월 13일부터 4월 10일까지 모노레일이 폐쇄된다고 했는데 바로 앞 문장에 모노레일을 재건축하기 때문이라는 이유가 나오므로 (B)가 정답이다. transit system은 버스, 기차 등을 망라하는 모든 운송 시스템을 의미한다.

어휘 be scheduled to do ~하기로 되어 있다 transit 수송, 교통 체계 extended 연장된 route 길, 경로

7.
올랜도 공항에 대해 나타나지 않은 것은 무엇인가?
(A) 올랜도 시내로 가는 버스 서비스를 이용할 수 있다.
(B) 현재의 모노레일은 구식이다.
(C) 공식 웹 사이트가 있다.
(D) 1개 이상의 터미널이 있다.

해설 NOT/True
Orlando Airport를 키워드로 지문을 검색한다. 올랜도 시내로 가는 버스에 대한 내용은 없으므로 (A)가 정답이다.

어휘 outdated 구식인, 낡은

8.
[1], [2], [3], [4]로 표시된 위치 중 다음 문장이 들어가기에 가장 적절한 곳은?
"모노레일 공사 진행 중에는 운행이 증편될 것입니다."
(A) [1]
(B) [2]
(C) [3]
(D) [4]

해설 문장 삽입
주어진 문장의 service는 free bus service(무료 버스 서비스)를 의미하므로, free bus service가 언급된 다음인 [3]에 오는 것이 적절하다. 따라서 (C)가 정답이다.

[9-12] 공지

> 젊은 기업가 주간
> ⁹ ¹¹ᶜ모리스타운은 3월 14일부터 21일까지 여덟 번째 연례 젊은 기업가 주간을 기념하게 됩니다. ¹¹ᴰ그 기간 동안, 모리스타운 지역사회는 우리 지역 기업들의 기업가 정신을 조명할 것입니다.
> ¹¹ᴮ소기업주들에 의해 운영되는 거의 모든 가게와 음식점들이 이 기간 동안 할인이나 판촉 행사를 할 예정입니다. ¹⁰ᴬMuriel's Diner는 스페셜 조식 샘플러를 가지고 5년 연속으로 행사에 참가합니다. ¹⁰ᴮKathy's Jewelry Boutique도 올해 다시 참가하며, 모든 구매에 대해 10% 할인을 제공합니다. ¹⁰ᶜ ¹⁰ᴰYuna's

Stationery는 처음으로 행사에 참여하며, 지난해 Viola & Me Crafts가 벌인 판촉 행사의 전철을 밟아 원 플러스 원 행사를 할 것입니다.

[12]관련 업체 및 이용 가능한 특별 할인에 대한 자세한 내용은 www.morristown.com을 확인하십시오. 무료 선물을 받을 수 있는 인쇄 가능한 쿠폰과 상품권도 찾을 수 있습니다. 지역의 기업을 지원하고 동시에 비용도 절감할 수 있는 기회가 여기 있습니다!

어휘 celebrate 기념하다, 축하하다 annual 연례의 period 기간 community 지역사회, 공동체 highlight 강조하다 entrepreneurial 기업가의 spirit 정신 promotion 판촉 diner 식당 consecutive 연속적인 sampler 샘플러, 시식용 음식 jewelry 보석류 purchase 구입(품) stationery 문구류 buy one, get one 원 플러스 원 follow in the footsteps of ~의 전철을 밟다 involved 관련된 unique 독특한, 독창적인

9.
공지의 목적은 무엇인가?
(A) 고객 문의에 답하기 위해
(B) 대중들에게 행사에 대해 알리기 위해
(C) 음식점의 개업을 광고하기 위해
(D) 여성 사업가들을 홍보하기 위해

해설 주제/목적
제목과 문두에서 젊은 기업가 주간이라는 행사를 알리고 있으므로 (B)가 정답이다.

어휘 inquiry 문의 alert 알리다, 주의를 환기하다 public 대중 promote 홍보하다

10.
공지에 따르면 젊은 기업가 주간에 새로 참여하는 업체는 무엇인가?
(A) Muriel's Diner
(B) Kathy's Jewelry Boutique
(C) Yuna's Stationery
(D) Viola & Me Crafts

해설 세부 사항
Yuna's Stationery가 처음으로 참여한다고 했으므로 (C)가 정답이다. Muriel's Diners는 5년 연속으로 참여하고, Kathy's Jewelry Boutique는 올해 다시 참여한다. 그리고 Viola & Me Crafts는 지난해에 참여했다.

11.
행사에 대해 나타난 것은 무엇인가?
(A) 업체들은 돈을 지불해야만 특집으로 소개될 수 있다.
(B) 젊은 기업가의 업체들이 모두 참가한다.
(C) 열린지 10년 이상 되었다.
(D) 지역의 업체들만을 조명한다.

해설 NOT/True
(A)에 대한 언급은 없고, 여덟 번째로 열렸다고 했으므로 (C)는 오답이다. 젊은 기업가들이 운영하는 업체가 전부 다 참여하는 것은 아니므로 (B)도 오답이다. 젊은 기업가 주간은 지역 내 업체들이 참여하는 행사이므로 (D)가 정답이다.

어휘 feature 특집 기사로 다루다 decade 10년

12.
[1], [2], [3], [4]로 표시된 위치 중 다음 문장이 들어가기에 가장 적절한 곳은?
"무료 선물을 받을 수 있는 인쇄 가능한 쿠폰과 상품권도 찾을 수 있습니다."
(A) [1]
(B) [2]
(C) [3]
(D) [4]

해설 문장 삽입
주어진 문장에 부사 even이 있으므로, 주어진 문장의 앞에 이미 어떤 혜택들이 소개되었다는 것을 유추할 수 있다. 웹 사이트에서 특별 할인에 관한 정보를 얻을 수 있다고 언급한 다음인 [4]가 가장 적절하다.

어휘 printable 인쇄 가능한 voucher 상품권, 쿠폰

UNIT 05 광고

빈출 유형 공략 01 본문 p.266

자격을 갖춘 후보자를 찾고 계신가요?
StarPoint Recruiters는 여러분이 찾고 있던 바로 그 업체입니다. 당사는 20년 이상 헤드헌팅 사업을 해 왔으며, 마케팅, 재무, 서비스, 경영 등의 여러 분야에서 전문 지식을 보유하고 있습니다.

우리는 다음과 같은 직원을 찾는 것으로 알려져 있습니다.
✓ 항상 시간을 엄수하는 직원
✓ 프로답게 복장을 갖추고 행동하는 직원
✓ 해당 분야에서 검증된 경력을 가진 직원
✓ 자신의 경력 계발에 진지하게 임하는 직원

당사의 전문 헤드헌터들에 대해 더 자세히 알고 싶으시면 4월 8일 오후 2시 설명회에 오시기 바랍니다. 설명회에서 당사의 최고경영자가 당사의 선발 과정과, 고객에게 최고의 후보자만을 추천하는 확실한 노하우에 대해 설명할 것입니다.

어휘 qualified 자격을 갖춘, 적임의 candidate 후보자, 지원자 recruiter 스카우터, 헤드헌터 expertise 전문 지식 field 분야 finance 재무 management 경영, 운영 on time 정각에, 제때에 professional 전문적인, 전문가의 manner 방법, 방식 verify 입증하다 career 경력 information session 설명회 selection 선정, 선발 ensure 확실히 하다, 보장하다 recommend 추천하다 client 고객

1.
StarPoint Recruiters가 후보자에 대해 약속하는 자질이 아닌 것은 무엇인가?
(A) 시간 엄수
(B) 관련 자격

(C) 효율성
(D) 적절한 복장

어휘 punctuality 시간 엄수   relevant 관련 있는, 적절한   qualification 자격(증)   efficiency 효율성   appropriate 적절한   attire 복장

빈출 유형 공략 02
본문 p.267

자막 제작자 구함!
Superb Subs는 영화, 텔레비전 프로그램, 인터넷 동영상 등의 다양한 매체용 자막을 제작할 최고의 직원들을 찾고 있습니다. 우리는 시험을 통과한 분들에게 무료 온라인 교육을 제공합니다. Superb Subs가 현재 찾고 있는 사람은 영어를 모국어로 하고 안정적으로 인터넷 접속이 되는, 본인의 컴퓨터와 헤드셋을 보유한 사람입니다.
Superb Subs에서 일하게 되면 여러분은 본인의 일정을 알아서 관리하게 됩니다. 하루에 1시간을 일할 수도 있고, 12시간 동안 일할 수도 있습니다. 또한 관심 있는 콘텐츠를 선택할 수 있습니다. 평균적인 Superb Subs 자막 제작자는 일하는 시간에 따라 주당 300달러에서 1,000달러를 법니다.
관심이 있으신가요? 오늘 www.superbsubs.com을 확인하고 지원하세요.

어휘 subtitle 자막   spectacular 멋진, 환상적인   a variety of 다양한   media 매체   trial test 시용 테스트   currently 현재, 지금   individual 사람   reliable 믿을 만한   access 접속   in charge of ~을 책임지는   interest 흥미롭게 하다   average 평균적인   depending on ~에 따라   apply 지원하다

2.
Superb Subs는 어떤 종류의 지원자를 찾고 있는가?
(A) 현재 자막을 작성하는 사람
(B) 여러 언어를 구사하는 사람
(C) 인터넷 연결이 좋은 사람
(D) 풀타임으로 일할 수 있는 사람

어휘 applicant 지원자   multiple 여럿의   connectivity 연결

ACTUAL TEST
본문 p.268

1. (A)	2. (C)	3. (D)	4. (B)	5. (C)
6. (A)	7. (C)	8. (B)	9. (A)	10. (B)
11. (A)				

[1-2] 온라인 광고

Yummy Vegan Foods
식단에서 동물성 제품을 배제하는 것에 관심이 있으세요?
보다 건강한 식사 방법을 찾고 있나요?
당신과 환경에 모두 이로운 맛있는 음식을 좋아하나요?

[1]당신이 이에 해당한다면 Yummy Vegan Foods를 드셔 보세요! 당신이 좋아하는 음식 중 얼마나 많은 것들이 더 건강에 좋은 채식주의 대안을 가지고 있는지 알게 되면 놀랄 것입니다.
[2]저희 웹 사이트를 방문하셔서 "vegancookies"라는 코드를 사용하시면 모든 주문에 대해 유제품이 들어 있지 않은 초콜릿칩 쿠키 6개를 받으실 수 있습니다!
[2]이 혜택은 12월 31일까지 유효하니 놓치지 마세요!

어휘 yummy 아주 맛있는   vegan 엄격한 채식주의자   remove 제거하다, 없애다   diet 식단   environment 환경   give ~ a try ~을 시도해 보다   dish 음식   alternative 대안   dairy-free 유제품이 들어 있지 않은   valid 유효한   miss out 놓치다

1.
광고의 목적은 무엇인가?
(A) 신규 고객을 유치하려고
(B) 신제품을 홍보하려고
(C) 새 메뉴를 선보이려고
(D) 새로 단장된 웹 사이트를 광고하려고

해설 주제/목적
Yummy Vegan Foods라는 제목 밑에 3개의 의문문으로 채식주의 음식에 대한 흥미를 고조시킨 후 자사 제품을 홍보하고 있으므로 고객을 유치하기 위한 목적의 광고라는 것을 알 수 있으므로 (A)가 정답이다.

어휘 attract 유치하다   showcase 소개하다   update 갱신하다, 업데이트하다

2.
연말까지 이용 가능한 것은 무엇인가?
(A) 배송료 할인
(B) 주간 식단
(C) 무료 디저트 제공
(D) 채식주의 요리책

해설 세부 사항
available과 end of the year를 키워드로 지문을 검색한다. end of the year는 지문에서 31 December(12월 31일)와 같이 나올 수 있다는 것을 염두에 둔다. 지문의 맨 끝에 This offer is valid until 31 December라고 나오는데, 앞쪽에서 this offer가 무엇인지 찾아보면 코드를 입력하면 받을 수 있는 무료 초콜릿칩 쿠키라는 것을 알 수 있다. 따라서 (C)가 정답이다.

어휘 available 이용 가능한   meal plan 식단   dessert 디저트   cookbook 요리책

[3-4] 광고

LAWRENCE 임대 아파트
침실 하나, 태평양이 내려다보이는 [3A]큰 창문, 널찍한 샤워 공간이 있는 욕실, [3C]최근에 보수된 식당과 주방 공간. [3B]대중교통과 지역 해변으로부터 수 분 거리에 위치. 110평방미터, 월세 1,400달러, 공과금 포함. 최소 1년의 임대 기간 요구됨. [4]계약

시 두 달 치 월세에 해당하는 보증금 지불 요. 8월 1일부터 입주 가능. 자세한 사항은 555-0124로 전화하세요.

어휘 for rent 임대용의 sizeable 꽤 큰, 상당한 크기의 overlook 내려다보다 spacious 넓은, 널찍한 renovate 수선하다, 보수하다 public transportation 대중교통 square meter 평방미터 monthly 매달, 월간 utility 공공요금, 공과금 minimum 최소한의 lease 임대 기간 security deposit 보증금 due 지불해야 하는

3.
광고에서 아파트에 대해 언급하지 않은 것은 무엇인가?
(A) 큰 창문이 있다.
(B) 대중교통에 가깝다.
(C) 최근에 보수되었다.
(D) 널찍한 침대가 있다.

해설 **NOT/True**
지문의 sizeable windows가 선택지에서 large windows로, public transportation이 public transit으로 패러프레이징되었다. 넓은 침대에 대한 언급은 없으므로 (D)가 정답이다.

어휘 mention 언급하다, 말하다 public transit 대중교통

4.
광고에 언급된 것은 무엇인가?
(A) 공과금은 임대료와 별도이다.
(B) 보증금이 필요하다.
(C) 아파트는 현재 비어 있다.
(D) 욕실에 욕조가 있다.

해설 **NOT/True**
utilities included가 있으므로 (A)는 오답, Available from August 1이 있으므로 (C)도 오답이고, (D)에 대한 언급은 없다. 두 달 치 월세에 해당하는 보증금이 필요하다고 했으므로 (B)가 정답이다.

어휘 utility bill 공과금 고지서 separate 분리된 unoccupied 비어 있는, 사람이 살고 있지 않은 tub 욕조

[5-7] 광고

"⁵창업하기"
Mitchell Consulting 창업자, Debra Mitchell 발표
11월 10일 수요일 오후 6시 30분부터 7시 30분까지
포 레인 2104번지 Les Amis 레스토랑

⁵창업에 대해 생각해 본 적이 있습니까? 어디서부터 시작해야 하는지 아시나요? 소기업주에게 가장 적합한 자원을 어디서 찾을 수 있을까요? 대출은 어떻게 확보할까요?
⁵Mitchell Consulting의 무료 세미나에서 비즈니스와 관련된 당신의 모든 질문에 대한 해답을 얻으세요. 소기업 전문가인 Debra Mitchell 씨가 사업을 시작하는 방법에 대해 발표를 할 것이며, 여러분의 모든 열정적인 질문에 답변할 것입니다.
Mitchell 씨는 Mitchell Consulting으로 가장 잘 알려져 있지만, 커피숍과 애완동물 미용실과 같은 몇 가지 다른 성공적인 벤처사업을 하고 있습니다. 그녀는 또한 〈처음부터 제대로 시작하라: 성공으로 가는 지침〉을 비롯한 여러 권의 자기 계발서를 쓴 저자이기도 합니다. 그녀는 사람들이 자기 자신의 열정을 따르도록 격려하기 위해 전국을 돌면서 연설과 발표를 하고 있습니다. 그녀는 다양한 재능과 관심사를 가지고 있으며, 새로운 업계로의 진출을 노리는 모든 사람들에게 분명 도움이 될 것입니다.
www.mitchellconsulting.com에서 이 행사에 등록하세요. 티켓에는 식사비가 포함되어 있지 않지만, ⁶세미나 도중 판매되는 Debra Mitchell의 모든 도서에 대해 50% 할인 쿠폰이 제공됩니다.

어휘 founder 설립자 resource 자원, 자산 secure 확보하다, 얻다 loan 대출(금) expert 전문가 give a presentation 발표하다 get started (일을) 시작하다 groom 동물의 털을 다듬다 self-help book 자기 계발서 inspire 고무하다, 영감을 불어넣다 passion 열정 register for ~에 등록하다 on sale 판매되는

5.
행사가 마련되는 이유는 무엇이겠는가?
(A) 업주들을 유치하기 위해
(B) 성공한 경영자를 축하하기 위해
(C) 사업을 새로 시작하는 사람들을 돕기 위해
(D) 사람들에게 대출을 받도록 장려하기 위해

해설 **추론/암시**
제목에서 예비 사업가들을 위한 것임을 밝힌 뒤 몇 개의 의문문으로 세미나의 주제가 무엇인지를 나열하고 있으므로 (C)가 정답이다.

어휘 organize 준비하다, 조직하다 attract 유치하다, 유인하다 executive 임원, 경영자 encourage 장려하다, 격려하다

6.
참가자들은 세미나에 참석하면 무엇을 받을 수 있는가?
(A) 할인
(B) Mitchell 씨와 일대일 만남
(C) 무료 식사
(D) 개인 맞춤 사업 계획

해설 **세부 사항**
attend와 seminar를 키워드로 지문을 검색한다. 동사 attend는 지문에서 participate in, register for 등으로 표현될 수 있다는 것을 염두에 두어야 한다. 마지막 단락에서 register for로 시작하는 문장이 나온 뒤 행사에 참여하면 받을 수 있는 혜택을 언급하고 있는데, 식사는 유료이지만, 도서에 대해 50% 할인을 받을 수 있다고 했으므로 (A)가 정답이다.

어휘 discount 할인 one-on-one 일대일 personalized 개인 맞춤의

7.
[1], [2], [3], [4]로 표시된 위치 중 다음 문장이 들어가기에 가장 적절한 곳은?
"그녀는 다양한 재능과 관심사를 가지고 있으며, 새로운 업계로의 진출을 노리는 모든 사람들에게 분명 도움이 될 것입니다."
(A) [1]
(B) [2]

(C) [3]
(D) [4]

해설 문장 삽입
주어진 문장의 she는 Debra Mitchell을 의미하며, 주어진 문장의 성격상 Debra Mitchell에 대한 홍보 성격의 글이 끝난 후에 오는 것이 자연스럽다. 따라서 저자이자 사업가이며 전국을 순회하는 강연자라는 소개를 한 다음인 [3]에 오는 것이 가장 자연스럽다.

어휘 wide array of 다수의   talent 재능

[8-11] 광고

> [8]애틀랜틱 시티에서 당신이 꿈꾸던 집을 임대하세요
>
> [8]여름이 몇 달 남지 않은 지금이야말로 여러분의 휴가 계획을 세울 때입니다. 애틀랜틱 시티에서 여러분의 하루 하루를 보내는 것보다 더 좋은 방법이 있을까요? 아름다운 바다 경치를 누릴 수 있고, 많은 카지노 중 한 곳에서 행운을 시험해 볼 수도 있고, 지역에서 가장 좋은 음식점들 몇 곳에서 맛있는 식사를 즐길 수도 있습니다.
>
> 여러분의 거처를 좁은 호텔방으로 제한하는 대신, 넓고 프라이빗한 주택을 빌리는 것이 휴가를 떠나기에 가장 좋은 방법입니다. 호텔에 지불하게 될 비용의 [9]일부분만 내고 호화롭고 잘 관리된 집에서 지낼 수 있습니다.
>
> 우리의 임대 프로그램은 다음과 같은 것을 제공합니다.
> ✓ [10C]짧게는 1박에서 길게는 수개월 동안 대여
> ✓ 모든 투숙객의 도착 전 대청소
> ✓ 세면도구, 침구 및 수건 완비
> ✓ [10A]대규모 단체 및 장기 투숙에 대한 할인
> ✓ [10D]임차인 보험
>
> [11]www.rentalhomesac.com에서 여러분이 꿈꾸던 별장의 가상 투어를 해보세요. 오늘 숙박을 예약하시려면 저희 직원에게 555-1198로 전화하세요.

어휘 limit 제한하다   luxurious 호화로운, 고급스러운   fraction 부분, 일부   stock (재고를) 갖추다   toiletries 세면도구   bedding 침구   renter 임차인, 세입자   insurance 보험   virtual 가상의   representative 대리인, 직원

8.
광고의 대상자는 누구인가?
(A) 애틀랜틱 시티 주민
(B) 휴양객
(C) 부동산 중개업자
(D) 호텔 지배인

해설 주제/목적/대상
제목과 본문의 첫 번째 문장에서 휴가를 계획하는 사람들을 위한 광고라는 것을 알 수 있으므로 (B)가 정답이다.

어휘 target audience 광고 대상자   seasonal 계절적인   real estate agent 부동산 중개인

9.
두 번째 단락 세 번째 줄의 'fraction'과 의미가 가장 가까운 것은?
(A) 부분
(B) 단체
(C) 분열
(D) 끝

해설 동의어 찾기
호텔을 이용하는 비용의 '일부'를 내고 주택을 빌릴 수 있다는 내용이므로 '부분'이라는 뜻의 part가 의미상 가장 가깝다. 따라서 (A)가 정답이다.

10.
프로그램의 특징으로 언급되지 않은 것은 무엇인가?
(A) 대규모 단체에 대한 요금 할인
(B) 숙박 도중 무료 청소 서비스
(C) 다양한 임대 기간
(D) 우발적인 피해에 대한 보호

해설 NOT/True
지문에서 프로그램의 장점이 나열된 부분을 선택지와 대조한다. 지문의 Discounts for larger groups가 선택지에서 Cheaper rates for large parties로, Rentals for as short as one night or as long as several months가 Rentals for various lengths of time으로, Renters insurance가 Protection against accidental damages로 패러프레이징되었다. 도착 전에만 대청소를 해줄 뿐 숙박 도중 청소를 해준다는 내용은 없으므로 (B)가 정답이다.

어휘 feature 특징   rate 요금   various 다양한   accidental 우발적인   damage 피해

11.
임대용 주택에 대해 어떻게 더 많은 정보를 얻을 수 있는가?
(A) 웹 사이트를 방문함으로써
(B) 광고에 응답함으로써
(C) 사무실에 들름으로써
(D) 온라인 후기를 읽음으로써

해설 세부 사항
웹 사이트에서 가상 투어를 할 수 있다고 했으므로 (A)가 정답이다.

어휘 respond 응답하다, 대응하다   stop by 잠깐 들르다   review 후기

UNIT 06 웹페이지, 양식, 후기

빈출 유형 공략 01   본문 p.276

> Trejo Bay Resort에 대금을 지불해 주셔서 감사합니다. 자세한 내용은 하단을 참조해 주십시오.
>
> 오늘 날짜: 5월 2일
> 예약 날짜: 8월 10일~22일
> 합계액: 2,580달러 *
> 지불한 계약금 (5월 2일): 120달러, 신용카드 XXXX-XXXX-XXXX-8774
> 잔금: 2,460달러

고객: Robert Muntz

*장기 투숙에 대한 10% 할인이 반영됨

여행 계획이 변경되면 저희에게 가능한 한 빨리 알려 주십시오. 취소 수수료는 예약일에 얼마나 임박하여 취소되었는지에 따라 계산됩니다. 이 정책에 대해 더 자세히 읽으시려면 여기를 클릭하세요.

어휘 detail 세부 사항 reservation 예약 total 합계 deposit 보증금, 계약금 outstanding 미지불된 balance 잔액, 잔고 reflect 반영하다 extended 연장된 notify 알리다, 통지하다 cancellation 취소 calculate 계산하다 based on ~에 따라

1.
Trejo Bay Resort에 대해 암시된 것은 무엇인가?
(A) 오래 투숙하면 할인해 준다.
(B) 무료 취소를 허용한다.
(C) 두 개 이상의 지점이 있다.
(D) 정기적으로 정책을 변경한다.

빈출 유형 공략 02
본문 p.277

Motley Solutions
콜터 가 772번지
더블린, 아일랜드

고객 유형:	재방문
고객 성명:	Earl Clevenger
이메일 주소:	e.clevenger@qmail.com
전화 번호:	555-0127
복사 개수:	500
컬러/흑백:	컬러

여기에 사양서를 첨부하세요:
소고기 육포_광고

추가 정보:
치즈와 고기 축제가 지역에서 열리기 때문에 축제를 위해 설치하는 육포 판매대를 광고하고 싶습니다. 이 양식에 첨부한 광고의 컬러 사본 500장이 필요합니다. 지난번에 주문했을 때는 전단지에 광택이 충분히 나지 않았으니, 인쇄할 때 좀 더 광택이 나는 종이를 사용해 주세요. 가격을 알려주시면 송금해 드리겠습니다.

어휘 copy 복사, 한 부 black and white 흑백 attach 첨부하다 specifications 사양 beef jerky 육포 stall 판매대, 노점 set up 설치하다 form 양식 flyer 전단지 glossy 윤이 나는 provide 제공하다 transfer 송금하다, 이체하다

2.
Clevenger 씨는 왜 양식을 작성했는가?
(A) 행사에 등록하기 위해
(B) 서비스를 요청하기 위해
(C) 민원을 제기하기 위해
(D) 의견을 주기 위해

ACTUAL TEST
본문 p.278

1. (C) **2.** (A) **3.** (B) **4.** (B) **5.** (D)
6. (B) **7.** (A) **8.** (C) **9.** (A) **10.** (C)
11. (B) **12.** (C)

[1-2] 웹페이지

Martin's Drop Off and Fly

| 홈 | 오시는 길 | 자주 묻는 질문 | 연락하기 |

Martin's Drop Off and Fly에 오신 것을 환영합니다. 당사는 공항에서 가까운 거리에 위치해 있으며 장기 주차를 위한 최상의 조건을 제공합니다. [1]아래 양식을 작성하시어 우리가 고객님의 차량을 위한 공간을 확보할 수 있도록 해주시기 바랍니다. 수용 능력이 제한되어 있기 때문에 사전 예약을 권장합니다. [2]A터미널에서부터 C터미널까지를 모두 경유하는 무료 셔틀 서비스가 10분마다 출발합니다. 보다 자세한 정보는 자주 묻는 질문 탭을 참조하세요. 구체적인 질문은 연락하기 탭에 있는 의견란에 해 주세요.

성명: Sarah Souza
항공사와 항공편 번호: Speedy Airways PX98620
주차할 날짜 및 대략적인 시간:
2월 20일 금요일 오후 6시 30분
차를 되찾아갈 날짜 및 대략적인 시간:
3월 3일 화요일 오후 1시 45분

어휘 directions 길 안내 a short distance from ~로부터 조금 떨어진 거리 deal 거래 조건 long-term 장기간의 fill out 작성하다, 기입하다 reserve 예약하다, 잡아 두다 capacity 용량, 수용 능력 limited 제한된 advance reservation 사전 예약 complimentary 무료의 shuttle service 왕복 운행 direct (편지 등을) 보내다 specific 구체적인 comment 의견 approximate 대략적인

1.
양식은 무엇에 이용되는가?
(A) 정식으로 민원 제기하기
(B) 택시 운행 일정 잡기
(C) 주차 공간 확보하기
(D) 항공권 검색하기

해설 세부 사항
공항 이용객들에게 차량 주차 공간을 제공하는 업체의 광고 글이다. 미리 주차 공간을 예약하기 위해 양식을 작성하라고 했으므로 (C)가 정답이다.

패러프레이징 a space for your car → a parking spot

어휘 issue 발급하다 formal 공식적인, 정식의 complaint 불만, 민원 schedule 일정을 잡다 secure 확보하다 parking spot 주차 공간

2.
셔틀에 대해 무엇이 나타나 있는가?
(A) 요금이 없다.

(B) 두 개의 터미널을 운행한다.
(C) 예약이 필요하다.
(D) 일정이 불규칙하다.

해설 **NOT/True**
shuttle을 키워드로 지문을 검색한다. 지문의 Complimentary shuttle service에서 complimentary는 무료라는 뜻으로 free의 동의어이므로 (A)가 정답이다. 셔틀은 A에서 C까지 세 개의 터미널을 운행하므로 (B)는 오답이고, 예약에 관한 언급은 없으며, 10분마다 규칙적으로 출발한다고 했으므로 (C), (D)도 오답이다.

어휘 fare (교통) 요금 require 요구하다, 필요로 하다
reservation 예약 irregular 불규칙한

[3-5] 후기

> McKenzie 양복점
> 후기 작성자: Cheryl Wright
> 평점(5점 만점): 4.5
>
> 저는 최근에 켄웨이 빌딩에 있는 McKenzie 양복점에서 처음으로 서비스를 이용했습니다. 주인인 Antonio McKenzie 씨는 저를 따뜻하게 맞아 주셨고 제 요구 조건을 잘 들어주셨습니다. ³그분과 그분의 두 아드님이 직원인데, 오래된 의복을 다루는 일에 대해 무척 해박하더군요. 저는 빈티지 숍에서 산 옷을 가져갔습니다. 그 옷은 표백제로 얼룩이 져서 천 조각 하나를 교체해야 했습니다. 완성된 옷이 저에게 다시 돌아왔을 때 그것은 새것처럼 보였습니다. ⁴옷감을 구하는 것이 거의 불가능한데도 불구하고 그분들이 옷감과 정확히 일치하는 천을 찾아냈다는 데 무척 놀랐습니다.
>
> 서비스가 매우 만족스러웠지만 한 가지 짚고 넘어가야 할 점이 있습니다. ⁵그 작업을 마치는 데 걸린 시간은 2주였는데, 업계 평균의 약 두 배였습니다. 이 점 때문에 필요한 서비스에 대해서는 미리 계획을 세우는 게 좋을 것 같습니다.

어휘 recently 최근에 greet 맞다, 환영하다 make up ~을 이루다, 구성하다 staff 직원 knowledgeable 해박한 deal with ~을 다루다 garment 의복, 옷 vintage 빈티지의, 연대가 오래 된 panel 판, 조각 replace 교체하다 stain 얼룩지게 하다 bleach 표백제 complete 완성하다 match 일치하는 것 fabric 천, 직물 point out 지적하다 turnaround 작업을 완료해서 회송하는 데 걸리는 시간

3.
McKenzie 양복점에 대해 암시된 것은 무엇인가?
(A) 최근에 켄웨이 빌딩으로 이전했다.
(B) 가족 사업이다.
(C) 서비스 선택의 폭을 넓혔다.
(D) 빈티지 옷을 판매한다.

해설 **추론/암시**
지문의 'He and his two sons, who make up the staff'에서 Antonio McKenzie와 그의 두 아들이 직원이라고 나오므로 가족이 운영하는 업체라는 것을 알 수 있다. 따라서 (B)가 정답이다.

어휘 move to ~로 이사하다 expand 확장하다, 확대하다 selection 선택, 선정 for sale 판매용의

4.
Wright 씨는 무엇에 대해 놀랐는가?
(A) 저렴한 수선 비용
(B) 희귀한 원단의 조달
(C) 세척제의 효과
(D) 큰 직원 규모

해설 **세부 사항**
surprised를 키워드로 지문을 검색해야 한다. 지문 중반부에 surprised의 유의어인 shocked가 나오고 그 뒤에 Ms. Wright가 놀란 이유가 나온다. 오래되어 구하기 힘든 원단을 찾아냈다는 것에 놀랐다고 했으므로 (B)가 정답이다.

패러프레이징 nearly impossible to find → rare

어휘 affordable (가격이) 알맞은, 입수 가능한 source 공급자를 찾다 rare 희귀한, 드문 effectiveness 효과

5.
[1], [2], [3], [4]로 표시된 위치 중 다음 문장이 들어가기에 가장 적절한 곳은?
"이 점 때문에 필요한 서비스에 대해서는 미리 계획을 세우는 게 좋을 것 같습니다."
(A) [1]
(B) [2]
(C) [3]
(D) [4]

해설 **문장 삽입**
주어진 문장의 this는 필요한 서비스를 미리 계획하도록 만드는 것이므로 시간과 관련이 있다는 것을 알 수 있다. 따라서 작업이 업계 평균의 두 배가 걸린다고 말하며 작업 속도를 지적한 문장 다음인 [4]에 들어가는 것이 가장 적합하다.

[6-8] 웹페이지

> ⁶Auckland Regal 호텔은 Orange River 부속건물의 건설이 공식적으로 완료되었음을 알리게 되어 기쁩니다. 호텔의 이 새로운 공간은 뉴질랜드에서 가장 현대적이고 고급스러운 디자인을 가지고 있습니다. 연회장, 회의실에 더해 행사장도 있어서 특별한 행사를 위해 여러분이 원하시는 모든 요구에 부응할 수 있습니다. 또한 호텔에 2박 이상을 예약한 손님들은 대규모 모임에 대해 할인을 받게 될 것입니다.
>
> 새로운 객실 외에, 저희 호텔에서 자부심을 가지고 제공하고 있는 것들입니다.
> • 폭넓은 룸서비스 메뉴
> • 온수 욕조가 있는 실내 및 실외 수영장
> • 저렴한 비용으로 이용할 수 있는 24시간 운동 시설
> • 보안이 유지되는 무료 인터넷 접속이 가능한 카페
> • ⁷로비에서 무료로 제공되는 차와 쿠키
>
> Auckland Regal 호텔은 대중교통, 관광지, 그리고 쇼핑 센터 근처에 편리하게 위치해 있습니다. 보다 자세한 것은 reservations@regalhotels.com으로 연락하세요.

어휘 wing 부속건물 officially 공식적으로 luxurious 고급스러운 ballroom 연회장 cater to ~을 충족시키다 in addition to

~외에 extensive 방대한, 폭넓은 indoor 실내의 tub 욕조
access 접속 gym 체육관, 헬스클럽 fee 요금, 비용
complimentary 무료의 public transportation 대중교통
tourist attraction 관광지

6.
주로 누구를 위한 정보인가?
(A) 잠재 투자자
(B) 도시의 방문객
(C) 호텔 직원
(D) 현지 투어 가이드

해설 **대상**
호텔 부속 건물의 완공을 알리며 호텔을 홍보하고 있으므로, 방문객들을 위한 홍보성 글임을 알 수 있다. 따라서 (B)가 정답이다.

어휘 intend 의도하다 potential 잠재적인 investor 투자자
local 지역의

7.
호텔은 투숙객에게 무엇을 무료로 제공하는가?
(A) 가벼운 다과
(B) 헬스장 이용
(C) 룸서비스
(D) 회의 장비

해설 **세부 사항**
free를 키워드로 지문을 검색한다. free의 동의어인 complimentary가 나오며 쿠키와 차를 무료로 제공한다고 했으므로 (A)가 정답이다.

패러프레이징 tea and cookies → light refreshments

어휘 refreshments 간식

8.
[1], [2], [3], [4]로 표시된 위치 중 다음 문장이 들어가기에 가장 적절한 곳은?
"또한 호텔에 2박 이상을 예약한 손님들은 대규모 모임에 대해 할인을 받게 될 것입니다."
(A) [1]
(B) [2]
(C) [3]
(D) [4]

해설 **문장 삽입**
In addition(또한)으로 보아 호텔을 홍보하는 내용 뒤에 이어지는 문장임을 알 수 있다. 새로 완공된 부속건물에 대한 홍보가 끝나고 객실 외의 서비스 홍보가 시작되기 전인 [3]에 들어가는 것이 가장 적절하다.

어휘 in addition 또한, 게다가 book 예약하다 gathering 모임

[9-12] 후기

"문제가 생기기 전까지는 훌륭한 서비스"
⁹Theresa Kirby
⁹저는 우리 회사가 제작하는 비디오 게임을 홍보합니다. 저의 주요 업무 중 하나는 광고 계약을 협상해서 체결하는 것입니다. ¹⁰우리는 전 세계에 상품을 판매하기 때문에 이러한 계약서가 정확하게 번역되는 것이 필수적이며, 그래서 저는 AGP 번역을 이용합니다. 저는 AGP 번역팀이 얼마나 빨리 번역 프로젝트를 마치는지에 항상 감탄해 왔습니다. 그들은 또한 제가 의도한 것을 완전히 이해했는지 확인하기 위해 최종안을 제공하기 전에 가끔 질문을 해오기도 합니다. 그들은 20개의 언어를 전문으로 하기 때문에, 저는 같은 회사를 다양한 프로젝트에 이용할 수 있습니다.

서비스의 그러한 측면은 항상 훌륭하지만, ¹¹저의 고객 서비스 문제가 얼마나 형편없이 처리되는지를 보고 놀랐습니다. 제가 요청하지 않은 프로젝트에 대해 제 계정에 예상치 못한 요금이 청구되었다는 것을 알았습니다. 저는 이메일로 고객 서비스팀에 연락했습니다. ¹²회사에서 영업일 기준으로 3일 이내에 연락을 하겠다는 자동 응답 회신을 받았습니다. 실상은 전혀 그렇지 않았습니다. 일주일 후, 저는 후속 이메일을 보냈고 그 후 며칠 후에 또 다른 이메일을 보냈습니다. 거의 한 달이 지난 후에야 AGP 번역의 누군가가 마침내 제 계정을 보고 요금을 환불해 주었습니다. 이같이 유감스러운 경험으로 인해 저는 다른 번역 업체를 알아보게 되었습니다.

어휘 issue 문제 promote 판촉하다, 홍보하다 main 주된, 주요한
negotiate 협상하다 secure 확보하다 contract 계약
essential 필수적인 accurately 정확하게 translate 번역하다
impressed 깊은 인상을 받은 draft 원고, 초안 ensure 보장하다, 확실하게 하다 completely 완전히 intend 의도하다
specialize in ~을 전문으로 하다 a variety of 다양한 poorly 형편없이, 좋지 못하게 handle 다루다, 처리하다 notice 알아차리다
account 계정, 계좌 contact 연락하다 automated 자동화된
get in touch 연락하다 follow-up 후속의 refund 환불하다
option 선택(권)

9.
Kirby 씨는 누구이겠는가?
(A) 마케팅 관리자
(B) 제품 검사자
(C) 비디오 게임 디자이너
(D) 회계사

해설 **추론/암시**
Theresa Kirby는 후기를 작성한 사람인데, 첫 문장에서 자신의 업무는 비디오 게임을 홍보하고 광고 계약을 체결하는 것이라고 했으므로 (A)가 정답이다.

어휘 tester 검사자, 시험관 accountant 회계사, 경리

10.
Kirby 씨에 대해 사실인 것은 무엇인가?
(A) 번역팀에 많은 질문을 한다.
(B) 종종 업무차 출장을 가야 한다.
(C) 법적 서류를 위해 서비스를 이용한다.
(D) 두 개 이상의 언어를 구사한다.

해설 **NOT/True**
광고 계약서를 정확하게 번역하기 위해 AGP 번역을 이용한다고 했

으므로 (C)가 정답이다.

패러프레이징 contracts → documents

어휘 legal 법적인, 법률의

11.
Kirby 씨는 어떤 문제점을 언급하는가?
(A) 고객 서비스팀이 아는 것이 별로 없었다.
(B) 자신의 민원이 즉시 처리되지 않았다.
(C) 번역 비용이 급격하게 올랐다.
(D) 정책 변경을 통보받지 못했다.

해설 세부 사항
Ms. Kirby는 두 번째 단락 전반에 걸쳐 AGP 번역이 고객 서비스 민원을 처리하는 방식에 실망해서 다른 번역 회사를 알아보게 되었다고 했으므로 (B)가 정답이다.

패러프레이징 customer service issue → complaint / handled → addressed

어휘 knowledgeable 아는 것이 많은, 박식한 address 처리하다 promptly 즉시 dramatically 극적으로, 급격히 inform 알리다, 통보하다 policy 정책, 방침

12.
[1], [2], [3], [4]로 표시된 위치 중 다음 문장이 들어가기에 가장 적절한 곳은?
"실상은 전혀 그렇지 않았습니다."
(A) [1]
(B) [2]
(C) [3]
(D) [4]

해설 문장 삽입
주어진 문장만으로는 This가 가리키는 것이 무엇인지 짐작하기 쉽지 않다. 이럴 경우 빈칸에 차례로 주어진 문장을 넣어보고 문맥이 자연스럽게 이어지는 것을 선택하는 것도 하나의 방법이다. 주어진 문장을 [3]에 넣어보면, This가 가리키는 것이 앞문장에 나온 회사의 자동 응답 내용임을 알 수 있다. 이것이 지켜지지 않았고 그 뒤로 거의 한 달 동안 민원이 처리되지 않았다는 내용이 이어지므로 문맥이 가장 자연스럽다.

어휘 not ~ at all 전혀 ~ 아닌 case 경우, 사례

UNIT 07 다중 지문

빈출 유형 공략
본문 p.286

수신: Oliver Gilbert 〈olivergilbert@gahaenterprises.net〉
발신: 에딘버그 스타디움 〈service@edinburgstadium.com〉
날짜: 12월 12일
제목: 개인 특별석

Gilbert 씨,

내년도에 에딘버그 스타디움의 개인 특별석을 예약해 주셔서 감사합니다. 이 이메일은 귀하께서 #B12 특별석을 배정받았음을 확인하기 위한 것이며, 이 특별석은 최대 20명까지 수용할 수 있습니다. 귀하가 원하시는 대로 특별석을 꾸미실 수 있으며, 당일에 경기나 다른 행사가 없더라도 특별석을 사용하실 수 있습니다. 귀하는 1월 2일부터 12월 31일까지 특별석을 이용하시게 됩니다.

개인 특별석 회원들께는 다양한 VIP 활동을 제공합니다. 예를 들어, 귀하는 경기가 끝난 후 홈팀 선수 중 한 명과 만나는 시간을 가지실 수 있습니다. [1-1]귀하께서 저희 스타디움에 오신 것을 환영하는 의미로 첫 VIP 활동 시 30% 할인이 제공됩니다. 조기 예약을 권장합니다.

Ronny Anderson
에딘버그 스타디움, 고객 서비스

어휘 book 예약하다 upcoming 다가오는, 곧 있을 confirm 확정하다 assign 배정하다 accommodate 수용하다, 부응하다 up to ~까지 decorate 장식하다, 꾸미다 have access to ~에 출입할 수 있다 a range of 다양한 meet-and-greet (유명인을) 만나는 session (특정한) 시간 athlete 운동선수

VIP 활동 요청 양식

성명: Oliver Gilbert
특별석 번호: B12
이메일: olivergilbert@gahaenterprises.net
요청 날짜: 2월 13일
행사: [2-1]Edinburg Tigers의 투수 Joseph Pollard와의 만남
참고: VIP 활동은 이용 가능한 범위가 제한되어 있습니다. 원하시는 날짜를 순서대로 나열해 주시면 저희가 최선을 다해 맞춰드리겠습니다.

[2-3]1순위 선택	3월 31일, 홈팀 vs. Hazelwood Knights
2순위 선택	4월 14일, 홈팀 vs. Grand Rapids Lions
3순위 선택	4월 6일, 홈팀 vs. Wakefield Tornadoes

요청을 받으면 영업일로 2일 이내에 이메일을 보내드리겠습니다.

어휘 form 양식 note 메모 limited 제한된 availability 이용 가능성 list 목록을 작성하다 prefer 선호하다 order 순서 business day 영업일

수신: Oliver Gilbert 〈olivergilbert@gahaenterprises.net〉
발신: 에딘버그 스타디움 〈service@edinburgstadium.com〉
날짜: 2월 14일
제목: 귀하의 VIP 활동 요청
첨부 파일: VIP#02895

Gilbert 씨,

에딘버그 스타디움에서 VIP 활동을 요청해 주셔서 감사합니다.

²⁻²Joseph Pollard와의 시간에서, 귀하께서 제안하신 날짜 중 1순위 선택에 일정을 잡을 수 있음을 알려드리게 되어 기쁩니다. 귀하의 계정에는 이미 요금이 청구되었습니다. 이 거래에 대한 영수증을 첨부하였으니 확인해 주십시오. ¹⁻²저희의 특별가를 통해 30% 할인을 받으셨다는 것을 알게 되실 것입니다. 행사 동안에는 추가 비용 없이 가벼운 다과가 제공될 것입니다. 그 이상의 음식이나 음료를 주문하고 싶으시면 최소한 행사 3일 전까지 제게 알려 주십시오.

Ronny Anderson
에딘버그 스타디움, 고객 서비스

어휘 attachment 첨부 파일 inform 알리다 schedule 일정을 잡다 account 계정 charge 부과하다 receipt 영수증 transaction 거래 note 주목하다 special offer 특가 refreshments 간식 additional 추가적인 beyond ~을 넘어서 at least 적어도, 최소한

1.
Gilbert 씨에 대해 무엇이 암시되었는가?
(A) 내년도 특별석 이용을 갱신하기를 원한다.
(B) 손님 명단을 바꿔야 한다.
(C) 처음으로 VIP 행사를 예약하고 있다.
(D) 이전 행사에 대해 초과 지불했다.

어휘 renew 갱신하다 overpay 초과 지급하다 previous 이전의

2.
Gilbert 씨는 언제 Joseph Pollard를 만나겠는가?
(A) 3월 31일
(B) 4월 6일
(C) 4월 14일
(D) 4월 22일

ACTUAL TEST
본문 p.288

| 1. (C) | 2. (D) | 3. (B) | 4. (A) | 5. (C) |
| 6. (B) | 7. (C) | 8. (B) | 9. (C) | 10. (C) |

[1-5] 기사 & 이메일

새크라멘토 (10월 7일)—트럭 운송 회사인 Marinello는 80대의 새 트럭들을 자사의 차량 목록에 추가한다고 발표했다. ¹,²프레몬트에서 국내 생산되는 Colchester는 하이브리드 엔진을 특징으로 하기 때문에 보다 친환경적이다. ⁵⁻¹트럭들은 사용 전 검사를 위해 본사로 보내질 것이다.

Marinello는 지난 5년 동안 꾸준히 성장해 왔으며 업계 선두주자가 되기 위한 발걸음을 내딛고 있다. "²이 새로운 차량들은 친환경적이고 휘발유에 드는 비용을 줄여줄 것이기 때문에 우리는 기쁘게 이 새로운 차량에 투자했습니다."라고 회사의 대표인 Leah Byrd 씨가 말했다. "30대의 차량에 냉장 시스템을 장착하는 것이 우리의 ³목표입니다. 나머지는 일정 온도로 보관할 필요가 없는 물품을 배송할 것입니다."

어휘 trucking 트럭 운송 addition 추가 fleet (회사의) 보유 차량 domestically 국내에서 manufacture 제조하다, 생산하다 feature 특징으로 하다 hybrid 하이브리드의 environmentally friendly 환경 친화적인 headquarters 본사 inspection 검사 steadily 꾸준히 be on pace 보조를 맞추다 thrilled 아주 기쁜 vehicle 차량 reduce 줄이다 spending 지출 gasoline 휘발유 representative 대표 aim 목적, 목표 equip A with B A에 B를 갖추다 unit 구성 단위, 1개 refrigeration 냉장 provide 제공하다 temperature 온도

수신: Rahul Marwah ⟨r.marwah@swansonmetals.com⟩
발신: Walter Donovan ⟨donovan_wal@marinello.com⟩
날짜: 10월 30일
제목: 배송

Marwah 씨,

귀하의 지속적인 거래에 감사드리며, 저희 배송 서비스가 충분히 만족스럽기를 바랍니다. 귀하는 현재 저희의 예전 배송 트럭으로 정기 배송을 받고 계십니다. ⁴하지만 저희의 최신 모델 트럭으로 바꾸시는 게 좋을 것 같습니다. 최신 모델이 약간 더 크기 때문에 안에 더 많은 물품을 넣을 수 있고, 따라서 배송 횟수를 줄일 수 있습니다.

⁵⁻²트럭들이 얼마 전에 포틀랜드에서 안전 점검을 마쳤습니다. 따라서 빠르면 다음 주에 세일럼에 있는 귀하의 창고로 가는 다음 번 배송에 사용될 수 있을 것입니다. 추가 물품 때문에 트럭에서 물건을 하역하는 데 시간이 더 필요할 것입니다. 이렇게 하기를 원하시면 저에게 알려주시기 바랍니다.

Walter Donovan
Marinello 물류 관리자

어휘 ongoing 계속 진행 중인 patronage 후원, 단골 거래 currently 현재 switch to ~으로 바꾸다 slightly 약간 fit 적합하게 하다, 꼭 맞다 result in ~한 결과를 낳다 therefore 그러므로 warehouse 창고 unload 하역하다 additional 추가적인

1.
Colchester는 무엇인가?
(A) 승합차
(B) 화물선
(C) 트럭 모델
(D) 냉장고 브랜드

해설 세부 사항
첫 번째 지문부터 Colchester를 키워드로 검색한다. 하이브리드 엔진을 장착한 트럭이라는 것을 알 수 있으므로 (C)가 정답이다.

어휘 passenger 승객 cargo 화물 refrigerator 냉장고

2.
Colchester에 대해 나타난 것은 무엇인가?
(A) 전 세계적으로 판매된다.
(B) Marinello에 의해 만들어졌다.
(C) 업계에서 인기가 있다.

(D) 연료비를 절감할 것이다.

해설 세부 사항

Marinello 관계자의 말인 'will reduce our spending on gasoline'에서 휘발유에 들어가는 연료비를 절약할 것임을 알 수 있다. 따라서 (D)가 정답이다. Marinello는 트럭 운송 회사이지, 트럭 제조사가 아니므로 (B)는 오답이고, (A)나 (C)와 관련된 내용은 나와 있지 않다.

어휘 industry 업계, 산업　save 절약하다　fuel 연료

3.

기사에서, 두 번째 단락 네 번째 줄의 'aim'과 의미상 가장 가까운 것은?

(A) 방향
(B) 의도
(C) 요구 사항
(D) 세트

해설 동의어 찾기

'It is our aim ~ refrigeration system.'을 해석하면 '~하는 것이 우리의 목표이다'라는 뜻이다. 선택지 중에서 '목표'와 의미가 가장 비슷한 것은 (B) intention이다.

4.

이메일의 목적은 무엇인가?

(A) 변화를 장려하기 위해
(B) 배달 시간을 확인하기 위해
(C) 지연을 해명하기 위해
(D) 주문을 변경하기 위해

해설 주제/목적

'However, I think you should switch to our newest truck model.'에 이메일의 발신자가 수신자에게 전하고 싶은 메시지가 드러난다. 'you should ~'는 강력히 권유할 때 쓰는 표현이다. 신형 트럭 모델로 바꿀 것을 권유했으므로 (A)가 정답이다.

어휘 recommend 추천하다, 권장하다　delay 지연　modify 변경하다

5.

Marinello의 본사는 어디에 위치해 있겠는가?

(A) 새크라멘토
(B) 프리몬트
(C) 포틀랜드
(D) 세일럼

해설 두 지문 연계_추론/암시

Marinello와 headquarters를 키워드로 지문을 검색한다. 첫 번째 지문의 'The trucks will be sent to the company's headquarters for inspection before being put to use'에서 트럭들이 검사를 받기 위해 회사의 본사로 보내질 것이라는 내용이 나왔고, 두 번째 지문의 'The trucks have just finished their safety inspections in Portland'에서 트럭들이 포틀랜드에서 검사를 마쳤다고 했으므로 회사의 본사는 포틀랜드에 있다는 것을 유추할 수 있다. 따라서 (C)가 정답이다.

어휘 be located 위치해 있다

[6-10] 전단지 & 이메일 & 이메일

Carolina Cleaning
렉싱턴에서 30년 가까이 영업을 하고 있습니다!

[6]복도나 로비와 같이 임차인들을 위한 주요 구역들을 전문적으로 청소함으로써 여러분의 건물이 최상의 상태로 보이도록 유지하세요. 정기적인 청소는 여러분의 투자 자산이 제 상태로 유지하는 데 도움이 될 뿐만 아니라 건물 내에 거주하는 모든 사람들에게 즐거운 분위기를 제공합니다. 여러분의 필요에 가장 적합한 서비스 패키지 상품을 선택할 수 있습니다.

알뜰 청소 상품: 복도와 로비의 카펫을 매일 진공청소기로 청소 및 먼지 제거

[8-2]표준 청소 상품: 알뜰 청소 상품에 포함된 모든 서비스 및 공용 구역의 쓰레기 처리 및 식물에 물 주기

표준 청소 플러스 상품: 표준 청소 상품에 포함된 모든 서비스 및 1층 창문의 내외부 청소

종합 청소 상품: 위에 열거된 모든 서비스 및 임차인의 퇴거 시 호실의 전면적인 청소와 매년 공용 구역의 카펫에 대한 스팀 청소

여러분의 특정한 요구 조건에 따라 견적을 받으려면 info@carolinacleaning.com으로 연락하세요.

어휘 serve 근무하다, 봉사하다　tenant 세입자, 임차인　hallway 복도　professionally 전문적으로　maintain 유지하다　investment 투자(물)　enjoyable 즐거운, 유쾌한　atmosphere 분위기　on site 건물 내의, 현장의　select 선택하다　package 패키지 상품　suit 어울리다, 적합하다　vacuum 진공청소기로 청소하다　dust 먼지를 털다　removal 제거　water 물을 주다　move out 이사를 나가다, 퇴거하다　annually 해마다　quote 견적　specific 특정한

발신: richardatwood@whittingtonltd.com
수신: info@carolinacleaning.com
날짜: 9월 9일
제목: 청소 서비스 요청

담당자 귀하:

저는 렉싱턴에 아파트 건물 두 채를 소유하고 있으며, 귀사의 청소 서비스를 이용하는 것을 고려하고 있습니다. 귀사의 홍보 전단지를 보았는데, [7]귀사가 오랫동안 영업을 해오셨기 때문에 특히 귀사를 고용할 의향이 있습니다.

[10-2]작업은 베드포드 근처의 말렛 아파트와 잭슨 인근의 밸리 아파트에서 이루어질 것입니다. 각 건물은 5층이고 1층에 로비가 있습니다. [8-1]귀사의 청소 팀이 매일 복도와 로비에서 먼지를 털고 진공청소기로 청소해 주시면 좋겠습니다. 그리고 쓰레기를 수거하고, 로비에 있는 몇 개의 화분도 관리해 주셨으면 합니다.

제가 결정을 내릴 수 있도록 가능한 빠른 시일 내에 비용 견적을 주시기 바랍니다.

Richard Atwood

어휘 promotional 홍보의　flyer 전단지　be in business 사업에 종사하다　carry out 수행하다, 실시하다　neighborhood 인근, 주변　story 층　collect 모으다, 수거하다　cost estimate 견적서　at one's earliest convenience 가능한 한 빨리

발신: info@carolinacleaning.com
수신: richardatwood@whittingtonltd.com
날짜: 9월 10일
제목: 회신: 청소 서비스 요청
첨부 파일: 추천서1

Atwood 씨,

Carolina Cleaning의 서비스에 관심을 가져주셔서 감사합니다. 귀하께 작업에 대한 가격 견적을 제공할 기회를 가졌으면 좋겠습니다. ⁹언제 직접 방문드릴 시간이 되는지 알려주시기 바랍니다. 우리 청소 직원 중 한 명이 청소가 필요한 구역의 크기를 측정하고 상태를 판단할 수 있습니다.

¹⁰⁻¹ 그 사이에, 저희 서비스에 만족하신 고객 중 한 명인 Courtney Armstrong 씨의 추천서를 첨부하오니 부담 없이 읽어보시기 바랍니다. 그분은 말렛 아파트 바로 길 건너편에 있는 가스토니아 아파트 단지의 소유자입니다.

귀하의 답장을 기다리겠습니다

Danielle Snyder
Carolina Cleaning, 영업 관리자

어휘 attachment 첨부 파일 testimonial 추천서, 추천의 글 in-person 직접의 assess 평가하다, 판단하다 in the meantime 그동안 attached 첨부된 apartment complex 아파트 단지

6.
전단지의 대상 고객은 누구이겠는가?
(A) 은행원
(B) 건물주
(C) 소매점 관리자
(D) 구직자

해설 추론/암시
flyer는 첫 번째 지문이므로 첫 번째 지문의 내용을 확인한다. your buildings에서 대상이 건물주라는 것을 알 수 있으므로 (B)가 정답이다.

7.
Atwood 씨는 Carolina Cleaning의 어떤 점을 특히 좋아하는가?
(A) 친환경적인 방식을 사용한다.
(B) 좋은 평가를 받았다.
(C) 자리를 잡은 업체이다.
(D) 가격이 저렴하다.

해설 세부 사항
Atwood를 키워드로 삼는다. Atwood는 두 번째 지문의 발신인이므로 두 번째 지문에서 단서를 찾아야 한다. 'was especially interested in hiring your company since you have been in business for a long time'에서 오랜 사업 경력 때문에 Carolina Cleaning을 고용하고 싶다고 했으므로 (C)가 정답이다.

어휘 eco-friendly 친환경적인 practice 방식, 관행 review 후기 well-established 확립된, 기초가 튼튼한 affordable 저렴한,

(가격이) 알맞은

8.
Atwood 씨는 어떤 서비스 상품을 이용하겠는가?
(A) 알뜰 청소 상품
(B) 표준 청소 상품
(C) 표준 청소 플러스 상품
(D) 종합 청소 상품

해설 두 지문 연계_추론/암시
두 번째 지문에서 Richard Atwood가 언급한 것은 'dust and vacuum the hallways and lobbies each day(매일 복도와 로비에서 먼지를 털고 진공청소기로 청소하다)', collect our trash and take care of a few potted plants in the lobbies(쓰레기를 수거하고, 로비에 있는 몇 개의 화분도 관리하다)'이다. 첫 번째 지문에서 해당 서비스에 해당하는 패키지 상품을 찾아보면 Standard Cleaning이 그에 해당하므로 (B)가 정답이다.

9.
Snyder 씨는 Atwood 씨에게 무엇을 해달라고 요청하는가?
(A) 계약서에 서명하기
(B) 자신에게 건물 치수를 보내기
(C) 언제 시간이 되는지 알려 주기
(D) 몇 장의 사진을 제공하기

해설 세부 사항
Ms. Snyder는 세 번째 지문의 발신인이므로 세 번째 지문에서 해당 정보를 검색한다. Carolina Cleaning의 직원이 언제 방문할 수 있는지를 문의하고 있으므로 (C)가 정답이다.

어휘 contract 계약(서) measurement 치수 availability (사람이) 시간이 나는지의 여부 provide 제공하다

10.
Armstrong 씨에 대해 암시된 것은 무엇인가?
(A) 전에 잭슨 인근에 살았다.
(B) 말렛 아파트로 입주하는 것에 관심이 있다.
(C) 베드포드 인근에 건물을 소유하고 있다.
(D) Atwood 씨와 방문 일정을 잡을 것이다.

해설 두 지문 연계_추론/암시
Ms. Armstrong은 세 번째 지문에 등장하는 이름인데, 'She is the owner of the Gastonia Apartment Complex, which is right across the street from the Mallett Apartments.'에서 가스토니아 아파트 단지의 소유자이며, 그 아파트 단지는 말렛 아파트의 건너편에 있다는 정보가 나온다. 두 번째 지문의 'the Mallett Apartments in the Bedford neighborhood'에서 말렛 아파트는 베드포드 인근에 있다는 것을 알 수 있으므로, 가스토니아 아파트도 베드포드에 있다는 것을 추론할 수 있다. 따라서 (C)가 정답이다.

어휘 move into ~에 입주하다

실전 모의고사

실전 모의고사 1회
본문 p.294

101. (A)	102. (B)	103. (C)	104. (B)	105. (A)
106. (C)	107. (D)	108. (D)	109. (C)	110. (A)
111. (D)	112. (B)	113. (A)	114. (C)	115. (B)
116. (D)	117. (D)	118. (A)	119. (C)	120. (A)
121. (A)	122. (C)	123. (A)	124. (A)	125. (C)
126. (A)	127. (C)	128. (B)	129. (C)	130. (D)
131. (A)	132. (C)	133. (C)	134. (C)	135. (C)
136. (A)	137. (C)	138. (C)	139. (D)	140. (A)
141. (C)	142. (C)	143. (B)	144. (C)	145. (C)
146. (A)	147. (C)	148. (C)	149. (B)	150. (C)
151. (C)	152. (B)	153. (C)	154. (C)	155. (C)
156. (B)	157. (C)	158. (C)	159. (A)	160. (C)
161. (C)	162. (D)	163. (D)	164. (D)	165. (A)
166. (C)	167. (C)	168. (A)	169. (B)	170. (C)
171. (D)	172. (C)	173. (C)	174. (C)	175. (B)
176. (D)	177. (D)	178. (D)	179. (C)	180. (B)
181. (C)	182. (C)	183. (B)	184. (C)	185. (C)
186. (C)	187. (D)	188. (C)	189. (C)	190. (C)
191. (D)	192. (C)	193. (C)	194. (B)	195. (C)
196. (A)	197. (C)	198. (B)	199. (B)	200. (C)

101. 인칭대명사 [소유격]
해석 소비자들은 그들이 환경에 미치는 영향을 인식해야 한다.

해설 빈칸은 뒤의 명사 impact를 수식하는 자리이므로 명사를 수식할 수 있는 소유격인 (A) their가 정답이다.

어휘 consumer 소비자 be aware of ~을 인지하다 impact 영향 environment 환경

102. 형용사 어휘 punctual
해석 강의는 오후 6시 정각에 시작하므로, 청중들은 시간을 엄수하는 것이 중요하다.

(A) 긴급한 (B) 시간을 엄수하는 (C) 짧은 (D) 즉각적인

어휘 lecture 강의 audience member 청중

103. 명사 자리
해석 Kelsey 씨는 고객에게 배터리를 과다하게 충전하는 것의 위험에 대해 설명했다.

해설 빈칸 앞에 관사 the가 있으므로, 빈칸에는 관사의 수식을 받는 명사가 와야 한다. 따라서 명사인 (C)가 정답이다.

어휘 danger 위험 overcharge 지나치게 충전하다, 과다 청구하다

104. 전치사 from
해석 일기 예보에서는 이른 아침부터 밤늦게까지 폭우가 내린다고 예보했다.

(A) ~에 (B) ~부터 (C) ~에 (D) ~ 사이에

해설 '이른 아침부터 밤늦게까지'라는 의미가 되어야 문맥상 자연스러우므로, until과 함께 '~부터 …까지'라는 의미로 자주 쓰이는 전치사 (B)가 정답이다. (D)는 '(둘) 사이에'라는 뜻의 전치사로 뒤에 A and B의 형태가 오므로 오답이다.

어휘 weather forecast 일기 예보 predict 예측하다

105. 동사 자리 + 과거 시제
해석 최근에 Kobayashi Motors에서 차량을 구입하셨다면, 당사 웹 사이트를 방문하여 차량이 리콜되지 않았는지 확인하십시오.

해설 빈칸은 앞의 부사 recently의 수식을 받으면서 뒤의 a vehicle을 목적어로 갖는 동사 자리이므로 (A) bought와 (B) buy가 정답 후보이다. 시간 부사 recently(최근에)는 과거 시제 또는 완료 시제와 어울려 쓰이므로, 과거 시제인 (A)가 정답이다.

어휘 recently 최근에 vehicle 차량 make sure 확인하다, 확실히 하다 recall 회수하다, 리콜하다

106. 명사 자리 [동사의 목적어]
해석 현장 관리자는 공장에서 가동이 원활하게 돌아가도록 유지한다.

해설 빈칸은 〈keep + 목적어 + 목적격 보어〉의 구조에서 동사 keep의 목적어 자리이므로 명사가 들어가야 한다. 선택지 중에서 명사는 operations(운영)와 operative(직공, 정보원)가 있는데, 목적격 보어 run(작동시키다)과 의미상 통하는 것은 operations 이므로 (C)가 정답이다.

어휘 floor manager 현장 관리자 operation 운영 smoothly 순조롭게

107. 부사 어휘 regularly
해석 Pete's Paninis는 식당에 오는 손님들이 식당의 메뉴에 계속해서 관심을 갖도록 하기 위해 정기적으로 메뉴를 교체한다.

(A) 단결하여 (B) 바르게 (C) 표면적으로 (D) 정기적으로

해설 빈칸은 뒤의 동사 changes를 수식하는 부사 자리로, change its menu(메뉴를 바꾸다)를 의미상 자연스럽게 수식할 수 있는 부사는 (D) regularly밖에 없다.

어휘 diner 식사하는 손님 offering 제공물, 팔 물건

108. 형용사 자리 [분사]
해석 Ichigawa Pet Store는 매장에서 보유한 점박이 이구아나들로 유명하다.

해설 빈칸은 뒤의 명사 iguanas를 수식하는 형용사 자리이므로, 형용사처럼 쓰이는 현재분사 (C)와 과거분사 (D)가 정답 후보가 된다. spotted는 '반점이 있는'이라는 의미로 iguanas를 문맥상 적절히 수식할 수 있으므로 (D)가 정답이다.

109. 부사 자리 [숫자 수식]
해석 호텔에서 공항까지의 택시 요금은 약 15달러이다.

해설 빈칸이 없어도 문장이 완벽하므로 빈칸은 부사 자리이다. 따라서 부사 (C)가 정답이다. 숫자 앞에서 숫자를 수식하는 부사에는 approximately 외에도 roughly(대략), about(약), almost(거의), nearly(거의) 등이 있다.

어휘 fee 요금   approximately 약, 대략

110. 부사 어휘 still

해설 건물 재설계를 위한 몇 달간의 기획 후에도, Lenape 씨는 여전히 어느 방향으로 가야 할지 확신하지 못하고 있다.
(A) 여전히 (B) 전에 (C) 나중에 (D) 그 밖에

해설 빈칸은 부정문에서 형용사 certain을 수식하는 부사 자리이다. '여전히 확신하지 못하다'라는 의미가 되어야 문맥상 자연스러우므로 (A)가 정답이다.

어휘 redesign 재설계   direction 방향

111. 부정대명사 one

해설 모든 지원자들을 인터뷰한 후, 우리는 그 역할에 가장 적합할 것이라고 생각하는 사람을 선택할 것이다.

해설 빈칸 앞에 정관사 the가 있고 빈칸 뒤에 주격 관계대명사 that이 있는 것으로 보아 빈칸에는 선행사 역할을 하는 명사나 대명사가 와야 한다. 문맥상 앞서 나온 candidates 중 한 명이라는 의미가 되어야 자연스러우므로 (D)가 정답이다.

어휘 candidate 후보자, 지원자   fit 적합하다   role 역할

112. 명사 어휘 revision

해설 장난감 시제품에 대한 사용자 테스트는 대대적인 수정이 필요하다는 결과를 이끌어냈다.
(A) 규모 (B) 수정 (C) 일탈 (D) 상기시키는 것

해설 빈칸 앞의 형용사 major의 수식을 받으면서 문맥에 적절한 명사 어휘를 찾아야 한다. 사용자 테스트를 하는 목적이면서, 아직 출시되지 않은 prototype(시제품) 테스트 결과와 연관 지을 수 있는 것은 '제품의 수정'이므로 (B)가 정답이다.

어휘 prototype 시제품, 견본   result in 결과적으로 ~이 되다
major 대다수의, 주요한

113. 전치사 between

해설 우리의 고객은 그들의 새로운 광고 캠페인을 위해 현대적인 디자인과 전통적인 디자인 사이에서 하나를 선택하는 데 어려움을 겪었다.
(A) ~ 사이에 (B) ~로서 (C) ~라는 것 (D) ~인지 (아닌지)

해설 빈칸 뒤에 명사구(the modern design and the traditional design)가 온 것으로 보아 빈칸은 전치사 자리임을 알 수 있으므로 (A) between과 (B) as가 정답 후보가 된다. 뒤에 나온 명사구의 형태가 A and B이므로 between과 함께 쓰여 between A and B(A와 B 사이에)가 되는 것이 적절하다. 따라서 (A)가 정답이다. (C)와 (D)는 접속사로서 명사구를 이끌 수 없으므로 오답이다.

어휘 client 고객   have difficulty doing ~하는 데 어려움을 겪다
modern 현대적인   traditional 전통적인   advertising campaign 광고 캠페인

114. 동사 어휘 wonder

해설 호기심 많은 고객들은 어떻게 Real Recyclables가 낡은 재료로 그렇게 고급 제품을 만들 수 있는지 종종 궁금해 한다.
(A) 숙고하다 (B) 제안하다 (C) 궁금하다 (D) 경쟁하다

해설 빈칸은 뒤의 명사절(how Real Recyclables is able to make such high-quality products from old materials)을 목적어로 취하는 동사 자리로, '어떻게 Real Recyclables가 낡은 재료로 그렇게 고급 제품을 만들 수 있는지 종종 궁금해 한다'고 해석하는 것이 문맥상 자연스러우므로 (C)가 정답이다.

어휘 curious 호기심이 많은   high-quality 고급의   material 재료

115. 부사 자리 [동사 수식]

해설 Lola's Apparel은 틀림없이 남아메리카에서 가장 성공한 소매점 체인 중 하나이다.

해설 빈칸을 제외해도 문장의 필수 성분이 모두 갖춰져 있으므로 빈칸은 수식어 자리임을 알 수 있는데, 빈칸 앞에 동사 is가 온 것으로 보아 빈칸에는 이를 수식하는 부사가 와야 한다. 따라서 부사인 (B)가 정답이다.

어휘 arguably 거의 틀림없이   successful 성공한   retail chain 소매점 체인

116. 전치사구 regardless of

해설 오토바이 운전자는 숙련도에 상관없이 헬멧을 착용해야 한다.

해설 빈칸은 뒤의 명사 skill level을 목적어로 취하는 전치사 자리로서, 전치사 of와 함께 regardless of(~에 상관없이)의 형태로 쓰이는 (D)가 정답이다. (A)는 접속부사, (B)는 접속사이므로 뒤에 〈주어+동사〉가 와야 한다.

어휘 be required to do ~하도록 요구받다

117. 명사 어휘 transaction

해설 은행은 고객들에게 낭비를 하지 않기 위해 해외여행을 하는 동안 모든 거래를 기록해 둘 것을 권고한다.
(A) 예방 (B) 주의 (C) 환경 (D) 거래

해설 keep track of의 목적어가 되면서 bank와 의미 연관성을 갖는 명사 어휘를 찾아야 한다. 선택지 중에서 해당 조건을 만족시키는 것은 (D) transactions밖에 없다.

어휘 advise 충고하다   keep track of ~을 기록하다, 추적하다
travel abroad 해외여행을 하다   avoid 피하다   overspending 낭비

118. 명사 어휘 surplus

해설 등산화 재고가 남아돌아서 KLP Camping은 대대적인 세일을 하고 있다.
(A) 여분, 잉여 (B) 유형 (C) 제한 (D) 집중, 중앙 집권

해설 대대적인 세일을 하는 것은 여분의 상품을 소진하기 위한 목적도 있으므로 선택지 중에서 (A)가 정답이다.

어휘 hiking boots 등산화

119. 형용사 자리 [주격 보어]

해석 MHG & Sons의 최고경영자는 항상 새로운 아이디어에 마음이 열려 있는데, 그 아이디어들이 신입 사원으로부터 나오더라도 그러하다.

해설 빈칸은 주어인 MHG & Sons' CEO의 성격이나 상태를 나타낼 수 있는 주격 보어 자리이며, 뒤의 전치사 to와 어울려 쓰여야 한다. 이 같은 조건을 만족시키는 것은 형용사인 (C) open이다.

어휘 come from ~에서 나오다   new recruit 신입 사원

120. 부사 어휘 everywhere

해석 Krazy Kola는 오지를 비롯해서 세계 어디서나 볼 수 있는 것 같다.
(A) 어디서나 (B) 때때로 (C) 결과적으로 (D) 게다가, 더욱이

해설 빈칸은 앞의 동사구 can be found를 수식하기에 적합한 부사가 들어갈 자리이다. 전치사구인 including remote parts of the world(세계의 오지를 비롯해서)와 의미가 통하는 부사 어휘는 (A) everywhere이다.

어휘 including ~을 포함하여   remote 외딴

121. 명사 어휘 excursion

해석 Tingley Travel은 최대 30명의 단체를 위한 유럽 여행 상품을 소개했다.
(A) 여행 (B) 합의 (C) 기관 (D) 성과

해설 주어인 Tingley Travel 및 빈칸 뒤의 전치사구인 to Europe과 의미 연관성이 있는 것은 (A)이다.

어휘 introduce 소개하다, 도입하다   up to ~까지

122. 형용사 어휘 assembled

해석 우리의 서비스를 통해 고객들은 이제 그들의 주거 공간을 위해 완전히 조립된 가구를 주문할 수 있다.
(A) 제안된 (B) 발견된 (C) 조립된 (D) 나열된

해설 빈칸 앞의 부사 fully의 수식을 받으면서 빈칸 뒤의 명사 furniture를 수식할 수 있는 형용사 어휘를 찾아야 한다. fully assembled는 하나의 단어처럼 furniture를 수식하는 표현이므로 (C)가 정답이다.

어휘 order 주문하다   fully 완전히   furniture 가구

123. 접속사 once

해석 거래가 일단 완료되면 이체를 요청한 사람은 입금을 확인하는 메시지를 받게 될 것이다.
(A) 일단 ~하면 (B) 비록 ~이지만 (C) 여전히 (D) ~하는 동안

해설 빈칸은 두 개의 절을 연결하는 접속사 자리로, 문맥상 '거래가 완료되면'이라는 의미가 되어야 자연스럽다. 따라서 '일단 ~하면'이라는 의미의 접속사인 (A)가 정답이다. (B)는 양보의 의미를 나타내는 접속사로 문맥상 적절하지 않다.

어휘 transaction 거래   complete 완료된   request 요청하다   transfer 이체   confirm 확인하다   deposit 입금, 예금

124. 부사 자리 [동사 수식]

해석 그 연구는 요가를 꾸준히 한 참가자들이 그렇지 않은 참가자들보다 더 나은 유연성을 보고했다는 것을 증명했다.

해설 빈칸은 주격 관계대명사절 안의 동사 practiced를 수식하는 부사 자리이므로 (A)가 정답이다.

어휘 prove 증명하다   participant 참가자   practice 연습하다   consistently 꾸준히   report 보고하다, 알리다   flexibility 유연성

125. 분사구문

해석 질문을 받았을 때, 직원들은 DFT International에서 일하는 것을 좋아하는 주된 이유 중 하나로 탄력적 근무 시간을 꼽았다.

해설 접속사 when 뒤에 절이 와야 하는데 주어와 동사가 없는 것으로 보아 주어가 생략된 분사구문임을 알 수 있다. 따라서 과거분사인 (C)와 현재분사인 (D)가 정답 후보가 된다. 직원들이 질문을 받은 것이므로, 생략된 주어 employees와 동사 ask는 수동의 관계에 있다. 따라서 과거분사인 (C)가 정답이다.

어휘 employee 직원   state ~을 분명히 말하다   flexible 탄력적인

126. 접속사 considering

해석 Kay 씨는 새로운 직장에서 여러 사람 앞에서 말하는 것이 처음이었다는 점을 고려하면 발표를 잘했다.
(A) ~을 고려하면 (B) 그러나 (C) 마치 ~인 것처럼 (D) ~하도록

해설 빈칸은 빈칸 앞뒤의 절을 연결하는 접속사 자리로, '발표를 잘 했다 / 여러 사람 앞에서 말하는 것이 처음이었다'라는 의미이므로 '~을 고려하면'이라는 의미의 접속사 (A)가 적절하다. (B)는 역접의 의미를 나타내는 접속사로 문맥상 적절하지 않다.

어휘 presentation 발표   attempt 시도

127. 부사 어휘 upstairs

해석 폐기되는 모든 기밀 파일은 위층에 있는 방에서 수거되어 파쇄된다.
(A) 도처에 (B) 어디(로)든지 (C) 위층에서 (D) 가까이

해설 빈칸을 제외해도 문장이 완전하므로 빈칸은 부사 자리이며, 문맥상 빈칸 앞의 장소를 나타내는 부사구 in a room의 의미를 보충하기에 가장 적절한 것은 (C) upstairs이다.

어휘 discard 폐기하다   confidential 기밀   collect 수집하다   shred 파쇄하다, 조각조각으로 찢다

128. 전치사 against

해석 병가를 3일 더 포함하도록 회사 방침을 바꾸는 것에 대한 논란은 없는 것 같다.
(A) ~ 때문에 (B) ~에 대한 (C) ~ 동안 (D) ~처럼

해설 빈칸 뒤에 동명사구(changing the company policy to include three extra sick days)가 온 것으로 보아 빈칸은 전치사 자리임을 알 수 있으므로 (B) against, (C) during, (D) as가 정답 후보가 된다. 문맥상 '회사 방침을 바꾸는 것에 대한 논란'이라는 의미가 자연스러우므로 (B)가 정답이다.

어휘 argument 논란, 논쟁   policy 방침   include 포함하다   sick day 병가

129. 동사 어휘 donate

해석 벨뷰의 주민들에게는 지역 동물 보호소에 오래된 이불이나 베개 등을 기부하는 것이 장려된다.
(A) 임대하다 (B) (입장을) 허락하다 (C) 기부하다 (D) 이동시키다

해설 빈칸 앞의 are encouraged to(~하는 것이 장려되다)와 어울려 '지역 동물 보호소에 기부하는 것이 장려되다'라는 의미가 자연스러우므로 (C)가 정답이다.

어휘 resident 주민 be encouraged to *do* ~하도록 권장되다 local 지역의 animal shelter 동물 보호소

130. 동사 어휘 narrate
해석 Choi 씨의 목소리가 가장 좋았기 때문에 그가 프로젝트의 내레이션을 맡았다.
(A) 유지하다 (B) 드러내다 (C) 목표로 삼다 (D) 내레이션을 하다
해설 선택지 중에서 voice(목소리)와 의미 연관성이 있는 것은 (D) narrating이다.
어휘 be in charge of ~을 맡다, 담당하다

131-134 이메일

> 수신: Simone Onochie
> 발신: customerservice@sportshere.com
> 날짜: 3월 29일
> 제목: 귀하의 최근 주문 (번호 8744463628)
>
> Onochie 씨,
>
> Sports Here!에서 주문해 주셔서 감사합니다. 귀하의 캐러멜 색 나일론 반바지가 발송되었습니다. [131]영업일 기준으로 3~4일 이내에 택배 물품을 받으실 수 있을 것입니다. 배송 상황을 확인하시려면 www.sportshere.com/myorder/track으로 이동하여 주문 번호를 입력하십시오.
>
> 저희 제품이 마음에 드실 것으로 확신하지만, 고객 만족을 보장하기 위해 www.sportshere.com/survey에서 간단한 설문 조사를 작성해 주실 것을 [132]요청드립니다. 저희 고객님들의 소중한 의견 덕분에, 저희는 훌륭한 서비스를 제공[133]할 수 있습니다. 설문 조사를 [134]완료하신 뒤에는, 다음 주문 시 10% 할인을 받을 수 있는 쿠폰이 귀하의 이메일로 발송될 것입니다. 즐거운 쇼핑하세요!
>
> Sports Here! 고객 서비스

어휘 recent 최근의 order 주문; 주문하다 shorts 반바지 ship 발송하다 status 상태, 상황 head over to ~로 이동하다 input 입력하다 guarantee 보장하다 satisfaction 만족 fill out ~을 작성하다 survey 설문 조사 valuable 소중한 feedback 의견, 반응 provide 제공하다

131. 알맞은 문장 고르기
(A) 영업일 기준으로 3~4일 이내에 택배 물품을 받으실 수 있을 것입니다.
(B) 죄송하지만 교환은 가능하지 않습니다.
(C) 환불하시려면 아무 Sports Here! 매장에 영수증을 가져오세요.
(D) 귀하의 교환품이 발송되면 이메일을 보내드리겠습니다.
해설 빈칸 앞에서 고객이 주문한 상품이 발송되었다고 했고, 빈칸 뒤에서 배송 상황을 확인하는 방법을 알려 주고 있으므로 빈칸에는 택배 물품을 언제 받을 수 있는지 알리는 내용이 오는 것이 적절하다. 따라서 (A)가 정답이다.

어휘 package 소포, 택배 business day 영업일 available 이용 가능한 receipt 영수증 refund 환불 replacement 교체, 대체

132. 동사 자리+현재 시제
해설 빈칸 앞에 문장의 주어 we가 있고, 빈칸 뒤에 명사절이 나오고 있으므로 빈칸은 명사절을 목적어로 취하는 동사 자리이다. 앞쪽의 등위접속사 but에 의해 앞의 절과 연결되므로, 시제는 앞의 절과 동일하게 현재 시제가 되어야 한다. 따라서 (B)가 정답이다.

133. 형용사 어휘 able
(A) 조심하는 (B) 감당할 수 있는 (C) ~할 수 있는 (D) 허용된
해설 빈칸 앞의 are와 빈칸 뒤의 to와 함께 어울려 be able to *do*(~할 수 있다)로 쓰이는 (C)가 정답이다. 문맥상으로도 고객들의 소중한 의견 덕분에 훌륭한 서비스를 '제공할 수 있다'고 하는 것이 가장 적절하다.

134. 동사 어휘 complete
(A) 완료하다 (B) 시연하다 (C) 설명하다 (D) 출판하다
해설 빈칸 뒤에서 할인 쿠폰이 이메일로 발송될 것이라고 했으므로, 문맥상 빈칸이 포함된 부분은 '설문 조사를 완료한 뒤에'라는 의미가 되는 것이 자연스럽다. 따라서 (A)가 정답이다.

135-138 안내문

> Riley's Café의 프라이빗 룸은 사적인 만남이 필요한 모든 경우에 예약할 수 있습니다. 바로 가까이에 있는 Riley's의 커피와 간식의 [135]편의를 이용하면서 스터디 모임, 회식 모임, 기타 축하 모임을 가지세요. 시간대를 [136]신청하시려면 www.rileyscafe.com/reservation을 방문하세요. 원하시는 시간대가 비어 있다면 예약이 확정됩니다. 10달러의 보증금이 요구됩니다. 만약 계획하고 있는 특정한 행사가 있으시다면, 기회를 놓치지 않기 위해 룸을 한참 전에 예약하는 것을 적극 [137]권장드립니다. [138]아울러 고객님들이 직접 뒷정리를 하셔야 한다는 것을 알려드립니다.
>
> 여러분을 모실 수 있기를 기대합니다!

어휘 private 개인의, 사적인 book 예약하다 session (특정 활동을 위한) 시간 celebration 축하 행사 reservation 예약 time slot 시간대 confirm 확정하다 deposit 보증금 specific 특정한 in advance 미리

135. 명사 어휘 convenience
(A) 놀라움 (B) 구출 (C) 편의 (D) 결정
해설 빈칸 앞의 with the와 빈칸 뒤의 of와 어울려 자연스러운 문맥을 이루는 명사가 와야 한다. 문맥상 'Riley's의 커피와 간식의 편의'를 이용하면서 필요한 모임이나 행사를 하라는 내용이 자연스러우므로 (C)가 정답이다.

136. to부정사 [부사 역할]
해설 빈칸 앞의 문장이 완전한 것으로 보아, 빈칸 이하는 문장을 수식하는 부사 역할의 어구임을 알 수 있다. 문맥상으로도 '시간대를 신청하려면' 웹 사이트를 방문하라는 의미이므로, 부사 역할을 하면

서 목적을 나타낼 수 있는 to부정사가 적절하다. 따라서 (A)가 정답이다.

137. 동사 어휘 encourage
(A) 보장하다 (B) 권장하다 (C) 암시하다 (D) 부인하다

해설 빈칸 뒤에서 기회를 놓치지 않기 위해 룸을 미리 예약하라고 했으므로, 문맥상 빈칸이 포함된 부분은 '매우 권장된다'라는 의미가 되는 것이 자연스럽다. 따라서 (B)가 정답이다.

138. 알맞은 문장 고르기
(A) 아울러 고객님들이 직접 뒷정리를 하셔야 한다는 것을 알려드립니다.
(B) 그러므로, 여러분은 돈을 많이 쓰게 될 것을 예상하셔야 합니다.
(C) 오늘 개업식에 와 주셔서 감사합니다.
(D) 질문에 올바르게 답하는 참가자들은 상품을 받게 될 것입니다.

해설 글의 전반에 걸쳐 프라이빗 룸에 대한 소개 및 예약 방법 등을 알려 주고 있으므로, 빈칸에도 프라이빗 룸과 관련된 내용으로 이용상의 주의 사항이 나오는 것이 적절하다. 따라서 (A)가 정답이다.

어휘 additionally 또한, 게다가   note 주의하다, 유념하다   cleanup 청소, 뒷정리   anticipate 예상하다   contestant (대회 등의) 참가자   correctly 정확히, 바르게

139-142 공지

> Markswell 직원 여러분은 주목해 주십시오:
>
> 다음 주 목요일인 6월 27일에 우리가 현재 건물의 9층으로 이전할 예정이라는 것을 다시 한번 알려 드립니다. 책상, 컴퓨터, 프린터, 의자 등 대형 물품은 모두 이삿짐 직원들이 ¹³⁹담당할 것입니다. 그러나 개인 물품은 개인별로 옮겨야 합니다. 여러분의 새로운 공간으로 이동하실 ¹⁴⁰때, 물건들을 다시 정리하기 전에 그곳을 먼저 청소할 것을 권합니다. ¹⁴¹또한, 사고가 나지 않도록 다른 사람들의 움직임에 주의해 주십시오. ¹⁴²이번 이동이 가능한 한 순조롭게 진행되도록 합시다. 협조해 주셔서 감사합니다.

어휘 reminder 상기시키는 것   current 현재의   mover 이사업체 (직원)   personal 개인의   individual 개인의   basis 기준, 근거   reorganize 재조직하다, 재정리하다   cooperation 협조

139. 수동태 + 미래 시제
해설 빈칸에 들어갈 알맞은 태와 시제를 가진 동사를 고르는 문제이다. handle이 타동사임에도 빈칸 뒤에 목적어가 없고, 주어가 All large items로서 처리되는 대상이므로 수동태인 (D)가 정답이다.

140. 접속사 when
(A) ~할 때 (B) ~처럼 (C) 게다가 (D) ~한 곳에

해설 빈칸 이하는 주어가 생략된 분사구문임을 알 수 있는데, 분사구문을 만들 때 접속사를 생략하지 않을 수 있으므로 빈칸은 접속사 자리임을 알 수 있다. 문맥상 '새로운 공간으로 이동할 때'라는 의미가 되는 것이 자연스러우므로 '~할 때'라는 뜻의 접속사 (A)가 정답이다.

141. 연결어 / 접속부사 additionally
(A) 그러나 (B) 그러므로 (C) 또한 (D) 마찬가지로

해설 선택지를 보니 빈칸은 연결어 자리로, 빈칸이 포함된 문장의 앞 문장은 물건들을 다시 정리하기 전에 새로운 공간을 청소하라는 내용이고, 빈칸이 포함된 문장은 사고가 나지 않도록 주의하라는 내용이다. 이 두 문장은 모두 새로운 공간으로 이동할 때 주의할 점을 말하고 있으므로, 추가의 의미를 나타내는 (C)가 정답이다.

142. 알맞은 문장 고르기
(A) 이번 이동이 가능한 한 순조롭게 진행되도록 합시다.
(B) 휴가 신청서를 제출하는 것을 잊지 마세요.
(C) 안내 데스크에 있는 상자에 여러분의 의견을 남겨 주세요.
(D) 여러분의 노고 덕분에 이전을 아주 잘 했습니다.

해설 글의 전반에 걸쳐 사무실 이전 시 유의할 점을 알려 주고 있으며, 빈칸 뒤에서 협조에 감사하다며 글을 마무리하고 있으므로, 빈칸에는 이전과 관련된 내용이 오는 것이 적절하다. 따라서 (A)가 정답이다. (D)는 이전을 끝낸 다음에 할 수 있는 말이므로 오답이다.

어휘 transition 이동, 이행   submit 제출하다   suggestion 제안(서)

143-146 회람

> 수신: 전 직원
> 발신: Mai Hoan, Central Records 소유주
> 제목: 오픈 마이크 책임자
> 날짜: 4월 17일
>
> 모든 직원 여러분,
>
> 이 발표는 내일 신문에 실릴 예정이지만, 여러분 모두에게 먼저 알려 드리고 싶었습니다. 지난 토요일 오픈 마이크의 ¹⁴³성공에 이어 Central Records는 매월 오픈 마이크 시리즈를 개최하기로 결정했습니다. 그렇기 때문에 우리는 월례 행사를 기획하고 진행할 오픈 마이크 책임자를 찾고 있습니다. 선발된 지원자는 6월 오픈 마이크를 ¹⁴⁴시작으로, 이어지는 모든 오픈 마이크 행사에서 일을 계속하게 될 것입니다.
>
> ¹⁴⁵이것은 초보자가 맡을 직책이 아니라는 것을 알아 두시기 바랍니다. 전에 밴드와 함께 현장에서 일한 경력이 필수입니다. ¹⁴⁶관심 있는 Central Records 직원들은 지원할 것을 적극 권장합니다. 직책에 대한 더 자세한 내용을 원하시면 저에게 연락하세요.
>
> Mai Hoan

어휘 coordinator 책임자, 조정자   announcement 발표   feature ~을 특집으로 하다   aware 알고 있는   host 개최하다   monthly 매월의   organize 기획하다   carry out 실행하다   candidate 지원자, 후보자   subsequent 그 후의, 뒤이은   essential 필수적인, 매우 중요한   contact 연락하다   detail 세부 사항   position (일)자리, 직위

143. 명사 어휘 success
(A) 압력 (B) 성공 (C) 불만 (D) 놀라움

해설 빈칸 뒤에서 Central Records가 매월 오픈 마이크 시리즈를 개최하기로 결정했다는 것에서 지난 토요일 오픈 마이크가 '성공'

했음을 추측할 수 있다. 따라서 (B)가 정답이다.

144. 동사 자리 + 미래 시제
해설 글의 전반부에서 매월 오픈 마이크 시리즈를 개최하기로 결정했고, 월례 행사의 책임자를 찾고 있다는 내용이 나온다. 따라서 빈칸이 포함된 문장은 선발된 사람은 6월 행사와 이후의 모든 행사에서 일을 '시작할 것이다'라는 내용이 되는 것이 자연스럽다. 따라서 미래 시제인 (A)가 정답이다.

145. 알맞은 문장 고르기
(A) 우리는 행사를 얼마나 자주 개최할지 아직 결정 중입니다.
(B) 면접단은 후보자들에게 깊은 인상을 받았습니다.
(C) 이것은 초보자가 맡을 직책이 아니라는 것을 알아 두시기 바랍니다.
(D) 모든 사람들이 오픈 마이크 공연을 즐기는 것처럼 보였습니다.
해설 빈칸 앞의 문장에서 오픈 마이크 행사 책임자로 선발되면 6월과 그 이후의 행사에서 일을 시작할 것이라고 했고, 빈칸 뒤의 문장에서는 전에 밴드와 함께 일했던 경력이 필요하다는 점을 언급했으므로, 빈칸에는 오픈 마이크 행사 책임자의 자격 요건에 관한 내용이 오는 것이 적절하다. 따라서 초보자가 할 수 있는 일이 아니라는 내용의 (C)가 정답이다.
어휘 interview panel 면접단 be impressed with ~에 깊은 인상을 받다 note 유념하다 entry-level 초보의, 말단의 performance 공연

146. 형용사 어휘 interested
(A) 관심 있는 (B) 의심 받는 (C) 일류의 (D) 관찰되는
해설 빈칸 뒤의 Central Records staff를 수식하는 형용사 어휘를 고르는 문제이다. 빈칸 뒤에서 직원들에게 지원을 장려하고 있고, 세부적인 내용을 원하면 자신에게 연락하라는 내용이 나온다. 따라서 '관심 있는' 직원들이 해야 할 일을 언급하는 문장임을 알 수 있으므로 (A)가 정답이다.

147-148 공지

Moncrieff Suitcase 고객 여러분은 주목해 주십시오!
낭비를 줄이기 위한 노력의 일환으로 [147]Moncrieff Suitcase에서는 이제 자사 제품군에 있는 모든 품목에 대한 수리를 제공할 것입니다. 예를 들어, 망가진 손잡이, 고장 난 지퍼, 그리고 빠진 바퀴를 교체할 수 있습니다. 새 여행 가방을 사는 데 드는 비용의 일부만으로 여행 가방을 수리 받으세요. 전문가인 [148]Joseph Osburne 씨가 화요일부터 토요일까지 현장에 있을 예정입니다. 그가 여러분의 가방을 검사하고, 작업이 시작되기 전에 [148]무료 견적을 내드릴 수 있습니다.

어휘 suitcase 여행 가방 as part of ~의 일환으로 as part of ~의 일환으로 effort 노력 reduce 줄이다 repair 수리 product 제품 line (상품의) 종류 replace 교체하다 damaged 손상된 fix 수리하다 fraction 부분, 일부 specialist 전문가 on site 현장에 inspect 검사하다 quote 견적

147. 공지가 작성된 이유는 무엇인가?
(A) 새로운 서비스를 발표하기 위해

(B) 보증 제공을 홍보하기 위해
(C) 여행 가방 쇼핑에 대한 조언을 하기 위해
(D) 인기 있는 제품을 소개하기 위해
해설 주제/목적
글의 목적은 대개 지문 도입부에 제시된다. Moncrieff Suitcase에서 자사 제품군의 모든 품목에 대해 수리를 제공할 것이라고 알리고 있으므로 (A)가 정답이다.
패러프레이징 will now offer repairs → announce a new service
어휘 promote 홍보하다 warranty 보증

148. Osburne 씨가 고객들에게 제공할 것은 무엇인가?
(A) 매장 쿠폰 코드
(B) 제품 시연
(C) 무료 비용 견적
(D) 판매 영수증
해설 세부 사항
Joseph Osburne을 키워드로 지문을 검색한다. 지문의 하단에 Joseph Osburne의 이름이 나온 후, 그가 무료 견적을 내줄 수 있다고 했으므로 (C)가 정답이다.
패러프레이징 free quote → free cost estimate
어휘 voucher 쿠폰, 할인권 demonstration 시연 estimate 견적 receipt 영수증

149-150 이메일

수신: Lori Carmona ⟨lcarmona@duncanfashions.com⟩
발신: Howard Monroe ⟨howard@gloryincorporated.com⟩
날짜: 1월 8일
제목: Glory 주식회사

Carmona 씨,

Glory 주식회사는 매년 당사의 서비스가 만족스러운지 확인하고 [149]우리 고객들의 비즈니스를 지원할 수 있는 가능한 방법을 찾기 위해 각각의 고객들과 간단한 전화 미팅을 갖고 있습니다. 저희는 해외 지사에서 근무할 직원들을 채용하는 것이 어려울 수 있다는 것을 알고 있습니다. [150]그렇기 때문에 저희는 귀사의 공석에 제안 드리는 모든 사람의 경력과 능력을 철저히 조사하여 가장 숙련된 인재들만 귀사에 연결해 드립니다.
언제 전화를 드리면 좋을지 알려 주세요.

Howard Monroe

어휘 incorporated 주식회사 satisfactory 만족스러운 identify 찾다, (신원 등을) 알아보다 assist 돕다 support 지원하다, 지지하다 hire 채용하다 branch 지사, 지점 thoroughly 철저히 investigate 조사하다 career 직업, 경력 background 배경 put forward 제안하다 experienced 경험 있는, 노련한 convenient 편리한

149. Monroe 씨가 Carmona 씨와 전화 통화를 마련하려는 이유는 무엇인가?
(A) 투자 기회를 알아보기 위해
(B) 그녀의 회사의 요구 사항을 가늠하기 위해

(C) 새로운 서비스를 소개하기 위해
(D) 몇몇 지사 방문을 준비하기 위해

해설 세부 사항
질문의 phone call을 키워드로 지문을 검색하여 phone meeting을 찾았다면 그 문장을 해석한다. 전화 미팅을 갖는 이유로 고객의 비즈니스를 지원할 수 있는 가능한 방법을 찾기 위함이라고 언급했으므로, Howard Monroe는 Lori Carmona가 속한 회사의 요구를 가늠하기 위해 그녀와 전화 통화를 하려는 것을 알 수 있다. 따라서 (B)가 정답이다.

패러프레이징 identify possible ways that we can assist in supporting their business → assess her company's needs

어휘 investment 투자   assess 평가하다, 가늠하다

150. Monroe 씨의 업체는 Carmona 씨의 업체를 어떻게 돕겠는가?
(A) 패션 동향을 조사함으로써
(B) 해외 지사에 대한 세금 자문을 제공함으로써
(C) 직책에 적합한 직원을 모집함으로써
(D) 새 사무실 건물을 찾음으로써

해설 세부 사항
질문에는 특별한 키워드가 없으므로, 도움을 주는 것과 관련된 내용을 찾아야 한다. 고객들의 비즈니스를 지원하기 위해 Carmona 씨의 업체의 공석에 숙련된 사람들을 제안하는 것이라고 했으므로 (C)가 정답이다.

패러프레이징 connecting you with the most experienced people → recruiting qualified staff members

어휘 trend 동향, 트렌드   recruit 채용하다, 모집하다   qualified 적격의, 자격을 갖춘   property 부동산

151-152 기사

레이크우드 (3월 3일)—레이크우드 시는 웨스트베리 다리를 건너는 운전자들이 곧 통행료를 지불해야 할 것이라고 발표했다. 최근 시 의회 회의에서 격렬한 토론이 있은 후, 11 대 3의 투표로 요금을 부과한다는 결정이 내려졌다. 요금소 설치 작업은 3월 20일부터 시작되며 ¹⁵¹요금 부과는 3월 31일부터 시작된다. 자동차와 오토바이는 다리를 건너는 데 4달러를 지불하게 될 것이다. 그보다 크기가 큰 차량은 크기에 따라 요금이 부과되며, 대형 화물 트럭은 다리를 건너려면 20달러까지 지불하게 될 것이다.

40년도 더 이전에 시에 의해 건설된 이래로, 웨스트베리 다리는 모든 운전자에게 무료였다. 하지만, ¹⁵²다리의 과도한 사용은 점점 더 빈번하게 보수를 해야 할 필요성의 원인이 되었다. 이러한 비용 상승으로, 의회는 다리에 자금을 마련할 방법을 찾을 수밖에 없었다.

'통행료 자동 결제' 시스템이 검토되고 있으며, 지역 주민들에게 4월 20일 의회 회의에서 이에 대한 의견을 공유하도록 권장하고 있다.

어휘 toll 통행료, 요금   vigorous 활발한, 격렬한   debate 토론, 논쟁   council 의회, 협의회   impose 부과하다   install 설치하다

charge 요금; (요금을) 청구하다   according to ~에 따라   oversized 특대의, 너무 큰   freight 화물   up to ~까지   contribute to ~에 기여하다, ~의 원인이 되다   increasingly 점점 더   have no choice but to do ~할 수밖에 없다   fund ~에 자금을 대다   fast pass system 통행료 자동 결제 시스템

151. 새로운 규정이 발효되는 시기는 언제인가?
(A) 3월 3일
(B) 3월 20일
(C) 3월 31일
(D) 4월 20일

해설 세부 사항
new regulation, go into effect 등을 키워드로 지문을 검색한다. 요금 부과는 3월 31일부터 시작된다고 했으므로 (C)가 정답이다.

패러프레이징 begin → go into effect

152. 기사에 따르면, 당국자들이 변경을 하도록 만든 것은 무엇인가?
(A) 과적 화물 트럭
(B) 증가하는 수리 비용
(C) 법인세 부족
(D) 환경 단체의 압력

해설 세부 사항
다리의 과도한 사용으로 보수의 필요성이 증가했고, 이에 따른 비용 상승으로 인하여 의회가 다리 보수를 위한 자금을 마련할 방법을 찾을 수밖에 없었다고 했으므로 (B)가 정답이다.

패러프레이징 these rising costs → Increasing repair costs

어휘 overload 과적하다   lack 부족, 결핍   business tax 법인세   pressure 압력

153-154 문자 메시지

Victoria Melrose (오전 9:05)
안녕하세요, Ethan, Oscar. ¹⁵³우리가 오늘 11시에 팀 회의를 갖기로 한 것으로 알고 있는데, 대신 2시에 시간 괜찮으세요?

Oscar Prentice (오전 9:06)
물론이죠. 그 시간에 갈 수 있습니다.

Ethan Clayborn (오전 9:08)
저도요. 회의실 예약에 문제가 있었나요?

Victoria Melrose (오전 9:09)
아니오, 하지만 ¹⁵³Jamie가 진료 예약이 있어요. 저는 아무도 회의에 빠지지 않았으면 좋겠거든요.

Oscar Prentice (오전 9:10)
맞는 말이에요. 그런데 ¹⁵⁴제가 안건을 이미 출력했는데, 안건에는 11시라고 되어 있어요. 원하시면 다시 출력할 수 있어요.

Victoria Melrose (오전 9:11)
고마워요, 하지만 그럴 필요는 없어요.

어휘 be supposed to do ~하기로 되어 있다, ~해야 하다

reserve 예약하다 conference 회의, 학회 medical 의학의, 의료의 appointment 예약, 약속 miss 놓치다 make sense 이치에 맞다 agenda 안건, 의제

153. Melrose 씨가 회의 시간을 변경하기를 원하는 이유는 무엇인가?
(A) 그녀는 자료를 준비하지 않았다.
(B) 직원 한 명이 그 시간에 참석할 수 없다.
(C) 회의실이 중복 예약되었다.
(D) 고객이 변경을 요청했다.

해설 세부 사항
Melrose 씨는 11시에는 Jamie가 진료 예약 때문에 회의에 올 수 없기 때문에 회의 시간을 변경하기를 원한다. 따라서 (B)가 정답이다.

어휘 material 자료 double-booked 중복 예약된 client 고객

154. 오전 9시 11분에, Melrose 씨가 "그럴 필요는 없어요"라고 쓸 때 그녀는 무엇을 의미하겠는가?
(A) 자신의 진료 예약을 변경할 수 있다.
(B) 이미 회의 장소를 선정했다.
(C) 현재의 문서를 사용할 수 있다.
(D) 프린터를 교체할 필요가 없다.

해설 의도 파악
의도 파악 문제는 바로 앞의 내용을 확인해야 한다. "that's not necessary"는 '그럴 필요는 없다'라는 뜻으로, 바로 앞에서 Oscar Prentice가 안건을 다시 출력할 수 있다고 한 말에 대한 응답이다. 즉, 안건을 다시 출력할 필요가 없고 현재 문서를 사용할 수 있다는 의미로 한 말이므로 (C)가 정답이다.

어휘 current 현재의, 지금의 replace 교체하다, 대체하다

155-157 설명서

Macon 신발
Macon 양가죽 슬리퍼 관리법

구매해 주셔서 감사합니다. 올바른 관리를 통해 귀하의 Macon 양가죽 슬리퍼를 오랫동안 신으실 수 있습니다.

슬리퍼를 신기 전에, 슬리퍼의 스웨이드 겉면에 [155]보호 스프레이를 사용하는 것을 추천합니다. 그렇게 하면 수분이 들어오는 것을 막는 장막이 만들어집니다. 스프레이 통에 있는 지침을 따르시고, 필요하면 스프레이를 다시 뿌리세요. [156D]슬리퍼를 신지 않을 때는 제공된 판지 슈트리를 사용하십시오. 슬리퍼의 모양을 유지할 수 있도록 각각의 슬리퍼 안쪽에 하나씩 넣으세요.

때를 제거하려면, 슬리퍼의 바깥쪽을 와이어 브러시로 부드럽게 솔질하세요. 디자인을 [157]망칠 수 있으니, [156B]슬리퍼의 자수 부분은 솔질을 하지 마십시오. 잘 안 지워지는 얼룩은 부드러운 면포를 백식초에 적셔 그 부분을 가볍게 두드리세요. 천연 양가죽은 냄새를 빨아들이는 경향이 있기 때문에 [156A]슬리퍼를 자주 환기시켜 주세요. 이것은 특히 야외에서 효과적이지만, [156C]그늘에서 해야 합니다. 그렇지 않으면 장시간 햇빛에 노출되어 색이 바랠 수 있습니다.

어휘 sheepskin 양가죽 purchase 구입, 구매 last 지속되다

오래가다 protective 보호하는 exterior 외부, 외면 barrier 장막 maintain 유지하다 remove 제거하다 brush 솔질하다; 솔, 빗 gently 부드럽게 embroider 수를 놓다 spoil 망치다 dip 담그다, 적시다 dab 가볍게 두드리다 have a tendency to do ~하는 경향이 있다 absorb 흡수하다 odor 냄새 air out 환기시키다 effective 효과적인 prolonged 장기간의 exposure 노출 fade 색이 바래다

155. 회사가 스프레이 사용을 추천하는 이유는 무엇인가?
(A) 표면을 세척하기 쉽게 하기 위해
(B) 냄새를 줄이기 위해
(C) 습기를 막기 위해
(D) 색바램을 줄이기 위해

해설 세부 사항
spray를 키워드로 지문을 검색한다. 보호 스프레이를 사용하면 물이 들어오는 것을 막는 장막을 만들 것이라며 스프레이 사용을 추천하고 있으므로, (C)가 정답이다.

패러프레이징 prevent water from getting in → keep moisture out

어휘 surface 표면 keep ~ out ~이 들어가지 않게 하다 moisture 습기, 수분

156. 설명서에 조언으로 언급되지 않은 것은 무엇인가?
(A) 정기적으로 슬리퍼를 환기시키기
(B) 자수를 부드럽게 솔질하기
(C) 슬리퍼를 직사광선에 두지 않기
(D) 사용 후에 삽입물을 넣기

해설 NOT/True
슬리퍼의 자수 부분을 솔질하지 말라고 했으므로 이와 반대되는 내용인 (B)가 정답이다.

패러프레이징 (A) frequently → regularly / (C) it must be done in the shade → Keeping the slippers out of direct sunlight / (D) use the cardboard wedges, Place one inside each slipper → Putting an insert in

어휘 regularly 정기적으로, 주기적으로 embroidery 자수 direct sunlight 직사광선

157. 세 번째 단락 두 번째 줄의 어휘 "spoil"과 의미상 가장 가까운 것은?
(A) 탐닉하다
(B) 손상시키다
(C) 실망시키다
(D) 부패하다

해설 동의어
spoil the design은 문맥상 '디자인을 망치다'라는 의미이며, 선택지 중 '망치다'와 의미상 가장 유사한 (B)가 정답이다.

158-160 공지

[158]Titan 연례 기술 학회의 모든 연사 여러분께 안내 말씀 드립니다:

¹⁵⁸도착하시면 행사 기획자인 Alana Sheppard 씨에게 도착 사실을 알려 주셔야 합니다. 접수처에 있는 직원이 그녀를 찾을 수 있는 곳을 알려 줄 수 있을 것입니다. Sheppard 씨가 여러분의 발표 자료를 받아서 나중에 나눠줄 것입니다. ¹⁵⁸그녀는 또한 여러분을 무대로 안내하여 그곳에서 음향 확인을 하고 슬라이드쇼가 제대로 작동하는지 확인할 수 있도록 해 드릴 것입니다. 연단 배치 등의 특별한 요청 사항이 있으면 그녀에게 알려 주세요. 그다음 날 신문사에서 행사에 대한 기사를 ¹⁵⁹실을 예정이라서 〈블룸필드 헤럴드〉에서 나온 사진작가가 행사 도중 사진을 찍을 예정임을 알아 두시기 바랍니다.

¹⁵⁸모든 발표자는 자신의 차례가 될 때까지 무대 밖에 있겠지만, 무대 뒤에서 다른 발표를 볼 수도 있습니다. ¹⁶⁰발표가 끝난 뒤, 모든 참가자에게 연회장에서 저녁 식사가 제공될 예정입니다. 특별한 테이블과 좌석이 여러분을 위해 따로 마련되어 있을 것입니다. 여러분의 이름표를 찾아보시면 됩니다.

문제나 우려되는 사항이 있으면 555-3019번으로 Sheppard 씨에게 전화해 주십시오. 감사합니다.

어휘 annual 매년의, 연례의 arrival 도착 report (도착을) 알리다 registration 등록 presentation 발표 distribute 나누어 주다, 배포하다 direct 안내하다, 알려 주다 properly 제대로, 적절히 request 요청, 요구 사항; 요청하다 placement 놓기, 배치 podium 연단 article 기사 presenter 발표자 participant 참가자 banquet hall 연회장 reserve (자리 등을) 따로 잡아두다 issue 문제, 사안 concern 걱정, 관심사

158. 공지가 작성된 이유는 무엇인가?
(A) 행사의 자원봉사자를 모집하기 위해
(B) 학회 직원에게 업무를 할당하기 위해
(C) 발표자들에게 절차에 대해 알리기 위해
(D) 참가자들에게 규칙을 상기시키기 위해

해설 주제/목적
이 공지의 목적은 글의 전반에 걸쳐 나타나 있다. 여러 단서들을 종합해 보면, 연례 기술 학회의 연사들에게 안내를 하겠다면서 행사가 어떻게 진행될지 그 절차를 알리고 있다. 따라서 (C)가 정답이다.

패러프레이징 speakers → presenters

어휘 recruit 모집하다, 선발하다 volunteer 자원봉사자 assign 할당하다 task 과제 inform 알리다 procedure 절차, 과정 remind 상기시키다 regulation 규정

159. 첫 번째 단락 일곱 번째 줄의 "carry"와 의미상 가장 가까운 것은?
(A) 게재하다
(B) 잡다
(C) 수송하다
(D) 받아들이다

해설 동의어 찾기
carry가 포함된 the newspaper will carry an article은 '신문에서 기사를 실을 예정이다'라는 의미이므로, carry는 '(기사 등을) 게재하다, 싣다'라는 의미로 쓰였다. 선택지 중 이와 의미상 유사한 (A)가 정답이다.

160. Titan 연례 기술 학회에 대해 시사된 것은 무엇인가?
(A) 사업주들만을 대상으로 열린다.
(B) 매년 같은 장소에서 개최된다.
(C) 참석자들을 위한 식사가 포함된다.
(D) 사전 등록을 필요로 하지 않는다.

해설 NOT/True
발표가 끝난 뒤 모든 참가자에게 저녁 식사가 제공될 것이라고 했으므로 학회에는 참가자들을 위한 식사가 포함될 것임을 알 수 있으므로 (C)가 정답이다.

패러프레이징 all participants will be served dinner → includes a meal for attendees

어휘 exclusively 독점적으로, 배타적으로 site 장소, 현장 attendee 참석자 advance 사전의

161-163 기사

오거스타 (2월 10일)—오거스타 시는 지역 경제를 지탱하기 위해 지역에 새로운 기업들을 유치하려고 열심히 노력해 왔다. ¹⁶¹그러한 기업 중 하나인 인테리어 디자인 회사 Chic Choices는 웨인즈버로에 있는 현 사무실에서 이곳 오거스타의 하일랜드 오피스 단지에 있는 한 상가 건물로 이전할 계획을 발표했다. 이 회사는 최소 15명의 정규직 직원을 보유할 것으로 예상되며 성수기에는 임시직 직원이 추가로 고용될 예정이다. 이 회사 소유주인 Angela Strom 씨는 ¹⁶¹가능한 한 많은 상품에 지역 공급업체를 이용하고자 애쓰고 있는데, 이는 사업으로 인해 창출되는 수익의 대부분이 오거스타에 남게 된다는 것을 의미한다.

Chic Choices는 현재 주택 수선을 전문으로 하고 있지만, 상가 프로젝트로도 확장할 계획이 있으며, 이것은 ¹⁶¹훨씬 더 많은 일자리 창출을 의미할 수 있다. 수선 과정은 ¹⁶²Wave-360이라 불리는 이 회사 고유의 소프트웨어 프로그램을 통해 간편해졌다. 방의 사진들은 프로그램에 업로드될 수 있다. 그런 다음 방을 컴퓨터 이미지로 '장식'하여 ¹⁶²프로젝트를 시작하기 전에 방이 어떻게 보일지 고객이 볼 수 있게 해 준다. 그러나 이 회사는 컴퓨터 이미지 작업만 하는 것은 아니다. ¹⁶³회사는 고객들이 카펫, 타일, 페인트 등을 둘러볼 수 있도록 2,500 평방피트의 전시장을 가지게 될 것이다. 회사의 현재 전시장은 그 크기의 절반도 안 된다. 이제 사람들은 이제까지보다 더 많은 수의 견본을 확인할 수 있다.

어휘 attract 끌어들이다 economy 경제 current 현재의 commercial 상업의 unit 한 가구, 한 개 additional 추가의 temporary 임시의 peak season 성수기 be dedicated to ~에 전념하다[헌신하다] supplier 공급업체 as ~ as possible 가능한 한 ~한[하게] revenue 수익, 수입 generate 창출하다 specialize in ~을 전문으로 하다 renovation 보수, 수선 expand 확장하다 as well 또한, 역시 unique 고유의, 독특한 decorate 장식하다 virtually 가상으로, 컴퓨터 이미지로 showroom 전시장 browse 둘러보다

161. 기사는 주로 무엇에 관한 것인가?
(A) 회사 창업자의 이력
(B) 인테리어 디자인 업계의 동향

(C) 한 회사 이전의 이점
(D) 지역 기업 정책의 변경 사항

해설 주제/목적
기사 전반에서 Chic Choices라는 회사의 이전으로 인해 예상되는 이점에 대해 설명하고 있으며, 이는 오거스타 지역 경제의 활성화 및 일자리 창출을 가져올 것임을 알 수 있다. 따라서 (C)가 정답이다.

패러프레이징 move → relocation

어휘 benefit 이점, 혜택   relocation 이전

162. Wave-360 프로그램이 사용자에게 허용하는 것은 무엇인가?
(A) 주택 수선 비용 계산하기
(B) 방의 정확한 사진 찍기
(C) 색상 조합 추천 받기
(D) 방에 대한 잠재적인 변경 사항 보기

해설 세부 사항
Wave-360을 키워드로 지문을 검색한다. 고객은 컴퓨터 이미지로 바뀐 방의 모습을 볼 수 있다고 했으므로 (D)가 정답이다.

패러프레이징 view → see

어휘 calculate 계산하다   accurate 정확한   recommendation 추천   combination 조합   potential 잠재적인

163. [1], [2], [3], [4]로 표시된 위치 중 다음 문장이 들어가기에 가장 적절한 곳은?
"이제 사람들은 이제까지보다 더 많은 수의 견본을 확인할 수 있다."
(A) [1]
(B) [2]
(C) [3]
(D) [4]

해설 문장 삽입
주어진 문장은 부사 now(이제)로 시작하므로, 주어진 문장 앞에는 이전의 상황을 묘사하는 내용이 나와야 알맞다. 따라서 전에는 전시장 규모가 2,500 평방피트의 절반도 되지 않았다는 내용의 뒤인 [4]에 들어가는 것이 가장 알맞다.

164-167 이메일

발신: Sebastian Dwyer
수신: Gabrielle Redmond
날짜: 4월 8일
제목: Ainsley 저택
첨부 파일: Ainsley 저택 사진

Gabrielle,

¹⁶⁴제가 드디어 Ainsley 저택을 방문할 기회가 생겼는데, 우리 광고를 찍기에 아주 좋은 장소일 수도 있을 거라고 생각합니다. 그 역사적인 건물은 외관이 인상적이에요. ¹⁶⁵ᶜ집 앞에 있는 분수대가 작동해서 평화로운 분위기를 자아내죠. 건물의 뒤편을 이용하는 것도 하나의 방법이 될 겁니다. ¹⁶⁵ᴮ몇 개의 청동상뿐만 아니라 ¹⁶⁵ᴰ큰 바위 정원이 있어요. 오늘 밤 서리가 내릴 것으로 예상되어 ¹⁶⁵ᴬ화단이 덮여 있었지만, 화단은 괜찮아 보일 거예요.

저택이 주요 고속도로와 매우 가까운 곳에 위치해 있기 때문에, 지나가는 차량들로 인해 소음이 너무 심하지 않을까 걱정했습니다. 다행히 수풀이 길게 늘어서 있어 이는 문제가 되지 않아요. ¹⁶⁶그러나 그 부지에 있는 나무들 중 일부는 그다지 건강해 보이지 않아요. 제가 이에 대해 직원과 이야기해 보니, 변색된 부분을 제거하기 위해 다듬을 수 있다고 합니다.

이 장소의 사용료에 ¹⁶⁷맞추기 위해, 우리는 모든 촬영을 반나절 안에 끝내도록 노력해야 합니다. 많은 기획이 필요하겠지만, 그렇게 하면 예산을 넘지 않을 수 있을 겁니다. 다음 회의에서 이 문제를 더 논의합시다.

Sebastian Dwyer

어휘 manor 영주의 저택   site 장소   shoot 촬영하다   commercial 광고; 상업의   impressive 인상적인   fountain 분수   operational 사용 중인, 가동 중인   rear 뒤쪽   option 선택(할 수 있는 것)   B as well as A A뿐만 아니라 B도(= not only A but also B)   statue 조각상   flowerbed 화단   frost 서리   located 위치한   concerned 걱정하는   pass by 옆을 지나가다   fortunately 다행히   bush 덤불   property 부동산, 건물   trim 다듬다, 손질하다   discolored 변색된   contain 억제하다, 포함하다   stay within budget 예산을 벗어나지 않다

164. 이메일의 목적은 무엇인가?
(A) 관광지를 추천하기 위해
(B) 회사 야유회를 제안하기 위해
(C) 상업용 부동산 구입에 반대하기 위해
(D) 촬영지에 대한 지지를 나타내기 위해

해설 주제/목적
목적 문제의 단서는 대개 지문 도입부에 제시된다. Ainsley 저택을 방문할 기회가 생겼는데, 광고를 찍기에 좋은 장소라고 생각한다고 말하며 지문 전반에 걸쳐 이 장소가 촬영에 적합한 이유를 설명하고 있으므로 (D)가 정답이다.

패러프레이징 site for shooting → filming site

어휘 recommend 추천하다   attraction 관광지, 명소   outing 야유회   oppose 반대하다   express 나타내다, 표현하다

165. Dwyer 씨가 직접 본 것이 아닌 것은 무엇인가?
(A) 화단
(B) 조각상
(C) 분수대
(D) 바위 정원

해설 NOT/True
지문에서 (B), (C), (D)에 대한 내용은 확인할 수 있으나, 화단이 덮여 있었다고 했으므로 화단은 직접 보지 못했음을 알 수 있다. 따라서 (A)가 정답이다.

166. Dwyer 씨가 직원에게 제기한 문제점은 무엇인가?
(A) 부지를 빌리는 비용이 너무 비싸다.
(B) 나무들의 상태가 좋지 않다.
(C) 교통 소음이 매우 지장을 준다.
(D) 건물에 페인트칠을 해야 한다.

해설 세부 사항
employee를 키워드로 지문을 검색하면 staff member를 찾을 수 있는데, 나무들 중 일부가 그다지 건강해 보이지 않아서 이에 대해 직원과 이야기했다고 했으므로 (B)가 정답이다.

패러프레이징 do not look very healthy → are in poor condition

어휘 disruptive 지장을 주는

167. 세 번째 단락 첫 번째 줄의 "contain"과 의미상 가장 가까운 것은?
(A) ~으로 구성되다
(B) 억제하다
(C) 유지하다
(D) 에워싸다

해설 동의어 찾기
contain이 포함된 부분은 '사용료에 맞추기 위해 모든 촬영을 반나절 안에 끝내도록 노력해야 한다'라는 의미이므로, contain은 '억제하다'라는 의미로 쓰였다. 선택지 중 이와 의미상 가장 유사한 (B)가 정답이다.

168-171 온라인 채팅

> Caroline Ingram (오후 5:12)
> 직원 안내서를 다시 작성하는 데 도움을 주셔서 고마워요. ¹⁷⁰금요일 늦은 시간인 걸 알지만, 다음 주 수요일에 신입 사원들이 오기 때문에 모두의 업무가 계속해서 제대로 진행되고 있는지 확인하고 싶었어요. ¹⁶⁸저는 회사 연혁에 대한 문구 작성을 끝냈으니, 필요하면 다른 걸 도와드릴 수 있어요.
>
> Eric Hale (오후 5:14)
> 모든 규정이 최신 정보인지는 제가 확인했습니다. 특히 사내 위원회의 업무 방식이 바뀌기도 해서요. 아직 교정을 봐야 하지만 오늘 퇴근하기 전에 보내 드릴 수 있어요.
>
> Andre Silva (오후 5:15)
> 시설 정보도 대부분 완료되었지만 ¹⁶⁹도움이 좀 필요해요. 제 컴퓨터에 디자인 프로그램이 설치되어 있지 않아서 건물 지도를 그릴 수 없어요.
>
> Caroline Ingram (오후 5:16)
> 그건 괜찮아요, Andre. ¹⁷⁰제가 어제 지도를 업데이트했으니 회사 웹 사이트에 있는 것을 사용하시면 됩니다.
>
> Eric Hale (오후 5:17)
> 이번 인쇄 작업량이 많을 거예요. 우리가 월요일 오후에 최종안을 제출하면 익일 서비스를 받을 수 있도록 ¹⁷¹누군가가 인쇄소에 전화해야 합니다.
>
> Andre Silva (오후 5:18)
> 제가 할게요.

어휘 rewrite 다시 쓰다 handbook 안내서 task 업무, 과제 on track 제대로 진행되고 있는 internal 내부의 committee 위원회 proofread 교정을 보다 facility 시설 complete 완료하다 install 설치하다 update 업데이트하다, 가장 최근의 정보를 알려 주다 ensure ~을 확실히 하다, 보증하다 overnight 야간의, 익일의 submit 제출하다 draft 원고, 초안

168. Ingram 씨는 무엇에 관해 썼는가?
(A) 회사 배경
(B) 직장 규정
(C) 시설 정보
(D) 직원 복지

해설 세부 사항
지문에서 Ingram이 작성한 글을 검색한다. 회사 연혁 관련 문구를 다 썼다고 했으므로 (A)가 정답이다.

패러프레이징 company history → business's background

169. Silva 씨가 도움을 필요로 하는 이유는 무엇인가?
(A) 업무에 대한 교육을 받지 않았다.
(B) 적절한 소프트웨어를 보유하고 있지 않다.
(C) 끝내야 할 다른 급한 프로젝트가 있다.
(D) 중요한 파일을 잃어버렸다.

해설 세부 사항
Silva가 쓴 글에서 assistance를 키워드로 검색한다. assistance는 help 등으로 패러프레이징될 수 있다는 것을 염두에 둔다. Andre Silva는 도움이 필요하다고 말하면서 디자인 프로그램이 없어서 건물 지도를 그릴 수 없다고 했으므로 (B)가 정답이다.

패러프레이징 program → software

어휘 train 훈련하다, 교육하다 urgent 긴급한

170. Ingram 씨가 지도를 온라인상에 업데이트한 때는 언제인가?
(A) 월요일
(B) 수요일
(C) 목요일
(D) 금요일

해설 세부 사항
update a map을 키워드로 Ingram이 쓴 문장을 검색한다. 어제 지도를 업데이트했다고 했는데, 첫 번째 줄에서 Caroline Ingram이 (지금은) 금요일 늦은 시간이라고 했으므로, 어제는 목요일이었음을 알 수 있다. 따라서 (C)가 정답이다.

171. 오후 5시 18분에, Silva 씨가 "제가 할게요"라고 쓸 때 그는 무엇을 의미하겠는가?
(A) 그는 초안을 교정 볼 것이다.
(B) 그는 프린터를 수리할 것이다.
(C) 그는 오리엔테이션에 참석할 것이다.
(D) 그는 업체에 연락할 것이다.

해설 의도 파악
의도 파악 문제는 바로 앞의 내용을 확인해야 한다. "I'm on it."은 '내가 하겠다'라는 뜻인데, 바로 앞에서 Eric Hale이 누군가가 인쇄소에 전화해야 한다고 말한 것에 대한 Silva 씨의 답변이므로, 본인이 인쇄소에 전화하겠다는 의미로 한 말임을 알 수 있다. 따라서 (D)가 정답이다.

패러프레이징 call the print shop → contact a business

어휘 contact 연락하다 business 업체

172-175 기사

세계적 도전에 나선 IFSA
Jeremiah Roark 작성

샌디에이고 (3월 20일)—172국제식품안전협회(IFSA)는 8월 3일부터 5일까지 40개국 이상에서 온 전문가, 정책 입안자, 기업주들이 모이는 연례 회의를 개최할 것이다. 회의는 전 세계 모든 사람들에게 안전한 식품을 보장하는 데 도움이 되는 관례를 제정하고 따르는 방법을 교육할 것이다. IFSA는 173D해당 분야의 사람들이 만나서 그들의 지식을 공유할 수 있는 기회를 마련하여 공공과 민간 부문 모두에서 협력 관계를 증진시킬 수 있기를 기대한다. 일련의 발표와 워크숍은 173A첨단 기술을 선보여 참가자들이 미래를 대비하고, 173B업계가 소비자들에게 더욱 신뢰받도록 할 예정이다.

광범위한 참여를 보장하고 불필요한 이동으로 인한 오염을 줄이기 위해 175회의는 전적으로 화상으로 개최될 것이다. 참가자들은 안정적인 인터넷 연결만 필요할 뿐이다. 그들은 생방송으로 활동을 보고 실시간으로 의견을 말할 수 있을 것이다. 나중에 IFSA 웹 사이트에서 회의의 일부를 다시 볼 수 있는 기회도 있을 것이다.

"저는 올해 행사를 기대하고 있습니다"라고 Arbor 슈퍼마켓의 주인인 174Uta Holzman 씨가 말했다. "작년에 얻은 통찰력은 매우 유용했고, 이미 제 사업에 적용했습니다. 하지만 저는 그저 한 개인일 뿐입니다. 세계 인구가 이처럼 빠르게 증가하고 있는 상황에서 174우리는 식품 안전 문제를 해결하기 위한 공동의 노력이 필요한데, 그 때문에 이와 같은 회의가 있다는 것이 기쁩니다."

IFSA는 또한 내년 행사를 계획하고 있으니, 자신의 전문 지식을 제공하고자 하는 사람은 a.lucchesi@ifsa.org로 Angelica Lucchesi에게 연락하는 것을 권한다.

어휘 take on ~을 떠맡다 bring together 모이게 하다 specialist 전문가 policymaker 정책 입안자 enact (법을) 제정하다 practice 관례, 관행, 실천 foster 증진하다 partnership 협력, 제휴 sector 부문 a series of 일련의 showcase 소개하다, 진열하다 cutting-edge 최첨단의 trustworthy 신뢰할 수 있는 widespread 널리 퍼진, 광범위한 participation 참가 entirely 전적으로 videoconference 화상 회의를 하다 stable 안정적인 look forward to ~을 고대하다 insight 통찰력 invaluable 매우 유용한, 귀중한 apply 적용하다, 지원하다 individual 개인; 개인의 coordinated 통합된, 협조된 look ahead to ~을 앞두다, ~을 내다 보다 contribute 제공하다, 기여하다 expertise 전문 지식

172. 기사의 목적은 무엇인가?
(A) 업계에서 주는 상의 수상자를 발표하려고
(B) 새로운 규제의 필요성을 강조하려고
(C) 교육적인 사업 행사를 홍보하려고
(D) 식품 공급의 안전 문제를 강조하려고

해설 주제/목적
목적 문제의 단서는 대개 지문 도입부에 제시된다. 국제식품안전협회(IFSA)가 안전한 식품 보장을 위한 관례를 제정하고 따르는 방법을 가르치는 연례 회의를 개최할 것이라고 했으므로 (C)가 정답이다.

패러프레이징 conference → event

어휘 winner 수상자 award 상 emphasize 강조하다 regulation 규정 promote 홍보하다 highlight 강조하다 supply 공급

173. IFSA의 목표로 나타나 있지 않은 것은 무엇인가?
(A) 신기술 도입
(B) 소비자 신뢰 구축
(C) 해당 부문의 일자리 증대
(D) 인적 네트워크 형성 기회 창출

해설 NOT/True
일자리 증대에 관해서는 언급된 바가 없으므로 (C)가 정답이다.

패러프레이징 (A) showcase cutting-edge technology → Introducing new technology / (B) make the industry more trustworthy for consumers → Building consumer trust / (D) a chance to meet and share their knowledge → Creating networking opportunities

어휘 introduce 도입하다, 소개하다 trust 신뢰 networking 인적 네트워크 형성

174. Holzman 씨에 대해 사실인 것은 무엇인가?
(A) 전문 분야는 식품 처리 절차이다.
(B) 사업이 꾸준히 성장하고 있다.
(C) 사람들이 협력에 집중해야 한다고 생각한다.
(D) 공공 부문에서 일하고 싶어 한다.

해설 NOT/True
Holzman을 키워드로 검색한다. 세 번째 단락의 끝에서 식품 안전 문제를 해결하기 위한 공동의 노력이 필요하다고 했으므로 (C)가 정답이다.

패러프레이징 we need a coordinated effort → people should focus on working together

어휘 procedure 절차, 과정 steadily 꾸준히

175. [1], [2], [3], [4]로 표시된 위치 중 다음 문장이 들어가기에 가장 적절한 곳은?

"그들은 생방송으로 활동을 보고 실시간으로 의견을 말할 수 있을 것이다."

(A) [1]
(B) [2]
(C) [3]
(D) [4]

해설 문장 삽입
주어진 문장은 화상 회의에 관한 것이므로, 회의는 전적으로 화상으로 개최되며, 참가자들은 안정적인 인터넷 연결만 있으면 된다는 내용 다음인 [2]에 들어가는 것이 적절하다.

176-180 회람 & 양식

회람
수신: 기획 위원들
발신: Hilda Geiger

제목: 환급 절차
날짜: 4월 19일

¹⁷⁶우리는 5월 10일 도쿄 지사에서 오는 방문객들의 도착에 대비하고 있으므로, 여러분들에게 Acosta Finance의 환급 방침에 대해 다시 한번 상기시켜 드리고자 합니다. ¹⁷⁶이처럼 중요한 회사 대표자들을 위해 환영 연회를 준비할 때 회사의 환급 방침을 유념하시기 바랍니다. ¹⁷⁷법인 카드는 부서장들에게만 발급되므로 다른 직원들은 물품 대금을 먼저 직접 지불하고 환급을 요청해야 합니다. ¹⁷⁹⁻¹10달러 미만의 소액 거래는 양식을 제출하면 현금으로 환급됩니다. 그 금액을 초과하는 금액은 여러분의 다음 번 급여와 같은 날에 은행 계좌로 입금됩니다.

예산을 반드시 염두에 두시기 바랍니다. 환영회는 우리 연간 행사 예산의 10% 이상을 ¹⁷⁸차지해서는 안 됩니다. 그렇지 않으면 연말에 직원 감사 행사를 일부 취소해야 할 수도 있습니다. 할당된 업무 중 확실하지 않은 사항이 있으면 저에게 직접 연락하시거나, 다음 행사 기획 회의에서 부담 없이 그에 대해 말씀하세요.

이 위원회에서 여러분의 노고에 감사드립니다.

어휘 committee 위원회 reimbursement 상환, 환급 procedure 절차 remind 상기시키다 make arrangements for ~을 준비하다 reception 환영 연회 representative 대표(자) keep ~ in mind ~을 염두에 두다 issue 발행하다, 발급하다 pay for ~에 대한 값을 지불하다 transaction 거래 cash 현금 form 양식 account 계좌 paycheck 급여 budget 예산 make up ~을 차지하다 cancel 취소하다 appreciation 감사 assign 할당하다 directly 직접

¹⁸⁰Acosta Finance 직원 지출 양식

이름: Sheila Hale
제출 날짜: 5월 3일
구매 이유: 환영회
승인자: Hilda Geiger

구매 일자	금액	업체명	명세
5월 1일	238.50달러	Diaz Catering	음식 주문
5월 1일	¹⁷⁹⁻²5.95달러	Party Palace	풍선
5월 2일	34.99달러	Ace Printing	환영 현수막
5월 2일	55달러	Lena Electronics	휴대용 스피커
5월 2일	11.25달러	¹⁸⁰A2B 택시	쇼핑센터로 이동
5월 2일	12.85달러	¹⁸⁰A2B 택시	사무실로 복귀

¹⁸⁰상기 구매에 대한 모든 영수증을 포함시키세요.

어휘 expense 경비, 지출 submission 제출 purchase 구입, 구매 approve 승인하다 banner 현수막 portable 휴대용의 include 포함하다 receipt 영수증

176. Geiger 씨는 5월 10일에 무슨 일이 있을 것이라고 말하는가?
(A) 새로운 회사 정책이 시행될 것이다.
(B) 새로운 직원이 소개될 것이다.
(C) 몇몇 구직자들이 면접을 볼 것이다.
(D) 몇몇 VIP 손님들이 사무실을 방문할 것이다.

해설 세부 사항
May 10을 키워드로 지문을 검색한다. 도쿄 지사에서 방문객들이 도착하며, 이들이 회사의 중요한 대표자들이라고 했으므로 (D)가 정답이다.

패러프레이징 visitors → guests

어휘 policy 정책, 방침 go into effect 발효되다, 실시되다 job candidate 구직자, 입사 지원자

177. 법인 카드에 대해 언급된 것은 무엇인가?
(A) 사용자가 영수증을 보관할 필요는 없다.
(B) 부서장들에게만 발급된다.
(C) 곧 위원들에게 지급될 것이다.
(D) Geiger 씨의 사무실에서 수령할 수 있다.

해설 세부 사항
company credit cards를 키워드로 지문을 검색한다. 법인 카드는 부서장들에게만 발급된다고 했으므로 (B)가 정답이다.

패러프레이징 department directors → department heads

어휘 department head 부서장 pick up 찾다, 수령하다

178. 회람에서, 두 번째 단락 첫 번째 줄의 "make up"과 의미상 가장 가까운 것은?
(A) 준비하다
(B) 발명하다
(C) 동의하다
(D) ~으로 구성되다

해설 동의어 찾기
make up이 포함된 make up more than 10% of our annual event budget은 '우리 연간 행사 예산의 10% 이상을 차지하다'라는 뜻이므로, make up은 '~을 차지하다'라는 의미로 쓰였다. 선택지 중 이와 의미가 가장 유사한 (D)가 정답이다.

179. Hale 씨의 다음 번 급여에 포함되지 않을 업체 비용은 무엇인가?
(A) Diaz Catering
(B) Party Palace
(C) Ace Printing
(D) Lena Electronics

해설 두 지문 연계_세부 사항
Hale과 next paycheck을 키워드로 지문을 검색한다. 첫 번째 지문에서 next paycheck이 들어간 문장 근처를 살펴보면 10달러 미만의 소액 거래는 현금으로 환급되고, 10달러를 초과하는 금액은 다음 급여와 같은 날에 은행 계좌로 지급된다고 했다. 그리고 Hale 씨는 두 번째 지문의 작성자인데, 지출 항목 중에서 10달러 미만의 금액은 Party Palace라는 것을 알 수 있다. 즉, Party Palace의 금액은 급여일에 지급되는 것이 아니라 즉시 현금으로 환급되므로 (B)가 정답이다.

180. Hale 씨가 5월 3일에 했을 것 같은 일은 무엇인가?
(A) 신용카드 명세서 사본을 작성했다

(B) 교통비 영수증을 제출했다
(C) 다른 위원에게 연락했다
(D) 쇼핑센터로 이동했다

해설 추론/암시

Hale과 May 3을 키워드로 지문을 검색한다. 두 번째 지문에서 Sheila Hale은 5월 3일에 직원 지출 양식을 제출했고, 그 중에는 A2B 택시를 타고 쇼핑센터와 사무실 사이를 이동한 교통비 지출 내역이 있다. 표 하단에 모든 영수증을 포함시키라고 했으므로 5월 3일에 제출한 것 중에는 교통비 영수증이 포함되어 있다는 것을 유추할 수 있으므로 (B)가 정답이다.

어휘 copy 사본 statement 입출금 내역서 transportation 교통수단

181-185 웹페이지 & 이메일

[181]식품 산업은 경쟁이 매우 치열하며, 여러분이 만드는 제품에 대한 브랜드 충성도를 높이는 가장 좋은 방법은 일관성을 제공하는 것입니다. [181]Ryrie Supplies의 실리콘 베이킹 매트가 있으면 고른 열전도를 보장할 수 있어 매번 동일한 결과를 얻을 수 있습니다. [182]당사의 매트는 화씨 영하 40도까지 냉동하거나 화씨 480도까지 가열할 수 있으므로, 여러분의 작업에 필요한 것이 무엇이든지 간에 균열이나 용해는 발생하지 않으니 안심하셔도 됩니다. 저희 매트는 아래와 같이 다양한 사이즈로 구입 가능합니다.

모델명	Gaffney	[184-2]Jimna	Marloo	Quinton
폭	35 cm	30 cm	42 cm	40 cm
길이	20 cm	42 cm	62 cm	55 cm
두께	0.75 mm	0.65 mm	0.95 mm	0.80 mm

어휘 competitive 경쟁적인, 경쟁력 있는 loyalty 충성심 consistency 일관성 even 고른, 균일한 distribution 분배, 분포 rest assured (that) (~임을) 확신해도[믿어도] 된다 crack 갈라지다, 금이 가다 melt 녹다, 용해하다 no matter what 비록 ~이 …라고 하더라도 available 구할 수 있는 a variety of 다양한 width 폭, 너비 length 길이 thickness 두께

수신: Erma Shahan <ermashahan@ryriesupplies.com>
발신: Walter Davila <w_davila@miramarinc.com>
[183]날짜: 6월 19일
제목: Miramar 주식회사 주문

Shahan 씨,

저희는 이번에는 평소처럼 주문을 넣지는 않을 것임을 알려 드리고 싶습니다. [183]다음 달에 새로운 관리자가 입사할 예정이라, 현재 우리의 주문이 모두 보류된 상태입니다. [184-1]저희는 귀사의 가장 얇은 매트를 약 6개월 동안 사용해 왔고, 그것에 매우 만족합니다. 다만 우리는 내년에 출시할 신제품을 현재 개발 중인데, 좀 더 두꺼운 것이 좋을 것 같습니다. [185]Quinton 모델 샘플 몇 개를 보내 주실 수 있나요? 물론, 어떤 것이 가장 적합한지 알아보기 위해 몇 군데 다른 회사의 제품들을 실험해 볼 것입니다.

Walter Davila

어휘 on hold 보류되어 release 출시하다 experiment 실험하다 suitable 적합한

181. Ryrie Supplies의 제품이 사용될 것 같은 곳은 어디인가?
(A) 보관 시설
(B) 제약 공장
(C) 업소용 주방
(D) 금융 기관

해설 추론/암시

Ryrie Supplies를 키워드로 지문을 검색하면 첫 번째 지문에 food industry와 baking mats from Ryrie Supplies가 나오므로 Ryrie Supplies의 제품은 음식을 다루는 업체의 주방에서 사용된다고 유추할 수 있다. 따라서 (C)가 정답이다.

어휘 storage 보관, 저장 pharmaceutical 제약의 commercial 상업의 financial 금융의 institution 기관

182. Ryrie Supplies의 제품에 대해 시사된 것은 무엇인가?
(A) 저장 공간을 절약하기 위해 둥글게 말 수 있다.
(B) 특수 장갑을 끼고 다루어야 한다.
(C) 재활용 재료로 만들어진다.
(D) 광범위한 온도를 견딜 수 있다.

해설 NOT/True

첫 번째 지문에서 Ryrie Supplies의 매트는 화씨 영하 40도에서 영상 480도까지의 온도를 견딜 수 있다고 했으므로 (D)가 정답이다.

어휘 roll (둥글게) 말다 handle 다루다, 처리하다 recycled 재활용된 material 물질, 재료 withstand 견디다 a wide range of 광범위한

183. Davila 씨에 따르면, 새로운 관리자가 Miramar 주식회사에서 근무하기 시작할 시기는 언제인가?
(A) 6월
(B) 7월
(C) 6개월 후
(D) 내년

해설 추론/암시

Davila가 발신인인 두 번째 지문을 new manager를 키워드로 검색한다. 다음 달에 새로운 관리자가 입사할 예정이라고 했는데, 이 메일을 보낸 날짜가 6월이므로 7월에 새 관리자가 근무를 시작할 것임을 유추할 수 있다. 따라서 (B)가 정답이다.

184. Miramar 주식회사에서 현재 사용하고 있는 모델은 무엇인가?
(A) Gaffney
(B) Jimna
(C) Marloo
(D) Quinton

해설 두 지문 연계_세부 사항

model, Miramar, use 등을 키워드로 지문을 검색한다. 두 번째 지문에서 Walter Davila는 자신의 회사가 가장 얇은 매트를 사용해 왔다고 했는데, 첫 번째 지문의 표를 보면 가장 얇은 모델은 Jimna이므로 (B)가 정답이다.

185. Davila 씨에 대해 암시된 것은 무엇인가?
(A) 새로운 배송 주소를 사용해야 한다.
(B) 곧 회사를 떠날 것이다.
(C) 시험삼아 다른 브랜드를 사용해 볼 계획이다.
(D) 현재 제품에 불만이 있다.

해설 추론/암시
Davila가 발신자인 두 번째 지문을 검색한다. Quinton 모델의 샘플을 보내달라고 요청했고, 어떤 것이 가장 적합한지 알아보기 위해 몇 군데 다른 회사의 제품을 가지고 실험해 볼 것이라고 했으므로, 지금 쓰는 것과는 다른 브랜드를 시험삼아 써볼 계획임을 유추할 수 있다. 따라서 (C)가 정답이다.

패러프레이징 experiment → try

어휘 shipping 배송 dissatisfied 불만족한

186-190 이메일 & 일정 & 이메일

수신: Derosa 주식회사 전 직원
발신: Priya Kapil
날짜: 6월 8일
제목: 무료 워크숍

직원 여러분,

다음 달에 우리 회사는 일련의 전문성 개발 워크숍을 개최할 것입니다. [186]워크숍은 저녁에 열릴 것이기 때문에, 여러분의 일상적인 업무에는 지장이 없을 것입니다. 출장 뷔페 식사가 제공될 것입니다. 각각의 워크숍 강의에 대해, 시간을 절약하기 위해 [187]여러분이 미리 살펴봐야 하는 몇 가지 자료 글과 안내 책자가 있습니다. 여러분의 출석은 연간 성과 평가에 긍정적인 영향을 미칠 것입니다.

워크숍에 관심이 있으신 분은 [188-1]참가자 등록을 담당하고 있는 Masaru Akita 씨에게 m.akita@derosa.com으로 이메일을 보내 주시기 바랍니다.

감사합니다.

Priya Kapil

어휘 professional 전문적인 take place 개최되다, 일어나다 interruption 중단, 방해 cater 출장 뷔페를 제공하다 session 교육 시간 packet 꾸러미, 책자 look over ~을 살펴보다 in advance 미리 attendance 참석 have an effect on ~에 영향을 미치다 positive 긍정적인 performance 성과, 공연 evaluation 평가 be in charge of ~을 맡다[담당하다] register 등록하다

Derosa 주식회사 직원들을 위한 전문성 개발 기회			
날짜	발표자	제목	메모
7월 6일	Brandon Thomas, 마케팅 부장	타인에게 영향을 미치는 방법	이러한 기술로 전문적인 관계를 구축하고 팀을 이끈다.
7월 13일	[188-2]Masaru Akita, 대리	직장 내의 변화 탐색하기	새로운 상황에 빠르게 적응하는 능력을 향상시킨다.
7월 20일	Priya Kapil, 인사부장	시간 관리 조언	맡은 역할이 무엇이든 간에 주어진 일정을 최대한 활용한다.
[189-2]7월 26일	Veronica Shapiro, 총괄 이사	창의적인 문제 해결	문제가 발생할 때 '새로운 사고를 하는 법'을 배운다.

어휘 presenter 발표자 influence 영향을 미치다; 영향 technique 기술, 기법 navigate 길을 찾다, 항해하다 improve 향상시키다 adapt to ~에 적응하다 management 관리 make the most of ~을 최대한 활용하다 think outside the box 새로운 사고를 하다 arise 일어나다, 발생하다

수신: Priya Kapil
발신: Aurora Reutter
[189-1]날짜: 7월 27일
제목: 워크숍

Kapil 씨,

회사의 전문성 개발 기회를 기획하신 귀하와 다른 분들께 감사드립니다. [189-1]저는 어제 교육 시간에 많은 것을 배웠습니다. 저는 강사가 〈비즈니스 블라스트〉라는 책에서 사용한 예시들이 마음에 들었습니다. 사실, 제 토론 그룹의 구성원들은 매달 첫 번째 화요일 점심시간에 만나서 책에 있는 나머지 활동들을 끝까지 해 볼 계획입니다. 다른 직원들도 원한다면 참여할 수 있도록 [190]이 일시적인 모임을 회사의 온라인 달력에 공지해 주시겠습니까?

감사합니다!

Aurora Reutter

어휘 instructor 강사 work through 끝까지 해내다 activity 활동 temporary 일시적인, 임시의

186. 첫 번째 이메일에서 워크숍에 대해 암시된 것은 무엇인가?
(A) 워크숍은 약 한 시간 동안 계속될 것이다.
(B) 참가자들은 마지막에 평가서를 작성할 것이다.
(C) 근무 시간이 아닌 시간에 열릴 것이다.
(D) 주로 관리팀을 대상으로 한다.

해설 추론/암시
워크숍은 저녁에 열릴 것이라서 일상적인 업무에 지장이 없을 것이라고 한 것으로 보아, 근무 시간 외의 시간에 열릴 것임을 유추할 수 있다. 따라서 (C)가 정답이다.

패러프레이징 in the evenings → outside of business hours

어휘 approximately 약, 대략 evaluation 평가(서) business hours 영업시간 mainly 주로 aim 겨냥하다, 목표로 하다 management 경영, 관리

187. 참가자들이 워크숍 전에 해야 할 일은 무엇인가?
(A) 발표자들에게 질문 보내기
(B) 식이 제한 사항을 제출하기

(C) 상사의 승인 받기
(D) 몇 가지 읽기 자료 검토하기

해설 세부 사항
prior to the workshops를 키워드로 지문을 검색한다. prior to는 before, in advance 등으로 패러프레이징될 수 있다는 것을 염두에 둔다. 첫 번째 지문에서 미리 살펴봐야 할 자료글과 안내 책자가 있다고 했으므로 (D)가 정답이다. 지문의 in advance가 질문에서 prior to로 패러프레이징되었다.

패러프레이징 look over → review / articles and information packets → reading materials

어휘 dietary 음식의, 식이의 restriction 제한 supervisor 상사, 감독자 approval 승인 review 검토하다

188. 등록 업무를 맡은 사람은 누구인가?
(A) 총괄 이사
(B) 대리
(C) 인사부장
(D) 마케팅 부장

해설 두 지문 연계_세부 사항
responsible for registration을 키워드로 지문을 검색한다. 첫 번째 지문의 끝부분에서 in charge of registering participants라는 표현이 나오며 담당자가 Masaru Akita라는 것을 알 수 있다. 두 번째 지문에서 Masaru Akita를 검색하면 표에서 Masaru Akita의 직급은 assistant manager로 나오므로 (B)가 정답이다.

189. Reutter 씨가 참석했던 워크숍은 무엇인가?
(A) 타인에게 영향을 미치는 방법
(B) 직장 내의 변화 탐색하기
(C) 시간 관리 조언
(D) 창의적인 문제 해결

해설 두 지문 연계_추론/암시
Reutter를 키워드로 지문을 검색한다. 세 번째 지문의 발신인인 Aurora Reutter가 자신은 어제 교육 시간에 많은 것을 배웠다고 말한다. 세 번째 지문의 날짜를 확인하면 7월 27일이므로 7월 26일에 Aurora Reutter가 참석한 워크숍 제목을 찾아야 한다. 두 번째 지문의 표에서 7월 26일을 검색하면 그날 있었던 워크숍의 제목은 Creative Problem-Solving이므로 (D)가 정답이다.

190. Reutter 씨가 Kapil 씨에게 하도록 요청한 것은 무엇인가?
(A) 그룹 구성원의 명단을 제공하기
(B) 회의 공간을 예약하기
(C) 온라인에 안내문 게시하기
(D) 워크숍 주제를 제안하기

해설 세부 사항
다중 지문의 마지막 문제의 단서는 대개 마지막 지문에 나온다. 발신인인 Reutter 씨가 수신인인 Kapil 씨에게 한 요청은 맨 끝에 나오는데, 모임을 회사 온라인 달력에 공지해 줄 것을 요청했으므로 (C)가 정답이다.

어휘 reserve 예약하다 post 게시하다

191-195 이메일 & 웹페이지 & 광고

수신: 디자인팀 〈design@orono.net〉
발신: Joan Elliot 〈jelliot@orono.net〉
날짜: 10월 30일
제목: 신규 직원

디자인팀 여러분,

우리 팀의 신입 직원인 Marianne Noland 씨를 맞이하게 되어 기쁩니다. 그녀는 그래픽 디자인 작업을 하여 Jerome Perez 씨가 우리의 O700 제품에 대한 증가하는 수요를 따라잡을 수 있도록 도울 것입니다. Marianne은 본인의 프리랜서 그래픽 디자인 업체를 운영하고 있기 때문에 ¹⁹³⁻¹Orono에서는 파트타임으로만 근무할 예정입니다. 그녀는 가끔 사무실에서 일할 것이지만, ¹⁹¹Orono를 위한 대부분의 프로젝트는 재택으로 할 것입니다.

우리는 우리 회사에 대한 Marianne의 기여 가능성에 대해 기대하고 있습니다. 그녀는 Prima Group을 비롯한 비영리 단체들뿐만 아니라 상업 프로젝트에 있어서도 인상적인 업무 포트폴리오를 가지고 있는데, ¹⁹⁵⁻¹Prima Group은 그녀가 친구들 두 명과 함께 설립했습니다.

¹⁹²우리는 11월 4일 오전 9시 30분에 휴게실에서 조촐한 환영회를 열 예정입니다. 차와 커피, 도넛이 제공되며, Marianne이 간단한 자기소개를 할 것입니다. 여러분 모두 Marianne을 만날 수 있는 기회를 갖기를 바랍니다. 회답은 안 하셔도 됩니다. 정해진 시간에 휴게실로 오시면 됩니다.

감사합니다.

Joan Elliot

어휘 demand 수요 freelance 프리랜서로 일하는 work part-time 파트타임으로 근무하다 occasionally 가끔 majority 대부분, 대다수 potential 잠재적인 contribution 기여 portfolio 작품집, 포트폴리오 nonprofit organization 비영리 단체 found 설립하다 break room 휴게실 serve 제공하다 briefly 간단히 RSVP 회답을 하다; 회답 요망 appointed 정해진, 지정된

Noland Design
여러분의 비즈니스와 예산에 맞는 맞춤형 그래픽 디자인!

소개: Marianne Noland는 크랜퍼드 대학교에서 그래픽 디자인 학사 학위를 받았습니다. 그녀는 프리랜서로 3년간 일하면서 고객들로부터 좋은 평가를 받고 있습니다. 그녀는 최근에 ¹⁹³⁻²가전제품을 생산하는 대기업에서 파트타임으로 근무하기 시작하면서 인기 있는 O700 제품의 사용 설명서를 디자인하고 있습니다. 프로젝트에 대한 도움이 필요하시면 연락하셔서 무료 상담 및 가격 견적을 받으시기 바랍니다.

어휘 custom 주문한, 맞춤의 suit 맞다 bachelor's degree 학사 학위 producer 생산업체 appliance 가전제품 instruction manual 사용 설명서 get in touch 연락을 취하다 consultation 상담 estimate 견적

> **Prima Group 자원봉사자 모집 행사**
> **12월 8일 일요일 오후 3시**
> **McCormack 홀 103호**
>
> 3년 전, ¹⁹⁵⁻²그린빌에서 나고 자란 세 명의 친구들은 그들이 자란 마을의 아이들이 예술을 접할 수 있도록 하는 방법을 찾고 싶어 했습니다. ¹⁹⁴ ¹⁹⁵⁻²그들은 학교의 예술 프로그램을 위한 기금을 모으는 것을 돕기 위해 Prima Group을 만들었습니다. Prima Group은 현재 더 많은 자원봉사자들을 찾고 있습니다. 모집 행사에는 자원봉사 코디네이터들은 물론 창립자들도 참석하여 여러분의 질문에 답하고 여러분의 실력과 관심사에 가장 맞는 역할을 찾을 것입니다. 그곳에서 뵙기를 바랍니다!

어휘 volunteer 자원봉사자 recruitment 모집 drive (조직적인) 운동 accessible to ~에 접근이 쉬운 founder 설립자, 창립자

191. 이메일에서 Noland 씨에 대해 나타난 것은 무엇인가?
(A) 전에는 비영리 단체에서만 일했다.
(B) 가족이 운영하는 회사에 채용되었다.
(C) Perez 씨를 대신할 것이다.
(D) Orono에서는 주로 원격 근무를 할 것이다.

해설 NOT/True
첫 번째 지문에서 Noland 씨에 대해 언급된 내용을 검색하며 선택지와 대조해 본다. Orono의 대부분의 프로젝트를 재택으로 할 것이라고 했으므로 (D)가 정답이다.

패러프레이징 be done from home → work remotely

어휘 previously 전에, 이전에 replace 대체하다, 대신하다 work remotely 원격[재택] 근무를 하다

192. 11월 4일 행사에서 무슨 일이 일어나겠는가?
(A) Noland 씨가 짤막한 담화를 할 것이다.
(B) Noland 씨가 상을 받을 것이다.
(C) 식사가 제공될 것이다.
(D) 직원이 승진할 것이다.

해설 세부 사항
November 4를 키워드로 지문을 검색하면, 첫 번째 지문의 후반부에서 11월 4일에 Marianne Noland가 간단한 자기소개를 할 것이라고 했으므로 (A)가 정답이다. 이날 제공되는 차, 커피, 도넛 등은 식사가 아니라 다과에 불과하므로 (C)는 오답이다.

패러프레이징 briefly introduce herself → give a brief talk

어휘 give a talk 연설하다 brief 짧은, 짤막한 promote 승진시키다

193. Orono의 업종은 무엇인가?
(A) 잡지사
(B) 가전제품 제조업체
(C) 건설 회사
(D) 의류 소매점

해설 두 지문 연계_추론/암시
Orono를 키워드로 지문을 검색하면, 첫 번째 지문에서 Marianne Noland가 Orono에서 파트타임으로 근무할 예정이라는 단서를 찾을 수 있다. 그리고 두 번째 지문에서 Marianne Noland가 가전제품 생산업체에서 파트타임으로 근무하기 시작했다는 소개 내용이 나오는데, 이를 종합해 보면, Orono는 가전제품 생산업체임을 알 수 있으므로 (B)가 정답이다.

패러프레이징 producer of appliances → appliance manufacturer

194. 광고에 의하면, Prima Group이 목표로 하는 것은 무엇인가?
(A) 마을에 미술관을 열기
(B) 미술 교육을 위한 기금을 제공하기
(C) 전시회를 통해 화가들을 지원하기
(D) 노인들을 위한 미술 수업을 열기

해설 세부 사항
세 번째 지문인 광고에서 Prima Group의 목표를 검색해 본다. 학교의 예술 프로그램을 위한 기금을 모으는 것을 돕기 위해 Prima Group을 만들었다고 했으므로 (B)가 정답이다.

패러프레이징 help raise money for art programs in schools → Provide funding for art education

어휘 funding 자금 (제공) exhibition 전시회 host 개최하다, 주최하다

195. Noland 씨에 대해 사실일 것 같은 것은 무엇인가?
(A) 강사로 자원해서 일한다.
(B) Prima Group의 자원봉사 코디네이터이다.
(C) 그녀의 고향은 그린빌이다.
(D) 그녀의 업체는 Prima Group에 기부했다.

해설 두 지문 연계 추론/암시
Noland를 키워드로 지문을 검색하면, 첫 번째 지문에서 Marianne Noland가 친구 두 명과 함께 비영리 단체인 Prima Group을 설립했다고 했고, 마지막 지문에서 Prima Group을 설립한 세 친구들은 그린빌에서 나고 자랐다고 했다. 따라서 Marianne Noland의 고향이 그린빌임을 알 수 있으므로 (C)가 정답이다.

패러프레이징 born and raised in Greenville → Her hometown is Greenville

어휘 volunteer 자원하다 instructor 강사 hometown 고향 donate 기부하다

196-200 안내 책자 & 이메일 & 이메일

> **Sunshine Tours**
>
> Sunshine Tours는 수십 년간 관광객들과 로크미어 섬의 모험 정신을 공유해 왔습니다. ¹⁹⁶18세 이상을 대상으로 하는 우리의 흥미로운 투어는 경험이 풍부한 가이드가 이끌며, 그들 대부분은 섬의 지역민들입니다. 투어는 일부 공휴일을 제외하고 매일 운영되며, ¹⁹⁷모두 도시락과 음료, 그리고 간식이 포함됩니다.
>
> 수상 관광 (B039)
> 느긋이 휴식을 취하면서 물에서 바라보는 특별한 전망을 통해 아름다운 로크미어 섬의 경치를 감상하세요! 보트에서 해변의 멋진 사진들을 얻을 수 있는 섬의 몇몇 장소를 방문합니다. 표준 요금: 70달러 / 액자에 넣은 단체 사진 포함: 75달러

¹⁹⁹⁻²언더 더 씨 (S013)
이 스노클링 투어는 지역의 해양 야생 동물을 가까이서 볼 수 있게 해 줍니다. ¹⁹⁹⁻²애시비 코브, 샌디 베이, 그리고 솔 베이를 방문하게 됩니다. 또한 모든 참가자에게 수중 디지털 카메라를 제공하여 수영하면서 각자 자신만의 독특한 사진을 담을 수 있습니다. 표준 요금: 85달러 / ²⁰⁰⁻²디지털 카메라 대여 포함: 90달러

트레일블레이저(T074)
자전거를 타고 경치 좋은 숲속을 지나 섬에 살고 있는 놀라운 동식물을 발견해 보세요. 표준 요금: 55달러 / 짚라인 체험 포함: 80달러

어센트 어드벤처(A085)
이 암벽 등반 투어에서 숨 막히는 바다의 경치를 즐기세요. 이 투어는 힘들지만 그만한 가치가 있습니다! 표준 요금: 125달러 / 추가 안전 교육 포함 (초보자 필수): 145달러

어휘 adventurist 모험주의적인; 모험주의자 for decades 수십 년간 operate 운영하다 excluding ~을 제외하고 sightseeing 관광 gorgeous 멋진 scenery 경치 perspective 관점, 시각 underwater 수중의 capture 포착하다, ~을 붙잡다 scenic 경치 좋은 zipline 짚라인 breathtaking 숨 막히는, 굉장한 additional 추가의

¹⁹⁹⁻¹수신: Darlene Amos; Glenn Roth
발신: Maurice Stotler
¹⁹⁹⁻¹날짜: 8월 3일
제목: 투어

안녕하세요, Darlene, Glenn!
¹⁹⁹⁻¹내일 투어와 관련하여, ¹⁹⁸ ¹⁹⁹⁻¹두 분이 평소에는 애시비 코브를 먼저 가시는 것으로 알고 있는데, 고객이 대신 샌디 베이를 먼저 방문해 달라고 요청했습니다. 단체원들 중 일부는 경험이 없어서 장비에 익숙해지기 위해 더 얕은 물에서 먼저 수영을 하고 싶어 하기 때문에, ¹⁹⁸저는 이에 동의했습니다. Darlene, 보험 목적으로 이 기록이 필요하기 때문에, 그들이 도착하면 참가자 명단에 있는 각 사람의 이름을 확인하도록 하세요. 그리고 Glenn, 당신이 곧 보트 면허를 갱신할 거라는 걸 알고 있는데, 그걸 받으면 복사본을 보내 주세요. 감사해요!

Maurice Stotler

어휘 regarding ~와 관련하여 inexperienced 경험 없는 shallow 얕은 get used to ~에 익숙해지다 equipment 장비 insurance 보험 purpose 목적 renew 갱신하다 license 면허

수신: Christina Chavez
발신: Maurice Stotler
날짜: 8월 3일
제목: Sunshine Tours
첨부 파일: sunshinetours_map.pic

Chavez 씨,
Sunshine Tours에 예약해 주셔서 다시 한번 감사드립니다!
²⁰⁰⁻¹내일 투어에 대해 귀하가 지불하신 1인당 90달러의 대금을

받았습니다. 출발지까지 어떻게 가는지 보여 주는 지도를 첨부해 드리니 확인해 주시기 바랍니다. 투어 후에 일행이 그 지역에서 함께 저녁 식사를 할 거라고 말씀하셨죠? 귀하의 투어 가이드가 귀하의 요구와 예산에 따라 추천해 드릴 수 있습니다.
즐거운 시간 되세요!
Maurice Stotler
Sunshine Tours, 예약 관리자

어휘 payment 지불, 대금 departure 출발 mention 말하다, 언급하다

196. Sunshine Tours에 대해 언급된 것은 무엇인가?
(A) 투어는 성인들만을 대상으로 한다.
(B) 10년 전에 설립되었다.
(C) 주로 보트 여행을 인솔한다.
(D) 대규모 단체에게 할인을 제공한다.

해설 **세부 사항**
다중 지문의 첫 번째 문제에 대한 단서는 첫 번째 지문에 나올 가능성이 크다. 첫 번째 지문에서 18세 이상을 대상으로 하는 투어라고 했으므로 (A)가 정답이다. 첫 번째 지문에 for decades(수십 년 동안)라고 나오므로 (B)는 오답이고, 첫 번째 지문에 보트 여행을 비롯한 다양한 상품이 나오므로 (C)도 오답이다. (D)에 관한 내용은 나오지 않는다.

패러프레이징 for ages 18 and up → for adults only

어휘 intend 의도하다 found 설립하다

197. Sunshine Tours의 모든 투어에 대해 시사된 것은 무엇인가?
(A) 출발지가 같다.
(B) 식사가 포함된다.
(C) 하루 종일 계속된다.
(D) 항상 두 명의 직원들에 의해 운영된다.

해설 **NOT/True**
첫 번째 지문에서 모든 투어에는 도시락이 포함된다고 했으므로 (B)가 정답이다.

패러프레이징 a packed lunch → a meal

어휘 run 운영하다

198. Stotler 씨가 첫 번째 이메일을 보낸 이유는 무엇인가?
(A) Roth 씨의 보트 면허 사본을 보내기 위해
(B) 직원들에게 변경 사항을 알리기 위해
(C) Amos 씨에게 참가자 명단을 제공하기 위해
(D) 초과 근무에 대해 투어 가이드들에게 감사를 표하기 위해

해설 **주제/목적**
첫 번째 이메일에서 단서를 검색한다. 고객이 애시비 코브 대신 샌디 베이를 먼저 방문해 달라고 요청했고, Stotler 씨가 이에 동의했다는 정보가 나온다. 즉, 투어 순서에 변경이 있음을 알리고 있으므로 (B)가 정답이다.

어휘 inform 알리다 appreciation 감사 work extra hours 초과 근무를 하다

199. 8월 4일에 Amos 씨와 Roth 씨가 배정된 투어는 무엇인가?
(A) B039
(B) S013
(C) T074
(D) A085

해설 두 지문 연계_추론/암시
August 4를 키워드로 지문을 검색한다. 두 번째 지문에서 이메일의 날짜가 8월 3일인데 내일, 즉 8월 4일 투어를 언급하면서 애시비 코브, 샌디 베이 등의 지명이 함께 나오고 있다. Ashby Cove, Sandy Bay 등의 지명을 키워드로 다른 지문을 검색하면 첫 번째 지문에서 해당 지명이 나오는 투어는 Under the Sea (S013)이므로 (B)가 정답이다.

200. Chavez 씨의 단체에 대해 암시된 것은 무엇인가?
(A) 그들은 평소보다 늦게 도착할 것이다.
(B) 투어를 다른 사람들에게 추천했다.
(C) 특수 카메라를 사용하고 싶어 한다.
(D) 단체 사진을 찍고 싶어 한다.

해설 두 지문 연계_추론/암시
다중 지문의 마지막 문제의 단서는 주로 마지막 지문에서 나온다. Chavez를 키워드로 지문을 검색하면, 세 번째 지문의 수신인이 Christina Chavez이고, 1인당 90달러인 투어를 신청했음을 알 수 있다. $90을 키워드로 다른 지문을 검색하면 첫 번째 지문에서 수중 디지털 카메라 대여를 포함한 비용이 90달러임을 알 수 있다. 이를 통해 Chavez 씨의 단체는 특수 카메라를 사용하려고 하는 것을 유추할 수 있으므로 (C)가 정답이다.

패러프레이징 underwater digital camera → special cameras

어휘 recommend 추천하다 take a photo 사진을 찍다

실전 모의고사 2회 본문 p.322

101. (D)	102. (A)	103. (C)	104. (B)	105. (C)
106. (B)	107. (A)	108. (B)	109. (A)	110. (C)
111. (D)	112. (A)	113. (B)	114. (D)	115. (A)
116. (C)	117. (B)	118. (B)	119. (A)	120. (B)
121. (D)	122. (A)	123. (B)	124. (B)	125. (B)
126. (C)	127. (A)	128. (A)	129. (C)	130. (C)
131. (B)	132. (C)	133. (C)	134. (B)	135. (C)
136. (A)	137. (C)	138. (D)	139. (C)	140. (C)
141. (B)	142. (D)	143. (C)	144. (B)	145. (C)
146. (C)	147. (C)	148. (C)	149. (C)	150. (C)
151. (C)	152. (B)	153. (B)	154. (C)	155. (D)
156. (C)	157. (C)	158. (C)	159. (C)	160. (C)
161. (C)	162. (C)	163. (C)	164. (C)	165. (B)
166. (D)	167. (A)	168. (C)	169. (C)	170. (A)
171. (D)	172. (C)	173. (C)	174. (C)	175. (C)
176. (B)	177. (D)	178. (C)	179. (B)	180. (A)
181. (C)	182. (C)	183. (D)	184. (C)	185. (C)
186. (C)	187. (A)	188. (A)	189. (C)	190. (D)
191. (B)	192. (B)	193. (C)	194. (C)	195. (D)
196. (C)	197. (C)	198. (A)	199. (C)	200. (A)

101. 동사 자리+수 일치
해석 Cardwell 씨는 BNH 주식회사의 부회장직을 흔쾌히 수락했다.

해설 빈칸은 부사 happily의 수식을 받으며 the position of vice president를 목적어로 갖는 동사 자리이므로 현재 시제인 (C)와 과거 시제인 (D)가 정답 후보이다. 주어인 Mr. Cardwell은 3인칭 단수여서 현재 시제일 경우 동사 뒤에 -(e)s가 필요하므로 (C)는 오답이다. 따라서 (D)가 정답이다.

어휘 happily 기꺼이 position 직위, 위치 incorporated 주식회사

102. 접속사 but
해석 일기 예보에서는 이번 주말에 비가 온다고 하지만, 카운티 박람회는 예정대로 계속될 것이다.

(A) 하지만 (B) 혹은 (C) (왜냐하면) ~이므로 (D) 그래서

해설 빈칸은 빈칸 앞뒤의 절을 연결하는 접속사 자리로, 해석하면 '주말에 비가 온다 / 카운티 박람회는 예정대로 계속될 것이다'라는 의미이므로 두 개의 절은 의미상 역접 관계를 형성한다. 따라서 역접의 접속사 (A)가 정답이다. (C)는 이유를 나타내는 접속사, (D)는 결과를 나타내는 접속사로 문맥상 적절하지 않다.

어휘 weather forecast 일기 예보 county 카운티, 자치군 fair 박람회, (농축산물) 품평회 as scheduled 예정대로

103. 소유격
해석 AX Shipping이 우리의 주문을 맞출 수 없다면 회사는 새로운 유통업체를 찾아야 한다.

해설 선택지를 통해 인칭대명사의 알맞은 격을 고르는 문제임을 알수 있다. 빈칸이 fulfill의 목적어로 쓰인 명사 orders 앞에 위치하므로, 명사를 수식하는 한정사 역할의 소유격 (C)가 정답이다.

어휘 distributor 판매 대리점, 유통업자 fulfill an order 주문품을 조달하다

104. 전치사 from
해석 이 레스토랑의 국제적인 메뉴에는 20개국 이상에서 온 요리들이 있다.

(A) ~까지 (B) ~에서 (C) ~처럼 (D) ~ 안으로

해설 문맥상 '20개국 이상에서 온 요리들'이라는 의미가 되어야 자연스러우므로, '~에서'라는 뜻의 전치사인 (B)가 정답이다.

어휘 cosmopolitan 국제적인, 전 세계적인

105. 명사 자리
해석 마케팅 팀의 목표는 대중의 마음에 오래 가는 인상을 남기는 것이다.

해설 빈칸 앞에 관사 a와 형용사 lasting이 있으므로 빈칸에는 이 둘의 수식을 동시에 받으면서 to부정사인 to leave의 목적어 역할을 하는 명사가 와야 한다. 따라서 명사인 (C)가 정답이다.

어휘 goal 목표 lasting 영속적인, 지속적인 impression 인상 audience 청중, 관객

106. 형용사 such
해석 Herzberg 씨는 포장에서의 그렇게 작은 변화가 회사 매출에 큰 영향을 미칠 수 있다는 것에 놀랐다.

(A) ~이므로 (B) 그렇게 (C) 그렇게 (D) ~로(서)

해설 빈칸은 that절의 주어를 이루므로 접속사인 since, so, as 등은 올 수 없다. 문맥상 '그렇게 작은 변화'라는 의미가 되는 것이 자연스러운데, 빈칸 다음에 〈a[an]+형용사+명사〉가 와서 '그렇게 ~한 …'라는 의미를 나타낼 수 있는 것은 형용사인 (B)이다. 〈such a[an]+형용사+명사〉를 하나의 표현으로 기억하자. so가 부사로 쓰일 경우 〈so+형용사+a[an]+명사〉의 순서로 나온다는 것도 알아 두자.

어휘 packaging 포장 make an impact on ~에 영향을 미치다

107. 명사 자리
해석 Everlasting Pillows의 부드러움이 그 브랜드를 그렇게 인기 있게 만드는 요인이다.

해설 빈칸 앞에 정관사 the, 빈칸 뒤에 전치사 of가 있으므로 빈칸은 뒤에 있는 전치사구의 수식을 받는 명사 자리이다. 따라서 명사인 (A)와 (D)가 정답 후보이다. 'Everlasting Pillows의 부드러움'이라는 의미가 자연스러우므로 정답은 (A)이다. '부드럽게 하기'라는 의미의 (D)는 문맥에 맞지 않으므로 오답이다.

어휘 pillow 베개 popular 인기 있는

108. 접속사 now that
해석 우리의 연간 목표가 정해졌기 때문에 회사는 마침내 앞으로 나아갈 수 있다.

(A) ~뿐만 아니라 (B) ~이기 때문에 (C) 무엇보다도 (D) ~ 때문에

해설 빈칸에 알맞은 접속사를 찾는 문제로, 빈칸 앞뒤의 의미 관계를 따져 보아야 한다. 연간 목표가 정해지는 것은 회사가 전진할 수 있는 이유가 되므로, 이유를 나타내는 접속사인 (B)가 정답이다. (D) 또한 이유를 나타내지만 전치사구이므로 오답이다.

108

어휘 yearly 연간의   move forward 전진하다

109. 명사 자리 [전치사의 목적어]
해석 요리사인 Charles Pinto는 연말까지 고급 레스토랑을 개장하기 위해 자신의 최대의 경쟁자와 협력하고 있다.

해설 빈칸에는 빈칸 앞에 있는 〈소유격+형용사〉인 his biggest의 수식을 받으면서 전치사 with의 목적어 역할을 하는 명사가 와야 한다. 따라서 명사인 (A)가 정답이다.

어휘 join forces with ~와 협력하다   competitor 경쟁자   high-class 고급의

110. 부사 어휘 soon
해석 5년 이상의 공사 끝에 Westbury Mall은 마침내 곧 개장할 것이다.
(A) 후에 (B) 그때 (C) 곧 (D) 바로

해설 빈칸이 없어도 완전한 문장을 이루므로 빈칸은 부사 자리이다. 빈칸이 포함된 문장이 미래 시제이므로 '곧, 조만간' 문을 열 것이라는 뜻이 되어야 알맞다. 따라서 (C)가 정답이다.

어휘 construction 건설, 공사

111. 부정대명사 nothing
해석 아무것도 Charles 씨의 기업가 정신을 막을 수 없었고, 그것이 그가 서른 살이 되기 전에 세 개의 업체를 개업한 이유이다.

해설 빈칸에 알맞은 대명사를 찾는 문제이다. 빈칸은 문장의 주어 자리이므로 대명사인 (C)와 (D)가 정답 후보이다. (C) Neither는 '둘 중 어느 것도 ~아닌'이란 뜻으로 문맥상 neither가 가리키는 특정 대상이 없으므로 적절하지 않다. 따라서 (D)가 정답이다.

어휘 entrepreneurial spirit 기업가 정신

112. 명사 어휘 knowledge
해석 고도의 전문 지식을 가진 사람만이 이 자리에 지원해야 한다.
(A) 지식 (B) 활동 (C) 대비, 조항 (D) 이전

해설 빈칸 앞의 highly specialized의 수식을 받아 의미가 통해야 하므로 '고도의 전문 지식'이라는 뜻을 이루는 (A)가 정답이다.

어휘 highly 고도로   specialized 전문적인, 전문화된   apply for ~에 지원하다

113. 소유격
해석 우리의 새 인턴사원은 재능이 있지만, 가끔 자신의 아이디어에 자신감이 부족할 때가 있다.

해설 선택지를 통해 인칭대명사의 알맞은 격을 고르는 문제임을 알 수 있다. 사람 주어인 Our new intern을 가리키는 소유격 인칭대명사는 (B)이다.

어휘 intern 인턴사원   talented 재능이 있는   lack ~이 없다[부족하다]   confidence 자신감

114. 동사 어휘 convince
해석 P&K Realtors의 직원들은 상사를 설득하여 겨울 휴가 동안 하루를 더 쉴 수 있도록 해주기를 원했다.
(A) 포함시키다 (B) 참다 (C) 놀라게 하다 (D) 설득하다

해설 빈칸에 들어갈 동사는 뒤에 목적어 their boss와 이어지는 to부정사구를 목적어 보어로 한다. '상사가 휴가를 하루 더 줄 수 있도록 설득하다'라는 뜻이 되어야 적절하므로 (D)가 정답이다. 〈convince+목적어+to부정사〉는 '목적어가 ~하도록 설득하다'라는 뜻이다.

어휘 extra 추가의, 여분의   day off 쉬는 날

115. 형용사 any
해석 하실 말씀이나 우려되는 점이 있으시면 제안함에 넣어 주세요.
(A) 무슨, 어떤 (B) 저 (C) 저것들의 (D) 모든

해설 빈칸이 If로 시작하는 조건절에 속해 있으므로 '어떤 ~라도'라는 뜻으로 부정형용사인 any가 들어가야 적절하므로 (A)가 정답이다.

어휘 comment 의견, 논평   concern 걱정, 관심사   suggestion 제안

116. 전치사 beside
해석 우체국은 모퉁이에 있는 오래된 은행 옆에 있는 건물이다.
(A) ~ 안으로 (B) ~에 대하여 (C) ~ 옆에 (D) (셋 이상의) ~ 사이에

해설 문맥상 '은행 옆에 있는 건물'이라는 의미가 되어야 자연스러우므로, '~ 옆에'라는 뜻의 전치사로 쓰이는 (C)가 정답이다. (D)는 뒤에 복수 명사가 오므로 오답이다.

어휘 post office 우체국   corner 모퉁이

117. 명사 자리
해석 Newman Fashion은 자사의 정장과 넥타이에 최상의 품질을 보장하는 특별한 소재를 사용한다.

해설 빈칸 앞에 관사 a와 형용사 special이 있으므로 빈칸에는 이 둘의 수식을 받으면서 동사 uses의 목적어 역할을 하는 명사가 와야 한다. 따라서 명사인 (B)가 정답이다.

어휘 material 재료, 직물   ensure 보장하다   quality 품질   suit 정장   tie 넥타이

118. 부사 자리 [동사 수식]
해석 맞춤 케이크를 만들 때, Carmen 씨는 항상 디자인과 글자들을 완벽하게 배열한다.

해설 빈칸 없이도 문장이 완전하므로 빈칸은 동사 aligns를 수식하는 부사 자리이다. 따라서 부사인 (B)가 정답이다.

어휘 custom 맞춤, 주문 제작한   align 정렬하다, 가지런히 만들다

119. 전치사 below
해석 온도가 화씨 40도 미만이면 시멘트는 제대로 경화되지 않을 것이다.
(A) ~ 아래에 (B) ~의 옆에 (C) ~ 동안 (D) ~ 옆에

해설 주어진 선택지들 중 온도와 함께 쓰일 수 있는 것은 (A)뿐이다. 문맥상으로도 '화씨 40도 미만'이라는 의미가 되어야 자연스러우므로 '~ 아래에'라는 뜻의 전치사로 쓰이는 (A)가 정답이다.

어휘 temperature 온도, 기온   degree (온도의 단위인) 도, 정도   Fahrenheit 화씨의   cement 시멘트   cure 경화하다   properly 제대로

120. 재귀대명사 [재귀 용법]
여행자들은 취소나 지연으로 인한 금전적 손실로부터 스스로를 지키기 위해 보험에 가입해야 한다.

해설 빈칸은 to protect의 목적어 자리인데, 빈칸이 가리키는 것은 주어인 travelers 외에는 찾을 수 없다. 따라서 재귀 용법으로 쓰인 재귀대명사 (B)가 정답이다.

어휘 insurance 보험 financial 금융의, 재정적 loss 손실 delay 지연

121. to부정사 [명사적 용법]
해석 Lawson 씨의 목표는 보통 사람이 단번에 자기 회사의 로고를 알아보도록 하는 것이다.

해설 빈칸은 빈칸 앞의 동사 is의 보어 자리로, 빈칸 뒤에 소유격 대명사 her가 이어지고 있으므로 형용사인 (A)와 명사인 (B)는 제외된다. 빈칸 앞의 for the average person을 의미상의 주어로 하고 빈칸 뒤의 her company's logo를 목적어로 취할 수 있는 동명사나 to부정사가 올 수 있으므로 (D)가 정답이다.

어휘 goal 목표 average 평균의, 보통의 recognize 알아보다, 인식하다 without a second thought 두 번 생각할 것도 없이 바로, 단번에

122. 형용사 자리 [분사]
해석 참석자들은 강의 전에 유용한 정보가 들어 있는 유인물 꾸러미를 가져가라는 말을 들었다.

해설 빈칸부터 information까지가 빈칸 앞의 package of handouts를 수식하는 구조로, 빈칸에는 현재분사 (A)와 과거분사 (D)가 들어갈 수 있다. useful information을 목적어로 취하여 '유용한 정보가 들어 있는 유인물 꾸러미'라는 능동의 의미를 나타내는 것이 자연스러우므로 현재분사인 (A)가 정답이다.

어휘 attendee 참석자 remind 상기시키다 pick up 집다, 찾다 package 꾸러미 handout 유인물

123. 명사 어휘 receipt
해석 물품 영수증이 있는 고객은 물품을 쉽게 교환 또는 환불할 수 있을 것이다.
(A) 선택권 (B) 영수증 (C) 항구 (D) 가능성

해설 물품의 교환이나 환불과 관련된 것이므로 '영수증'을 뜻하는 (B)가 정답이다.

어휘 exchange 교환하다 refund 환불하다 easily 쉽게

124. 형용사 어휘 factual
해석 출판사는 정보가 대중에게 공개되기 전에 그것이 사실인지 확인해야 한다.
(A) 동등한 (B) 사실인 (C) 국내의 (D) 상대적인

어휘 publisher 출판사 release 공개하다 public 대중

125. 부사 어휘 properly
해석 Royal 씨는 지난번 호텔 카드키가 제대로 작동하지 않았기 때문에 새 호텔 카드키는 제대로 작동하길 바랐다.
(A) 새로 (B) 제대로 (C) 행복하게 (D) 빠르게

해설 동사 work와 어울려 쓰이는 부사를 고르는 문제이다. '제대로 작동하다'라는 뜻이 되어야 적절하므로 (B)가 정답이다. work properly(제대로 작동하다)는 자주 쓰이는 표현이므로 통째로 기억해두자.

어휘 work 작동하다 last 지난 malfunction 제대로 작동하지 않다

126. 형용사 어휘 favorable
Perfume Palace의 개발자들은 대다수의 테스터들이 호의적인 평가를 할 때까지 그들의 새로운 향수 제조 화학식을 수정했다.
(A) 적격인 (B) 영구적인 (C) 호의적인 (D) 실용적인

해설 향수 제조 화학식을 수정하는 것은 좋은 평가를 받기 위함이므로 '호의적인'이라는 뜻의 (C)가 정답이다.

어휘 developer 개발자 modify 수정하다 formula 공식, 화학식 scent 향기 majority 대다수, 대부분 review 평가

127. 형용사 자리 [분사]
해석 Higgins 씨는 JN Electronics와의 합병 제안의 세부 내용에 대해 우려하고 있다.

해설 빈칸은 빈칸 뒤의 명사 merger를 수식하는 형용사 자리이거나 merger와 함께 복합명사를 이루는 명사 자리이다. proposal merger와 proposition merger는 복합명사를 이루지 못하므로 (B), (C)는 오답이다. 따라서 형용사 역할을 하는 과거분사 (A)와 현재분사 (D)가 정답 후보인데, 합병은 제안하는 주체가 아니라 제안되는 대상이므로 수동의 의미를 나타내는 (A)가 정답이다.

어휘 be concerned about ~에 대해 걱정하다 specifics 세부 내용 proposed 제안된 merger 합병

128. 명사 어휘 boundary
해석 시더빌과 플레전트 타운의 경계는 한 줄로 늘어서 있는 아름다운 데이지 꽃으로 표시되어 있다.
(A) 경계 (B) 차이 (C) 수당 (D) 규정

해설 '한 줄로 늘어선 데이지 꽃으로 표시되는' 것이라고 했으므로 '경계(선)'을 뜻하는 (A)가 정답이다.

어휘 mark 표시하다 row 줄, 열 daisy 데이지 꽃

129. 형용사 자리
해석 Flomo 씨는 자사 제품을 홍보하는 광고용으로 매우 단순한 디자인을 선호한다.

해설 빈칸은 뒤의 명사 designs를 수식하는 형용사 자리이므로 형용사인 (D)가 정답이다.

어휘 prefer 선호하다 simplistic 지나치게 간단한[단순한] advertisement 광고 promote 홍보하다 product 제품

130. 명사 어휘 dimension
해석 가구를 주문하기 전에 집의 치수를 정확히 측정하세요.
(A) 보험 (B) 깊이 (C) 치수 (D) 사생활

해설 가구를 주문할 때 필요한 것은 집의 '치수'이므로 (C)가 정답이다.

어휘 measure 측정하다 precisely 정확하게 order 주문하다 furniture 가구

131-134 정보

귀하의 모든 운동의 필요성에 Channing's Sporting Goods를 선택해 주셔서 감사합니다. 저희 품질관리팀은 처음 세 번의 검사에서 이상을 놓칠 **131**경우를 대비하여 완벽을 기하기 위해 네 번 검품합니다. **132**이 같은 세심함이 저희 회사가 다른 판매자와는 다른 특별한 점입니다. 이 때문에 Channing's Sporting Goods는 고객의 민원을 거의 받지 않지만, 민원을 받으면 최대한 신속하게 처리하고 있습니다. 어떤 이유로든 주문에 불만이 있는 경우, 당사 고객 서비스 팀에 연락하시면 귀하의 요청이 즉시 **133**처리될 것입니다. 저희는 소중한 고객님들을 위한 모범적인 서비스를 제공하기 위해 필요한 것 **134**이상을 해 드리기를 원하므로 환불 및 교환을 위한 무료 반품 배송을 기꺼이 제공합니다.

어휘 athletic 운동의 quality 품질 quadruple-check 4번 검사하다 perfection 완벽 abnormality 이상, 비정상 slip through ~을 빠져나가다 complaint 불만, 불평 dissatisfied 불만인 contact 연락하다 handle 처리하다 right away 즉시 refund 환불 exchange 교환 exemplary 모범적인

131. 접속사 in case
(A) ~ 때문에 (B) ~할 경우에 대비하여 (C) ~을 통해 (D) ~하자마자

해설 빈칸 뒤에 〈주어+동사〉가 이어지는 것으로 보아, 빈칸은 접속사 자리이므로 전치사인 (C)는 오답이다. '이상을 놓칠 경우에 대비하여 제품을 네 번 검사한다'는 의미가 자연스러우므로 빈칸 앞의 just와 함께 쓰여 '~할 경우에 대비하여'라는 뜻을 나타내는 접속사 (B)가 정답이다.

132. 알맞은 문장 고르기
(A) 공장의 일자리는 종종 지역 신문에 게시됩니다.
(B) 저희는 현재 모든 운동화에 20% 할인을 제공 중입니다.
(C) 이 같은 세심함이 저희 회사가 다른 판매자와는 다른 특별한 점입니다.
(D) 저희 브랜드는 눈길을 끄는 스타일로 유명합니다.

해설 제품을 네 번 검사한다고 한 빈칸 앞 문장의 내용을 This attention to detail로 받아 '이 같은 세심함이 다른 판매자와 구별되는 특별한 점이다'라는 내용이 이어지는 것이 자연스럽다. 빈칸 뒤의 Because of this의 this 또한 This attention to detail을 가리키므로 정답은 (C)이다.

어휘 set A apart from B A를 B와 구별하다[차별화하다] eye-catching 눈길을 끄는

133. 수동태+미래 시제
해설 빈칸은 your request를 주어로 하는 동사가 들어갈 자리이므로 (D)는 오답이다. 빈칸 뒤에 목적어가 없고, 내용상 문장의 주어인 '요청'은 처리하는 주체가 아니라 처리를 받는 대상이므로 수동태인 (A)와 (C)가 정답 후보이다. 문맥상 '요청이 즉시 처리될 것이다'라는 의미가 되어야 자연스러우므로 미래 시제인 (A)가 정답이다.

134. 전치사 어휘 above
(A) 그 다음에 (B) 주위에 (C) 가까이 (D) ~을 넘어

해설 빈칸 앞의 동사 go와 어울려 빈칸 뒤의 what is necessary를 목적어로 취해 의미가 통하는 전치사를 골라야 한다. go above가 '~을 넘어서다, ~ 이상을 하다'라는 뜻으로 '필요한 것 이상을 해주다'라는 의미가 되므로 (D)가 정답이다.

135-138 이메일

발신: Adorlee Lambert 〈a.lambert@fashionnow.net〉
수신: Russell Fluet 〈russell_fluet@ragstorussell.com〉
날짜: 11월 20일
제목: Rags to Russell 특집

Fluet 씨,

귀하의 패션 상점인 Rags to Russell이 〈파인 패션 매거진〉에 의해 올해의 파리 20대 신흥 패션 브랜드 중 하나로 선정되었음을 알려 드리게 되어 기쁩니다. 저희는 오는 1월호에 귀하의 업체를 **135**특집으로 다룰 것입니다. 저희 목록에는 패션 업계 최고의 **136**벤처 업체들만 포함되어 있어서, 이것은 평생 단 한 번뿐인 기회입니다.

귀하의 특집 기사를 생생하게 살리기 위해, 귀하와 귀하의 매장 사진을 저희 잡지에 싣고 싶습니다. **137**저희는 전면 컬러의 고해상도 이미지를 찾고 있습니다. 저희는 늦어도 12월 10일**138**까지 그것을 받아야 합니다. 사진 촬영에 문제가 있으면 저희에게 알려주세요. 기꺼이 도와드리겠습니다

감사합니다. 축하드립니다!

Adorlee Lambert
〈파인 패션 매거진〉 편집장

어휘 boutique 부티크, 양품점 select 선정하다 emerge 드러나다, 부상하다 upcoming 다가오는, 곧 있을 issue (정기 간행물의) 호; 문제, 쟁점 include 포함하다 industry (특정 분야의) 산업, 업계 once-in-a-lifetime 평생 단 한 번뿐인 opportunity 기회 bring ~ to life ~을 활기 넘치게 하다 at the latest 늦어도 editor-in-chief 편집장

135. 동사 자리+능동태
해설 빈칸은 your business를 목적어로 가지는 동사 자리로, 주어인 We는 동사 feature의 주체이므로 빈칸에는 능동태 동사가 와야 한다. 빈칸 앞에 will be가 있는 것으로 보아 미래진행형임을 알 수 있다. 따라서 (C)가 정답이다.

136. 명사 어휘 venture
(A) 벤처 기업 (B) 민주 국가 (C) 별미 (D) 독점 상품

해설 빈칸 앞의 최상급 the finest의 수식을 받는 명사 어휘를 고르는 문제이다. 바로 앞 문장의 your business와 의미 연관성이 있는 (A)가 정답이다.

137. 알맞은 문장 고르기
(A) 귀하가 보유한 최고의 의류 품목의 샘플을 보내는 걸 잊지 마세요.
(B) 대상은 5천 달러 이상의 가치가 있습니다.
(C) 저희는 전면 컬러의 고해상도 이미지를 찾고 있습니다.
(D) 저희가 귀하의 업체에 몇 장의 사본을 보내겠습니다.

해설 빈칸 앞의 문장에서 잡지에 사진을 싣고 싶다고 했고, 빈칸 뒤

의 문장에서는 늦어도 12월 10일까지 그것을 받아야 한다고 했으므로, 빈칸에는 사진에 대한 내용이 오는 것이 적절하다. 따라서 (C)가 정답이다.

어휘 worth ~의 가치가 있는   high-resolution 고해상도의

138. 전치사 by
(A) ~을 통해 (B) ~에 (C) ~에서 (D) ~까지
해설 빈칸 뒤에 날짜(10 December)가 나오는 것으로 보아 시간을 나타내는 단어 앞에 쓰여 '~까지'라는 뜻의 전치사로 쓰이는 (D)가 정답이다.

139-142 이메일

> 발신: Muhammed Sayid ⟨m_sayid@ncf.org⟩
> 수신: 전 직원 ⟨stafflist@ncf.org⟩
> 제목: NCF의 신임 본부장
> 날짜: 8월 14일
>
> NCF 팀 및 협력사 여러분께:
>
> 이사회가 Thomas Silva 씨를 국립아동기금의 신임 본부장으로 채용하기로 139결정했음을 여러분 모두에게 알려 드리게 되어 기쁩니다. Silva 씨는 비영리 분야에서 관리 및 지역사회 조직화 활동으로 잘 알려져 있습니다.
>
> Silva 씨는 가장 최근에 Saint Mark's 암 연구 센터에서 일했고 그 단체를 위해 수백만 달러를 모금하는 것을 도왔습니다. Saint Mark's에서, 그는 수백 명의 자원봉사자들과 직원들을 담당했고 140운영이 순조롭게 이루어지도록 했습니다. 141우리는 그의 전문 지식이 우리 팀에도 긍정적으로 기여할 것이라고 확신합니다.
>
> Silva 씨가 막 새 사무실 준비를 마쳤으니, 근무 중에 잠시 시간을 내어 그에게 142자기소개를 해 주세요.
>
> Muhammed Sayid
> 국립아동기금 이사장

어휘 inform 알리다   board of directors 이사회   nonprofit 비영리의   community 지역 사회   organize 조직하다   cancer 암   research 조사, 연구   raise 모으다   organization 조직, 단체   be in charge of ~을 담당하다   volunteer 자원봉사자   make sure 확실하게 하다   smoothly 순조롭게   set up 설치하다, 준비하다

139. 동사 자리 + 현재완료 시제
해설 빈칸은 the board of directors를 주어로 하고 to hire ~ director를 목적어로 갖는 동사 자리이므로 (A)와 (B)가 정답 후보가 된다. 이미 채용한 신임 본부장을 소개하는 내용이므로 현재완료 시제인 (B)가 정답이다.

140. 명사 어휘 operations
(A) 수리 (B) 운영 (C) 발표 (D) 경험

141. 알맞은 문장 고르기
(A) 2차 면접 합격을 축하드립니다.
(B) 우리는 그의 전문 지식이 우리 팀에도 긍정적으로 기여할 것이
(C) 수리가 끝났음을 알려 드리게 되어 기쁩니다.
(D) 특별히 부탁드릴 게 있어서 글을 씁니다.

해설 빈칸 앞에서 Mr. Silva의 경력 사항과 주요 업적을 언급했으므로, 빈칸에는 그와 관련된 내용이 이어지는 것이 자연스럽다. 따라서 Mr. Silva가 팀에 긍정적으로 기여할 것이라는 희망을 피력하는 (B)가 정답이다.

어휘 Congratulations 축하합니다   expertise 전문 지식   contribute 기여하다   positively 긍정적으로   renovation 수리, 보수   request a favor 부탁하다

142. 재귀대명사 [재귀 용법]
해설 빈칸은 동사 introduce의 목적어 자리인데, 빈칸이 가리킬 수 있는 대상은 명령문의 주어로 생략되어 있는 you이므로, 주어와 목적어 자리인 빈칸이 일치함을 알 수 있다. 따라서 재귀 용법으로 쓰인 재귀대명사 (D)가 정답이다.

143-146 전단

> 사모아 국립관광공사 방문객 무료 입장권
>
> 사모아 국립관광공사(SNTO)에서 특별 공지를 해 드립니다. SNTO는 이 전단의 뒷면에 열거된 업체들과 143함께 관광객들이 문화적으로 중요한 여러 명소에 무료로 입장할 수 있도록 하는 새로운 프로그램을 후원하기 위해 협력해 왔습니다. 우리는 한정된 예산으로 우리나라의 유구한 역사를 탐험하고자 하는 분들을 위해 사모아를 매력적인 관광지로 만드는 것을 144목표로 합니다. 145주요 볼거리에는 타푸아 반도 열대 우림 보호 구역, 사모아 박물관, 그리고 유명 작가인 Robert Louis Stevenson 씨의 옛집 투어 등이 포함됩니다.
>
> 입장권을 받으시려면 당사 웹사이트 www.snto.org/culturepass를 확인하시거나 공항에 있는 저희 부스를 방문하십시오. 146입장권은 최대 일주일 동안 사용하실 수 있습니다.

어휘 announcement 공지, 발표   list 열거하다   flyer (광고·안내용) 전단   collaborate 협력하다   sponsor 후원하다   a number of 많은   culturally 문화적으로   significant 중요한   attraction 명소, 볼거리   inviting 매력적인   destination 목적지, 관광지   on a budget 한정된 예산으로   explore 탐험하다   peninsula 반도   rainforest 열대 우림   preserve 보호 구역   famed 유명한   former 예전의   claim 얻다, 주장하다

143. 전치사 along with
(A) ~와는 달리 (B) ~의 도처에 (C) ~와 함께 (D) ~에도 불구하고
해설 문장의 동사가 has collaborated(협력했다)이므로 SNTO는 열거된 업체들과 함께 일하고 있다는 것을 알 수 있으므로, '~와 함께'라는 뜻의 전치사 (C)가 정답이다.

144. 동사 자리 [수 일치]
해설 빈칸은 주어 We 뒤에 오는 동사 자리이므로 (A)와 (D)가 정답 후보인데, 주어가 복수 명사이므로 복수 동사인 (A)가 정답이다.

145. 형용사 어휘 featured
(A) 은퇴한 (B) 발견된 (C) 호화로운 (D) 주요한

해설 빈칸 뒤의 명사 attractions를 수식하기에 의미상 적절한 형용사를 골라야 한다. '주요 명소'라는 의미가 되는 것이 적절하므로 '주요한'이라는 뜻의 (D)가 정답이다.

146. 알맞은 문장 고르기
(A) 지속적인 후원에 감사드립니다.
(B) 귀하가 저희 호텔에 투숙하시길 고대합니다.
(C) 입장권은 최대 일주일 동안 사용하실 수 있습니다.
(D) 현금과 카드는 모두 허용되는 결제 수단입니다.

해설 빈칸 앞의 문장에서 입장권을 받는 방법을 언급하고 있으므로, 입장권에 관한 부연 설명을 하는 내용이 이어지는 것이 자연스럽다. 따라서 (C)가 정답이다.

어휘 appreciate 감사히 여기다 consistent 지속적인 patronage 애용, 후원 acceptable 받아들여지는

147-148 계약서

Kennewick Communications
네트워크 서비스 공급자 계약서

고객 이름: Lily Cronin
주소: 필드크레스트 레인 1406번지, 오마하, 네브래스카 68102
패키지 유형: 광섬유 광대역 회선   개통일: 3월 15일
설치비: 35달러   월 사용료: 85달러
계약 기간: 1년   지불 유형: 계좌 이체

Kennewick Communications의 고객이 되어 주셔서 감사합니다. 귀하에게 이 지역에서 가장 빠르고 신뢰할 수 있는 인터넷 서비스를 제공해 드리게 되어 기쁩니다. 기사가 댁을 방문하여 필요한 장비를 가져다 드리고 서비스를 구축해 드릴 것입니다. 첫 세 달 동안의 월 이용료는 68달러인데, 그것은 정상 요금에서 20% 할인된 금액입니다. 그리고 이 기간 이후에는 저희가 특별 판촉을 제공하지 않는 한 요금에 더 이상의 할인은 적용되지 않을 것입니다. [147]귀하는 첫 세 달 동안 위약금 없이 계약을 해지하실 수 있습니다. [148]서비스에 기술적인 문제를 겪으실 경우 555-4331번으로 저희에게 전화해 주십시오.

서명: Lily Cronin
날짜: 3월 10일

어휘 provider 공급자 agreement 계약(서), 동의 fee 요금, 수수료 contract 계약(서) term 기간 transfer 이체; 이전하다 reliable 믿을 수 있는 region 지역 technician 기술자, 기사 property 부동산, 건물 equipment 장비 regular 보통의, 평상시의 period 기간 further 더 이상의, 추가 apply 적용하다 promotion 판촉 cancel 취소하다 penalty 벌금, 위약금

147. 계약을 취소하는 고객에 대해 언급된 것은 무엇인가?
(A) 모든 장비를 반납해야 한다.
(B) 20%의 수수료가 부과될 것이다.
(C) 첫 3개월 내에 무료로 취소할 수 있다.
(D) 기술적인 문제가 있을 때 취소할 수 있다.

해설 세부 사항
첫 세 달 동안 위약금 없이 계약을 해지할 수 있다고 했으므로 (C)가 정답이다.

패러프레이징 cancel your contract without penalty during the first 3 months → cancel for free in the first three months

148. Cronin 씨가 제공된 번호로 전화를 하게 될 이유는 무엇인가?
(A) 주소를 변경하기 위해
(B) 계약을 해지하기 위해
(C) 문제를 알리기 위해
(D) 새로운 거래를 문의하기 위해

해설 세부 사항
서비스에 문제가 있으면 전화하라고 했으므로 (C)가 정답이다.

패러프레이징 technical issues → a problem

149-150 문자 메시지

Belle Chauvet [오후 4:18]
안녕하세요, Ernest. [149]당신에게 파리 여행 참가자 명단이 있나요?

Ernest Lessard [오후 4:20]
[150]6월 3일에 실시되는 것을 말씀하시는 건가요?

Belle Chauvet [오후 4:21]
네, 그거예요.

Ernest Lessard [오후 4:22]
네, 총 23명입니다. [149]지난번처럼 막바지 예약이 있을 수도 있어서 호텔에 미리 알려 놨어요. 금요일에 모두에게 여행 일정표를 보낼 계획입니다.

Belle Chauvet [오후 4:24]
잘하셨어요! 제게 명단을 전달해 주시고 변경 사항이 있으면 나중에 알려 주시겠어요?

어휘 participant 참가자 take place 일어나다, 열리다 in total 전체로, 합계하여 last-minute 막바지의, 마지막 순간의 inform 알리다 itinerary 여행 일정 forward 전달하다, 보내다

149. 화자들이 근무할 것 같은 업종은 무엇인가?
(A) 교육 기관
(B) 여행사
(C) 은행
(D) 호텔

해설 추론/암시
파리 여행 참가자 명단을 언급하면서, 막바지 예약에 대비하여 호텔에 미리 알렸다거나 여행 일정표를 보낼 계획이라는 등의 내용을 통해 화자들은 여행업체 직원들임을 추론할 수 있다. 따라서 (B)가 정답이다.

150. 오후 4시 21분에, Chauvet 씨가 "네, 그거예요"라고 쓰는 이유는 무엇인가?
(A) 그녀는 파리 방문에 관심을 나타내고 있다.
(B) 그녀는 Lessard 씨가 맞다고 말하고 있다.
(C) 그녀는 업무를 제시간에 끝내겠다고 약속한다.
(D) 그녀는 Lessard 씨의 사업 계획에 동의한다.

해설 의도 파악

의도 파악 문제는 바로 앞의 내용을 확인해야 한다. 6월 3일에 실시되는 파리 여행의 참가자 명단을 말하는 거냐는 Ernest Lessard의 질문에 이같이 답했으므로 Ernest Lessard의 말이 맞다는 것을 나타내고 있다. 따라서 (B)가 정답이다.

151-152 메모

전반적으로, 저는 [151]월례 리뷰 절차를 위해 보내 주신 커피 그라인더의 특징에 만족했습니다. 갈린 원두의 크기가 일정했는데, 이는 컵마다 추출률이 동일할 것이라는 의미입니다. 저는 알기 쉬운 조립 설명서가 마음에 들었습니다. [152]하지만 수거함의 모양 때문에 그 안에 청소용 스펀지를 집어넣기가 어려웠습니다. 그 점은 개선될 수 있다고 생각합니다. 그래도 큰 사이즈는 정말 마음에 들었고, 많은 고객들이 좋아할 것 같습니다. 제가 염려하는 또 다른 부품은 손잡이였습니다. 그것은 매우 얇은 플라스틱으로 만들어진 것 같아서 원두를 갈 때 쉽게 부러질 수 있습니다.

Mona Yang

어휘 overall 전반적으로 feature 특징 grind 갈다 consistent 일관된 extraction 추출 rate 비율 assembly 조립 instructions (사용) 설명서 collection 수집, 수거 chamber (특정 목적용) 실(室), 공간 improve 개선하다 appreciate 높이 평가하다 component 요소, 부품 concern ~을 걱정스럽게[우려하게] 만들다

151. Yang 씨에 대해 암시된 것은 무엇인가?
(A) 커피 그라인더를 반품하고 싶어 한다.
(B) 커피숍을 소유하고 있다.
(C) 정기적으로 의견을 제공한다.
(D) 장치의 부품 하나를 잃어버렸다.

해설 추론/암시

Mona Yang은 메모의 작성자로서, 첫 번째 문장의 our monthly review process를 통해 매월 어떤 제품에 대해 분석하고 의견을 제공한다는 것을 추론할 수 있으므로 (C)가 정답이다.

패러프레이징 review → feedback

152. Yang 씨가 수거함에 대해 언급하는 것은 무엇인가?
(A) 충분히 크지 않다.
(B) 청소하기 어려웠다.
(C) 플라스틱으로 만들어야 한다.
(D) 쉽게 깨질 수 있다.

해설 세부 사항

collection chamber를 키워드로 지문을 검색하면, 수거함의 모양 때문에 청소용 스펀지를 넣기가 어려웠다고 했으므로, 청소가 용이하지 않았음을 유추할 수 있다. 따라서 (B)가 정답이다.

153-154 편지

Thurman 씨,

전국환경책임협회(NAER)는 국내 건설 산업에 있어 친환경적인 실천을 앞장서서 지지하고 있습니다. 매년, '지속 가능한 엔지니어링 상'을 통해 우리는 혁신적인 방법을 사용하여 지구의 자원을 최대한 활용하는 기업을 표창하고 있습니다. 귀하가 그 분야의 전문가이기에, [153]지속 가능한 디자인과 건축을 가장 잘 대표하는 건물에 대한 귀하의 의견을 듣고 싶습니다.

며칠 후, 투표용지를 받게 되실 텐데 [153]수상 자격이 있다고 생각하시는 건물을 세 개까지 지명하실 수 있습니다. [154]후보 지명 과정에 참여하시려면 양식을 작성한 후 제공된 봉투에 넣어 우리에게 반송해 주시기 바랍니다.

문의 사항이 있으시면 저는 555-8205번으로 통화 가능합니다.

Vivian Demott

어휘 leading 선도적인 advocate 옹호자, 지지자 eco-friendly 친환경적인 practice 실천, 관행 construction 건설 sustainable 지속 가능한 recognize 표창하다, 인정하다 innovative 혁신적인 method 방법 make the best use of ~을 최대한 활용하다 resource 자원 ballot 투표용지 nominate 지명[추천]하다 deserve ~을 받을 만하다 recognition 인정, 표창 participate in ~에 참여하다 complete 작성하다, 완료하다 envelope 봉투

153. Demott 씨가 Thurman 씨에게 요청하는 것은 무엇인가?
(A) 추천서
(B) 혁신적인 건물들의 목록
(C) 그의 업적에 대한 요약
(D) 행사 참석 확인

해설 세부 사항

혁신적인 기업을 표창한다고 하면서, 그러한 취지에 부합하는 건물을 지명해 달라고 요청하고 있으므로 (B)가 정답이다.

패러프레이징 the buildings that represent the best of sustainable design and construction → innovative buildings

154. Thurman 씨는 요청에 어떻게 응답해야 하는가?
(A) 전화 설문 조사를 완료함으로써
(B) Demott 씨를 만남으로써
(C) 웹 사이트를 방문함으로써
(D) 우편으로 양식을 반송함으로써

해설 세부 사항

후보 지명 과정에 참여하려면 양식을 작성하여 봉투에 넣어 반송해 달라고 했으므로 (D)가 정답이다.

패러프레이징 send it back to us in the envelope provided → returning a form by mail

155-157 제품 소개

[155]Paintstop은 벽에 곰팡이가 생기는 것을 막도록 특별히 만들어진 페인트 첨가제입니다. 이것은 욕실이나 주방 등 습기가 차기 쉬운 곳에 안성맞춤입니다. Paintstop을 사용하시려면 [156]50밀리리터 용기를 아크릴 및 오일 페인트 등의 2.5리터 페인트 통에 섞기만 하면 됩니다.

[155]Paintstop은 곰팡이 포자를 죽이며, 포자가 다시 생기지 않

는 것을 보장합니다. 그 효과는 페인트의 수명 동안 지속됩니다. 또한 157페인트 색상을 다소 연하게 만드는 경쟁사 제품과 달리, Paintstop은 본연의 색상을 유지시켜 줍니다.

Paintstop으로 보기 흉하고 건강에 해로운 곰팡이와 작별하세요!

어휘 additive 첨가제 mold 곰팡이 prone to ~의 경향이 있는 dampness 습기 such as ~와 같은 spore 홀씨, 포자 effectiveness 효과 last 지속되다 competitor 경쟁자, 경쟁업체 slightly 약간 preserve 보존하다 unsightly 보기 흉한

155. Paintstop은 무엇을 하도록 만들어졌는가?
(A) 방의 습도를 감소시키기
(B) 곰팡이로 인한 얼룩을 제거하기
(C) 페인트를 더 오래 지속시키기
(D) 곰팡이 증식을 방지하기

해설 세부 사항
Paintstop은 벽에 곰팡이가 생기지 않도록 만들어진 페인트 첨가제로, 곰팡이 포자를 죽인다고 나와 있으므로 (D)가 정답이다.

패러프레이징 stop mold from growing, kills mold spores and ensures that they will not return → Prevent the growth of mold

156. 제품 설명에 따르면, Paintstop에 대해 사실인 것은 무엇인가?
(A) 정기적으로 덧발라야 한다.
(B) 서로 다른 종류의 페인트에 사용할 수 있다.
(C) 페인트의 건조 시간을 늦춘다.
(D) 2.5리터 통으로 판매된다.

해설 NOT/True
아크릴, 오일 페인트 등 어떤 페인트 통에든 섞기만 하면 된다고 나와 있으므로 여러 종류의 페인트에 사용할 수 있음을 알 수 있다. 따라서 (B)가 정답이다.

157. Paintstop은 시중에 나와 있는 다른 제품과 어떻게 다른가?
(A) 벽에 바르기 더 쉽다.
(B) 빛에 의해 손상되지 않는다.
(C) 페인트 색상을 바꾸지 않는다.
(D) 해로운 성분이 들어 있지 않다.

해설 세부 사항
other products on the market을 키워드로 지문을 검색하면, our competitors' products가 있는 문장에서 경쟁사 제품은 페인트 색상을 연하게 만들지만, Paintstop은 본연의 색깔을 유지시킨다고 했으므로 (C)가 정답이다.

패러프레이징 preserves the true color → does not alter paint colors

158-160 설명서

158Zamora Manufacturing에서 Z-880 전기 드릴을 구입해 주셔서 감사합니다. 드릴이 제대로 작동하도록 정비해 두면 작동 중 드릴의 안전성은 물론 드릴의 성능도 유지할 수 있습니다.

159사용 후 드릴은 마른 천으로 닦아서 원래 보관함에 보관해야 합니다. 그렇게 하면 중요한 공기구멍들을 막을 수 있는 불필요한 먼지로부터 드릴을 보호하게 됩니다. 드릴을 장기간 보관할 계획이면 배터리를 제거해야 합니다.

장치를 충전할 때는 배터리를 충전기에서 제거하기 전에 160배터리가 완전히 충전되었는지 확인하십시오. 이것은 녹색 불로 표시될 것입니다. 적어도 6개월마다 배터리를 완전히 방전시키세요. 이렇게 하시면 배터리 수명을 연장하는 데 도움이 됩니다. 드릴을 최대한 활용하기 위한 팁과 요령은 www.zamora.com/z-880에서 확인하십시오.

어휘 purchase 구입, 구매 electric 전기의 keep ~ in order ~을 정돈해 두다 maintain 유지하다 performance 성능 in operation 가동 중 wipe down ~을 말끔히 닦다 air vent 공기구멍, 환기구 charge 충전하다 run out 다 떨어지다 completely 완전히 extend 연장하다 get the most out of ~을 최대한 활용하다

158. 설명서가 대상으로 하는 사람은 누구이겠는가?
(A) 상점 직원
(B) 안전 검사관
(C) 제조 직원
(D) 전동 공구 소유자

해설 대상
문두를 검색하면, 전기 드릴을 구입해 주셔서 고맙다고 하는 것으로 보아, 전기 드릴을 갖고 있는 사람을 대상으로 하는 설명서임을 유추할 수 있다. 따라서 (D)가 정답이다.

패러프레이징 electric drill → power tool

159. 제품 보관에 권장되는 것은 무엇인가?
(A) 공기구멍 내 먼지 확인하기
(B) 먼저 젖은 천으로 닦기
(C) 매번 배터리 분리하기
(D) 딸려 있는 용기를 사용하기

해설 세부 사항
동사 storing을 키워드로 지문을 검색하면, 드릴은 사용 후 마른 천으로 닦아서 원래의 보관함에 보관하라고 했으므로, (D)가 정답이다.

패러프레이징 its original case → the container that came with it

160. [1], [2], [3], [4]로 표시된 위치 중 다음 문장이 들어가기에 가장 적절한 곳은?
"이것은 녹색 불로 표시될 것입니다."
(A) [1]
(B) [2]
(C) [3]
(D) [4]

해설 문장 삽입
주어진 문장의 This가 가리키는 것은 배터리 충전 상황이므로, 배터리가 완전히 충전되었는지 확인하라는 내용 다음인 [3]의 자리에 들

어가는 것이 적절하다. 따라서 (C)가 정답이다.

161-163 이메일

수신: 전체 고객 목록
발신: Soltero Spa
날짜: 4월 10일
제목: 취소

Soltero Spa 고객님께,

Soltero Spa에서는 모든 고객님이 원하시는 시술을 편리한 시간에 받으실 수 있도록 하려고 합니다. ¹⁶¹5월 1일부터는 예약일로부터 24시간 이내에 취소 시 시술비의 30%에 해당하는 수수료를 부과하기 시작할 것입니다. 이 정책으로 고객님들이 일정 변경에 대해 일찍 알려 주도록 하여 다른 고객님께 그 예약일을 제공할 수 있게 되기를 바랍니다. 이는 저희 서비스에 대한 높은 수요를 감당하도록 해주는 데 있어 ¹⁶²매우 중요합니다. ¹⁶³저희 건물에 5개의 새로운 시술실을 추가함으로써 시술 일정을 잡기 위한 긴 대기 시간이 줄어들었지만, 이 새로운 규정이 훨씬 더 많은 도움이 되기를 바랍니다.

William Soltero
Soltero Spa 소유주

어휘 customer 고객 cancellation 취소 treatment 치료, 시술 convenience 편의, 편리 charge (요금을) 청구하다 appointment 예약, 약속 encourage 권장[장려]하다 critical 대단히 중요한 keep up with ~을 따라잡다 demand 수요

161. 이메일이 작성된 이유는 무엇인가?
(A) 취소에 대해 사과하기 위해
(B) 약속을 변경하기 위해
(C) 정책 변경을 알리기 위해
(D) 새로운 시술을 소개하기 위해

해설 **주제/목적**
주제/목적 문제는 문두를 검색한다. 5월 1일부터 예약일로부터 24시간 이내 취소 시 수수료를 부과할 예정이라면서 변경되는 정책을 알리고 있으므로 (C)가 정답이다.

162. 첫 번째 단락 다섯 번째 줄의 어휘 'critical'과 의미상 가장 가까운 것은?
(A) 긴급한
(B) 문제가 있는
(C) 부정적인
(D) 중요한

해설 **동의어 찾기**
critical이 포함된 부분은 '저희 서비스에 대한 높은 수요를 감당하도록 해주는 데 있어 매우 중요하다'라는 의미이다. critical은 '매우 중요한'이라는 의미로 쓰였으므로 (D)가 정답이다.

163. Soltero Spa에 대해 암시된 것은 무엇인가?
(A) 건물 확장 공사를 끝냈다.
(B) 영업시간을 연장할 것이다.
(C) 정기적으로 직원들을 훈련시킨다.
(D) 전화로 예약을 받는다.

해설 **추론/암시**
건물에 5개의 새로운 시술실을 추가했다고 했으므로, 건물 확장 공사가 있었다는 것을 유추할 수 있다. 따라서 (A)가 정답이다.

164-167 기사

홈 오피스 환경 자금 지원

오클랜드(1월 8일)—그 어느 때보다 많은 사람들이 재택근무를 함에 따라 기업들은 원격 근무자들과의 의사소통 방식뿐만 아니라 ¹⁶⁴그들을 지원하는 방식도 조정하고 있다. 많은 기업들이 따르는 새로운 추세는 직원들에게 홈 오피스 예산을 제공하는 것이다. ¹⁶⁷회사 내의 많은 역할을 사무실 밖에서 수행할 수 있다. 하지만 모든 사람이 제대로 된 환경을 갖추고 있는 것은 아니다. ¹⁶⁷따라서 기업들은 직원들이 생산성을 유지하기 위해 사용할 수 있는 모든 도구, 즉 책상, 사무실 의자, 심지어 커피 머신과 같은 구매품에 대한 자금을 제공하기 시작하고 있다.

"저는 홈 오피스를 만들기 위해 제 자금을 쓸 필요가 없어서 기뻤습니다."라고 Conifer Enterprises의 영업 사원인 ¹⁶⁵Albert Steiner 씨가 말했다. "¹⁶⁵저는 고객들과 영상 통화를 자주 하기 때문에, 제게는 전문적으로 보이는 공간을 배경으로 두는 것이 중요합니다."

"이것은 우리가 직원들을 지원할 수 있는 또 다른 방법입니다."라고 Elysian의 인사부장인 ¹⁶⁶Patricia Miller 씨가 설명했다. "우리는 직원들에게 우리가 그들을 소중하게 여기고 그곳이 어디든 그들을 위해 편안한 근무 환경을 만들어 주고 싶다는 것을 보여 주기 위해 ¹⁶⁶작년에 홈 오피스 예산을 제공하기 시작했습니다. 그것은 가장 숙련되고 경험이 많은 직원들이 우리 회사에 오래 머물 수 있도록 하는 중요한 요소입니다."

어휘 fund 자금을 제공하다; 자금 adjustment 조정 communicate 의사소통하다 remote 원격의 support 지원하다 perform 수행하다 tool 도구 productivity 생산성 representative 대표(자) background 배경 value 소중하게 여기다

164. 기사가 작성된 이유는 무엇인가?
(A) 직원 야유회에 자금 지원을 권고하기 위해
(B) 원격 근무의 장점을 설명하기 위해
(C) 최근에 도입된 직원 복지 혜택을 설명하기 위해
(D) 생산성 문제에 대해 조언을 하기 위해

해설 **주제/목적**
지문 도입부에서 원격 근무자들을 지원하기 위해 기업들이 직원들에게 홈 오피스 예산을 제공한다고 했고, 기사 전반에 걸쳐 이와 관련된 내용이 이어지고 있으므로 (C)가 정답이다.

165. Steiner 씨에 대해 사실인 것은 무엇인가?
(A) 사람들이 작업 공간을 설치하는 것을 돕는다.
(B) 고객들과 온라인으로 대화한다.
(C) 사무실에서 일하는 것을 선호한다.
(D) Conifer Enterprises의 신입 직원이다.

해설 **NOT/True**
Steiner를 키워드로 지문을 검색하면, Albert Steiner는 고객들과 영상 통화를 자주 한다고 했으므로 (B)가 정답이다.

패러프레이징 have video calls with clients → speaks with clients online

166. Miller 씨의 회사가 작년에 변화를 준 이유는 무엇인가?
(A) 더 작은 사무실로 이전하기 위해
(B) 주가를 높이기 위해
(C) 운영비를 절감하기 위해
(D) 재능 있는 직원들을 놓치지 않기 위해

해설 세부 사항
Miller 씨는 숙련되고 경험 많은 직원들이 회사에 오래 머물 수 있도록 작년에 홈 오피스 예산을 제공하기 시작했다고 했으므로 (D)가 정답이다.

패러프레이징 making sure the most skilled and experienced staff members stay with our company → To retain talented staff

167. [1], [2], [3], [4]로 표시된 위치 중 다음 문장이 들어가기에 가장 적절한 곳은?
"하지만 모든 사람이 제대로 된 환경을 갖추고 있는 것은 아니다."
(A) [1]
(B) [2]
(C) [3]
(D) [4]

해설 문장 삽입
주어진 문장의 setup이 가리키는 것을 찾아야 한다. setup은 홈 오피스 환경을 의미하므로, 기업들이 홈 오피스 예산을 제공하고 있다는 내용이 나온 다음인 [1]에 들어가는 것이 적절하다. 또한 주어진 문장에 이어지는 문장은 기업들이 환경이 제대로 갖추어져 있지 않은 직원들의 사무실 밖 근무를 돕기 위해 자금을 제공하기 시작했다는 내용이므로 문맥적으로도 적절하다.

168-171 웹페이지

| 홈 | 부스 대여 | 사진 갤러리 | 연락처 |

1월 2일 업데이트됨

내슈빌 페스티벌에서 여러분의 물품을 선보이세요! 참가자 수가 지난 몇 년간 꾸준히 증가하고 있으며, ¹⁶⁸도자기와 뜨개질 의류, 가정용 장식품 등 수작업으로 만든 물품에 관한 최대 규모의 전시 행사입니다. 축제는 1년에 세 번 열립니다. ¹⁶⁹부스 대여 신청은 2월 15일(봄 축제), 5월 15일(여름), 7월 15일(가을)까지 접수해야 합니다. 전에 축제에서 전시를 한 적이 있는 업체에는 부스 선정 우선권이 주어집니다. ¹⁷¹ᶜ부스 대여료는 다양하며 부스 크기에 따라 계산됩니다.

여러분의 부스를 계획할 때, 부스가 정리가 잘 되어 있고 매력적이어야 한다는 점에 유의하십시오. 테이블 덮개와 장식을 권장합니다. 강풍이 불 때 위험해질 수 있기 때문에 ¹⁷¹ᴮ튼튼하고 견고한 텐트만 허용됩니다. 가격은 물품에 명확하게 표시되어야 하며, 모든 표지판은 전문적인 방식으로 인쇄되어야 합니다.

모든 부스는 축제 당일 오전 8시에 문을 열 준비가 되어야 하고 ¹⁷⁰오후 7시(뒷마당)나 오후 8시(건물 내부)까지 오픈 상태를 유지해야 합니다. ¹⁷¹ᴬ축제 시간 동안 부스에서 일하는 사람이 적어도 한 명은 있어야 합니다.
부스 대여 신청은 여기를 클릭하세요.

어휘 showcase 선보이다, 전시하다 attendance 참석자 수 exhibition 전시(회) pottery 도자기 decoration 장식(품) application 신청, 지원 exhibit 전시하다 priority 우선권 selection 선정, 선택 vary 다양하다, 다르다 calculate 계산하다 based on ~에 근거하여 heavy-duty 매우 튼튼한 sturdy 튼튼한, 견고한 professionally 전문적으로 rear 뒤쪽의 courtyard 마당, 뜰

168. 내슈빌 페스티벌에서 판매되는 것은 무엇이겠는가?
(A) 현지에서 재배한 농산물
(B) 수공예품
(C) 원예용품
(D) 중고 장비

해설 추론/암시
수작업으로 만든 물품으로는 최대 규모라고 했으므로 (B)가 정답이다.

패러프레이징 items made by hand such as pottery, knitted clothing, household decorations, and more → Handmade crafts

169. 여름 축제 부스 신청 마감일은 언제인가?
(A) 1월 2일
(B) 2월 15일
(C) 5월 15일
(D) 7월 15일

해설 세부 사항
deadline, summer festival 등의 키워드로 지문을 검색하면, 부스 대여 신청은 여름의 경우 5월 15일까지라고 나와 있으므로 (C)가 정답이다.

170. 내슈빌 페스티벌에 대해 암시된 것은 무엇인가?
(A) 실내와 실외 전시 공간을 모두 갖추고 있다.
(B) 올해 처음으로 시작될 것이다.
(C) 직원들은 자원봉사로 일한다.
(D) 수익금은 자선 단체에 기부될 것이다.

해설 추론/암시
뒷마당은 오후 7시, 건물 내부는 오후 8시까지 오픈 상태를 유지해야 한다고 했으므로, 실내와 실외에 모두 전시 공간이 있음을 유추할 수 있다. 따라서 (A)가 정답이다.

패러프레이징 in the rear courtyard, inside the building → indoor and outdoor exhibition spaces

171. 축제의 부스에 대해 사실이 아닌 것은 무엇인가?
(A) 항상 직원이 배치되어 있어야 한다.
(B) 경량 텐트는 허용되지 않는다.
(C) 비용은 부스의 크기에 따라 결정된다.
(D) 표지판은 사전에 승인받아야 한다.

해설 **NOT/True**
표지판을 사전에 승인받아야 한다는 내용은 나와 있지 않으므로 (D)가 정답이다.

패러프레이징 (A) There must be at least one person working at the booth during the festival hours → They must be staffed at all times / (B) Heavy-duty and sturdy tents only will be accepted → Lightweight tents are not allowed / (C) Fees for booth rental vary and are calculated based on the booth size → The cost depends on the size of the booth

172-175 온라인 채팅

> Sam Aubry (오전 10:03)
> Mary, Daniel, 오늘 바빠요? 제 프레젠테이션에 시각 자료를 추가해 줄 사람이 필요해요. 오늘 제가 외부에서 열리는 워크숍에 가야 하는데 프로젝트 마감일이 다가오고 있거든요.
>
> Mary Shin (오전 10:04)
> 제가 할 수 있어요.
>
> Sam Aubry (오전 10:05)
> 고마워요! ¹⁷²우리 서비스의 개요에 관한 것으로, 고객을 대신하여 입사 지원자를 모집하고 심사하는 방법에 대해 설명하는 거예요.
>
> Daniel Bingham (오전 10:06)
> ¹⁷³그런데 당신은 보통은 준비성이 철저하잖아요, Sam. 어쩌다가 시간이 부족하게 된 거예요?
>
> Sam Aubry (오전 10:07)
> 마감일이 갑자기 앞당겨졌어요.
>
> Mary Shin (오전 10:08)
> 그렇군요. 염두에 두고 있는 사진 스타일이 있다면 알려 주세요.
>
> Daniel Bingham (오전 10:09)
> 그렇군요.
>
> Sam Aubry (오전 10:10)
> 당신이 가장 좋아 보인다고 생각하는 거라면 뭐든지요, Mary.
>
> Mary Shin (오전 10:11)
> 알겠어요. ¹⁷⁴프레젠테이션에 관해서 말인데요, 당신이 우리 기존 고객들 중 한 명으로부터 홍보용 추천서를 받을 계획이었던 것으로 알고 있어요. 그걸 할 시간이 있었나요?
>
> Sam Aubry (오전 10:12)
> 안타깝지만 없었어요.
>
> Daniel Bingham (오전 10:13)
> ¹⁷⁵제가 점심 식사 후에 Lowe 씨를 만날 예정이거든요. 제가 그분께 우리를 위해 추천의 글을 써 달라고 부탁할게요. 그녀는 우리의 서비스에 매우 만족하고 있기 때문에, 분명히 우리를 돕는 것을 마다하지 않을 거예요.

어휘 off-site 현장 밖의, 외부의 outline 개요 recruit 모집하다 screen 가려내다 candidate 후보자, 지원자 on behalf of ~을 대신[대표]하여 organized 체계적인 run out of ~을 다 써버리다 deadline 마감일 endorsement (상품에 대한) 공개적인 지지, 홍보성 추천 unfortunately 안타깝게도 testimonial 추천서, 추천 후기

172. 화자들이 근무하는 곳은 어디이겠는가?
(A) 렌터카 사무실
(B) 취업 알선 업체
(C) 연구소
(D) 금융 컨설팅 회사

해설 **추론/암시**
Sam Aubry가 고객을 대신하여 입사 지원자를 모집하고 심사하는 서비스에 대해 설명하는 프레젠테이션 준비에 도움을 요청하고 있으므로, 화자들은 취업 알선 업체에서 근무하고 있음을 유추할 수 있다. 따라서 (B)가 정답이다.

173. Aubry 씨에 대해 암시된 것은 무엇인가?
(A) 새로운 팀원이다.
(B) 곧 직업을 바꿀 계획이다.
(C) 보통은 상세한 계획을 세워서 일한다.
(D) 판매를 완료할 수 없었다.

해설 **추론/암시**
10:06에 Daniel Bingham이 'you're usually so organized, Sam'이라고 말한 것으로 보아 Sam Aubry는 organized한 사람, 즉 계획적으로 일하는 사람이라는 것을 추론할 수 있으므로 (C)가 정답이다.

어휘 switch 바꾸다 detailed 상세한 complete 완료하다, 끝내다

174. 오전 10시 12분에, Aubry 씨가 "안타깝지만 없었어요"라고 쓸 때 그는 무엇을 암시하는가?
(A) 그는 대화를 이해하지 못한다.
(B) 그는 점심 후에 Lowe 씨를 만날 수 없다.
(C) 그는 동료들에게 보고서를 보낼 수 없다.
(D) 그는 너무 바빠서 업무를 처리하지 못했다.

해설 **의도 파악**
바로 앞에서 Mary Shin이 "Did you have time to do that?"이라고 물었는데 그에 대한 답변으로 이렇게 말했으므로 that이 의미하는 것을 찾아야 한다. that은 바로 앞문장에 나온 to get an endorsement from one of our current clients를 의미하므로, Sam Aubry는 고객들의 추천서를 받을 시간이 없었다고 말하는 것이다. 따라서 그것을 task로 패러프레이징한 (D)가 정답이다.

175. Bingham 씨가 오늘 오후에 하려고 계획하는 것은 무엇인가?
(A) 워크숍에 참석하기
(B) 사진 검색하기
(C) 고객에게 부탁하기
(D) 프레젠테이션 연습하기

해설 **세부 사항**
Daniel Bingham은 Lowe 씨를 만나서 추천서를 써 달라고 부탁하겠다고 했고, 서비스에 매우 만족하고 있다고 한 것으로 보아 Lowe 씨가 고객임을 알 수 있다. 따라서 (C)가 정답이다.

176-180 이메일 & 기사

> 수신: Callum Baxter
> 발신: Phoebe Hagai

날짜: 5월 8일
제목: 제안서 논의

Baxter 씨,

우리 택시에서 동영상 스크린을 제거하는 것에 대해 논의할 수 있도록 회의를 마련하고 싶습니다. ¹⁷⁶대부분의 승객들은 시끄러운 동영상에 매우 짜증이 난다고 알리고 있고, 음 소거 버튼이 있는데도 종종 작동하지 않습니다. 우리는 일주일에 여러 번 이에 대한 지적을 받습니다. 동영상이 광고를 통해 수익을 창출한다는 것은 이해하지만, ¹⁷⁸동영상 스크린에 대한 불만이 우리 웹사이트에서 가장 자주 언급되는 문제이므로, 이제는 이익을 내기 위해 다른 ¹⁷⁷접근법을 사용해야 할 때입니다.

이 스크린들은 결제에도 사용되므로 기본적인 신용 카드 판독기로 대체되어야 한다고 생각합니다. ¹⁸⁰⁻¹우리는 더 많은 단체 승객들을 수용할 수 있도록 승합차를 몇 대 구입하는 것도 고려해야 합니다. 또한, 이제는 전기 자동차에 투자하기 시작할 때입니다. 저는 위에서 말한 제 제안의 모든 부분에 대해 당신과 논의하기를 고대하고 있습니다.

Phoebe Hagai

어휘 set up 준비하다 remove 제거하다 irritated 짜증이 난 mute 무언의, 말 없는 comment 논평, 의견 generate 만들어 내다 revenue 수익 approach 접근법 complaint 불만 common 흔한 payment 지불 replace 대체하다 accommodate (차·배 등이 손님을) 태우다, 수용하다 in addition 게다가, 덧붙여 invest in ~에 투자하다 electric vehicle 전기 자동차 look forward to doing ~하기를 고대하다 proposal 제안

Clover Taxis가 새로운 전환을 맞이하다
Georgina Willis 작성

(5월 27일)—Clover Taxis는 많은 비난을 받아 온 차량 뒷좌석의 스크린을 제거하고 신용 카드 판독기로 대체한다는 계획을 발표했다. ¹⁸⁰⁻²또한, 업체는 자사의 보유 차량에 보통 크기의 4도어 전기 자동차 택시 20대를 구입할 자금을 마련했다. ^{179B}이 차량들은 쉽게 알아볼 수 있도록 겉에 이전과 동일한 녹색과 흰색 페인트가 입혀질 것이다. ^{179A}Clover Taxis는 또한 가장 바쁜 시간대를 처리할 더 많은 기사를 고용할 것이다. ^{179C}이러한 변화로 요금이 소폭 인상되겠지만, 여전히 이 업체는 가격 면에서 경쟁사보다 약간 낮은 수준을 유지한다.

어휘 take a new turn 새로운 국면이 전개되다 criticize 비판[비난]하다 secure 확보하다, 안전하게 하다 funding 자금 fleet (한 기관이 소유한 전체 비행기·버스·택시 등의) 무리 recognizable 알아볼 수 있는 cover 떠맡다, 덮다 result in 결과적으로 ~가 되다 increase 증가; 증가하다 fare (교통) 요금 slightly 약간 competitor 경쟁자 in terms of ~ 면에서

176. 이메일에 따르면, Hagai 씨의 회사가 자주 받는 민원은 무엇인가?
(A) 업체의 높은 택시 승차 요금
(B) 동영상 스크린의 소리
(C) 에어컨의 부족
(D) 신용 카드 처리 문제

해설 세부 사항
complaints를 키워드로 첫 번째 지문을 검색하면, 승객들이 시끄러운 동영상에 짜증을 내고 그에 대해 지적한다고 했으므로 (B)가 정답이다.

패러프레이징 the noisy videos → The sound of the video screens

177. 이메일에서, 첫 번째 단락 다섯 번째 줄의 어휘 'approach'와 의미상 가장 가까운 것은?
(A) 움직임
(B) 통로
(C) 도착
(D) 방법

해설 동의어 찾기
approach가 포함된 부분은 문맥상 '이익을 내기 위해 다른 접근법을 사용해야 할 때이다'라는 의미로, approach가 '접근법'이라는 의미로 쓰였다. 선택지 중 이와 의미상 가장 유사한 (D)가 정답이다.

178. Clovers Taxis 고객들에 대해 암시된 것은 무엇인가?
(A) 그들은 회의에 초대된다.
(B) 그들은 고객 보상 프로그램에 등록할 수 있다.
(C) 그들은 온라인에서 의견을 공유한다.
(D) 그들은 주로 광고를 통해 업체에 대해 알게 되었다.

해설 추론/암시
동영상 스크린에 대한 불만이 웹 사이트에서 가장 자주 언급되는 문제라고 했으므로 고객들이 온라인에서 의견을 공유한다는 것을 유추할 수 있다. 따라서 (C)가 정답이다.

패러프레이징 the most common issue mentioned on our Web site → feedback online

179. 기사에 따르면, Clover Taxis가 그대로 유지할 계획인 것은 무엇인가?
(A) 택시 기사 수
(B) 차량 외관
(C) 서비스 이용 가격
(D) 텔레비전 기술

해설 세부 사항
Clover Taxis는 새로운 택시에도 겉에 똑같은 색깔의 페인트를 입힐 것이라고 했으므로 (B)가 정답이다.

패러프레이징 the outside → exterior appearance

어휘 vehicle 차량 exterior 외부의 appearance 겉모습, 외양

180. Hagai 씨에 대해 암시된 것은 무엇인가?
(A) 자신의 제안의 일부를 거절당했다.
(B) 전에 택시 기사였다.
(C) 업체의 경쟁사를 조사할 것이다.
(D) Baxter 씨와 함께 차량 몇 대를 점검했다.

해설 두 지문 연계_추론/암시
이메일에서 발신인인 Phoebe Hagai가 한 말을 확인하면, Phoebe Hagai는 승합차 구입을 고려해야 한다고 했으나, 기사에서는 보통 크기의 전기 자동차를 구입할 자금을 확보했다고 했을 뿐,

승합차 구입에 대한 언급은 없다. 따라서 Phoebe Hagai의 제안 내용 중 일부가 거절되었음을 유추할 수 있으므로 (A)가 정답이다.

181-185 이메일 & 이메일

수신: Houghton 은행 직원
발신: Fen Lang
날짜: 10월 4일
제목: 직원 유니폼

직원들께:

11월 1일, Houghton 은행의 유니폼이 ¹⁸²ᴬ현재의 연회색 유니폼에서 짙은 감색으로 바뀌게 됩니다. ¹⁸²ᴰ그렇더라도 소재는 여전히 여러분에게 익숙한 가벼운 면이 될 것입니다. ¹⁸¹우리는 직원들이 필요한 물품을 직접 주문하도록 Uniworld Supplies와 협정을 맺었습니다. 그렇게 하기 위해서는 www.uniworldsupplies.com을 방문하셔서 우리 은행의 여섯 자리 코드인 856227을 입력하시면 주문 페이지로 이동합니다. 이용할 수 있는 네 가지 옵션이 있습니다:

세트 1: 긴팔 셔츠, 바지
¹⁸³⁻²세트 2: 반팔 셔츠, 바지, 카디건
세트 3: 긴팔 셔츠, 스커트
세트 4: 반팔 셔츠, 스커트, 카디건

¹⁸⁵⁻¹각각의 세트의 가격은 100달러이며, 은행에서 여러분의 계정으로 100달러를 입금할 것입니다. 이 한도 이상은 여러분이 사비로 유니폼을 주문하실 수 있습니다. ¹⁸²ᶜ배송은 최대 5일이 걸릴 수 있으므로 10월 26일까지 주문하도록 하십시오.

Fen Lang

어휘 lightweight 가벼운, 경량의 be used to ~에 익숙하다 make arrangements with ~와 협정을 맺다 directly 직접 input 입력하다 available 이용할 수 있는 sleeve 소매 trousers 바지 cardigan 카디건 credit 입금하다 account 계정, 계좌 at one's own expense 사비로

수신: Chelsea Moss 〈moss.c@houghtonbank.com〉
발신: Uniworld Supplies 〈orders@uniworldsupplies.com〉
날짜: 10월 20일
제목: 주문 번호 045935

Moss 씨,

귀하의 거래에 감사드립니다! 유감스럽게도 현재 저희는 귀하가 요청하신 대로 ¹⁸⁵⁻²완전한 두 세트를 보내 드릴 수 없습니다. ¹⁸³⁻¹저희는 완전한 세트의 일부인 반팔 셔츠 두 벌과 바지 두 벌을 발송했습니다. ¹⁸⁴주문하신 나머지 상품은 재입고되는 대로 발송됩니다. 이로 인해 불편을 끼쳐 드려 죄송합니다.

Uniworld Supplies 팀

어휘 unfortunately 유감스럽게도 request 요청하다 remainder 나머지 ship 발송하다 in stock 재고가 있는 inconvenience 불편 cause 일으키다, 야기하다

181. Lang 씨에 따르면, 직원들이 직원 유니폼을 주문할 때 해야 하는 일은 무엇인가?
(A) 은행의 우편 주소 사용하기
(B) 환급을 위해 영수증을 보관하기
(C) 회사 코드 입력하기
(D) 상사의 승인 받기

해설 세부 사항
Fen Lang이 발신인인 첫 번째 이메일을 검색하면, 직원들은 유니폼을 주문할 때 웹 사이트를 방문하여 여섯 자리 코드를 입력해야 한다고 했으므로 (C)가 정답이다.

패러프레이징 input the six-digit code for our bank → Input a company code

182. Houghton 은행 유니폼에 대해 사실이 아닌 것은 무엇인가?
(A) 이전과 색상이 달라질 것이다.
(B) 최소 세 벌로 구성된다.
(C) 도착하는 데 5일이 걸릴 수도 있다.
(D) 가벼운 천으로 만들어진다.

해설 NOT/True
uniforms를 키워드로 지문을 검색하면, Houghton 은행 유니폼은 연회색에서 짙은 감색으로 바뀔 것이고, 배송이 최대 5일이 걸릴 수 있으며, 가벼운 면으로 만들어진다고 했다. 옵션을 보면 Set 1, 3은 두 벌로 구성되어 있으므로 최소 세 벌이라고 한 (B)는 사실이 아니다. 따라서 (B)가 정답이다.

183. Moss 씨가 주문했을 것 같은 옵션은 무엇인가?
(A) 세트 1
(B) 세트 2
(C) 세트 3
(D) 세트 4

해설 두 지문 연계_추론/암시
두 번째 이메일에서 Uniworld Supplies는 Chelsea Moss에게 세트의 일부인 반팔 셔츠와 바지를 발송했다고 했으며, 나머지 상품은 재입고되는대로 발송하겠다고 했다. 첫 번째 이메일에서 반팔 셔츠와 바지가 포함된 것은 Set 2이므로 (B)가 정답이다.

184. 두 번째 이메일의 목적은 무엇인가?
(A) 지연을 알리기 위해
(B) 새로운 물품을 소개하기 위해
(C) 지불을 확인하기 위해
(D) 환불을 제공하기 위해

해설 주제/목적
주문한 물품의 일부 발송 사실과, 나머지 물품은 재입고되는 대로 발송된다고 알리는 것이 이메일의 목적이므로 정답은 (A)이다.

185. Moss 씨에 대해 암시된 것은 무엇인가?
(A) 물품의 손상을 발견했다.
(B) 사이즈를 잘못 주문했다.
(C) 주문품의 일부에 대해 돈을 낼 것이다.
(D) 환불을 요청해야 한다.

해설 두 지문 연계_추론/암시
첫 번째 이메일에서 100달러 한도 이상의 유니폼은 사비로 주문할 수 있다고 했다. 두 번째 이메일에서 Chelsea Moss는 두 세트를

주문했음을 알 수 있으므로 1개 세트에 대해 개인적으로 비용을 지불할 것이다. 따라서 (C)가 정답이다.

186-190 기사 & 웹페이지 & 이메일

에드먼턴 (1월 16일)—[186]에드먼턴에 기반을 둔 Hartland Design Institute(HDI)가 이제 새로운 소유주를 맞게 되었다. 이 기관은 Albright International에 매각되었다. 회사의 대변인인 Luan Melo 씨는 어제 언론 브리핑에서 이 사실을 확인해 주었다. "우리는 학생들이 진로 목표를 달성하는 데 도움이 되는 강좌를 운영하는 기회를 갖게 되어 기쁩니다. [187]지난 몇 년 동안 디자인 업계 내 경쟁이 크게 증가했기 때문에 디자이너들은 많은 사람들 사이에서 두각을 보일 수 있는 기술을 갖추는 것이 필수적입니다."라고 Melo 씨는 말했다.

그러한 변화에도 불구하고, 수업 일정에는 차질이 없을 것이며, 교수진은 대체로 그대로 유지될 것이다. [188-1]학생들이 기대하는 한 가지 개선점은 6월에 온라인 수업을 추가한다는 계획이다.

최신 정보를 원하면 www.hartlanddesign.ca를 방문하면 된다.

어휘 institute 전문 교육 기관, 협회 based in ~에 기반을 둔 ownership 소유(권) spokesperson 대변인 confirm 확인해 주다 operate 운영하다 achieve 성취하다, 이루다 competition 경쟁 industry 업계, 산업 significantly 크게, 상당히 essential 필수적 equip 갖추다 stand out 두드러지다 despite ~에도 불구하고(= in spite of) interruption 방해, 중단 faculty 교수진 improvement 개선점

| 홈 | 등록 | 교수진 | 연락처 |

Hartland Design Institute (HDI)

[188-2]3월 10일부터 시작되는 봄 학기 등록이 이제 시작되었습니다! 강좌는 선착순으로 수강할 수 있으므로 조기 등록을 추천합니다. 전체 강좌 목록은 아래를 참조하십시오. 강좌 설명을 읽고 강좌 시간을 보시려면 MORE DETAILS를 클릭하세요. 수업료 10%에 해당하는 보증금을 등록 시 납부하셔야 합니다. 나머지는 강좌 첫날까지 내셔야 합니다.

B048 제품 포장
강사: Lucio Napolitano   MORE DETAILS
G051 [188-2][189] 고급 광고 디자인 *
강사: Oliva Baldwin   MORE DETAILS
G052 [188-2][189] 고급 광고 디자인 *
강사: Saita Heida   MORE DETAILS
P115 [190-2]로고 디자인 (인증 획득)
강사: Wyatt Dobson   MORE DETAILS
T236 [189]Skyrock Illustrator (인증 획득)
강사: Antoine Yates   MORE DETAILS
T237 [189]Skyrock Illustrator (인증 획득)
강사: Delmina Greco   MORE DETAILS
[188-2] * 온라인 강좌

어휘 register 등록; 등록하다 contact 연락; 연락하다 enrollment 등록 term 학기, 용어, 말 on a first-come, first-served basis 선착순으로 description 설명 deposit 보증금 due (돈을) 지불해야 하는 instructor 강사 advanced 고급의 certification 증명, 인증

수신: <contact@hartlanddesign.ca>
발신: <rcuomo@bealsmail.ca>
제목: 메시지
날짜: 3월 26일

Hartland Design Institute 귀하,

저는 귀사의 이메일 시스템에 발생한 오류를 알려 드리고자 합니다. 저는 현재 귀 기관에서 수업을 듣고 있지만, 업무가 겹쳐서 3월 30일에 참석하지 못할 것입니다. [190-1]저는 제 강사인 Wyatt Dobson 씨에게 이메일을 보내려고 했지만, 제 이메일이 전달되지 못했다는 자동 메시지를 받았습니다. 제가 수업에 참석하지 못할 것이라는 것과 다른 학생들도 그와 연락하는 데 어려움을 겪고 있을 수 있다는 것을 Dobson 씨에게 주지시켜 주시겠어요?

감사합니다.

[190-1]Rosa Cuomo

어휘 be in attendance 참석하다 due to ~ 때문에 conflict 갈등, 상충

186. 기사의 주된 내용은 무엇인가?
(A) 업계의 현재 경향
(B) 에드먼턴에서의 사업 기회
(C) 교육 기관의 매각
(D) 기관의 이전

해설 주제/목적
주제/목적은 지문의 앞부분에 나오며, 다중 지문의 첫 번째 문제의 단서는 첫 번째 지문에 나오는 편이다. 기사 초반에 HDI가 Albright International에 매각된 사실을 밝히고 있으므로 (C)가 정답이다.

패러프레이징 under new ownership, The institute was sold → The sale of an educational institution

187. 기사에서 Melo 씨가 시사하는 것은 무엇인가?
(A) 한 분야의 경쟁이 더 치열해지고 있다.
(B) 지역의 임금이 오르고 있다.
(C) 강좌의 인기가 높아지고 있다.
(D) 기업들이 요구 사항을 바꾸고 있다.

해설 NOT/True
기사에서 Melo 씨의 말을 인용한 부분을 보면, 디자인 업계 내 경쟁이 크게 증가했다는 말을 하고 있으므로 (A)가 정답이다.

패러프레이징 Competition within the design industry has increased significantly → A field is becoming more competitive

188. HDI에 대해 암시된 것은 무엇인가?
(A) 예상보다 빨리 온라인 수업을 제공한다.
(B) 개원이 지연되었다.

(C) 조기 등록하는 학생들에게 할인을 제공한다.
(D) 봄 학기에 더 많은 수업을 추가할지도 모른다.

해설 두 지문 연계_추론/암시
기사 지문의 후반부에 6월에 온라인 수업 추가 계획이 있다고 했고, 웹페이지에서는 3월 10일부터 시작되는 봄 학기에 몇 개의 온라인 강좌가 있음을 알 수 있다. 이를 통해 HDI는 기존의 계획보다 빨리 온라인 수업을 제공하고 있음을 유추할 수 있으므로 (A)가 정답이다.

189. 웹페이지에 따르면, HDI의 강좌에 대해 사실인 것은 무엇인가?
(A) 모두 마지막에 인증서를 제공한다.
(B) 새로운 학생들을 위한 공간이 없다.
(C) 어떤 강좌는 같은 강사가 가르친다.
(D) 어떤 강좌는 한 학기에 두 번 이상 제공된다.

해설 NOT/True
웹페이지 지문의 수업 목록에서 고급 광고 디자인과 Skyrock Illustrator는 2개씩 개설되어 있으므로 (D)가 정답이다.

190. Cuomo 씨에 대해 암시된 것은 무엇인가?
(A) HDI에서 다른 강좌를 수료했다.
(B) 원격으로 수업을 듣고 있다.
(C) HDI에서 일자리를 원한다.
(D) 로고 디자인에 관심이 있다.

해설 두 지문 연계_추론/암시
Rosa Cuomo가 쓴 이메일에서 그녀가 수강하는 강좌의 강사가 Wyatt Dobson임을 알 수 있는데, 웹페이지를 검색하면 Wyatt Dobson은 로고 디자인 강사이므로 Rosa Cuomo는 로고 디자인 강좌를 수강한다는 것을 알 수 있다. 그러므로 (D)가 정답이다.

191-195 청구서 & 이메일 & 이메일

Emerald Landscaping
굿원 로 2478번지
포트 로더데일, 플로리다 33311
www.emeraldlandscaping.net

날짜: 9월 1일   청구서 번호: 06581
고객: Ridenour Consulting   대표자: Shirley Lusk
전화: 555-5781
이메일: luskshirley@ridenourconsulting.com

날짜	서비스 내역	요금
8월 3일	잔디 깎기 (¹⁹¹클라크스빌 지점)	850달러
	잔디 깎기 (¹⁹¹심슨 지점)	600달러
	¹⁹⁵⁻²비료 처리 (클라크스빌 지점)	200달러
8월 13일	잔디 깎기 (클라크스빌 지점)	850달러
	잔디 깎기 (심슨 지점)	600달러
	¹⁹²⁻²라일락 덤불 심기 (클라크스빌 지점)	550달러
8월 23일	잔디 깎기 (클라크스빌 지점)	850달러
	잔디 깎기 (심슨 지점)	600달러
	나무 손질 (심슨 지점)	1200달러
	소계:	6300달러
	계정 잔고:	350달러
	미지불액:	5950달러

어휘 landscaping 조경   invoice 청구서, 송장   representative 대표   fertilizer 비료   treatment 처리, 처치   subtotal 소계   balance due 미지불액, 지불해야 할 돈

¹⁹²⁻¹발신: Shirley Lusk 〈luskshirley@ridenourconsulting.com〉
수신: Emerald Landscaping 〈contact@emeraldlandscaping.net〉
날짜: 9월 3일
제목: 8월 서비스

Emerald Landscaping 귀하,

저는 귀사에서 Ridenour Consulting에 보낸 가장 최근 청구서에 오류가 있음을 알리고자 합니다. ¹⁹²⁻¹우리는 지난달에 라일락 덤불을 심기로 계획했지만, 이 일은 전혀 실행되지 않았습니다. 하지만 저희가 어제 받은 청구서를 살펴보니 이 서비스에 대한 요금이 적혀 있었습니다. 계산서에서 이 요금을 제외하고 가급적 빨리 갱신된 청구서를 보내 주십시오. 우리는 그 후에 즉시 지불을 할 수 있을 것입니다.

감사합니다.

Shirley Lusk
Ridenour Consulting

어휘 carry out 실행하다   charge 요금   at one's earliest convenience 가급적 빨리

¹⁹³ ¹⁹⁴발신: Alan Gilliam 〈agilliam@emeraldlandscaping.net〉
수신: Shirley Lusk 〈luskshirley@ridenourconsulting.com〉
날짜: 9월 4일
제목: 귀하의 Emerald Landscaping 문의 사항
첨부 파일: 청구서_06581_수정

Lusk 씨,

어제 귀하의 가장 최근 계산서와 관련된 문제에 대해 저희에게 이메일을 보내 주셔서 감사합니다. ¹⁹³회계부서를 대표하여 이번 실수에 대해 죄송하다는 말씀을 드리고 싶습니다. ¹⁹⁴평소에 라일락 덤불을 공급하는 업체가 갑자기 폐업하여 귀하께서 요청하신 덤불을 심지 못했다는 것을 작업반장으로부터 확인했습니다. 만약 귀하께서 향후 서비스를 다시 예약하기를 원하신다면, 새로운 공급업체 덕분에 언제든지 그 작업을 해드릴 수 있습니다.

수정된 청구서를 첨부했습니다. ¹⁹⁵⁻¹사과의 의미로, 귀하께서 8월에 받았던 것과 같은 무료 비료 처리를 제공해 드리고자 합니다. 이것은 3개월에 한 번 권장되는 사항이기 때문에 11월로 예정될 것입니다.

귀하의 이해와 성원에 감사드립니다.

Alan Gilliam

어휘 inquiry 문의 regarding ~에 관하여 on behalf of ~을 대표[대신]하여 go out of business 폐업하다 rebook 다시 예약하다 amend 수정하다 by way of ~의 수단[방법]으로써 apology 사과 patronage 애용, 후원

191. 청구서에서 Ridenour Consulting에 대해 시사된 것은 무엇인가?
(A) 8월에 쿠폰을 사용했다.
(B) 지점이 두 곳 이상이다.
(C) 일주일에 한 번 잔디 깎기 서비스를 이용한다.
(D) 나무를 제거해 달라고 요청했다.

해설 NOT/True 문제
Ridenour Consulting에 제공한 청구서의 서비스 내역에 클라크스빌 지점과 힉슨 지점이 나와 있으므로 Ridenour Consulting은 두 곳 이상의 지점이 있음을 알 수 있다. 따라서 (B)가 정답이다. 잔디 깎기 서비스는 10일 간격으로 이용했으므로 (C)는 오답이다.

192. Lusk 씨는 자신이 얼마나 더 청구 받았다고 생각하는가?
(A) 350달러
(B) 550달러
(C) 600달러
(D) 850달러

해설 두 지문 연계_세부 사항
Lusk를 키워드로 지문을 검색하면, 두 번째 지문의 발신인인 Shirley Lusk는 라일락 덤불을 심지 않았는데 이에 대한 요금이 청구되었다고 했다. 청구서에서 라일락 덤불 심기를 검색하면 그에 대한 요금은 550달러이므로 (B)가 정답이다.

193. Gilliam 씨의 직업은 무엇이겠는가?
(A) 수리 기사
(B) 작업반장
(C) 회계 담당자
(D) 운전기사

해설 추론/암시
Alan Gilliam이 보낸 이메일에서 회계부서를 대표하여 사과한다고 했으므로, 그는 회계부서에서 일하는 것을 알 수 있다. 따라서 (C)가 정답이다.

194. Gilliam 씨에 따르면, 서비스에 문제를 일으킨 것은 무엇인가?
(A) 악천후
(B) 장비 고장
(C) 예기치 않은 폐업
(D) 직원 일정 문제

해설 세부 사항
Gilliam을 키워드로 지문을 검색하면, 세 번째 지문의 발신인인 Alan Gilliam은 라일락 덤불 공급업체의 폐업으로 인해 서비스에 문제가 생겼음을 알리고 있으므로 (C)가 정답이다.

패러프레이징 our usual supplier of lilac bushes suddenly went out of business → An unexpected business closure

195. Lusk 씨에 대해 암시된 것은 무엇인가?
(A) 그녀의 이메일에 대한 답장을 당일에 받았다.
(B) 잔디에 비료를 더 자주 줘야 한다는 조언을 받았다.
(C) Emerald Landscaping과의 계약이 11월에 만료된다.
(D) 그녀의 회사는 200달러 상당의 무료 서비스를 받을 것이다.

해설 두 지문 연계_추론/암시
Alan Gilliam이 보낸 이메일에서 그는 사과의 의미로 Shirley Lusk가 8월에 받았던 비료 처리 서비스를 무료로 제공하겠다고 했는데, 청구서에서 해당 서비스를 찾아보면 비용이 200달러이므로 Shirley Lusk의 회사는 200달러에 해당하는 서비스를 무료로 받을 것임을 유추할 수 있다. 따라서 (D)가 정답이다.

패러프레이징 free fertilizer treatment → free service

196-200 목록 & 이메일 & 후기

부동산 목록: 호숫가 산장, 건축 중
[196] 위치: Swan Estates (바셀 호수 북쪽)
연락처: Frank Clements, 555-4701

Swan Estates에서 휴식을 취하면서 호숫가의 삶을 즐기세요! 저희 호화로운 산장은 여름에는 호수에서 활동을 즐기고 [196] 겨울에는 근처에 있는 Hickory Hills 리조트에서 스키를 탈 수 있어 연중 휴가에 안성맞춤입니다.

Violet과 Sage 모델에는 보트 전용 개인 부두가 있습니다. Marigold 모델은 참나무 바닥과 대리석 조리대를 특징으로 합니다. [197] Lily 모델에는 놀이터 기구를 설치할 공간이 있는 넓은 뒷마당이 있습니다. 옵션 중 가장 작은 Iris 모델은 에너지 효율이 좋고 아늑합니다.

[197] 완공된 산장: 판매 준비 완료

산장 번호	모델 종류	침실	화장실
4A	Violet	4개	2개
8B	Sage	3개	2개
[199-2] 15A	Marigold	2개	2개
18D	Iris	2개	1개

어휘 property 부동산, 건물 cabin 산장, 오두막 construction 건설, 공사 in progress 진행 중인 location 위치, 장소 estate (저택이 있는 대규모) 사유지, 토지 luxury 호화로운 year-round 연중 내내 activity 활동 include 포함하다 private 개인의 dock 부두 feature ~의 특징을 이루다 flooring 바닥 granite 대리석, 화강암 countertop 주방용 조리대 spacious 넓은

수신: Karl Reynolds 〈karl@swanestates.com〉
[198] 발신: Hannah Baek 〈baekh@barrington1.com〉
날짜: 4월 4일
제목: 호숫가 산장

Reynolds 씨,

[198A] 저희 오빠가 최근에 Swan Estates 산장을 구입했는데 훌륭하다고 해서 저도 하나 구입하고 싶습니다. [198D] 저는 그 지역에서 꽤 먼 곳에 살고 있기 때문에, 둘러보러 가기 전에 구입 가능 여부를 확인하고 싶습니다. [198C] [199-1] 휴가 때에만 산장을 사용할

계획이라 침실 두 개면 충분할 것입니다. 그래도 화장실이 두 개 있는 게 더 편할 것 같아서 두 개의 화장실이 있는 걸 선호합니다. ²⁰⁰⁻¹저는 이번 주 금요일이나 토요일인 4월 8일이나 9일, 또는 다음 주말 토요일이나 일요일인 4월 16일이나 17일에 산장을 둘러볼 수 있습니다. 이 이메일 주소로 제게 연락하시면 됩니다.

대단히 고맙습니다.

Hannah Baek

어휘 availability 이용 가능성, 구입 여부 convenient 편리한

부동산 후기: Swan Estates

저는 Swan Estates의 산장을 구입했고, 처음부터 끝까지 그 과정에 만족했습니다. Karl Reynolds 씨는 우리에게 몇 개의 다른 산장을 둘러보게 해 주셨고, 우리의 모든 질문에 대답해 주셨습니다. 산장 자체는 잘 지어졌고 아름다운 환경에 위치해 있습니다. ²⁰⁰⁻²딱 한 가지 구매자들이 유의해야 할 것은, 평일에만 둘러볼 수 있다는 것입니다. 이 점은 산장을 방문하려고 직장에 휴가를 내고 싶지 않은 사람들에게는 어려울 수 있습니다.

Hannah Baek

어휘 process 과정 from start to finish 처음부터 마지막까지 situate 위치시키다 setting 환경 note 주의하다

196. Swan Estates에 대해 사실인 것은 무엇인가?
(A) 거주자를 위한 보트 대여를 포함한다.
(B) 아직 방문객들에게 개방되지 않았다.
(C) 공원이 내려다보인다.
(D) 스키 리조트 근처에 있다.

해설 NOT/True
Swan Estates를 키워드로 지문을 검색하면, 첫 번째 지문에서 겨울에는 근처에 있는 Hickory Hills 리조트에서 스키를 탈 수 있다고 했으므로 (D)가 정답이다.

패러프레이징 ski at nearby Hickory Hills Resort → near a ski resort

197. 아직 건축 중인 Swan Estates 산장의 종류는 무엇인가?
(A) Sage
(B) Marigold
(C) Lily
(D) Iris

해설 세부 사항
첫 번째 지문인 목록에 나온 산장 모델 중, 공사가 끝나 판매 준비가 된 산장은 Violet, Sage, Marigold, Iris이며, Lily의 이름은 보이지 않으므로 (C)가 정답이다.

198. 이메일에서 Baek 씨에 대해 시사된 것은 무엇인가?
(A) 그녀의 가족 구성원이 Swan Estates를 추천했다.
(B) 그녀의 오빠는 그녀와 함께 산장에 투자할 것이다.
(C) 일 년 내내 산장을 이용할 계획이다.
(D) 바셀 호수의 다른 지역 근처에 산다.

해설 NOT/True
Baek 씨가 보낸 이메일에서 자신의 오빠가 최근에 Swan Estates 산장을 구입하고 그것이 훌륭하다고 말했다고 했으므로 (A)가 정답이다.

199. Baek 씨에게 가장 잘 맞는 Swan Estates 산장은 무엇이 겠는가?
(A) 4A
(B) 8B
(C) 15A
(D) 18D

해설 두 지문 연계_세부 사항
이메일에서 Hannah Baek은 침실 두 개에 화장실 두 개를 선호한다고 했는데, 목록에서 침실 두 개와 화장실 두 개인 모델은 Marigold로서 산장 번호는 15A이므로 (C)가 정답이다.

200. Baek 씨는 언제 산장을 둘러보았겠는가?
(A) 4월 8일
(B) 4월 9일
(C) 4월 16일
(D) 4월 17일

해설 두 지문 연계_추론/암시
이메일에서 Hannah Baek은 이번 주 금요일이나 토요일, 또는 다음 주 토요일이나 일요일에 산장을 둘러볼 수 있다고 했는데, 후기에서 산장은 평일에만 둘러볼 수 있다고 했다. 따라서 Hannah Baek은 금요일인 4월 8일에 산장을 둘러보았을 것으로 유추할 수 있으므로 (A)가 정답이다.

실전 모의고사 3회				본문 p.350
101. (C)	102. (A)	103. (A)	104. (D)	105. (B)
106. (B)	107. (C)	108. (A)	109. (C)	110. (A)
111. (C)	112. (A)	113. (A)	114. (C)	115. (D)
116. (B)	117. (B)	118. (B)	119. (A)	120. (B)
121. (C)	122. (C)	123. (C)	124. (B)	125. (D)
126. (B)	127. (C)	128. (C)	129. (C)	130. (D)
131. (A)	132. (C)	133. (C)	134. (B)	135. (A)
136. (C)	137. (C)	138. (C)	139. (C)	140. (A)
141. (D)	142. (C)	143. (D)	144. (C)	145. (C)
146. (A)	147. (C)	148. (A)	149. (B)	150. (C)
151. (D)	152. (C)	153. (D)	154. (C)	155. (A)
156. (B)	157. (D)	158. (C)	159. (C)	160. (C)
161. (D)	162. (A)	163. (D)	164. (C)	165. (C)
166. (C)	167. (C)	168. (C)	169. (A)	170. (C)
171. (D)	172. (C)	173. (D)	174. (A)	175. (B)
176. (C)	177. (C)	178. (C)	179. (B)	180. (A)
181. (D)	182. (A)	183. (D)	184. (A)	185. (B)
186. (A)	187. (B)	188. (C)	189. (D)	190. (B)
191. (D)	192. (D)	193. (C)	194. (C)	195. (B)
196. (C)	197. (B)	198. (A)	199. (D)	200. (B)

101. 형용사 any
해석 Peacock 씨는 경기장 밖에서 어떤 주차 공간도 찾을 수 없었다.
(A) 다른 것들 (B) 그것의 (C) 무슨, 어떤 (D) 아무도
해설 빈칸은 parking spots를 수식하는 형용사 자리이며 부정문을 만드는 unable이 있으므로 부정형용사인 (C)가 정답이다.
어휘 parking spot 주차 공간   stadium 경기장

102. 동사 어휘 promote
해석 광고판은 주요 고속도로 근처에 위치한 식당을 홍보하는 좋은 방법이다.
(A) 홍보하다 (B) 기념하다 (C) 줄이다 (D) 할인하다
어휘 billboard (옥외) 광고판   located ~에 위치한   highway 고속도로

103. 동사 자리
해석 보통의 포레스트 빌 주민은 매년 도서관에서 세 권의 책을 빌린다.
해설 빈칸은 주어인 The average Forest Ville resident 뒤에 오는 동사 자리이므로 현재 시제의 동사 형태인 (A)가 정답이다.
어휘 average 평균의, 보통의   resident 거주자, 주민   borrow 빌리다   each year 매년

104. 명사 자리
해석 Lawrence 주식회사의 주식 분석 보고서는 단편 소설에 해당하는 길이이다.
해설 빈칸은 주격 보어 역할을 하면서 빈칸 뒤의 전치사구 of a short novel의 수식을 받는 명사 자리이므로 명사인 (D)가 정답이다.
어휘 stock 주식, 재고(품)   analysis 분석   length 길이   short novel 단편 소설

105. 부사 어휘 always
해석 위대한 정치가들은 항상 유권자들의 말에 귀를 기울이고 그들에게 가장 최선인 것을 하려고 노력한다.
(A) 다음에 (B) 항상 (C) ~하는 동안 (D) ~을 포함하여
해설 빈칸은 뒤의 동사 listen을 수식하기에 적합한 부사가 들어갈 자리이다. 위대한 정치가들의 특성을 묘사하는 문장이므로 유권자들의 말에 '항상' 귀를 기울인다는 내용이 되어야 자연스럽다. 따라서 (B)가 정답이다.
어휘 politician 정치가   voter 유권자, 투표자

106. 형용사 어휘 experienced
해석 가장 경험이 풍부한 지원자들만이 면접을 볼 기회를 가질 것이다.
(A) 빈번한 (B) 경험이 풍부한 (C) 닫힌 (D) 재정 지원을 받는
어휘 candidate 후보자, 지원자   chance 기회, 가능성   interview 면접을 보다, 인터뷰를 하다

107. 명사 어휘 indication
해석 빨간색 배터리 아이콘은 휴대폰을 충전해야 한다는 것을 나타내는 표시이다.
(A) 허용 (B) 접근성 (C) 표시 (D) 예시
어휘 icon (컴퓨터) 아이콘   charge 충전하다

108. 부정대명사 each
각각의 팀이 부여받은 과제를 제시간에 완수한다면 프로젝트는 성공할 것이다.
(A) 각자 (B) 둘 다 (C) 누군가 (D) 모든 것
해설 빈칸은 부사절의 주어인 team을 수식하고 있으므로, 단수 명사를 수식할 수 있는 한정사 each가 정답이다. (B)는 뒤에 복수 명사가 와야 하므로 오답이다. '누군가'를 의미하는 부정대명사 (C)와 '모든 것'을 의미하는 부정대명사 (D) 또한 오답이다.
어휘 assign 배정하다   task 과제   on time 제시간에

109. 전치사 to
해석 새 소프트웨어에 문제가 있는 직원은 IT 부서에 말씀하세요.
(A) 가까이에 (B) ~의 옆에 (C) ~에게 (D) ~에서
해설 문맥에 알맞은 전치사를 고르는 문제이다. 빈칸에는 앞의 동사 speak과 함께 speak to로 쓰여 '~에게 말을 하다'라는 의미를 나타내는 to가 들어가는 것이 알맞다. 따라서 (C)가 정답이다.
어휘 issue 문제, 사안   department 부서

110. 형용사 자리 [형용사+명사]
해석 Molly's Candles는 다른 양초 제조업체들과 차별화되는 독특한 향을 가진 제품들을 판매한다.
해설 전치사 with의 목적어로 쓰인 명사 scents를 수식할 수 있는 것은 형용사이므로 (A)가 정답이다.
어휘 distinct 뚜렷한, 독특한   scent 향기   set ~ apart from ~을 …와 차별화하다

125

111. 동사 어휘 support
해석 그 대학의 학장들은 학생들을 최대한 지원하기 위해 오리엔테이션에 참석할 것이다.
(A) 상상하다 (B) 상호 작용하다 (C) 지원하다 (D) 상의하다
어휘 dean (대학의) 학장 as best one can 할 수 있는 데까지, 최선을 다하여

112. 부사 자리 [형용사 수식]
해석 PK Realtors는 지역의 다른 부동산 중개업자에 비해 상대적으로 수수료가 저렴하다.
해설 빈칸 없이도 문장이 완전하므로 빈칸은 빈칸 뒤의 형용사 cheaper를 수식하는 부사 자리이다. 따라서 부사인 (A)가 정답이다.
어휘 realtor 부동산업자 comparatively 비교적, 상대적으로 commission 수수료 rate 비율

113. 명사 어휘 workshop
해석 그린빌 시 의회는 사업 확장을 노리는 소기업들을 위한 무료 워크숍을 개최할 것이다.
(A) 워크숍 (B) 표 (C) 정책 (D) 발표
어휘 city council 시 의회 host 개최하다 expand 확장하다

114. 형용사 자리 [형용사＋명사]
해석 Hermes's Restaurant는 훌륭한 서비스와 아주 맛있는 요리로 유명하다.
해설 빈칸은 소유격 its와 명사 service 사이이므로 뒤의 명사 service를 수식하는 형용사 자리이다. 따라서 형용사인 (C)가 정답이다.
어휘 be known for ~으로 유명하다, ~으로 알려져 있다 delectable 아주 맛있는 cuisine 요리

115. 동사 어휘 circle
해석 추수 감사절 퍼레이드는 다음 주 목요일에 마을 전체를 두 바퀴 돌 것이다.
(A) 뛰어오르다 (B) 거닐다 (C) 절뚝거리다 (D) 돌다, 선회하다
해설 빈칸 뒤 around와 어울려 circle around(~의 둘레를 돌다)로 쓰이는 (D)가 정답이다. 문맥상으로도 마을 전체를 두 바퀴 '돌 것이다'라고 하는 것이 가장 적절하다.
어휘 Thanksgiving Day 추수 감사절 parade 퍼레이드, 가두 행진

116. 부사 어휘 already
해석 오전 10시밖에 안 되었지만, Hardy Bakery는 이미 그날 판매할 신선한 빵이 다 팔려 나갔다.
(A) 곧 (B) 이미 (C) 자주 (D) 결코 ~않다
어휘 even though 비록 ~이지만 sell out of ~을 다 팔아버리다

117. 동사 자리＋수동태
해석 그 아파트 건물은 2년 전에 철거된 이후 버려져 있다.
해설 빈칸 앞의 it은 앞에 나온 The apartment building을 대신하는 대명사로, 빈칸은 동사 자리이다. 빈칸 뒤에 타동사 demolish의 목적어가 없고, 문맥상으로도 아파트는 '철거되는' 대상이므로 수동태인 (B)가 정답이다.
어휘 abandon 버리다 demolish 철거하다, 파괴하다

118. 형용사 어휘 unknown
해석 무슨 이유인지 모르지만, 고객들은 보통 크기의 지갑보다 소형 지갑을 선호하는 것 같았다.
(A) 정확한 (B) 알려지지 않은 (C) 부정확한 (D) 흥미진진한
어휘 prefer A to B B보다 A를 선호하다 purse 지갑

119. 부사 자리 [동사 수식]
해석 난방기의 온도 설정은 기기 전면의 버튼을 이용해 쉽게 조절할 수 있다.
해설 빈칸을 제외해도 문장이 완전하므로 빈칸은 동사 adjusted를 수식하는 부사 자리이므로 (A)가 정답이다.
어휘 temperature 온도 setting 설정 adjust 조절하다, 조정하다

120. 접속사 vs. 부사
해석 이 한정판 레코드는 사인이 들어간 포스터와 사진집이 함께 제공된다.
(A) 다음에 (B) ~와 (C) ~ 이후로 (D) ~와 함께
해설 빈칸 앞뒤로 두 개의 명사구인 a signed poster와 a photo book이 이어지고 있으므로, 빈칸에는 구와 구를 대등하게 연결하는 등위 접속사인 (B)가 들어가야 한다.
어휘 limited edition 한정판 vinyl record 레코드, 음반 come with ~이 함께 딸려 나오다

121. 형용사 자리
해석 프로젝트 관리자에게 있어 고객 불만을 적절히 처리하는 것은 매우 중요하다.
해설 전치사 of의 목적어로 쓰인 명사 importance를 수식할 수 있는 것은 형용사이므로, 빈칸 앞 전치사 of, 빈칸 뒤 명사 importance와 함께 어울려 of critical importance(아주 중요한)로 쓰이는 (C)가 정답이다.
어휘 properly 적절히 address 처리하다 complaint 불만

122. 부사 어휘 fondly
해석 Bennett 씨의 팀원들은 그의 은퇴 기념 만찬에서 즐거웠던 추억을 나눌 때 그에 대해 호의적으로 말했다.
(A) 거의 ~하지 않다 (B) 모호하게 (C) 애정을 가지고 (D) 단호하게
해설 speak fondly of는 '~에 대해 호의적으로[좋게] 말하다'라는 뜻이다.
어휘 share 나누다, 공유하다 retirement 은퇴, 퇴직

123. 형용사 자리 [the＋형용사의 최상급]
해석 Groover Tech의 새로운 스마트폰은 그 회사가 지금까지 작업한 것 중 가장 비밀스러운 프로젝트이다.
해설 빈칸 앞에 the와 연결될 수 있으려면 명사인 (A)나 형용사의 최상급인 (C)가 가능하다. (A)는 '스마트폰이 비밀주의이다'라는 뜻

이 되므로 의미상 적절하지 않다. 따라서 의미상으로도 어울리는 (C)가 정답이다.

어휘 secretive 비밀스러운 work on 작업하다 so far 지금까지

124. 형용사 자리 [주격 보어]
해석 대부분의 구매자들은 올해 SuperSwim의 수영복 상품에 관심이 있는 것 같다.

해설 빈칸은 주어인 Most buyers의 상태를 보충 설명하는 주격 보어 자리로, 문장의 동사인 seem은 〈seem+형용사〉로 쓰여 '~ 인 것 같다'라는 의미를 나타낼 수 있으므로 빈칸에는 형용사가 들어가야 한다. 또한, 빈칸 뒤의 전치사 in과 함께 어울려야 하므로 interested in(~에 관심이 있는)의 형태로 쓰이는 (B)가 정답이다.

어휘 buyer 구매자 seem ~인 것 같다, ~인 것처럼 보이다 bathing suit 수영복 option 선택(권), 선택할 수 있는 것

125. 접속사 although
해석 지역 주민들은 Pete's Coffee를 즐겼지만, 그 업체는 근처에 계속 문을 여는 주요 프랜차이즈 가맹점들과 경쟁하는 데 어려움을 겪었다.

(A) 따라서 (B) ~ 때문에 (C) ~이므로 (D) 비록 ~이지만

해설 빈칸은 앞뒤의 절을 연결해 주는 접속사 자리로 선택지 중에서 접속사는 (C)와 (D)이다. 지역 주민들이 Pete's Coffee를 즐기는데 Pete's Coffee가 경쟁에서 어려움을 겪는 것은 모순된 결과이므로 양보의 접속사 (D)가 정답이다. (A)는 접속 부사이므로 절을 연결하는 역할을 할 수 없고, (B)는 구전치사이므로 뒤에 절이 올 수 없다.

어휘 local 현지인, 주민 have trouble *doing* ~하는 데 어려움을 겪다 major 주요한 franchise 프랜차이즈 nearby 근처에

126. 전치사 before
해석 면접 전에, Delgado 씨는 채용 위원회에게 이상적인 후보자로 보였다.

(A) ~하자마자 (B) ~ 전에 (C) 꼭 ~처럼 (D) 거의

해설 빈칸 뒤에 명사구(his interview)가 온 것으로 보아 빈칸은 전치사 자리이므로 (B)와 (C)가 정답 후보이다. 문맥상 '면접 전에'라는 의미가 되어야 자연스러우므로 '~ 전에'라는 뜻의 전치사 (B)가 정답이다. (A)는 접속사, (D)는 부사이므로 오답이다.

어휘 appear ~처럼 보이다 ideal 이상적인 committee 위원회

127. 접속사 vs. 전치사
해석 신중하게 점검을 한 후, 정비공은 미등을 제외하고 차의 모든 것이 제대로 작동하고 있다는 것을 알았다.

(A) 비록 ~이지만 (B) (셋 이상의) 사이에 (C) ~을 제외하고
(D) ~ 때문에

해설 문맥에 어울리는 접속사 또는 전치사를 고르는 문제이다. 빈칸 뒤에 명사구(the taillights)가 왔으므로 빈칸은 전치사 자리이다. 따라서 (B)와 (C)가 정답 후보이다. 문맥상 '미등을 제외하고 모든 것이 제대로 작동한다'라는 의미가 되어야 자연스러우므로 구전치사 (C)가 정답이다.

어휘 inspection 점검, 검사 mechanic 정비공 properly 제대로 taillight 미등

128. 부사 자리 [형용사, 분사 수식]
해석 롤러코스터 조작 담당자들은 모든 탑승객들이 좌석에 단단히 고정되도록 해야 한다.

해설 빈칸 없이도 문장이 완전하므로 빈칸은 빈칸 앞의 secured를 수식하는 부사 자리이다. 따라서 부사인 (C)가 정답이다.

어휘 operator (기계 등의) 조작자, 운영자 passenger 탑승객 secure 고정시키다 tightly 단단히, 꽉

129. 명사 자리 [형용사+명사]
해석 이 차는 시중의 다른 어떤 차도 능가하는 비할 데 없는 속도를 자랑한다.

해설 빈칸은 빈칸 뒤의 주격 관계대명사절의 선행사이면서 빈칸 앞의 형용사 unparalleled의 수식을 받는 명사 자리이다. 따라서 명사인 (A)와 (D)가 가능한데, (A) speeding은 '속도위반'이라는 뜻이므로 적절하지 않다. 문맥상으로도 의미가 적절한 (D)가 정답이다.

어휘 boast 자랑하다, 뽐내다 unparalleled 비할 데 없는 outperform 능가하다 on the market 시중에 나온

130. 구전치사 prior to
해석 비즈니스에 관한 강좌를 듣기 전에, Alfaro 씨는 어떻게 회사를 시작할지 전혀 몰랐다.

(A) ~ 다음에 (B) ~ 때문에 (C) 아직 (D) ~ 전에

해설 빈칸 뒤에 동명사구가 있으므로 빈칸에는 전치사가 와야 한다. 문맥상 '강좌를 듣기 전에'라는 의미가 되어야 알맞으므로 (D)가 정답이다.

어휘 take a course 강의를 듣다 have no idea 전혀 모르다

131-134 이메일

> 수신: 여러 수신자들
> 발신: Lovely Closet <information@lovelycloset.com>
> 제목: 모바일 앱 문제
> 날짜: 4월 28일
>
> 소중한 고객님께:
>
> 저희 Lovely Closet은 고객님들을 위한 헌신적인 서비스에 자부심을 가지고 있습니다. 저희는 최고급 의류를 가장 좋은 가격에 제공하는 데 헌신하고 있기 [131]때문에 전국 최고의 의류 쇼핑 앱입니다. 유감스럽게도, 저희는 현재 저희의 모바일 앱 관련 문제를 [132]처리하고 있습니다. [133]이용자들께서 안정적인 인터넷 환경에서도 앱을 사용하지 못하고 계십니다. 저희는 IT 부서와 이 문제를 논의했고, 그들은 그것을 고치려 노력하고 있습니다. [134]당분간은 저희 웹 사이트를 사용하여 멋진 패션을 찾고 주문하세요. 불편을 끼쳐드린 점을 사과드리며, 가능한 한 빨리 애플리케이션이 실행되도록 할 것을 약속드립니다.
>
> Pavel Lee
> Lovely Closet 최고경영자

어휘 multiple 다수의, 여러 recipient 받는 사람, 수령인 valued 소중한 consumer 소비자, 고객 pride *oneself* on ~에 대해 자부심을 느끼다 dedicated 헌신적인 be committed to ~에 헌신[전념]하다 garment 의류, 옷 deal with (문제·과제 등을) 처

리하다 at the moment 지금 discuss 논의하다 feel free to do 마음대로[거리낌 없이] ~하다 place an order 주문하다 apologize 사과하다 inconvenience 불편

131. 접속사 because
(A) ~ 때문에 (B) ~인 것처럼 (C) 그렇지만 (D) ~에도 불구하고

해설 빈칸에 알맞은 접속사를 찾는 문제로, 빈칸 앞뒤의 의미 관계를 따져 보아야 한다. 빈칸 뒤의 최고급 의류를 가장 좋은 가격에 제공하는 데 헌신적인 것은 전국 최고의 의류 쇼핑 앱이 된 이유가 되므로, '~ 때문에'라는 뜻으로 이유를 나타내는 접속사 (A)가 정답이다.

132. 동사 자리 + 현재 시제
해설 주어 we 뒤에 동사가 없으므로 빈칸은 동사 자리이다. 따라서 (B)와 (C)가 정답 후보이다. 문장 맨 뒤의 부사구 at the moment는 현재 시제와 어울려 쓰이므로, 현재진행형인 (C)가 정답이다.

133. 알맞은 문장 고르기
(A) 저희는 문제의 원인을 찾지 못하고 있는 것 같습니다.
(B) 이용자들께서 안정적인 인터넷 환경에서도 앱을 사용하지 못하고 계십니다.
(C) 이용자들은 경쟁사의 앱 디자인을 선호한다고 알렸습니다.
(D) 저희는 이 앱 작업을 한 지 이제 5년이 되었습니다.

해설 빈칸 앞에서 모바일 앱 관련 문제를 언급했고, 빈칸 뒤에서 IT 부서가 그 문제를 고치고 있다는 내용이 나오므로 빈칸에는 그 문제에 대한 구체적인 내용이 들어가야 한다. 따라서 (B)가 정답이다.

어휘 source 근원, 원천 stable 안정적인

134. 부사 어휘 for now
(A) 그렇지 않으면 (B) 당분간은 (C) 마찬가지로 (D) 결국

135-138 안내문

> Gizo Technology는 이제 자사 전자제품이 구입일로부터 최소 3년 동안 135새것처럼 잘 작동할 것을 보장합니다. 136이 새로운 보증은 저희의 예전 품질 보증에 2년을 추가한 것입니다. 이 보증은 Gizo Technology의 매장, 공인 137대리점, 그리고 우리 웹 사이트에서 판매되는 모든 제품에 적용됩니다. 보증 기간 중인 제품 중 제대로 작동하지 않는 제품은 저희 공장 중 한 곳으로 직접 발송하시어 수리나 교환을 받을 수 있습니다. 가능하다면, 유효한 영수증을 동봉하여 138원래 포장에 넣어 저희에게 제품을 발송해 주십시오.

어휘 guarantee 보증하다 electronics 전자 기기 as good as new 새것같이 좋은 date of purchase 구입일 warranty (품질) 보증서 apply to ~에 적용하다 authorized 공인된 malfunction 오작동하다 ship 발송하다 directly 곧장, 직접 repair 수리 exchange 교환 packaging 포장 valid 유효한 receipt 영수증

135. 형용사 자리
해설 빈칸 앞 as good as와 함께 어울려 쓰여 '새것같이 좋은'이라는 의미를 나타낼 수 있는 단어는 형용사 new이다. 따라서 (A)가 정답이다. as good as new를 하나의 어구로 기억해 두자.

136. 알맞은 문장 고르기
(A) 모든 제품은 평생 품질 보증이 딸려 있습니다.
(B) 제품 견본을 구하시려면 담당자에게 말씀하십시오.
(C) 이 새로운 보증은 저희의 예전 품질 보증에 2년을 추가한 것입니다.
(D) 우리의 신형 배터리는 전보다 에너지 효율적입니다.

해설 자사 전자제품이 3년 동안 새것같이 잘 작동할 것을 보장한다는 앞 문장의 내용을 This new guarantee로 받아 새로운 보증에 대해 설명하는 내용이 이어지는 것이 적절하다. 또한, 빈칸 뒤에서 이를 This warranty로 받아 부연 설명하고 있으므로 (C)가 정답이다.

어휘 lifetime 평생의 representative 판매원, 대표(자) add 더하다 previous 이전의, 예전의

137. 명사 자리 [형용사+명사]
해설 빈칸은 빈칸 앞 형용사 authorized의 수식을 받는 명사 자리이므로 (A)와 (C)가 정답 후보이다. '공인 대리점'이라는 의미가 자연스러우므로 (C)가 정답이다. '유통'이라는 의미의 명사 (A)는 문맥에 맞지 않으므로 오답이다.

138. 형용사 자리 [한정사+형용사+명사]
해설 빈칸 앞에 소유격 its가 있고 빈칸 뒤에 명사 packaging이 있으므로 빈칸은 명사를 수식할 수 있는 형용사 자리이다. 따라서 형용사인 (D)가 정답이다.

139-142 공지

> Pricilla's Home Garden Supplier는 소중한 고객님들을 위해 새로운 것을 준비하고 있습니다. 매장의 일부분을 보수할 예정으로, 이 부분은 쇼핑객들에게 일시적으로 폐쇄될 것입니다. 5월 17일부터 화분 코너가 공사에 들어갈 139예정입니다. 140이에 따라 보수 기간 동안 매장의 이 코너에서는 씨앗과 비료를 구입하실 수 없을 것입니다. 리모델링은 5월 26일까지는 끝나게 되어 있습니다. 저희 인테리어 디자인 직원들과 관리자들은 141며칠 동안 차질이 빚어져도 결국에는 노력할 가치가 있을 것이라고 믿고 있습니다.
>
> 142보수 공사가 끝난 후, 특별 기념행사가 있을 것입니다. 이 기간 동안, 고객님들은 무료로 초보자용 식물 세트와 씨앗을 받으실 수 있을 것입니다. 고객님들은 또한 희귀한 파리지옥풀 경품 추첨에 참가하실 수 있습니다.

어휘 renovate 개조하다, 보수하다 temporarily 일시적으로 potted plant 화분에 심은 식물 department (상품별) 매장, 코너 under construction 공사 중인 fertilizer 비료 available 구할 수 있는 renovation 개조, 보수 disruption 혼란, 분열 in the end 결국 kit 한 세트 raffle 추첨 rare 희귀한, 드문 Venus flytrap 파리지옥풀

139. 동사 자리 + 수동태
해설 빈칸은 the potted plants department를 주어로 하는 동사 자리이므로 (B)와 (C)가 정답 후보이다. 빈칸 뒤에 slate의 목적어가 없고, 문맥상으로도 '공사될 예정이다'라는 의미가 자연스러우므로 수동태인 (C)가 정답이다. slate가 '(일정을) 계획하다'라는

의미로 쓰일 때는 주로 수동태 형태를 취한다는 것을 알아 두자.

140. 연결어/접속 부사 consequently
(A) 따라서 (B) ~ 때문에 (C) 그 후 (D) 놀랍게도

해설 문장 맨 앞에 콤마로 분리되어 올 수 있는 것은 부사이다. 접속사인 (B)를 제외하고 접속 부사인 (A)와 (C), 부사인 (D)가 가능하다. '화분 코너 공사가 예정되어 있다'는 내용의 앞 문장은 원인, '보수 기간 동안 이 코너에서 씨앗과 비료를 구입할 수 없을 것이다'는 내용의 뒤 문장은 결과에 해당하므로, 인과관계를 나타내는 (A)가 정답이다.

141. 형용사 자리 [한정사 + 형용사 + 명사]
(A) 결코 ~ 않다 (B) 작은 (C) (양이) 적은 (D) (수가) 적은

해설 빈칸 앞에 부정관사 a가 있고 빈칸 뒤에 명사구 days of disruption이 있으므로 빈칸은 명사(구)를 수식할 수 있는 형용사 자리이다. 따라서 부사인 (A)는 오답이다. 나머지 선택지들 중 빈칸 뒤에 오는 가산명사의 복수형 days를 수식할 수 있는 것은 few뿐이므로 (D)가 정답이다.

142. 알맞은 문장 고르기
(A) 고객들은 쿠폰을 가져오는 것이 권장됩니다.
(B) 매장 전체가 이틀 동안 문을 닫을 것입니다.
(C) 보수 공사가 끝난 후, 특별 기념행사가 있을 것입니다.
(D) 인조 잔디는 요청하는 즉시 구할 수 있습니다.

해설 빈칸 뒤에 고객들에게 무료로 주어지는 것과 참가할 수 있는 경품 추첨 관련 내용이 나오는 것으로 보아 빈칸에는 특별 기념행사가 있을 것이라는 내용이 나오는 것이 자연스럽다. 따라서 (C)가 정답이다.

어휘 artificial 인공의 turf 잔디 upon request 요청하는 즉시

143-146 기사

브리즈번 (10월 20일)—Fast 사는 오늘 연례 스포츠카 쇼케이스를 발표했다. Fast 사의 대변인인 Elizabeth Hawkins 씨에 따르면, 이 회사의 143연례 행사는 업계에서 가장 우수하고 가장 빠른 자동차를 부각시키는 데 전념한다. 올해는 몇몇 새로운 판매업체들뿐만 아니라 몇몇 친숙한 기업들도 합류할 것이다. 특히 관심을 끄는 차들 중 하나는 태양 에너지만으로 달리는 신형 Manfrin 6000이다. 144이 차는 변화하는 업계 표준을 반영하고 있다. "방문객들은 자동차 전시회 기간 동안 환경에 초점을 두고 있음을 보게 되리라고 기대할 수 있습니다."라고 Hawkins 씨는 말했다. "145그들은 소개된 모든 차들이 대단히 친환경적이라는 것을 알면 기쁠 것입니다. 각 제조사는 환경에 미치는 영향이 적은 차량을 만드는 방법에 대한 국제 146규정을 따랐으며, 구매자들께서 이를 높이 평가해 주시길 바랍니다."

어휘 reveal 밝히다, 알리다 annual 연례의 spokesperson 대변인 be dedicated to ~에 전념하다 highlight 강조하다, 돋보이게 하다 industry 산업, 업계 familiar 친숙한 corporation 기업 as well as ~뿐만 아니라 vendor 판매자 brand-new 신형의, 신제품의 entirely 전적으로, 완전히 solar energy 태양 에너지 environmental 환경의 auto show 자동차 전시회 feature 출연하다, ~의 특징을 이루다 exceptionally 예외적으로, 대단히 eco-friendly 친환경적인 manufacturer 제조사 reduced 줄어든, 감소한 impact 영향 appreciate ~을 높이 평가하다, 고마워하다

143. 형용사 어휘 yearly
(A) 잦은 (B) 가끔의 (C) 매달의 (D) 매년 있는

해설 첫 번째 문장에 나온 annual Sports Car Showcase를 패러프레이징한 표현을 찾아야 한다. annual은 yearly와 유의어 관계에 있으므로 (D) yearly가 정답이다.

144. 알맞은 문장 고르기
(A) 도로에 있는 대부분의 차량은 스포츠카가 아니다.
(B) 이 차는 변화하는 업계 표준을 반영하고 있다.
(C) 수력 발전 에너지는 몇몇 산업들 사이에서 인기가 있다.
(D) 가격은 웹 사이트에서 알 수 있다.

해설 빈칸 앞의 brand-new Manfrin 6000을 This car로 받아 '이 차는 변화하는 업계 표준을 반영한다'는 내용으로 이어지는 것이 자연스럽다. 빈칸 뒤에 쇼케이스에 나온 차들의 친환경적인 특징을 언급하는 것 또한 '변화하는 업계 표준'과 관련된 내용이므로 (B)가 정답이다.

어휘 hydroelectric 수력 발전의

145. 인칭대명사 They
(A) 그것 (B) 그녀 (C) 그들 (D) 그

해설 빈칸은 문장의 주어 자리로, 빈칸 앞 문장의 주어인 Visitors를 대신하는 인칭대명사가 들어가야 하므로 3인칭 복수형 인칭대명사인 (C)가 정답이다.

146. 명사 자리 [형용사 + 명사]
해설 빈칸은 빈칸 앞 형용사 global의 수식을 받으면서, 동시에 빈칸 뒤 on부터 environment까지의 전치사구의 수식을 받는 명사 자리이다. 따라서 (A)가 정답이다.

147-148 광고

잭슨타운 GRACE 컨트리클럽
148C5월 14일 개장

저희 Grace 컨트리클럽은 벨 파크웨이 84번지에 있는 저희의 최신 부지에서 열릴 개장식에 모든 관심 있는 레저 애호가들이 저희와 함께 하도록 초대하고자 합니다. 147저희의 최고급 시설, 탁월한 서비스, 그리고 독특한 세계 요리를 직접 경험해 보십시오.

특별 할인: 회원 가입 첫 2개월 동안 10% 할인 혜택을 누리십시오! 이 혜택은 148B신규 회원에게만 제공되며 148D다른 할인과 결합할 수 없습니다. 본 할인은 148C개장일로부터 7월 15일까지 148A모든 Grace 컨트리클럽 가맹점에서 유효합니다.

더 많은 정보를 원하시면 www.gracecountryclub.com/jacksontown을 방문하시거나, 가이드 투어를 하는 동안 저희 부지에 직접 오셔서 보시기 바랍니다.

어휘 grand opening 개장, 개점 enthusiast (~에) 열심인 사람, 광, 팬 facility 시설 exceptional 뛰어난, 특별한 unique 독특

한 cuisine 요리 for oneself 스스로 offer 할인, 제안 membership 회원의 지위[신분, 자격] combine 결합하다 valid 유효한 franchise 가맹점, 프랜차이즈 premises 부지, 구내

147. 잭슨타운 Grace 컨트리클럽에 대해 시사된 것은 무엇인가?
(A) 첫 번째 가맹점이다.
(B) 일주일에 5일 문을 연다.
(C) 이국적인 요리를 제공한다.
(D) 회원 가입은 필요하지 않다.

해설 NOT/True
독특한 세계 요리를 경험해 보라고 했으므로 이국적인 요리를 제공함을 알 수 있다. 따라서 (C)가 정답이다.

패러프레이징 unique international cuisine → exotic dishes

148. 특별 할인에 대해 언급되지 않은 것은 무엇인가?
(A) 잭슨타운 지점에만 적용된다.
(B) 재가입 회원에게는 유효하지 않다.
(C) 2개월 동안 계속된다.
(D) 다른 쿠폰과 함께 사용할 수 없다.

해설 NOT/True
모든 Grace 컨트리클럽 가맹점에 적용된다고 했으므로 (A)가 정답이다.

어휘 apply to ~에 적용되다 branch 지점, 지사 last 지속되다, 계속되다

149-150 메모

> 손님,
> 로스앤젤레스와 Murray 호텔에서 즐거운 시간을 보내시기 바랍니다. 저희는 귀하를 손님으로 모시게 되어 기쁩니다. ¹⁵⁰ᴬ오전 6시부터 11시까지 로비 옆 식당에서 ¹⁵⁰ᶜ무료 조식이 제공됩니다. 매일 제공되는 조식에는 다양한 페이스트리, 스크램블드에그, 토스트, 과일, 그리고 소시지가 포함됩니다. 커피와 차도 드실 수 있습니다. ¹⁴⁹ ¹⁵⁰ᴮ6월 18일에는 그날 오후에 열리는 학회를 준비하기 위해 조식이 제공되지 않을 것임을 알려 드립니다. 그러나, 손님들은 조식 시간에 무료 룸서비스를 주문하여 식사를 받으실 수 있습니다.
> Gwen Alton
> Murray 호텔 지배인

어휘 complimentary 무료의 adjacent to ~에 인접한 include 포함하다 an assortment of 여러 가지의 pastry 페이스트리 in order to do ~하기 위하여 meal 음식, 식사

149. 메모의 목적 중 하나는 무엇인가?
(A) 손님들에게 수리를 알리기 위해
(B) 식사 서비스 변경을 설명하기 위해
(C) 공개 행사를 공지하기 위해
(D) 개인 초대장을 발송하기 위해

해설 주제/목적
6월 18일에 무료 조식 대신 무료 룸서비스 식사가 제공될 것임을 알리고 있으므로 (B)가 정답이다.

어휘 inform 알리다 renovation 수리, 보수 invitation 초대(장)

150. 조식에 대해 사실인 것은 무엇인가?
(A) 정오까지 이용할 수 있다.
(B) 6월 18일에 이용할 수 없다.
(C) 무료로 제공된다.
(D) 계속 새롭게 바뀐다.

해설 NOT/True
무료 조식이 제공된다고 했으므로 (C)가 정답이다.

패러프레이징 complimentary → for free

151-152 이메일

> 수신: Angela Vasquez 〈a.vasquez@vestaltd.com〉
> 발신: Mickey McAlister 〈m.mcalister@vestaltd.com〉
> 날짜: 6월 3일
> 제목: 안내 책자
>
> 안녕하세요, Angela.
>
> ¹⁵¹제가 안내 책자의 최종안과 함께 보내 드린 파일을 열어 보지 못하셨다니 유감입니다. 최신 버전의 Doc-Reader 소프트웨어를 갖고 계신가요? 그렇지 않다면 그것이 문제의 원인일 수 있습니다. 제가 나중에 안내 책자의 인쇄본을 가져다 드리겠습니다.
>
> ¹⁵²안내 책자에서 제가 새로 단장된 부엌과 넓은 뒷마당에 특히 주목하도록 했다는 것을 알게 되실 겁니다. 저는 이런 것들이 구매자들의 마음에 들 수 있는 특징이 될 것이고, 이것은 우리 팀이 이 부동산에 대해 가장 좋은 가격을 받는 데 도움이 될 것이라고 생각합니다. 안내 책자의 내용을 확인하시는 대로, 다음 주에 부동산을 확인하고 싶어 하시는 매수 희망자 중 한 명인 Bryant 씨에게 그것을 보내겠습니다.
>
> Mickey

어휘 brochure 안내 책자 final draft 최종안 version 버전, 판 drop off 가져다주다 draw attention to ~에 주목하게 하다 feature 특징 appeal to ~의 마음에 들다 property 부동산, 건물 confirm 확인하다 content 내용(물) prospective 예비의, 유망한 check out 확인하다

151. McAlister 씨가 Vasquez 씨의 파일에 문제가 있었다고 생각하는 이유는 무엇인가?
(A) 그것은 컴퓨터 바이러스를 포함하고 있었다.
(B) 그것은 다른 폴더로 경로가 재설정되었다.
(C) 그녀는 잘못된 파일명을 사용했다.
(D) 그녀의 소프트웨어가 예전 버전일지도 모른다.

해설 세부 사항
McAlister 씨는 Vasquez 씨가 최신 버전의 Doc-Reader 소프트웨어가 없어서 파일을 열지 못했을지도 모른다고 언급했으므로 (D)가 정답이다.

어휘 contain 포함하다 redirect 새로운 방향으로 돌리다 outdated 구식의, 시대에 뒤진

152. McAlister 씨의 직업은 무엇이겠는가?
(A) 건설 노동자
(B) 건축가
(C) 부동산 중개인
(D) 집주인

해설 추론/암시
Mickey McAlister는 자신이 안내 책자에 넣은 내용을 언급하며 그것이 구매자들의 마음에 들 만한 특징이라고 했고, 이로 인해 부동산 가격을 잘 받을 수 있을 것이라고 한 것으로 보아 부동산 중개인임을 유추할 수 있다. 따라서 (C)가 정답이다.

153-154 문자 메시지

> Angelica Robinson (오전 11:49):
> 안녕하세요, James. ¹⁵³정육점에서 소 옆구리살을 찾고 있는데, 구할 수 있는 고깃덩어리가 아무것도 마음에 안 들어요. ¹⁵⁴어젯밤에 남은 게 있는지 확인해 줄래요? 남은 게 없으면, 다른 부위의 소고기를 사야 할 것 같아요.
>
> James Gorski (오전 11:56):
> 다 떨어진 것 같네요. ¹⁵³주방장님께 말씀드릴게요.
>
> Angelica Robinson (오전 11:57):
> 정말 고마워요.
>
> James Gorski (오후 12:01):
> ¹⁵³주방장님께서 부챗살이나 목살이 좋은 대용품이 될 거라고 말씀하셨어요. 손님들이 주문을 할 때 알려 드려야 할 것 같아요.
>
> Angelica Robinson (오후 12:03):
> 문제없습니다. 고마워요!

어휘 butcher 정육점 (주인) flank steak 플랭크 스테이크 ≪소의 옆구리 부위의 살점, 또는 그 스테이크≫ cut (동물에서 잘라 낸 고기) 덩어리 flat iron steak 플랫 아이언 스테이크 ≪상대적으로 저렴하나 맛이 좋은 부챗살≫ chuck steak 척 스테이크, 암소 목살 substitute 대용품 inform 알리다 place an order 주문하다

153. Gorski 씨가 일할 것 같은 업체는 무엇인가?
(A) 식료품점
(B) 행사 기획사
(C) 옷 가게
(D) 음식점

해설 추론/암시
Gorski 씨는 정육점에서 소고기를 사고 있는 Robinson 씨와 통화 중인데, 주방장과 이야기하여 원래 사려던 소고기 부위가 아닌 다른 부위를 사기로 하고, 손님들이 주문하기 전에 알려야 할 거라고 했으므로, Gorski 씨는 음식점에서 일하는 직원임을 추론할 수 있다. 따라서 (D)가 정답이다.

154. 오전 11시 56분에, Gorski 씨가 "다 떨어진 것 같네요"라고 쓸 때 그는 무엇을 의미하는가?
(A) 일할 수 있는 다른 사람이 아무도 없다.
(B) 일부 저장품이 다 떨어졌다.
(C) 마감일이 지났다.
(D) 손님이 없다.

해설 의도 파악
의도 파악 문제는 제시된 문장의 앞뒤 문장에서 단서를 찾는다. 제시된 문장은 어젯밤 남은 소고기가 있는지 확인해 달라는 Robinson 씨의 요청에 대한 대답이므로 (B)가 정답이다.

어휘 supplies 저장품 run out (공급품이) 다 떨어지다 deadline 마감 기한

155-157 공지

> Tarry Town Tea Society 회원 여러분, 주목하십시오.
>
> 다음 주 토요일, Tarry Town Tea Society는 새로운 차향인 샤프란 차를 소개할 예정입니다. 이 매우 인기 있는 향신료는 아주 많은 건강상의 이점을 제공하는 맛있는 차를 만들어 냅니다. 여러분의 지속적인 성원에 대한 감사의 표시로, ¹⁵⁵저희는 Tea Society 회원들이 우리 모임에서 일반 대중보다 한 달 먼저 그 차를 시음하실 수 있도록 결정했습니다.
>
> 또한, 시내에 있는 커피숍 가맹점에서 Tarry Town Tea Society 회원증을 보여 주시면 할인된 가격으로 샤프란 차를 한 잔 받으실 수 있습니다. ¹⁵⁷골드 등급과 다이아몬드 등급 회원에게는 주문하신 차와 함께 원하는 디저트도 무료로 제공됩니다. 플래티넘 회원들께는 집에 가져가 차나 요리용으로 사용할 수 있도록 작은 봉지에 담은 정품 샤프란을 드립니다.
>
> 이 Tea Society 행사는 오늘 시작됩니다. ¹⁵⁶특별 행사 날짜에 대한 자세한 내용을 원하시면 당사 웹 사이트 www.tarrytowntea.com/members를 방문해 주십시오.

어휘 society 협회 introduce 소개하다 flavor 향미, 맛 saffron 샤프란 sought-after 인기 있는, 수요가 많은 spice 향신료 a myriad of 무수한 appreciation 감사 continued 지속적인 general public 일반 대중 reduced 줄인, 할인한 rate 요금, 가격 detail 세부 사항

155. 모든 Tarry Town Tea Society 회원들이 이용할 수 있는 것은 무엇인가?
(A) 독점적으로 제공되는 음료
(B) 비공개 파티
(C) 새로운 종류의 디저트
(D) 진귀한 향신료들

해설 세부 사항
Tea Society 회원들이 일반인보다 한 달 먼저 샤프란 차를 시음할 수 있도록 정했다고 했으므로 (A)가 정답이다.

패러프레이징 tea → drink

어휘 exclusive 독점적인, 전용의 rare 드문, 진귀한

156. 공지에 따르면, 웹 사이트에서 구할 수 있는 것은 무엇인가?
(A) 할인 코드
(B) 일정
(C) 조리법
(D) 인쇄 가능한 전단

해설 세부 사항
특별 행사 날짜에 대한 자세한 내용을 원하면 웹 사이트를 방문하라고 했으므로 (B)가 정답이다.

패러프레이징 more details about special event dates → schedule

어휘 printable 인쇄 가능한 flyer 전단지

157. [1], [2], [3], [4]로 표시된 위치 중 다음 문장이 들어가기에 가장 적절한 곳은?

"플래티넘 회원들께는 집에 가져가 차나 요리용으로 사용할 수 있도록 작은 봉지에 담은 정품 샤프란을 드립니다."

(A) [1]
(B) [2]
(C) [3]
(D) [4]

해설 문장 삽입

주어진 문장은 플래티넘 회원이 받을 혜택에 관한 내용인데, 골드 등급에서 다이아몬드 등급, 그리고 플래티넘 등급으로 갈수록 혜택의 범위가 커지고 있으므로, 골드 등급과 다이아몬드 등급 회원의 혜택을 언급한 다음인 [4] 자리에 오는 것이 자연스럽다. 따라서 (D)가 정답이다.

어휘 authentic 진품인

158-159 기사

Onio 공장이 새로운 모습을 얻게 되다

3월 26일―한때 파스타 제조 능력으로 알려졌던 Onio 공장이 올봄에 대대적인 변신을 하고 있다. ¹⁵⁸시 의회는 버려진 공장을 음식점, 의류와 기타 품목을 판매하는 매장, 그리고 라이브 공연을 위한 두 개의 무대가 있는 쇼핑몰로 탈바꿈하기 위해 노력하고 있다.

¹⁵⁸공장은 기업의 새로운 사무실 공간을 만들기 위해 거의 철거될 뻔했지만 지역 주민들이 그 제안에 반발했다. ¹⁵⁹지역사회 구성원들은 이 공장이 50년 넘게 운영되어 왔기 때문에 이곳을 역사적인 건물로 보고 있다. 그처럼 강력한 반대가 있은 뒤, 시 공무원들은 현재의 계획을 따르기로 결정했다.

"Onio는 한때 전국에서 가장 큰 파스타 공장 중 하나였습니다"라고 Aurora Larsen 시장이 말했다. "사람들이 더 많은 사무직 일자리를 선택했을 때, Onio는 결국 문을 닫았습니다. 고맙게도, 이 새로운 프로젝트는 건물에 다시 활기를 불어넣을 것입니다. 새로워진 공간이 주민들이 좋은 먹거리와 쇼핑, 그리고 공연을 즐길 수 있는 안전한 장소가 되길 바랍니다."

어휘 look 외관, 모양 pasta 파스타 capability 능력 makeover (모양의) 단장 council 의회 turn A into B A를 B로 바꾸다 abandoned 버려진 pedestrian 보행자 mall 쇼핑몰 demolish 철거하다 corporate 기업의 protest 항의하다, 반대하다 view 보다 landmark 랜드마크, 주요 지형지물 be in operation 운영되다 note 언급하다 mayor 시장 opt for ~을 선택하다 eventually 결국 breathe life into ~에 새로운 기운을 불어넣다 performance 공연

158. 공장에 대한 현재 계획으로 언급되지 않은 것은 무엇인가?
(A) 공연을 위한 공간
(B) 식당
(C) 기업의 사무실

(D) 소매점

해설 NOT/True

공장을 음식점과 매장, 공연 공간이 있는 쇼핑몰로 바꾸려고 한다고 나와 있지만, 회사 사무실과 관련된 계획은 주민들의 반대로 무산된 예전 계획이므로 (C)가 정답이다.

패러프레이징 (A) two stages for live shows → Performance spaces / (B) restaurants → Dining establishments / (D) stores selling clothing and other goods → Retail shops

159. Onio 공장에 대해 암시된 것은 무엇인가?
(A) 운영 중인 가장 큰 파스타 공장이다.
(B) 문을 연 지 1세기가 넘었다.
(C) 현대 기술에 의해 대체되었다.
(D) 시민들에게 중요하다.

해설 추론/암시

지역사회 구성원들이 이 공장을 역사적인 건물로 보고 있다고 했으므로 (D)가 정답이다.

어휘 replace 대신하다, 대체하다 significant 중요한

160-163 회람

회람

수신: 고객 서비스 팀
발신: 고객 서비스 관리자, Adriano Fonti
날짜: 10월 13일

다음 주는 Mike's Hardware에서 열리는 첫 번째 고객 서비스 감사 주간입니다. ¹⁶⁰다음 주 내내 여러분을 위한 특별한 행사가 계획되어 있습니다. ¹⁶¹우리는 올해 탁월함과 양질의 서비스에 대한 여러분의 헌신에 대해 여러분 모두에게 감사를 드리기 위해 이 행사를 갖습니다. 경영진은 각 고객 서비스 담당자에 대한 훌륭한 평가를 들었고, 우리는 더할 나위 없이 자부심을 느꼈습니다. Kevin's Woodworks와의 협업이 다소 어려웠지만, 우리 직원들은 그럼에도 힘을 합쳐 고객들이 기대해 온 놀라운 서비스를 제공했습니다. 경영진은 모두의 헌신과 전문성에 깊은 인상을 받았습니다.

월요일 아침에 우리는 Henry's Café에서 모두를 위해 개인 맞춤형 배달 주문을 받을 것입니다. ¹⁶²화요일에는 과일 접시와 다양한 페이스트리를 아침 식사로 이용할 수 있습니다. 수요일에 우리는 점심으로 피자를 배달받을 것입니다. 목요일에, 우리는 El Quesadilla에서 각자 메뉴를 선택하여 저녁 식사를 할 것입니다. ¹⁶³그리고 마지막으로 금요일에는 퇴근 후 친목을 도모하기 위해 동네 술집에 갈 것입니다. 술값은 회사에서 각각 두 잔씩 지불할 것입니다.

여러분 모두 회사에서 마련한 것들에 즐거운 시간이 되길 바랍니다!

어휘 throughout ~ 내내 commitment 헌신 excellence 우수, 탁월(성) quality 양질의 management 경영, 경영진 collaboration 협업 a bit 다소, 약간 pull together 함께 일하다, 협력하다 dedication 헌신 professionalism 전문성 platter (음식을 차려 내는 데 쓰는 큰 서빙용) 접시 an assortment of 여러 가지의 optional 선택적인, 마음대로 선택 가능한 happy hour (회사의 비공식) 친목 시간 in store 준비되어

160. Fonti 씨가 이 회람을 작성한 이유는 무엇인가?
(A) 직원의 의견을 묻기 위해
(B) 향후 교육 시간을 논의하기 위해
(C) 일련의 행사에 관해 상세히 설명하기 위해
(D) 직원들을 나무라기 위해

해설 주제/목적
지문 도입부에서 고객 서비스 직원들을 위한 특별 행사가 계획되어 있다고 언급했고, 행사에 대한 구체적인 내용이 이어지고 있으므로 (C)가 정답이다.

패러프레이징 special events → a series of events

어휘 training session 교육   give details 상세히 말하다   a series of 일련의   scold 나무라다, 꾸짖다

161. Mike's Hardware에 대해 암시된 것은 무엇인가?
(A) 이달의 직원상이 있다.
(B) 사업이 잘 안 되고 있다.
(C) 소유주가 사업을 매각하는 것을 고려하고 있다.
(D) 직원들에게 감사하고 있다.

해설 NOT/True
Mike's Hardware는 고객 서비스 직원들에게 감사하기 위해 감사 주간을 연다고 했으므로 (D)가 정답이다.

패러프레이징 thank each of you → appreciates its staff members

162. 오전에 행사가 열리는 날은 언제인가?
(A) 화요일
(B) 수요일
(C) 목요일
(D) 금요일

해설 세부 사항
화요일 아침에 아침 식사를 받고, 수요일은 점심으로 피자를 배달 받고, 목요일은 저녁 식사, 금요일은 퇴근 후 술집에 갈 것이라고 했으므로 오전에 행사가 열리는 날은 화요일이다. 따라서 (A)가 정답이다.

163. [1], [2], [3], [4]로 표시된 위치 중 다음 문장이 들어가기에 가장 적절한 곳은?
"술값은 회사에서 각각 두 잔씩 지불할 것입니다."
(A) [1]
(B) [2]
(C) [3]
(D) [4]

해설 문장 삽입
지문 후반부를 보면 월요일부터 금요일까지 시간 순서대로 일어날 일을 설명하고 있다는 것을 알 수 있다. 주어진 문장은 금요일에 술집에 간 후에 일어날 상황이므로 [4] 자리에 들어가는 것이 적절하다. 따라서 (D)가 정답이다.

164-167 설명서

Cregar

Cregar 고객들은 품질과 스타일을 중시하며, 우리가 시즌마다 새로 선보이는 물품들을 기대하고 있습니다. 매출을 극대화하기 위해서는 우리 매장이 무엇을 제공할 수 있는지 보여 주고, [165]고객들이 우리의 가죽 핸드백, 벨트 등을 포함하는 라이프스타일을 상상할 수 있도록 돕는 것이 중요합니다. [164]매장 전시를 꾸밀 때는 이야기를 담아야 합니다. 상품은 시선을 사로잡고 매력적인 방식으로 배치되어야 합니다. 물품에 포함된 모든 표시는 간략해야 하며, 표시의 색상은 제품과 어울려야 합니다. [166]진열대에 놓는 물품의 수를 제한하세요. 그렇지 않으면 고객들의 주의가 너무 산만해져 우리가 고객에게 보여 주려고 하는 것에 고객이 주의를 기울이지 못할 위험이 있습니다. 가장 중요한 제품을 입구 근처에 배치하고, 선반 주변이 [167]깨끗하게 유지되도록 하십시오.

어휘 value 중시하다   look forward to *doing* ~하기를 고대[기대]하다   maximize 극대화하다   display 전시, 진열   merchandise 상품   eye-catching 눈길을 끄는   arrange 배치하다   attractive 매력적인   sign 표시   include 포함하다   complement 보완하다, 어울리다   limit 제한하다   otherwise 그렇지 않으면   run the risk of ~의 위험이 있다   distracted 주의가 산만한   place 놓다, 배치하다   entrance 입구   shelving unit 선반

164. 설명서는 누구를 대상으로 작성되었겠는가?
(A) Cregar 고객들에게 연락하는 영업 사원들
(B) Cregar 진열대를 설치하는 직원들
(C) Cregar 제품을 구매한 고객들
(D) Cregar 상품 개발자들

해설 대상
매장 전시에 대한 지침을 담고 있으므로 (B)가 정답이다.

패러프레이징 creating store displays → set up Cregar displays

어휘 contact 연락하다   set up 설치하다

165. Cregar가 판매하는 것은 무엇이겠는가?
(A) 가전제품
(B) 화장품
(C) 액세서리
(D) 소프트웨어

해설 추론/암시
판매하는 제품으로 가죽 핸드백과 벨트를 언급한 것으로 보아 액세서리 판매업체임을 유추할 수 있다. 따라서 (C)가 정답이다.

패러프레이징 leather handbags, belts → accessories

166. 설명서에서 적은 수의 물품을 사용하도록 조언하는 이유는 무엇인가?
(A) 업무에 소요되는 시간을 줄여 준다.
(B) 훨씬 더 적은 공간을 필요로 한다.
(C) 고객의 관심을 집중시키는 데 도움이 될 수 있다.
(D) 프로젝트의 전체 비용을 절감한다.

해설 **세부 사항**
진열대에 놓을 물품의 수를 제한하지 않으면 고객들의 주의가 산만해져 보여 주고자 하는 것에 집중하지 못할 위험이 있다고 했다. 이는 바꿔 말하면, 물품의 수를 제한해야 고객의 관심을 집중시킬 수 있다는 의미이므로 (C)가 정답이다.

패러프레이징 pay attention → focus customers' attention

어휘 reduce 줄이다 task 업무, 과제 space 공간 overall 전반적인

167. 첫 번째 단락 열 번째 줄의 어휘 "clear"와 의미상 가장 가까운 것은 무엇인가?
(A) 순수한
(B) 이해할 수 있는
(C) 비어 있는
(D) 분명한

해설 **동의어 찾기**
clear가 포함된 부분은 문맥상 '선반 주변이 깨끗하게 유지되도록 해라'라는 의미이므로, clear는 '~이 없는'이라는 의미로 쓰였다. 선택지 중 이와 의미상 가장 유사한 (C)가 정답이다.

168-171 온라인 채팅

Beatrice Iden (오후 4:14) 안녕하세요, 여러분. 주말이 오기 전에 모두들 잘 되고 있는지 확인하고 싶었어요. **169** Eric, Kloud 백화점과의 회의는 어땠어요?

Eric Neely (오후 4:16) 잘됐습니다! **168** 그들은 초도 주문으로 우리의 2인용 텐트 500개를 구입하기로 합의했어요. 서명된 계약서가 제 바로 앞에 있어요.

Beatrice Iden (오후 4:17) 잘됐군요! 오늘 수고하셨어요.

Kenneth Wolf (오후 4:21) 축하해요! 이것으로 당신이 두 달 연속으로 최고 영업 사원이 된 것 같은데요.

Susan Kuzma (오후 4:22) 정말 잘됐어요, Eric. **171** 사무실에 도착해서 영수증을 모두 제게 주시면 출장비 환급을 신청해 드릴게요.

Eric Neely (오후 4:23) 그게 확실해요, Kenneth? **170** Jamie Hill이 불과 얼마 전에 엄청난 매출을 올렸다고 들었어요.

Beatrice Iden (오후 4:25) **170** Jamie의 고객들이 마지막 순간에 마음을 바꿨답니다. 다른 회사가 더 나은 할인을 제공하고 있었기 때문에 그들은 그곳과 거래하기로 결정했어요.

Eric Neely (오후 4:26) 너무 안됐네요. **171** 아, 도와줘서 고마워요, Susan.

Susan Kuzma (오후 4:27) 천만에요!

어휘 check in with (확인하기 위해) ~와 연락하다 contract 계약(서) in a row 연속하여 receipt 영수증 put in the request for ~을 신청하다 reimbursement 환급 land 차지하다, 획득하다 sale 매출, 판매 at the last minute 마지막 순간에 discount 할인

168. 글쓴이들이 종사할 것 같은 업종은 무엇인가?
(A) 여행 기획
(B) 프로그래밍
(C) 직원 교육
(D) 캠핑 장비 판매

해설 **추론/암시**
백화점에 텐트 판매 사실을 알리는 것으로 보아, 캠핑 용품을 판매하는 사람들임을 유추할 수 있으므로 (D)가 정답이다.

169. Iden 씨의 직함은 무엇이겠는가?
(A) 영업 관리자
(B) 비서
(C) 인사부장
(D) 마케팅 이사

해설 **추론/암시**
Beatrice Iden은 Eric Neely에게 고객과의 회의 결과를 묻고, Jamie Hill의 업무 성과를 알리는 등 부서의 전반적인 판매 업무 관련 정보를 제공하는 것으로 보아 영업을 담당하는 관리자임을 유추할 수 있다. 따라서 (A)가 정답이다.

170. Hill 씨에 대해 시사된 것은 무엇인가?
(A) 최근에 입사했다.
(B) 상임 이사이다.
(C) 판매를 완결 짓지 못했다.
(D) 곧 회사를 옮길 것이다.

해설 **NOT/True**
Hill 씨의 고객이 마지막 순간에 마음을 바꿔 다른 회사와 거래하기로 결정했으므로, Hill 씨는 거래를 완성하지 못했음을 알 수 있다. 따라서 (C)가 정답이다.

어휘 recently 최근에 join 합류하다 executive 임원 switch 바꾸다, 전환하다

171. 오후 4시 27분에, Kuzma 씨가 "천만에요!"라고 쓸 때 그녀는 무엇을 암시하는가?
(A) 공급업체와의 협상이 잘 되었다.
(B) 그녀의 컴퓨터가 정상적으로 작동하고 있다.
(C) 그녀는 하루가 끝나서 기쁘다.
(D) 그녀는 Neely 씨를 돕는 것을 마다하지 않는다.

해설 **의도 파악**
"No problem"은 '천만에요, 문제없어요'라는 뜻으로, 영수증을 제출하면 출장비 환급을 신청해 주겠다는 Kuzma 씨의 말에 Neely 씨가 고맙다고 하자 이에 Kuzma 씨가 괜찮다는 의미로 대답한 말이다. 따라서 (D)가 정답이다.

어휘 function 작동하다 normally 정상적으로

172-175 이메일

수신: stafflist@milton-data.com
발신: williamsc@milton-data.com
날짜: 9월 6일
제목: 회사 수련회

직원 여러분,

지난달 회사 수련회에 적극적으로 참여해 주신 여러분에게 감사드립니다. 여러분 모두 즐거운 시간 보내셨기를 바랍니다. ¹⁷²이 연례 행사는 다른 부서의 직원들과 협력 관계를 구축하는 데 있어 중요한 일부분입니다. 그것은 또한 우리가 미래에 대한 회사의 사명에 집중할 수 있는 기회를 줍니다.

¹⁷³제가 직원 의견 카드에 있는 여러분들의 답변을 검토했는데, 여러분의 답변을 보다 자세히 설명해 주셨으면 좋겠습니다. 이 답변들은 내년도 수련회 기획에 도움이 될 것입니다. 다음 질문에 대해 이메일로 답변해 주십시오.

- 선정된 장소의 장점과 단점은 무엇이었습니까?
- 어떤 시간이 가장 좋았고 그 이유는 무엇입니까?
- 내년 의제에 추가되었으면 하는 활동이나 주제는 무엇입니까?
- 주제에 대해 발표하는 것에 관심이 있나요? 그렇다면, 당신의 전문 분야는 무엇입니까?

¹⁷⁴성수기에는 저렴한 가격에 우리가 필요로 하는 공간을 제공하는 장소를 찾기 어렵기 때문에 저는 벌써부터 내년도 장소 예약을 알아보고 있습니다. 하지만, 저는 여러분의 답변을 먼저 듣고 싶습니다. 그러므로 저는 여러분이 가급적 빨리 답변해 주실 것을 요청합니다. 여러분의 답변에 미리 감사드립니다. ¹⁷⁴ ¹⁷⁵그 답변들은 제가 내년도 수련회에 필요한 계획을 세우는 데 도움이 될 것입니다.

Clara Williams

어휘 retreat 야유회, 단합대회 participation 참가, 참여 cooperative 협력하는 department 부서 review 검토하다 response 답변 elaborate on ~에 대해 상세히 말하다 venue (행사) 장소 agenda 의제 present 발표하다 expertise 전문성, 전문 지식 affordable 적당한 가격의, 저렴한 peak season 성수기 in advance 미리

172. 회사 수련회에 대해 시사된 것은 무엇인가?
(A) 올해는 평소보다 더 길었다.
(B) 매년 7월에 열린다.
(C) 부서 간의 팀워크를 촉진한다.
(D) 몇 개의 지사들을 소집한다.

해설 NOT/True
다른 부서와 협력 관계를 구축하는 데 있어 중요하다고 했으므로 (C)가 정답이다.

패러프레이징 building cooperative relationships with staff in different departments → facilitates teamwork among departments

어휘 facilitate 촉진하다 bring together 소집하다, 모이게 하다

173. 직원 의견 카드에 대해 암시된 것은 무엇인가?
(A) Williams 씨는 아직 그것들을 읽지 않았다.
(B) 그것들은 몇 가지 잘못된 정보를 포함하고 있었다.
(C) 그것들은 회사의 관리자들에게만 보내어졌다.
(D) 참가자들의 긴 답변은 들어 있지 않았다.

해설 추론/암시
employee comment card를 키워드로 지문을 검색하면, 이메일의 작성자는 직원들에게 보다 자세한 답변을 요청하고 있다. 즉, 직원 의견 카드에 적힌 내용은 길지 않다는 의미이므로 (D)가 정답이다.

어휘 contain 포함하다 include 포함하다 participant 참가자

174. Williams 씨는 왜 즉각적인 의견을 요청하는가?
(A) 그녀는 곧 예약할 계획이다.
(B) 그녀는 몇 명의 이사들을 만날 것이다.
(C) 그녀는 할인을 이용하기를 원한다.
(D) 그녀는 승진을 기다리고 있다.

해설 세부 사항
직원들의 답변을 듣고 그것을 반영하여 내년도 수련회 장소를 예약할 것이라고 했으므로 (A)가 정답이다.

패러프레이징 book → make a reservation

어휘 make a reservation 예약하다 board members 이사진 take advantage of ~을 이용하다 promotion 승진

175. Williams 씨는 누구이겠는가?
(A) 웹 사이트 개발자
(B) 행사 책임자
(C) 건물주
(D) 회사 투자자

해설 추론/암시
수련회 계획을 세우고 예약을 하는 사람은 수련회 관련 업무를 책임지고 있는 사람이므로 (B)가 정답이다.

패러프레이징 retreat → event

176-180 광고 & 이메일

맞춤 명함

Sakai Printers는 자사의 새로운 웹 사이트인 www.sakaiprinters.com을 알리게 되어 기쁩니다. ¹⁷⁶고객들은 이제 직접 저희 매장에 오거나 이메일을 보내는 것 외에도, 온라인으로 저희를 방문하여 주문하실 수 있습니다. 저희의 새로운 시스템을 이용하면 사진을 업로드하고, 자신만의 명함을 디자인하고, 클릭 몇 번으로 현관 앞까지 주문하실 수 있습니다.

다음과 같은 다양한 옵션이 있습니다:

종류	상세 설명	최소 주문 수량
베이직	기본 경량지	50장
스탠더드	일반 재질 종이, 매끄러운 질감	50장
¹⁷⁸⁻²프리미엄	고급 재질 종이, 다양한 색상 가능	100장
럭셔리	최고급 재질, 다양한 색상과 금테	150장

¹⁷⁷각각의 옵션의 견본을 받으려면 주문 전에 저희에게 이메일로 연락 주시기 바랍니다.

어휘 custom-made 맞춤의 business card 명함 in addition to ~에 더하여 in person 직접 doorstep 현관 description 설명 minimum 최소의 lightweight 경량의 texture 질감, 감촉 contact 연락하다

135

수신: customerservice@sakaiprinters.com
발신: deon_hogg@perfectpetgoods.com
날짜: 1월 19일
제목: 회신: 주문 6754
[180]첨부 파일: NewLogo_PerfectPetGoods

관계자 귀하:

제 주문을 잠시 중단하고 [179]명함이 인쇄되기 전에 디자인을 변경할 수 있게 해 주셔서 정말 감사드립니다. [178-1]비록 제가 최소 수량을 주문하기는 했지만, 사용할 수 없는 명함이 100장 있다면 유감스러웠을 것입니다.

이전 이메일에서 언급했듯이, [179]실수로 구버전의 회사 로고를 웹 사이트에 업로드했습니다. [180]이 이메일에 업데이트된 버전을 첨부하였으니, 새로운 이미지를 사용하여 제 주문을 계속 진행해 주세요. [180]새로운 파일에 문제가 있다면 알려 주세요.

다시 한번 감사드립니다!

Deon Hogg

어휘 attachment 첨부 파일 pause 중단하다 allow 허락하다 unfortunate 유감스러운, 불행한 mention 언급하다 previous 이전의 accidentally 잘못하여 attach 첨부하다 issue 문제, 사안

176. Sakai Printers에 대해 언급된 것은 무엇인가?
(A) 다섯 종류의 명함을 제공한다.
(B) 오프라인 매장이 없다.
(C) 이메일로 주문을 받는다.
(D) 새로 개업한 업체이다.

해설 세부 사항
고객들이 직접 방문하거나 이메일을 보내는 대신 온라인으로 주문할 수 있다고 했으므로, 직접 방문, 이메일 주문, 온라인 주문의 세 가지 방법 모두로 주문을 받는다는 사실을 알 수 있다. 따라서 (C)가 정답이다.

어휘 physical 물리적인, 실재하는 location 위치, 장소

177. 광고에 따르면, 고객들이 이메일을 통해 할 수 있는 것은 무엇인가?
(A) 고객 경험에 대한 의견 제출하기
(B) 서비스에 대해 질문하기
(C) 견본 명함 요청하기
(D) 환불이나 교환 요청하기

해설 세부 사항
e-mail을 키워드로 첫 번째 지문을 검색하면, 지문의 말미에서 각 옵션의 견본을 받으려면 이메일로 연락하라고 했으므로 (C)가 정답이다.

패러프레이징 a sample of each option → sample cards
어휘 submit 제출하다 feedback 의견, 피드백 refund 환불

178. Hogg 씨가 주문했을 것 같은 명함의 종류는 무엇인가?
(A) 베이직
(B) 스탠더드

(C) 프리미엄
(D) 럭셔리

해설 두 지문 연계_추론/암시
두 번째 지문에서 Hogg 씨는 최소 수량이 100장인 명함을 주문했음을 알 수 있다. 첫 번째 지문에서 최소 수량이 100장인 명함의 종류를 찾아보면 Premium이므로 (C)가 정답이다.

179. Hogg 씨가 명함의 로고를 교체하기를 원하는 이유는 무엇인가?
(A) 색상이 잘 어울리지 않았다.
(B) 디자인이 예전 것이었다.
(C) 크기가 너무 컸다.
(D) 배치가 정렬되어 있지 않았다.

해설 세부 사항
Hogg 씨는 명함이 인쇄되기 전에 디자인을 변경할 필요가 있었는데, 이는 구버전의 회사 로고를 웹 사이트에 업로드했기 때문이다. 따라서 (B)가 정답이다.

패러프레이징 the old version of my company's logo → Its design was outdated

어휘 match 어울리다 placement 배치 misaligned 정렬이 제대로 안 된

180. 이메일에서, 두 번째 단락 네 번째 줄의 어휘 "issues"와 의미상 가장 가까운 것은 무엇인가?
(A) 문제
(B) 종이
(C) 공책
(D) 기록

해설 동의어 찾기
issues는 문맥상 '문제점'을 의미하므로 (A)가 정답이다.

181-185 웹페이지 & 이메일

알렌타운 시 워크숍

여러분의 시를 출간하기를 늘 바라셨나요? 대중들이 감상하기를 기다리는 시가 한가득 있나요? 그렇다면, 알렌타운 시 워크숍(APW)에 신청하는 것을 고려해 보세요.

APW는 시인 지망생들과 활동 중인 시인들이 함께 모여 아이디어를 교환하고 더 나은 작가로 부상할 수 있는 기회입니다. [184-2]지난 12년 동안, APW는 전국의 작가들이 창의적인 목소리를 내도록 도왔습니다. 동료 워크숍, 공개 시 낭송을 즐기고, 〈Allentown Quarterly〉지에 작품을 발표하고 싶다면 다음번 워크숍 신청을 고려해 보십시오.

• [181B]워크숍은 6월 13일부터 6월 30일까지 주중에 개최됩니다.
• 각 강의는 오전 10시부터 오후 4시까지 열리며, 정오에 한 시간 반의 점심 휴식 시간이 있습니다.
• [181C]수업료는 1,299달러이며 6월 1일까지 전액을 납부해야 합니다.
• 필요가 입증된 분들에게는 금전적 지원이 제공됩니다.
• [181D]각 강의의 정원은 8명입니다.

신청 방법:
[181A]4월 1일까지 [182]5페이지에서 10페이지 분량의 시와 300 단어 이하의 자기소개서를 apply@allentownpoets.org로 보내 주십시오. 신청서의 양이 많아서 합격자들만 회신을 받게 되실 것입니다.

어휘 publish 출판하다 a stack of 한무더기의 appreciate 감상하다 public 대중; 공개적인 consider 고려하다 apply for ~에 지원[신청]하다 opportunity 기회 aspiring 장차 ~가 되려는 practicing 현역으로 활동하고 있는 gather 모이다 emerge 부상하다, 생겨나다 peer 동료 tuition 수업료 pay in full 전액을 지불하다 financial 재정적인 aid 지원, 원조 demonstrate 입증하다 cap (액수의) 한도를 정하다 autobiographical 자전적인 statement 진술(서) no more than ~ 이하 due to ~ 때문에 volume 분량 application 지원(서) response 대답, 회신

[184-1] 발신: Marie Owen ⟨m.owen@allentownpoets.org⟩
수신: Jasper Fultz ⟨jasper_fultz@jmail.com⟩
날짜: 5월 3일
제목: [183]축하합니다! 선정되셨습니다
첨부파일: 학생 양식

Fultz 씨,

제 이름은 Marie Owen이고, 저는 알렌타운 시 워크숍의 강사 중 한 명입니다. [183]귀하가 올해 시 워크숍에 합격하셨음을 알려 드리게 되어 기쁩니다. 우리 위원회는 특히 귀하의 작문 샘플에 담긴 심상에 깊은 인상을 받았습니다.

[184-1]저에 대해 말씀 드리자면, 저는 APW가 시작된 이후로 계속 가르치고 있습니다. 저는 세 권의 시집을 썼고 제 시 중 몇 편은 전 세계에 배포되는 출판물에 실렸습니다.

이 이메일에 첨부된 학생 양식을 작성해서 저에게 다시 보내 주시거나 6월 1일까지 알렌타운 예술 아카데미에 가져다주시기 바랍니다. 6월 13일 우리의 첫 수업 날 귀하를 만나기를 고대합니다. 며칠 내로 [185]제가 이메일로 첫 번째 과제를 보낼 테니 잘 챙겨보시기 바라며, 그것은 강의 첫날까지는 끝내셔야 합니다.

Marie Owen

어휘 instructor 강사 committee 위원회 particularly 특히 imagery 이미지, 심상 collection (시·노래 등의) 모음집 feature ~을 특별히 포함하다 distribute 배포하다, 유통하다 publication 출판물 complete 완성하다 drop off 가져다주다 keep an eye out for ~이 있는지 지켜보다, 살펴보다 assignment 과제, 숙제

181. 웹페이지에 따르면, 시 강의에 대해 사실인 것은 무엇인가?
(A) 신청 마감일은 6월 1일이다.
(B) 강의는 일주일에 세 번이다.
(C) 수업료는 강의 첫날까지 내야 한다.
(D) 강의에는 최대 8명의 학생이 있다.

해설 NOT/True
강의 정원이 8명이라고 했으므로 (D)가 정답이다. 강의 신청 마감일은 4월 1일이고, 강의는 주중에 열리므로 월요일부터 금요일까지 일주일에 다섯 번이며, 수업료는 6월 1일까지 내야 한다고 했으므로 (A), (B), (C)는 오답이다.

패러프레이징 Each class is capped at eight students → Classes have a maximum of eight students

어휘 deadline 마감 due 지불해야 하는 a maximum of 최대의

182. 신청서에 포함되어야 하는 것은 무엇인가?
(A) 간단한 자기소개
(B) 이력서
(C) 전문적인 사진
(D) 출판된 시

해설 세부 사항
신청하려면 시와 300단어 이하의 자기소개서를 보내라고 했으므로 (A)가 정답이다.

패러프레이징 an autobiographical statement of no more than 300 words → a short self-description

183. Owen 씨의 이메일의 목적은 무엇인가?
(A) 친구가 활동을 신청하도록 설득하기 위해
(B) 자신의 수많은 수상 내역을 말하기 위해
(C) 지원자를 면접에 부르기 위해
(D) 합격자를 축하하기 위해

해설 주제/목적
이메일의 제목이 축하한다는 내용이고, 합격을 알리게 되어 기쁘다고 했으므로 (D)가 정답이다.

어휘 convince 설득하다 successful applicant 합격자

184. Owen 씨에 대해 암시된 것은 무엇인가?
(A) APW에서 12년 동안 가르치고 있다.
(B) Fultz 씨의 작품을 읽은 유일한 사람이다.
(C) 수십 편의 시집을 썼다.
(D) Fultz 씨와 밀접한 관계를 맺고 있다.

해설 두 지문 연계_추론/암시
Owen 씨가 쓴 이메일에서 그녀는 APW가 시작된 이후 계속 가르치고 있다고 했고, 웹페이지에서 APW는 12년 동안 열렸다고 나와 있으므로 Owen 씨는 APW에서 12년 동안 가르치고 있음을 유추할 수 있다. 따라서 (A)가 정답이다.

패러프레이징 I have been teaching at the APW since it began → She has taught at APW for 12 years

어휘 dozens of 수십의

185. Fultz 씨가 하도록 요청받은 것은 무엇인가?
(A) 또 다른 작문 샘플 보내기
(B) 강의 과제에 대비하기
(C) 재정적인 지원을 찾아보기
(D) 수업료를 즉시 지불하기

해설 세부 사항
Marie Owen이 며칠 내로 첫 번째 과제를 보낼 테니 잘 챙겨보라고 했으므로 (B)가 정답이다.

186-190 웹페이지 & 온라인 양식 & 조사 결과

| 홈 | 음원 샘플 | 서비스 소개 | 후기 | 연락처 |

40개 이상의 언어를 구사하는 5천 명 이상의 성우를 보유한 Custom Voice는 여러분의 프로젝트를 도울 준비가 되어 있습니다. 우리는 성우 경험이 있는 원어민들만을 고용하고 있으며, [186]성우들은 우리 녹음실이나 여러분이 선택한 장소에서 여러분의 텍스트를 녹음할 수 있습니다. 우리는 수십 년 동안 높은 수준의 담화 및 노래 녹음을 제공해 왔습니다. [187]그리고 이제 우리의 녹음 기사들은 자연음, 교통 소음, 날씨 관련 소리와 같은 녹음된 소리들을 추가로 넣을 수 있습니다.

[189-2]A 서비스: 한 명의 성우로 구어체 담화 음성 녹음. 회사 내 레이션, 오디오북 및 전화 안내 멘트에 적합.
B 서비스: 두 명 이상의 성우로 구어체 담화 음성 녹음. 광고 및 이러닝 자료에 사용되는 가장 인기 있는 서비스.
C 서비스: 한 명의 가수로 노래 녹음. 시엠송과 교육용 노래에 인기 만점.
D 서비스: 두 명 이상의 가수로 노래 녹음. 소프라노, 알토, 테너, 베이스 가능. 상업용 음악 앨범 제작시 백 보컬 추가 가능.

모든 음악 녹음은 최소 48시간 전에 가사와 악보가 제공되어야 한다는 것을 유념해 주세요. 비용 견적을 보시려면 우리의 프로젝트 개요 양식에 귀하의 프로젝트에 대한 세부 정보를 작성해 주십시오.

어휘 description 묘사, 서술   review 후기   voice actor 성우   language 언어   native speaker 모국어 사용자, 원어민   record 녹음하다   text 글, 문서   on location 현지에서   site 위치, 장소   for decades 수십 년간   additional 추가의   corporate 기업의   narration 내레이션   telephone prompt 전화 녹음 메시지   commercial 광고   material 자료   jingle 시엠송   backup vocal 백 보컬   lyric 가사   sheet music 악보   in advance 사전에, 미리   cost estimate 비용 견적   complete 작성하다   overview 개요   form 양식   details 세부 사항

Custom Voice: 프로젝트 개요 양식

성명: [188]Gavin Barrett
날짜: 3월 16일

귀하의 프로젝트 및 요구 사항에 대한 개요를 제공해 주십시오:
[188]제가 눌어붙지 않는 취사도구를 몇 가지 개발했는데, [189-1]그것을 세척하는 방법을 설명하는 동영상에서 내레이션을 해줄 성우가 한 명 필요합니다. 대본 길이는 대략 350단어입니다. [190-1]성우는 남성이었으면 좋겠고, 제 광고 타깃층을 위해 영국식 억양을 선호합니다. 가능하다면 일주일 내에 이 프로젝트를 끝내고 싶습니다.

어휘 needs 요구 사항   nonstick 눌어붙지 않는   pots and pans 취사도구   voiceover (화면 밖의) 해설 소리   instruction 지시   approximately 대략   male 남성의; 남성   prefer 선호하다   UK 영국(= United Kingdom)   accent 억양   target audience 광고 타깃

Custom Voice: Gavin Barrett 씨 프로젝트에 이용 가능한 연기자

이름	연령대	남성/여성	상세 설명
Trisha Blanchard	20-29	여성	경력 3년의 미국인 가수 겸 성우
[190-2]Salvador Campanella	40-49	[190-2]남성	많은 애니메이션 영화 연기 경력이 있는 [190-2]영국인 성우 겸 가수
Kirby Garrison	30-39	남성	경력 10년의 미국인 성우
Bonnie Walsh	40-49	여성	오디오북과 기업체 내레이션으로 알려진 영국인 성우

모든 성우는 해당 언어의 원어민들입니다.

어휘 performer 연기자   available 이용 가능한   age bracket 연령대   perform 연기하다   animated film 애니메이션 영화

186. Custom Voice에 대해 암시된 것은 무엇인가?
(A) 직원들은 업무상 출장을 갈 수 있다.
(B) 개인적인 용도로만 녹음을 한다.
(C) 고객들을 위해 녹음 대본을 작성할 수 있다.
(D) 몇 년 전에 설립되었다.

해설 추론/암시
첫 번째 문제에 대한 단서는 보통 첫 번째 지문에 나온다. 첫 번째 지문에서 성우들은 프로젝트를 의뢰한 고객들이 정한 장소에서 녹음을 할 수 있다고 했으므로 (A)가 정답이다.

어휘 found 설립하다

187. Custom Voice에서 이제 이용 가능한 새로운 서비스는 무엇인가?
(A) 창작곡 쓰기
(B) 음향 효과 추가하기
(C) 다양한 억양 제공하기
(D) 빠른 서비스 제공하기

해설 세부 사항
이제 녹음 기사들이 자연음, 교통 소음, 날씨 관련 소리와 같은 음향 효과를 넣을 수 있다고 했으므로 (B)가 정답이다.

패러프레이징 put in additional recorded sounds → Adding sound effects

어휘 original 독창적인   add 더하다, 추가하다   sound effect 음향 효과   supply 공급하다   provide 제공하다

188. Barrett 씨에 대해 사실인 것은 무엇인가?
(A) 하루 만에 작업이 끝나기를 원한다.
(B) 전에 Custom Voice를 이용한 적이 있다.
(C) 몇 가지 취사도구를 고안했다.
(D) 대본의 길이를 줄이기를 원한다.

해설 NOT/True
Barrett을 키워드로 지문을 검색하면 두 번째 지문의 작성자가

Gavin Barrett이고 nonstick pots and pans를 개발했다고 했으므로 (C)가 정답이다.

패러프레이징 created → designed / pots and pans → cookware

어휘 overnight 밤 사이에   cookware 취사도구   shorten 줄이다

189. Barrett 씨에게는 어떤 Custom Voice 서비스가 가장 맞겠는가?
(A) A 서비스
(B) B 서비스
(C) C 서비스
(D) D 서비스

해설 두 지문 연계_추론/암시
두 번째 지문에서 작성자인 Gavin Barrett은 동영상에서 내레이션을 해줄 성우가 한 명 필요하다고 했는데, 첫 번째 지문에서 한 명의 성우와 내레이션에 해당하는 것은 Service A이므로 (A)가 정답이다.

190. Barrett 씨의 프로젝트에 가장 적합한 사람은 누구인가?
(A) Trisha Blanchard
(B) Salvador Campanella
(C) Kirby Garrison
(D) Bonnie Walsh

해설 두 지문 연계_추론/암시
두 번째 지문에서 Gavin Barrett은 영국 억양을 사용하는 남성 성우를 원한다고 했는데, 세 번째 지문에서 그러한 조건에 부합하는 사람은 Salvador Campanella이므로 (B)가 정답이다.

191-195 웹페이지 & 이메일 & 이메일

http://www.atterburydesigns.com/client_portfolio			
홈	요금	**191** 거래처 포트폴리오	연락처

191 아래 링크를 클릭하여 저희 거래처의 웹 사이트를 둘러 보세요.

191 192-2 통신	부동산	음식 서비스	광업
• Passaic Phones	• Rose Johnson Realty	• Holloway	• Tampa Industrial
• RB Telecom	• Home Street	• Lee's Steakhouse	• Prospect Mining
• **192-2** Granillo	• Maxi-Move	• Beans Coffee Shop	

어휘 portfolio 포트폴리오, 목록   communications 정보 통신
real estate 부동산   mining 광업

수신: Daniel McClellan 〈dmcclellan@mail-storage.net〉
발신: Leah Atterbury 〈leah@atterburydesigns.com〉
날짜: 9월 18일

제목: 오스틴에서 인사드립니다

McClellan 씨,

어떻게 지내세요? 잘 지내고 계시길 바라요. 저는 Cartwright Design Institute에서 학업을 마친 후, **193** Howarth Services에서 1년 정도 일했습니다. 새로운 디자인 기술을 활용하고 고객과 잘 소통하는 방법을 배울 수 있는 좋은 기회였습니다. 하지만, **193** 회사가 샌디에이고로 이전했을 때, 저는 오스틴에 머물기로 결정했어요.

일을 그만둔 후, **192-1** 저는 Granillo를 위한 웹 사이트를 만드는 것을 시작으로 제 회사를 설립했습니다. 그 일을 시작으로, 저는 서서히 더 많은 고객을 상대하게 되었고, 다행히도 그 어느 때보다 바쁘게 지내고 있습니다. 그래서 글을 쓰게 됐는데요. **195-2** 업무상 분명히 많은 웹 디자이너들을 알고 계실 거라고 생각합니다. 저를 위해 프리랜서로 일할 수 있는 사람을 추천해 주실 수 있는지 궁금합니다. 이것은 제가 업무량을 따라잡는 데 도움이 될 겁니다. 어떤 도움이라도 주시면 정말 감사하겠습니다.

대단히 감사합니다.

Leah

어휘 greeting 인사   institute 기관, 협회   put ~ to use ~을 이용하다   communicate 의사소통하다   quit 그만두다   launch 시작하다   take on ~을 떠맡다   fortunate 운 좋은, 다행인   keep up with ~에 뒤지지 않다, 따라잡다   workload 업무량, 작업량   appreciate 감사하다

수신: Leah Atterbury 〈leah@atterburydesigns.com〉
194 발신: Daniel McClellan 〈dmcclellan@mail-storage.net〉
날짜: 9월 20일
제목: 회신: 오스틴에서 인사드립니다

안녕하세요 Leah,

잘 지내고 계시다니 기쁩니다. **194** 당신이 졸업한 지 몇 달 후에 저는 Cartwright Design Institute를 떠났답니다. 저는 현재 사진 스튜디오에서 일하고 있습니다. 그 이후로 오랜 시간이 지났지만 저는 가끔 디자인 학교에서 근무했던 시절을 생각합니다.

저는 여전히 당신의 분야에서 꽤 많은 연락처를 가지고 있습니다. **195-1** 555-7801번으로 Joel Duncan 씨에게 연락하세요. 제 생각에 그가 바로 당신이 찾고 있는 사람일 것 같아요. 제가 도울 수 있는 다른 방법이 있다면 알려 주세요.

행운을 빌어요.

Daniel

어휘 currently 현재, 지금   quite a few 상당히 많은   field 분야, 현장   get in touch with ~와 연락을 취하다   exactly 정확히, 바로

191. Atterbury Designs에 대해 사실인 것은 무엇인가?
(A) 최근에 부동산 업계에서 일하기 시작했다.
(B) 소규모 업체들을 전문으로 한다.
(C) 약 1년 전에 설립되었다.

139

(D) 여러 업종에 거래처를 두고 있다.

해설 **NOT/True**
다중 지문의 첫 번째 문제에 대한 단서는 첫 번째 지문에서 나오는 편이다. Atterbury Designs의 웹페이지에 있는 거래처의 포트폴리오를 살펴보면, 통신, 부동산, 음식 서비스, 광업 등으로 업종이 다양하므로 (D)가 정답이다.

어휘 specialize in ~을 전문으로 하다   launch 시작하다, 개시하다

192. Atterbury Designs의 첫 거래처의 업종은 무엇이었는가?
(A) 통신 회사
(B) 부동산 회사
(C) 음식 서비스 회사
(D) 광업 회사

해설 **두 지문 연계_세부 사항**
두 번째 지문에서 Leah Atterbury는 Granillo의 웹 사이트를 만드는 것으로 시작해서 회사를 설립했다고 했는데, Granillo를 키워드로 다른 지문을 검색하면 첫 번째 지문에서 Granillo가 통신 회사로 나오므로 (A)가 정답이다.

193. Atterbury 씨가 Howarth Services에 대해 시사하는 것은 무엇인가?
(A) 샌디에이고에서 설립되었다.
(B) 직원들에게 1년 계약을 제안한다.
(C) 더 이상 오스틴에서 영업을 하지 않는다.
(D) 직원들이 재택근무를 할 수 있도록 해 준다.

해설 **추론/암시**
첫 번째 이메일에서 Atterbury 씨는 Howarth Services가 오스틴에서 샌디에이고로 이전했을 때 오스틴에 머물기로 했다고 했으므로, 그 회사는 더 이상 오스틴에서 사업을 하지 않는다는 것을 유추할 수 있다. 따라서 (C)가 정답이다.

어휘 found 설립하다   contract 계약(서)   operate 운영하다
work remotely 원격 근무하다, 재택근무하다

194. McClellan 씨는 누구이겠는가?
(A) Atterbury 씨의 예전 동료
(B) Cartwright Institute의 소유주
(C) Atterbury 씨의 예전 교사
(D) Howarth Services의 직원

해설 **추론/암시**
Daniel McClellan은 두 번째 이메일의 발신자로서, Leah Atterbury와 같은 시기에 Cartwright Design Institute에 있었고, 그곳에서 근무하던 시절을 생각한다고 했으므로, Cartwright Design Institute의 교사였다는 것을 추론할 수 있다. 따라서 (C)가 정답이다.

어휘 former 예전의   coworker 동료

195. Atterbury 씨가 Duncan 씨에게 전화할 이유는 무엇이겠는가?
(A) 그의 업체를 위한 웹페이지를 디자인하기 위해
(B) 그에게 취업 기회를 제안하기 위해
(C) 추천서를 요청하기 위해
(D) 사무실 공간에 대해 문의하기 위해

해설 **두 지문 연계_추론/암시**
Duncan을 키워드로 지문을 검색하면 세 번째 지문에 Joel Duncan이라는 이름이 나오고, 이메일의 발신인인 Daniel McClellan이 수신인인 Leah Atterbury에게 Duncan에게 연락할 것을 제안하고 있다는 것을 알 수 있다. 다른 지문에서 그 이유를 찾아보면, 두 번째 지문에서 Leah Atterbury는 Daniel McClellan에게 프리랜서로 일할 웹 디자이너를 추천해 달라고 했으므로, Daniel McClellan은 Joel Duncan을 추천하고 있다는 것을 알 수 있다. 따라서 Leah Atterbury는 Joel Duncan에게 프리랜서 일자리를 제안하기 위해 전화할 것임을 유추할 수 있으므로 (B)가 정답이다.

어휘 reference letter 추천서

196-200 이메일 & 일정표 & 이메일

수신: 전 직원
발신: Richard Rhodes
날짜: 12월 2일
제목: 새 소식

여러분,

Belfour 주식회사를 대표해서 반가운 소식을 알려드립니다. 우리 회사는 지난 1년 동안 멈출 기미도 없이 괄목할 만한 성장을 했습니다. 지난달만 해도 [197]뉴로텀 지역에서만 열 번이 넘는 영업 전략 워크숍을 진행할 수 있었습니다.

이러한 긍정적인 추세로 인해, [196]우리는 팀에 새로운 워크숍 발표자 두 명을 채용하기로 결정했습니다. Robin Niva 씨는 디지털 마케팅 전문가이며 6년 이상의 경험을 가지고 있습니다. [199-2]Tai Tsuda 씨는 우리의 의료 영업 권위자가 될 텐데, 그는 15년 이상의 의료 교육 경력을 가지고 있습니다. 이 두 사람이 다음 달 중에 워크숍을 개최하기 시작할 것입니다.

두 분이 Belfour 주식회사 가족이 된 걸 환영해 주세요!

대표 이사 Richard Rhodes

어휘 on behalf of ~을 대신[대표]하여, ~을 위해서   outstanding 두드러진, 뛰어난   growth 성장   sign 표시, 징후   conduct 실시하다   strategy 전략   positive 긍정적인   trend 추세, 동향
presenter 발표자   authority 권위자, 권위

Belfour 주식회사 교육 일정 기획안 1월 둘째 주				
강의 제목	날짜	길이	장소	발표자
효과적인 이메일 광고	[200-2]1월 6일	[200-2]종일	[198A]뉴로텀 컨벤션 센터	Robin Niva
흥미로운 광고 카피 만들기	1월 7일	[198D]반일	[198A]뉴로텀 컨벤션 센터	Joseph Bronston

시제품 판매하기	1월 8일	종일	뉴로텀 연구 병원	Tai Tsuda
199-1 주치의에게 호소하는 방법	199-1 1월 9일	198D 반일	뉴로텀 가족 병원	추후 공지 예정

어휘 propose 제안하다 effective 효과적인 advertising 광고(하기) create 만들어 내다 experimental product 시제품 appeal to ~에 호소하다 family doctor 주치의

수신: Richard Rodes 〈richardr@belfourinc.net〉
200-1 발신: Ning Ma 〈ningma@sellme.com〉
날짜: 1월 7일
제목: 워크숍

Rhodes 씨,

200-1 Sell.me의 저희 직원 몇 명이 1월 6일과 7일에 귀사의 교육 과정에 참석했습니다. 저는 피드백을 제공하고 요구 사항도 제안하고자 합니다.

저희 직원들은 복잡한 주제를 고려할 때 반나절 과정이 다소 짧은 것 같다고 생각했습니다. 그러나, 200-1 종일 세미나는 시간상 문제가 있었고 훨씬 더 짧아도 될 것 같았습니다.

뿐만 아니라, 주차 관련 문제도 있었습니다. 참가자들을 위한 전용 주차장이 없어 일부 직원들은 행사장에 제시간에 도착하기 위해 고군분투했고, 차를 주차하기 위해 비싼 요금까지 내야 했습니다. 이 문제에 대한 해결책을 찾아 주시면 대단히 감사하겠습니다.

시간을 내 주셔서 감사합니다.

Ning Ma, Sell.me 최고경영자

어휘 considering ~을 고려하면 complex 복잡한 further 뿐만 아니라, 게다가 concern 우려, 걱정 reserved 남겨 둔, 지정의 participant 참가자 struggle 투쟁하다, 분투하다 venue 장소 solution 해결책

196. 첫 번째 이메일의 목적은 무엇인가?
(A) 직원들을 회의에 초대하기 위해
(B) 회사의 미래 성장을 계획하기 위해
(C) 새 직원들을 소개하기 위해
(D) 새 지점의 개장을 발표하기 위해

해설 주제/목적
새로운 워크숍 발표자 두 명을 채용하기로 했다면서 이들을 소개하고 있으므로 (C)가 정답이다.

어휘 conference 회의, 학회

197. Belfour 주식회사가 전문으로 하는 분야는 무엇이겠는가?
(A) 텔레마케팅
(B) 영업 교육
(C) 의료 기술
(D) 디지털 교육

해설 추론/암시
Belfour 주식회사의 교육 일정을 보면 주로 영업 및 마케팅과 관련된 강의들로 이루어져 있으므로 영업 교육을 전문으로 한다고 유추할 수 있다. 따라서 (B)가 정답이다.

패러프레이징 sales strategies workshops → sales training

198. 일정표에서 워크숍에 대해 시사하는 것은 무엇인가?
(A) 어떤 워크숍은 같은 장소에서 열린다.
(B) 하루 종일 몇 번의 휴식이 있다.
(C) 모두 같은 사람이 이끈다.
(D) 보통 하루 종일 지속된다.

해설 NOT/True
뉴로텀 컨벤션 센터에서 열리는 강의가 두 개이므로 (A)가 정답이다. 반일 동안 지속되는 강의가 전체 강의의 절반이므로 (D)는 오답이다.

어휘 break 휴식 last 지속되다, 계속되다

199. 1월 9일 워크숍을 이끌 사람은 누구이겠는가?
(A) Rhodes 씨
(B) Niva 씨
(C) Bronston 씨
(D) Tsuda 씨

해설 두 지문 연계_추론/암시
일정표에서 1월 9일 워크숍은 '주치의에게 호소하는 방법'으로 의료 관련 강의인데, 첫 번째 이메일에서 Tai Tsuda가 의료 영업 권위자라고 했으므로 그가 해당 워크숍 진행자로 적임임을 알 수 있다. 따라서 (D)가 정답이다.

200. Ma 씨가 직원들의 교육 경험에 대해 암시하는 것은 무엇인가?
(A) 그들은 완전히 만족했다.
(B) 1월 6일 워크숍은 너무 길었다.
(C) 주차를 쉽게 할 수 있었다.
(D) 주제들은 재미없었다.

해설 두 지문 연계_추론/암시
두 번째 이메일에서 발신인인 Ma 씨는 자사 직원들이 1월 6일과 7일에 교육을 들었는데, 종일 세미나는 훨씬 더 짧아도 될 것 같았다며 시간상의 문제를 거론하고 있다. 일정표를 보면, 1월 6일과 7일 중 종일 강의는 1월 6일 강의였다. 이를 통해 Ma 씨의 직원들이 1월 6일 워크숍이 너무 길었다고 느꼈음을 유추할 수 있으므로 (B)가 정답이다.

패러프레이징 could have been much shorter → was too long

어휘 completely 완전히 readily 손쉽게

정답 및 해설

에듀윌 토익 READING RC
정답 및 해설

고객의 꿈, 직원의 꿈, 지역사회의 꿈을 실현한다

에듀윌 도서몰 book.eduwill.net
- 부가학습자료 및 정오표: 에듀윌 도서몰 → 도서자료실
- 교재 문의: 에듀윌 도서몰 → 문의하기 → 교재(내용, 출간) / 주문 및 배송

업계 최초 대통령상 3관왕, 정부기관상 19관왕 달성!

2010 대통령상   2019 대통령상   2019 대통령상

대한민국 브랜드대상 국무총리상   국무총리상   문화체육관광부 장관상   농림축산식품부 장관상   과학기술정보통신부 장관상   여성가족부장관상

서울특별시장상   과학기술부장관상   정보통신부장관상   산업자원부장관상   고용노동부장관상   미래창조과학부장관상   법무부장관상

- **2004**
  서울특별시장상 우수벤처기업 대상
- **2006**
  부총리 겸 과학기술부장관 표창 국가 과학 기술 발전 유공
- **2007**
  정보통신부장관상 디지털콘텐츠 대상
  산업자원부장관 표창 대한민국 e비즈니스대상
- **2010**
  대통령 표창 대한민국 IT 이노베이션 대상
- **2013**
  고용노동부장관 표창 일자리 창출 공로
- **2014**
  미래창조과학부장관 표창 ICT Innovation 대상
- **2015**
  법무부장관 표창 사회공헌 유공
- **2017**
  여성가족부장관상 사회공헌 유공
  2016 합격자 수 최고 기록 KRI 한국기록원 공식 인증
- **2018**
  2017 합격자 수 최고 기록 KRI 한국기록원 공식 인증
- **2019**
  대통령 표창 범죄예방대상
  대통령 표창 일자리 창출 유공
  과학기술정보통신부장관상 대한민국 ICT 대상
- **2020**
  국무총리상 대한민국 브랜드대상
  2019 합격자 수 최고 기록 KRI 한국기록원 공식 인증
- **2021**
  고용노동부장관상 일·생활 균형 우수 기업 공모전 대상
  문화체육관광부장관 표창 근로자휴가지원사업 우수 참여 기업
  농림축산식품부장관상 대한민국 사회공헌 대상
  문화체육관광부장관 표창 여가친화기업 인증 우수 기업
- **2022**
  국무총리 표창 일자리 창출 유공
  농림축산식품부장관상 대한민국 ESG 대상